The Bilingual Mental Lexicon

BILINGUAL EDUCATION & BILINGUALISM
Series Editors: Nancy H. Hornberger, *University of Pennsylvania, USA* and
Colin Baker, *Bangor University, Wales, UK*

Bilingual Education and Bilingualism is an international, multidisciplinary series publishing research on the philosophy, politics, policy, provision and practice of language planning, global English, indigenous and minority language education, multilingualism, multiculturalism, biliteracy, bilingualism and bilingual education. The series aims to mirror current debates and discussions.

Full details of all the books in this series and of all our other publications can be found on http://www.multilingual-matters.com, or by writing to Multilingual Matters, St Nicholas House, 31-34 High Street, Bristol BS1 2AW, UK.

BILINGUAL EDUCATION & BILINGUALISM
Series Editors: Nancy H. Hornberger, *University of Pennsylvania, USA* and Colin Baker, *Bangor University, Wales, UK*

The Bilingual Mental Lexicon
Interdisciplinary Approaches

Edited by
Aneta Pavlenko

MULTILINGUAL MATTERS
Bristol • Buffalo • Toronto

Library of Congress Cataloging in Publication Data
A catalog record for this book is available from the Library of Congress.
The Bilingual Mental Lexicon: Interdisciplinary Approaches
Edited by Aneta Pavlenko.
Bilingual Education and Bilingualism: 70
Includes bibliographical references and index.
1. Bilingualism–Psychological aspects.
2. Lexicology–Psycological aspects. I. Pavlenko, Aneta, 1963-
P115.4.B53 2009
404'.2019–dc22 2008035194

British Library Cataloguing in Publication Data
A catalogue entry for this book is available from the British Library.

ISBN-13: 978-1-84769-125-5 (hbk)
ISBN-13: 978-1-84769-124-8 (pbk)

Multilingual Matters
UK: St Nicholas House, 31-34 High Street, Bristol BS1 2AW, UK.
USA: UTP, 2250 Military Road, Tonawanda, NY 14150, USA.
Canada: UTP, 5201 Dufferin Street, North York, Ontario M3H 5T8, Canada.

The policy of Multilingual Matters/Channel View Publications is to use papers that are natural, renewable and recyclable products, made from wood grown in sustainable forests. In the manufacturing process of our books, and to further support our policy, preference is given to printers that have FSC and PEFC Chain of Custody certification. The FSC and/or PEFC logos will appear on those books where full certification has been granted to the printer concerned.

Typeset by Datapage International Ltd.
Printed and bound in Great Britain by the Cromwell Press Ltd.

Contents

Contributors

Jeanette Altarriba (PhD in Cognitive Psychology, Vanderbilt University, 1990) is Professor of Psychology at the University at Albany, State University of New York, Albany, NY, USA. She is co-editor, with Roberto Heredia, of two volumes, *Bilingual Sentence Processing* (Elsevier, 2002) and *An Introduction to Bilingualism: Principles and Processes* (Routledge, 2008). Her research interests include bilingual language processing, second language acquisition, and emotion, attention and cognition. Her current work studies how monolingual and bilingual speakers represent emotion-related words through the use of both implicit and explicit measures.

Dana Basnight-Brown is a doctoral student in Cognitive Psychology at the University at Albany, State University of New York, Albany, NY, USA. Her research interests include second language acquisition, bilingual semantic processing, morphological processing in monolinguals and bilinguals, perception of foreign accent, emotion representation across languages and cross-cultural psychology.

Peter Ecke (PhD in Second Language Acquisition and Teaching, University of Arizona, USA, 1996) is Associate Professor at the University of Arizona, USA. He is a faculty member in the Department of German Studies and the Interdisciplinary PhD Program in Second Language Acquisition and Teaching. He directs the department's Basic Language Program and its Summer-Study-in-Leipzig-Germany Program. His research interests include the multilingual lexicon, vocabulary acquisition, and L2 learners' errors and word finding problems, particularly, the tip-of-the-tongue phenomenon.

Marianne Gullberg (PhD in Linguistics, Lund University, Sweden, 1998) holds positions at the Max Planck Institute for Psycholinguistics and at Radboud University Nijmegen, the Netherlands. Together with A. Özyürek she also heads the Nijmegen Gesture Centre. Her research targets second language acquisition and multilingual processing and language use, with particular attention to implicit learning, discourse and the semantic-conceptual interface.

Scott Jarvis (PhD in Linguistics, Indiana University, USA, 1997) is Associate Professor of Linguistics at Ohio University, USA. He is the co-author (with Aneta Pavlenko) of the book *Crosslinguistic Influence in Language and Cognition* (Routledge, 2008). His research concentrates on issues related to the investigation of cross-linguistic influence and the measurement of language proficiency. Currently he is the Associate Editor for the journal *Language Learning*.

Barbara Köpke (PhD in Linguistics, University of Toulouse-Le Mirail, France, 1999) is Associate Professor at the Department of Language Science of the University of Toulouse-Le Mirail, Toulouse, France. Together with Monika Schmid, she has edited two collections of papers and a special edition of the *Journal of Neurolinguistics* on first language attrition. Her research focuses on neuro- and psycholinguistics of first language attrition, in particular on the role of working memory in language attrition.

Viorica Marian (PhD in Psychology, Cornell University, USA, 2000) is Associate Professor of Communication Sciences and Disorders, Psychology and Cognitive Science at Northwestern University, USA. Her research focuses on bilingualism/multilingualism and the brain's ability to accommodate multiple languages and is funded by the National Science Foundation and the National Institutes of Health. Using cognitive, behavioral and neurological measures, she studies spoken and written language processing and the relationship between language and memory.

Renata Meuter (D Phil in Experimental Psychology, University of Oxford, UK, 1994) is a Senior Lecturer in the School of Psychology and Counseling and a member of the Institute of Health and Biomedical Innovation, Queensland University of Technology, Brisbane, Australia. She also has research collaborations with the Centre for Accident Research and Road Safety, Queensland. Her research interests focus on language selection and control in multilinguals, the relationship between control and aspects of language processing, as well as on factors determining task performance in different operational settings affected by monotony (such as driving and baggage screening).

Aneta Pavlenko (PhD in Linguistics, Cornell University, USA, 1997) is Professor at the College of Education, Temple University, Philadelphia, USA. She is the author of *Emotions and Multilingualism* (Cambridge University Press, 2005, winner of the BAAL Book Prize), editor of *Bilingual Minds* (Multilingual Matters, 2006) and co-author (with Scott Jarvis) of *Crosslinguistic Influence in Language and Cognition* (Routledge, 2008). Her research examines the relationship between language, emotions and cognition in bilingualism and second language acquisition.

Monika Schmid (PhD in English Language and Linguistics, Heinrich Heine University, Dusseldorf, Germany, 2000) is Rosalind Franklin Fellow and senior lecturer in English Language at the Rijksuniversiteit, Groningen, the Netherlands. Her research examines psycholinguistic and sociolinguistic aspects of first language attrition. She has been awarded a VENI-scholarship for a large-scale study of language attrition of German migrants in English- and Dutch-language settings and is currently heading a multilateral investigation into the development of multilingual proficiency.

Robert W. Schrauf (PhD in Medical Anthropology, Case Western Reserve University, USA, 1995) is Associate Professor of Applied Linguistics at the Pennsylvania State University, USA. He completed postdoctoral training in Cognitive Psychology at Duke University. Prior to his appointment at Penn State, he was an Assistant Professor at the Feinberg School of Medicine at Northwestern University. His research concerns the cognitive processes of bilingual autobiographical memory in younger and older adults, bilingualism and cognitive aging, and applied linguistics and health sciences. He is president of the Association for Anthropology and Gerontology and Associate Editor of the *Journal of Cross-Cultural Gerontology*.

Preface: Time for New Metaphors?

ANETA PAVLENKO

In 1992, I entered graduate school with a clear idea of what I wanted to study. Two pilot studies later, it turned out that the research questions I wanted to ask were not particularly interesting – they had easy and unsurprising answers. By my second year of study, I was at a loss as to what I wanted to research. One day as I was browsing through new acquisitions in the library, I came across an unassuming blue paperback entitled *The Bilingual Lexicon*, edited by Robert Schreuder and Bert Weltens (1993). A few pages into the book, I was hooked. To this day, I remember the thrill of reading De Groot's and Kroll's chapters on words and concepts in the bilingual lexicon and realizing this was it, this was the area to which I wanted to contribute most.

Later on, conversations with colleagues confirmed that mine was not a unique experience – Harris' (1992) volume *Cognitive Processing in Bilinguals* and Schreuder and Weltens' (1993) collection have sparked new interest in bilingualism, motivating numerous scholars to examine bilingual processing and the relationship between forms and meanings in bilinguals' languages. The research conducted in the decade that followed has been analyzed and synthesized in Kroll and De Groot's (2005) comprehensive *Handbook of Bilingualism: Psycholinguistic Approaches*. The present volume aims to complement their collection by showcasing interdisciplinary approaches to the study of the bilingual lexicon.

The volume opens with a chapter by Renata Meuter discussing contributions from neurolinguistic and neurophysiological research to the study of the bilingual lexicon. Moving from the brain to the mind, Robert Schrauf presents a neurocognitive view of the mental lexicon and of its interaction with autobiographic memory and the distributed self. Viorica Marian considers audio-visual integration in bilingual language processing, and the contribution of new technologies, such as eye tracking, to our understanding of this process. The two chapters that follow are dedicated to semantic representation and processing. Jeanette Altarriba and Dana Basnight-Brown draw on evidence from traditional reaction-time-based psycholinguistic tasks, while Scott Jarvis considers the implications of studies of cross-linguistic influence. Conceptual representation and processing are considered in the next two chapters. Aneta Pavlenko examines bilinguals' concepts in the light of evidence from elicited narratives and sorting and categorization tasks, while Marianne Gullberg argues for the importance of considering the evidence from gesture studies. The last two chapters are dedicated to bilingual lexical retrieval. Peter Ecke takes a synchronic perspective on the issue and reviews studies of the tip-of-the-tongue phenomenon, while Monika Schmid and Barbara Köpke take a diachronic perspective and examine the evolution of the bilingual lexicon over the life-span of individuals, focusing on first language attrition.

To ensure overall coherence, all volume contributors were asked to address the following questions: (1) What research questions are currently asked in the study of the bi- and multilingual lexicon in your area of expertise? (2) What methods of inquiry are used in your area to address these questions? (3) What are the key findings and what are their implications for our understanding of the structure of the bi- and multilingual mental lexicon? (4) What do you see as the key directions for future inquiry?

Each question was asked with a specific purpose. Explicit reflections on the key research questions are useful because they give readers an idea of what we want to know and an understanding of how questions about the bilingual lexicon may vary by the area of inquiry, how different areas of inquiry may answer the same questions in different ways, and – most importantly – what questions have and have not yet been asked and answered across different research areas.

Detailed reviews of methodological approaches explain how we know what we know and in doing so help to demystify methodology. Novice researchers often feel apprehensions about conducting research in this field, if they have not been trained in a particular laboratory to use specific approaches. The purpose of this collection is to provide clear, step-by-step, methodological guidance for researchers who do not have readily available mentors, but would like to try their hand at bilingual lexicon research as well as for researchers who wish to add new approaches to their methodological repertoires.

Summaries of the main findings and their implications clarify what we know, while directions for future inquiry outline what we do not know and would like to know. These summaries and reflections also reveal limitations of previous research and point to promising areas for future inquiry. In the present volume, three sets of limitations reappear across chapters. The first set involves the study participants. The contributors argue that many studies in the field favor sequential or late bilinguals and overgeneralize the findings of these studies to all bilinguals. Another problem is the focus on bilingualism even in studies with individuals who know and use more than two languages. The second set of limitations involves the combinations of languages commonly used in the bilingual lexicon research: many preliminary conclusions have been reached on the basis of studies with languages that use Latin alphabets. The third set involves the stimuli: most research to date has focused on concrete words and cognates, thus offering little information about the processing of other types of words. Even more importantly, this research has examined the processing of decontextualized words, thus providing little insight into how words are processed in context.

The contributors agree that future research needs to examine the multilingual lexicon because the influence of certain factors, such as the order of language acquisition, cannot be fully understood by studying bilinguals only (see also Jarvis' chapter). They also agree that theories and hypotheses have to be tested across different groups of bi- and multilingual speakers, because their levels of proficiency and language trajectories could differentially affect their performance – thus there may be no single bi- and multilingual lexicon, but rather bi- and multilingual lexicons. Studies also have to consider different types of words, such as emotion words or polysemous words (see also Altarriba & Basnight-Brown's chapter), different language combinations, such as languages with different orthographic systems or tonal and nontonal languages (see also Marian's chapter), and speech-sign combinations that could inform us about the nature of the bimodal lexicon.

The main contribution of the present volume to research in the area is in familiarizing the readers with interdisciplinary approaches to the study of the bilingual lexicon in context. Marian points to ways of incorporating visual contexts; Schrauf places words within the context of autobiographic memory; Jarvis, Pavlenko and Gullberg consider words in the context of oral and written discourse; Gullberg also underscores the embodied nature of language production. This emphasis on the context stems from increasing concerns about ecological validity of theories and models in the field and has important implications for applicability of bottom-up models of bilingual processing (for an in-depth discussion see Marian's chapter).

Some chapters in the volume also question the very premises – and metaphors – of the current inquiry. Schrauf argues that in the study of memory metaphors from the cognitive neuroscience, such as activation and (re)construction, have greater explanatory power than information processing metaphors, such as storage, representation or retrieval. Similar arguments are put forth by Marian who favors emergentist metaphors in the study of audio-visual integration in bilingual processing. Drawing on Spivey (2007), Marian argues that the bilingual lexicon is best conceived as a process, rather than a state, because states require stasis, while patterns of neural activation in the brain are always in flux. A dynamic approach to the mental lexicon is also taken in Pavlenko's chapter. Adopting Barsalou's (2003) view of concepts, Pavlenko argues that conceptual representations – similar to memories – function in a context-dependent manner, where different representations may be activated by the same words in different communicative settings.

This change of metaphors has important implications for future research on the bilingual lexicon and for questions asked with regard to representation and processing. A stable permanent representation accessed selectively or non-selectively becomes but a phantom, in this approach, because distributed representations do not exist in a pure state – rather they emerge, assemble and reassemble to serve the needs of particular tasks. In turn, development is seen not as a change in representations per se, but as a change in the speaker's ability to assemble a particular representation for a particular purpose within a particular span of time. Consequently, we no longer ask either/or questions, because the answer to the questions about shared versus separate representations or selective versus non-selective access is invariably 'it depends' – certain contexts and tasks will activate separate selectively accessed representations, while others may activate representations non-selectively. Instead, we can articulate new questions: under what conditions is access (non)selective? What factors trigger particular types of representations? What circumstances affect development of distributed representations? It is my sincere hope that the questions raised in this volume will inspire a new generation of researchers in the same way that Schreuder and Weltens' volume inspired many of us.

To conclude, I would like to thank all of the volume contributors for their extreme professionalism, promptness, openness and flexibility that made working on this volume a pleasure and an honor. I also want to thank everyone who generously contributed their time and expertise to the peer-review process: Panos Athanasopoulos, Benedetta Bassetti, Michele Bishop, Kees De Bot, Gessica De Angelis, Jean-Marc Dewaele, Tamar Gollan, Catherine Harris, Barbara Malt, Steve McCafferty, Elena

Schmitt, Jyotsna Vaid and all of the volume contributors. Thanks to all of you, this volume is a truly collaborative endeavor.

References

Barsalou, L. (2003) Situated simulation in the human conceptual system. *Language and Cognitive Processes* 18, 513–562.

Harris, R. (ed.) (1992) *Cognitive Processing in Bilinguals*. Amsterdam: North Holland.

Kroll, J. and De Groot, A.M.B. (eds) *Handbook of Bilingualism: Psycholinguistic Approaches*. Oxford: Oxford University Press.

Schreuder, R. and Weltens, R. (eds) (1993) *The Bilingual Lexicon*. Amsterdam: John Benjamins.

Spivey, M. (2007) *The Continuity of Mind*. Oxford/New York: Oxford University Press.

Chapter 1

Neurolinguistic Contributions to Understanding the Bilingual Mental Lexicon

RENATA MEUTER

Introduction

Many bilinguals will have had the experience of unintentionally reading something in a language other than the intended one (e.g. MUG to mean *mosquito* in Dutch rather than a receptacle for a hot drink, as one of the possible intended English meanings), of finding themselves blocked on a word for which many alternatives suggest themselves (but, somewhat annoyingly, not in the right language), of their accent changing when stressed or tired and, occasionally, of starting to speak in a language that is not understood by those around them. These instances where lexical access appears compromised and control over language behavior is reduced hint at the intricate structure of the bilingual lexical architecture and the complexity of the processes by which knowledge is accessed and retrieved. While bilinguals might tend to blame word finding and other language problems on their bilinguality, these difficulties per se are not unique to the bilingual population. However, what is unique, and yet far more common than is appreciated by monolinguals, is the cognitive architecture that subserves bilingual language processing. With bilingualism (and multilingualism) the rule rather than the exception (Grosjean, 1982), this architecture may well be the default structure of the language processing system. As such, it is critical that we understand more fully not only how the processing of more than one language is subserved by the brain, but also how this understanding furthers our knowledge of the cognitive architecture that encapsulates the bilingual mental lexicon.

The neurolinguistic approach to bilingualism focuses on determining the manner in which the two (or more) languages are stored in the brain and how they are differentially (or similarly) processed. The underlying

1

assumption is that the acquisition of more than one language requires at the very least a change to or expansion of the existing lexicon, if not the formation of language-specific components, and this is likely to manifest in some way at the physiological level. There are many sources of information, ranging from data on bilingual aphasic patients (Paradis, 1977, 1985, 1997) to lateralization (Vaid, 1983; see Hull & Vaid, 2006, for a review), recordings of event-related potentials (ERPs) (e.g. Ardal *et al.*, 1990; Phillips *et al.*, 2006), and positron emission tomography (PET) and functional magnetic resonance imaging (fMRI) studies of neurologically intact bilinguals (see Indefrey, 2006; Vaid & Hull, 2002, for reviews). Following the consideration of methodological issues and interpretative limitations that characterize these approaches, the chapter focuses on how the application of these approaches has furthered our under-standing of (1) selectivity of bilingual lexical access, (2) distinctions between word types in the bilingual lexicon and (3) control processes that enable language selection.

1. Methodological Issues

Studies focusing on the neurophysiological correlates of bilingual language processing often are more concerned with localization and lateralization than with the consideration of how behavioral and physiological data converge to inform our understanding of the bilingual lexicon. (For reviews of select areas see Abutalebi *et al.*, 2005; Fabbro, 2001b; Hull & Vaid, 2005; Vaid & Hull, 2002.) Important insights have been gleaned from the closer observation of bilingual aphasics (Fabbro, 2001a; Paradis, 2004). In addition, a number of studies have provided PET and hemodynamic evidence, as well as ERP correlates, for lexical organization and access (e.g. De Bleser *et al.*, 2003; Phillips *et al.*, 2006), semantic organization (e.g. Halsband *et al.*, 2002) and issues of control (e.g. Rodriguez-Fornells *et al.*, 2006) in the bilingual lexicon. It is important to be mindful of the strengths and limitations of each approach and how they may be optimally applied.

1.1. Bilingual aphasia

Early forays into the bilingual brain intrigued us with descriptions of the many different recovery patterns observed in multilingual aphasia. For example, some patients demonstrated selective recovery of either the first learned or most familiar language (Pitres, 1895; see also Albert & Obler, 1978; Paradis, 1977, 1997). Others showed pathological switching between languages (Fabbro *et al.*, 2000) and selective, antagonistic recovery patterns (Aglioti *et al.*, 1996; Aglioti & Fabbro, 1993). Inferences drawn from aphasic deficits involve a reverse extrapolation to a(n assumed) premorbid state of intact linguistic functioning. However, often little is known about the patient's language history and consequently a retrospective comparison is potentially flawed. Such information is critically important because age and manner of acquisition, and premorbid language use and proficiency would have affected the patient's performance in each language post-injury.

Those concerns aside, the seductive aspect of this approach is that patterns of language performance (both intact and impaired) suggest selective damage to (or preservation of) one or more language components or processing pathways. Following a modular approach to cognitive architecture (cf. Fodor, 1983; Shallice, 1988), dissociations in performance can be taken to reflect an underlying cognitive architecture characterized by subcomponents that can be impaired selectively. However, it is difficult to determine the source of the cognitive deficit and which task components are adversely affected, because it is unclear whether the cause is a circumscribed lesion or more extensive damage, or whether the deficit results from abnormal functioning elsewhere or even reflects intact residual functioning in the lesioned area (see also Green & Price, 2001).

When testing bilingual aphasics, the degree of similarity between the languages spoken is often ignored and there is a tendency to use concrete items. Yet we know that concrete and abstract items are processed differently (e.g. De Groot & Nas, 1991; Dong *et al.*, 2005). An explicit comparison of bilingual aphasic performance on such items would yield important insights, and so would contrasting the processing of cognates and noncognates, also known to be differently represented (Sánchez-Casas & García-Albea, 2005). Cognates have been used in attempts to improve language functioning in bilingual aphasics, on the assumption that reinforcing cross-linguistic form and meaning overlap should encourage cross-linguistic generalization (e.g. Kohnert, 2004).

While studies of bilingual aphasia have provided valuable insights into localization of language function, they have been less immediately helpful in informing models of bilingual language processing. Case studies tend to be descriptive and the patterns of language performance observed often are not interpreted within an existing processing framework nor used to test the validity of any such framework (for a more detailed discussion, see Gollan & Kroll, 2001). Green and Price (2001) recommended combining the traditional clinical neurolinguistic approach with functional imaging, thus enabling a direct comparison of normal and aphasic bilinguals.

Importantly, the use of neuroimaging techniques reveals not only the regions involved in the execution of components of a task (without, however, being able to determine which regions are essential), but also the interaction between them. When applying this approach to patients, it becomes possible to ascertain (for example) whether the observed deficit is due to differences in neuronal areas recruited for the task or to the use of different cognitive strategies, or whether control of language performance is compromised because of deficits in neural areas believed to mediate such control (such as the anterior cingulate). Limitations aside, several case histories can be interpreted in the light of existing models of the bilingual lexicon and inform those same models.

1.2. ERPs and imaging studies

Valuable contributions have been made by imaging and ERP studies of bilingual language processing. Their comparison, however, is often limited by the heterogeneity of participants (in terms of proficiency, and age and manner of acquisition), the wide range of tasks used, the lack of appropriate comparison groups and the variety of languages spoken. Inconsistencies between PET and fMRI findings in particular may be due also to differences in technology.

In PET studies, data is averaged across participants. Findings are therefore more difficult to interpret and detail is lost in reduced spatial resolution. Thus, if regions of activation potentially correlated with distinct language components are anatomically close, it may not be possible to distinguish between them using PET. With fMRI, on the other hand, individual data can be considered and spatial resolution is superior (see Abutalebi *et al.*, 2005, for a review). A difficulty affecting hemodynamic methods generally is how to interpret increased (differential) activation. Is it just that, activation, or are inhibitory processes occurring elsewhere contributing to the pattern? (See also Fabbro, 2001b.) Furthermore, activation in a certain region does not *ipso facto* imply that the area is necessary for task execution nor does lack of (differential) activation imply lack of involvement. Subtraction methods may simply obscure the possibility that the same region might be implicated in several of the task components (cf. Green & Price, 2001). However, careful comparisons across tasks can reveal areas that are differentially active. Given existing knowledge about cognitive processes believed to be subserved by those areas and knowledge of the task components, converging evidence may be obtained for the existence of those components.

The particular strength of ERP scalp recordings is that they are online measures of brain activity that is directly (and temporally) linked to cognitive processes and allow the various properties of linguistic stimuli to be indexed. One primary language indicator is the N400, a negative ERP component with a central scalp distribution and a peak amplitude at approximately 400 ms after the appearance of a word. The N400 is used to index aspects of semantic processing in sentence context as well as that of individual words, within and between languages. In response to semantic violations, a larger (i.e. more negative) N400 is typically observed (e.g. Ardal *et al.*, 1990). Lexical aspects, such as word frequency, can also be indexed by N400, which is larger for words of lower frequency (Kutas & Van Petten, 1990). A repetition priming effect is captured in reduced N400 amplitudes (e.g. Rugg *et al.*, 1995). Another measure sometimes used is the phonological mismatch negativity (PMN), an ERP component with an earlier peak between 250 and 350 ms post stimulus-onset and elicited when phonological processing is carried out. Its distribution is more fronto-central (cf. Phillips *et al.*, 2006).

Form and meaning can be varied both within and between languages, and the careful evaluation of ERP components can determine whether these linguistic variations are processed differently. A phenomenon such as adaptation can be applied embedded in repetition priming within and between languages, allowing inferences to be drawn about the level at which words are processed by common or shared cognitive processes. This methodology is predicated on the demonstration that repetition of information results in attenuated neuronal responses. For example, neurons in the visual system reduce their response to repeated occurrences of the same stimulus (adaptation), but might fire as strongly to a repeat stimulus of which just one aspect has been changed (Grill-Spector & Malach, 2001). Useful insights have been gained using this technique (e.g. Phillips *et al.*, 2006).

1.3. Summary

Optimal information comes from converging evidence from different methodologies, especially where cognitive deficit due to a prescribed brain injury dovetails with activation in the same, undamaged region when the task is performed successfully in an intact person. But some caveats remain. Importantly, for these techniques to be maximally effective they should be combined with a thorough understanding of the cognitive underpinnings of the tasks to be performed and the research tools used. Careful evaluation of aphasic performance and use of ERP recordings and imaging techniques within a well-articulated cognitive framework can provide supporting evidence for the existence of distinct cognitive processes underlying bilingual task performance and further our knowledge regarding lexical access, word type distinction and control in the bilingual lexicon.

2. Selectivity of Bilingual Lexical Access

There is general consensus that bilingual lexical access is characterized by non-selectivity (e.g. De Groot *et al.*, 2000; Dijkstra & Van Heuven, 1998, 2002). Such non-selectivity has been found to operate for orthographic (e.g. De Groot & Nas, 1991) and phonological codes (e.g. Duyck, 2005; Jared & Kroll, 2001; Nas, 1983). More strikingly, even when the other language is not mentioned or used in the task, behavioral responses are affected (Dijkstra *et al.*, 2000).

One model that incorporates non-selective access is the Bilingual Interactive Activation (BIA) model (Dijkstra & Van Heuven, 1998). A model of bilingual word recognition, it assumes rich interconnectedness between lexical representations within and across languages, with bidirectional inhibitory and excitatory links between feature, letter, word and language levels. Candidate words are activated independently of language membership – the embodiment of non-selective lexical access. In an extension of the BIA model, BIA + (Dijkstra & Van Heuven, 2002), control over language selection is implemented via a task/decision system, a function previously assigned to language nodes. Instead, their function – together with orthography, phonology and semantics – is to indicate language membership. Integration across the different levels of representation further extends non-selective access beyond orthography.

Cross-linguistic effects are not always obtained (Gerard & Scarborough, 1989; Rodriguez-Fornells *et al.*, 2002; Scarborough *et al.*, 1984), an inconsistency easily explained by differences in tasks and materials used. For example, context effects (such as list composition and task demands) can constrain lexical access to a degree (cf. Dijkstra, 2005). Seemingly less easily accounted for is the cross-linguistic facilitatory effect of noncognate translation equivalents (Costa & Caramazza, 1999; Costa *et al.*, 1999; Gollan *et al.*, 2005). If inhibitory processes operate to enable the selection of a word in the appropriate language by deselecting the other language (as is assumed in the BIA model and Green's (1998) Inhibitory Control (IC) model), all words in the other language should be inhibited, including translation equivalents. The facilitation observed instead suggests selective access of only those entries that are specific to the required response language (for a critical discussion, see La Heij, 2005). Observations from bilingual aphasics, as well as neurophysiological data, have informed the debate to varying degrees.

2.1. Bilingual aphasia

Patterns of selective recovery reported throughout the literature (Fabbro, 2001a; Paradis, 1977) would suggest that the bilingual's languages are not only organized separately, but also accessed independently and selectively. However, a fair proportion of recovery patterns include cases with parallel recovery. Also, reports of involuntary switching in bilingual patients even when this is inappropriate (and known to be inappropriate even by the patients) suggest instead that lexical access is non-selective (Fabbro *et al.*, 2000; Goral *et al.*, 2006). Whichever word or phrase reaches selection threshold first is selected, the decision driven by content- rather than language-appropriateness. Control implications are discussed later in the chapter.

Some studies with bilingual aphasics, particularly those involving rehabilitation, use techniques that are premised on a bilingual lexicon that is at least partly integrated. Accordingly, it is possible to prime information in the other language through the use of cognates (Kohnert, 2004), although improvement in the trained language typically is more pronounced. Such findings suggest non-selectivity, in that information provided in L_A nonetheless activates associated L_B items. Treatment studies are not consistent in their findings (e.g. Galvez & Hinckley, 2003), however inconsistencies can be accounted for by differences in cross-linguistic overlap (Kohnert, 2004; Lalor & Kirsner, 2001b; Roberts & Deslauriers, 1999). Furthermore, recovery patterns may be affected by premorbid proficiency (Edmonds & Kiran, 2006). Recent ERP and fMRI studies provide further important contributions to this discussion.

2.2. Imaging studies and ERPs

Evidence from hemodynamic and ERP studies overwhelmingly supports the non-selective access position. For example, when fairly fluent Dutch–English bilinguals decided whether triplets of letter strings (e.g. *HOUSE-ANGEL-HEAVEN* versus *ZAAK* (business)-*ANGEL-HEAVEN*) were all legal words in English and/or Dutch (De Bruijn *et al.*, 2001), reliable N400 amplitude reductions for L2 targets (*HEAVEN*) primed by interlingual homographs (*ANGEL* (*sting* in Dutch)) indicated that the alternative L2 meaning also received automatic activation. While the language of the first word provided a uniquely English or Dutch context (e.g. *HOUSE* or *ZAAK* (business)), both readings of the homograph were activated, suggesting that language nodes merely tag language identity and a task/decision system exercises control (Dijkstra & Van Heuven, 2002).

Non-selective access was also seen when highly proficient Dutch–English bilinguals performed an English lexical decision task on interlingual homographs preceded by semantically related (*HEAVEN-ANGEL*) or unrelated (*HOUSE-ANGEL*) English primes (Kerkhofs *et al.*, 2006). Both reaction time (RT) and N400 patterns showed facilitation if the prime was semantically related to the target's reading in English but also in the irrelevant Dutch language. More revealingly, the degree of facilitation was affected by the frequency of the homograph's alternate readings. Greater effects were obtained for high frequency English readings and low frequency Dutch readings.

Yet further evidence for non-selectivity comes from a study of fluent English–French bilinguals who performed an auditory word repetition task and a translation priming task (Phillips *et al.*, 2006). Five-word sequences were presented in which the first four words were identical repetitions (R). The fifth word was identical (control), a translation equivalent (skirt (R)-*jupe*), or unrelated (skirt (R)-window) or related in meaning (skirt (R)-pants) and presented in the same or other language (skirt (R)-*pantalon*). For within language repetitions both the degree of adaptation and the N400 distribution were virtually identical for both languages. Translations from an L2 repeated sequence to the L1 (L2 → L1: backward translation) showed only a strong PMN effect, reflecting the lexical and phonological changes. The lack of an N400 effect indicated that when processing an L2 word, its L1 translation was activated. However, for forward translation (L1 → L2) the PMN/N400 pattern was similar to that observed for a change of meaning (and form) within L1, suggesting that neither the phonological form nor the conceptual representation of the L2 translation were accessed. Similar observations were made using fMRI adaptation (Klein *et al.*, 2006b).[1] The findings are indicative of automatic non-selective lexical access of L1 when processing L2, but not vice versa. Thus, at least in the auditory modality, non-selective access of L2 and L1 occurs but only when processing the weaker language. Lexical access therefore appears to be modulated by relative proficiency. Given these findings, it is conceivable that Kerkhofs *et al.* (2006) would have obtained a similar lack of facilitation of the homographs' L2 reading had the task been carried out in L1.

At first glance the aforementioned studies suggest a glaring inconsistency. However, whether or not L2 is automatically activated may have as much to do with task requirements as with the stimuli used. For example, on a language-specific go-no go task[2] with Catalan–Spanish bilinguals and Spanish-speaking monolinguals,[3] differences in N400 amplitude (increased for low frequency compared to high frequency items) revealed that only words in the target language were processed semantically (Rodriguez-Fornells *et al.*, 2002). No frequency effects were registered for words (all noncognates) from the non-target language, suggesting they were not processed beyond the orthographic stage. Thus, the language-specific nature of the stimuli (in contrast to the homographs used by Kerkhofs *et al.* (2006)) allowed early selection to occur. Consistent with the role of task control schemas (IC model) and the task/decision system (BIA+ model), a change in task, such as that used by De Bruijn *et al.* (2001), shows that information related to both languages is processed if both are important in carrying out the required task.

2.3. Summary

ERP and fMRI methodology, perhaps more so than studies of bilingual aphasia, have advanced our understanding of the extent to which meanings common to both languages are accessed in parallel and at which stage the selection is made. Important advances have been made through the combination of more rigorous experimental design, structured to test specific cognitive predictions. This approach should be continued and extended, with greater and consistent use of experimental paradigms that allow for neurolinguistic verification of the independent contribution of task demands and language-specific characteristics on lexical selection. Overwhelmingly the data favor non-selective access. However, cross-linguistic overlap, relative proficiency, as well as language context (see also Elston-Güttler *et al.*, 2005) may constrain lexical selection.

3. Word Type Distinctions

As regards the structure of the bilingual lexicon, the evidence favors common conceptual representations, with varied conceptual overlap across languages (e.g. De Groot, 1992a, 1992b, 2000; Francis, 2005; Poulisse, 1997). Initially it was assumed that the same conceptual representations were accessed for both languages, a reasonable assumption given evidence such as cross-linguistic semantic priming effects even with vastly differing orthographies (e.g. Chen & Ng, 1989). However, many of the earlier studies tended to use concrete nouns as stimuli, and we now know that there are important differences related to word type that have implications for representation at the semantic and conceptual level.[4]

An important framework for the investigation of word type distinctions is provided by the Distributed Feature model developed by De Groot and others (De Groot, 1992a, 1992b, 1993; De Groot & Comijs, 1995; Van Hell & De Groot, 1998a, 1998b, see also Kroll & De Groot, 1997). Here a distinction is made between concrete and abstract nouns, and between cognates and noncognates. Specifically, concrete nouns and cognates are more similar in meaning across languages. Consistent with these classifications, when the targets are concrete nouns or cognates, marked advantages have been found across a range of tasks for translation and recognition (e.g. Caramazza & Brones, 1979; De Groot, 1992a, 1992b; De Groot & Nas, 1991; Van Hell & De Groot, 1998a, 1998b). By contrast, the representation of abstract nouns (such as *honor*) is assumed to be largely determined by the context that, in bilinguals, can be dramatically different. An alternative model holds that cognates, by virtue of their shared morphology, are clustered in the lexicon, irrespective of language membership. Noncognates, in contrast, are lexically distributed (Kirsner *et al.*, 1993). Importantly, meaning further determines organization (Lalor & Kirsner, 2001a). The main question centers on whether the linguistic functions of the words determine how they are represented lexically.

No explicit claims are made about other classes of words, such as the noun/verb distinctions, that have been reported in monolinguals (e.g. De Bleser & Kauschke, 2003; Luzzatti *et al.*, 2006). Determining the psychological reality of these in bilinguals is complicated by the fact that, depending on the languages in question, a number of words might cross noun-verb classes and may or may not share meaning (e.g. *wave* (as in *to wave* or *a wave* in the sea, different meanings) versus *sleep* (both a verb and a noun, related meanings)). In addition, proficiency variably affects processing and, in bilinguals, is reflected in the underlying conceptual representations for verbs (Segalowitz & de Almeida, 2002). Neurolinguistic evidence has shed further light on the psychological reality of word type distinctions.

3.1. Bilingual aphasia

Studies that have used paradigms involving verb generation from nouns or have looked at processing differences between nouns and verbs in patients are few, but these few do indicate a distinction. One report shows an early, highly proficient bilingual Catalan–Spanish Alzheimer patient, LPM, to be similarly impaired in both languages in naming line drawings (e.g. *broom*) compared to generating the associated verb (e.g. *sweeping*) (Hernández *et al.*, 2007). A similar dissociation did not occur in comprehension, suggesting that (1) conceptual representations were intact and accessed equally in both languages and (2) a lexically-based distinction exists between nouns and verbs. Similarly, when cued with sign language, a bilingual British sign language (BSL)-English user, Maureen, was able to produce spoken English nouns but not verbs (Marshall *et al.*, 2005).

Cognate status did not affect performance in L1 for LPM (Hernández *et al.*, 2007), but there was a non-significant tendency for better performance with cognates in L2, a pattern consistent with Phillips *et al.* (2006). A cognate effect is found in bilingual aphasic patients (e.g. Ferrand & Humphreys, 1996) and training with cognates facilitates recovery in bilingual aphasia (Kohnert, 2004), suggesting shared word characteristics. Lalor and Kirsner (2001b) similarly showed superior performance in a multilingual aphasic (L1 Greek), tested in Italian and English. English, but not Italian, was formally acquired. Naming and lexical decision performance was superior for cognates. However, while these studies support a cognate/noncognate distinction, the relative contribution of shared meaning, orthography and phonology has not as yet been determined.

Evidence for an abstract/concrete distinction is also not unequivocal. For example, when asked to translate bidirectionally between pairs of his three languages (L1 Hebrew, L2 English and L3 French), a trilingual aphasic, EC, showed longer RTs for abstract (as compared to concrete) words, but only when translating from L2 to L1 (Goral *et al.*, 2006). It should be noted that, while the concrete words crossed word classes (e.g. *hammer*), the abstract words did not and also had unique meanings (e.g. *truth*). Here again we see the pattern repeated of non-selective access but only for backward translation (consistent with Phillips *et al.*, 2006).

Aphasic evidence then supports a distinction between concrete nouns and verbs, and between cognates and noncognates. Any distinction between abstract and concrete words must be classified by indexing conceptual equivalence across languages (Goral *et al.*, 2006; Kroll & Tokowicz, 2001) and so too for cognates. In drawing any conclusions from the data, factors such as relative premorbid proficiency as well as cross-linguistic overlap must be taken into consideration.

3.2. Imaging studies and ERPs

While evidence from PET and fMRI studies provides support for common conceptual representations across languages – as inferred from marked similarities in cortical activation and distribution (Chee *et al.*, 2000, 2003; Halsband *et al.*, 2002; Illes *et al.*, 1999; Klein *et al.*, 1999) – few studies allow us to determine distinctions between classes of words. Often data is averaged across word types (e.g. Illes *et al.*, 1999), the focus is on grammatical function (Ullman, 2006; Weber-Fox & Neville, 2001) or predominantly concrete nouns are used (e.g. Chee *et al.*, 2000, 2001; Klein *et al.*, 2006b).

A notable exception is a PET study with fairly proficient Flemish–French bilinguals in Belgium who covertly named pictures with cognate or noncognate labels separately in each language (De Bleser *et al.*, 2003). Activation patterns revealed differences only for noncognate naming in the weaker L2, specifically in the ventral and dorsal regions of the left inferior frontal gyrus and anteriorally to the inferotemporal region, believed to reflect greater difficulty in L2 lexical retrieval post-semantically. However, as the authors point out, it is conceivable also that the L2 noncognates might be less well defined conceptually. Furthermore, although naming accuracy during the PET phase could not be established, the behavioral data showed marked differences in L2 naming efficiency, especially for noncognates, suggesting that many lexical entries did not exist or were accessible only via direct connections with their L1 counterparts (cf. Kroll & Stewart, 1994). Importantly, however, the lack of any differences for cognates suggests that these are similarly represented across languages (De Groot, 1993).

Evidence regarding the concrete/abstract distinction is inconclusive. For example, when late Finnish–English bilinguals memorized and verbally recalled pairs of unrelated words (both either highly imageable or abstract) separately in both languages, memory retrieval in both languages and for both word types was associated with similar levels of bilateral prefrontal as well as precuneus activation and, in L1, Broca's area was equally activated (Halsband *et al.*, 2002). Thus, both word types appear to be processed similarly, in direct contrast with other observations (De Groot, 1993). However, the task used here was not explicitly designed to look at word type effects and the use of PET may have failed to capture more subtle differences as could be measured using ERPs.

3.3. Summary

With respect to the nature of lexical representations then, neurolinguistic evidence supports the cognate/noncognate distinction. Recent behavioral evidence suggests that their representation in the lexicon might best be characterized as based on morphological similarities (Lalor

& Kirsner, 2001a; Sánchez-Casas & García-Albea, 2005), but as yet there is no neurolinguistic evidence to support this contention. Evidence supporting verb/noun distinctions is thus far restricted to studies of bilingual aphasia, while the abstract/concrete distinction is not unequivocally supported. Future research could explore further the representation of different word types in bilingual lexical organization through the systematic evaluation of semantic, phonological, orthographic, morphological and functional components.

4. Control in Language Selection

The importance of control over language selection is most obvious when bilinguals inadvertently switch between languages. Such involuntary intrusions can be accounted for by differences in levels of activation across languages (e.g. Poulisse & Bongaerts, 1994), however some form of top-down control is required to enable the willed selection of a response in L_A and to minimize interference from L_B. The way in which language selection is accomplished is perhaps best set out in the IC model (Green, 1986, 1993, 1998). Other, equally relevant models have been proposed by De Bot and colleagues (De Bot, 1992; De Bot & Schreuder, 1993) and by Poulisse and colleagues (Poulisse, 1997; Poulisse & Bongaerts, 1994). (For a recent discussion, see La Heij, 2005.)

Within the IC model, control is exerted through the inhibition of the 'other language' task schema when speaking L_A. Upon a switch back to L_B, this generalized inhibition of L_A must be undone, a process associated with a measurable cost. Behavioral evidence supports this idea (Costa & Santesteban, 2004; Meuter & Allport, 1999), showing language switch costs directly related to relative proficiency: a paradoxically larger cost is observed when switching back to the stronger L1. The lack of similar asymmetry for L1/L3 switches in fluent (early) bilinguals prompted the suggestion that these bilinguals had developed a control ability to facilitate language switching generally (Costa & Santesteban, 2004; Costa *et al.*, 2006). However, confounds between age of acquisition (AoA) and relative proficiency effects make it difficult to determine the relative importance of either factor (but see Meuter & Milner, 2007).

It is nonetheless conceivable that bilingual language control relies on a select set of cognitive processes that are better honed or perhaps altogether different (as determined by AoA or proficiency) because of increased multiple language use. (See also Rodriguez-Fornells *et al.* (2006) for a recent review.) Ideally, comparisons should be made between early and late proficient and nonproficient bilinguals on a range of cognitive tasks, including language selection and switching tasks. Given the evidence that the processing of languages with very different characteristics in either phonological realization (e.g. Klein *et al.*, 2001; Tham *et al.*, 2005) or orthographic representation (Gollan *et al.*, 1997) appear to activate different cortical areas, it is conceivable that individuals regularly controlling such disparate languages might show qualitatively different control abilities. When orthography unambiguously cues language, reduced interference is experienced in a Stroop task (Fang *et al.*, 1981) and significantly smaller switch costs are experienced (Meuter & Tan, 2003). Whether such advantages result from increased control ability, over and above a language-specificity effect, might be resolved by the inclusion of alinguistic switch tasks. Comparisons across studies (e.g. Tan *et al.*, 2001; Tham *et al.*, 2005) reveal differences between monolinguals and bilinguals when processing similar tasks, suggesting that experience impacts differentially on brain organization. The question to be asked is whether available neurolinguistic evidence can distinguish between the possible solutions offered to account for selection.

4.1. Bilingual aphasia

The importance of control processes is highlighted in bilingual aphasic patients. Fabbro *et al.* (2000) reported on a Friulan–Italian patient who, while linguistically intact and fully conscious of which language to speak, was nonetheless unable to control his language output (similar cases of uncontrolled language switching have been reported by Aglioti *et al.*, 1996; Fabbro, 1999). One recovery pattern, alternate antagonism with paradoxical translation (Paradis *et al.*, 1982), further suggests that the language usage pattern may be related primarily to changes in accessibility. Green's (1998) IC model accounts for such patterns by assuming that what is lost is the ability to wilfully control language selection (and not the language itself).

Unfortunately, patient reports are often incomplete and primarily descriptive, making it difficult to interpret the deficits. One notable attempt to move beyond the descriptive level was a detailed discussion of patient EM (Gollan & Kroll, 2001), previously described by Aglioti and colleagues (Aglioti *et al.*, 1996; Aglioti & Fabbro, 1993). EM, bilingual in Venetian (a spoken Italian dialect) and Italian (acquired formally but used infrequently), showed relatively intact performance in L2 Italian while her ability to use the L1 was markedly impaired. Specifically, contrary to normal bilingual performance, EM was better at forward translation (L1 to L2). Partial damage to a control mechanism could account for this pattern, because EM showed evidence of paradoxical translation (still requiring some access to L1) of which one explanation could be the incomplete inhibition of L1. However, given the possibility that manner of acquisition might determine how grammatical and lexical aspects of language are represented (Paradis, 2004; Ullman, 2001), it is conceivable that, for EM, preinjury control processes favored forward translation and what we observe is intact functioning. Only a comparison with adequate controls would help resolve this issue.

Such comparisons were made for an English–Urdu bilingual non-aphasic frontal lobe patient, FK (Meuter *et al.*, 2002). While perfectly able to name Arabic numerals in either language in a number-naming task, FK made a number of errors when required to switch languages, especially when L2 was the required response language. FK instead produced a significant number of erroneous responses in L1, many more than the bilingual controls. This error pattern, combined with a normal RT pattern, suggests that FK's monitoring ability was compromised. He was no longer able to control and inhibit responses from the stronger L1 when L2 needed to be spoken.

4.2. Imaging studies and ERPs

Patterns of brain activity similarly reveal relative control in bilingual language selection. Not surprisingly, changes in task requirements, stimuli and relative proficiency determine the patterns observed. For example, English–Spanish bilinguals showed no differences in the processing of English codeswitched sentences and unilingual English sentences (Moreno *et al.*, 2002). The codeswitched data showed less of a cost (as indexed by N400) than did lexical (within-language) switches. These data do not suggest increased control implications for bilinguals, at least not in comprehension, however greater proficiency in L2 Spanish allowed the earlier detection of a switch and facilitated its processing.

The pattern changes when voluntary and deliberate shifts of language are made. Two fMRI studies of Spanish–English bilinguals by Hernandez and colleagues (Hernandez *et al.*, 2000, 2001) revealed increased dorsolateral prefrontal activity when switching between languages. Importantly, Hernandez *et al.* (2001) found that this increased activation was less marked when executing a within-language switch task. These results suggest that the need to prevent interference from a competing language requires additional executive control processing (see also Price *et al.*, 1999; Rinne *et al.*, 2000; Rodriguez-Fornells *et al.*, 2006). Consistent herewith, increased activation was found in the inferior frontal regions for speakers who needed to operate in a language-selective manner (Rodriguez-Fornells *et al.*, 2002). Importantly, this increased activation was observed only for those speakers for whom the two languages were part of the task.

In a recent study using magneto-encephalography (MEG), Bialystok *et al.* (2005) found evidence relating speeded responses to somewhat different brain regions in bilinguals (mostly left hemisphere inferior and superior frontal regions, as well as cingulate and temporal regions) compared to monolinguals (mid-frontal), suggesting the possibility that executive function and control in bilinguals is at the very least enhanced if not developed somewhat differently. In some cases, activation of areas (such as those in the frontal lobes) has been related explicitly to differences in relative proficiency in the two languages, with poorer proficiency requiring greater control for task execution (e.g. Chee *et al.*, 2001). While AoA and proficiency were confounded here, recent findings suggest that greater proficiency results in organic changes (Mechelli *et al.*, 2004). It is therefore conceivable that changes in control ability may extend beyond greater efficiency generally.

4.3. Summary

Overwhelmingly the data support an account such as that provided by the IC model (Green, 1998). Neurolinguistic evidence points at control processes regulating bilingual performance. Comparing bilingual tasks with monolingual ones revealed differences specifically related to language selection (Hernandez *et al.*, 2001). However, comparative studies are required, with the inclusion of alinguistic switching tasks, to determine whether the apparent superior control ability is unique to bilinguals and how it is affected by proficiency, age and/or manner of acquisition. Only then will we be able to determine whether bilinguals refine and hone general purpose control processes that provide cognitive advantage (e.g. Bialystok *et al.*, 2004), or whether these control processes are unique to bilinguals. Few studies directly compare bilinguals with monolinguals, thus making it difficult to draw inferences about additional processes recruited for bilingual language processing (but see Tham *et al.*, 2005). Also, to date, studies focus more globally on control over language per se, rather than more specifically on control of components of language processing (see also Gollan & Kroll, 2001).

Conclusions

Neurolinguistic research, when combined with tight experimental control, provides a powerful means to obtain convergent evidence for the structure of the bilingual mental lexicon. Data from bilingual aphasia, as well as recording and imaging techniques, simultaneously increase our understanding of the processes that underlie the observed behavior and suggest other avenues of exploration.

The available evidence supports the non-selective access account, even for nonproficient bilinguals. Importantly, the data confirms that translation equivalents and alternate meanings are activated (e.g. De Bruijn *et al.*, 2001; Phillips *et al.*, 2006). That this occurs when bilinguals are passively listening to words demonstrates the highly interactive nature of the lexicon and underscores the importance of bottom-up processing as incorporated in the BIA+ model (Dijkstra & van Heuven, 2002). The asymmetrical effects seen with nonproficient bilinguals support one of the central assumptions in the Revised Hierarchical (RH) Model (cf. Kroll & Tokowicz, 2005) in which low L2 proficiency is reflected in direct lexical connections with L1 equivalents. However, contrary to the tenets of that model, conceptual representations were also activated (Phillips *et al.*, 2006), and it is clear that both relative proficiency and cross-linguistic overlap constrain lexical selection.

The cognate/noncognate distinction is the one typically used to determine lexical overlap, but studies have largely been confined to related languages and have not considered phonological effects. Rather than focusing on the cognate/noncognate distinction, a more fruitful approach might be to use cross-linguistic homographs, homophones or even pseudohomophones (e.g. Duyck, 2005). The distinction between abstract and concrete items received no support: one issue there might be the difficulty in controlling for other embedded word type effects (e.g. noun-verb cross-overs). Morphological effects with cognates (Lalor & Kirsner, 2001a; Sánchez-Casas & García-Albea, 2005) suggest that other factors might determine the uniqueness of specific classes of items and the inclusion of such items as part of the stimuli would shed further light on this issue.

There is much scope for more directed research into the control processes subserving language selection. At present we cannot be certain that the observed patterns are unique to bilinguals and represent the formation of fundamentally different control processes, or whether existing control processes are simply better honed. It is likely that a range of factors impact on the development of such control processes and where they are specific to language they are likely to be determined by age and manner of acquisition, relative proficiency, language use and linguistic overlap. The data fairly consistently point to proficiency as the determining factor in efficient language use (e.g. Phillips *et al.*, 2006; but see Kotz & Elston-Güttler, 2004).

Green and Price (2001) cogently argue for an approach that applies imaging methodology to the study of bilingual aphasics and a few have moved in that direction (e.g. Meinzer *et al.*, 2007). When doing so it is critical that the tasks used are well understood, both at a cognitive and a neurophysiological level, and a clear theoretical framework is applied. Of equal importance is the inclusion of appropriate controls. Particularly when testing patients, a comparison with intact matched bilinguals is invaluable but such controls are mostly lacking. Only when these measures are taken can assumptions about the structure of the bilingual lexicon be tested and challenged.

Notes

1. This finding is inconsistent with the RH model (Kroll & Stewart, 1994), where the processing of the weaker L2 – in nonproficient bilinguals – is believed to occur via direct lexical connections with L1.
2. The language-specific go-no go task requires bilinguals to press a button to words in one language while ignoring pseudowords and words in the other language.
3. N.B. All participants were recruited from German universities. It follows that German was mastered to some degree of competency to allow university-level studies, effectively rendering the bilinguals trilingual and the mono-linguals bilingual (see also Dijkstra & Van Heuven, 2006; Grosjean *et al.*, 2003). The trilinguals used their two stronger languages, while the bilinguals used only L1.
4. Not included is the representation of emotion words in the bilingual lexicon (Altarriba & Bauer, 2004).

References

Abutalebi, J., Cappa, S. and Perani, D. (2005) What can functional neuroimaging tell us about the bilingual brain? In J. Kroll and A.M.B. De Groot (eds) *Handbook of Bilingualism: Psycholinguistic Approaches* (pp. 497–515). Oxford: Oxford University Press.

Aglioti, S., Beltramello, A., Girardi, F. and Fabbro, F. (1996) Neurolinguistic and follow-up study of an unusual pattern of recovery from bilingual subcortical aphasia. *Brain* 119, 1551–1564.

Aglioti, S. and Fabbro, F. (1993) Paradoxical selective recovery in a bilingual aphasic following subcortical lesions. *NeuroReport* 4, 1359–1362.

Albert, M. and Obler, L. (1978) *The Bilingual Brain: Neurophysiological and Neurolinguistic Aspects of Bilingualism*. New York: Academic Press.

Altarriba, J. and Bauer, L. (2004) The distinctiveness of emotion concepts: A comparison between emotion, abstract, and concrete words. *American Journal of Psychology* 117 (3), 389–410.

Ardal, S., Donald, M., Meuter, R., Muldrew, S. and Luce, M. (1990) Brain responses to semantic incongruity in bilinguals. *Brain and Language* 39 (2), 187–205.

Bialystok, E., Craik, F.I.M., Grady, C., Chau, W., Ishii, R., Gunji, A. *et al.* (2005) Effect of bilingualism on cognitive control in the Simon task: Evidence from MEG. *NeuroImage* 24 (1), 40–49.

Bialystok, E., Craik, F., Klein, R. and Viswanathan, M. (2004) Bilingualism, aging, and cognitive control: Evidence from the Simon task. *Psychology and Aging* 19 (2), 290–303.

Caramazza, A. and Brones, I. (1979) Lexical access in bilinguals. *Bulletin of the Psychonomic Society* 13, 212–214.

Chee, M.W.L., Hon, N., Lee, H.L. and Soon, C.S. (2001) Relative language proficiency modulates BOLD signal change when bilinguals perform semantic judgements. *NeuroImage* 13 (6, Supplement 1), 1155–1163.

Chee, M.W., Soon, C.S. and Lee, H.L. (2003) Common and segregated neuronal networks for different languages revealed using functional magnetic resonance adaptation. *Journal of Cognitive Neuroscience* 15 (1), 85–97.

Chee, M.W.L., Weekes, B., Lee, K.M., Soon, C.S., Schreiber, A., Hoon, J.J. *et al.* (2000) Overlap and dissociation of semantic processing of Chinese characters, English words, and pictures: Evidence from fMRI. *NeuroImage* 12 (4), 392–403.

Chen, H.C. and Ng, N.L. (1989) Semantic facilitation and translation priming effects in Chinese-English bilinguals. *Memory & Cognition* 17, 454–462.

Costa, A. and Caramazza, A. (1999) Is lexical selection in bilingual speech production language-specific? Further evidence from Spanish-English and English-Spanish bilinguals. *Bilingualism: Language and Cognition* 2 (3), 231–244.

Costa, A., Miozzo, M. and Caramazza, A. (1999) Lexical selection in bilinguals: Do words in the bilingual's two lexicons compete for selection? *Journal of Memory and Language* 41 (3), 365–397.

Costa, A. and Santesteban, M. (2004) Lexical access in bilingual speech production: Evidence from language switching in highly proficient bilinguals and L2 learners. *Journal of Memory and Language* 50 (4), 491–511.

Costa, A., Santesteban, M. and Ivanova, I. (2006) How do highly proficient bilinguals control their lexicalization process? Inhibitory and language-specific selection mechanisms are both functional. *Journal of Experimental Psychology: Learning Memory and Cognition* 32 (5), 1057–1074.

De Bleser, R., Dupont, P., Postler, J., Bormans, G., Speelman, D., Mortelmans, L. *et al.* (2003) The organization of the bilingual lexicon: A PET study. *Journal of Neurolinguistics* 16 (4), 439–456.

De Bleser, R. and Kauschke, C. (2003) Acquisition and loss of nouns and verbs: Parallel or divergent patterns? *Journal of Neurolinguistics* 16 (2/3), 213.

De Bot, K. (1992) A bilingual production model: Levelt's speaking model adapted. *Applied Linguistics* 13, 1–24.

De Bot, K. and Schreuder, R. (1993) Word production and the bilingual lexicon. In R. Schreuder and B. Weltens (eds) *The Bilingual Lexicon* (pp. 191–214). Amsterdam: John Benjamins.

De Bruijn, E., Dijkstra, T., Chwilla, D. and Schriefers, H. (2001) Language context effects on interlingual homograph recognition: Evidence from event-related potentials and response times in semantic priming. *Bilingualism: Language and Cognition* 4 (2), 155–168.

De Groot, A.M.B. (1992a) Bilingual lexical representation: A closer look at conceptual representations. In R. Frost and L. Katz (eds) *Orthography, Phonology, Morphology, and Meaning* (pp. 389–412). Amsterdam: Elsevier.

De Groot, A.M.B. (1992b) Determinants of word translation. *Journal of Experimental Psychology: Learning, Memory, and Cognition* 18 (5), 1001–1018.

De Groot, A.M.B. (1993) Word-type effects in bilingual processing tasks: Support for a mixed-representational system. In R. Schreuder and B. Weltens (eds) *The Bilingual Lexicon* (pp. 27–51). Amsterdam: John Benjamins.

De Groot, A.M.B. (2000) On the source and nature of semantic and conceptual knowledge. *Bilingualism: Language and Cognition* 3 (1), 7–9.

De Groot, A.M.B. and Comijs, H. (1995) Translation recognition and translation production: Comparing a new and an old tool in the study of bilingualism. *Language Learning* 45 (3), 467–509.

De Groot, A.M.B., Delmaar, P. and Lupker, S. (2000) The processing of interlexical homographs in translation recognition and lexical decision: Support for non-selective access to bilingual memory. *Quarterly Journal of Experimental Psychology. A, Human Experimental Psychology* 53 (2), 397–428.

De Groot, A.M.B. and Nas, G.L.J. (1991) Lexical representation of cognates and noncognates in compound bilinguals. *Journal of Memory and Language* 30 (1), 90–123.

Dijkstra, T. (2005) Bilingual visual word recognition and lexical access. In J. Kroll and A.M.B. De Groot (eds) *Handbook of Bilingualism: Psycholinguistic Approaches* (pp. 179–201). Oxford: Oxford University Press.

Dijkstra, T., Timmermans, M. and Schriefers, H. (2000) On being blinded by your other language: Effects of task demands on interlingual homograph recognition. *Journal of Memory and Language* 42 (4), 445–464.

Dijkstra, T. and Van Heuven, W.J.B. (1998) The BIA model and bilingual word recognition. In J. Grainger and A. Jacobs (eds) *Localist Connectionist Approaches to Human Cognition* (pp. 189–225). Hillsdale, NJ: Lawrence Erlbaum.

Dijkstra, T. and Van Heuven, W.J.B. (2002) The architecture of the bilingual word recognition system: From identification to decision. *Bilingualism: Language and Cognition* 5, 175–197.

Dijkstra, T. and Van Heuven, W.J.B. (2006) On language and the brain – Or on (psycho)linguists and neuroscientists? Commentary on Rodriguez-Fornells *et al. Language Learning* 56 (1), 191–198.

Dong, Y., Gui, S. and MacWhinney, B. (2005) Shared and separate meanings in the bilingual mental lexicon. *Bilingualism: Language and Cognition* 8 (3), 221–238.

Duyck, W. (2005) Translation and associative priming with cross-lingual pseudohomophones: Evidence for nonselective phonological activation in bilinguals. *Journal of Experimental Psychology: Learning, Memory, and Cognition* 31 (6), 1340–1359.

Edmonds, L.A. and Kiran, S. (2006) Effect of semantic naming treatment on crosslinguistic generalization in bilingual aphasia. *Journal of Speech, Language, and Hearing Research* 49 (4), 729–748.

Elston-Güttler, K., Gunter, T. and Kotz, S. (2005) Zooming into L2: Global language context and adjustment affect processing of interlingual homographs in sentences. *Cognitive Brain Research* 25 (1), 57–70.

Fabbro, F. (1999) *The Neurolinguistics of Bilingualism*. Hove, UK: Psychology Press.

Fabbro, F. (2001a) The bilingual brain: Bilingual aphasia. *Brain and Language* 79 (2), 201–210.

Fabbro, F. (2001b) The bilingual brain: Cerebral representation of languages. *Brain and Language* 79 (2), 211–222.

Fabbro, F., Skrap, M. and Aglioti, S. (2000) Pathological switching between languages following frontal lobe lesion in a bilingual patient. *Journal of Neurology, Neurosurgery, and Psychiatry* 68, 650–652.

Fang, S.P., Tzeng, O.J. and Alva, L. (1981) Interlanguage versus interlanguage Stroop effects in two types of writing systems. *Memory & Cognition* 9, 609–617.

Ferrand, L. and Humphreys, G. (1996) Transfer of refractory states across languages in a global aphasic patient. *Cognitive Neuropsychology* 13, 1163–1191.

Fodor, J. (1983) *The Modularity of Mind*. Cambridge, MA: MIT Press.

Francis, W. (2005) Bilingual semantic and conceptual representation. In J. Kroll and A.M.B. de Groot (eds) *Handbook of Bilingualism: Psycholinguistic Approaches* (pp. 251–267). Oxford: Oxford University Press.

Galvez, A. and Hinckley, J. (2003) Transfer patterns of naming treatment in a case of bilingual aphasia. *Brain and Language* 87 (1), 173–174.

Gerard, L. and Scarborough, D. (1989) Language-specific access of homographs by bilinguals. *Journal of Experimental Psychology: Learning, Memory, and Cognition* 15, 305–315.

Gollan, T., Forster, K. and Frost, R. (1997) Translation priming with different scripts: Masked priming with cognates and noncognates in Hebrew-English bilinguals. *Journal of Experimental Psychology: Learning, Memory, and Cognition* 23 (5), 1122–1139.

Gollan, T. and Kroll, J. (2001) Bilingual lexical access. In B. Rapp (ed.) *The Handbook of Cognitive Neuropsychology: What Deficits Reveal about the Human Mind* (pp. 321–345). Philadelphia, PA: Psychology Press.

Gollan, T., Montoya, R., Fennema-Notestine, C. and Morris, S. (2005) Bilingualism affects picture naming but not picture classification. *Memory & Cognition* 33 (7), 1220–1234.

Goral, M., Levy, E., Obler, L. and Cohen, E. (2006) Cross-language lexical connections in the mental lexicon: Evidence from a case of trilingual aphasia. *Brain and Language* 98 (2), 235–247.

Green, D. (1986) Control, activation, and resource: A framework and a model for the control of speech in bilinguals. *Brain and Language* 27 (2), 210–223.

Green, D. (1993) Towards a model of L2 comprehension and production. In R. Schreuder and B. Weltens (eds) *The Bilingual Lexicon* (pp. 249–277). Amsterdam: John Benjamins.

Green, D. (1998) Mental control of the bilingual lexico-semantic system. *Bilingualism: Language and Cognition* 1 (2), 67–81.

Green, D. and Price, C. (2001) Functional imagining in the study of recovery patterns in bilingual aphasia. *Bilingualism: Language and Cognition* 4 (2), 191–201.

Grill-Spector, K. and Malach, R. (2001) fMRI-adaptation: A tool for studying the functional properties of human cortical neurons. *Acta Psychologica* 107, 293–321.

Grosjean, F. (1982) *Life with Two Languages: An Introduction to Bilingualism.* Cambridge, MA: Harvard University Press.

Grosjean, F., Li, P., Münte, T. and Rodriguez-Fornells, A. (2003) Imaging bilinguals: When the neurosciences meet the language sciences. *Bilingualism: Language and Cognition* 6 (2), 159–165.

Halsband, U., Krause, B., Sipilä, H., Teräs, M. and Laihinen, A. (2002) PET studies on the memory processing of word pairs in bilingual Finnish-English subjects. *Behavioral Brain Research* 132 (1), 47–57.

Hernandez, A.E., Martinez, A. and Kohnert, K. (2000) In search of the language switch: An fMRI study of picture naming in Spanish-English bilinguals. *Brain and Language* 73 (3), 421–431.

Hernandez, A.E., Dapretto, M., Mazziotta, J. and Bookheimer, S. (2001) Language switching and language representation in Spanish-English bilinguals: An fMRI study. *NeuroImage* 14 (2), 510–520.

Hernández, M., Costa, A., Sebastián-Gallés, N., Juncadella, M. and Reñé, R. (2007) The organization of nouns and verbs in bilingual speakers: A case of bilingual grammatical category-specific deficit. *Journal of Neurolinguistics* 20 (4), 285–305.

Hull, R. and Vaid, J. (2005) Clearing the cobwebs from the study of the bilingual brain: Converging evidence from laterality and electrophysiological research. In J. Kroll and A.M.B. de Groot (eds) *Handbook of Bilingualism: Psycholinguistic Approaches* (pp. 480–496). Oxford: Oxford University Press.

Hull, R. and Vaid, J. (2006) Laterality and language experience. *Laterality* 11 (5), 436–464.

Illes, J., Francis, W., Desmond, J., Gabrieli, J., Glover, G., Poldrack, R. *et al.* (1999) Convergent cortical representation of semantic processing in bilinguals. *Brain and Language* 70 (3), 347–363.

Indefrey, P. (2006) A meta-analysis of hemodynamic studies on first and second language processing: Which suggested differences can we trust and what do they mean? *Language Learning* 56, 279–304.

Jared, D. and Kroll, J. (2001) Do bilinguals activate phonological representations in one or both of their languages when naming words? *Journal of Memory and Language* 44 (1), 2–31.

Kerkhofs, R., Dijkstra, T., Chwilla, D. and de Bruijn, E. (2006) Testing a model for bilingual semantic priming with interlingual homographs: RT and N400 effects. *Brain Research* 1068 (1), 170–183.

Kirsner, K., Lalor, E. and Hird, K. (1993) The bilingual lexicon: Exercise, meaning and morphology. In R. Schreuder and B. Weltens (eds) *The Bilingual Lexicon* (pp. 215–248). Amsterdam: John Benjamins.

Klein, D., Milner, B., Zatorre, R., Zhao, V. and Nikelski, J. (1999) Cerebral organization in bilinguals: A PET study of Chinese-English verb generation. *Neuroreport: For Rapid Communication of Neuroscience Research* 10 (13), 2841–2846.

Klein, D., Zatorre, R.J., Milner, B. and Zhao, V. (2001) A cross-linguistic PET study of tone perception in Mandarin Chinese and English speakers. *NeuroImage* 13 (4), 646–653.

Klein, D., Watkins, K., Zatorre, R.J. and Milner, B. (2006a) Word and nonword repetition in bilingual subjects: A PET study. *Human Brain Mapping* 27 (2), 153–161.

Klein, D., Zatorre, R., Chen, J-K., Milner, B., Crane, J., Belin, P. *et al.* (2006b) Bilingual brain organization: A functional magnetic resonance adaptation study. *NeuroImage* 31 (1), 366–375.

Kohnert, K. (2004) Cognitive and cognate-based treatments for bilingual aphasia: A case study. *Brain and Language* 91 (3), 294–302.

Kotz, S. and Elston-Güttler, K. (2004) The role of proficiency on processing categorical and associative information in the L2 as revealed by reaction times and event-related brain potentials. *Journal of Neurolinguistics* 17 (2–3), 215–235.

Kroll, J. and De Groot, A.M.B. (1997) Lexical and conceptual memory in the bilingual: Mapping form to meaning in two languages. In A.M.B. De Groot and J. Kroll (eds) *Tutorials in Bilingualism: Psycholinguistic Perspectives* (pp. 169–199). Mahwah, NJ: Lawrence Erlbaum.

Kroll, J. and Stewart, E. (1994) Category interference in translation and picture naming: Evidence for asymmetric connection between bilingual memory representations. *Journal of Memory and Language* 33 (2), 149–174.

Kroll, J. and Tokowicz, N. (2001) The development of conceptual representation for words in a second language. In J. Nicol (ed.) *One Mind, Two Languages: Bilingual Language Processing* (pp. 49–71). Oxford: Blackwell.

Kroll, J. and Tokowicz, N. (2005) Models of bilingual representation and processing: Looking back and to the future. In J. Kroll and A.M.B. De Groot (eds) *Handbook of Bilingualism: Psycholinguistic Approaches* (pp. 531–553). Oxford: Oxford University Press.

Kutas, M. and Van Petten, C. (1990) Electrophysiological perspectives on comprehending written language. In P. Rossini and F. Mauguiere (eds) *New Trends and Advanced Techniques in Clinical Neurophysiology. Journal of Electroencephalography and Clinical Neurophysiology* Supplement 41, 155–167. Amsterdam: Elsevier.

La Heij, W. (2005) Selection processes in monolingual and bilingual lexical access. In J. Kroll and A.M.B. De Groot (eds) *Handbook of Bilingualism: Psycholinguistic Approaches* (pp. 289–307). Oxford: Oxford University Press.

Lalor, E. and Kirsner, K. (2001a) The representation of 'false cognates' in the bilingual lexicon. *Psychonomic Bulletin & Review* 8 (3), 552–559.

Lalor, E. and Kirsner, K. (2001b) The role of cognates in bilingual aphasia: Implications for assessment and treatment. *Aphasiology* 15 (10–11), 1047–1056.

Luzzatti, C., Aggujaro, S. and Crepaldi, D. (2006) Verb-noun double dissociation in aphasia: Theoretical and neuroanatomical foundations. *Cortex* 42 (6), 875–883.

Marshall, J., Atkinson, J., Woll, B. and Thacker, A. (2005) Aphasia in a bilingual user of British sign language and English: Effects of cross-linguistic cues. *Cognitive Neuropsychology* 22 (6), 719–736.

Mechelli, A., Crinion, J., Noppeney, U., O'Doherty, J., Ashburner, J., Frackowiak, R. *et al.* (2004) Structural plasticity in the bilingual brain: Proficiency in a second language and age at acquisition affect grey-matter density. *Nature* 431 (7010), 757.

Meinzer, M., Obleser, J., Flaisch, T., Eulitz, C. and Rockstroh, B. (2007) Recovery from aphasia as a function of language therapy in an early bilingual patient demonstrated by fMRI. *Neuropsychologia* 45 (6), 1247–1256.

Meuter, R. and Allport, A. (1999) Bilingual language switching in naming: Asymmetrical costs of language selection. *Journal of Memory and Language* 40 (1), 25–40.

Meuter, R., Humphreys, G. and Rumiati, R. (2002) The frontal lobes and bilingual language switching: Modulatory control in language selection. *International Journal of Bilingualism* 6, 109–124.

Meuter, R. and Milner, K. (2007) Effects of age of acquisition and relative proficiency on language switching. Paper presented at the 6th International Symposium on Bilingualism, Hamburg, Germany.

Meuter, R. and Tan, C. (2003) A comparative study of the role of language-specificity and language mode in determining language switch costs. Paper presented at the 4th International Symposium on Bilingualism, Tempe, AZ.

Moreno, E., Federmeier, K. and Kutas, M. (2002) Switching languages, switching palabras (words): An electrophysiological study of code switching. *Brain and Language* 80 (2), 188–207.

Nas, G. (1983) Visual word recognition in bilinguals: Evidence for a cooperation between visual and sound based codes during access to a common lexical store. *Journal of Verbal Learning and Verbal Behavior* 22 (5), 526–534.

Paradis, M. (1977) Bilingualism and aphasia. In H. Whitaker and H.A. Whitaker (eds) *Studies in Neurolinguistics* (Vol. 3; pp. 65–121). New York: Academic Press.

Paradis, M. (1985) On the representation of two languages in one brain. *Language Sciences* 7 (1), 1–39.

Paradis, M. (1997) The cognitive neuropsychology of bilingualism. In A.M.B. De Groot and J. Kroll (eds) *Tutorials in Bilingualism: Psycholinguistic Perspectives* (pp. 331–354). Mahwah, NJ: Lawrence Erlbaum.

Paradis, M. (2004) *A Neurolinguistic Theory of Bilingualism*. Amsterdam: John Benjamins.

Paradis, M., Goldblum, M-C. and Abidi, R. (1982) Alternate antagonism with paradoxical translation behavior in two bilingual aphasic patients. *Brain and Language* 15 (1), 55–69.

Phillips, N., Klein, D., Mercier, J. and de Boysson, C. (2006) ERP measures of auditory word repetition and translation priming in bilinguals. *Brain Research* 1125 (1), 116–131.

Pitres, A. (1895) Aphasia in polyglots. In M. Paradis (ed.) *Readings on Aphasia in Bilinguals and Polyglots* (pp. 26–49). Montreal: Didier.

Poulisse, N. (1997) Language production in bilinguals. In J. Kroll and A.M.B. De Groot (eds) *Tutorials in Bilingualism: Psycholinguistic Perspectives* (pp. 201–224). Mahwah, NJ: Lawrence Erlbaum.

Poulisse, N. and Bongaerts, T. (1994) First language use in second language production. *Applied Linguistics* 15, 36–57.

Price, C., Green, D. and von Studnitz, R. (1999) A functional imaging study of translation and language switching. *Brain: A Journal of Neurology* 122 (12), 2221–2235.

Rinne, J., Tommola, J., Laine, M., Krause, B., Schmidt, D., Kaasinen, V. *et al.* (2000) The translating brain: Cerebral activation patterns during simultaneous interpreting. *Neuroscience Letters* 294 (2), 85–88.

Roberts, P. and Deslauriers, L. (1999) Picture naming of cognate and non-cognate nouns in bilingual aphasia. *Journal of Communication Disorders* 32 (1), 1–23.

Rodriguez-Fornells, A., Balaguer, R. and Münte, T. (2006) Executive control in bilingual language processing. *Language Learning* 56, 133–190.

Rodriguez-Fornells, A., Rotte, M., Heinze, H.J., Nösselt, T. and Münte, T. (2002) Brain potential and functional MRI evidence for how to handle two languages with one brain. *Nature* 415 (6875), 1026–1029.

Rugg, M., Doyle, M. and Wells, T. (1995) Word and nonword repetition within- and across-modality: An event-related potential study. *Journal of Cognitive Neuroscience* 7, 209–227.

Sánchez-Casas, R. and García-Albea, J. (2005) The representation of cognate and noncognate words in bilingual memory: Can cognate status be characterized as a special kind of morphological relation? In J. Kroll and A.M.B. De Groot (eds) *Handbook of Bilingualism: Psycholinguistic Approaches* (pp. 226–250). Oxford: Oxford University Press.

Scarborough, D., Gerard, L. and Cortese, C. (1984) Independence of lexical access in bilingual word recognition. *Journal of Verbal Learning and Verbal Behavior* 23 (1), 84–99.

Segalowitz, N. and de Almeida, R. (2002) Conceptual representation of verbs in bilinguals: Semantic field effects and a second-language performance paradox. *Brain & Language* 81 (1–3), 517–531.

Shallice, T. (1988) *From Neuropsychology to Mental Structure*. Cambridge: Cambridge University Press.

Tan, L.H., Feng, C-M. and Fox, P.T. (2001) An fMRI study with written Chinese. *Neuroreport* 12 (1), 82–88.

Tham, W., Rickard Liow, S., Rajapakse, J., Choong Leong, T., Ng, S., Lim, W. *et al.* (2005) Phonological processing in Chinese-English bilingual biscriptals: An fMRI study. *NeuroImage* 28 (3), 579–587.

Ullman, M. (2001) The neural basis of lexicon and grammar in first and second language: The declarative/procedural model. *Bilingualism: Language and Cognition* 4 (2), 105–122.

Ullman, M. (2006) The declarative/procedural model and the shallow structure hypothesis. *Applied Psycholinguistics* 27 (1), 97–105.

Vaid, J. (1983) Bilingualism and brain lateralization. In S. Segalowitz (ed.) *Language Functions and Brain Organization* (pp. 315–339). New York: Academic Press.

Vaid, J. and Hull, R. (2002) Re-envisioning the bilingual brain using functional neuroimaging: Methodological and interpretative issues. In F. Fabbro (ed.) *Advances in the Neurolinguistics of Bilingualism* (pp. 315–355). Udine, Italy: Forum.

Van Hell, J. and De Groot, A.M.B. (1998a) Conceptual representation in bilingual memory: Effects of concreteness and cognate status in word association. *Bilingualism: Language and Cognition* 1 (3), 193–211.

Van Hell, J. and De Groot, A.M.B. (1998b) Disentangling context availability and concreteness in lexical decision and word translation. *Quarterly Journal of Experimental Psychology A: Human Experimental Psychology* 51 (1), 41–63.

Weber-Fox, C. and Neville, H. (2001) Sensitive periods differentiate processing of open- and closed-class words: An ERP study of bilinguals. *Journal of Speech, Language, and Hearing Research* 44 (6), 1338–1354.

Chapter 2

The Bilingual Lexicon and Bilingual Autobiographical Memory: The Neurocognitive Basic Systems View

ROBERT W. SCHRAUF

Introduction

The bilingual lexicon and bilingual autobiographical memory intersect at the point where words trigger memories and memories are experienced as language events. In the laboratory, this link is operationalized by the ubiquitous use of cue words to trigger autobiographical memories. While some research has attempted to identify which cue-word properties are most efficient at triggering autobiographical memories, little work has addressed whether word properties have any systematic effect on the phenomenological properties of autobiographical memories. One intriguing exception is work on the *language-specificity effect*, which finds that particular personal memories are associated with one or the other of the bilingual's languages. In addition, despite significant advances in empirical research and theoretical reflection concerning neurocognitive models of lexicosemantic memory and autobiographical memory, little work has addressed the intersection of these in the act of word-cued autobiographical memory. These two themes – the relation between psycholinguistic word properties and bilingual autobiographical memory and the reframing of that relation in neuroscientific terms – form the subject of this chapter.

1. The Neurocognitive View of Memory

In recent years, several authors have argued that models of cognition should move beyond the boxes-and-arrows approach of information-processing systems and towards an approach based on neural processing and brain anatomy. The information-processing approach is based on the computer as a model of cognition, which promotes the notion of abstract information: '...information that either is the same for the whole mind or is used to integrate the output of more specialized modules, that is abstract and propositional, and that does not depend on the unique functions and properties of each basic system' (Rubin, 2006: 277). Alternative models based on neuroanatomy and findings in cognitive neuroscience have been proposed for both semantic and episodic memory. Both are important in this context because semantic memory grounds lexicosemantic cuing in autobiographical memory and episodic memory grounds the retrieval and formation of memories.

In the case of semantic memory, Barsalou (1999) argues that most accounts of the relation between perception and cognition have assumed that perceptual information in specific sensory systems is transformed by the mind into amodal, abstract information that is then manipulated by higher-order cognitive processes. Against this view, he argues that no neural evidence exists to support such transduction, and that there is no coherent account that can explain how such amodal information is mapped back onto perceptual states. He proposes an alternative account in which acts of perception activate appropriate sites in the sensory cortex, resulting in neural representations that can be selectively activated and manipulated as 'perceptual symbols'. In short, no separate, amodal class of information is necessary to explain cognition.

Applied to language, such a view implies that the sensory representations that serve as the referents ('meanings') of words are also stored in neuronal networks in the sensory cortices and not in some amodal, conceptual store. This is the upshot of Pulvermuller's (1999) work on the neural representations of word classes (e.g. grammatical function words, concrete content words, words with visual referents and words referring to actions). In this account, phonological and lexical forms of words are represented in neuronal assemblies in the perisylvian cortex, but different classes of words show different patterns of activation. Function words, such as articles, auxiliary verbs, conjunctions, etc. are represented almost exclusively in the perisylvian cortex and strongly left-lateralized. Content words (e.g. words with visual referents and/or words referring to activities) are also phonologically and lexically represented in the perisylvian cortex, but have multiple, bilateral links to other areas of the cortex that represent their acoustic, auditory, olfactory and somato-sensory referents. Thus, for instance, emotion words show links to the limbic system; action words show links to the motor, premotor and prefrontal cortex; pain words show links to the somatosensory cortex, and so on.

Perhaps the most compelling evidence for this view of lexicosemantic memory comes from neuroimaging evidence that shows that the same sensory areas are active when participants remember objects as when they perceive such objects (Nyberg *et al.*, 2000; Wheeler *et al.*, 2000). For example, when participants manipulate information about animals, visual areas are active, and when they perform mental tasks with tools, motor and somatosensory areas become active (Damasio *et al.*, 1996; Rossler *et al.*, 1995).

The relevance of this work on lexicosemantic memory for studies of autobiographical memory resides in the fact that the vast majority of such studies are driven by words-as-cues. (This is true of *all* of the research on bilingual autobiographical memory.) This is the Crovitz-Schiffman (1974) word-cue technique in which participants hear or see a word, retrieve the semantic referent of that word, and then use that meaning (referent) to search for a personal memory. Current models of autobiographical memory tend to reduce the information in this cue to an amodal, symbolic representation, which is then delivered to the auto-biographical search mechanism (Conway & Pleydell-Pearce, 2000; Conway & Rubin, 1993). The search (or memory retrieval) mechanism works as follows.

The participant in an autobiographical memory experiment receives a cue word (e.g. *horse*) with the instruction to retrieve a specific memory, typically an event that happened on one day and within a few hours. The mental retrieval process involves elaborating the search criteria and moving through a mental hierarchy in search of a memory that matches the criteria. The search criteria include (minimally): (1) a memory related to the self, (2) that occurred on one day, (3) that contains visual imagery and (4) that is associated with the cue (*horse*). The mental hierarchy of autobiographical memory is thought to consist of higher levels corresponding to lifetime periods or overarching themes (e.g. *when I used to visit Mike in Kentucky*), middle levels corresponding to generic memories (e.g. *horseback riding on weekends*) and lower levels correspond-ing to a specific memory (e.g. *the time the horse ran off with me*). At the very lowest level of the hierarchy is event-specific knowledge (e.g. *brown horse, rocky trail, feeling of fright*, etc.). Note that this lowest level again reflects information-processing models because the pooled somatosensory, sensory and emotional details of an autobiographical memory are all stored in an undifferentiated, amodal box labeled 'event-specific knowledge' (Conway & Rubin, 1993). In sum, in the information-processing view, a cue word triggers an amodal, symbolic referent (lexicosemantic memory) that is then taken up into the autobiographical retrieval process, resulting in a search through the mind and ultimately the elaboration of a remembered event composed of amodal, symbolic event-specific knowledge.

In the same way that Barsalou (1999) and Pulvermuller (1999) have argued that a neurocognitive view should replace the information-processing view in lexicosemantic retrieval, so Rubin and colleagues have argued that a neurocognitive view should replace the information-processing paradigm in autobiographical memory. They propose the *basic-systems model of episodic memory* (Greenberg & Rubin, 2003; Rubin, 1998, 2005, 2006; Rubin *et al.*, 2003; Schrauf & Rubin, 2000). In brief, this model envisions the retrieval of an autobiographical memory, from the moment of cue to the full mental experience of a past event (typically 5–10 seconds), as the integration of information from key component systems (visual, spatial, auditory, linguistic, emotional and narrative) located in specific areas of the brain. As with the neurocognitive view of semantic memory, the basic-systems model of episodic memory empha-sizes the neural integration of information from specific brain sites corresponding to different kinds of information – each with its own schema-driven organization (Rubin, 2006). By implication, if we take seriously the notion that information in the brain is represented in neural networks in the sensory, somatosensory, motor, prefrontal cortices (and so on), then we may need to rethink the intersection between semantic cue and autobiographical search-and-retrieval.

2. Word-cued Autobiographical Memory in the Basic-systems Model

What might word-cued autobiographical memory look like in the neurocognitive basic-systems model? As a first foray into the territory, the discussion centers on highly imageable cue words with clear sensory referents and leaves both abstract and emotion cue words (or indeed the emotionality of cues) for a future effort. Prior research on lexicosemantic memory shows that concrete, emotion and abstract words have different mental representations (Altarriba, 2006), which could conceivably affect their role as cues in autobiographical retrieval, but for the purposes of this paper, we restrict attention to concrete, imageable words. Let us return to the example given above, and assume that an individual is asked to retrieve an autobiographical memory in response to the cue word *horse*. (It seems to matter little whether the cue word is heard and decoded phonologically, or read and decoded orthographically, since current research (e.g. Hillis, 2001) suggests equivalent access to the underlying semantic referents.) As noted above, the evidence suggests that linguistic decoding, whether phonological or orthographic, is left-lateralized in the brain and localized in the perisylvian cortices. However, the linked coactivation of neuronal assemblies in the sensory cortices takes place in both hemispheres (Pulvermuller, 1999). Thus, *horse* activates neuronal assemblies that represent lexical forms in the perisylvian cortex, which in turn are linked to neuronal assemblies in the visual cortices of the occipital and inferior temporal lobes that represent object and sensory properties. Obviously, activation of neuronal assemblies in the visual cortex in response to *horse* need not imply that a full-blown mental image of *horse* floods consciousness every time the word is encountered, but rather that *horse* triggers some subset of the neuronal assembly in the visual cortex regularly associated with the word.

Meanwhile, the individual begins a mental search for a personal memory related to *horse*. This involves the explicit memory system, associated with the medial temporal lobes (MTL), which are responsible for binding information into events at the moment the events are encoded into memory, and the search-and-retrieval system, associated with the frontal areas, which is responsible for the selection and temporary storage of information during the retrieval process. In fMRI studies (Cabeza *et al.*, 2004; Rubin, 2006) and PET studies (Conway, 2001; Conway *et al.*, 1999) that track the time course of memory retrieval and formation, these MTL and frontal areas show considerable activation from the moment of the cue to the moment of memory capture, after which their activation decreases. Conversely, areas of the brain that represent sensory knowledge, such as the visual cortex, show lower levels of activation until the moment of memory capture and then increasing activation afterwards. (These lower levels of activation may represent the activation of neuronal assemblies associated with the visual object cue word.) As both behavioral and neuropsychological evidence demonstrate, visual information is a critical component in autobiographical retrieval (Brewer, 1992; Brewer & Pani, 1996; Larsen, 1998; Schrauf, 2003). For instance, patients who have experienced loss of visual memory (suffering from visual memory deficit amnesia) show a loss of autobiographical memories (Greenberg & Rubin, 2003; Rubin & Greenberg, 1998).

In essence, retrieval of a memory to a cue word involves a certain amount of 'bottom-up' processing in which sensory areas of the brain are activated early on as a result of access to modality-specific semantic referents (e.g. whatever low-level activation corresponds to visual referents triggered by *horse*), while top-down processes are massively moved online to search for a memory-related-to-the-self and involving these neural representations of *horse*. Hence, it seems likely that the presentation of the cue word for a visual object triggers a low-level activation of neuronal assemblies in the visual cortex (sensory activation), and then, as autobiographical retrieval progresses to the full capture of a memory, additional and massive activation takes place in the visual cortices (additional sensory activation). As top-down and bottom-up processes converge, a memory satisfying the specified criteria (i.e. involving *horse* and related-to-the-self) emerges and additional sensory and other information is activated as the memory is fully retrieved. Relevant brain areas are the visual cortex (visual imagery), ventral visual stream, from occipital through inferior temporal cortex (object information), dorsal visual stream, through occipital and parietal lobes (spatial imagery), the limbic system (emotion) and so on.

3.   Psycholinguistic Properties of Cue Words and the Phenomenological Properties of Autobiographical Memories

Given that the cue word triggers activation in the sensory cortices, which is then taken up into the actual memory, we might ask about the relation between the psycholinguistic properties of cue words and the phenomenological and metacognitive properties of autobiographical retrieval. Previous research on words-as-cues has focused on how the psycholinguistic properties of words affect processes in autobiographical memory, such as retrieval latency, age-of-episode and the temporal specificity of the memory.

Robinson (1976) investigated three classes of words: activity words (verbs), object words (nouns) and affect words (adjectives). He found shortest latencies with object and activity cues. Almost as a class apart, emotion cues took longer to recall, generally commemorated more recent events and had less temporal specificity (participants recalled fewer temporal details than for events cued by object or activity cues). Interestingly, recent research on words in semantic memory has shown that emotion words are represented differently in the mind than either concrete or abstract words, and that certain non-emotion words (e.g. coffin, gun) possess a certain valence and arousal (Altarriba, 2006). Thus, emotion words, or non-emotion words with definite valence or arousal effects, could affect autobiographical recall in particular ways.

In more recent work on cue properties, Rubin and Schulkind (1997) investigated ratings of imagery, concreteness, meaningfulness, goodness, emotionality and corpus frequency of 124 words (Rubin, 1980) when used as cues for autobiographical recalls. Results demonstrated that words with higher ratings of imageability, concreteness and meaningfulness triggered autobiographical memories with shorter latencies and triggered older memories. Emotionality, goodness and frequency did not have marked effects on retrieval latencies or age-of-episode in autobiographical memory.

However, little research has investigated whether the *psycholinguistic properties* of words-as-cues correlate with the *phenomenological properties* of remembered events. (As noted above, in this paper cues are limited to highly imageable words, in part because the evidence from existing studies of cue-word effects is clear concerning concrete words, but mixed concerning abstract and emotion words.) Given this methodological restriction to imageable cues, we ask: does a highly imageable cue word trigger a very vivid visual memory? This might be predicted from the convergence of bottom-up activation of information in the sensory cortices (from the cue word) and top-down processes of autobiographical retrieval and the formation of a full-blown autobiographical memory. Or not. In a protocol analysis of the steps followed by participants from cue to autobiographical memory, Schrauf (2003) found that participants focused especially on the visual information in the cue, but that the relation between the sensory referent of the cue and the role that the sensory referent played in the resulting memory were not necessarily tightly linked. Participants *used* sensory referents to troll through memory in search of an incident that was linked to the cue, but often used additional and oblique associations to the cue to improve search.

In other words, a highly imageable cue word (corresponding to a highly imageable sensory referent) might generate an autobiographical memory that is very vivid or an autobiographical memory that is vague and 'known' rather than remembered and re-experienced. Thus, for instance, the cue word *horse* could trigger a very vivid memory of being saddle-sore and tired after riding during a Memorial Day parade in the rain at age 11 or it could trigger a vague memory of having to clean out a stall on any one of a dozen occasions. Horse might be a highly imageable cue word, but it may or may not trigger a highly imageable memory, and in fact the memory may or may not include a horse as part of the content. In effect, the available research would predict a weak correlation between cue properties (e.g. imageability, concreteness, etc.) and properties of autobiographical memories (e.g. visual and auditory vividness).

The one striking exception to this relation between lexical cue and autobiographical memory occurs in studies of bilingual autobiographical memory that find a robust relation between the bilingual lexicon and the memories retrieved. Here, the evidence supports *language-specific autobiographical retrieval*. Two lines of research point to this conclusion. One series of studies shows that, when presented with a cue word in the first language (L1), bilinguals tend to recall an L1 memory, and when presented with a word in the second language (L2), they recall an L2 memory (Marian & Neisser, 2000; Matsumoto & Stanny, 2006). Another series of experiments shows that memories that come to mind in L1 in fact represent experiences that took place in the L1, and memories that come to mind in L2 represent experiences that took place in L2 (Larsen *et al.*, 2002; Schrauf, 2000, 2003; Schrauf & Rubin, 1998, 2000, 2003, 2004). This literature suggests a fairly robust relation between the bilingual lexicon and autobiographical memories. The question is: how might we articulate such links on the basis of what we know about the brain? Before moving on to this question, however, we examine the behavioral evidence concerning the relation between the psycholinguistic properties of word cues and the phenomenological properties of memories in bilingual autobiographical memory. To date, no empirical research has addressed this question.

4. Specific Questions About Word Cues in Autobiographical Recall

Given the overarching importance of visual information in autobio-graphical memory, the strategy here is to compare the effects of highly imageable cue words and purely visual cues (pictures), then to consider the effects of cue words with variable imageability and finally to move on to the effects of the language(s) of those cues. In the following, it is important to bear in mind that cue word imageability refers to the imageability of the semantic referent, which acts upon autobiographical retrieval, but is not the same as the autobiographical memory, which also has variable imageability as a phenomenological property.

4.1. Question 1: Do word cues versus picture cues have differential effects?

Prior research on semantic memory suggests that imageable words (meaning that their referents are imageable) activate the same areas in the cortex that are activated in the presence of those objects (e.g. Nyberg *et al.*, 2000). Given these findings, we might predict that using pictorial representations of objects as cues for autobiographical memory would be roughly the same as using imageable words. After all, a picture of an object and the name of that object both activate the same area of the cortex, and in either case an initial stimulus must be processed (word versus picture). To my knowledge, no prior research has directly compared pictures and labels as cues, and therefore the issue deserves an empirical test. Of particular interest here is retrieval latency in response to the two kinds of cues. If latencies are equivalent, this would add support for, but not prove that, from the viewpoint of autobiographical retrieval, pictorial versus verbal cuing has similar effects via their visual referents.

4.2. Question 2: Do psycholinguistic properties of word cues affect the phenomenological properties of autobiographical recalls?

A second question concerns the psycholinguistic properties of words-as-cues. In contrast to pictures-as-cues, which cannot be more or less imageable or concrete because they are by definition images and concrete, words-as-cues *do* vary in their imageability and concreteness. As noted above, previous research has indeed confirmed that higher imageability and concreteness correlate with shorter retrieval latencies and more remote versus recent memories (Rubin & Schulkind, 1997). What has not been examined is whether the imageability and concreteness, as well as other subjective properties of cue words (such as pleasantness or familiarity), correlate with the phenomenological properties of the autobiographical memory cued by that word. Our current view of autobiographical retrieval, as outlined above, is that cue words enter into cyclical retrieval as one of a number of elements comprising the search criteria. That is, there are any number of reconstructions of remembered events that may satisfy the criteria, and this suggests a one-to-many mapping between a cue and potential memories. In turn, this means that many other factors may enter into the selection of the final autobiographical memory (e.g. social context, intent of the person remembering). Thus, it does not seem likely that subjective properties of a cue (imageability, concreteness, pleasantness or familiarity) will be highly predictive of the phenomenological properties of the actual autobiographical memory that it triggers. Again, however, the possibility merits an empirical test.

4.3. Question 3: Does the specific language of the cue word have an effect on autobiographical recalls?

A third question concerns the relation between the language of the cue and the resulting autobiographical memory. As noted above, the available research on bilingual autobiographical memory points to clear language effects (Larsen *et al.*, 2002; Marian & Neisser, 2000; Matsumoto & Stanny, 2006; Schrauf, 2000, 2003; Schrauf & Rubin, 1998, 2000, 2003, 2004). However, previous studies have looked for effects by pooling cues by language (i.e. compared all memories cued by all Spanish words against all memories cued by all English words) and have not attended to whether the same cue word will have differential effects via its two translation equivalents. Thus, in the study described below, the language of the cue is manipulated via translation equivalents in a repeated measures design that holds constant the semantic referent. This attempt to control for all factors other than language cannot be completely successful because translation equivalents never map perfectly onto one another. Nevertheless, a credible test can be conducted if the lexical entries in question are restricted to simple, highly imageable, concrete objects (e.g. cloud, eye, knife, etc.) where semantic overlap from language to language is arguably quite high (De Groot, 1993; De Groot & Poot, 1997; Schrauf & Durazo-Arvizu, 2006; Schrauf & Rubin, 2004).

5. The Behavioral Evidence: A Psycholinguistic Study of Autobiographical Cues in L1

5.1. Sample

The data for these analyses come from a larger study concerning the effects of immigration, second language acquisition and the resulting bilingualism on autobiographical retrievals of Puerto-Rican Spanish–English bilinguals and the emotional content of those memories (Schrauf & Hoffman, 2007; Schrauf & Rubin, 2004). This larger study compared autobiographical retrievals of Puerto-Rican Spanish–English bilinguals living in the USA with the autobiographical retrievals of their age-matched monolingual Spanish-speaking counterparts on the island of Puerto Rico. Immigrant ($n = 30$) and island ($n = 25$) samples were matched on age ($M = 69.3$, $SD = 6.9$ versus $M = 72.1$, $SD = 5.3$) and education ($M = 7.1$, $SD = 3.9$ versus $M = 6.1$, $SD = 3.5$). However, socio-economic status was higher for immigrants (annual $10,000–19,999) than for islanders (annual $\leq$ $10,000; $z = 4.50$, $p < 0.001$). Average age-at-immigration for the immigrants was 22.1 years ($SD = 7.1$) and ranged between 15 and 38. In the analyses presented below, no differences were found between islanders and immigrants. Rather, the data from both groups are pooled to provide more statistical power. The exception, of course, is the explicitly bilingual analysis corresponding to question three, which involves only immigrant participants.

5.2. Procedures

All immigrant participants took the Spanish and English versions of two subtests of the Woodcock-Muñoz Language Survey (Picture Naming and Analogies), while islanders took only the Spanish versions of the two subtests. On the Spanish subtests, immigrants and islanders did not differ on Picture Naming ($t(52) = 1.24$, n.s.), but differed on the Analogies subtest, with immigrants having higher scores than islanders ($t(52) = 4.0$, $p < 0.001$). Among immigrants, a comparison of Spanish versus English scores showed higher performance in Spanish versus English on Picture Naming ($t(28) = 2.22, p < 0.05$) and in Spanish versus English on Analogies ($t(28) = 4.0, p < 0.001$).

Immigrant participants were tested in four sessions. The language of the sessions (instruction, cues and memory report) alternated between Spanish versus English (counterbalanced across participants) so that each participant did two sessions in English and two sessions in Spanish. Islanders participated in two sessions, both in Spanish. In each session, participants received between 12 and 20 cues (with the pace set by the participant). In response to each cue card, participants were asked to think of a personal memory, something that happened to them or something they did, from any time in life (from remote past to very recent) and of any importance (from trivial to highly significant). Memories were verbally reported and audiotaped.

Immediately after each memory, individuals were asked if the memory came to them in no language, Spanish, English or both. After retrieving the entire set of memories for a particular session, participants provided the following ratings of phenomenological properties on seven-point Likert scales. 'I can feel now what I felt then...' (emotional intensity). 'I can see it in my mind...' (visual detail). 'I can hear myself or other people speaking...' (auditory detail). For these variables, ratings were: $1 =$ nothing, $3 =$ vaguely, $5 =$ distinctly, $7 =$ as clearly as if it were happening right now. 'I have talked about this event...' (rehearsal) was rated on the following scale: $1 =$ not at all, $3 =$ sometimes, $5 =$ many times, $7 =$ as often as any event in my life. 'This experience changed my life...' (significance) was rated on the following scale: $1 =$ not at all, $4 =$ some, $7 =$ completely. The reaction time for each retrieval was recorded via stopwatch from the moment the participant saw the cue to the moment he or she began speaking.

5.3. Picture and word cues

Memory stimuli, whether words or pictures, possess 'properties' in a psychological sense because participants are observed to react to them in patterned ways. In most instances, of course, there is no direct access to participants' reactions to cues, and so we must rely on participant ratings. Further, since all participants in this study are consecutive bilinguals who began learning English at immigration, only Spanish norms for Spanish words can be used. The psychological properties of English words, normed on individuals for whom English is their first language, have no established empirical bearing for individuals for whom English is a second language. Also, because this is secondary analysis of an existing study, the following additional limitations apply.

In the original study, memory cues consisted of pictures from the Snodgrass and Vanderwaart (1980) set and their corresponding labels (words). The cue set consisted of 110 distinct cues (each with a picture and word version) chosen from the larger 260 Snodgrass set by selecting pictures with the highest *H*-scores (percentage of participants producing the most common name) in the Spanish version of the Snodgrass set (Sanfeliu & Fernandez, 1996). *H*-scores were used to ensure (to the extent possible) that participants were in fact responding to the same under-lying meaning of picture and word cues. No study in Spanish exists that reports the psycholinguistic properties of the names of the pictures in the Snodgrass set. Thus, an existing word norming study in Spanish had to be mined for words that would correspond to those in the Snodgrass set. Algarabel (1996) provides psycholinguistic norms for 1917 Spanish words, including word frequency, imageability, meaningfulness, concreteness, familiarity and pleasantness. Forty-five of the words in the Algarabel set match pictures in the Snodgrass set. Because for methodological reasons the cues were restricted to words with corresponding pictures in the Snodgrass set, the ranges of psycholinguistic values are somewhat restricted: imageability (4.00–6.63), concreteness (4.04–6.87), familiarity (3.57–6.71) and pleasantness (2.14–6.30). The analyses reported below are therefore restricted to the 45 cues (each with pictorial and word formats) for which norms are available. The unit of analysis is the cue word and all analyses concern only Spanish cues.

5.4. Results

5.4.1. Question 1

The first question asks: does cuing with words versus pictures have differential effects on either the process of autobiographical retrieval or the memories generated? This question was tested by assessing whether retrievals in response to picture versus word cues were faster or different phenomenologically in some way. This analysis was conducted on the pooled data from both islanders and immigrants. A matched pairs t-tests with alpha set at $p < 0.01$ to control for multiple comparisons showed no significant differences between memories cued by pictures versus memories cued by words for logged reaction times ($t(44) = 1.55$), visual detail ($t(44) = 0.08$), auditory detail ($t(44) = 0.67$), emotional intensity ($t(44) = 0.67$), the significance of the event ($t(44) = 0.23$) or frequency of rehearsal ($t(44) = 1.76$).

These analyses suggest that there are no differences in autobiographical retrievals when they are cued by words versus pictures. Given that behavioral and neuropsychological research clearly demonstrates that visual information predominates in autobiographical memory, this lack of superiority for visual versus linguistic cues is curious. Of course, it is difficult to theorize on the basis of null results, and one possible reason for the finding is that both word and picture cues were mixed in the same sessions (and not blocked). Nevertheless, pending additional research, these results suggest two likely conclusions. First, the lack of differences in retrieval latencies for autobiographical memories cued by pictures versus words suggests that whatever variation there is in the time-course of autobiographical retrieval has little to do with whether cues are linguistic or non-linguistic. Second (and not surprisingly), cue modality seems to have no effect on the phenomenological properties of the actual memories (visual detail, auditory detail, emotionality, etc.). Apparently, *how* the sensory imagery associated with the cue is activated is not a critical factor either for the process or for the product of remembering.

5.4.2. Question 2

The second question asks whether the psycholinguistic properties of word cues are predictive of the phenomenological properties of autobiographical memories. In fact, they are not. Table 2.1 displays correlations between Spanish word properties (imageability, concreteness, pleasantness or familiarity) and phenomenological properties of memories (numbers of memories, logged reaction times, visual detail, auditory detail and emotional intensity). In analyses of the Spanish word cues on pooled data from bilinguals and monolinguals, with alpha set to $p < 0.01$ to control for multiple comparisons, no correlation emerged as significant, and in fact many ran in directions opposite to what might be expected. Analogous to the previous analysis, these results suggest that the amount and kind of sensory information activated by a word cue

Table 2.1 Correlations between word cue properties and phenomenological properties of autobiographical memories

	Imageability	*Concreteness*	*Familiarity*	*Pleasantness*
Numbers of memories	− 0.27	− 0.21	− 0.06	0.12
Log RT	0.08	− 0.19	0.11	0.10
Visual detail	− 0.17	0.07	− 0.09	− 0.27
Auditory detail	− 0.03	0.09	0.01	− 0.23
Emotional intensity	− 0.09	0.02	− 0.06	− 0.17

does not enter into the amount and kind of sensory information activated by the corresponding autobiographical memory. The most reasonable account is that information activated by the cue is taken up by the search-and-retrieval process as part of the search criteria, but is markedly recontexualized in the final memory.

5.4.3. Question 3

The third question concerns whether the language of the cue word (Spanish or English) is related to the 'language of the memory'. While manipulating the language of the cue is quite simple, identifying the 'language of a memory' is not. Various methods have been adopted, and these have been reviewed elsewhere (Schrauf & Durazo-Arvizu, 2006). In this study, memories were categorized by the participants, who were asked (for each memory) whether it came to them in no language, Spanish, English or both languages. Leaving aside non-linguistic and 'both' language memories, matched pairs t-tests on numbers of Spanish memories cued by Spanish versus English cues showed no significant effect of cue language on Spanish memories ($t(44) = 1.52$, n.s.; Figure 2.1). However, numbers of English memories cued by English words were higher than numbers of English memories cued by Spanish words ($t(44) = 3.40$, $p < 0.01$; Figure 2.2). This asymmetry, according to which the language-specificity effect is seen primarily in the second language, is probably the result of the significantly higher average number of Spanish memories per cue ($M = 6.53$, $SD = 3.29$) than English memories per cue ($M = 0.84$, $SD = 0.85$), reflecting participants' higher proficiency in Spanish versus English and their living in linguistically isolated

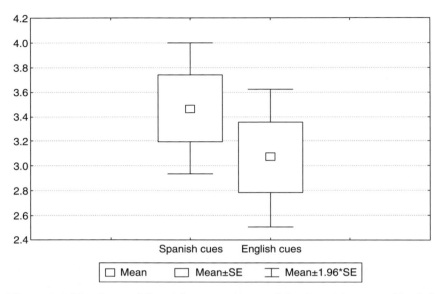

Figure 2.1 Numbers of Spanish memories cued by Spanish versus English words.

neighborhoods. Given these circumstances, the effect of English cues on English memories is notable.

In sum, it would seem that the bilingual lexicon has few effects on autobiographical retrieval, with the crucial exception of the language-specificity effect. More precisely, there are few if any direct effects of the psycholinguistic properties of words on the phenomenological properties of the resulting autobiographical memories. Words that cause greater activation of sensory information, or that trigger more intense emotional responses, do not cue memories that are more vivid or more emotionally intense than words with less potency. But the language of the words in the bilingual lexicon does seem to have consistent effects. Words in L1 are more likely to trigger memories in L1. Words in L2 are more likely to trigger memories in L2.

6. How Does the Language of the Cue Trigger a Language-specific Memory?

To sharpen this question, it is important to keep in mind the critical differences between these two mental tasks. Lexicosemantic retrieval is

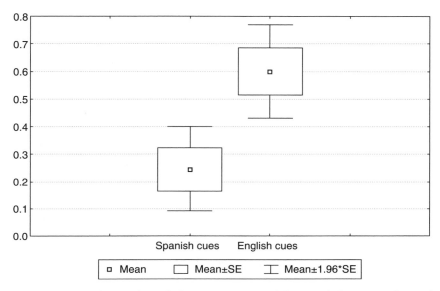

Figure 2.2 Numbers of English memories cued by English versus Spanish words.

an automatic process, clearly outside conscious control, that occurs in milliseconds. Autobiographical retrieval as operationalized in the laboratory is an effortful, controlled process, to some extent available to conscious monitoring, which takes about 5–10 seconds. Autobiographical retrievals in response to cues may or may not include the semantic referents of those cues and do not seem to benefit from the sensory properties of those cues. Thus, the two retrieval processes would seem to be largely independent of one another (at least serially so), again with the one exception that the language of the cue word is more likely to trigger an autobiographical memory related to that language than not. What might explain this language-specificity effect?

6.1. The language tag hypothesis

To date, the literature on bilingual autobiographical memory has evoked Tulving's (1972, 1983) encoding specificity to explain bilingual autobiographical memory. Encoding specificity is the theory that successful retrieval involves a match between information in the retrieval cue and information stored in the encoded engram. In this account, the language spoken at the time of the event (first language or second language or both) becomes a feature of the mnemonic trace, and is reactivated at the time of retrieval. In work on list recall and repetition blindness, Altarriba and Soltano (1996) have argued that, as bilinguals store concepts across languages, they also associate 'language tags' with the concepts that correspond to the language in which the concepts were presented in the lists. Applied to bilingual autobiographical memory, this suggests that personal memories also have some kind of 'language tag' associated with them.

But what would this look like? One possibility is that all of the bilingual's autobiographical memories that are subsequently identified as being either L1 or L2 memories actually contain words as part of the content of the memory (conversation, writing, inner speech). There is some evidence for this. Schrauf and Rubin (2000) had bilinguals identify each memory as having come to them in no language, L1, L2 or both and rate each recall for presence of voices and presence of written words. Memories in L1, L2 or both languages showed higher rates of 'presence of voices' than memories recalled in no language, but non-linguistic memories also in fact contained 'voices' and some linguistic memories did not. Interestingly, there was little recall of written words as part of the content of any memories.

6.2. The search criteria hypothesis

Another possibility, heretofore unexamined in the literature, is that the language of the cue acts as a constraint on recall strategy. That is, the specific language of the cue (L1 or L2) becomes part of the search criteria and activates search through lifetime periods or through a class of generic memories in which that language was spoken or experienced. Once the search process has identified a lifetime period or class of generic memories with strong associations to one or the other language, the likelihood of retrieving a language congruent memory is increased. For instance, given the cue word *caballo* (*horse*), I think of fieldwork in Spain (a lifetime period), and riding a horse in the Three Kings Parade in the little neighborhood where I lived for a year (the specific memory).

Thus, language tags may not be necessary. This possibility has yet to be tested. Perhaps the strongest indication that something like this is the case is the composition of the bilingual samples of existing studies. A brief review of the literature in bilingual autobiographical memory shows that every published study has involved consecutive bilinguals who learned their L1 first and only later learned their L2, usually in late childhood or adolescence. The one exception is found in Schrauf (2003) in which half the sample was simultaneous bilinguals. Table 2.2 shows the studies to date and the mean ages-at-immigration for participants. In effect, no study has systematically considered simultaneous bilinguals who learned both L1 and L2 from birth. This is significant because the division of life into two broad periods corresponding to a monolingual early period and a bilingual later period provides a potent mental shortcut for memory search. That is, the language of the cue can easily trigger a search through one of two lifetime periods distinctively associated with one or the other language. In fact, all studies with consecutive bilinguals show a bias to recall L1 memories to L1 cues from earlier in life when L1 was the only language spoken, even though participants continue to speak the L1 after immigration and encode L1 autobiographical memories after immigration. At any rate, the issue awaits empirical verification.

One important test of this hypothesis would be to assess the bilingual autobiographical memory of simultaneous bilinguals who would not enjoy this simple dichotomization of life into an early monolingual and later bilingual period. However, even a simultaneous bilingual would have classes of memories (generic memories) that could be distinguished by culture and language. For example, if the L1 is associated with a particular experiential domain, such as family or religion, whereas the L2 is associated with another domain, such as professional activities, these different domains could easily facilitate the classification of memories by language.

7. The Language-specificity Effect and the Neurocognitive Basic-systems Model

What might it mean at the level of the brain to filter search through a lifetime period or generic class of memories? Let us return to the basic systems account of episodic memory (Rubin, 2005, 2006). At the encoding of events into memory, the MTLs form links between areas of the brain that are simultaneously active. Thus, concurrent neuronal activations for visual information (visual cortex), object information (ventral visual stream, from occipital through inferior temporal cortex), spatial information (dorsal visual stream, through occipital and parietal lobes), auditory information (auditory cortex) and so on, are all bound together by the MTLs as an 'event'. Further, although we may not entirely understand at the level of the brain what it means to say that this event is

Table 2.2 Mean age-at-immigration of bilingual autobiographical memory samples

Study	Bilingual group	n	Mean age at study (SD)	Mean age-at-immigration (SD) or other information
Marian and Neisser (2000)	Russian–English	20	21.8 (4.1)	14.2 (2.9)
Matsumoto and Stanny (2006)	Japanese–English	18	22.7 (2.65)	Eight international, three exchange, seven intensive English students
Larsen *et al.* (2002)	Polish–Danish	20	Group 1: 51.4 (2.55)	Group 1: 24.10 (1.8)
			Group 2: 61.4 (3.34)	Group 2: 33.6 (2.7)
Schrauf (2004)	Spanish–English	10	19.1 (1.37)	Five immigrants: ages 4–11
				Five born in USA to Hispanic parents
Schrauf and Rubin (1998)	Spanish–English	12	64.58 (2.93)	28 (5.7)
Schrauf and Rubin (2000)	Spanish–English	8	65.63 (2.77)	28.0 (6.02)
Schrauf and Rubin (2004)	Spanish–English	30	69.35 (6.9)	22.13 (7.1)

subjectively recorded as 'my experience', nevertheless, this information too must be integrated into the encoding of the event. After all, an autobiographical memory is by definition a memory with explicit reference to the self (Brewer, 1986). In this neurocognitive, basic-systems model, 'the self is a collection of highly developed schemata, in several of the basic systems, that maintain the relatively stable characteristics of the individual... The self's neural location is thus highly distributed' (Rubin, 2006: 292). However and wherever these higher-level schemata are activated in the brain, their activation is subject to the same MTLs binding as the rest of the experienced event.

The neural activations that are bound together at the moment of encoding the memory (e.g. riding a horse during the Three Kings Parade in Spain) include both event-specific information (e.g. brown horse, cool weather, etc.) and activations of higher-order schemata as well (e.g. doing fieldwork in Spain). At retrieval, these higher-order schemata are activated first and trigger the cascade toward the assembly of information originally bound together by the MTLs. All that is needed to explain the language-specific effect in bilingual autobiographical memory is a link between the language of the cue and one or the other of the higher-order schemata. The Spanish word *caballo* and 'doing fieldwork in Spain' provide just such a connection, without appealing to a language tag in the actual singular memory. An association between language of the cue and higher-level schemata (e.g. just being in Spain) is sufficient.

Note that this hypothesis does not eliminate the language-specific effect in bilingual autobiographical memory, since that effect simply describes either the likelihood of retrieving a memory congruent with the language of the cue, or of retrieving a memory in the language in which it was encoded. It does, however, suggest that language (in the sense of the specific languages of the bilingual) does not constitute a fundamental organizing principle of autobiographical memory. This follows the notion that autobiographical memories are not stable collections of features stored in the mind or the brain.

For example, talking with friends about getting saddle sore while riding horses, I might recall the experience of riding a horse for two hours in Spain. Or, talking to a group of friends about cultural differences in Christmas customs, I might remember the costumes of the Three Kings who were riding horses in the local Christmas procession in which I participated while in Spain. The underlying event is the same, but the memories need not share an identical core. My recall of being saddle sore may not involve remembering the costumes of the Three Kings at all, and my memory of the Three Kings may not involve my being on the horse. (In a Wittgensteinian sense, the different accounts bear a 'family resemblance' to one another.) In this sense, there is no underlying store of autobiographical memories, and hence there are no preformed units that might have as one of their features an L1 or L2 language tag. Hence, there are no L1 versus L2 memories. Memory is not organized linguistically in this fashion. The more likely view is that the language-specific memory effect is caused by an association of the language of the cue with some generic class of memories associated with speaking and/ or hearing that language.

These conclusions are tentative in that the current study relies exclusively on concrete, imageable cue words. It is possible that more abstract, less imageable cues, or cue words referring to interior psychic states or emotions would function in some different way. Such possibilities deserve empirical treatment. However, the current data suggest that, from the information-processing viewpoint, the language of the cue becomes part of the search criteria and triggers search through a lifetime period or set of generic memories associated with the individual's speaking the language of the cue. From the neurocognitive view, the explanation is the same, except that the emphasis is on the activation of higher-order neural schemata distributed across the brain (i.e. whatever neuroscientists are likely to eventually represent as the 'self' in the brain).

At the level of scientific metaphor, however, there are some advantages to moving away from information-processing metaphors to metaphors from cognitive neuroscience. Greenberg and Rubin (2003: 689) note that: 'The first claims that memories are stored at encoding and later retrieved. The second maintains that the mind/brain changes with experience, so that it will respond differently when exposed to stimuli in the future'. On the one hand, metaphors of storage and retrieval do seem to imply that 'items' are deposited and classified and await delivery to some central staging area. In the case of autobiographical memories, this is misleading since memories are selectively reconstructed at each recall. Further, the storage and retrieval metaphor invokes the amodal character of information in the brain since 'items' are treated similarly throughout the mind and at varying levels of mental hierarchy. On the other hand, the cognitive science metaphors of 'activation' across 'neural networks' imply a phased change of activation in response to stimuli, which strengthens some connections (excitation) and weakens others (inhibition). As Rubin (2005, 2006) points out, each area of the cortex has its own schemata, representing previous activations, from which new selective activations are made as a memory is reconstructed.

Conclusion

This chapter represents the attempt to think through the relation between the bilingual lexicon and bilingual autobiographical memory from the perspective of a neurocognitive model of memory. In effect, two kinds of memory retrieval are at issue: lexicosemantic retrieval (the cue word) and autobiographical retrieval (a personal memory). Neurocognitive models of lexicosemantic retrieval suggest that retrieval of word meaning involves activation extending from neural representations of the word in the perisylvian cortex to the same cortical areas that are associated with actual experience of the semantic referents of that word (Barsalou, 1999; Pulvermuller, 1999). The neurocognitive, basic-systems model of episodic memory suggests that encoding an event involves laying down neural representations of the concurrent visual, auditory, haptic, etc. information in the sensory cortices and the binding together of this information by the MTLs. When the event is remembered (retrieved), this information is reintegrated by the MTLs and frontal lobes (Greenberg & Rubin, 2003; Rubin, 2006).

Interestingly, although the activation of sensory information occurs as a result of lexicosemantic retrieval (the cue), such activation does not necessarily play a role in the fully formed autobiographical memory that is triggered by it. A close look at the relation between psycholinguistic properties of cue words (e.g. imageability, pleasantness) and the phenomenological properties of personal memories (e.g. vividness, emotion) shows no systematic relation. Vivid cues do not necessarily produce vivid memories. The exception to this case (seen only in bilinguals) is the language of the cue. The analysis of cue language reported in this chapter, as well as previous research, shows a tendency for cue language to predict language of autobiographical retrieval.

This language-specificity effect has usually been explained by a version of encoding specificity, termed here the language tag hypothesis (Larsen *et al.*, 2002; Marian & Neisser, 2000; Matsumoto & Stanny, 2006; Schrauf, 2000; Schrauf & Rubin, 1998, 2004). This is the assumption that autobiographical memories have as one of their stored features the language spoken at the time of the event. However, this smuggles into the model the notion that autobiographical memories are stored, stable collections of particular kinds of information, and this does not concur with current theory or empirical findings. Rather, autobiographical memories seem to be reconstructions driven by the particularities of the information in the cue, the purpose of retrieval and the current 'working self' (Conway & Pleydell-Pearce, 2000).

An alternative account would locate the effect of the language of the cue earlier in the memory retrieval process. This search criterion hypothesis suggests that the language of the cue activates a higher-order representation of the self as speaker-hearer of the language, which in turn activates memories associated with that self-schema. This hypothesis awaits empirical confirmation in the laboratory, but a careful look at existing studies of bilingual autobiographical memory shows that the majority of participants in such studies have been consecutive bilinguals for whom life divides more or less neatly into an L1 period (usually prior to immigration) and an L1–L2 period (post-immigration). This broad bifurcation of the self across two time periods would provide a potent clue to how the search criterion hypothesis might be operating.

The implementation of this approach in the neurocognitive, basic-systems model requires theorizing about how the self is represented at the level of the brain. One view is that the self is distributed across the brain as the interweaving of higher-order schemata in sensory, somato-sensory, motor, affective and linguistic areas of neural representation. This is hypothetical, and also requires additional investigation.

In the end, this extended reflection on the relation between the bilingual lexicon and bilingual autobiographical memory steps back from any attempt to find direct links between words in the lexicon and the memories that are cued by them. More specifically, these reflections place in grave doubt the notion that the language of a cue word matches something language-specific in the remembered event. In fact, by assuming a neurocognitive view, the chapter recasts both word representation and autobiographical memories as networks of activation in the brain with multiple, varied and often circuitous (to us) pathways between them. In particular, the connection between the bilingual lexicon (words) and bilingual autobiographical memory (remembered experiences) is not simply a question of overlapping neuronal assemblies. Rather, retrieval is mediated through higher-order patterns of activation (lifetime periods or life themes) and the neural networks representing the bilingual 'selves who speak' (or spoke) these languages during those lifetime periods. This shifts the question away from how a word in either of the bilingual's two languages triggers a language-specific memory to how such word triggers a language-specific self that in turn triggers a language-specific memory. These are promising avenues of research for a young field of investigation.

References

Algarabel, S. (1996) Indices de interes psicolinguistico de 1917 palabras castellanas [Psycholinguistic indices for 1,917 Spanish words]. *Cognitiva* 8, 43–88.

Altarriba, J. (2006) Cognitive approaches to the study of emotion-laden and emotion words in monolingual and bilingual memory. In A. Pavlenko (ed.) *Bilingual Minds: Emotional Experience, Expression, and Representation* (pp. 232–256). Clevedon: Multilingual Matters.

Altarriba, J. and Soltano, E. (1996) Repetition blindness and bilingual memory: Token individuation for translation equivalents. *Memory and Cognition* 24 (6), 700–711.

Barsalou, L. (1999) Perceptual symbol systems. *Behavioral and Brain Sciences* 22, 577–660.

Brewer, W. (1986) What is autobiographical memory? In D. Rubin (ed.) *Autobiographical Memory* (pp. 25–49). Cambridge: Cambridge University Press.

Brewer, W. (1992) Phenomenal experience in laboratory and autobiographical memory tasks. In M. Conway, D. Rubin, H. Spinnler and W. Wagenaar (eds) *Theoretical Perspectives on Autobiographical Memory* (pp. 31–51). Dordrecht: Kluwer.

Brewer, W. and Pani, J. (1996) Reports of mental imagery in retrieval from long-term memory. *Consciousness and Cognition* 5, 265–287.

Cabeza, R., Prince, S., Daselaar, S., Greenberg, D., Budde, M., Dolcos, F. *et al.* (2004) Brain activity during episodic retrieval of autobiographical and laboratory events: An fMRI study using a novel photo paradigm. *Journal of Cognitive Neuroscience* 16 (9), 1583–1594.

Conway, M. (2001) Sensory-perceptual episodic memory and its context: Autobiographical memory. In A. Baddeley, M. Conway and J. Aggleton (eds) *Episodic Memory: New Directions in Research* (pp. 53–70). Oxford: Oxford University Press.

Conway, M. and Pleydell-Pearce, C. (2000) The construction of autobiographical memories in the self-memory system. *Psychological Review* 107, 261–288.

Conway, M. and Rubin, D. (1993) The structure of autobiographical memory. In A. Collins, S. Gathercole, M. Conway and P. Morris (eds) *Theories of Memory* (pp. 103–137). Hillsdale, NJ: Lawrence Erlbaum.

Conway, M., Turk, D., Miller, S., Logan, J., Nebes, R., Meltzer, C. *et al.* (1999) A positron-emission tomography (PET) study of autobiographical memory retrieval. *Memory* 7 (5/6), 679–702.

Crovitz, H. and Schiffman, H. (1974) Frequency of episodic memories as a function of their age. *Bulletin of the Psychonomic Society* 4, 517–551.

Damasio, H., Grabowski, T., Tranel, D., Hichwa, R. and Damasio, A. (1996) A neural basis for lexical retrieval. *Nature* 380, 499–505.

De Groot, A.M.B. (1993) Word-type effects in bilingual processing tasks: Support for a mixed representational system. In R. Schreuder and B. Weltens (eds) *The Bilingual Lexicon* (pp. 27–51). Amsterdam: John Benjamins.

De Groot, A.M.B. and Poot, R. (1997) Word translation at three levels of proficiency in a second language: The ubiquitous involvement of conceptual memory. *Language Learning* 47 (2), 215–264.

Greenberg, D. and Rubin, D. (2003) The neuropsychology of autobiographical memory. *Cortex* 39, 687–728.

Hillis, A. (2001) The organization of the lexical system. In B. Rapp (ed.) *The Handbook of Cognitive Neuropsychology: What Deficits Reveal about the Human Mind* (pp. 185–210). Philadelphia, PA: Taylor & Francis.

Larsen, S. (1998) What is it like to remember? On phenomenal qualities of memory. In C. Thompson, D. Herrman, D. Bruce, J. Read, D. Payne and M. Toglia (eds) *Autobiographical Memory: Theoretical and Applied Approaches* (pp. 163–190). Mahwah, NJ: Lawrence Erlbaum.

Larsen, S., Schrauf, R., Fromholt, P. and Rubin, D. (2002) Inner speech and bilingual autobiographical memory: A Polish-Danish cross-cultural study. *Memory* 10 (1), 45–54.

Marian, V. and Neisser, U. (2000) Language-dependent recall of autobiographical memories. *Journal of Experimental Psychology: General* 129 (3), 361–368.

Matsumoto, A. and Stanny, C.J. (2006) Language-dependent access to autobiographical memory in Japanese-English bilinguals and US monolinguals. *Memory* 14 (3), 378–390.

Nyberg, L., Habib, R., Tulving, E., McIntosh, A., Cabeza, R. and Houle, S. (2000) Large-scale neurocognitive networks underlying episodic memory. *Journal of Cognitive Neuroscience* 12, 163–173.

Pulvermuller, F. (1999) Words in the brain's language. *Behavioral and Brain Sciences* 22, 253–336.

Robinson, J. (1976) Sampling autobiographical memory. *Cognitive Psychology* 8, 578–595.

Rossler, F., Heil, M. and Hennighausen, E. (1995) Distinct cortical activation patterns during long term memory retrieval of verbal, spatial, and color information. *Journal of Cognitive Neuroscience* 7, 51–65.

Rubin, D. (1980) 51 properties of 125 words: A unit analysis of behavior. *Journal of Verbal Learning and Behavior* 19, 736–755.

Rubin, D. (1998) Beginnings of a theory of autobiographical remembering. In C. Thompson, D. Herrman, D. Bruce, J. Read, D. Payne and M. Toglia (eds) *Autobiographical Memory: Theoretical and Applied Perspectives* (pp. 47–67). Mahwah, NJ: Lawrence Erlbaum.

Rubin, D. (2005) A basic systems approach to autobiographical memory. *Current Directions in Psychological Science* 14 (2), 79–83.

Rubin, D. (2006) The basic systems model of episodic memory. *Perspectives in Psychological Science* 1 (4), 277–311.

Rubin, D. and Greenberg, D. (1998) Visual memory-deficit amnesia: A distinct amnesic presentation and etiology. *Proceedings of The National Academy of Sciences* 95, 5413–5416.

Rubin, D., Schrauf, R. and Greenberg, D. (2003) Belief and recollection of autobiographical memories. *Memory and Cognition* 31 (6), 877–886.

Rubin, D. and Schulkind, M. (1997) Properties of word cues for autobiographical memory. *Psychological Reports* 81, 47–50.

Sanfeliu, M. and Fernandez, A. (1996) A set of 254 Snodgrass-Vanderwart pictures standardized for Spanish: Norms for name agreement, image agreement, familiarity, and visual complexity. *Behavior Research Methods, Instruments, and Computers* 28 (4), 537–555.

Schrauf, R. (2000) Bilingual autobiographical memory: Experimental studies and clinical cases. *Culture & Psychology* 6 (4), 387–417.

Schrauf, R. (2003) A protocol analysis of retrieval in autobiographical memory. *International Journal of Bilingualism* 7 (3), 235–256.

Schrauf, R. and Durazo-Arvizu, R. (2006) Bilingual autobiographical memory and emotion: Theory and methods. In A. Pavlenko (ed.) *Bilingual Minds: Emotional Experience, Expression, and Representation* (pp. 284–311). Clevedon: Multilingual Matters.

Schrauf, R. and Hoffman, L. (2007) The effects of revisionism on remembered emotion: The valence of older, voluntary immigrants' pre-migration memories. *Applied Cognitive Psychology* 21, 895–913.

Schrauf, R. and Rubin, D. (1998) Bilingual autobiographical memory in older adult immigrants: A test of cognitive explanations of the reminiscence bump and the linguistic encoding of memories. *Journal of Memory and Language* 39 (3), 437–457.

Schrauf, R. and Rubin, D. (2000) Internal languages of retrieval: The bilingual encoding of memories for the personal past. *Memory and Cognition* 28 (4), 616–623.

Schrauf, R. and Rubin, D. (2003) On the bilingual's two sets of memories. In R. Fivush and C. Haden (eds) *Autobiographical Memory and the Construction of a Narrative Self: Developmental and Cultural Perspectives* (pp. 121–145). Mahwah, NJ: Lawrence Erlbaum.

Schrauf, R. and Rubin, D. (2004) The 'language' and 'feel' of bilingual memory: Mnemonic traces. *Estudios de Sociolinguistica* 5 (1), 21–39.

Snodgrass, J. and Vanderwaart, M. (1980) A standardized set of 260 pictures: Norms for name agreement, image agreement, familiarity, and visual complexity. *Journal of Experimental Psychology: Human Learning and Memory* 6 (2), 174–215.

Tulving, E. (1972) Episodic and semantic memory. In E. Tulving (ed.) *Organization of Memory* (pp. 381–403). New York: Academic Press.

Tulving, E. (1983) *Elements of Episodic Memory.* Oxford: Clarendon Press.

Wheeler, M., Peterson, S. and Buckner, R. (2000) Memory's echo: Vivid remembering reactivates sensory-specific cortex. *Proceedings of the National Academy of Sciences of the United States of America* 97, 11125–11129.

Chapter 3

Audio-visual Integration During Bilingual Language Processing

VIORICA MARIAN

Introduction

Despite the fact that bilingual language processing generally takes place in complex natural environments with multiple simultaneous modes of input, laboratory studies of bilingualism rarely consider the multimodal nature of bilingual language comprehension. For bilingual as well as monolingual listeners, multimodal input includes both linguistic input (such as the phonological and orthographic forms of a word), as well as non-linguistic input (such as seeing the face of the speaker or the objects in the listener's immediate surrounding environment). While the interaction between phonology and orthography has received consideration in psycholinguistic studies of bilingual language processing, research on cross-modal audio-visual sensory integration in bilinguals is more limited. In general, audio-visual integration in bilinguals has yet to receive careful consideration in the literature. The objective of this chapter is to contribute to the understanding of how bilingual language processing is impacted by multimodal integration and audio-visual interaction. To accomplish this goal, two bodies of literature are considered. The first incorporates paradigms that consider multimodal integration of auditory and visual input during language comprehension and discusses them within the context of bilingualism. The second focuses on evidence suggesting that orthographic and phonological information interact during bilingual spoken and written language comprehension. The chapter also reviews existing models of bilingual language processing that may be able to account for audio-visual interaction, and draws implications for representation in the bilingual mental lexicon.

1. Audio-visual Integration During Language Processing

One of the most striking phenomena illustrating the interaction between auditory and visual modalities during spoken language comprehension is the McGurk effect (McGurk & MacDonald, 1976). The McGurk effect refers to the finding that if listeners are played the sound /ba/ auditorily, while presented visually with a face that is pronouncing /ga/, they will report hearing the sound /da/. As counterintuitive as this seems, this effect is very robust and consistent (e.g. Van Wassenhove *et al.*, 2007) and, in fact, many lecturers now include it as an easy-to-replicate demo in their undergraduate courses. The McGurk effect demonstrates that listeners constantly combine input from the two modalities when perceiving language. In general, in healthy individuals, language processing is cross-modal, with input from the auditory and visual modalities interacting as one hears, reads, writes or pronounces words.

The cross-modal nature of language processing can be traced to the cortical level. For example, cortical areas typically associated with speech processing have been found to be active during observation of visual articulatory movement (Calvert *et al.*, 1997, 2000; Campbell *et al.*, 2001; Nishitani & Hari, 2002). Similarly, neural responses to speech sounds in a modality-specific region of the auditory cortex appear to be modified by the simultaneous visual presentation of letters (e.g. Van Atteveldt *et al.*, 2004). Integration of auditory and visual information appears to happen so early in the processing stream that it can be detected even at the level of the brainstem (Musacchia *et al.*, 2006). Musacchia and associates (2006) found that seeing facial movement (lip-reading) changed the amplitude of the brainstem response to acoustic speech and suggested that the brain showed enhanced responses to auditory-visual stimuli relative to the sum of unimodal responses.

The role of visual input during spoken language processing is clear when one considers findings that visual input alone, in the absence of any auditory information, can be sufficient for listeners to determine what language a speaker is using. For instance, Ronquest and Hernandez (2005) asked participants to watch visual-only speech stimuli and decide if the language spoken was Spanish or English. They found that listeners were able to identify the language correctly well above chance, simply by watching the speaker's face. Moreover, speech perception is improved not only by viewing the mouth/lip movements, but also by having access to a view of the top of the head only (e.g. Davis & Kim, 2006) and to head movements (e.g. Munhall *et al.*, 2004). Although these latter effects are smaller than those observed for watching lip movements, it is striking that such visual information significantly enhances language comprehension. This suggests that listeners are adept at perceiving visual input during language processing, and integrate it with auditorily perceived input.

Interestingly, while both monolinguals and bilinguals can distinguish a language by visual correlates of speech alone, bilinguals seem to do so with greater accuracy than monolinguals, but only for languages they know (Soto-Faraco *et al.*, 2007). Soto-Faraco and associates (2007) found that Spanish–Catalan bilinguals were very successful at discriminating Spanish and Catalan based on visual information alone (watching the speaker's face), Spanish monolinguals were able to do so less success-fully, while Italian–English bilinguals were unable to differentiate Spanish and Catalan. This suggests that previous experience is instru-mental in shaping the way listeners recognize and rely on visual information during spoken language comprehension. This experience is likely largely automatic and not consciously monitored by the speaker or listener. Because bilinguals' experiences are more varied and exten-sive, they may be more adept at interpreting input from the visual modality during language processing and may be more skilled at relying on both modalities during language comprehension.

This suggestion is consistent with findings from the speech perception literature. Consider, for instance, a study by Sumby and Pollack (1954) who found that reliance on visual properties during speech processing increases as the signal-to-noise ratio (SNR) decreases (i.e. as the speech signal becomes weaker in relation to the noise around it). Viewing a speaker's articulatory movements is known to particularly benefit a listener's ability to understand speech in noisy environments. The gain from viewing visual articulation relative to an auditory-alone condition can be up to threefold under certain SNRs (Ross *et al.*, 2007). Specifically, Ross and associates (2007) found that multisensory integration was maximally beneficial at intermediate SNR levels. Where exactly bilingual language comprehension falls on the SNR continuum is likely influenced by many factors, such as language proficiency, degree of accented speech, similarity between the two languages, etc. However, overall, the SNR is likely to be lower in bilinguals (especially in their weaker language) because their decreased ability to perceive sound contrasts in a non-native language may yield a larger 'noise' category (e.g. Bradlow & Bent, 2002; Bradlow & Pisoni, 1999). As a result, bilingual and multi-lingual listeners, especially those with lower language proficiency, may be more likely to rely on the speaker's face when listening to speech, in order to boot-strap information that they cannot access auditorily. This suggestion is consistent with the 'inverse effectiveness' principle of multisensory integration, according to which the gain from viewing articulatory movements is most pronounced when auditory input is decreased relative to noise (Ross *et al.*, 2007).

Taking into account SNRs, spoken language comprehension in bilinguals is likely to rely even more on cross-modal integration than in monolinguals, with visual information supplementing auditory input. This greater reliance on multimodal input when processing auditory information may explain why non-native speakers sometimes experience greater difficulties comprehending their less-proficient language over the telephone and why native speakers have greater difficulty comprehending accented speech over the telephone. In fact, the argument that over-the-telephone conversations are negatively impacted by the speaker's linguistic background have been used to deny employment to non-native speakers and have been upheld in court rulings (e.g. *Clau v. Uniglobe* and *Guillen v. Dufour*, in Munro, 1998), with the tribunal commissioner asserting that 'he knew from personal experience that accented speech was hard to understand on the phone' (Munro, 1998: 141). Although much of the evidence on intelligibility over the telephone is anecdotal, it is consistent with evidence that intelligibility of foreign speech is negatively impacted by noise (e.g. Munro, 1998).

Consequently, it might be argued that speakers of multiple languages may be especially likely to rely on and be impacted by cross-modal integration when processing linguistic input. Previous research shows that visual speech information can even be used to help distinguish sounds in a second language that cannot be perceived using auditory input alone. For instance, Navarra and Soto-Faraco (2007) have found that adding visual information about lip movements could enhance Spanish speakers' ability to distinguish between the Catalan sounds /ɛ/ and /e/. Specifically, while Spanish-dominant bilinguals were unable to distinguish between the two Catalan sounds based on auditory-only information, they were able to perceive the contrast when visual information about lip movements was added (Catalan-dominant bilinguals were able to differentiate between the two sounds in both conditions). The authors concluded that visual speech information enhances second language perception by way of multisensory integration. This idea that nonproficient speakers rely more on cross-modal input when processing language is consistent with evidence from the second language acquisition literature showing that bimodal input benefits implicit and explicit memory (Bird & Williams, 2002), speaking performance (Borras & Lafayette, 1994) and language learning (Danan, 1992; Vanderplank, 1988).

Another line of convincing evidence supporting the cross-modal nature of bilingual spoken language processing comes from psycholinguistic studies using eye tracking. Initially, the eye-tracking methodology (e.g. Tanenhaus *et al.*, 1995) was adapted for use with bilinguals to test whether bilinguals process their two languages sequentially or in parallel (e.g. Marian, 2000; Marian & Spivey, 2003a, 2003b; Spivey & Marian, 1999). In a typical experimental set-up, bilinguals were presented with a display of objects, including one whose name (e.g. *chair*) overlapped across languages with the name of another object in the display (e.g. *cherepaha*, Russian for 'turtle') (Figure 3.1). When instructed to pick up the *chair*, Russian–English bilinguals made eye movements to the *cherepaha* significantly more often than to control objects. Such findings suggest that, during early stages of processing, unfolding auditory input activates multiple word alternatives within and between languages. The influence of sublexical phonological overlap on word processing remains

Figure 3.1 Sample display from an eye-tracking study of spoken word recognition in bilinguals. The display shows a light bulb, a chair, a ruler and a turtle. The Russian word for turtle is *cherepaha* (the 'che' overlaps with 'chair'). Studies show that when instructed in English to pick up the chair, Russian–English bilinguals frequently look at the turtle. Similarly, when instructed in Russian to pick up the turtle, Russian–English bilinguals frequently look at the chair. Monolinguals do not show these effects.

apparent until the lexical decision stage. Such gradual activation, leading up to word selection, is consistent with auditory word recognition models (e.g. Luce & Pisoni, 1998; Marslen-Wilson, 1987; McClelland & Elman, 1986) and indicates that a bilingual's two languages remain active in parallel and that bilinguals simultaneously map phonemic input onto both of their lexicons (with it cascading to higher levels of representation, e.g. Blumenfeld & Marian, 2007; Marian *et al.*, 2008) as a word unfolds in real time.

These findings have since been replicated and extended in eye-tracking studies with Dutch–English bilinguals (Weber & Cutler, 2004), Japanese–English bilinguals (Cutler *et al.*, 2006), French–German bilinguals (Weber & Paris, 2004) and Spanish–English bilinguals (Canseco-Gonzalez, 2005; Ju & Luce, 2004). They have shown that the visual environment comes into play both on microscales, such as computer screens (e.g. Blumenfeld & Marian, 2007; Weber & Cutler, 2004) and on macroscales, such as actual objects in the surrounding environment (e.g. Marian & Spivey, 2003a, 2003b; Spivey & Marian, 1999). Across languages and experimental designs, these eye-tracking studies not only support parallel processing of both languages during spoken word comprehension, but also suggest that the visual array surrounding a bilingual listener in real-world settings interacts with auditory input to influence language comprehension.

Specifically, as a word unfolds, incoming auditory input is combined online with incoming visual input and the two sources mutually interact to exclude options that are not plausible in at least one modality, thus making the recognition process faster and more efficient than it would be unimodally. In other words, the two modalities work together to facilitate comprehension, with the spoken word recognition component incrementally decoding the speech signal, mapping it onto multiple plausible lexical items as the word unfolds, and finally zeroing in on one specific lexical item with partial matches no longer activated. At the same time, the visual modality speeds up the process in a top-down fashion by limiting the options that the auditory input can map onto. Alternatively, the visual modality may increase activation of the target via the additional pathway, so that the cumulative effect of both modalities makes activation of the target more robust and faster. This highly interactive, highly dynamic process happens online in a matter of milliseconds and is a testimony to the astounding human linguistic capacity. Just as monolingual language comprehension is a 'hungry' process (Spivey, 2007), where the system continuously and insatiably seeks and integrates new information, so is the bilingual system one in which expectations about the upcoming input continuously influence the computation of probabilities for what is likely to come next. This 'hunger' is a well-fitting description for the opportunistic cognitive processes that constantly integrate signals across modalities and information sources and, in the case of bilinguals, also across languages.

In fact, bilingualism may be one of a number of experiences that can influence how auditory and visual information is integrated crossmodally. Another interesting example comes from music. Kraus (2007) suggested that a hallmark of the musician's brain is enhanced multisensory processing and that musicians neurally combine audio-visual information more precisely than nonmusicians in the auditory brainstem early in the processing stream. This work suggests that previous experience (in this case, with music) can influence neural patterns of multisensory integration and has important implications for bilinguals, a group whose previous experience with other languages may yield similar outcomes. For instance, both groups (musicians and bilinguals) are 'auditory experts', in the sense that they receive a lot of rich and varied auditory input that they often have to integrate with other modalities, visual or sensorimotor, very quickly online (see also Mechelli *et al.*, 2004).

In future research, it would be interesting to examine empirically whether bilingual and multilingual speakers who have extensive practice with more than one language show the same type of neurological changes in the auditory brainstem and similar performance advantages as those exhibited in research with musicians (see Wong *et al.*, 2007, for an example of advantages in musicians). These advantages may be more pronounced for bilinguals whose experience with audio-visual integration is more diverse due to speaking languages that vary more, for example, when one language is alphabetic and the other logographic, or when one language is tonal and the other is not (for studies of neural changes as a result of acquiring a tonal language, see Krishnan *et al.*, 2005; Wang *et al.*, 2003). Another question for future empirical research with bilinguals is whether this greater experience with integrating sensory input across multiple modalities translates to other advantages in the cognitive system. It is possible that a greater experience with cross-modal integration constitutes one of the sources on which a bilingual advantage builds, and works alongside or cumulatively with other sources examined by bilingualism scholars, such as cognitive control (e.g. Ben-Zeev, 1977) and inhibition skills (e.g. Bialystok, 2005, 2006, for a review, see Cook, 1997). Future research exploring the role of cross-modal integration alongside and vis-à-vis other sources of bilingual advantage may be fruitful.

In sum, previous research has shown that language comprehension relies on cross-modal integration from the auditory and visual modalities, and that this is especially true for bilinguals, whose SNR may be lower. Sources of visual input include visual information about the speaker and visual information about the surrounding environment. Eye-tracking studies suggest that, during language comprehension, auditory input is continuously coupled with and augmented by visual input. Bilinguals rely on cross-modal integration as a matter of course to enhance intelligibility (sometimes even to perceive sounds that cannot be discriminated unimodally) and to speed-up comprehension, and they do so continuously and automatically during language use.

2. Interaction Between Phonology and Orthography During Language Processing

In addition to cross-modal integration, some evidence for audio-visual interaction comes from studies that focus on the interplay between phonology and orthography during language processing. Although visual word recognition is often conceived of as processing written input, it is in fact the case that the auditory shape of the word (i.e. its phonetic and phonological form) also becomes active during orthographic decoding. That is, when reading a word, the reader automatically coactivates the auditory form of the visual input, regardless of whether the latter is alphabetic or logographic. Some evidence of phonological involvement in reading comes from monolingual studies showing that regular letter-to-phoneme mappings are read faster than irregular letter-to-phoneme mappings. For example, the word *mint* has regular letter-to-phoneme mappings for -*int* that are consistent with the majority of words including this letter sequence (e.g. *hint*, *stint*, *interesting*, etc). In contrast, the word *pint* has irregular letter-to-phoneme mappings for –*i*- in -*int* (pronounced /aI/ as in *mile* and *kind*) and therefore takes longer to process (e.g. Baron & Strawson, 1976). Other evidence comes from studies of cross-modal priming, which consistently find that written primes facilitate performance on auditory tasks, i.e. previous exposure to the visual form of a stimulus facilitates recognition of that stimulus when presented auditorily (e.g. Berry *et al.*, 1997; Lovemann *et al.*, 2002; McClelland & Pring, 1991). Moreover, empirical evidence suggests that a word's phonological similarity to other words influences its recognition in the visual modality (e.g. Dijkstra *et al.*, 1999; Ferrand & Grainger, 1994; Perfetti & Bell, 1991; Van Orden, 1987; Van Orden *et al.*, 1988).

In the bilingual literature, a number of studies have examined the role of phonology in visual word recognition (e.g. Doctor & Klein, 1992; Lam *et al.*, 1991; Nas, 1983). Increased phonological similarity has been found to influence bilingual language processing. For example, studies of masked phonological priming (i.e. the prime was presented too briefly for the subject to be consciously aware of it) revealed facilitative interlingual homophone priming from both the native to the non-native language, and from the non-native to the native language (e.g. Brysbaert *et al.*, 1999; Van Wijnendaele & Brysbaert, 2002). In contrast, cross-linguistic form primes (i.e. the participant was consciously aware of perceiving the phonological prime) have been found to inhibit target words in the native language (e.g. Silverberg & Samuel, 2004) and in the non-native language (e.g. Dijkstra *et al.*, 1999; Nas, 1983). These differences in results likely emerged because the masked priming tasks that yielded facilitation had activated sublexical phonological representations only, while lexical decision tasks that yielded cross-linguistic inhibition had activated both lexical and sublexical representations. Together, both facilitatory and inhibitory types of evidence suggest that phonology and phonological overlap play a notable role in orthographic decoding and impact both lexical and sublexical processing in bilingual visual word recognition.

Moreover, studies of bilingual visual word recognition have found that the phonological form of a word is activated not only for the target language, but also for the non-target language (e.g. Dijkstra *et al.*, 1999; Van Wijnendaele & Brysbaert, 2002). Furthermore, the phonology of the non-target language is activated not only when the two languages share orthography (for a review, see Doctor & Klein, 1992), but also when the two orthographic systems are distinct, further confirming the interactive nature of the bilingual mental lexicon. For instance, English-Hebrew bilinguals (Tzelgov *et al.*, 1990) and Mandarin-English bilinguals (Chen & Ho, 1986), tested with a cross-linguistic Stroop task, experienced interference from the non-target language. Because all stimuli were presented only visually and because the two languages did not share orthography, any cross-linguistic interference observed in these bilingual Stroop studies (e.g. Chen & Ho, 1986; Tzelgov *et al.*, 1990) indicated that this interference was driven by non-target language phonology, thus suggesting that the orthography-to-phonology mappings activated the phonological system of the non-target language.

With the increased use of eye-movement monitoring to study bilingual language processing during reading (e.g. Altarriba *et al.*, 1996, 2001; McDonald & Thompson, 2006), eye-tracking technology also prompted research on bilingual visual word recognition. For example, Kaushans-kaya and Marian (2007) provided evidence for activation of both the phonological and orthographic forms of a word during bilingual language processing in a study that tracked eye movements of Russian–English bilinguals during a Picture-Word Interference task. Specifically, bilinguals were asked to name pictures presented on a computer-screen in the presence of written words or pseudowords that appeared elsewhere on the same screen, while their eye movements were recorded. The picture label and the words/pseudowords overlapped across languages in orthography, phonology or both. Eye movements to written words that competed cross-linguistically with a target were taken as indicative of parallel activation during the comprehension component of the task. During picture naming, reaction time differences for words and pseudowords that shared orthography/phonology compared to words and pseudowords that did *not* share orthography/phonology were taken as indicative of parallel activation during the production component of the task. Results showed that both the auditory form and the written form of the target and the non-target language were activated during this combined word recognition and naming task. These findings were interpreted as supporting a non-selective view of bilingual language processing in which both languages are active in parallel, but they also provide support for automatic online audio-visual integration during bilingual language comprehension and production.

In addition to visual word recognition, coactivation of both written and auditory forms of a word has been found during auditory language comprehension. Although less intuitive, it is clearly the case that the orthographic shape of a word is frequently activated during spoken language processing. For instance, auditory primes have been found to influence performance on written word processing tasks (e.g. Lovemann *et al.*, 2002). Moreover, bimodal (auditory and written) presentation of information has been found to impact performance during auditory language processing tasks and to improve word recognition in mono-lingual speakers, as well as in bilingual speakers (Dijkstra *et al.*, 1993; Erdener & Burnham, 2005; Frost *et al.*, 1988; Massaro *et al.*, 1990). Other support for the role of orthography in spoken word recognition comes from monolingual studies that find that auditory word recognition is influenced not only by phonological neighborhood size, but also by orthographic neighborhood size (e.g. Ziegler *et al.*, 2003). The term *orthographic neighborhood* refers to all words that differ by one letter from the target word, whereas the term *phonological neighborhood* refers to all words that differ by one phoneme from the target word. Studies that have manipulated the size of the orthographic neighborhood of a word during an auditory word recognition task have found that neighborhood size influences recognition rates.

In sum, psycholinguistic studies have demonstrated that phonological information influences written word processing and orthographic information influences auditory word processing (e.g. Van Orden & Goldinger, 1994; Van Orden *et al.*, 1990). The finding that bilinguals process phonological and orthographic information in parallel during visual and auditory word recognition lends further support to a bilingual language processing system that is highly interactive across languages and modalities.

3. Modeling Audio-visual Integration During Bilingual Language Processing

Computational models of bilingual language processing currently include the Bilingual Interactive Activation model (BIA and its modified version BIA +) (Dijkstra *et al.*, 1998; Dijkstra & Van Heuven, 2002; Van Heuven *et al.*, 1998), the Bilingual Activation Verification model (BAV) (Grainger, 1993), the Bilingual Interactive Model of Lexical Access (BIMOLA) (Grosjean, 1997), the Semantic Orthographic and Phonological Interactive Activation model (SOPHIA) (Van Heuven, 2000) and the Self-Organizing Model of Bilingual Processing (SOMBIP) (Li & Farkas, 2002). New models are continuously being developed.

An example of a typical early model of bilingual language processing is the BAV model, shown in Figure 3.2 (Grainger, 1993). The BAV is a model of bilingual visual word recognition modeled after the mono-lingual Activation Verification model (Paap *et al.*, 1982). According to this model, a given letter string activates all lexical representations that share letters in the same position as the stimulus, and the greater the number of shared letters, the higher the activation level of the corresponding lexical representation. In the BAV, incoming orthographic information initially activates lexical representations in both languages independently of language context. The most strongly activated of these representations form two separate candidate sets in each lexical system. Language context information then comes into play during selection/verification processes. This information guides the verification process to the appropriate lexical system and thus diminishes the number of possible candidates by half.

Although the BAV allows initial parallel access to lexical representa-tions in both languages, it does posit two distinct lexical systems in

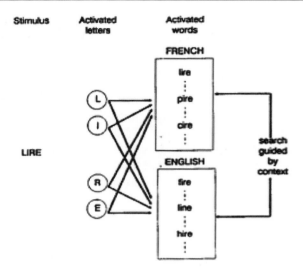

Figure 3.2 A graphic representation of the Bilingual Activation Verification (BAV) model (based on Grainger, 1993)

bilinguals. The utility of separate lexical systems for the two languages remains a matter of debate and is inconsistent with some of the more recent empirical evidence suggesting an integrated lexical system in bilinguals (for instance, the BAV cannot account for cross-language neighborhood effects, e.g. Grainger & Dijkstra, 1992; Grainger *et al.*, 1992). As it is, the model works at the letter level, but not at the feature level (the feature level stores separate visual letter features and precedes letter recognition), and can be used to account for results from languages that share orthography, but not from languages with different ortho-graphies. In order for the BAV to account for audio-visual interaction and for languages that do not share orthographies, it would have to be revised to include a phonological component and a feature component, both of which would interact bidirectionally with the letter component. Without such revisions, the BAV is representative of what early models of bilingual language processing looked like: none of them incorporated the interplay between phonology and orthography and between audio-visual sensory input. However, efforts to do so have been undertaken in recent years and are considered next.

As far as accounting for the interaction between phonology and orthography during word recognition, current monolingual models typically incorporate a phonological processing component (e.g. Coltheart *et al.*, 2001; Seidenberg & McClelland, 1989). Moreover, some monolingual accounts of auditory speech perception also incorporate an orthographic component (e.g. Dijkstra *et al.*, 1995; Frauenfelder *et al.*, 1990; Ziegler *et al.*, 2003). Although models of bilingual *spoken* word recognition have not yet included the orthographic form of the input, bilingual models of *visual* word recognition have started to incorporate the phonological form of the word. For instance, the BIA+ model (Dijkstra & Van Heuven, 2002) shown in Figure 3.3 is one model of bilingual visual word recognition that incorporates the role of phonology during bilingual reading and has been implemented computationally.

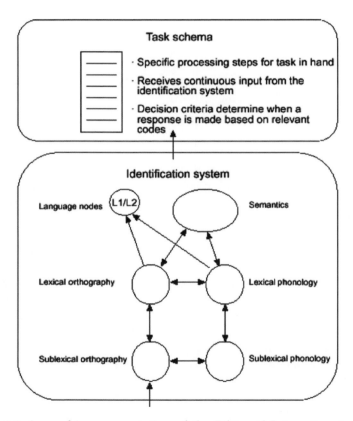

Figure 3.3 A graphic representation of the Bilingual Interactive Activation Plus (BIA+) model (based on Dijkstra & Van Heuven, 2002).

The BIA+ constitutes a revision and enhancement of the original BIA model (Dijkstra & Van Heuven, 1998), which in turn was modeled after the Interactive Activation model of visual word recognition in monolinguals proposed by McClelland and Rumelhart (1981). The BIA+ model consists of four representational levels: a feature level, a letter level, a word level and a supralexical 'language node' (Dijkstra *et al.*, 1998). Activation in the BIA+ model takes place bidirectionally both within and between levels. The model is interactive in the sense that higher-level nodes can now send input to lower-level nodes, in addition to previously postulated bottom-up input.

In the BIA+, sensory input from orthographic stimuli activates feature representations in memory. The feature representations send activation to letter representations, which in turn send activation to lexical representations in both languages. These lexical representations then send activation to the supralexical language nodes. An activated language node sends back excitatory feedback to all the lexical nodes in that language, and those lexical nodes in turn send excitatory feedback to their component letters. Activation of the language node in the BIA+ is influenced by previous lexical recognition. A previously recognized word in L1 increases the activation level of the L1 language node and decreases the activation level of the L2 language node. As a result, the activation level of all words in the L1 increases, while the activation level of all words in the L2 decreases. It is through this feedback process from language nodes to word nodes that the BIA+ explains how bilingual subjects limit interference from the non-target language.

The BIA+ model suggests that almost immediately following the initial non-selective activation phase, language context information allows the suppression of context-incompatible lexical representations via top-down inhibitory connections from language nodes to word representations. In this way, the BIA+ can account for the occurrence of cross-language interference and for the fact that bilinguals are able to keep such interference to a minimum by using language context. In addition, the BIA+ model (Dijkstra & Van Heuven, 2002) postulates separate nodes for lexical and sublexical *phonological* information, as well as for lexical and sublexical *orthographic* information. This ability to incorporate the interplay between phonology and orthography during visual language processing is a major strength of the BIA+ model, yielding an elegant account of audio-visual integration in terms of phonological and orthographic linguistic input. The BIA+ model was not, however, designed to integrate other forms of linguistically relevant visual information, such as items in the surrounding visual environment.

In fact, none of the existing models of bilingual language processing currently accommodate cross-modal audio-visual interaction such as that described in the first section of this chapter. Thus, beyond the integration of phonology and orthography, there remains a need to model the interplay of auditory and visual input during bilingual spoken language comprehension in complex visual environments. One model of monolingual language processing that can be adapted particularly well to reflect bilingual processing is Marslen-Wilson's COHORT model. The original COHORT model (Marslen-Wilson & Welsh, 1978) is based on the assumption that word recognition takes place on the basis of analyzing all words that match the onset of a target word (see Figure 3.4, panel A). For example, as a spoken word unfolds over time, listeners may initially coactivate the words *marker, marble,* and *mop* (among others) upon hearing *m-*, rule out *mop* after hearing *mar-* and identify the target word as *marker* after hearing *mark-*.

According to the COHORT model, recognition takes place in two stages. During the first stage, all words that exactly match the onset of a

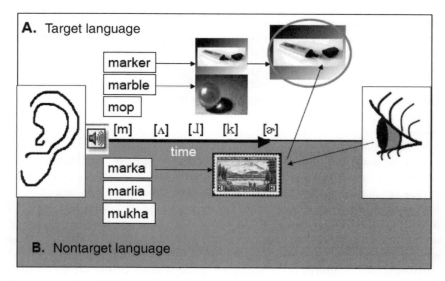

Figure 3.4 Unfolding of the acoustic signal, and cohort activation within and across languages, as indexed by eye movements. Panel A illustrates Marslen-Wilson's COHORT model (1987) in a monolingual scenario (Tanenhaus *et al.,* 1995). Panel B extends the model to a bilingual scenario, as proposed by Marian (2000) and Blumenfeld and Marian (2007).

target word are activated, generating the word-initial cohort. Words that do not match the onset do not enter the cohort, are not activated and do not compete for recognition. The second stage is a deactivation stage during which the cohort members that do not match subsequent sensory input are eliminated from the cohort as more input is received. The cohort members do not have any effect upon each other; therefore, neither the number nor the frequency of the cohort members affects the time course of word recognition in this early model. Only the final cohort members that match the target word the longest determine word recognition. Thus, the COHORT model predicts recognition of a given word on the basis of analyzing its cohort members. The status of words is binary, i.e. the words are either in or out of the cohort. All processing takes place online and in parallel. The activated lexical competitors at any given time are the words that match, and are aligned with, the target word. The recognition point of a presented word corresponds to the moment that the word becomes unique with respect to the other words in the lexicon. The model can make precise and testable predictions about the time course of word recognition. One shortcoming of the COHORT model is the binary status of the cohort words, where the matching between acoustic input and each member of the cohort is an all-or-none process. Another major problem with the COHORT model seems to be its failure to take into account that the number and the frequency of the cohort members affect the time course of word recognition. Both number and frequency effects have been observed repeatedly in monolingual language processing (e.g. Luce *et al.*, 1990), as well as in bilingual language processing (e.g. Beauvillain & Grainger, 1987). To address these shortcomings, the initial model was modified to the COHORT II model.

The COHORT II model (Marslen-Wilson, 1987), like the COHORT, is a strictly bottom-up model, with no top-down effects involved in access or selection. It retains the fundamental characteristics of a cohort-based word recognition model, but differs from the original model in a few important ways. First, the cohort membership is increased to include words that mismatch the sensory input to some degree. The advantage of this modification is that the proposed system is more tolerant of minor deviations in the input; the disadvantage is that the cohort set is now not clearly specified. Second, the model allows for different levels of activation for the cohort members, depending upon their fit with the input and their frequency. The advantage of this modification is that it expresses the varying degree of match between the input and the different competitors; the disadvantage is that it does not specify how word frequency and the degree of match with the input determine activation. Finally, the model is more explicit on the issue of sublexical representations. The advantage of this modification is that now recognition is based on feature matrices, mapping features directly onto lexical units, with no intermediate phoneme decision. Consequently, cohorts can be activated whose initial phoneme differs from that of the input but has partial feature overlap. Thus, while the COHORT model makes clear and testable predictions, it makes several simplifying assumptions that are not always accurate with respect to lexical processing. COHORT II fits better with what we know about lexical processing, but is not clear about the competitor set and cannot always predict the time course of word recognition (Frauenfelder, 1996).

To account for bilingual language processing, the COHORT II model needs to be modified to postulate activation of initial cohorts in both languages (see Figure 3.4, panel B). A Bilingual COHORT model would assume that as the listener perceives auditory input, lexical items from both languages are activated in parallel, resulting in a combined bilingual cohort that extends across the two languages. In the end, as the auditory input unfolds, only the appropriate target is selected, as it is in a monolingual context. A Bilingual COHORT model can successfully accommodate findings from the bilingual empirical literature showing that both languages are activated in parallel in a bilingual, while at the same time incorporating the interplay between the auditory and visual modalities during spoken word recognition in naturalistic environments. That is, in everyday language comprehension, the auditory pathway is rarely the only source of input; rather, the listener is typically situated in complex visual environments with the visual pathway providing additional input that may or may not be related to the auditory input (for example, when words have multiple meanings, as is the case of homophones within and across languages, processing of auditory input is augmented by visual input that is congruent with the relevant word meaning).

The proposed Bilingual COHORT model could account for bilinguals relying more on visual information during auditory processing relative to monolinguals. For example, parallel visual access could be posited and modeled after Seidenberg and McClelland's (1989) triangle model of reading, where all words are processed by a single system containing distributed orthographic, phonological and semantic codes. In the Bilingual COHORT model, integration of the auditory and visual information would likely take place at an intermediate stage, perhaps with amplification of auditory information that is consistent with the visual input. The same could be true for orthography, as in the case of subtitles, where one experiences amplification of auditory input that is consistent with the subtitles. Such multimodal parallel access would be active in both monolinguals and bilinguals, but in bilinguals it might result in greater reliance on the other modality when input from one modality is incomplete or noisy.

Despite its advantages, the proposed Bilingual COHORT model still has the drawback of an entirely bottom-up, feed-forward architecture. Although the model seems to account well for the initial stages of cross-linguistic parallel activation of lexical items in bilinguals, its strictly feed-forward architecture may not allow for any contextual effects on processing. For example, in the case of exact homonyms, the lexical items in both languages are activated, but only one of the two is chosen as the target word, depending upon linguistic context. One way to accommodate these kinds of data is to incorporate 'language tags' in the model to specify the language in use, similar to the language tags postulated by the BIA model (Dijkstra & Van Heuven, 1998) or the Inhibitory Control (IC) model (Green, 1998). Another way would be to postulate the existence of a language node. Or, if the model is a connectionist one, the selectivity could be further explained by higher initial probabilities of the vector of lexical nodes in the active language (e.g. by residual activation from prior use). Mathematically, that could be expressed by adding a positive constant to the nodes in the active language, increasing their baseline activation. The connectionist model may also incorporate variations in the strength of the weights between items by language, to account for higher activation of the target language than activation of the non-target language. In this case, stronger connection weights between sublexical and lexical levels in the native language could account for auditory input mapping more strongly onto the native system than onto the non-native one. In the same vein, a language node account may also influence selectivity by increasing pathway strength or increased activation from the language node associated with the stronger language.

Each of these solutions may work to different degrees, and efforts are currently underway to develop a computational, interactive model of bilingual spoken language processing that would adequately account for audio-visual interaction (laterally within levels, as well as bottom-up and top-down between levels). A Bilingual COHORT model, like any other bilingual model, should also be able to accommodate mixed language input. In any case, one problem that models of bilingual spoken language processing are guaranteed to encounter is the difficulty of accounting for identification when the phonemes and features do not carry much overlap in the two languages, as is often the case (even when the perceptual categories of the bilingual are not sensitive to these differences, their existence in the input must be accounted for computationally). This problem, however, is not unique to bilingual processing. Models of monolingual language processing are also plagued by the difficulty of accounting for differences among speakers (accents, voice properties) and variability in the rate of speech, ambient noise, etc.

Even with these changes and caveats, the Bilingual COHORT model remains very limited. Its scope is much narrower than that of, for instance, BIA +. In an ideal world, a global model that would combine the different foci and strengths of existing bilingual models would be particularly desirable. This global model of bilingualism would combine BIA + ability to allow for interaction between phonology and orthography during written comprehension, SOMBIP and BIMOLA relevance to spoken comprehension, Bilingual COHORT model ability to integrate non-linguistic visual information as the word unfolds, the Revised Hierarchical Model's (RHM) (Kroll & Stewart, 1994) focus on links between forms and concepts, and IC focus on control of the two languages. This, of course, is a tall order, and one that cannot currently be implemented. However, with further development of computational tools and additional knowledge about the bilingual cognitive architecture, it is only a matter of time until a comprehensive model of bilingual language processing can be developed. After all, the capacity of bilingual models has notably increased in the 10 years between BAV and BIA +, and it is not unreasonable to expect that a few more decades of modeling would produce further strides. Until then, the task of modeling bilingualism is broken down into multiple smaller components (e.g. written comprehension, spoken comprehension, production, non-linguistic visual input, control, concepts). (In addition to the original texts, concise summaries of the models discussed here, along with their graphic representations, can be found in a number of recent review papers, including a thorough overview of computational models by Thomas and Van Heuven (2005) and a historical review of bilingual cognitive models by Kroll and Tokowicz (2005).)

Conclusions: Audio-visual Integration and Representation in the Bilingual Mental Lexicon

In sum, it is clear that audio-visual integration is an inherent part of bilingual language processing, be it integration of auditory and visual modalities or integration of phonological and orthographic word-forms. Bilingual models of language processing are beginning to account for the role of phonology during visual word recognition, but they have yet to address the role of orthography during auditory word recognition. The COHORT model (Marslen-Wilson, 1987; Marslen-Wilson & Welsh, 1978) of monolingual language processing is one model that can be adapted to allow for bimodal integration during bilingual spoken language processing. However, a model of audio-visual integration during bilingual language comprehension would have to allow for both – the cross-modal interaction between auditory and visual input and the interplay between phonology and orthography. Such a model will also need to be able to account for the fact that, by its very nature, bilingualism is not a static phenomenon, but a dynamic, developmental process, which undergoes changes continuously. As the level of proficiency or the manner of acquisition change, so do language processing and representation. The concept of a dynamically evolving bilingual system has previously been incorporated in the RHM (Kroll & Stewart, 1994) and the SOMBIP (Li & Farkas, 2002). Both of these models have posited changes in the representation of the second language, and in the relationship between the first and second languages, as proficiency levels change. Although neither the RHM nor the SOMBIP address the issue of audio-visual integration in bilinguals, they provide valuable insights into developmental factors (such as changes in proficiency levels) that have to be incorporated into a multimodal integration model of bilingual language processing.

The recognition that language comprehension is a cross-modal, interactive process carries implications for representation in the bilingual mental lexicon. It suggests that, as linguistic input unfolds, it becomes integrated across modalities incrementally and thus, its representation in the bilingual mental lexicon is constantly changing and evolving. This 'in-flux' state is inevitable, as language comprehension is a continuous, never static, process. In his book, *The Continuity of Mind*, Spivey (2007: 206) describes the mental representations of sentences, words and phonemes as *a process* and not *a thing*, and writes the following about language comprehension:

> ... there is no point in time when the mental trajectory through state space, which is propelled by a combination of environmental sensory input and goal-oriented expectations, stops and stands still. It is always in motion. The patterns of neural activation in the brain are in perpetual flux. An important consequence of this temporal continuity of mind is that there can be no mediating states (e.g., Dietrich & Markman, 2003), because states require stasis. ...these dynamic

patterns, or continuous processes… are not states, and therefore cannot be static symbols that are discretely separable from one another in time or in representational space. What this means is that language is not a string of symbols whose grammatical relationships are encoded by discrete hierarchical structures in an encapsulated linguistic module. Language, like the rest of perception and cognition, is a continuous trajectory through a high-dimensional state space…

Though these statements are both sensible and intuitive, they in fact carry revolutionary implications for the way we think about representations in the bilingual mental lexicon. Current models of bilingual language organization and processing do not allow for this continuity of mental states and instead idealize representations in the bilingual mental lexicon as discrete states. The need to describe mental representations in the bilingual lexicon as dynamic, continuous processes is the likely next step in the psycholinguistics of bilingualism. In general, as bilingualism scholars, we need to move away from unimodal perspectives of bilingual language processing and recognize that language comprehension in the real world is a combination of multiple sources of input that interact to form a final composite interpreted by the brain. In essence, we hear with our brain and not with our ears, as the McGurk effect (described at the beginning of this chapter) so elegantly shows. As research on bilingual language processing moves from the laboratory to the real world, it becomes increasingly clear that studies and models of bilingualism need to reflect and to be rooted in the understanding that language is a multimodal and dynamic process.

Acknowledgements

Preparation of this chapter was supported in part by grants NSF-BCS-0418495 and NICHD-1R03HD046952-01A1. I thank Henrike Blumenfeld, Margarita Kaushanskaya, Melissa Baese, Caroline Engstler, Aneta Pavlenko and the anonymous reviewers for helpful comments and suggestions.

References

Altarriba, J., Kambe, G., Pollatsek, A. and Rayner, K. (2001) Semantic codes are not used in integrating information across eye fixations in reading: Evidence from fluent Spanish-English bilinguals. *Perception & Psychophysics* 63, 875–890.

Altarriba, J., Kroll, J., Sholl, A. and Rayner, K. (1996) The influence of lexical and conceptual constraints on reading mixed-language sentences: Evidence from eye fixations and naming times. *Memory and Cognition* 24, 477–492.

Baron, J. and Strawson, C. (1976) Use of orthographic and word-specific knowledge in reading words aloud. *Journal of Experimental Psychology: Human Perception and Performance* 2, 386–393.

Beauvillain, C. and Grainger, J. (1987) Accessing interlexical homographs: Some limitations of a language-selective access. *Journal of Memory and Language* 26, 658–672.

Ben-Zeev, S. (1977) The influence of bilingualism on cognitive strategy and cognitive development. *Child Development* 48, 1009–1018.

Berry, D., Banbury, S. and Henry, L. (1997) Transfer across form and modality in implicit and explicit memory. *The Quarterly Journal of Experimental Psychology* 50A (1), 1–24.

Bialystok, E. (2005) Consequences of bilingualism for cognitive development. In J. Kroll and A.M.B. De Groot (eds) *Handbook of Bilingualism: Psycholinguistic Approaches* (pp. 417–432). Oxford: Oxford University Press.

Bialystok, E. (2006) Effect of bilingualism and computer video game experience on the Simon task. *Canadian Journal of Experimental Psychology* 60 (1), 68–79.

Bird, S. and Williams, J. (2002) The effect of bimodal input on implicit and explicit memory: An investigation into the benefits of within-language subtitling. *Applied Psycholinguistics* 23, 509–533.

Blumenfeld, H. and Marian, V. (2007) Constraints on parallel activation in bilingual spoken language processing: Examining proficiency and lexical status using eye-tracking. *Language and Cognitive Processes* 22 (5), 1–28.

Borras, I. and Lafayette, R. (1994) Effects of multimedia courseware subtitling on the speaking performance of college students of French. *The Modern Language Journal* 78, 61–65.

Bradlow, A. and Bent, T. (2002) The clear speech effect for non-native listeners. *Journal of the Acoustical Society of America* 112 (1), 272–284.

Bradlow, A. and Pisoni, D. (1999) Recognition of spoken words by native and non-native listeners: Talker-, listener- and item-related factors. *Journal of the Acoustical Society of America* 106 (4), 2074–2085.

Brysbaert, M., Van Dyck, G. and Van de Poel, M. (1999) Visual word recognition in bilinguals: Evidence from masked phonological priming. *Journal of Experimental Psychology: Human Perception and Performance* 25, 137–148.

Calvert, G., Bullmore, E., Brammer, M., Campbell, R., Williams, S., McGuire, P. *et al.* (1997) Activation of auditory cortex during silent lipreading. *Science* 276, 593–596.

Calvert, G., Campbell, R. and Brammer, M. (2000) Evidence from functional magnetic resonance imaging of cross-modal binding in the human hetero-modal cortex. *Current Biology* 10, 649–657.

Campbell, R., MacSweeney, M., Surguladze, S., Calvert, G., McGuire, P., Suckling, J. *et al.* (2001) Cortical substrates for the perception of face actions: An fMRI study of the specificity of activation for seen speech and for meaningless lower-face acts. *Cognitive Brain Research* 12, 233–243.

Canseco-Gonzalez, E. (2005) 'Carpet or Carcel' effects of speaker type, fluency, and language mode on bilingual lexical access. *Abstracts of the 5th International*

Symposium on Bilingualism (pp. 156–157). Barcelona, Spain: Universidad Autonoma de Barcelona.

Chen, H.C. and Ho, C. (1986) Development of Stroop interference in Chinese-English bilinguals. *Journal of Experimental Psychology: Learning, Memory, and Cognition* 12, 397–401.

Clau v. Uniglobe Pacific Travel (1995) *Canadian Human Rights Reporter* 23, D/515–D/518.

Coltheart, M., Rastle, K., Perry, C., Langdon, R. and Ziegel, J. (2001) DRC: A dual route cascaded model of visual word recognition and reading aloud. *Psychological Review* 108, 204–256.

Cook, V. (1997) The consequences of bilingualism for cognitive processing. In A.M.B. De Groot and J. Kroll (eds) *Tutorials in Bilingualism: Psycholinguistic Perspectives* (pp. 279–300). Hillsdale, NJ: Lawrence Erlbaum.

Cutler, A., Weber, A. and Otake, T. (2006) Asymmetric mapping from phonetic to lexical representations in second-language listening. *Journal of Phonetics* 34, 269–284.

Danan, M. (1992) Reversed subtitling and dual coding theory: New directions for foreign language instruction. *Language Learning* 42 (4), 497–527.

Davis, C. and Kim, J. (2006) Audio-visual speech perception off the top of the head. *Cognition* 100, B21–B31.

Dietrich, E. and Markman, A. (2003) Discrete thoughts: Why cognition must use discrete representations. *Mind and Language* 18, 95–119.

Dijkstra, A., Frauenfelder, U. and Schreuder, R. (1993) Grapheme-phoneme interaction in a bimodal detection task. *Journal of Experimental Psychology: Human Perception and Performance* 19 (5), 1–20.

Dijkstra, A., Grainger, J. and Van Heuven, W. (1999) Recognition of cognates and interlingual homographs: The neglected role of phonology. *Journal of Memory and Language* 41, 496–518.

Dijkstra, A., Roelofs, A. and Fiews, S. (1995) Orthographic effects on phoneme monitoring. *Canadian Journal of Experimental Psychology* 49 (2), 264–271.

Dijkstra, A. and Van Heuven, W. (1998) The BIA-model and bilingual word recognition. In J. Grainger and A. Jacobs (eds) *Localist Connectionist Approaches to Human Cognition* (pp. 189–225). Mahwah, NJ: Lawrence Erlbaum.

Dijkstra, A. and Van Heuven, W. (2002) The architecture of the bilingual word recognition system: From identification to decision. *Bilingualism: Language and Cognition* 5, 175–197.

Dijkstra, A., Van Heuven, W. and Grainger, J. (1998) Simulating cross-language competition with the Bilingual Interactive Activation model. *Psychologica Belgica* 38, 177–196.

Doctor, E. and Klein, D. (1992) Phonological processing in bilingual word recognition. In R. Harris (ed.) *Cognitive Processing in Bilinguals* (pp. 237–252). Amsterdam: Elsevier.

Erdener, V. and Burnham, D. (2005) The role of audiovisual speech and orthographic information in non-native speech production. *Language Learning* 55 (2), 191–228.

Ferrand, L. and Grainger, J. (1994) Effects of orthography are independent of phonology in masked form priming. *The Quarterly Journal of Experimental Psychology* 47A, 365–382.

Frauenfelder, U. (1996) Computational models of spoken word recognition. In T. Dijkstra and K. de Smedt (eds) *Computational Psycholinguistics: AI and Connectionist Models of Human Language Processing* (pp. 114–138). London: Taylor & Francis.

Frauenfelder, U., Segui, J. and Dijkstra, A. (1990) Lexical effects in phoneme processing: Facilitatory or inhibitory? *Journal of Experimental Psychology: Human Perception and Performance* 16 (1), 77–91.

Frost, R., Repp, B. and Katz, L. (1988) Can speech perception be influenced by simultaneous presentation of print? *Journal of Memory and Language* 27, 741–755.

Grainger, J. (1993) Visual word recognition in bilinguals. In R. Schreuder and B. Weltens (eds) *The Bilingual Lexicon* (pp. 11–26). Amsterdam: John Benjamins.

Grainger, J. and Dijkstra, T. (1992) On the representation and use of language information in bilinguals. In R. Harris (ed.) *Cognitive Processing in Bilinguals* (pp. 207–220). Amsterdam: Elsevier.

Grainger, J., O'Regan, J., Jacobs, A. and Segui, J. (1992) Neighborhood frequency effects and letter visibility in visual word recognition. *Perception & Psychophysics* 51, 49–56.

Green, D. (1998) Mental control of the bilingual lexico-semantic system. *Bilingualism: Language and Cognition* 1, 67–81.

Grosjean, F. (1997) Processing mixed language: Issues, findings, and models. In A.M.B. De Groot and J. Kroll (eds) *Tutorials in Bilingualism: Psycholinguistic Perspectives* (pp. 225–254). Hillsdale, NJ: Lawrence Erlbaum.

Guillen v. R. Dufour Enterprises Ltd. (1995) Unpublished decision. British Columbia Council of Human Rights.

Ju, M. and Luce, P. (2004) Falling on sensitive ears: Constraints on bilingual lexical activation. *Psychological Science* 15, 314–318.

Kaushanskaya, M. and Marian, V. (2007) Non-target language recognition and interference in bilinguals: Evidence from eye tracking and picture naming. *Language Learning* 57, 119–163.

Kraus, N. (2007) Music experience shapes subcortical sensory circuitry. Paper presented at the Music Cognition Colloquium, Northwestern University School of Music.

Krishnan, A., Xu, Y., Gandour, J. and Cariani, P. (2005) Encoding of pitch in the human brainstem is sensitive to language experience. *Cognitive Brain Research* 25, 161–168.

Kroll, J. and Stewart, E. (1994) Category interferences in translation and picture naming: Evidence for asymmetric connection between bilingual memory representation. *Journal of Memory and Language* 33, 149–174.

Kroll, J. and Tokowicz, N. (2005) Models of bilingual representation and processing. In J. Kroll and A.M.B. De Groot (eds) *Handbook of Bilingualism: Psycholinguistics Approaches* (pp. 531–553). Oxford: Oxford University Press.

Lam, A., Perfetti, C. and Bell, L. (1991) Automatic phonetic transfer in bidialectal reading. *Applied Psycholinguistics* 12, 299–311.

Li, P. and Farkas, I. (2002) A self-organized connectionist model of bilingual processing. In R. Heredia and J. Altarriba (eds) *Bilingual Sentence Processing* (pp. 59–88). North Holland: Elsevier Science.

Lovemann, E., van Hoff, J.C. and Gale, A. (2002) A systematic investigation of same and cross modality priming using written and spoken responses. *Memory* 10 (4), 267–276.

Luce, P. and Pisoni, D. (1998) Recognizing spoken words: The neighborhood activation model. *Ear & Hearing* 19, 1–36.

Luce, P., Pisoni, D. and Goldinger, S. (1990) Similarity neighborhoods of spoken words. In G. Altmann (ed.) *Cognitive Models of Speech Perception: Psycholinguistic and Computational Perspectives* (pp. 122–147). Cambridge, MA: MIT Press.

Marian, V. (2000) Bilingual language processing: Evidence from eye-tracking and functional neuroimaging. Unpublished doctoral dissertation, Cornell University.

Marian, V. and Spivey, M. (2003a) Competing activation in bilingual language processing: Within- and between-language competition. *Bilingualism: Language and Cognition* 6, 97–115.

Marian, V. and Spivey, M. (2003b) Bilingual and monolingual processing of competing lexical items. *Applied Psycholinguistics* 24, 173–193.

Marian, V., Blumenfeld, H. and Boukrina, O. (2008) Sensitivity to phonological similarity within and across languages: A native/non-native asymmetry in bilinguals. *Journal of Psycholinguistic Research* 37, 141–170.

Marslen-Wilson, W. (1987) Functional parallelism in spoken word recognition. *Cognition* 25, 71–102.

Marslen-Wilson, W. and Welsh, A. (1978) Processing interactions and lexical access during word-recognition in continuous speech. *Cognitive Psychology* 10, 29–63.

Massaro, D., Cohen, M. and Thompson, L. (1990) Visible language in speech perception: Lipreading and reading. *Visible Language* 22, 8–31.

McClelland, A. and Pring, L. (1991) An investigation of cross-modality effects in implicit and explicit memory. *Quarterly Journal of Experimental Psychology* 43A, 19–33.

McClelland, J. and Elman, J. (1986) The TRACE model of speech perception. *Cognitive Psychology* 18, 1–86.

McClelland, J. and Rumelhart, D. (1981) An interactive activation model of context effects in letter perception: Part 1. An account of basic findings. *Psychological Review* 88, 375–407.

McDonald, S. and Thompson, J. (2006) Using eye-tracking to contrast lexical-level and conceptual-level connections in the bilingual lexicon. Unpublished manuscript. School of Philosophy, Psychology, and Language Sciences, University of Edinburgh.

McGurk, H. and MacDonald, J. (1976) Hearing lips and seeing voices: A new illusion. *Nature* 264, 746–748.

Mechelli, A., Crinion, J., Noppeny, U., O'Doherty, J., Ashburner, J., Frackowiak, R. *et al*. (2004) Structural plasticity in the bilingual brain: Proficiency in a second language and age at acquisition affect grey-matter density. *Nature* 431 (7010), 757.

Munhall, K., Jones, J., Callan, D., Kuratate, T. and Vatikiotis-Bateson, E. (2004) Visual prosody and speech intelligibility – Head movement improves auditory speech perception. *Psychological Science* 15, 133–137.

Munro, M. (1998) The effects of noise on the intelligibility of foreign-accented speech. *Studies in Second Language Acquisition* 20, 139–154.

Musacchia G., Sams, M., Nicol, T. and Kraus, N. (2006) Seeing speech affects acoustic information processing in the human brainstem. *Experimental Brain Research* 168, 1–10.

Nas, G. (1983) Visual word recognition in bilinguals: Evidence for a cooperation between visual and sound based codes during access to a common lexical store. *Journal of Verbal Learning and Verbal Behavior* 22, 526–534.

Navarra, J. and Soto-Faraco, S. (2007) Hearing lips in a second language: Visual articulatory information enables the perception of secondary language sounds. *Psychological Research-Psychologische Forschung* 71, 4–12.

Nishitani, N. and Hari, R. (2002) Viewing lip forms: Cortical dynamics. *Neuron* 19, 1211–1220.

Paap, K., Newsome, S., McDonald, J. and Schvaneveldt, R. (1982) An activation-verification model for letter and word recognition: The word-superiority effect. *Psychological Review* 89, 573–594.

Perfetti, C. and Bell, L. (1991) Phonemic activation during the first 40 ms of word identification: Evidence from backward masking and priming. *Journal of Memory & Language* 30 (4), 473–485.

Ronquest, R. and Hernandez, L. (2005) Lip-reading skills in bilinguals: Some effects of L1 on visual-only language identification. *Research on Spoken Language Processing, Progress Report 27*. Indiana University, Bloomington, IN.

Ross, L., Saint-Amour, D., Leavitt, V., Javitt, D. and Foxe, J. (2007) Do you see what I am saying? Exploring visual enhancement of speech comprehension in noisy environment. *Cerebral Cortex* 17, 1147–1153.

Seidenberg, M. and McClelland, J. (1989) A distributed, developmental model of word recognition and naming. *Psychological Review* 96, 523–568.

Silverberg, S. and Samuel, A. (2004) The effect of age of second language acquisition on the representation and processing of second language words. *Journal of Memory and Language* 51, 381–398.

Soto-Faraco, S., Navarra, J., Weikum, W., Vouloumanos, A., Sebastian-Galles, N. and Wereker, J. (2007) Discriminating language by speech-reading. *Perception & Psychophysics* 69, 218–231.

Spivey, M. (2007) *The Continuity of Mind*. Oxford/New York: Oxford University Press.

Spivey, M. and Marian, V. (1999) Cross-talk between native and second languages: Partial activation of an irrelevant lexicon. *Psychological Science* 10, 281–284.

Sumby, W. and Pollack, I. (1954) Visual contribution to speech intelligibility in noise. *Journal of the Acoustical Society of America* 26, 212–215.

Tanenhaus, M., Spivey-Knowlton, M., Eberhard, K. and Sedivy, J. (1995) Integration of visual and linguistic information in spoken language comprehension. *Science* 268, 632–634.

Thomas, M. and Van Heuven, W. (2005) Computational models of bilingual comprehension. In J. Kroll and A.M.B. De Groot (eds) *Handbook of Bilingualism: Psycholinguistics Approaches* (pp. 202–225). Oxford, NY: Oxford University Press.

Tzelgov, J., Henik, A. and Leiser, D. (1990) Controlling Stroop interference: Evidence from a bilingual task. *Journal of Experimental Psychology* 16, 760–771.

Van Atteveldt, N., Formisano, E., Goebel, R. and Blomert, L. (2004) Integration of letters and speech sounds in the human brain. *Neuron* 43, 271–282.

Van Heuven, W. (2000) Visual word recognition in monolingual and bilingual readers: Experiments and computational modeling. PhD thesis, University of Nijmegen.

Van Heuven, W., Dijkstra, T. and Grainger, J. (1998) Orthographic neighborhood effects in bilingual word recognition. *Journal of Memory and Language* 39, 458–483.

Van Orden, G. (1987) A rows is a rose: Spelling, sound and reading. *Memory and Cognition* 15, 181–198.

Van Orden, G. and Goldinger, S. (1994) Interdependence of form and function in cognitive systems explains perception of printed words. *Journal of Experimental Psychology: Human Perception and Performance* 20, 1269–1291.

Van Orden, G., Johnston, J. and Hale, B. (1988) Word identification in reading proceeds from spelling to sound to meaning. *Journal of Experimental Psychology: Learning, Memory, and Cognition* 14, 371–386.

Van Orden, G., Pennington, B. and Stone, G. (1990) What do double dissociations prove? *Cognitive Science* 25, 111–172.

Van Wassenhove, V., Grant, K. and Poeppel, D. (2007) Temporal window of integration in auditory-visual speech perception. *Neuropsychologia* 45, 598–607.

Van Wijnendaele, I. and Brysbaert, M. (2002) Visual word recognition in bilinguals: Phonological priming from the second to the first Language. *Journal of Experimental Psychology: Human Perception and Performance* 28, 616–627.

Vanderplank, R. (1988) The value of teletext subtitles in language learning. *ELT Journal* 42 (4), 272–281.

Wang, Y., Sereno, J., Jongman, A. and Hirsch, J. (2003) fMRI evidence for cortical modification during learning of Mandarin lexical tones. *Journal of Cognitive Neuroscience* 15, 1–9.

Weber, A. and Cutler, A. (2004) Lexical competition in non-native spoken-word recognition. *Journal of Memory and Language* 50, 1–25.

Weber, A. and Paris, G. (2004) The origin of the linguistic gender effect in spoken-word recognition: Evidence from non-native listening. Poster presented at the 26th Annual Meeting of the Cognitive Science Society, Chicago, IL.

Wong, P., Skoe, E., Russo, N., Dees, S. and Kraus N. (2007) Musical experience shapes human brainstem encoding of linguistic pitch patterns. *Nature Neuroscience* 10, 420–422.

Ziegler, J., Muneaux, M. and Grainger, J. (2003) Neighborhood effects in auditory word recognition: Phonological competition and orthographic facilitation. *Journal of Memory and Language* 43, 779–793.

Chapter 4

An Overview of Semantic Processing in Bilinguals: Methods and Findings

JEANETTE ALTARRIBA and DANA M. BASNIGHT-BROWN

Introduction

Among the various levels of linguistic processing that characterize human language, semantics is the area that is most concerned with the representation and processing of meaning. If an individual possesses knowledge of multiple languages, the ways in which each of those languages represents and stores meaning, and the relationship between languages lead to interesting questions regarding the interaction between language, memory and perception. The current chapter will provide a brief overview of the methods that have been used to examine semantic processing in bilingual speakers (e.g. word priming, semantic categorization, Stroop task) and recent research using these methods. Moreover, semantics itself will also be examined in terms of two different word types that are used to describe meaning and have received quite a bit of attention – cognates versus noncognates. The nature of the processing of these word types across languages will also be discussed in light of recent studies that examine the processing of those words across a bilingual's languages. Finally, this chapter will summarize a few main findings with regards to semantic processing that any model would need to account for in providing a comprehensive account of memory representation for bilingual speakers. Our review of the tasks used in this area of inquiry will not be comprehensive, rather we will focus on recent research findings and reveal the current understanding regarding the usefulness of the methods in question.

1. Semantic Representation and Processing

It is important to delimit how semantic representations are distinct from their underlying conceptual ones. Pavlenko (1999) indicates that there are issues of concern that arise when the terms *semantic* and *conceptual* are used interchangeably. While words may share features of semantic meaning and may even be interchangeable across languages (such as the word *silla* in Spanish and its translation *chair* in English), there are other cases in which words that seem to share meaning actually represent different underlying concepts in the two languages. Other words may exist in one language only. For example, the English word *privacy* has no translation equivalent in Russian (Pavlenko, 1999; see also Altarriba, 2003, for examples from Spanish).

Pavlenko (1999) notes that words carry with them three basic components: lexical (word form), semantic (explicit information that relates words to other words) and conceptual (non-linguistic multimodal information, based on world knowledge) (see also chapters by Jarvis and Pavlenko, this volume). Although the three components may be inter-related, they are not interchangeable. Moreover, it is the final component – the conceptual one – that leads to the argument that while lexical entries across a bilingual's lexicons may share basic word meaning (i.e. semantics), it cannot be assumed that they also share an underlying concept (Altarriba, 2000).

The nature and existence of these levels of representation have been the focus of much debate for well over two decades (see e.g. De Groot, 1992, 1993; Francis, 2005; Kroll & Stewart, 1994; Kroll & Tokowicz, 2001; Potter *et al.*, 1984). In the present chapter, the terms *semantic* and *conceptual* will be used to refer to a general level of *meaning*, and thus, can be viewed as interchangeable for the purposes of the current discussion. This level of mental representation for words, phrases and the like is distinguished from a *lexical* level of representation – one that refers to the orthographic or phonological representations. We will also pay attention to the *automaticity* with which mental representations are processed and accessed from memory. Given that automaticity constitutes one of the cornerstones of contemporary cognitive psychology (see e.g. Ashcraft, 2005; Neely & Kahan, 2001), the following section will discuss a variety of cognitive tasks used to explore automaticity and the representation of semantic and lexical information in bilinguals.

2. Findings from Multiple Cognitive Tasks

2.1. Semantic and translation priming across languages

For more than three decades, cognitive psychologists have used the priming paradigm to explore how lexical forms and semantics are represented in memory. In this experimental approach, participants are presented with one or two letter strings on a computer screen. Responses can be measured in two ways. In a *lexical decision task*, individuals are instructed to decide if the letter string is a real word or a nonword (a fake word that is usually phonologically possible in the language that is being studied, e.g. *blit* in English). Participants press one of two keys to denote what type of word (real word versus nonword) has been presented. In a *pronunciation task*, participants say the presented word out loud into a microphone. In both types of tasks, the amount of time needed to respond to each word is recorded and measured in milliseconds (ms). Most semantic priming tasks are constructed so that one word (i.e. prime) appears first, followed by a second word (i.e. target) that is either related or unrelated to the prime word. In most cases, participants are instructed to respond only to the target word. The basic *priming effect*, reported when this paradigm was first used, is that participants were faster to respond to words that were semantically related or commonly associated with each other. For example, pairs of words (presented simultaneously) like *nurse-doctor* and *bread-butter* were recognized faster than pairs that were unrelated, like *doctor-butter* and *bread-nurse* (Meyer & Schvaneveldt, 1971). Therefore, the basic concept behind this paradigm is that when a word is recognized, not only is its meaning automatically activated, but activation spreads to those words that are semantically related to or associated with the presented word. Based on this theory of *spreading activation*, the activation spreads along all pathways, diminishing in strength as the number of pathways increases (Collins & Loftus, 1975).

This experimental paradigm is widely used because it allows one to explore how words are connected or stored in memory, and to determine whether certain processes occur automatically or under conscious control. With regards to bilingual language processing, the priming task can be used to examine the presentation and storage of two languages by presenting participants with cross-language word pairs. For example, if one were testing Spanish–English bilinguals, the prime word *pencil* may be followed by the target word *goma* (eraser). In this case, the prime and target pair *pencil-goma* is presented in the second language (L2)-first language (L1) direction; however, most cross-language priming experiments include equal numbers of word pairs presented in the L1-L2 direction. In addition, translation word pairs (e.g. *pencil-lápiz*) have also been used in many cross-language priming studies (translation priming is sometimes referred to as *repetition priming* in the literature; see e.g. Zeelenberg & Pecher, 2003).

To date, there have been roughly a dozen semantic priming studies and a dozen translation priming studies conducted with bilingual speakers at different proficiency levels whose L2 was English and whose L1s included Spanish (Altarriba, 1990, 1992; Schwanenflugel & Rey, 1986), Chinese (Chen & Ng, 1989; Jiang, 1999; Jiang & Forster, 2001; Keatley *et al.*, 1994), Dutch (De Groot & Nas, 1991; Keatley & de Gelder, 1992; Keatley *et al.*, 1994) and Hebrew (Tzelgov & Eben-Ezra, 1992). Overall, the results suggest that semantic and translation facilitation can be found for cross-language word pairs, revealing that bilinguals can and do access the semantic representations in both of their languages, even across highly dissimilar orthographies (see Altarriba & Basnight-Brown, 2007, for a complete listing of the outcomes reported from all cross-language priming studies). Two trends are observed in this literature: (1) facilitation for translation word pairs is typically larger than for semantically related word pairs and (2) facilitation for prime-target pairs presented in the L2-L1 direction is often smaller in magnitude (or nonexistent) when compared to facilitation in the L1-L2 direction.

Even though it does appear that semantic meanings in both languages can be activated, and certainly the degree of activation increases as one's proficiency in the L2 increases (Altarriba & Canary, 2004; Basnight-Brown & Altarriba, 2007; Finkbeiner *et al.*, 2004), the automaticity surrounding the activation of semantics in the L2 must be interpreted cautiously. Several methodological factors may influence the outcomes, including (1) stimulus onset asynchrony (SOA), i.e. the amount of time between the prime and target presentation, (2) relatedness proportion (RP), i.e. the proportion of related to unrelated trials in each word list and (3) nonword ratio (NWR), i.e. the proportion of nonword to word trials in each word list. These factors vary greatly across studies, making it difficult to draw clear conclusions from these experiments (see Altarriba & Basnight-Brown, 2007, for an in-depth discussion of these factors).

Several studies have attempted to control some of these factors (e.g. Dong *et al.*, 2005; Jiang, 1999; Jiang & Forster, 2001). For example, Jiang and colleagues tested Chinese–English bilinguals using a masked priming paradigm (Forster & Davis, 1984), where prime words were preceded by a *forward mask* (i.e. a row of cross hatches), a variation of the priming task often used to decrease prime visibility, thereby providing a stronger role for unconscious, subliminal processing in mediating responses. Facilitation in the lexical decision task was observed for cross-language word pairs presented in the L1-L2 direction (Jiang, 1999), but not in the L2-L1 direction (Jiang, 1999; Jiang & Forster, 2001; see Forster & Jiang, 2001 for further explanation), replicating the asymmetry reported in previous studies. However, when the task was changed to an episodic priming task (i.e. bilinguals classified words as *old* or *new* after a study phase), significant L2-L1 priming was reported, leading the authors to suggest that L2 words are represented in episodic memory and L1 words are stored in lexical memory (Jiang & Forster, 2001).

More recently, Finkbeiner and associates (2004) proposed a different account to describe the mechanisms responsible for the asymmetrical priming effects reported. In a study with stimuli in Japanese (L1) and English (L2), they found non-significant translation priming in the L2-L1 direction and significant within-language priming for L2-L2 words. They argued that the absence of L2-L1 priming was not caused by the inability to process L2 primes under masked conditions (because L2-L2 priming was observed), and introduced an alternative account based on the number of senses belonging to a word. The Sense Model, put forth by Finkbeiner and associates (2004), is based on the idea that many words have language-specific senses or meanings that are usually not taken into account when creating and interpreting bilingual research. For example, the word *ball* in English and *balón* in Spanish are direct translations of each other, but *ball* can have several meanings or senses (*a football* or *basketball, a dance, 'having a ball', ball bearings, ball of one's foot*, etc.), while in Mexican Spanish *balón* is mainly used to describe *a volleyball, basketball* or *soccer ball* (R. Heredia, personal communication, 2007).

The researchers argue that each of the senses belonging to a word in the L1 and L2 are stored separately in semantic memory and the magnitude of facilitation observed in priming tasks is influenced by the number of senses of each word. Because many bilinguals (particularly the adolescent bilinguals in Finkbeiner *et al.*'s study) are typically more proficient in their L1 compared to their L2, they most likely know the range of senses associated with the L1 word, whereas they may not know all the senses associated with the L2 word. According to this model, facilitation increases as the 'proportion of primed to unprimed senses' of the target word increases. Therefore, significant facilitation in the L1-L2 direction occurs because L1 primes activate a high proportion of senses in the L2. In the opposite direction (L2-L1), there are fewer L1 senses activated by an L2 prime because L2 proficiency is weaker than it is in L1, and as a result, many of the L1 senses are never activated because they are not associated with the L2 translation (Finkbeiner *et al.*, 2004).

Basnight-Brown and Altarriba (2007) examined semantic and translation priming in Spanish–English bilinguals using unmasked (Experiment 1) and forward masked (Experiment 2) priming procedures. When prime words were unmasked and the SOA length was short (100 ms), significant facilitation was observed in the L1-L2 and L2-L1 directions for both the semantic and translation word pairs, with the magnitude of the effect being larger for those pairs that were direct translations of each other. When the experimental conditions were constrained further and prime words were forward masked, reliable facilitation was only observed for the translation word pairs (in both language directions). The absence of an asymmetry for translations in this experiment was interpreted as being due to bilingual participants' learning trajectories. Whereas many of the studies that have reported asymmetrical effects have used adolescent bilinguals (i.e. those who learned their L2 at the age of 12 or 13), the Spanish–English bilinguals in this study were early bilinguals who learned their L2 on average at the age of five. Most interestingly, the results reveal that when experimental conditions are constrained, semantic meanings in both of a bilingual speaker's languages can be activated to some degree. However, as postulated by the Sense Model, the level of proficiency modulates the degree of this activation.

Lastly, characteristics of the word stimuli used in cross-language priming experiments have also been shown to influence whether or not the effect is observed. Under masked prime conditions, Schoonbaert *et al.* (2006) reported significant facilitation in both language directions for Dutch and English translations. However, semantic priming in both language directions was detected only for concrete word pairs (not for abstract words), suggesting that characteristics of the word stimuli play an important role in word recognition.

2.2. Categorization task

Categorization tasks are used to examine how categories and their exemplars are organized in memory. In this task, participants are presented with prime and target words in the same manner as in traditional semantic priming; however, rather than making a lexical decision, participants must determine if the word belongs to a specific category. For example, at the start of each trial, a semantic category name (e.g. *fruit*) is presented in capital letters on the computer screen to cue the participant to the category of interest. This cue is then followed by the presentation of a traditional prime-target trial (e.g. *manzana–apple*, where *manzana* is the Spanish translation of *apple*, see Grainger & Frenck-Mestre, 1998) for which the participant must determine if the presented target word is a member of the given category.

Recently, categorization tasks have become the focal point of much discussion because the outcomes of studies employing these tasks differ from outcomes of studies that employ semantic and translation priming studies previously reported, suggesting task differences. Grainger and Frenck-Mestre (1998) were the first to observe such differences in a study designed to compare/contrast semantic categorization with the lexical decision task in English–French bilinguals (all primes were masked). When the lexical decision task was used, they observed no L2-L1 facilitation, replicating other semantic and translation priming studies. In contrast, when the categorization task was used, significant L2-L1 translation priming was observed, a finding that has recently been replicated when the same task was used with Japanese–English bilinguals (Finkbeiner *et al.*, 2004, Experiments 1–3).

Based on the findings from Grainger and Frenck-Mestre (1998) and Finkbeiner *et al.* (2004), it appears that the asymmetry present in lexical decision (predominantly in adolescent bilinguals) is absent in semantic categorization. This finding has also been explained in terms of the Sense Model, where the activation of a category is said to allow the bilingual to 'filter out' any senses of the word that are irrelevant to the category, thereby allowing priming to occur to a greater degree (Finkbeiner *et al.*, 2004; see also Wang & Forster, 2006).

In contrast to the typical categorization task and lexical decision response described above, Segalowitz and de Almeida (2002) used a creative variation of the speeded categorization task to examine how bilinguals store and access category exemplars in their two languages. In this task, late English–French bilinguals determined whether words presented (e.g. *to jump*, *desire*) were verbs of motion or verbs denoting a psychological state. Initially, the results indicated that participants were faster and more accurate in L1 than in L2. However, a different pattern emerged when the same words were used in an arbitrary classification task (i.e. words were randomly determined to belong to one of two categories, category A or category B, regardless of their semantic meaning). Prior to the experimental task, the bilinguals learned the classifications for each word. This training was necessary because the categories were random and labeled with letters (A, B) so that underlying semantic meaning could not determine where items should be placed (e.g. *value* was a member of category A and *desire* a member of category B). In the experimental task, the bilinguals made key presses to denote whether the individually presented words belonged to category A or B. The theory behind this manipulation was that the random assignment of words to categories A or B would be easier in the L2 than in the L1 (where semantic representations tend to be stronger). Results indicated that the bilinguals were more accurate in L2 than in L1 (*L2 better than L1 effect*). This led the authors to conclude that experience, rather than semantics, may play more of a role in how late bilinguals represent their L2. One other issue not mentioned, but that certainly could also modulate the reported processing differences, is that L2 representations for action and psychological state verbs may have a lower degree of overlap with other words in memory (compared to the L1). Furthermore, only two types of verbs were used in this experiment. It would be interesting to explore the effect of other types of word stimuli on categorization using the same task.

Lastly, research aimed at the processes involved in the production of exemplars from a given category (e.g. *fruit, countries*) has revealed that Spanish–English bilinguals who generated exemplars in both languages produced the same numbers of exemplars as those bilinguals who generated exemplars in only one language (Gollan *et al.*, 2002). Because the use of two languages did not reveal an increase in generated exemplars, the authors concluded that interference between the two languages dampened any processing advantages available to those using two languages.

In conclusion, the use of categorization tasks has shed some light on how semantic information is represented in bilingual speakers. The research reviewed reveals that categorical priming is not sensitive to the language asymmetry often reported in the bilingual semantic priming literature, supporting the idea that bilinguals are able to process these words faster by filtering out irrelevant senses or unrelated meanings (Finkbeiner *et al.*, 2004; Grainger & Frenck-Mestre, 1998). This research also indicates that in the L1 (or in the dominant language), semantic meanings from category exemplars are more tightly connected than they are in the L2 (or in the weaker language) (Segalowitz & de Almeida, 2002), but that interference can occur between the two languages during the language production process (Gollan *et al.*, 2002).

2.3. Picture-naming tasks

In *picture-naming tasks*, a picture is shown on the computer screen and participants are asked to name the item depicted (in either the L1 or the L2). Once again, response times are measured for each response. These tasks are useful because they activate the appropriate semantic information directly (rather than just activating lexical links between the L1 and L2). In a study conducted by Hernandez and Reyes (2002), pictures of common objects (e.g. *airplane*) were presented multiple times and participants named the same pictures in the same language (within-language condition) or once in each language (between-language condition). The results revealed that translation priming was larger in magnitude for the within-language condition than for the between-language condition. Of greater interest was the finding that when a lag (i.e. greater time duration between repeated presentations of the pictures) was introduced, within-language priming decreased in magnitude, while between-language priming was not affected. This led the authors to conclude that different processes are responsible for within-language and between-language repetition picture naming. Specifically, the authors suggest that within-language processes rely on a stronger link between the semantic and lemma level (i.e. a mediating level connected to both the lexical store(s) and to semantic representations; see Kroll & De Groot, 1997), whereas between-language picture naming relies only on links between semantic and lexical levels.

Researchers using brain-imaging techniques also found differences in picture naming in bilinguals' two languages. When late Spanish–English bilinguals (i.e. those who learned the L2 English in their late teenage years) named pictures in both of their languages, functional magnetic resonance imaging (fMRI) data revealed increased brain activity when naming in the L2 as compared to the L1 (Hernandez & Meschyan, 2006), suggesting that lexical retrieval and production require more attention in the L2 than in the L1.

In an effort to examine whether age of acquisition or the chronological order in which items are learned is most influential in lexical-semantic development, Hirsch and associates (2003) had Spanish–English bilinguals name pictures of concrete objects (average age of acquisition of English was 11 years old). Then, the participants filled out a questionnaire asking them to rate the age at which they learned each English word depicted in the pictures. As expected, it was observed that words acquired earlier in the L2 learning process were named significantly faster than those learned later. This led the authors to suggest that the mapping between lexical and semantic information is stronger for words acquired earlier in the L2. What was most striking about this outcome was that regardless of the age of acquisition of the L2 (these were all adolescent bilinguals), the data suggest that chronological order plays an important role in determining L2 picture-naming speed.

In conclusion, picture stimuli are a useful addition to the word stimuli typically used to explore bilingual semantic memory because they require that individuals access semantic information directly and not through multiple lexical routes. Overall, current research using the picture-naming paradigm indicates that L2 and L1 picture naming do not occur in an identical manner. More specifically, L2 naming requires more attentional control, suggesting that semantic information is more deeply embedded in L1 representations. More work needs to be done in this area, particularly in light of the fact that all of the studies discussed previously examine the same bilingual group (Spanish–English bilinguals) and similar types of word stimuli (concrete items). It would be interesting to see if these findings generalize to different types of stimuli, testing conditions and languages, while also taking into account the chronological order in which items are acquired, a variable often ignored in past studies.

2.4. The Stroop task

In the typical Stroop task, words that name colors (e.g. *red*, *blue*, *yellow*) are visually presented to participants, and their task is to name the color of the ink in which the words appear (Stroop, 1935). When the color of the ink matches the printed word, say *red* in red ink (the congruent condition), naming times are typically much faster than in the mismatched condition, *red* in blue ink (the incongruent condition). The probable cause of the interference is the difficulty in suppressing the articulation and production of the written word in favor of the name of the ink color. This difficulty in turn is often linked to the automaticity with which a proficient reader processes words in a familiar language.

In the bilingual version of this task, words may appear in one language, but responses are required in a different language. Thus, the word *red* in English may require the response *rojo* (red in Spanish) if it appears in red, or *azul* (blue in Spanish) if it appears in blue. Overall, color-naming interference is greater in within-language conditions compared to between-language conditions (Altarriba & Mathis, 1997; Chen & Ho, 1986; Mägiste, 1984, 1985; Preston & Lambert, 1969; Tzelgov *et al.*, 1990). This result stems from the fact that semantic meanings for color words in the L1 are more strongly coded than the same meanings in the L2. That is, L1 color words typically have a higher level of activation frequency within memory, due to the earlier age of acquisition of those words.

Lee and associates (1992) investigated Stroop interference effects within and between languages for three groups of children whose L1s were Chinese, Malay and Tamil, respectively, and whose L2 was English. The researchers hypothesized that interference effects should be diminished in the Chinese–English case due to overall differences in orthography and language structure between these two languages. However, the data revealed similar magnitudes of interference for all language combinations across the three groups of participants. Thus, orthography does not exert as strong an influence on the Stroop effect as does the meaning of the color words. Sumiya and Healy (2004) also reported significant between-language Stroop effects with Japanese and English color word stimuli that were also orthographically dissimilar. However, when loan words were used in Japanese, for those that bore a phonological similarity to their English counterparts (e.g. the words *blue* and *green*), interference was larger as compared to phonologically dissimilar cross-language stimuli. Thus, in contrast to orthography, phonology, together with semantics, plays a role in accessing cross-language items in the processing of color-word Stroop stimuli.

Altarriba and Mathis (1997) applied the Stroop task to the study of the semantic representations of newly acquired L2 words. They trained monolingual English speakers on a set of Spanish color words and then administered a Stroop task where the words were presented on a computer screen in Spanish and responses were required in English. Participants were asked to name the colors in which the words appeared. Since these novice learners had undergone a process of training that emphasized the semantic meanings of their newly acquired words (e.g. matching words to their definitions, selecting words in a sentence completion task, etc.), participants encoded the new words to such an extent that they produced significant Stroop interference effects in the incongruent, cross-language conditions. As the effects were not as strong as those displayed by a control group of highly proficient simultaneous and childhood Spanish–English bilinguals, Altarriba and Mathis (1997) concluded that the more proficient individuals are in their two languages, the greater the interference experienced within a bilingual Stroop task.

In more recent work, Stroop-like tasks have been used in the context of translation studies to examine the degree to which lexical entries in one language remain active while spoken responses are made in the other language. For example, Miller and Kroll (2002) instructed Spanish–English bilinguals to translate words from one language into the other. Shortly after the target word appeared, a distractor word also appeared on screen. This word appeared in the language of production and was related either to the meaning or to the form of the target word. Semantically related distractor words produced a Stroop-like interference effect in responding to the target stimuli. In contrast, distractor words with a high orthographic similarity to the target words produced facilitation in responding. This latter result appears to contradict that reported earlier for Stroop color-word naming (Altarriba & Mathis, 1997). However, one of the primary differences is the fact that in Miller and Kroll's (2002) study, the response involved the production of a translation equivalent, while in Altarriba and Mathis' (1997) study, the response involved the naming of color for color words. In the latter case, there is significantly more overlap between meanings than might be the case for basic translation equivalents.

Finally, researchers have applied the Stroop effect to the study of emotion word representation in bilinguals. Sutton and associates (2007) extended the emotional Stroop effect to the investigation of the automatic access of emotional components in Spanish and English words. They presented Spanish–English bilinguals with emotion words (e.g. *anger*) and neutral words (e.g. *floor*) in English and Spanish. The participants' task was to press one of two keys depending on the color of the word. Words appeared in either blue or green. The authors found that color naming was slower for the emotion-related items compared to the neutral condition. It appears that aspects of the emotional content of the word captured attention and produced interference in color naming, and this effect occurred similarly in both languages in this group of bilinguals. This study provided an automatic measure of selective attention to emotional information in words in more than one language. This relatively new effect deserves further replication and study in order to understand the constraints that surround the emotional Stroop effect in bilingual and multilingual populations (see also Altarriba, 2006, for an overview of the use of other related tasks in investigations of emotion word processing both within and between languages).

The evidence from the Stroop task in bilinguals reveals two things: (1) semantic representations in one language can automatically influence processing in a second language (it is difficult to keep the languages fully separate when completing this task) and (2) Stroop effects can be viewed diagnostically, since the greater the depth of semantic representation in one language, the stronger the emerging Stroop effects in that language. Stroop-like tasks in which individuals are asked to process information in one language while suppressing the influence of a different language indicate that semantic activation occurs for both languages whether or not the task demands require their activation. Stroop color-word interference has been demonstrated across a variety of languages, and has also been demonstrated recently in bilinguals from different age groups (Zied *et al.*, 2004). Zied and associates (2004) have demonstrated that whereas bilinguals who are dominant in one language may show greater interference in that language, balanced bilinguals demonstrate equivalent amounts of Stroop interference in both language directions. Again, as mentioned earlier, to the extent that bilinguals are balanced and L1 and L2 share a relatively similar age of acquisition, it is plausible that the frequency with which items in both languages have been encountered and processed is somewhat similar, lending itself to the possibility that processing occurs in similar ways in both languages.

Overall, it has been shown that word recognition in a second language is influenced by the characteristics of words, specifically the degree of semantic and/or orthographic overlap between the L2 word and its L1 translation. Furthermore, the number of translations that are shared or not shared by the L1 and L2 is also a factor that has been shown to influence word production (e.g. Tokowicz *et al.*, 2002).

2.5. Cognate processing tasks

Several studies in the field have examined the processing of cognates and noncognates by bilingual speakers. *Cognates* are words that are orthographically, phonologically and semantically similar (to some degree) (e.g. *music* and *música* in English and Spanish). *Noncognates* are words that may have the same or similar meanings, but differ in terms of orthography and phonology (for an in-depth discussion of this distinction and a comprehensive overview of the research, see De Groot, 1993; Sánchez-Casas & García-Albea, 2005). *False cognates* or *false friends*, in contrast, are words that share form, but not meaning, such as the word *red* in English (refers to the color) and Spanish (refers to a *net*).

The task most commonly used to examine the processing of these word types is the priming paradigm with lexical decision response (discussed earlier), because it allows researchers to examine whether cognates share a lexical representation or whether they are represented separately in each language. Theoretically, facilitation for cognate translations is interpreted as evidence of a shared lexical representation, while the absence of an effect for noncognate translations (e.g. *pencil-lápiz*) suggests that the two words have separate lexical representations.

Most of the studies specifically aimed at examining processing similarities and differences between cognates and noncognates have done so with Spanish–English (Cristoffanini *et al.*, 1986; Gerard & Scarborough, 1989; Scarborough *et al.*, 1984), Dutch–English (de Groot & Nas, 1991; Van Hell & De Groot, 1998), Italian–English (Lalor & Kirsner, 2001) and Spanish–Catalan bilinguals (see Sánchez-Casas & García-Albea,

2005). Several studies have reported facilitation only for cognates (Cristoffanini *et al.*, 1986; De Groot & Nas, 1991; Gerard & Scarborough, 1989; Sánchez-Casas *et al.*, 1992; Sánchez-Casas & García-Albea, 2005; Scarborough *et al.*, 1984). In addition, studies that used more constrained conditions, such as masking, which provide a more accurate account of how these words are processed, report larger magnitudes of facilitation for translations that are orthographically similar (De Groot & Nas, 1991; Sánchez-Casas *et al.*, 1992). The pattern of asymmetry observed is also consistent with that reported in the cross-language priming studies. Proficiency appears to modulate whether facilitation for cognates and noncognates is observed in both language directions (Sánchez-Casas & García-Albea, 2005).

In addition to the priming task, the processing of cognates/non-cognates has also been examined using other tasks and methods. For example, Van Hell and De Groot (1998) used an association task to explore differences in word production. Dutch–English bilinguals were presented with a word on the computer screen and were asked to say aloud the name of the first word associate that came to mind. Across languages, it was observed that production and later retrieval of these associations was easier for cognates than for noncognates. This cognate advantage has been replicated in the picture-naming task with bilingual aphasic patients, where pictures with cognate names were produced faster and were less sensitive to retrieval failures than those with noncognate names (Costa *et al.*, 2005; Roberts & Deslauriers, 1999).

Several studies have examined the processing of true cognates and false cognates. Data obtained from unmasked priming revealed the absence of a facilitatory effect for false cognates in English–Italian bilinguals (Lalor & Kirsner, 2001). García-Albea *et al.* (1996, cited in Sánchez-Casas & García-Albea, 2005) conducted a masked priming experiment where stimuli consisted of cognate, noncognate and false cognate word pairs in Spanish and English. The results revealed significant facilitation only for the cognate pairs (in both language directions) and non-significant effects for both the noncognates and the false cognates. Overall, this study reveals that cognate facilitation is (1) not simply the result of orthographic and phonological overlap (since no facilitation was observed for false friends) and (2) not the result of semantic overlap (since no facilitation was observed for noncognate translations). Most interestingly, these data imply that a convergence of orthographic and semantic effects is responsible for determining the organization of the bilingual lexicon.

Conclusions

This chapter outlined various research methods and findings that should be considered when developing any explanation, theory or model of bilingual semantic memory. The first finding comes from the semantic priming literature, where greater facilitation was observed for translation words pairs as compared to semantically related word pairs. More semantic overlap between translations is thought to be responsible for this outcome, a characteristic of cross-language relationships that is best taken into account by De Groot's (1992) Distributed Feature Model, where words with more semantic overlap across languages produce more facilitation, that is, faster processing.

A second consistent finding in this body of literature is the asymmetry in the size of the effects that was modulated by language direction and task. In the semantic priming literature, larger effects were reported in the L1-L2 direction as compared to the L2-L1 direction, where effects were smaller or nonexistent. However, when the semantic categorization task was used, asymmetries in the size of the effects were no longer found. Theoretically, the Revised Hierarchical Model (RHM) (Kroll & Stewart, 1994) predicts that processing asymmetries for each language direction should occur as a function of how strong the connections are between the L1 and L2 lexicons and conceptual store. However, the Sense Model suggested by Finkbeiner and colleagues (2004) may be more appropriate in explaining results for cross-language semantic priming studies. As suggested earlier, bilinguals may be aware of more meanings or senses of a word in their first (or dominant) language which would allow for greater L1-L2 processing, and which would decrease L2-L1 processing (if only a few senses are known in the L2, individuals will only activate a small percentage of L1 senses, thereby decreasing activation in the L2-L1 direction). Further, the Sense Model would suggest that when the categorization task is used, activation of the category allows the bilingual to 'filter out' any unrelated meanings or senses, which explains why asymmetries are not typically observed in that task.

The next set of findings emerging from the picture-naming task suggests that L1 and L2 picture naming do not occur in the same way, but rather that semantic representations are more highly connected to L1 lexical entries, as revealed in the priming outcomes. In addition, results from studies that have used the Stroop task revealed that (1) both languages of a bilingual are activated, to some extent, when processing stimuli in a single language and (2) semantic influence of one language on the processing of another occurs quite early in the L2 learning process (cf. Altarriba & Mathis, 1997). The finding that semantic information in one language can influence processing in the other is perhaps most interesting because this finding implies that bilingual language processing is non-selective at the early stages of processing. Theoretically, the issue of non-selectivity has been incorporated into the BIA (and BIA+) models of bilingual language processing (Dijkstra & van Heuven, 1998, 2002, see also Marian, this volume, for a more detailed description of these models and of non-selectivity in spoken word processing).

Finally, studies examining the representation and processing of cognates versus noncognates reveal that the advantages sometimes noted for cognate word processing are not solely due to the overlap that exists orthographically and sometimes phonologically between cognates. In fact, it seems that semantics plays an important role in the processing of cognate words, indicating that shared meaning is important to the mental architecture that describes the semantic and lexical representation for language in the bilingual mind. For this reason, it is important that future models of bilingual processing focus on how these different levels of processing – orthographic, phonological and semantic – interact and change as proficiency levels change.

Across all of the different paradigms described in the current chapter, it was consistently found that proficiency levels and frequency of use in each language are largely responsible for differences observed. One of the strengths of the RHM (Kroll & Stewart, 1994) is that it attempts to explain how one becomes bilingual and how the strength and direction of the connections between the different levels of representation emerge and progress as a second language is acquired. A comprehensive theory of bilingual processing and semantic development does need to be dynamic in nature and able to account for changes in fluency, proficiency and even maturation that a bilingual undergoes as their language abilities develop, but it also needs to consider non-selective aspects of processing across different modalities and word types (see Altarriba, 2000, for a similar argument). The current research sets the groundwork for the development of future theories that are much more integrated and comprehensive in their approach.

References

Altarriba, J. (1990) Constraints on interlingual facilitation effects in priming in Spanish-English bilinguals. Unpublished doctoral dissertation, Vanderbilt University.

Altarriba, J. (1992) The representation of translation equivalents in bilingual memory. In R. Harris (ed.) *Cognitive Processing in Bilinguals* (pp. 157–174). Amsterdam: Elsevier.

Altarriba, J. (2000) Language processing and memory retrieval in Spanish-English bilinguals. *Spanish Applied Linguistics* 4, 215–245.

Altarriba, J. (2003) Does *cariño* equal 'liking'? A theoretical approach to conceptual nonequivalence between languages. *International Journal of Bilingualism* 7, 305–322.

Altarriba, J. (2006) Cognitive approaches to the study of emotion-laden and emotion words in monolingual and bilingual memory. In A. Pavlenko (ed.) *Bilingual Minds: Emotional Experience, Expression and Representation* (pp. 232–256). Clevedon: Multilingual Matters.

Altarriba, J. and Basnight-Brown, D. (2007) Methodological considerations in performing semantic and translation priming experiments across languages. *Behavior Research Methods, Instruments, and Computers* 39, 1–18.

Altarriba, J. and Canary, T. (2004) Affective priming: The automatic activation of arousal. *Journal of Multilingual and Multicultural Development* 25, 248–265.

Altarriba, J. and Mathis, K. (1997) Conceptual and lexical development in second language acquisition. *Journal of Memory and Language* 36, 550–568.

Ashcraft, M. (2005) *Cognition* (4th edn). Upper Saddle River, NJ: Prentice Hall.

Basnight-Brown, D. and Altarriba, J. (2007) Differences in semantic and translation priming across languages: The role of language direction, age of acquisition, and language dominance. *Memory & Cognition* 35, 953–965.

Chen, H.C. and Ho, C. (1986) Development of Stroop interference in Chinese-English bilinguals. *Journal of Experimental Psychology: Learning, Memory, and Cognition* 12, 397–401.

Chen, H.C. and Ng, M.L. (1989) Semantic facilitation and translation priming effects in Chinese-English bilinguals. *Memory and Cognition* 17, 454–462.

Collins, A. and Loftus, E. (1975) A spreading activation theory of semantic processing. *Psychological Review* 82, 407–428.

Costa, A., Santesteban, M. and Caño, A. (2005) On the facilitatory effects of cognate words in bilingual speech production. *Brain and Language* 94, 94–103.

Cristoffanini, P., Kirsner, K. and Milech, D. (1986) Bilingual lexical representations: The status of Spanish-English cognates. *The Quarterly Journal of Experimental Psychology* 38A, 367–393.

De Groot, A.M.B. (1992) Determinants of word translation. *Journal of Experimental Psychology: Learning, Memory, and Language* 18, 1001–1018.

De Groot, A.M.B. (1993) Word-type effects in bilingual processing tasks. In R. Schreuder and B. Weltens (eds) *The Bilingual Lexicon* (pp. 27–51). Amsterdam: John Benjamins.

De Groot, A.M.B. and Nas, G. (1991) Lexical representation of cognates and noncognates in compound bilinguals. *Journal of Memory and Language* 30, 90–123.

Dijkstra, A. and Van Heuven, W. (1998) The BIA-model and bilingual word recognition. In J. Grainger and A. Jacobs (eds) *Localist Connectionist Approaches to Human Cognition* (pp. 189–225). Mahwah, NJ: Lawrence Erlbaum.

Dijkstra, A. and Van Heuven, W. (2002) The architecture of the bilingual word recognition system: From identification to decision. *Bilingualism: Language and Cognition* 5, 175–197.

Dong, Y., Gui, S. and MacWhinney, B. (2005) Shared and separate meanings in the bilingual mental lexicon. *Bilingualism: Language & Cognition* 8, 221–238.

Finkbeiner, M., Forster, K., Nicol, J. and Nakamura, K. (2004) The role of polysemy in masked semantic and translation priming. *Journal of Memory and Language* 51, 1–22.

Forster, K. and Davis, C. (1984) Repetition priming and frequency attenuation in lexical access. *Journal of Experimental Psychology: Learning, Memory, and Cognition* 10, 680–698.

Forster, K. and Jiang, N. (2001) The nature of the bilingual lexicon: Experiments with the masked priming paradigm. In J. Nicol (ed.) *One Mind: Two Languages* (pp. 72–83). Malden, MA: Blackwell.

Francis, W. (2005) Bilingual semantic and conceptual representation. In J. Kroll and A.M.B. de Groot (eds) *Handbook of Bilingualism: Psycholinguistic Approaches* (pp. 251–267). Oxford: Oxford University Press.

García-Albea, J., Sánchez-Casas, R. and Valero, T. (1996) Form and meaning contribution to word recognition in Catalan-Spanish bilinguals. Paper presented at the meeting of the Ninth Conference of the European Society for Cognitive Psychology, University of Wurzburg, Germany, September.

Gerard, L. and Scarborough, D. (1989) Language specific lexical access of homographs by bilinguals. *Journal of Experimental Psychology: Learning, Memory, and Cognition* 15, 305–315.

Gollan, T., Montoya, R. and Werner, G. (2002) Semantic and letter fluency in Spanish-English bilinguals. *Neuropsychology* 16, 562–576.

Grainger, J. and Frenck-Mestre, C. (1998) Masked priming by translation equivalents in proficient bilinguals. *Language and Cognitive Processes* 13, 601–623.

Hernandez, A. and Meschyan, G. (2006) Executive function is necessary to enhance lexical processing in a less proficient L2: Evidence from fMRI during picture naming. *Bilingualism: Language and Cognition* 9, 177–188.

Hernandez, A. and Reyes, I. (2002) Within and between language priming differ: Evidence from repetition of pictures in Spanish-English bilinguals. *Journal of Experimental Psychology: Learning, Memory, and Cognition* 28, 726–734.

Hirsh, K., Morrison, C., Gaset, S. and Carnicer, E. (2003) Age of acquisition and speech production in L2. *Bilingualism: Language and Cognition* 6, 117–128.

Jiang, N. (1999) Testing processing explanations for the asymmetry in masked cross-language priming. *Bilingualism: Language and Cognition* 2, 59–75.

Jiang, N. and Forster, K. (2001) Cross-language priming asymmetries in lexical decision and episodic recognition. *Journal of Memory and Language* 44, 32–51.

Keatley, C. and de Gelder, B. (1992) The bilingual primed lexical decision task: Cross-language priming disappears with speeded responses. *European Journal of Cognitive Psychology* 4, 273–292.

Keatley, C., Spinks, J. and de Gelder, B. (1994) Asymmetrical cross-language priming effects. *Memory and Cognition* 22, 70–84.

Kroll, J. and De Groot, A.M.B. (1997) Lexical and conceptual memory in the bilingual: Mapping form to meaning in two languages. In A.M.B. De Groot and J. Kroll (eds) *Tutorials in Bilingualism: Psycholinguistic Perspectives* (pp. 169–199). Mahwah, NJ: Lawrence Erlbaum.

Kroll, J. and Stewart, E. (1994) Category interference in translation and picture naming: Evidence for asymmetric connections between bilingual memory representations. *Journal of Memory and Language* 33, 149–174.

Kroll, J. and Tokowicz, N. (2001) The development of conceptual representation for words in a second language. In J. Nicol (ed.) *One Mind: Two Languages* (pp. 49–71). Malden, MA: Blackwell.

Lalor, E. and Kirsner, K. (2001) The representation of false cognates in the bilingual lexicon. *Psychonomic Bulletin & Review* 8, 552–559.

Lee, W.L., Wee, G.C., Tzeng, O. and Hung, D. (1992) A study of interlingual and intralingual Stroop effect in three different scripts: Logograph, syllabary, and alphabet. In R. Harris (ed.) *Cognitive Processing in Bilinguals* (pp. 427–442). Amsterdam: Elsevier.

Mägiste, E. (1984) Stroop tasks and dichotic translation: The development of interference patterns in bilinguals. *Journal of Experimental Psychology: Learning, Memory, and Cognition* 10, 304–315.

Mägiste, E. (1985) Development of intra- and interlingual interference in bilinguals. *Journal of Psycholinguistic Research* 14, 137–154.

Meyer, D. and Schvaneveldt, R. (1971) Facilitation in recognizing pairs of words: Evidence of a dependence between retrieval operations. *Journal of Experimental Psychology* 90, 227–234.

Miller, N. and Kroll, J. (2002) Stroop effects in bilingual translation. *Memory & Cognition* 30, 614–628.

Neely, J. and Kahan, T. (2001) Is semantic activation automatic? A critical re-evaluation. In H. Roediger, J. Nairne, I. Neath and A. Suprenant (eds) *The Nature of Remembering: Essays in Honor of Robert G. Crowder* (pp. 69–93). Washington, DC: American Psychological Association.

Pavlenko, A. (1999) New approaches to concepts in bilingual memory. *Bilingualism: Language & Cognition* 2 (3), 209–230.

Potter, M., So, K., Von Eckardt, B. and Feldman, L. (1984) Lexical and conceptual representation in beginning and proficient bilinguals. *Journal of Verbal Learning and Verbal Behavior* 23, 23–38.

Preston, M. and Lambert, W. (1969) Interlingual interference in a bilingual version of the Stroop color-word task. *Journal of Verbal Learning and Verbal Behavior* 8, 295–301.

Roberts, P. and Deslauriers, L. (1999) Picture naming of cognate and non-cognate nouns in bilingual aphasia. *Journal of Communication Disorders* 32, 1–23.

Sánchez-Casas, R., Davis, C. and García-Albea, J. (1992) Bilingual lexical processing: Exploring the cognate/non-cognate distinction. *European Journal of Cognitive Psychology* 4 (4), 293–310.

Sánchez-Casas, R. and García-Albea, J. (2005) The representation of cognate and noncognate words in bilingual memory. In J. Kroll and A.M.B. De Groot (eds) *Handbook of Bilingualism: Psycholinguistic Approaches* (pp. 226–250). Oxford: Oxford University Press.

Scarborough, D., Gerard, L. and Cortese, C. (1984) Independence of lexical access in bilingual word recognition. *Journal of Verbal Learning and Verbal Behavior* 23, 84–99.

Schoonbaert, S., Duyck, W. and Brysbaert, M. (2006) Concreteness effects in masked cross-language priming. Poster presented at the Fifth International Conference of the Mental Lexicon, Montreal, Canada, October.

Schwanenflugel, P. and Rey, M. (1986) Interlingual semantic facilitation: Evidence for a common representational system in the bilingual lexicon. *Journal of Memory and Language* 25, 605–618.

Segalowitz, N. and de Almeida, R. (2002) Conceptual representation of verbs in bilinguals: Semantic field effects and a second language performance paradox. *Brain and Language* 81, 517–531.

Stroop, J. (1935) Studies of interference in serial verbal reactions. *Journal of Experimental Psychology* 18, 643–662.

Sumiya, H. and Healy, A.F. (2004) Phonology in the bilingual Stroop effect. *Memory & Cognition* 32, 752–758.

Sutton, T., Altarriba, J., Gianico, J. and Basnight Brown, D. (2007) The automatic access of emotion: Emotional Stroop effects in Spanish-English bilingual speakers. *Cognition and Emotion* 21, 1077–1090.

Tokowicz, N., Kroll, J., De Groot, A.M.B. and Van Hell, J. (2002) Number-of-translation norms for Dutch-English translation pairs: A new tool for examining language production. *Behavior Research Methods, Instruments, and Computers* 34, 435–451.

Tzelgov, J. and Eben-Ezra, S. (1992) Components of the between language semantic priming effect. *European Journal of Cognitive Psychology* 4, 253–272.

Tzelgov, J., Henik, A. and Leiser, D. (1990) Controlling Stroop interference: Evidence from a bilingual task. *Journal of Experimental Psychology: Learning, Memory, and Cognition* 16, 760–771.

Van Hell, J. and De Groot, A.M.B. (1998) Conceptual representation in bilingual memory: Effects of concreteness and cognate status in word association. *Bilingualism: Language and Cognition* 1 (3), 193–211.

Wang, X. and Forster, K. (2006) Task effects in masked translation priming. Poster presented at the 5th International Conference of the Mental Lexicon, Montreal, CA, October.

Zeelenberg, R. and Pecher, D. (2003) Evidence for long-term cross-language repetition priming in conceptual implicit memory tasks. *Journal of Memory and Language* 49, 80–94.

Zied, K., Philipe, A., Karine, P., Valerie, H.T., Ghislaine, A., Arnaud, R. *et al.* (2004) Bilingualism and adult differences in inhibitory mechanisms: Evidence from a bilingual Stroop task. *Brain and Cognition* 54, 254–256.

Chapter 5
Lexical Transfer

SCOTT JARVIS

Introduction

This chapter deals with a phenomenon referred to as *lexical transfer*, which can be defined as the influence that a person's knowledge of one language has on that person's recognition, interpretation, processing, storage and production of words in another language. Following common conventions, I will use the terms 'transfer' and 'cross-linguistic influence' interchangeably to refer to this phenomenon (e.g. Jarvis & Pavlenko, 2008; Odlin, 1989). My focus in this chapter will be on the ways in which mental lexical representations and lexical processing procedures acquired through one language can affect a second language (L2) user's knowledge and use of words in another language. Most of the findings I will discuss come from research on L2 learners and bilinguals, but where possible, I will also review findings from studies on third- (L3) and fourth-language (L4) learners and multilinguals.

I begin in the first section by discussing some of the fundamental theoretical tenets that inform current thinking on lexical transfer. One of the primary tenets is that a person's knowledge of the form-related properties of a word (i.e. the way a word is pronounced and spelled in its various forms) is stored separately from the person's knowledge of the word's syntactic constraints and semantic associations, which in turn is stored separately from the person's conceptual knowledge. In the second section, I describe how these assumptions have shaped investigations into the structure and internal processes of the bilingual lexicon. Then, in the third section, I review the findings of studies that have investigated transfer related to the form-related properties of words (i.e. lexemic transfer), and in the fourth section I discuss transfer research related to the syntactic constraints and semantic associations of words in an L2 user's mental lexicon (i.e. lemmatic transfer). In the fifth section, I provide a brief summary of the types of methods that have been used in the investigation of lexical transfer, and in the final section, I conclude the chapter by recapping the primary findings related to lexical transfer and pointing to some areas where further research is crucially needed.

1. Lemmas and Lexemes

As Faerch *et al.* (1984), Nation (1990, 2001), Richards (1976), Ringbom (1987) and others have explained, knowing a word means the ability to recognize and retrieve the word from memory, and it also means knowing (1) how the word is spelled and pronounced in its various forms, (2) the word's meaning(s), (3) its grammatical class and syntactic constraints, (4) its collocations and syntagmatic associations (i.e. the words that it tends to co-occur with), (5) its lexical and conceptual associations (i.e. the words and meanings it is associated with that are not part of its collocational frame or denotational meaning) and (6) how frequently the word occurs in the language, how formal it is and in which registers of the language it can be used appropriately and conventionally. Cross-linguistic influence can and often does affect each of these dimensions of word knowledge and sometimes affects several dimensions at the same time.

Researchers working on lexical transfer are interested in discovering how these dimensions of word knowledge relate to one another in the mind, and how lexical transfer operates in the minds of those who know more than one language. One of the important theoretical assumptions that have influenced this line of inquiry is Garrett's (1975) claim that a word's syntactic and morphophonological specifications are stored separately from each other in the mind. Kempen and Huijbers (1983) and Kempen and Hoenkamp (1987) developed this idea into the distinction between *lemmas* and *lexemes* – terms that were already in use in the field of lexicography. In the theory put forward by Kempen and colleagues, 'a lexical entry's lemma specifies its semantic-syntactic properties, and the lexeme specifies its morphophonological properties' (Roelofs *et al.*, 1998: 220). This distinction and the details associated with it play a prominent role in Levelt's (1989; Levelt *et al.*, 1999) influential speech production model, and via Levelt they have been adopted by numerous other researchers investigating various aspects of both monolingual and bilingual knowledge and performance (see, e.g. De Bot, 2004 and Poulisse, 1999 for reviews of such research).

Lemmas and lexemes are distinct not only from each other, but also from mental concepts. *Concepts* reflect the level of thought and experiential knowledge, and they consist of various types of mental images, image schemas, mental scripts and forms of knowledge that are organized into structured categories of thought and categories of meaning (see, e.g. Lakoff, 1987; Murphy, 2002). Semantic representations, on the other hand, encompass mental links that map lemmas to concepts, as well as lemmas to other lemmas (e.g. synonyms, collocations) (cf. Francis, 2005; Pavlenko, 1999). Researchers are not always careful to distinguish between conceptual and semantic representations; for example, Levelt *et al.* (1999) use the term 'lexical concept' in a way that seems to include both types of representations. The present chapter does not deal with the conceptual level, so I will not seek to address this problem here (but see Pavlenko's chapter in this volume for an in-depth discussion of the importance of the distinction between semantic and conceptual knowledge).

The model developed by Levelt *et al.* (1999) characterizes lexical access in speech production as progressing through several sequential stages. The essence of this process is as follows: first, lexical concepts are 'activated as part of a larger message that captures the speaker's communicative intention' (1999: 3). The lexical concepts activated during this conceptual preparation stage subsequently select the lemmas with which they are linked in the person's mental lexicon. Through a series of subsequent stages in which morphosyntactic and phonological constraints and discursive information are taken into account, the selected lemmas progressively activate the relevant morphological, phonological and phonetic information and procedures that are needed for the speaker to produce the appropriate, corresponding lexemes (see also Costa, 2005).

The terms 'lemma' and 'lexeme' have not been used with complete consistency in the literature, and in fact in Levelt's own work, the use of these terms has changed over time. Following Kempen and Hoenkamp (1987), Levelt (1989) used the term 'lemma' to refer to both the syntactic and semantic properties of a word, but Roelofs (1992) and Levelt *et al.* (1999) later associated the term 'lemma' more specifically with the syntactic specifications of a word, while introducing the term 'lexical concept' to refer to a word's semantic properties. The distinction between lemmas and lexical concepts is not always necessary, however, and Levelt *et al.* (1999: 37 fn. 1) have said that 'even in our own writings we regularly use the term *lemma* in its original sense, in particular if the semantics/syntax distinction is not at issue'. In the present paper, I will use the term 'lemma' in its original sense, that of specification of semantic and syntactic properties, in order to capture with this single term the characteristics that lexico-semantic and lexico-syntactic transfer have in common. These characteristics differ from the patterns of transfer that can be found in the morphological, phonological and graphemic forms of words that learners and bilinguals produce. I will describe this latter type of transfer as occurring at the level of lexemes. Even though the term 'lexeme' has been gradually disappearing from the literature as theories have begun separating the lexeme level into multiple, finer-grained levels of representation (e.g. Dijkstra & Van Heuven, 2002; Levelt *et al.*, 1999), its use is still conventional (e.g. De Angelis, 2005a; Longoni *et al.*, 2005), and in the present paper I find it to be very useful for clarifying the distinction between the two broad types of lexical transfer just mentioned, which I will refer to as lemmatic transfer and lexemic transfer.

The scope of *lexemic transfer* includes both the phonological and graphemic structure of (a particular form of) a word. For example, for the word GO, it relates to a person's knowledge of how to pronounce and spell *go*, *goes*, *going*, *gone* and *went*. The scope of *lemmatic transfer*, on the other hand, relates to the semantic and syntactic properties of words. The semantic properties in question are (1) mental associations between lemmas and concepts, which account for phenomena such as polysemy and the semantic ranges of words and (2) mental associations between lemmas and other lemmas, which are fundamental to phenomena such as synonymy, antonymy and other types of word-word associations (see Ringbom, 2007: 27–28 for a discussion of word associations). Syntactic properties, by comparison, concern a word's specified syntactic category (e.g. noun, verb, etc.), its subcategorization frame (e.g. *thankful* is followed by a prepositional phrase beginning with *for*), and various other inherent syntactic specifications, such as the word's grammatical gender (cf. Roelofs, 1992). Some syntagmatic specifications of words – such as collocational knowledge (e.g. *birds chirp* but *geese honk* and *owls hoot*) and knowledge of the makeup of compound words (e.g. *billboard*), phrasal verbs (e.g. *look at*) and fixed expressions (e.g. *so to speak*) – involve syntactic and semantic specifications simultaneously, which indeed strengthens the rationale for treating words' syntactic and semantic specifications together under the umbrella of lemmatic transfer.

2.   The Bilingual Mental Lexicon

Although the *consequences* of lexical transfer – whether lexemic or lemmatic – can be seen in learners' and bilinguals' language use (such as in the lexical errors they produce), the transfer itself that results in these consequences generally takes place via one of the two following mental processes in the bilingual mental lexicon: (1) the formation of learned cross-linguistic associations and (2) processing interference. Learned cross-linguistic associations involve what have sometimes been described as interlingual identifications (Odlin, 1989; Weinreich, 1953) or, in other words, established mental links between stored representations of elements (e.g. lexemes or lemmas) from two (or more) different languages. Processing interference, on the other hand, can arise through the activation of words (lemmas or lexemes) in one language when the speaker is trying to use another language, and this can, in principle, happen independently of previously formed mental associations between specific pairs of words from two (or more) different languages. Now, it should also be acknowledged that besides learned cross-linguistic associations and processing interference, lexical transfer can also occur in the form of intentional and strategic uses of language, such as when a person switches to another language or borrows a lexeme from one language due to difficulties encountered while using another. However, I will not be concerned with intentional or strategic cases of transfer in this chapter, but will instead focus on unintended manifestations of lexical transfer arising from learned cross-linguistic associations and processing interference.

The field's understanding is still limited in relation to how learned cross-linguistic associations are formed and how they are represented in an L2 user's mental lexicon, but important groundwork has been laid through a number of studies. Two of the seminal studies in this area are Kroll and Stewart (1994) and De Groot *et al.* (1994), both of which used word-translation tasks with Dutch–English bilinguals to determine the nature of the links between L1 and L2 lexical representations. Kroll and Stewart (1994) found that their participants could translate from L2 English into L1 Dutch more quickly than from L1 Dutch into L2 English, and they interpreted these results as showing that translation from L1 to L2 involves concept mediation (i.e. a pathway of activation from the L1 word to its associated concept to the corresponding L2 word), whereas translation from L2 to L1 is unmediated, progressing directly from the L2 word to the L1 word. De Groot *et al.* (1994) confirmed that translation from L2 to L1 is generally faster than from L1 to L2, but they also found that the meaning of a word (i.e. concrete or abstract) affects the speed of translation in both directions, which suggests that meaning-related mental representations are activated to varying degrees regardless of the direction of translation. Their assumption was that the greater the degree to which meaning-related representations are activated, the more difficult it is (i.e. the longer it takes) to access a word's translation equivalent. Neither study made a distinction between lexemes and lemmas, nor between lemmas and concepts, so it is not clear whether the semantic effects these studies found were really the result of concept mediation versus simply semantic mediation at the lemma level.

Although these studies did not distinguish between lexemes and lemmas, later work by these and other researchers has explicitly addressed some of the ways that these two levels of lexical knowledge are represented in bilingual memory. Most of the relevant research relies on bilinguals' reaction times and error rates in tasks that involve word naming, word translation, word recognition, semantic categorization and lexical judgments, though some also involves neuroimaging (see, e.g. Abutalebi *et al.*, 2005). In some of these studies, a priming procedure is used where a word from one language is shown (sometimes in a way that prevents it from being consciously registered) just before the bilingual is to act on (e.g. translate or make a decision about) a word in another language. When cross-linguistic priming effects are found, this is taken as evidence of possible mental associations between words from the two languages and of the possible routes of activation between them – where '*activation* refers to the availability of representations at different levels of processing' (Costa, 2005: 309), and *route of activation* refers to the trail of successive mental representations that have thus become activated.

Summaries of current models of the bilingual lexicon can be found, among other places, in De Bot (2004), Francis (2005), Jiang (2000), Kroll and Tokowicz (2005) and Sánchez-Casas and García-Albea (2005). One is led to conclude from these models and from the empirical data they are based on, that mental connections can exist between words from different languages at each level of representation (i.e. lexemes, lemmas and concepts) and also across levels of representation (e.g. a lexeme from Language A can be mentally associated with a lemma from Language B). These models and the data they are based on also suggest that it is not so much a matter of where cross-linguistic lexical associations may be formed in the mind, but rather how strong those connections are, that determines the consequences they will have for lexical transfer. That is, a lexeme or lemma may have multiple connections (i.e. learned associations) with other mental lexical representations within and across languages, and the likelihood of a lexeme or lemma activating a lexeme or lemma from another language appears to depend not just on whether there already exists a cross-linguistic connection between them, but also on how strong that connection is in relation to the other connections with which it competes (see, e.g. Goral *et al.*, 2006). The strength of a connection may be affected by many factors, including frequency and recency of use, as well as the degree of similarity between the two lexical representations that are mentally connected (see, e.g. Michael & Gollan, 2005: 397–398).

Turning now from the effects of learned cross-linguistic associations to the effects of processing interference, it is pertinent to begin with the observation that research on cross-linguistic processing interference has been influenced substantially by the language-activation metaphor, with the current thinking being that both of a bilingual's languages can be active (or activated) simultaneously even when, on the surface, the bilingual is using only one of the two languages. The issue is, of course, far more complex than this, and Grosjean (1999) has pointed out that a bilingual's language mode at any given moment can be anywhere along a continuum from completely monolingual to completely bilingual depending on the context, the stimuli, the nature of the task and so forth. If Grosjean is correct, then it may be that bilinguals are always or nearly always somewhere between both extremes of the continuum, such that a nonselected language (i.e. the language that the bilingual is not currently receiving or producing) is never completely active or completely inactive in the mind. It is not completely clear what this means, however, and what matters for present purposes is not just the degree of activation of the language as a whole, but more particularly the level of activation of individual words within the nonselected language. In a summary of the relevant research, De Bot (2004: 23–24) states that 'access to words in the lexicon is non-selective, i.e. words from more than one language compete for activation both in production and perception, but a – still to be defined – minimal level of proficiency/activation is needed to have words from a language play a role in the selection process, i.e. their default level of activation should be high enough to make them competitive'. De Bot also explains that the overall level of activation of a language can have an important effect on the degree to which a particular word or set of words is activated, and that an activated word in one language can coactivate a word in another language with which it shares formal (phonological or orthographic) similarities (see also Sánchez-Casas & García-Albea, 2005). De Angelis (2005a) and Poulisse (1999) describe additional factors – including word frequency, grammatical class (i.e. whether it is a content or function word), language status (i.e. whether it is a word from the L1 or a later-learned language) etc. – that can affect a word's level of activation. The primary implication of this line of research for lexical transfer is that when the level of activation of a word in a nonselected language rises to the degree that it competes with a word in the selected language, the former may inadvertently intrude into the person's speech, may interfere with the person's ability to access the latter word or may result in a hybridized blend of both words. Documented examples of each of these possibilities will be discussed next.

3. Lexemic Transfer

The distinction between lexemic and lemmatic transfer is similar to Ringbom's (1987, 2001) distinction between formal and semantic transfer. Lexical errors involving formal transfer, in Ringbom's framework, include (1) the use of deceptive or false cognates (e.g. *Many offers of violence have not enough courage to speak about it*, reflecting influence from Swedish *offer* = 'victim'; Ringbom, 1987: 157), (2) unintentional language switches involving the use of words from the wrong language (e.g. *and then nog one* = 'and then another one', reflecting an accidental switch into Dutch; Poulisse, 1999: 148) and (3) coinages of new words by blending the formal properties of words from different languages (e.g. *We have the same clothers*, reflecting a blend of the English word *clothes* and the Swedish word *klä'der* = 'clothes'; Ringbom, 1987: 153). The first two categories involve the use of an inappropriate word (either the wrong word or a word from the wrong language), and the third category relates to transfer-induced errors in the pronunciation and spelling of words. I will discuss each of these types of lexemic transfer in the following paragraphs. Most of this discussion will focus on errors, given that it is errors that have received the bulk of attention in this area of research. However, it is important to acknowledge that lexemic transfer can be and often is positive, especially in the case of closely related languages and especially during comprehension (Odlin, 1989; Ringbom, 2007).

As already indicated, the first two categories of formal lexical transfer involve the use of an inappropriate word. As such, they could be characterized as cases of faulty word choice – or erroneous lemma selection – which might suggest lemmatic transfer instead of lexemic transfer. However, even though these types of transfer probably do extend to the lemma level, there is reason to believe that they are driven largely by lexemic factors. To understand how lexemic factors affect the choice of deceptive or false cognates, it is useful to consider a full range of cross-linguistic lexical relationships. As a starting point, we can distinguish between cross-linguistic pairs of words that are true historical cognates (e.g. English *house* and Swedish *hus*) and those that are not. Within each of these two divisions, we can then classify pairs of words according to whether they are the same, similar or dissimilar in terms of both form and meaning. This is what I have done in Table 5.1

Table 5.1 Genetic cognate relationships

		Form		
		Same	*Similar*	*Dissimilar*
Meaning	Same	Sw. *finger*	Sw. *fader*	Sw. *hjul*
		Eng. *finger*	Eng. *father*	Eng. *wheel*
	Similar	Sw. *offer* (victim; offer)	Sw. *ben* (leg; bone)	Sw. *täcka* (cover)
		Eng. *offer*	Eng. *bone*	Eng. *thatch*
	Dissimilar	Sw. *strand* (beach)	Sw. *gris* (pig)	Sw. växt (plant)
		Eng. *strand*	Eng. *grease*	Eng. *waist*

and Table 5.2 with pairs of Swedish and English words. Based on etymological information provided in the *Oxford English Dictionary*, the pairs of words in Table 5.1 are true historical cognates in the sense that each pair appears to have derived from a single word in the proto-Germanic language from which both English and Swedish have sprung. The pairs of words in Table 5.2, on the other hand, do not reflect a genetic relationship between English and Swedish, and the words in this table that are formally similar to each other are either loanwords in both languages (e.g. *radio*) or are similar only by coincidence (e.g. *kind*).

The terms 'deceptive cognates' and 'false cognates' are often substituted with the term 'false friends' in the scholarly literature, and if we define *false friends* as cross-linguistic word pairs that are (1) formally the same or similar and (2) semantically similar or dissimilar (but not the same), then we end up with eight types of false friends, which are illustrated in the bottom-left four cells in Table 5.1 and Table 5.2. The point I am trying to make is that false friends are not all of a single type. They can be true cognates, international loanwords or accidentally similar words, and their degree of cross-linguistic similarity can vary in relation to both form and meaning. As far as true cognates are concerned, research discussed by Sánchez-Casas and García-Albea (2005) has found that these have powerful priming effects such that they activate the forms and meanings of the target word (i.e. the translation equivalent of a cognate) just as quickly as does priming with the target word itself. Furthermore, this priming effect occurs even when the form and meaning of the prime are only loosely similar to the target word. By

Table 5.2 Nongenetic cognate relationships

		Form		
		Same	*Similar*	*Dissimilar*
Meaning	Same	Sw. *radio*	Sw. *terrass*	Sw. *mat*
		Eng. *radio*	Eng. *terrace*	Eng. *food*
	Similar	Sw. *student* (in college)	Sw. *pensel* (paintbrush)	Sw. *ǎka* (ride; drive)
		Eng. *student*	Eng. *pencil*	Eng. *ride*
	Dissimilar	Sw. *kind* (cheek)	Sw. *aktuell* (current)	Sw. *moln* (cloud)
		Eng. *kind*	Eng. *actual*	Eng. *hill*

contrast, noncognate false friends tend to have a priming effect only when they are formally identical or almost identical to the target word, and their effects on the activation of both the form and the meaning of the target word are more limited than is the case with true cognates.

Of course, L2 users do not always know the difference between true cognates, loanwords and accidentally similar words, and in the case of genetically closely related languages such as English and Swedish, the effects of all three may be essentially the same. However, in the case of more distant languages and genetically unrelated languages, L2 users do seem to be sensitive to the difference between cognates, international loanwords and accidentally similar words, and this sensitivity has an important impact on the number and types of errors they produce with false friends. Finnish speakers, for example, seem to be aware of the fact that there are no true cognates between English and Finnish, and thus they rarely produce lexical transfer errors involving a reliance on Finnish stock words that are, by accident, superficially similar to English words (e.g. Fi. *home* = 'mold', Fi. *into* = 'enthusiasm'). Finnish speakers also seem to be aware of the international loanwords that exist in Finnish (e.g. Fi. *auto* = 'automobile'; Fi. *bussi* = 'bus', Fi. *radio* = 'radio'; Fi. *televisio* = 'television'; Fi. *filmi* = 'film'; Fi. *presidentti* = 'president') – largely because loanwords tend to be phonotactically different from Finnish stock words – and Finnish speakers do tend to assume that these international loanwords have counterparts in English that are formally and semantically similar. In most cases, this assumption is correct, so this does not result in a large number of errors.

Although Finnish-speaking learners of English have less trouble with false friends than Swedish speakers do, this does not mean that Finnish speakers are inherently more cautious about this type of error. Ringbom (1987, 2001) has shown that Finnish speakers who know Swedish as an L2 or L3 produce a substantial number of errors in L2 or L3 English based on Swedish–English false friends and very few based on Finnish–English false friends. The reason for this probably has to do with the overall degree of similarity that the learners perceive between Swedish and English, on the one hand, versus Finnish and English, on the other (see Jarvis & Pavlenko, 2008; Ringbom, 2007), and it may also reflect the overall degree to which Swedish versus Finnish is activated in their minds while they are using English (cf. De Bot, 2004).

Levels of activation are also thought to play a prominent role in the second type of formal lexical transfer introduced at the beginning of this section: unintentional language switches. As I mentioned earlier, unintentional language switches involve the selection of a word from the wrong language, and this can be regarded as a type of slip of the tongue. This is the perspective that Poulisse (1999) took in her examination of 2000 slips of the tongue in L1 Dutch speakers' use of spoken L2 English. She found that 459 of the slips were L1 lexical intrusions, and the high number of these led Poulisse to conclude that the learners' L1 was mentally activated during their oral production of the L2. She also concluded that certain factors seem to raise the activation level of an L1 word during L2 production. For example, she found that L1 words that occur frequently in the L1, and also L1 words that have L2 cognates, are especially likely to intrude into a person's use of the L2. Another factor she noted is L2 proficiency, which she found decreases the likelihood of L1 lexical intrusions.

Poulisse's study of unintentional language switches dealt with L2 learners, but other studies, such as Cenoz (2001), Ringbom (1987, 2001) and Williams and Hammarberg (1998), have examined unintentional lexical intrusions in the speech and writing of language learners who know multiple languages. The study by Williams and Hammarberg (1998) investigated language switches produced by a learner of Swedish who had prior knowledge of English (native), German (near-native), French (advanced) and Italian (elementary). Using oral Swedish data elicited through interviews and picture description tasks, the researchers found that the learner frequently switched into both L1 English and L2 German, but very rarely into either French or Italian. Additionally, there was a substantial difference between her switches into English and her switches into German. Her switches into the L1 generally reflected metalinguistic comments, self-corrections and appeals for assistance, whereas her use of L2 German words in otherwise Swedish utterances generally served no identifiable pragmatic purpose. The researchers concluded that the learner's German lexicon was mentally activated to a fairly high level while she was speaking Swedish, but her L1 English was activated to a much lesser degree, as evidenced by the fact that English words rarely emerged as *unintentional* intrusions into her Swedish. The researchers attributed the strong activation of German to four important factors: (1) the learner was *highly proficient* in German, (2) German is *closely related* to Swedish, (3) the learner had used German *recently* and (4) German was *not the native language* of the learner. Regarding the second factor, studies by Cenoz (2001) and Ringbom (1987, 2001) confirm that trilingual users of English are far more likely to produce lexical intrusions from a related language (Spanish or Swedish) than from an unrelated language (Basque or Finnish). Regarding the fourth factor, Williams and Hammarberg assumed that learners have a higher propensity to suppress the activation level of the L1 than of a non-L1 language. There is some support for this assumption in the literature (see De Bot, 2004: 26–28), but Dewaele (1998) also provides some counter-evidence, which I will describe shortly.

In the meantime, it should again be noted that the overall level of activation of a language is no more important for lexical transfer than the levels of activation of specific words within that language. A study by De Angelis (2005a) illustrates this point quite clearly. She found that first-year university-level learners of Italian whose L1 was either English or Spanish and who had previously learned French as an additional language, were particularly susceptible to the unintentional intrusion of the French subject pronoun *il* ('he') in their use of Italian on a writing task. Although numerous other words from English, Spanish and French intruded into their use of Italian, the French word *il* was by far the most frequently occurring intrusion, accounting for approximately 19% of all lexical intrusions in their use of Italian, and also for approximately 44% of all lexical intrusions originating from French. Learners who had not learned French did not show this tendency at all. Among those who had learned French, it was the Spanish speakers who showed the greater tendency to use *il* as a subject pronoun in Italian. The corresponding word in Spanish is *el* ('he', 'the'), which is formally similar to the French *il*, but has a wider range of functions. The corresponding word in Italian is *lui* ('he'), but Italian does have a word *il* ('the'), which is identical in form to the intruding French word *il* and which carries one of the functions of the Spanish word *el*. In this particular case, it seems that the convergence of formal (lexemic) and functional (lemmatic) similarities between Spanish, French and Italian results in a particularly high activation level for the lexeme *il*, and increases its likelihood of being selected during language production.

The final type of formal lexical transfer introduced at the beginning of this section involves word coinages created by the combination of the formal properties of words from different languages (e.g. *If I found gold, I would be luckly* = 'If I found gold, I would be <u>happy</u>', influenced by Swedish *lycklig* = 'happy'; from Ringbom, 1987: 154). This is perhaps the type of lexemic transfer that most obviously involves the level of lexemes, given that it is specifically the forms of words that are modified through this type of transfer. In many cases, the coinages involve the blending of two clearly identifiable words from two different languages (e.g. the example of *luckly* given earlier), but sometimes they also entail the use of a word stem from one language with inflectional morphology from another (e.g. *All these wooden golves must be cleaned*, Sw. *golv* = 'floor'; Ringbom, 1987: 154) or even the modification of the word stem itself to make it seem like a word of the target language (e.g. *Don't walk under a stedge*, Sw. *stege* = 'ladder'; Ringbom, 1978: 89). Like the other types of formal lexical transfer that I have discussed so far, Ringbom (1978, 1987, 2001) found that blends and coinages are far more likely to involve related languages (Swedish and English) than unrelated ones (Finnish and English). A recent thesis by Meriläinen (2006) likewise shows that Finnish speakers rarely produce these types of errors by drawing on their knowledge of Finnish, although a few sparse examples can be found, mainly pertaining to loanwords (e.g. *The book tells about a man named Musashi who lived in feodalic Japan*, Fi. *feodaalinen* = 'feudal'; Meriläinen, 2006: 145; see Ringbom, 1978: 90 for additional relevant examples).

To what extent this type of transfer involves learned cross-linguistic lexical associations is not completely clear, but it does seem clear that levels of language activation – and therefore also processing interference – play a role. In fact, in a study on the use of 'lexical inventions' by Dutch-speaking learners of English and French, Dewaele (1998: 487) considered 'the proportion of lexical inventions from a particular language . . . to be an indicator of the level of activation of that language in the mind of the speaker'. Some of the participants had learned English before French, and the others had learned French before English. The focus of the study was on the participants' use of French in informal speaking tasks, and the purpose was to discover whether L1 Dutch or L2/L3 English is a stronger source of influence on the types of lexical blends they produce. The results of the study show 'that the French L2 speakers (who have English as an L3) transfer more from their L1 (Dutch) whereas the French L3 speakers transfer more from their L2 English' (Dewaele, 1998: 486–487). There were also a few cases where the transfer was from both Dutch and English simultaneously. These are intriguing findings concerning activation because they show, first of all, that words from more than one language at a time can be mentally activated during a person's use of the target language. Second, Dewaele's findings provide an important contrast to the findings of Williams and Hammarberg (1998) because they show that the nonselected language with the highest level of activation (i.e. the language intruding the most into the person's use of the target language) can be either the L1 or a post-L1 language, depending on factors such as the order in which the language was acquired in relation to the language currently being used.

To summarize, the three types of formal lexical transfer discussed in this section reflect lexeme-level links and processes, in the sense that they appear to be induced largely by formal cross-linguistic lexemic similarities and/or by levels of lexeme activation. Although learned cross-linguistic links between corresponding lexemes of different languages must certainly have an effect on the nature and occurrence of lexemic transfer, most of the evidence borne out in the empirical literature seems to point more toward processing interference (i.e. levels of activation) than toward interlingual identifications as the main cause of observable manifestations of lexemic transfer. The use of false friends may often reflect pre-existing mental associations between words that are superficially similar, but it seems clear that this is not always a necessary precondition, and it is also clear that false friends have important effects on language perception and comprehension independently of pre-existing interlingual identifications (e.g. Ringbom, 2007; Sánchez-Casas & García-Albea, 2005). As far as unintentional language switches are concerned, this appears to be caused largely by a high level of activation in the intruding lexeme independently of a possibly existing mental connection between the intruding lexeme and the target lexeme (cf. Poulisse, 1999; Williams & Hammarberg, 1998). Finally, concerning lexical blends and coinages, although it is possible that these may sometimes reflect the way a target lexeme is represented in the mental lexicon, it also seems quite likely that they are often created online due to processing interference from competing activated lexemes (cf. Dewaele, 1998).

4. Lemmatic Transfer

In the preceding section, I explained that the distinction between lexemic and lemmatic transfer is similar to Ringbom's (1987, 2001) distinction between formal and semantic transfer. This is especially true in relation to the correspondence between lexemic and formal transfer, but less so with regard to the correspondence between lemmatic and semantic transfer. To be sure, lemmatic transfer does encompass the types of semantic transfer that Ringbom describes, but it also extends beyond semantic transfer to include the collocational, morphological and syntactic constraints on words. The essence of what Ringbom means by semantic transfer, however, may nevertheless be very similar to the notion of lemmatic transfer. For example, in both his 1987 and 2007 books, he describes semantic transfer in terms of the learner's knowledge of the L2 system, which includes both grammar and vocabulary, and also includes collocational restrictions and links between words (e.g. Ringbom, 2007: 100). Additionally, one of the two types of semantic transfer he emphasizes involves calques (or literal translations of compound lexical items, such as *firestick* = 'match', from Fi. *tulitikku* = lit. 'fire stick'), which are inherently syntagmatic in nature given that they are not just a matter of form-meaning mapping, but also involve the way that multiple forms are brought together to convey a particular meaning.

Although there are potentially many types of lemmatic transfer, in this section I will concentrate on the following four: (1) semantic extensions, (2) calques, (3) collocational transfer and (4) subcategorization transfer. The first two are the types of semantic transfer that Ringbom (1987, 2001) has traditionally referred to, and the last two are other types of word-related transfer that have received a fair amount of attention in the literature. What combines all four categories is the notion that a person's knowledge of a lemma includes the word's semantic associations and syntactic constraints (e.g. De Bot, 2004; Kempen & Huijbers, 1983). For the purposes of this chapter, semantic associations can be thought of as mental links between a lemma and one or more concepts, and syntactic constraints can be thought of as mental links between lemmas. This is admittedly an oversimplification, but it nevertheless seems to be a useful metaphor. Drawing from this metaphor, we could say that semantic extensions are largely a matter of lemma-concept links, whereas the remaining three types of lemmatic transfer are more a matter of how lemmas are linked to one another (and to functional morphology and syntactic structures).

As far as semantic extensions are concerned, this term has actually been used to refer to two different types of meaning transfer whose differences are at times very subtle, but which are nevertheless quite important. One type is what I referred to earlier as conceptual transfer, and this is not so much a matter of how lemmas are linked to concepts, but instead of how those concepts themselves are constituted. Conceptual transfer is the topic of Chapter 6, so I will not deal with it further here. Instead, I will focus on semantic extensions only to the extent that they involve the ways that lemmas are linked to concepts. The clearest examples of these pertain to cases where polysemy is represented differently in one language than in another, such as in the following example from Meriläinen (2006: 92), where a Finnish-speaking learner of English, while writing an essay in English, has extended the meaning of the word *spin* in a Finnish-like manner: *the cat climbs beside man and lies down as near to man as possible starting to spin* (pro *purr*; Fi. *kehrä̈tä* = 'spin; purr'). The Finnish verb *kehrä̈tä* is polysemous in the sense that it is linked to two separate concepts: the concepts for spinning and purring. A plausible interpretation of what led to this error is that when learning the word *spin*, the learner who produced this error carried over the full set of semantic links (i.e. the lemma-concept mappings) from the Finnish word *kehrä̈tä* and applied them to *spin*. A slightly different interpretation has been offered by Jiang (2002, 2004), who found that Chinese speakers and Korean speakers are significantly faster at judging the relationship between pairs of English words that have a single translation equivalent in the L1 (e.g. *problem* and *question* are both translated as *wenti* in Chinese) than they are at judging the relationship between pairs of words that are semantically related but are represented by different words in the L1 (e.g. *interrupt* and *interfere* correspond to *daduan* and *ganrao*, respectively, in Chinese). Jiang's (2002) interpretation is that learners tend to associate L2 lexemes with L1 lemmas, which means that L1 and L2 lexemes (e.g. *problem* and *wenti*) become morphological variants of the same lemma (e.g. WENTI) (see Sánchez-Casas & García-Albea, 2005, for a similar account of how cognates are represented in bilingual memory). However, from the perspective adopted here, it seems that Jiang's results could be accounted for equally well by positing that L2 words that have a single translation in the L1 do have their own lemmas, but that these lemmas are linked to the same concept. Future research should be able to clarify which interpretation is more parsimonious by testing whether learners' knowledge of the polysemy, collocational constraints and subcategorization frames for corresponding words in the L1 and L2 differ – which would be evidence for separate lemmas.

Concerning calques (or loan translations), these have been widely documented in the literature. In many cases, they involve simple compound words that are transferred (or directly translated) from one language to another, such as *youngman* (for *bachelor*, from Swedish *ungkarl* = lit. 'young man'; Ringbom, 2001: 64) and *animaldoctor* (for *veterinarian*, from Finnish *elä'inlä'ä'kä'ri* = lit. 'animal doctor'; Meriläinen, 2006: 91). In other cases, they additionally involve more complex constructions and collocational constraints, as in the following example: *in farm lives dogs and cats, of course, maybe they both <u>spend</u> there <u>cat's days</u>* (for <u>lead an easy life</u>, from Finnish *viettä'ä' kissanpä'iviä'* = lit. 'spend cat's days'). One might argue that this last example is a matter of an idiom being transferred from the L1 to the L2, but in many respects, calques and transferred idioms (and other types of transferred fixed expressions) are similar phenomena in the sense that what is transferred is a blueprint for organizing multiple forms (words and morphemes) together in specific orders and within specific syntactic constructions in order to allow them to convey a specific intended message (see, e.g. Bongartz, 2002, for a more thorough treatment of compound constructions in a second language). Although the precise manner in which compound words, idioms and other types of fixed expressions are represented in the mental lexicon is not completely clear, it does seem clear within the framework adopted here that they must involve lemma-level associations, such as lemma-lemma connections and various syntactic specifications.

What is also particularly interesting about both semantic extensions and calques is that, unlike the types of lexemic transfer I discussed in the previous section, the types of lemmatic transfer I have discussed so far seem not to entail activation levels or processing interference, but learned interlingual identifications that affect the ways that L2 words (lemmas, in this case) are represented in the mental lexicon. Another thing that distinguishes lexemic transfer from the types of lemmatic transfer I have discussed so far is that the likelihood of lexemic transfer increases with the perceived similarities of the languages in question, but semantic extensions and calques are equally likely in cases where the languages are unrelated as they are in cases where the languages are closely related (Ringbom, 1987, 2001, 2007). A better predictor for the likelihood of semantic transfer is the learner's level of proficiency in the source language. This means that semantic transfer from L1 to L2 is generally more common than semantic transfer from L2 to L3 (Ringbom, 2001: 65–66), but it is important to recognize that semantic transfer can occur in multiple directions, even from the L2 to the L1 (see, e.g. Jarvis, 2003; Pavlenko & Jarvis, 2002). Ultimately, it may be that the likelihood of semantic transfer is less directly determined by the L2 user's overall proficiency in the source language than by the richness of that person's knowledge of the specific words that might produce transfer effects.

Moving next to collocational transfer, this is not generally treated as a type of semantic transfer in the literature, but it should be clear that it is closely related to calques, which are treated as a type of semantic transfer. In the earlier example where a Finnish-speaking learner of English used the phrase *spend cat's days* to mean 'lead an easy life', *cat's days* is the direct translation of a compound word in Finnish (*kissanpäiviä*), so this part of the phrase is clearly a calque. However, it could also be regarded as a collocation given that it involves two words that conventionally co-occur. The word *spend* (*viettää* in Finnish) is also part of the collocation, though somewhat more loosely in the sense that it is not part of a compound word and it does not have to occur immediately adjacent to the rest of the phrase. The point is that calques and collocational transfer are closely related phenomena (perhaps forming a continuum), and one of the advantages of the notion of lemmatic transfer is that it allows us to bring these two phenomena together under the same umbrella.

Collocational transfer has been investigated by numerous researchers, including Biskup (1992), Hasselgren (1994), James (1998), Latkowska (2006), Lesniewska (2006) and Meriläinen (2006), among others. The types of methods used for eliciting learners' knowledge of collocations have involved translation and fill-in-the-blank tasks, as well as unguided essays (in the case of Meriläinen). These studies have documented a great number of instances of collocational transfer and have confirmed that the lemma-lemma associations that learners have in their L1s are indeed often carried over to the corresponding lemmas in the L2 (e.g. *There is also people who wants to get married, do children and build a nice house*; for *have children*, from Finnish *tehdä lapsia* = lit. 'do/make children'). There is more to the story, however, and if we recognize phrasal verbs (e.g. *let down, put off*) as lexical collocations, then one additional, intriguing finding emerges, which is that learners whose L1s lack phrasal verbs (e.g. Finnish, Hebrew) tend to avoid using phrasal verbs in the L2, opting instead for one-word equivalents (e.g. *disappoint, postpone*) (Laufer & Eliasson, 1993; Sjöholm, 1995). Learners whose L1s do have phrasal verbs (e.g. Swedish) do not show the same aversion to using them in the L2 except in particular cases, such as when L2 phrasal verbs seem too L1-like. Similar to other negative consequences of lemmatic transfer, the avoidance of phrasal verbs by learners whose L1s do not have phrasal verbs tends to decrease with increasing levels of L2 proficiency (Sjöholm, 1995). However, proficiency does not completely prevent collocational transfer from occurring, and it has even been documented from an L2 to an L1 (e.g. Jarvis, 2003). Like other types of lemmatic transfer – but unlike lexemic transfer – language distance does not seem to reduce the likelihood of collocational transfer.

Finally, regarding subcategorization transfer, this pertains particularly to cases that, on the surface, are syntactic errors involving a headword (such as an adjective or verb) and its complement (such as a noun phrase or a prepositional phrase). In many of the relevant cases, the wrong type of complement is chosen, such as a prepositional phrase instead of a noun phrase (e.g. *She kissed with him* versus *She kissed him*) or a noun phrase instead of a prepositional phrase (e.g. *He was thinking his mother* versus *He was thinking about his mother*). In still other cases, the subcategorization transfer manifests itself not in the choice of the wrong type of complement, but in the choice of a wrong specific word within the complement (e.g. *late from an appointment* versus *late for an appointment*; Meriläinen, 2006: 135). Numerous instances of these types of transfer involving L1 influence on L2 have been documented by Adjémian (1983), Dušková (1969), Meriläinen (2006) and others, and they have also been documented in the reverse direction, from L2 to L1 (e.g. Jarvis, 2003; Pavlenko & Jarvis, 2002). All of these cases of subcategorization transfer reflect the influence of the syntactic specifications of headwords in one language on an L2 user's understanding and application of the syntactic specifications of corresponding headwords in another language.

Assuming that syntactic specifications are contained within a word's lemma (e.g. Levelt *et al.*, 1999), this clearly is a type of lemmatic transfer. Its relationship to other types of lemmatic transfer, such as semantic transfer, can be appreciated especially in light of a study by Helms-Park (2001), which investigates the expression of causation in L2 English by L1 speakers of Hindi–Urdu and Vietnamese. Causation works differently in each of these languages, and even differently with different words in the same language (e.g. the verb *boil* can be used both intransitively and as a causative transitive, as in *The potatoes boiled* and *I boiled the potatoes*; by contrast, *disappear* can be used as an intransitive but not as a causative transitive, as in *The ball disappeared* but not **I disappeared the ball*). Analyzing data collected with a picture-based production test, a picture-based multiple-choice test and a grammaticality judgment test, Helms-Park found that the speakers of Hindi–Urdu and Vietnamese differed significantly from each other in their use of causation in English, and did so in ways that were generally in line with the way causation is expressed in their L1s (although some intralingual overgeneralizations were also found). The relevance of this study to the present discussion is that causation represents an area where semantic associations and syntactic constraints (such as a verb's subcategorization specifications) both play a very prominent role in determining how a particular notion will be expressed. Once again, this lends credence to the idea that lexico-semantic and lexico-syntactic transfer are two sides of the same coin – a coin that the notion of lemmatic transfer seems to account for quite well.

The four types of lemmatic transfer that I have discussed in this section exhibit two important similarities that distinguish them from lexemic transfer. First, they do not appear to be constrained by language distance. This point has been made explicitly by Ringbom (1987, 2001) in relation to semantic extensions and calques, and the research I have reviewed on collocational transfer and subcategorization transfer suggests that it is true of these types of lemmatic transfer, as well. Second, none of the four types of lemmatic transfer I have discussed appears to be induced to any substantial degree by processing interference or activation levels – as was the case for lexemic transfer – but instead all four types of lemmatic transfer appear to result primarily from the ways that L2 users construct lexical representations in one language in accordance with their knowledge of corresponding words in another language.

5. Summary of Methods

The methods of data collection that have been used in the studies reviewed in this chapter include a range of techniques, from highly controlled receptive tasks where learners act on one word at a time, to relatively free and spontaneous production tasks involving longer texts or stretches of discourse. The more controlled methods include picture naming (e.g. seeing a picture of a bear and saying *bear*), picture classification (e.g. deciding whether various pictures represent things that are human-made versus natural), word naming (e.g. seeing the word *bear* and pronouncing it aloud), word translation (e.g. seeing *bear* and translating it into another language), lexical decision (e.g. deciding whether *uncle* refers to a male or female, deciding whether *problem* and *question* are similar), and various types of lexical preference tasks (e.g. multiple-choice tasks, fill-in-the-blank tasks) and also grammaticality judgment tasks (e.g. where an individual word or a multiword unit may be of the wrong form or carry the wrong meaning). Lexical priming and the measurement of reaction times are often used with tasks such as picture naming, word translation and lexical decision in order to test whether seeing or hearing a particular word from one language can facilitate the speed with which a person is able to perform the task with another word. These types of techniques are especially useful in the investigation of lexemic transfer, particularly as it pertains to the strength of connections between L1 and L2 lexemes relative to other types of representations (e.g. meaning representations) that lexemes may activate (for a summary of this type of research, see Kroll & Tokowicz, 2005). Some of these types of controlled tasks, such as lexical decision, are also used in neuroimaging studies in order to measure levels of brain activation and locations of neural activity (e.g. in order to probe further into the different levels of lexical knowledge and in order to test for differences between L1 and L2 knowledge) (see, e.g. Abutalebi *et al.*, 2005; Longoni *et al.*, 2005). Other types of controlled tasks, including lexical preference tasks and grammaticality judgment tasks, are often designed to elicit evidence of learners' lexico-semantic and/or lexico-syntactic knowledge (e.g. Hasselgren, 1994; Helms-Park, 2001), and these types of tasks tend to be better suited to investigating lemmatic transfer.

Methods for collecting free-production data include observations of natural language use and data elicited through oral interviews, written journals, written essays, and oral and written narrative descriptions of pictures and silent films. Free-production data often offer rich and contextualized evidence of both lexemic transfer (e.g. unintentional language switches and lexical blends) and lemmatic transfer (e.g. semantic extensions, calques, collocational transfer, subcategorization transfer) (see, e.g. Adjémian, 1983; Biskup, 1992; Ringbom, 1987).

A number of studies on lexical transfer have investigated the language use of people who know more than two languages. More of this type of research is crucially needed in the future because there are complex factors – such as the effects of cross-linguistic similarities, language proficiency and order of language acquisition – that affect lexical transfer but cannot be understood fully without examining speakers of more than two languages (e.g. De Angelis, 2005a, 2005b; Dewaele, 1998; Ringbom, 1987). Methodologically rigorous studies are relatively rare in transfer research, yet this is what is urgently needed if we are to develop a better understanding of how languages interact in the minds of language learners and true bi- and multilinguals (see Jarvis & Pavlenko, 2008, for an in-depth discussion of the principles of rigorous inquiry in transfer research).

Conclusions

The existing research on cross-linguistic effects in bilingual lexical representation and processing suggests that word knowledge involves three general levels of representation: lexemes, lemmas and concepts. As far as lexemes are concerned, mental links can be established between words within and across languages, and these links may also be formed within (e.g. lexeme to lexeme) and across levels of representation (e.g. lexeme to lemma). Lexemic representations and the links between them appear to be of varying strengths – depending on factors such as cross-linguistic similarity and frequency of use – and their strengths are believed to affect the degree to which they will be activated during the use of another language. When lexemes in the nonselected language are at a high level of activation, they can affect the speed of lexical processing and lexical decisions in the selected language (De Bot, 2004) and can also emerge as lexical intrusions into the selected language in the form of false friends, cross-linguistic lexical blends and unintentional language switches (e.g. Dewaele, 1998; Poulisse, 1999; Ringbom, 2001; Williams & Hammarberg, 1998).

Concerning lemmas, cross-linguistic effects also arise out of the associations that L2 users make between the lemmatic representations they have for the different languages they know. These associations, or interlingual identifications, affect the way that lexical knowledge is represented in the L2 user's mental lexicon, and their effects are seen particularly in the ways that a person maps words to meanings (i.e. lemmas to concepts) and words to other words (lemmas to lemmas). The effects of cross-linguistic influence in lemma-concept associations are especially evident in the semantic extensions that L2 users produce (e.g. Ringbom, 1987), whereas the effects of cross-linguistic influence in lemma-lemma associations are seen more in instances of collocational transfer (e.g. Hasselgren, 1994; Meriläinen, 2006). Calques represent a cross-linguistic effect that may involve both lemma-concept and lemma-lemma associations simultaneously. In subcategorization transfer, on the other hand, the role of lemma-concept associations seems minimal to nonexistent, and the role of lemma-lemma associations is unclear. Nevertheless, subcategorization transfer does clearly involve lemma-level syntagmatic constraints, as do calques and collocational transfer, and all four types of lemmatic transfer discussed in this chapter appear to be free from the factors that constrain lexemic transfer (i.e. levels of activation and language distance).

Future research is needed to confirm these findings and to settle some unresolved questions. One of the questions alluded to earlier is whether semantic transfer entails cross-linguistic influence in the links between lexemes and lemmas (Jiang, 2002), or between lemmas and concepts or both. Another series of questions concerns the nature of lexemic and lemmatic representations and the links between them. This is especially true of lemmatic representations, for which there remains a good deal of confusion about the nature of syntactic specifications and of how they are represented in the mind. We also need to know whether lemmatic representations can involve both implicit and explicit knowledge. We know that it is possible to have both implicit and explicit knowledge about the meanings, forms and syntactic specifications of words, but the question is whether both implicit and explicit knowledge can be stored within the lemma itself. Concerning the links between lexemes and lemmas, we need to know more about the nature of these links and about whether reaction times are a good indication of the strength of the links between them. Regarding lexical transfer, we need to know whether – particularly at the lemma level – this entails the transfer of a mapping blueprint (e.g. about how words are mapped to concepts) or the formation of associations between lemmas belonging to different languages, or whether it involves both (cf. De Angelis, 2005b). We also need to know what makes it possible for an L2 user to gradually overcome negative transfer effects at increasing levels of proficiency. Do L2 users eventually acquire the same types of representations of lexemes and lemmas that native speakers have, or do they develop different representations along with an ability to compensate for those differences during actual language use?

References

Abutalebi, J., Cappa, S. and Perani, D. (2005) What can functional neuroimaging tell us about the bilingual brain? In J. Kroll and A.M.B. De Groot (eds) *Handbook of Bilingualism: Psycholinguistic Approaches* (pp. 497–515). Oxford: Oxford University Press.

Adjémian, C. (1983) The transferability of lexical properties. In S. Gass and L. Selinker (eds) *Language Transfer in Language Learning* (pp. 250–268). Rowley, MA: Newbury House.

Biskup, D. (1992) L1 influence on learners' rendering of English collocations: A Polish/German empirical study. In P. Arnaud and H. Béjoint (eds) *Vocabulary and Applied Linguistics* (pp. 85–93). London: Macmillan.

Bongartz, C. (2002) *Noun Combination in Interlanguage: Typology Effects in Complex Determiner Phrases*. Tübingen, Germany: Niemeyer.

Cenoz, J. (2001) The effect of linguistic distance, L2 status and age on cross-linguistic influence in third language acquisition. In J. Cenoz, B. Hufeisen and U. Jessner (eds) *Cross-linguistic Influence in Third Language Acquisition: Psycholinguistic Perspectives* (pp. 8–20). Clevedon: Multilingual Matters.

Costa, A. (2005) Lexical access in bilingual production. In J. Kroll and A.M.B. De Groot (eds) *Handbook of Bilingualism: Psycholinguistics Approaches* (pp. 308–325). Oxford: Oxford University Press.

De Angelis, G. (2005a) Interlanguage transfer of function words. *Language Learning* 55, 379–414.

De Angelis, G. (2005b) Multilingualism and non-native lexical transfer: An identification problem. *International Journal of Multilingualism* 2, 1–25.

De Bot, K. (2004) The multilingual lexicon: Modelling selection and control. *The International Journal of Multilingualism* 1, 17–32.

De Groot, A.M.B., Dannenburg, L. and Van Hell, J. (1994) Forward and backward word translation by bilinguals. *Journal of Memory and Language* 33, 600–629.

Dewaele, J-M. (1998) Lexical inventions: French interlanguage as L2 versus L3. *Applied Linguistics* 19, 471–490.

Dijkstra, T. and Van Heuven, W. (2002) The architecture of the bilingual word recognition system: From identification to decision. *Bilingualism: Language and Cognition* 5, 175–197.

Dušková, L. (1969) On sources of errors in foreign language teaching. *International Review of Applied Linguistics* 7, 11–36.

Faerch, C., Haastrup, K. and Phillipson, R. (1984) *Learner Language and Language Learning*. Clevedon: Multilingual Matters.

Francis, W. (2005) Bilingual semantic and conceptual representation. In J. Kroll and A.M.B. De Groot (eds) *Handbook of Bilingualism: Psycholinguistics Approaches* (pp. 251–267). Oxford: Oxford University Press.

Garrett, M. (1975) The analysis of sentence production. In G. Bower (ed.) *The Psychology of Learning and Motivation* (Vol. 9; pp. 133–177). New York: Academic Press.

Goral, M., Levy, E.S., Obler, L.K. and Cohen, E. (2006) Cross-language lexical connections in the mental lexicon: Evidence from a case of trilingual aphasia. *Brain and Language* 98, 235–247.

Grosjean, F. (1999) The bilingual's language modes. In J. Nicol (ed.) *One Mind, Two Languages: Bilingual Language Processing* (pp. 1–25). Oxford: Blackwell.

Hasselgren, A. (1994) Lexical teddy bears and advanced learners: A study into the ways Norwegian students cope with English vocabulary. *International Journal of Applied Linguistics* 4, 237–260.

Helms-Park, R. (2001) Evidence of lexical transfer in learner syntax: The acquisition of English causatives by speakers of Hindi-Urdu and Vietnamese. *Studies in Second Language Acquisition* 23, 71–102.

James, C. (1998) *Errors in Language Learning and Use*. New York: Longman.

Jarvis, S. (2003) Probing the effects of the L2 on the L1: A case study. In V. Cook (ed.) *Effects of the Second Language on the First* (pp. 81–102). Clevedon: Multilingual Matters.

Jarvis, S. and Pavlenko, A. (2008) *Crosslinguistic Influence in Language and Cognition*. New York and London: Routledge.

Jiang, N. (2000) Lexical representation and development in a second language. *Applied Linguistics* 21, 47–77.

Jiang, N. (2002) Form-meaning mapping in vocabulary acquisition in a second language. *Studies in Second Language Acquisition* 24, 617–637.

Jiang, N. (2004) Semantic transfer and its implications for vocabulary teaching in a second language. *Modern Language Journal* 88, 416–432.

Kempen, G. and Hoenkamp, E. (1987) An incremental procedural grammar for sentence formulation. *Cognitive Science* 11, 201–258.

Kempen, G. and Huijbers, P. (1983) The lexicalization process in sentence production and naming: Indirect election of words. *Cognition* 14, 185–209.

Kroll, J. and Stewart, E. (1994) Category interference in translation and picture naming: Evidence for asymmetric connections between bilingual memory representations. *Journal of Memory and Language* 33, 149–174.

Kroll, J. and Tokowicz, N. (2005) Models of bilingual representation and processing: Looking back and to the future. In J. Kroll and A.M.B. De Groot (eds) *Handbook of Bilingualism: Psycholinguistic Approaches* (pp. 531–553). Oxford: Oxford University Press.

Lakoff, G. (1987) *Women, Fire, and Dangerous Things. What Categories Reveal about the Mind.* Chicago, IL: University of Chicago Press.

Latkowska, J. (2006) On the use of translation in studies of language contact. In J. Arabski (ed.) *Cross-linguistic Influences in the Second Language Lexicon* (pp. 210–225). Clevedon: Multilingual Matters.

Laufer, B. and Eliasson, S. (1993) What causes avoidance in L2 learning: L1-L2 differences, L1-L2 similarity, or L2 complexity? *Studies in Second Language Acquisition* 15, 35–48.

Lesniewska, J. (2006) Is cross-linguistic influence a factor in advanced EFL learners' use of collocations? In J. Arabski (ed.) *Cross-linguistic Influences in the Second Language Lexicon* (pp. 65–77). Clevedon: Multilingual Matters.

Levelt, W. (1989) *Speaking: From Intention to Articulation.* Cambridge, MA: MIT Press.

Levelt, W., Roelofs, A. and Meyer, A. (1999) A theory of lexical access in speech production. *Behavioral and Brain Sciences* 22, 1–37.

Longoni, F., Grande, M., Hendrich, V., Kastrau, F. and Huber, W. (2005) An fMRI study on conceptual, grammatical, and morpho-phonological processing. *Brain and Cognition* 57, 131–134.

Meriläinen, L. (2006) Lexical transfer errors in the written English of Finnish upper secondary school students. Unpublished Licenciate thesis, Department of English, University of Joensuu, Finland.

Michael, E. and Gollan, T. (2005) Being and becoming bilingual: Individual differences and consequences for language production. In J. Kroll and A.M.B. De Groot (eds) *Handbook of Bilingualism: Psycholinguistic Approaches* (pp. 389–407). Oxford: Oxford University Press.

Murphy, G. (2002) *The Big Book of Concepts.* Cambridge, MA: MIT Press.

Nation, I.S.P. (1990) *Teaching and Learning Vocabulary.* New York: Newbury House.

Nation, I.S.P. (2001) *Learning Vocabulary in Another Language.* Cambridge: Cambridge University Press.

Odlin, T. (1989) *Language Transfer: Cross-linguistic Influence in Language Learning.* Cambridge: Cambridge University Press.

Pavlenko, A. (1999) New approaches to concepts in bilingual memory. *Bilingualism: Language and Cognition* 2, 209–230.

Pavlenko, A. and Jarvis, S. (2002) Bidirectional transfer. *Applied Linguistics* 23, 190–214.

Poulisse, N. (1999) *Slips of the Tongue: Speech Errors in First and Second Language Production.* Amsterdam: John Benjamins.

Richards, J.C. (1976) The role of vocabulary teaching. *TESOL Quarterly* 10, 77–89.

Ringbom, H. (1978) The influence of the mother tongue on the translation of lexical items. *Interlanguage Studies Bulletin* 3, 80–101.

Ringbom, H. (1987) *The Role of the First Language in Foreign Language Learning.* Clevedon: Multilingual Matters.

Ringbom, H. (2001) Lexical transfer in L3 production. In J. Cenoz, B. Hufeisen and U. Jessner (eds) *Cross-linguistic Influence in Third Language Acquisition: Psycholinguistic Perspectives* (pp. 59–68). Clevedon: Multilingual Matters.

Ringbom, H. (2007) *The Importance of Cross-linguistic Similarity in Foreign Language Learning: Comprehension, Learning and Production.* Clevedon: Multilingual Matters.

Roelofs, A. (1992) A spreading-activation theory of lemma retrieval in speaking. *Cognition* 42, 107–142.

Roelofs, A., Meyer, A. and Levelt, W. (1998) A case for the lemma/lexeme distinction in models of speaking: Comment on Caramazza and Miozzo (1997). *Cognition* 69, 219–230.

Sánchez-Casas, R. and García-Albea, J. (2005) The representation of cognate and noncognate words in bilingual memory: Can cognate status be characterized as a special kind of morphological relation? In J. Kroll and A.M.B. De Groot (eds) *Handbook of Bilingualism: Psycholinguistic Approaches* (pp. 226–250). Oxford: Oxford University Press.

Sjöholm, K. (1995) *The Influence of Crosslinguistic, Semantic, and Input Factors on the Acquisition of English Phrasal Verbs: A Comparison Between Finnish and Swedish Learners at an Intermediate and Advanced Level.* Åbo, Finland: Åbo Akademi University Press.

Weinreich, U. (1953) *Languages in Contact.* The Hague: Mouton.

Williams, S. and Hammarberg, B. (1998) Language switches in L3 production: Implications for a polyglot speaking model. *Applied Linguistics* 19, 295–333.

Chapter 6

Conceptual Representation in the Bilingual Lexicon and Second Language Vocabulary Learning

ANETA PAVLENKO

Introduction

In the past decades, scholars have made great strides in under-standing how cross-linguistic differences play out in orthographic, phonological, morphosyntactic and lexical processing in the bilingual lexicon. There still remains, however, one area where cross-linguistic differences have not been sufficiently explored and integrated, namely the level of conceptual representation. Early studies of bilingualism had asked whether the two lexicons are linked to a shared conceptual store or two separate stores (Keatley, 1992). At present, most bilingual processing and representation models, with the exception of the Distributed Feature Model (DFM) (De Groot, 1992), assume that while phonological and morphosyntactic forms differ across languages, meanings and/or con-cepts are largely, if not completely, shared (cf. Costa, 2005; Kroll & Stewart, 1994). This assumption is justified by the fact that bilinguals can translate most words from one language to another, by the evidence of cross-linguistic semantic priming and by the interference from one language in picture naming in another (Kroll & Sunderman, 2003). Consequently, a central issue in theories of the bilingual lexicon had been *the mapping of form to meaning* (Kroll & De Groot, 1997: 169). Research on conceptual representation had focused on the links between word forms and meanings and examined factors that affect the speed of conceptual access and the strength of interlingual connections, but not the nature of the representation itself (De Groot, 2002; Kroll & Tokowicz, 2005).

Recently, there emerged a new line of research on concepts in the bilingual lexicon where the focus of attention shifted from links between word forms and concepts to the actual structure of *linguistic categories*, that is mental representations linked to word forms (*lexical concepts*) and grammatical notions (*grammatical concepts*) (Ameel *et al.*, 2005; Athanasopoulos, 2006, 2007, in press; Cook *et al.*, 2006; Malt & Sloman, 2003; Pavlenko, 2002a, 2003, 2008a; Stepanova Sachs & Coley, 2006; for an overview see Jarvis & Pavlenko, 2008). The key question in this research is not 'Is the conceptual store shared or separate?' but 'What is shared and what is separate in particular lexical concepts?' The central issue in this inquiry is *the mapping of forms to real-world referents*. Studies of lexical concepts in this paradigm ask: what is the structure of linguistic categories in the minds of monolingual speakers? That is, how are words mapped on to objects, events and actions in the real world? What are the similarities and differences between categories linked to transla-tion equivalents? How do bilinguals' categories compare to those of monolingual speakers of their respective languages?

The findings of these studies have important implications for models of the bilingual lexicon, because they challenge the shared store assumption, indicating a much more complex conceptual organization. The purpose of this chapter is to review these studies[1] and to present a model of the bilingual lexicon that reflects their findings. I will begin by explaining why studies using reaction-time-based tasks have failed to produce much information about representation of lexical concepts. Then, I will introduce methods used in the recent studies, synthesize their findings and reflect on their implications for existing models of concepts in the bilingual lexicon. Subsequently, I will put forth a Modified Hierarchical Model (MHM) that incorporates both earlier and more recent findings and aims to facilitate a transition from the first to the second stage of research on bilinguals' concepts. Both the discussion and the model are limited to the bilingual lexicon because empirical studies to date have not yet examined multilinguals' concepts. The terms *bilinguals* and *second language (L2) users* will be used interchangeably to refer to speakers of two languages. The term *L2 learners* will refer to people studying a second language, formally or informally.

1. Methodological Approaches to the Study of Bilinguals' Lexical Concepts

1.1. First stage: Psycholinguistic methods

Psycholinguistic studies of concepts in the bilingual lexicon commonly rely on a variety of reaction-time tasks, such as lexical decision, semantic priming, sentence priming, picture naming, translation, translation equivalent recognition, word association, semantic categorization and the Stroop interference task (De Groot, 1992; Kroll, 1993; Snodgrass, 1993;

see also Altarriba & Basnight-Brown, this volume). These tasks have been used to examine whether L1 and L2 words in the bilingual lexicon are linked to a common conceptual representation. In this paradigm, faster reaction times are taken to indicate stronger connections between word forms (*interlingual connections*), in turn stronger connections are attributed to shared meanings.

There exist, however, several problems with these assumptions and the methods used to test them. To begin with, it is not clear whether stronger connections are always – or exclusively – a function of shared meaning. For instance, in translation tasks a longer amount of time needed to translate a particular word is commonly taken to indicate a lower degree of shared meaning between the translation equivalents (De Groot, 1992, 1993, 1995). In reality, however, the strength of interlingual connections may be affected by a host of other factors, including bilinguals' levels of proficiency in the languages in question, the context of their acquisition, the context of their use, the level of activation of respective languages, similarity of word forms and the frequency of coactivation of particular word pairs (De Groot, 1995, 2002; Kroll & Tokowicz, 2005; Marian, this volume). In beginning and intermediate L2 learners, as well as in first language (L1) attriters (see Schmid & Köpke, this volume), connections between translation equivalents may be weak regardless of the objective similarity between their meanings (hence slower translation rate), while in expert bilinguals, such as simultaneous translators, connections may be strong even between partial equivalents (hence faster translation rate).

Consequently, it is not clear whether all reaction-time-based tasks access conceptual representations as they purport to do. Semantic priming constitutes an excellent example of such problematic task. It is often assumed that 'there should only be cross-language priming if both languages access a common conceptual memory representation' (Kroll, 1993: 57). Following this logic, De Groot and Nas (1991) argued that the presence of cross-language priming for English–Dutch cognates (e.g. *rose-roos*) and the absence of priming for noncognates (e.g. *bird-vogel*) suggest that cognates share conceptual representations and noncognates do not (see also De Groot, 1992, 1993). While these results have been replicated in several other studies, some studies also found priming for false cognates, suggesting that facilitation effects may also be a function of form similarity (for an up-to-date review of cognate representation studies, see Sánchez-Casas & García-Albea, 2005).

Finally, it is unclear whether weaker connections, as seen for example in the lack of semantic priming, can unambiguously indicate the lack of shared meaning. If the Dutch–English bilinguals in De Groot and Nas' (1991) study were asked to name a set of pictures or to sort them into the categories of *bird* and *vogel*, it is quite possible that the same pictures would have been named *bird* and *vogel*, which in turn would have indicated a shared representation. This in turn raises a question of what exactly is meant by a 'shared representation' – is representation 'shared' when the two words are mapped onto the same set of referents even if they do not prime each other?

These questions suggest that instead of inferring the degree of shared meaning from the strength of interlingual connections, future research needs to disambiguate the two and to investigate the relationship between them. Reaction-based tasks, developed for the study of language processing, are well-suited for examining the strength of interlingual connections, but do not offer us any means to examine the contents of linguistic categories and thus to determine the degree to which they are actually shared.

Several possible alternatives have been put forth in the psycholinguistic literature. One such alternative is a word-rating task, where participants rank the closeness of a set of words to a stimulus word (Dong *et al.*, 2005). Unfortunately, in this task as well the strength of the interlingual connection can be attributed to a variety of reasons. For instance, Dong and associates (2005) found that Chinese words *xin liang* (bride) and *hong se* (red) are more strongly linked than their English translation equivalents (because brides wear red in China), while English words *jealousy* and *green* are more strongly linked than their Chinese equivalents (because English speakers talk about turning *green with envy*). These links, however, are of different nature: the first link reflects implicit knowledge about the category and is therefore conceptual, while the second reflects a metaphoric extension of a color term and is therefore semantic (for a discussion of this distinction see section 3.2.2). Metaphoric extensions constitute an important aspect of L2 word knowledge (see also Jarvis, this volume), but do not form part of the actual contents of linguistic categories *jealousy* or *bride*. Thus, word ratings may reveal the strength of interlingual connections, but do not tell us much about the actual structure of linguistic categories (i.e. who counts as a bride? what does a prototypical bride look like? what situations elicit jealousy? etc.).

Another alternative is the similarity judgment task where bilinguals are asked to judge the similarity of meanings of translation equivalents in their respective languages (Moore *et al.*, 1999). This task avoids the problems linked to reaction-time inferencing yet it too displays a major theoretical flaw – conceptual representations are by their nature implicit, but the participants are engaged in a task that involves a metalinguistic judgment, and thus explicit memory (for a discussion of the implicit/ explicit distinction see section 3.2.3). Considering that most lay speakers lack metalinguistic knowledge about particularities of translation equivalence, it is not clear whether their subjective judgments are congruent with ways in which they actually use words. For instance, Dutch–French bilinguals may judge the Dutch *kom* and the French *bol* (both are roughly similar to the English 'bowl') to be near perfect translation equivalents, while their categorization patterns would indicate that the equivalence is only partial: the objects contained in the Dutch category *kom* are systematically divided between two categories in French, *bol* and *plat* (dish) (Ameel *et al.*, 2005; for evidence of dissociation between naming and similarity judgments see Stepanova Sachs & Coley, 2006).

This example leads me to another problem in traditional psycho-linguistic research, namely avoidance of cross-linguistic differences in selection of materials for picture naming and semantic categorization tasks, designed to study conceptual access (e.g. Caramazza & Brones, 1980; Chen, 1992; Dufour & Kroll, 1995; McElree *et al.*, 2000). To begin with, researchers commonly eliminate stimuli that do not have clear translation equivalents (e.g. McElree *et al.*, 2000). This elimination ensures stimulus comparability across languages, but distorts the picture of the bilingual lexicon that emerges from studies with such limited stimuli.

Secondly, studies of conceptual access commonly favor words that appear to share meanings (e.g. Caramazza & Brones, 1980) and in particular concrete words, assuming that appearances and functions of the entities they refer to 'will generally be the same in different language communities' (De Groot, 1995: 404). In reality, even when they are similar, linguistic categories linked to these words may not match fully: the category *chair* does not share all members with the categories *silla* (Spanish) or *chaise* (French), nor does the category *cup* share all members with the categories *taza* (Spanish) or *sefel* (Hebrew) (Ameel *et al.*, 2005; Graham & Belnap, 1986; Kronenfeld *et al.*, 1985; Malt *et al.*, 1999, 2003).

Additional problems appear in material selection for the picture-naming task, the only task in the traditional array that involves the actual mapping between words and their real-world referents. These tasks commonly involve single pictures, representing prototypical members of a particular category of objects or animals (e.g. Chen, 1992). The naming of such a picture does constitute evidence of conceptual access, but the use of a single category member, and a prototypical one at that, limits what we can infer. Since conceptual categories may share some but not all members, we can say that the representation is (partially) shared, but cannot determine the extent to which it is shared.

To sum up, it appears that in the first stage of the study of bilinguals' lexical concepts, the assumed reliability of psycholinguistic tasks may have been achieved at the expense of decreased content validity (Appel, 2000). The reliance on tasks involving decontextualized words and single pictures of prototypical objects, coupled with avoidance of cross-linguistic differences, may have created a somewhat skewed picture of the bilingual lexicon, because these circumstances are most likely to evoke the same representations in bilinguals' respective languages (Kroll & Tokowicz, 2005). This outcome is not surprising, because, with the exception of picture naming, reaction-time-based tasks were developed to examine the relationship between word forms, rather than between words and their real-world referents. Inferences based on reaction times have generated important information about the strength of interlingual connections yet it is not clear whether this strength can be unproblematically equated with the degree of shared meaning – the relationship between the two needs to be established, rather than assumed. Consequently, the time has come to disentangle the two and to examine lexical concepts in their own right.

1.2. Second stage: Cross-cultural research methods

Recent studies of bilinguals' linguistic categories rely on methodologies developed for cross-cultural inquiry in the fields of linguistic anthropology, cognitive and cultural psychology and applied linguistics. These approaches involve naming, categorization, sorting and narrative elicitation tasks that examine ways in which monolinguals and bilinguals' words are mapped to real-world referents.

Naming tasks, in this paradigm, differ from traditional picture-naming tasks in that they contain several pictures or videoclips that may be linked to a single word. Participants may be required to name: (1) colors represented by particular color chips or charts (e.g. Athanasopoulos, in press), (2) objects presented directly or via photographs (e.g. Ameel *et al.*, 2005; Malt *et al.*, 1999), (3) motion events presented via videoclips (e.g. Hohenstein *et al.*, 2006) or (4) abstract concepts or emotions elicited by particular scenarios (e.g. Stepanova Sachs & Coley, 2006). The purpose of these tasks is to establish the range of responses from relatively monolingual speakers of particular languages, to decide which exemplars or scripts may be prototypical for the category in question and which might be peripheral, and to find out how bilinguals' responses compare to those of monolingual speakers of their respective languages.

Categorization and *sorting tasks* ask participants to judge the similarity between: (1) color chips (e.g. Athanasopoulos, in press), (2) objects (e.g. Malt *et al.*, 1999), (3) objects and substances (e.g. Athanasopoulos, 2007; Cook *et al.*, 2006), (4) pictures (e.g. Athanasopoulos, 2006), (5) motion events (e.g. Gennari *et al.*, 2002) or (6) scripts (e.g. Stepanova Sachs & Coley, 2006). They differ from the semantic categorization task and the similarity judgment task described earlier in their focus on word referents.

Narrative elicitation tasks ask participants to retell a story they read, heard or inferred from a series of pictures or a videoclip (Pavlenko, 2002a, 2003, 2008a; Pavlenko & Driagina, 2007; for a more detailed discussion of narrative elicitation in the study of bilingualism, see Pavlenko, 2008b). Participants may also be asked to narrate while looking at a series of pictures or a videosegment, or to express reactions toward a particular narrative (Panayiotou, 2004). These tasks, traditionally used in the study of first language acquisition, applied linguistics and sociolinguistics, have recently been adopted in the study of the bilingual lexicon. Their purpose is to examine how monolingual and bilingual speakers name particular objects or events in context.

Together, these tasks have several advantages over traditional psycholinguistic tasks in the study of bilinguals' linguistic categories. The first is their ecological validity, which stems from the focus on the use of words in context and on the relationship between words and their real-world referents. The second is the sensitivity to cross-linguistic differences. For instance, using traditional psycholinguistic tasks, we may find that Russian–English bilinguals can easily access translation equivalents *glass/stakan* and *cup/chashka*, appropriately name pictures of prototypical cups and glasses and exhibit semantic priming effects in both directions. For some models, such performance is sufficient to posit semantic/conceptual equivalence within each word pair. A naming task will reveal, however, that this equivalence is limited to the shared prototypical exemplars, such as china *cups/chashki* with handles and *glasses/stakany* made out of glass. In turn, the placement of paper and plastic containers will vary depending on the language of the task. In the trial that uses English-language labels, the participants will place paper and plastic containers into the category of *cups*. In the Russian-language trial, the same objects would be placed into the category of *stakany* (glasses), because [GLASSNESS] in Russian is determined by shape, rather than by material. This task then reveals cross-linguistic differences where none were seen before and suggests that the representation of these translation equivalents is only partially shared.

The third advantage of these tasks is their ability to differentiate between two types of shared representations: (1) ones that mirror those of monolingual speakers and (2) ones that deviate from those of monolingual speakers and are shared as a result of conceptual transfer or convergence. To return to the example above, we cannot assume that all bilinguals will categorize paper and plastic containers in accordance with the constraints of the respective languages. In an English-language trial, L1 Russian-dominant bilinguals may place these containers into the category labeled *glasses*, rather than *cups*, and thus display L1 conceptual transfer. In turn, L2 English-dominant bilinguals may display L2 transfer in the Russian-language trial, placing the same containers into the category of *chashki* (cups), rather than *stakany* (glasses). In both cases the representations of the Russian and English translation equivalents are shared due to conceptual transfer and do not reflect monolinguals' lexical concepts.

To sum up, when it comes to the study of conceptual representation, tasks derived from cross-cultural inquiry transcend the limitations of reaction-time-based methods and allow us to examine ways in which bilinguals map their words onto real-world referents. Let us now examine the findings of research that employs these methods.

2. Recent Findings

2.1. Concepts

Undoubtedly, there are many more concepts than words and some concepts have no linguistic encoding in any language. The focus of the present discussion is exclusively on lexical concepts, that is linguistic categories linked to words (Malt *et al.*, 1999, 2003), that develop in the process of language socialization, with the aid of autobiographic and episodic memory. In the view adopted here, *lexical concepts* are seen as multimodal mental representations that include visual (mental imagery), auditory (sound), perceptual (texture) and kinesthetic (sensory-motor) information stored in implicit memory. These representations are dynamic and as such are subject to developmental changes and generational and individual differences, that is differences between speakers who may have had different experiences with, knowledge of, or expertise in the area in question (Murphy, 2002). Their distributed nature allows them to function in a context-dependent manner, whereby somewhat different representations may be activated by the same words in different communicative settings (see also Barsalou, 2003; Malt *et al.*, 2003). In similar settings, they may be quite systematic, allowing speakers of the same language to perform naming, identification, comprehension and inferencing tasks along similar lines (on systematicity of lexical choice in context, see Pavlenko & Driagina, 2007).

Cross-linguistic studies in cognitive psychology, cognitive linguistics and linguistic anthropology show that speakers of different languages rely on linguistic categories that may differ in structure, boundaries or prototypicality of certain category members (e.g. Levinson, 2003; Lucy, 1992a, 1992b; Malt *et al.*, 1999, 2003). This in turn means that translation equivalents are not always conceptual equivalents (cf. Panayiotou, 2006): some words may be in a relationship of partial (non)equivalence, and there are also words that have no conceptual equivalents in the other language. In what follows, I will discuss the consequences of these relationships for bilinguals' linguistic categories, distinguishing between objective differences (as seen in performance of monolingual or at least L1-dominant speakers of respective languages) and subjective representations in the minds of different types of bilingual speakers.

2.2. Conceptual equivalence

In the case of *conceptual equivalence* or *near equivalence*, linguistic categories mediated by languages A and B share both category structure and boundaries. Examples of such near equivalence come from a study by Ameel and associates (2005), where monolingual French and Dutch speakers and simultaneous Dutch–French bilinguals in Belgium performed a series of naming and sorting tasks with pictures of household objects. In experiments with monolingual speakers, the researchers found that all of the objects called *tas* in Dutch were put into the French category *tasse* (both are roughly similar to the English *cup*); this category also included two additional objects that are not called *tas* in Dutch. Similarly, all the objects called *bord* in Dutch were placed in the French category *assiette* (both are roughly similar to the English *plate*), except for one that would not be called *assiette*. The French category also included one object that would not be called *bord* in Dutch. Bilinguals named the same 14 drinking containers *tas* in Dutch and *tasse* in French, and the same 6 dishes *bord* in Dutch and *assiette* in French (one more dish called *bord* in Dutch was referred to as *bol* (bowl) in French).

Pavlenko's studies investigated conceptual equivalence in sequential bilinguals. In Pavlenko's (2002b) study, native speakers of English and Russian systematically used the words *upset* and *rasstroennaia* (upset, fem) to refer to a female character in narratives elicited by a short film, suggesting that the script portrayed in the film falls in the category of *upset* and *rasstroennaia* (more work is needed however to determine the range of scripts in these linguistic categories). Pavlenko and Driagina (2007) replicated the findings of this study with different groups of native speakers of Russian and English. They also found that American L2 learners of Russian described the character just as native speakers of Russian did, with the adjective *rasstroennaia* (upset, fem) and the corresponding verb *rasstroit'sia* (to become upset).

In a study that used a different short film as an elicitation stimulus, Pavlenko (2008a) found that in describing a character experiencing fear, L1 Russian speakers favored reflexive emotion verbs *ispugat'sia* (to get scared) and *boiat'sia* (to fear, to experience fear). L1 English speakers in the same context favored emotion adjectives or pseudo-participles such as *afraid*, *frightened* or *terrified*. These choices differed structurally but not conceptually – all belonged to the same domain of fear. Lexical choices made by L2 speakers of Russian and English mirrored for the most part those made by the target language speakers, suggesting that L2 speakers have internalized new structural patterns of emotion description, verbs in the case of L2 Russian and adjectives in the case of L2 English (for similar results see also Pavlenko & Driagina, 2007).

Together, these findings suggest that the relationship of conceptual equivalence or near equivalence presents no difficulties for L2 vocabulary learning, even in the case when the L1 and the L2 favor words from distinct grammatical categories (Pavlenko, 2008a; Pavlenko & Driagina, 2007). All the learners need to do is to link L2 word forms to already established lexical concepts. Provided the speakers subjectively perceive the concepts in question to be similar, positive L1 transfer will facilitate the process.

2.3. Partial (non)equivalence

Not all categories, however, are fully or nearly equivalent. Rather, many are in a relationship of partial (non)equivalence. In what follows, I will focus on one relationship of partial (non)equivalence, nesting, recognizing that there exist many more ways in which categories can partially overlap, such as e.g. cross-cutting (Malt *et al.*, 2003).

2.3.1. Nesting: Type 1

In the case of *nesting*, two or more categories of one language are subsumed, fully or partially, within a larger category in another language. I will differentiate between two types of nesting relationships here. In the next subsection, I will consider a case of a single category of one language roughly divided between two categories in another language. In what follows, I will examine a case when a smaller category of one language is subsumed within a larger category of another language.

This relationship between the categories can be found across a variety of domains. In the domain of containers, for instance, the English category *jar* is nested within the Spanish category *frasco* that also contains additional objects named *bottle* and *container* in English (Malt *et al.*, 2003). Similarly, the Russian category *chashka* is nested within a larger English-language category *cup* that additionally includes plastic and paper containers without handles used for hot and cold liquids, referred to as *stakanchiki* (little glasses) in Russian. In the domain of emotions, the Russian category *revnost'* is nested within the English category *jealousy* (Stepanova Sachs & Coley, 2006). *Revnost'* refers exclusively to scripts that involve intimate relationships or sibling rivalry, while *jealousy* may also refer to contexts where one experiences envy (e.g. 'I am so jealous of your trip to Hawaii').

Stepanova Sachs and Coley (2006) used naming and sorting tasks with short scripts describing jealousy- and envy-arousing situations to examine the relationship between *revnost'/jealousy* and *zavist'/envy* in monolingual Russian and English speakers and Russian–English bilinguals who learned English as teenagers or adults. On the naming task, monolingual Russian speakers differentiated categorically between scripts describing *revnost'* and *zavist'*, while monolingual English speakers judged both *envy* and *jealousy* as terms appropriate to describe the envy stories. Bilingual speakers responded according to the language of the task: in Russian they differentiated between *revnost'* and *zavist'* and in English they showed no such distinction with the envy stories. On the triad-sorting task, the participants were required to pick any two situations out of three that go together and explain why. In that task, all groups performed similarly except for the triad that included three kinds of situations: envy, jealousy and a control one. Russian monolinguals treated the three as different, while English monolinguals and Russian–English bilinguals grouped envy and jealousy situations together.

Overall, the results of the study showed that both Russian and English speakers can reliably differentiate between romantic jealousy and envy aroused by other people's possessions or good luck. At the same time, the scope of use of the English word *jealousy* was not limited to scripts involving romantic jealousy, as was the case for its Russian translation equivalent *revnost'* – rather this category also subsumed scripts involving *envy*. Consequently, English speakers see the boundaries between the two categories as fuzzy, while for Russian speakers *revnost'* and *zavist'* are categorically distinct. Sequential bilinguals displayed an ability to maintain the differences between the two categories and to perform according to the constraints of each language in the naming tasks, but their similarity judgments showed a blurring of the category boundary.

Their performance leads me to suggest that a nesting relationship may facilitate initial L2 learning via positive L1 transfer of the shared meaning. Eventually, L2 learners will need to adjust the boundaries of their linguistic categories, either expanding or narrowing them in accordance with the L2 constraints. Failure to readjust the boundaries appropriately would lead to instances of L1 conceptual transfer, where L2 objects or situations are named in accordance with the L1 category boundaries. This transfer would be particularly apparent in the cases where the L1 has a more expanded category, as for instance in American L2 learners of Russian who would refer to envy-arousing situations with the term *revnost'* (romantic jealousy).

In the case of successful restructuring, the boundaries of the L2 category are modified without changing the boundaries of the corresponding L1 category. As a result, speakers perform in accordance with the constraints of each language, as did bilinguals in Stepanova Sachs and Coley (2006). Alternatively, we may find partial restructuring taking place for some category members but not others, or convergence of two categories. In these two cases, L2 performance will be target-like only in some cases. Finally, with advanced L2 users and L1 attriters, we may also find that the boundaries of the L1 category have shifted under the influence of the L2, as seen on the triad-sorting task in Stepanova Sachs and Coley's (2006) study. Eventually, such boundary shift may lead to L2 conceptual transfer in the L1 performance (cf. Jarvis & Pavlenko, 2008).

2.3.2. Nesting: Type 2

In some cases, a single category of one language may subsume, fully or partially, two or more categories of another language. For instance, in the domain of color, the English category *blue* subsumes the categories differentiated by Russian and Greek speakers, respectively, as *goluboi* (Rus) or *ghalazio* (Gr) (roughly similar to *light blue*) and *sinii* (Rus) and *ble* (Gr) (roughly similar to *dark blue*) (Andrews, 1994; Athanasopoulos, in press). In the domain of containers, Ameel and associates (2005) found that 25 objects placed within the Dutch category *fles* (roughly similar to the English *bottle*) are split almost equally between the French categories *bouteille* (roughly similar to *bottle*) and *flacon* (small bottle). In the domain of emotions, the English category *to be angry* roughly corresponds to the Russian *zlit'sia* (to be experiencing anger in general) and *serdit'sia* (to be experiencing anger, to be actively cross, angry, mad at someone in particular) (Pavlenko & Driagina, 2007). In the domain of abstract categories, the English *to be* roughly corresponds to Spanish *ser* and *estar*, *to know* to French *savoir* and *connaître*, *to fall* to Finnish *pudota* (to fall from a higher to lower altitude) and *kaatua* (to fall from a vertical to a horizontal position) (Jarvis, 2003). In all of these cases, one language requires its speakers to make more fine-grained distinctions and to pay attention to contrasts not encoded in the other language.

In the minds of bilingual speakers, these linguistic categories may correspond to those of monolingual speakers of the L1 and L2. Alternatively, they may approximate the larger category, if this category is encoded in the dominant language. Several studies offer empirical support for the latter possibility. In the domain of furniture, Graham and Belnap (1986) established that native speakers of Spanish use the word *silla* to refer to objects which were perceived by native speakers of English as either *chairs* or *stools*, and the word *banco* to refer to objects that were differentiated by native speakers of English as either *stools* or *benches*.[2] Spanish-speaking L2 learners of English in the study did not differentiate systematically between *chairs*, *stools* and *benches*, relying instead on conceptual boundaries associated with the categories *silla* and *banco*. In the domain of containers, Ameel and associates (2005) found that Dutch–French bilinguals have a smaller category of *flacon* (small bottle) than monolingual French speakers and a larger category of *bouteille*, corresponding more closely to the category *fles* (both are roughly similar to *bottle*), in Dutch, the dominant language of the speakers.

In the domain of emotions, American L2 learners of Russian in Pavlenko and Driagina's (2007) study consistently described the behavior of a character in a film with the verb *serdit'sia* (to be experiencing anger, to be actively cross, angry, mad at someone in particular), while native speakers of Russian referred to the same character using the verb *zlit'sia* (to be experiencing anger in general), because it was not immediately clear why the main character was angry. The learners' lexical choice suggested that they had not yet internalized the differences between the two categories, whereby *serdit'sia* is a relational term, requiring a clear referent of the action/process of being angry, while *zlit'sia* is a process that is not necessarily directed toward anyone in particular.

Notably, the influence of the dominant language is not limited to that of the L1. Andrews' (1994) study shows that young Russian–English bilinguals living in the USA and dominant in L2 English are losing the categorical distinction between *sinii* and *goluboi* under the influence of the English *blue*. A somewhat different and intriguing result comes from Athanasopoulos' (in press) study of a similar contrast in Greek. The researcher found that the majority of advanced-level Greek–English bilinguals have shifted the focus (i.e. best example) of one of their L1 categories to the L2 category *blue*. At the same time, they have moved the focus of the other L1 category away from the L2 focus, thus maintaining the perceptual distance between the L1 category foci.

It appears then that in the process of L2 vocabulary learning, going from two or more linguistic categories to one may be relatively easy, even though the process may still require some adjustment (Athanasopoulos, in press; see also Gullberg, this volume). In contrast, going from one to many is a challenging process, whereby L2 learners need to restructure their conceptual representations in order to categorize objects, events and phenomena in accordance with the target-language constraints. Failure to internalize the distinctions required by the L2 would lead to instances of L1 conceptual transfer (Graham & Belnap, 1986; Jarvis & Pavlenko, 2008; Pavlenko & Driagina, 2007). Partial restructuring or convergence may lead to creation of categories that are distinct from those of either language (Ameel *et al.*, 2005). Successful conceptual restructuring allows bilinguals to perform in accordance with language-specific constraints in each language. Finally, bilinguals whose dominance had shifted to the L2 may display a blurring of categorical distinctions required by the L1 (Andrews, 1994; Jarvis, 2003) or a shift away from the L1 category prototypes (Athanasopoulos, in press).

2.4. Conceptual non-equivalence

In the case of *conceptual non-equivalence*, a linguistic category of one language does not have a counterpart in another language. In the domain of artifacts, for instance, American L2 learners of Russian may be unfamiliar with a *fortochka*, a small window pane on top of a window that can be opened to let some air in, common in Russian buildings. In turn, Russian L2 learners of English may have never encountered *rowhouses* or *rowhomes*, adjacent single-family dwellings, common in the Northeast of the USA and Canada. Even familiar objects may be grouped into language-specific categories. In the domain of containers, for instance, the Dutch category *bus* (roughly similar to *can*) does not appear to have a French counterpart, with objects called *bus* in Dutch spread over six French categories (Ameel *et al.*, 2005). In the domain of abstract categories, some languages may lack translation equivalents of the English *privacy* or *personal space* (Karasik *et al.*, 2005; Pavlenko, 2003).

Language-specificity was also found among emotion categories, such as the English *frustration*, the Russian *perezhivat'* (to suffer, to worry, to experience things keenly) (Pavlenko, 2002a, 2002b) or the Greek *stenahoria* (discomfort/sadness/suffocation) (Panayiotou, 2004).

Pavlenko (1997, 2003) used narrative elicitation to investigate the implications of the fact that *privacy* and *personal space* do not have translation equivalents in Russian. The study used two films portraying situations that could be potentially perceived as invasions of privacy or personal space. Four groups of participants recalled the films: (1–2) monolingual speakers of Russian and English, (3) Russian–English bilinguals residing in Russia who had never been to an English-speaking country (Group 1), and (4) Russian–English bilinguals residing in the USA (Group 2), with Group 2 performing recalls in both Russian and English. The researcher found that in English-language narratives, some English monolinguals and bilinguals in Group 2 used the terms *privacy* and *personal space* to describe the contents of the films (for replication of these results with a different stimulus, see Pavlenko, 2002a). In Russian-language narratives, bilinguals in Group 2 conveyed these concepts through lexical borrowing or loan translation, such as *on vtorgaetsia v ee odinochestvo* (he is invading her solitude). In contrast, Russian monolinguals and bilinguals in Group 1 never commented on the spatial proximity of the characters, not even to say that someone sat down too closely to someone else. During the debriefing procedure, several participants from Group 1 were able to define *privacy*, but they also acknowledged that they were not sure when and how to use this term. These results suggested that *privacy* and *personal space* do not have conceptual equivalents in Russian (for a similar argument see Karasik *et al.*, 2005).

In another set of studies, Pavlenko (2002a, 2002b) and Pavlenko and Driagina (2007) used narrative elicitation by two short films to investigate nonequivalent emotion words *frustration* and *perezhivat'* (to suffer, to worry, to experience things keenly). They found that monolingual Russian speakers systematically used the term *perezhivat'* to describe the feelings of the main characters in the films, while American L2 learners of Russian and Russian–English bilinguals residing in the USA did not use the term at all. During the debriefing procedure, several L2 learners recognized the word *perezhivat'* and stated that they 'studied it' but were still not sure how to use it. Some learners borrowed the word *frustration* into Russian to describe the main character, e.g. *kak chto-to ee frastriruet/frastrirovalo* (as if something frustrates/frustrated her) (Pavlenko & Driagina, 2007).

Together, these results suggest that the ability to define the word explicitly is not paramount to having a conceptual representation that allows L2 learners to map the new word onto its real-world referents. The reason for this is the dissociation between two types of memory, implicit and explicit: definitions learned explicitly are stored in explicit memory, while multimodal conceptual representations involving visual, kinesthetic and other types of information, need to be developed in implicit memory (see also section 3.2.3; Paradis, 1994). Consequently, words referring to novel objects, such as *fortochka*, are perhaps the easiest to acquire because they have tangible, easily perceivable referents. Abstract words, such as *privacy*, and emotion words, such as *frustration* or *perezhivat'*, may be more difficult because the learners need to appropriately identify the range of situations and contexts to which these words may apply. Consequently, the first possible L2 learning outcome in the case of conceptual non-equivalence is the presence of an explicit definition in the absence of a multimodal conceptual representation. Eventually, the learners may internalize the category partially, applying the word to a limited range of objects or situations. Finally, they may fully internalize the linguistic category and thus use the word spontaneously in the same range of contexts as native speakers of the target language, as Russian–English bilinguals in Group 2 did with *privacy* and *personal space* (Pavlenko, 2002a, 2003).

The presence of conceptual nonequivalents has implications not only for L2 learning but also for bilingual performance. In the studies discussed here, American L2 learners of Russian borrowed the L1 term *frustration* into their L2 Russian narratives (Pavlenko & Driagina, 2007). In turn, Russian–English bilinguals living in the USA referred to *privacy* and *personal space* not only in L2 English but also in L1 Russian, in the form of lexical borrowing and loan translation (Pavlenko, 2002a, 2003; for discussion of similar borrowing of L2 emotion terms by Greek–English bilinguals, see Panayioutou, 2004). These findings show that while some bilinguals use nonequivalents only in the appropriate language, others may use them as an interpretive category in the other language in the form of codeswitching or lexical borrowing, and yet others may pause, hesitate and stutter, searching for a nonexistent translation (Pavlenko, 1997, 2003).

2.5. Summary

Let us now summarize the findings of the studies discussed. The first finding involves the degree of difference across linguistic categories. Studies, focused on the relationship between words and their real-world referents, reveal pervasive cross-linguistic differences across all domains, including linguistic categories linked to concrete words (Ameel *et al.*, 2005; Graham & Belnap, 1986; Kronenfeld *et al.*, 1985; Malt *et al.*, 1999, 2003). These findings suggest that bilinguals need to develop partially different categories, if they are to use their languages in a target-like manner.

The second important finding involves the existence of two types of fully shared representations that have different implications for bilingual performance: (1) in the case of conceptual equivalence, they reflect those in the monolingual lexicons and lead to target-like performance (e.g. Pavlenko, 2008a; Pavlenko & Driagina, 2007) and (2) in the case of partial (non)equivalence, they are established as a result of conceptual transfer, convergence or partial restructuring and may lead to deviations from monolingual performance (Ameel *et al.*, 2005; Andrews, 1994; Athana-sopoulos, in press; Graham & Belnap, 1986; Pavlenko & Driagina, 2007).

The third and perhaps the most dramatic finding involves the nature of second language learning. Previously, it was commonly assumed that the goal of adult L2 learning was 'not to learn new concepts, but rather to acquire new mappings between concepts and second language words' (Kroll, 1993: 55). In contrast, the studies reviewed here reveal that at the center of L2 vocabulary learning are the processes of *conceptual restructuring*, that is readjustment of the category structure and bound-aries in accordance with the constraints of the target linguistic category, and *conceptual development*, that is development of new multimodal representations that allow speakers to map new words onto real-world referents similar to native speakers of the target language.

These processes manifest themselves differently at different stages of bilingual development. In the early stages, L2 learners may acquire an explicit definition or translation of a particular word. In the case of conceptual equivalence, this word will then be linked to its translation equivalent and to an already existing linguistic category. In the case of partial (non)equivalence, however, this linking may lead to erroneous performance (Graham & Belnap, 1986; Pavlenko & Driagina, 2007). In the case of conceptual non-equivalence, an explicit definition may exist in the absence of a multimodal conceptual representation, which means that L2 learners will not be able to use the words in the appropriate contexts (Pavlenko, 1997, 2003; Pavlenko & Driagina, 2007).

Both conceptual restructuring and development of new linguistic categories appear to be gradual processes. In the case of conceptual restructuring, for instance, Malt and Sloman (2003) established that with increases in the length of English language experience (measured both as the length of formal instruction and the length of time in the target language context), L2 users of English were better able to match native speakers' naming patterns for household objects and displayed more agreement with their object typicality judgments. Approximation of the L2 categories is not the only possible outcome of the process – lexical concepts may also undergo convergence whereby a single representation subserves both translation equivalents.

Given sufficient time and input, however, some L2 users succeed in conceptual restructuring and development, developing *conceptual fluency*, that is performance according to the constraints of the target-language categories. As a result, they may perform in a target-like manner in both languages (Stepanova Sachs & Coley, 2006). Bilinguals who experience a shift in dominance, may eventually exhibit the influence of L2 categories on their L1 performance (Andrews, 1994; Athanasopolos, in press; Pavlenko, 2002a, 2003; Stepanova Sachs & Coley, 2006).

Last but not least, it appears that the use of language-specific linguistic categories is not constrained to the language in which they originated – they may appear as an interpretive category in the bilingual's other language in the form of lexical borrowing, loan translation or code-switching (Panayiotou, 2004; Pavlenko, 2002a, 2003, 2008a; Pavlenko & Driagina, 2007).

3.   Models of the Bilingual Lexicon

3.1. Current models of the bilingual lexicon

Let us now examine the implications of the findings summarized above for models of the bilingual lexicon. Take, for instance, the classic example from Weinreich (1953), the word pair *book* (English) and *kniga* (Russian). Weinreich (1953) uses this word pair to illustrate three possible relationships in the bilingual lexicon: a shared conceptual representation (compound), two separate conceptual representations (coordinate) and a representation accessed via L1 (subordinate). The studies reviewed here suggest, however, that the type of representation depends not only on the learning trajectory but also, critically, on the actual relationship between the linguistic categories in question. From this perspective, the pair *book/kniga* can *only* be used to illustrate a single shared representation, or a relationship of conceptual equivalence, because Russian and English speakers name the same objects *books* and *knigi*.

Weinreich's model, however, ceased to be the dominant representation of the bilingual lexicon. To date, two models dominate the discussion of bilinguals' conceptual representations: the Revised Hierarchical Model

(RHM) (Kroll & Stewart, 1994; see Figure 6.1) and the Distributed Feature Model (DFM) (De Groot, 1992; see Figure 6.2). The RHM reflects two important findings in research on interlingual connections: (1) translation from L1 to L2 is faster than picture naming in the L2 and (2) translation from L2 to L1 is faster than from L1 to L2, in particular in novice learners; (e.g. Chen & Leung, 1989; Kroll & Curley, 1988; see also De Groot, 2002; Kroll & De Groot, 1997; Kroll & Tokowicz, 2005, for discussion of conflicting findings). These findings were interpreted to mean that in the early stages L2 words are more strongly connected to their L1 translation equivalents than to concepts and that conceptual access (as seen in the picture-naming task) takes place via the L1 equivalents (lexical mediation). As the L2 proficiency increases, the links between L2 words and concepts become stronger and learners begin to rely more on direct links (conceptual mediation) (for a discussion of the two mediation processes see also Potter *et al.*, 1984).

The unique strength of the RHM is in capturing the developmental change in linking between L2 and L1 word forms and lexical concepts. Unfortunately, this relinking reflects only the case of conceptual equivalence. The unified and stable nature of the conceptual store assumed in the RHM does not accommodate the cases of partial and

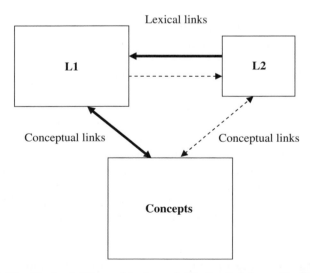

Figure 6.1 The Revised Hierarchical model (adapted from Kroll & Stewart, 1994)

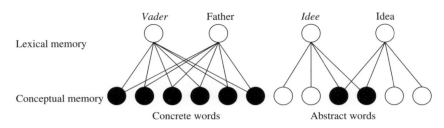

Figure 6.2 The Distributed Feature model (adapted from De Groot, 1992, 1993)

complete non-equivalence and does not allow us to differentiate between target- and non-target-like performance in mapping words to referents.

In turn, the primary strength of the DFM is attention to cross-linguistic differences. The model reflects the finding that bilinguals translate concrete words and cognates faster than abstract words (De Groot, 1992, 1993, 1995; De Groot *et al.*, 1994; Kroll & Stewart, 1994; Van Hell & De Groot, 1998). This finding is taken to mean that representations of concrete words and cognates are largely, if not completely, shared across languages while representations of abstract words share fewer semantic features.

Despite the fact that the model incorporates cross-linguistic differences, it does not easily accommodate the findings summarized above. To begin with, the model lacks a developmental component that would make predictions as to the learning of partial translation equivalents. Its second weakness is the reliance on the feature-based approach, which has been largely cast aside in contemporary cognitive psychology because it does not account for prototype and context-dependence effects (Murphy, 2002; see also De Groot, 1992: 406–408). These effects play an important role in L2 vocabulary learning and use. For instance, Ijaz (1986) demonstrated that in contexts where L1 and L2 words differ in peripheral meanings, L2 learners perform in a target-like manner with prototypical or core meanings, but display L1 transfer in peripheral meanings (see also Aitchison, 1994; Kellerman, 1978, 1983). These prototype effects, as well as differences in category structure and boundaries revealed in the studies discussed above, cannot be accommodated by the feature-based approach.

The third weakness of the DFM is the equation of the strength of interlingual connections with the degree of shared meaning. The problematic nature of this equation has already been discussed in section

1.1, yet one aspect of this issue deserves further discussion, namely conflation of word type and conceptual properties. Research in this paradigm suggests that the degree of overlap in concepts is determined by word frequency, cognate status and concreteness (De Groot, 1992, 1993, 1995, 2002). The first two, however, are lexical, not conceptual properties. Word frequency has no relation to conceptual structure (and vice versa), and neither does the cognate status *per se*. Rather, cognates, depending on the vagaries of their linguistic history, may be full, partial equivalents or nonequivalents, also known as false cognates (for an in-depth discussion of cognates see Jarvis, this volume; Sánchez-Casas & García-Albea, 2005).

At the same time, there is no doubt that cognate status may lead L2 learners to assume a shared meaning, even in the case of partial equivalence or false cognates (for a discussion of semantic priming by false cognates, see Sánchez-Casas & García-Albea, 2005). For instance, many American L2 learners of Spanish assume that *embarazada* (pregnant, fem) is a cognate of *embarrassed* and treat it as such. The DFM, however, offers no means of differentiation between shared representations reflecting similarity between linguistic categories of particular languages, and shared representations that derive from erroneous assumptions. The figure illustrating the model appears to reflect the relationship between particular linguistic categories, yet the studies in this paradigm examine the relationships in the minds of particular speakers, which, as demonstrated earlier, may or may not reflect monolinguals' linguistic categories.

The last weakness of the model is the assumption that concrete words share meanings, because they are translated faster than abstract words. This assumption is in contrast with the findings of studies that reveal numerous cross-linguistic differences in the naming of household objects, such as cups, bottles or dishes, by monolingual and bilingual speakers of French and Dutch (Ameel *et al.*, 2005), English, Spanish and Chinese (Graham & Belnap, 1986; Malt *et al.*, 1999, 2003) and English, Hebrew and Japanese (Kronenfeld *et al.*, 1985). These studies suggest that concrete words may also be linked to partially or completely distinct linguistic categories. These categories are not necessarily easy to readjust. For instance, Malt and Sloman (2003) found that even advanced L2 users of English do not fully approximate native speakers' patterns of naming household objects, a result that would not be predicted – and cannot be explained – by a model that assumes shared meanings of (high-frequency) concrete words.

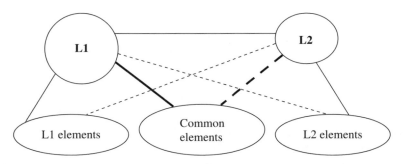

Figure 6.3 The Shared Asymmetrical Model (adapted from Dong *et al.*, 2005)

A more dynamic approach toward modeling L2 vocabulary learning and bilingual performance has been advanced by Dong *et al.* (2005). In the Shared Asymmetrical Model (SAM) put forth by these authors, the L1 and the L2 lexicons are linked to each other as well as to common conceptual elements, L1 elements and L2 elements (see Figure 6.3). The model succeeds in bringing together cross-linguistic differences and the vocabulary learning process, but it lacks clarity with regard to the nature and structure of conceptual representation (see section 1.1).

3.2. The Modified Hierarchical Model (MHM)

The MHM proposed here (see Figure 6.4) differs from the three models above, while attempting to retain their strengths.[3] In doing so, it aims to function as a transitional model, which preserves the earlier findings while asking new questions and positing new hypotheses. Building on the RHM (Kroll & Stewart, 1994), the MHM retains the developmental progression from lexical to conceptual mediation in L2 learning. It also retains the notion of shared and partially shared representations central to the DFM and the SAM. At the same time, the MHM differs from the other models in three important aspects outlined next.

3.2.1. Organization of the conceptual store

The first distinguishing aspect of the MHM is the organization of the conceptual store. While the RHM assumes a unified conceptual store, in the MHM conceptual representations may be fully shared, partially overlapping or fully language-specific: L1 and L2 categories in Figure 6.4 stand for conceptual nonequivalents and for language-specific aspects of partial equivalents. Recognition of language-specific lexical concepts,

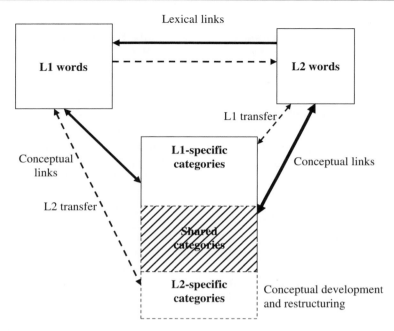

Figure 6.4 The Modified Hierarchical Model

such as *frustration* or *privacy*, differentiates the MHM also from the DFM and the SAM.

The inclusion of language-specific lexical concepts has interesting implications for theories of bilingual processing. It has been commonly assumed that the formulation of a message begins in the conceptualizer or the undifferentiated conceptual system and might activate lexical links in both languages of a bilingual (cf. Costa, 2005; Green, 1998). If we see some linguistic categories as language- and culture-specific, only one language may have the necessary word forms, while activation of lexical links in the other language would fail, producing breakdowns in fluency (Pavlenko, 1997, 2003). To use lexical concepts of one language as interpretive categories in another language, bilinguals may resort to codeswitching, lexical borrowing or loan translation (Panayiotou, 2004; Pavlenko, 1997, 2002a, 2003; Pavlenko & Driagina, 2007).

The activation process, in this view, becomes a two-way interaction between the mind and the environment, where linguistic and social contexts affect the conceptualizer, activating concepts and frames that are linked to one language, while inhibiting others and making them less relevant or at least less accessible. Several studies in cross-cultural psychology provide evidence of such context-dependent nature of bilingual cognition (e.g. Hong *et al.*, 2000; Ross *et al.*, 2002; Trafimow *et al.*, 1997).

Studies in bilingualism also suggest that bilingual performance varies across tasks, whereby the same speakers may perform in accordance with language-specific constraints on some tasks and display transfer in others (Jarvis, 2003; Stepanova Sachs & Coley, 2006; see also Gullberg's chapter on the discontinuities between verbal and gestural performance). This variation also supports the view of conceptual representation as a dynamic, distributed and emergent phenomenon that functions in a context-dependent manner (Barsalou, 2003; Malt *et al.*, 2003).

3.2.2. Conceptual transfer

The second distinguishing feature of the MHM is the recognition of the phenomenon of conceptual transfer, which in turn is predicated on the differentiation between semantic and conceptual levels of representation. The term *semantic representation* refers here to the largely implicit knowledge of: (1) the mapping between words and concepts determining how many concepts and which particular concepts are expressed by a particular word via polysemy or metaphoric extension and (2) connections between words, which account for phenomena such as collocation, word association, synonymy and antonymy (see also Jarvis, this volume; Jarvis & Pavlenko, 2008). This view locates semantic at the level of links between words and concepts, as well as words and other words, and is undoubtedly more narrow than that assumed in a lot of other work in linguistics and psychology. At the same time, it allows researchers to differentiate between errors made at the level of linking (semantic transfer) and those that involve the structure of conceptual categories (conceptual transfer).

To illustrate this difference, let us consider an example of a Finnish speaker who says in L2 English *He bit himself in the language* (meaning 'He bit himself in the tongue') (Ringbom, 2001: 64). Both the Finnish word *kieli* and the English word *tongue* are polysemic, meaning that they are linked to two distinct concepts, that of a human body part, tongue, and that of a means of communication, language. These concepts are clearly differentiated by the speakers of both languages. The error committed by the Finnish speaker consists in linking the Finnish word *kieli* to the high-frequency English word *language*, which refers only to the means of communication but not to the body part. This error is seen here as semantic transfer, because it occurred at the point of mapping words to concepts and does not involve the structure of conceptual categories (see also Jarvis & Pavlenko, 2008). In contrast, when an English speaker of L2 Russian asks for a *chashka* (roughly similar to *cup*) in reference to a drinking container made of paper, the transfer is not simply semantic (inappropriate link) but conceptual (inadequate knowledge of the structure of category *chashka*, which does not include plastic and paper containers). This reliance on the L1 linguistic category is viewed here as conceptual transfer because the transfer originates with multimodal conceptual representations.

To account for such non-target-like performance, MHM differentiates between two types of shared conceptual representations. The first, marked 'shared categories' in Figure 6.4, involves representations that are shared – or partially shared – by monolingual speakers of respective languages, and are represented in the same manner in the minds of bilingual speakers leading to target-like performance. No assumptions are made *a priori* as to which representations may be shared, rather the degree of sharedness is established empirically for particular word pairs. For instance, in the case of categories roughly corresponding to the English *cup*, the Dutch *tas* and the French *tasse* share category members (Ameel *et al.*, 2005), while the English *cup*, the Russian *chashka*, the Spanish *taza* and the Hebrew *sefel* overlap only partially (Graham & Belnap, 1986; Kronenfeld *et al.*, 1985).

The second type of shared representations involves those that are shared in the minds of individual bilinguals but do not coincide with monolinguals' representations and lead to non-target-like performance. The use of L2 words in accordance with L1 linguistic categories is seen here as L1 conceptual transfer; similarly, the use of L1 words in accordance with L2 linguistic categories is seen as L2 conceptual transfer.

The differentiation between semantic and conceptual levels of representation allows us to differentiate between the sources of transfer, conceptual versus semantic, and to consider what is involved in L2 acquisition in each case (see also Jarvis & Pavlenko, 2008). In the case of the semantic transfer example, the Finnish L2 learner of English needs to inhibit the link between the word *language* and the concept of the body part (tongue) and to link both lexical concepts (tongue and language) to the polysemic English word *tongue*. This process involves inhibition and relinking, but not conceptual restructuring. In the case of conceptual transfer, the English-speaking L2 learner of Russian needs to restructure linguistic categories corresponding to *chashka* (cup) and *stakan* (glass), transferring paper and plastic containers from the former to the latter.

3.2.3. L2 learning as conceptual restructuring

This restructuring takes us to the third and the most important distinguishing feature of the MHM, namely the view of L2 learning embedded in the model. While the RHM assumes that the goal of L2 vocabulary learning is the development of direct links between L2 words and concepts, the MHM views the main goal of L2 learning as conceptual restructuring and development of target-like linguistic categories (for a discussion of factors affecting conceptual restructuring and development in L2 learning, see Jarvis & Pavlenko, 2008: 150–151, 172–173).

This learning is seen as a gradual process, taking place in implicit memory. The term *implicit* refers here to the knowledge that individuals may not be aware of but which researchers can infer from their systematic verbal and non-verbal performance. This is the knowledge that drives spontaneous speech production. The term *explicit* refers to the metalinguistic knowledge of word definitions, grammar rules or translation equivalents that individuals are aware of and are capable of verbalizing on demand. The distinction between implicit and explicit knowledge and memory is commonly accepted in the fields of second language acquisition and bilingualism (N. Ellis, 1994; R. Ellis, 2006; Paradis, 1994, 2004), but it has not yet been incorporated into models of the bilingual lexicon. Yet it is an important distinction because in a second or additional language learned in the classroom, explicit knowledge may play a central role in verbal performance of beginning and intermediate students (Paradis, 1994).

The studies discussed earlier in the chapter reveal a dissociation between explicit and implicit knowledge in L2 learners, whereby the ability to translate and define language-specific linguistic categories does not automatically lead to the ability to use these words in context (Pavlenko, 1997, 2003; Pavlenko & Driagina, 2007). The same dissociation exists in the case of partial equivalents, such as the Spanish copula verbs *ser* and *estar*, both of which are translated in English as *to be*. These verbs are challenging for English-speaking L2 learners of Spanish, because they require differentiation between two types of being. For instance, *ser* may refer to more permanent states, such as character traits, and *estar* to temporary states, such as moods. Consequently, *ella es alegre* means 'she is happy, joyful' (a character trait), while *ella está alegre* means 'she is in a good mood, content, happy right now' (a temporary state). Early on in the learning process, students memorize the distinctions between the two and the contexts in which the verbs are commonly used. But is memorization of definitions and examples sufficient for target-like performance?

Empirical studies show that L2 learners' performance on the two copulas varies across contexts (De Keyser, 1990). In foreign language classroom tasks, such as fill-in-the-blanks, which allow sufficient time for information retrieval from explicit memory, learners may draw on the rules they memorized and demonstrate more or less target-like performance. In contrast, in spontaneous communication, where performance is time-constrained, *ser* is commonly overgeneralized; studies also show that *ser* is acquired first and used more correctly than *estar* even after several years of instruction (De Keyser, 1990; Geeslin, 2003; Ryan & Lafford, 1992). It appears then that many L2 learners map *ser* onto the L1 category of being and do not differentiate systematically between temporary and permanent states of being. To develop target-like categories corresponding to *ser* and *estar* in implicit memory, L2 learners require prolonged interaction with Spanish speakers. These findings suggest that researchers interested in conceptual representation and processing should not confuse explicit and implicit representations and should employ tasks that reveal implicit conceptual knowledge.

The distinctions between explicit and implicit, as well as semantic and conceptual knowledge, adopted here have three advantages for the study of the bilingual lexicon. First, they illuminate the sources of errors in L2 learners' performance, and in doing so contribute to the model's ecological validity. Second, they allow us to formulate new hypotheses with regard to L2 vocabulary learning and to ask, for instance, whether errors due to negative conceptual transfer may persist longer than errors due to negative semantic transfer because of the challenges involved in restructuring existing conceptual representations and developing new ones. Third, they force us to reconsider the applicability of different methods for the study of conceptual representation. In this view, neither word association tasks nor word similarity judgments access the level of implicit conceptual representation. Word associations reveal semantic links formed through polysemy, synonymy or collocation, while word similarity judgments reveal speakers' beliefs about language that may or may not be congruent with implicitly encoded linguistic categories that drive the naming process.

Conclusions and Implications

To conclude, let me begin by stating what I do not argue for. First, I do not argue that all models of bilingual processing should take into account cross-linguistic differences in linguistic categories. The models that would benefit most from incorporating these differences are developmental models of L2 vocabulary learning and models of the bilingual lexicon. Secondly, I do not argue that all models of the bilingual lexicon should differentiate between semantic and conceptual levels of representation, in particular according to the definitions presented here. Rather, I argue that lexical properties, such as word frequency, or semantic properties, such as polysemy, should not be confused with conceptual properties, and that tasks that examine interlingual connections do not necessarily illuminate the structure of conceptual representations. Third, I do not argue that all models of the bilingual lexicon should differentiate between explicit and implicit knowledge. Rather, I argue that tasks drawing on explicit knowledge cannot be used to examine implicit representations. Finally and most importantly, I do not argue that research driven by the RHM and the DFM did not contribute to the understanding of the bilingual lexicon. Rather, I argue that this research made important contributions to our understanding of interlingual connections. De Groot (1992, 1993) has also rightly argued that bilinguals' representations need not be of one type (compound, co-ordinate or subordinate), but may contain a mixture of representational formats. Now the time has come to move to the next stage of research on bilinguals' concepts, where the strength of interlingual connections is differentiated from the degree of shared meaning and where sharedness is established empirically, rather than assumed.

To facilitate the transition to this stage, I have put forth the MHM that brings another layer of depth to our understanding of the bilingual mental lexicon, positing that distinct conceptual equivalence relationships have different implications for L2 vocabulary learning:

(1) *conceptual equivalence* facilitates L2 vocabulary learning through positive transfer; the main learning task in this context is the establishment of links between L2 words and already existing concepts;

(2) *partial (non)equivalence* facilitates learning through partial overlap (positive transfer), yet also complicates it when learners assume complete equivalence and display negative transfer; the main L2 learning task in this context is conceptual restructuring;

(3) *non-equivalence* simultaneously complicates learning, as learners have to develop new categories, and facilitates it through the absence of competing representations; the L2 learning task here involves development of a new linguistic category that allows learners to map a new word onto real-world referents; this task

may be easier in the case of new objects and more challenging in the case of abstract or emotion categories.

Depending on the nature of the conceptual equivalence relationship and on the learner's trajectory, L2 learners may manifest: (1) positive L1 conceptual transfer (in the case of conceptual equivalence); (2) positive or negative L1 conceptual transfer (in the case of partial (non)equivalence); (3) internalization of new concepts or lack thereof (in the case of conceptual non-equivalence); and (4) conceptual restructuring (in the case of partial (non)equivalence). Conceptual restructuring, in turn, may result in: (1) coexisting representations, where speakers conform to the constraints of each language; (2) partial restructuring; (3) converging representations distinct from the categories mediated by languages A and B; and (4) shift toward the L2 category. Consequently, the shape of bilinguals' conceptual representations is affected by the equivalence relationship and, in the case of partial or complete (non)equivalence, by opportunities for L2 socialization.

This approach offers several productive directions for future inquiry. To begin with, the field can now examine the relationship between the strength of interlingual connections (as seen through priming or translation rates) and the degree of shared meaning between particular translation equivalents (as seen through naming, sorting and categorization tasks). Differentiating between the actual linguistic categories (as seen in monolinguals' performance) and the categories in the bilingual minds, this inquiry will further illuminate factors that affect the strength of interlingual connections and the shape of conceptual representations.

More importantly, we can now expand the focus of inquiry to include conceptual restructuring and development of new linguistic categories. The first direction for such inquiry is empirical study of the structure and boundaries of various linguistic categories, especially those linked to high-frequency words, across a variety of languages. The products of such inquiry, in a dictionary or web-format, would offer an excellent resource for foreign language teachers committed to highlighting areas of partial (non)equivalence. This inquiry could also illuminate areas where native speakers of a particular language are likely to agree and those where individual and generational differences might be particularly apparent.

The second important direction is longitudinal study of conceptual restructuring and development as seen through verbal and non-verbal performance of L2 learners tested regularly over a span of several years. To reach an in-depth understanding, these processes need to be studied in a variety of learners, classroom versus naturalistic, and in a variety of language combinations. Several hypotheses may be tested in such inquiry. First, we may hypothesize that the learning of conceptual equivalents will proceed faster than that of partial equivalents, and that the rate of learning of nonequivalents will depend on both their referents (i.e. whether they refer to easily identifiable objects, processes and phenomena) and opportunities for L2 socialization. Secondly, in the case of partial (non)equivalence, L2 learners may initially assume full equivalence, and display L1 conceptual transfer in their performance. Third, we may hypothesize that conceptual transfer may persist longer than semantic transfer due to difficulties involved in conceptual restructuring compared to relinking.

The differentiation between the three types of conceptual equivalence also has implications for FL and L2 instruction. More often than not, FL/L2 materials and curricula overlook cross-linguistic differences through their textual focus on translation equivalents and images produced by clip-art manufacturers (Read, 2003). These materials convey a view that L2 vocabulary learning takes place in the context of conceptual equivalence, which is not necessarily the case. Rather, vocabulary instruction should be differentiated depending on the conceptual equivalence relationship between the lexical items in question, as well as on the learners' proficiency level.

In the case of conceptual equivalence, L2 instruction should focus on strengthening the links between L2 words and their L1 translation equivalents through L2 production tasks, translation from L1 to L2 and other tasks that involve recall, rather than recognition, of L2 vocabulary items. Instruction at intermediate and advanced levels could also include metaphoric extensions of particular words that may or may not be the same across languages (Kellerman, 1978, 1983; see also Verspoor & Lowie, 2003).

In the case of partial (non)equivalence, L2 instruction should highlight the areas of similarity and difference and aid in conceptual restructuring. This instruction could involve consciousness-raising activities, such as explanations, discussions and exercises that introduce learners to cross-linguistic differences. It could also involve naming, sorting and categorization activities that allow learners to understand how various category members – be they objects, such as china, plastic, paper, and glass containers, or situations arousing particular feelings, such as jealousy or envy – might be referred to by native speakers of the target language.

Language corpora offer an excellent tool for such instruction, allowing learners to identify the range of contexts where particular words could be used. Thus, to understand how *problem* differs from *question*, Chinese L2 learners of English could consult English-language corpora, such as COBUILD (www.titania.cobuild.collins.co.uk) (Jiang, 2004). Similarly, to understand the difference between *zlit'sia* and *serdit'sia*, American L2 learners of Russian could consult Russian language corpora, such as www.ruscorpora.ru. (For an example of FL teaching materials that involve language corpora and exercises created specifically to advance conceptual restructuring in American L2 learners of Russian, see Pavlenko & Driagina, 2006.) The development of L2 categories could be further aided by exercises that involve visual representations. For instance, the Culturally Authentic Pictorial Lexicon of German (www.washjeff.edu/capl), developed by Shaughnessy (Read, 2003), features numerous pictures of German realia that can be used in naming and sorting activities, and in awareness-raising discussions.

Finally, in the case of conceptual non-equivalence, L2 instruction should facilitate the development of new concepts. This development could be facilitated through tasks that present learners with novel objects or ask them to interpret particular situations. Subsequent awareness-raising discussions could focus on cross-linguistic differences in the ways in which particular objects, events and phenomena are named, conceptualized and interpreted in the learners' respective languages.

Acknowledgements

I am very grateful for helpful suggestions and insightful comments on earlier versions of this chapter made by Panos Athanasopoulos, Peter Ecke, Scott Jarvis, Barbara Malt and Robert Schrauf. All errors and inconsistencies are exclusively mine.

Notes

1. The discussion here will focus on the studies of lexical concepts; for studies of bilinguals' grammatical concepts, see Athanasopoulos (2006, 2007), Cook *et al.* (2006), Jarvis and Pavlenko (2008); for discussion of the interface between structural and conceptual factors in the bilingual lexicon, see Pavlenko (2008a).
2. Due to the difference in tasks and materials, these findings are in stark contrast with those of Caramazza and Brones (1980) who claimed, on the basis of a semantic categorization task, that representations of furniture are shared in English and Spanish.
3. I fully recognize that the visual representation is but a metaphor for the L2 learning process, which cannot be captured in its entirety via boxes, circles and links. As pointed out by De Groot (1992: 389), one cannot help but

wonder whether 'rather than parsimoniously capturing its essence, these few strokes and dashes may do injustice to the complexity of reality'.

References

Aitchison, J. (1994) Understanding words. In G. Brown, K. Malmkjoer, A. Pollitt and J. Williams (eds) *Language and Understanding* (pp. 83–95). Oxford: Oxford University Press.

Ameel, E., Storms, G., Malt, B. and Sloman, S. (2005) How bilinguals solve the naming problem. *Journal of Memory and Language* 52, 309–329.

Andrews, D. (1994) The Russian color categories *sinij* and *goluboj*: An experimental analysis of their interpretation in the standard and emigre languages. *Journal of Slavic Linguistics* 2, 9–28.

Appel, R. (2000) Language, concepts, and culture: Old wine in new bottles? *Bilingualism: Language and Cognition* 3 (1), 5–6.

Athanasopoulos, P. (2006) Effects of the grammatical representation of number on cognition in bilinguals. *Bilingualism: Language and Cognition* 9 (1), 89–96.

Athanasopoulos, P. (2007) Interaction between grammatical categories and cognition in bilinguals: The role of proficiency, cultural immersion, and language of instruction. *Language and Cognitive Processes* 22 (5), 689–699.

Athanasopoulos, P. (in press) Cognitive representation of color in bilinguals: The case of Greek blues. *Bilingualism: Language and Cognition.*

Barsalou, L. (2003) Situated simulation in the human conceptual system. *Language and Cognitive Processes* 18, 513–562.

Caramazza, A. and Brones, I. (1980) Semantic classification by bilinguals. *Canadian Journal of Psychology* 34, 77–81.

Chen, H.C. (1992) Lexical processing in multilingual speakers. In R. Harris (ed.) *Cognitive Processing in Bilinguals* (pp. 253–264). Amsterdam: Elsevier.

Chen, H.C. and Leung, Y.S. (1989) Patterns of lexical processing in a non-native language. *Journal of Experimental Psychology: Learning, Memory, and Cognition* 15, 316–325.

Cook, V., Bassetti, B., Kasai, C., Sasaki, M. and Takahashi, J.A. (2006) Do bilinguals have different concepts? The case of shape and material in Japanese L2 users of English. *International Journal of Bilingualism* 10, 137–152.

Costa, A. (2005) Lexical access in bilingual production. In J. Kroll and A.M.B. De Groot (eds) *Handbook in Psycholinguistics of Bilingualism* (pp. 308–325). Oxford: Oxford University Press.

De Groot, A.M.B. (1992) Bilingual lexical representation: A closer look at conceptual representations. In R. Frost and L. Katz (eds) *Orthography, Phonology, Morphology, and Meaning* (pp. 389–412). Amsterdam: Elsevier.

De Groot, A.M.B. (1993) Word-type effects in bilingual processing tasks: Support for a mixed-representational system. In R. Schreuder and B. Weltens (eds) *The Bilingual Lexicon* (pp. 27–51). Amsterdam: John Benjamins.

De Groot, A.M.B. (1995) Determinants of bilingual lexicosemantic organization. *Computer Assisted Language Learning* 8 (2–3), 151–180.

De Groot, A.M.B. (2002) Lexical representation and lexical processing in the L2 user. In V. Cook (ed.) *Portraits of the L2 User* (pp. 32–63). Clevedon: Multilingual Matters.

De Groot, A.M.B., Dannenburg, L. and Van Hell, J. (1994) Forward and backward word translation by bilinguals. *Journal of Memory and Language* 33, 600–629.

De Groot, A.M.B. and Nas, G.L.J. (1991) Lexical representation of cognates and non-cognates in compound bilinguals. *Journal of Memory and Language* 30, 90–123.

De Keyser, R. (1990) From learning to acquisition: Monitoring in the classroom and abroad. *Hispania* 73 (1), 238–247.

Dong, Y., Gui, Sh. and MacWhinney, B. (2005) Shared and separate meanings in the bilingual mental lexicon. *Bilingualism: Language and Cognition* 8 (3), 221–238.

Dufour, R. and Kroll, J. (1995) Matching words to concepts in two languages: A test of the concept mediation model of bilingual representation. *Memory & Cognition* 23, 166–180.

Ellis, N. (ed.) (1994) *Implicit and Explicit Learning of Languages*. New York: Academic Press.

Ellis, R. (2006) Modelling learning difficulty and second language proficiency: The differential contributions of implicit and explicit knowledge. *Applied Linguistics* 27, 431–463.

Geeslin, K. (2003) A comparison of copula choice: Native Spanish speakers and advanced learners. *Language Learning* 53, 703–764.

Gennari, S., Sloman, S., Malt, B. and Fitch, T. (2002) Motion events in language and cognition. *Cognition* 83, 49–79.

Graham, R. and Belnap, K. (1986) The acquisition of lexical boundaries in English by native speakers of Spanish. *International Review of Applied Linguistics* 24, 275–286.

Green, D. (1998) Mental control of the bilingual lexico-semantic system. *Bilingualism: Language and Cognition* 1, 67–81.

Hohenstein, J., Eisenberg, A. and Naigles, L. (2006) Is he floating across or crossing afloat? Cross-influence of L1 and L2 in Spanish-English bilingual adults. *Bilingualism: Language and Cognition* 9 (3), 249–261.

Hong, Y., Morris, M., Chiu, C. and Benet-Martinez, V. (2000) Multicultural minds: A dynamic constructivist approach to culture and cognition. *American Psychologist* 55 (7), 709–720.

Ijaz, I.H. (1986) Linguistic and cognitive determinants of lexical acquisition in a second language. *Language Learning* 36, 401–451.

Jarvis, S. (2003) Probing the effects of the L2 on the L1: A case study. In V. Cook (ed.) *Effects of the Second Language on the First* (pp. 81–102). Clevedon: Multilingual Matters.

Jarvis, S. and Pavlenko, A. (2008) *Crosslinguistic Influence in Language and Cognition*. New York: Routledge.

Jiang, N. (2004) Semantic transfer and its implications for vocabulary teaching in a second language. *Modern Language Journal* 88 (3), 416–432.

Karasik, V., Prohvacheva, O., Zubkova, I. and Grabarova, E. (2005) *Inaia mental'nost'* [*A Different Mentality*]. Moscow: Gnosis.

Keatley, C. (1992) History of bilingualism research in cognitive psychology. In R. Harris (ed.) *Cognitive Processing in Bilinguals* (pp. 15–49). Amsterdam: North-Holland.

Kellerman, E. (1978) Giving learners a break: Native language intuitions as a source of predictions about transferability. *Working Papers on Bilingualism* 15, 59–92.

Kellerman, E. (1983) Now you see it, now you don't. In S. Gass and L. Selinker (eds) *Language Transfer in Language Learning* (pp. 112–134). Rowley, MA: Newbury House.

Kroll, J. (1993) Accessing conceptual representations for words in a second language. In R. Schreuder and B. Weltens (eds) *The Bilingual Lexicon* (pp. 53–81). Amsterdam: John Benjamins.

Kroll, J. and Curley, J. (1988) Lexical memory in novice bilinguals: The role of concepts in retrieving second language words. In M. Gruneberg, P. Morris and R. Sykes (eds) *Practical Aspects of Memory* (Vol. 2; pp. 389–395). London: Wiley.

Kroll, J. and De Groot, A.M.B. (1997) Lexical and conceptual memory in the bilingual: Mapping form to meaning in two languages. In A.M.B. De Groot and J. Kroll (eds) *Tutorials in Bilingualism: Psycholinguistic Perspectives* (pp. 169–199). Mawhah, NJ: Lawrence Erlbaum.

Kroll, J. and Stewart, E. (1994) Category interference in translation and picture naming: Evidence for asymmetric connections between bilingual memory representations. *Journal of Memory and Language* 33, 149–174.

Kroll, J. and Sunderman, G. (2003) Cognitive processes in second language learners and bilinguals: The development of lexical and conceptual representations. In C. Doughty and M. Long (eds) *The Handbook of Second Language Acquisition* (pp. 104–129). Malden, MA: Blackwell.

Kroll, J. and Tokowicz, N. (2005) Models of bilingual representation and processing: Looking back and to the future. In J. Kroll and A.M.B. De Groot (eds) *Handbook of Bilingualism: Psycholinguistic Approaches* (pp. 531–553). Oxford: Oxford University Press.

Kronenfeld, D., Armstrong, J. and Wilmoth, S. (1985) Exploring the internal structure of linguistic categories: An extensionist semantic view. In J. Dougherty (ed.) *Directions in Cognitive Anthropology* (pp. 91–110). Champaign, IL: University of Illinois Press.

Levinson, S. (2003) *Space in Language and Cognition: Explorations in Cognitive Diversity.* Cambridge: Cambridge University Press.

Lucy, J. (1992a) *Language Diversity and Thought. A Reformulation of the Linguistic Relativity Hypothesis.* Cambridge: Cambridge University Press.

Lucy, J. (1992b) *Grammatical Categories and Cognition. A Case Study of the Linguistic Relativity Hypothesis.* Cambridge: Cambridge University Press.

Malt, B. and Sloman, S. (2003) Linguistic diversity and object naming by non-native speakers of English. *Bilingualism: Language and Cognition* 6, 47–67.

Malt, B., Sloman, S. and Gennari, S. (2003) Universality and language specificity in object naming. *Journal of Memory and Language* 29, 20–42.

Malt, B., Sloman, S., Gennari, S., Shi, M. and Wang, Y. (1999) Knowing versus naming: Similarity and the linguistic categorization of artifacts. *Journal of Memory and Language* 40, 230–262.

McElree, B., Jia, G. and Litvak, A. (2000) The time course of conceptual processing in three bilingual populations. *Journal of Memory and Language* 42, 229–254.

Moore, C., Romney, A., Hsia, T. and Rusch, C. (1999) The universality of the semantic structure of emotion terms: Methods for study of inter- and intra-cultural variability. *American Anthropologist* 101 (3), 529–546.

Murphy, G. (2002) *The Big Book of Concepts*. Cambridge, MA: MIT Press.

Panayiotou, A. (2004) Bilingual emotions: The untranslatable self. *Estudios de Sociolinguistica* 5 (1), 1–19.

Panayiotou, A. (2006) Translating guilt: An endeavor of shame in the Mediterranean? In A. Pavlenko (ed.) *Bilingual Minds: Emotional Experience, Expression, and Representation* (pp. 183–208). Clevedon: Multilingual Matters.

Paradis, M. (1994) Neurolinguistic aspects of implicit and explicit memory: Implications for bilingualism and SLA. In N. Ellis (ed.) *Implicit and Explicit Learning of Languages* (pp. 393–419). San Diego, CA: Academic Press.

Paradis, M. (2004) *A Neurolinguistic Theory of Bilingualism*. Amsterdam: Benjamins.

Pavlenko, A. (1997) Bilingualism and cognition. Unpublished doctoral dissertation, Cornell University.

Pavlenko, A. (2002a) Bilingualism and emotions. *Multilingua* 21, 45–78.

Pavlenko, A. (2002b) Emotions and the body in Russian and English. *Pragmatics and Cognition* 10, 201–236.

Pavlenko, A. (2003) Eyewitness memory in late bilinguals: Evidence for discursive relativity. *International Journal of Bilingualism* 7 (3), 257–281.

Pavlenko, A. (2008a) Structural and conceptual equivalence in the acquisition and use of emotion words in a second language. *The Mental Lexicon* 3 (1), 91–120.

Pavlenko, A. (2008b) Narrative analysis in the study of bi- and multilingualism. In M. Moyer and Wei Li (eds) *The Blackwell Guide to Research Methods in Bilingualism*. Oxford: Blackwell.

Pavlenko, A. and Driagina, V. (2006) *Advanced-level Narrative Skills in Russian: A Workbook for Students and Teachers*. State College, PA: Center for Advanced Language Proficiency, Education, and Research. On WWW at www.calper.la.psu.edu.

Pavlenko, A. and Driagina, V. (2007) Russian emotion vocabulary in American learners' narratives. *Modern Language Journal* 91 (2), 213–234.

Potter, M., So, K-F., Von Eckardt, B. and Feldman, L. (1984) Lexical and conceptual representation in beginning and more proficient bilinguals. *Journal of Verbal Learning and Verbal Behavior* 23, 23–38.

Read, B. (2003) Professor's website uses photographs to teach the German language. *The Chronicle of Higher Education* 12 December, A31.

Ringbom, H. (2001) Lexical transfer in L3 production. In J. Cenoz, B. Hufeisen and U. Jessner (eds) *Cross-linguistic Influence in Third Language Acquisition: Psycholinguistic Perspectives* (pp. 59–68). Clevedon: Multilingual Matters.

Ross, M., Xun, W.Q.E. and Wilson, A. (2002) Language and the bicultural self. *Personality and Social Psychology Bulletin* 28, 1040–1050.

Ryan, J. and Lafford, B. (1992) Acquisition of lexical meaning in a study abroad environment: SER and ESTAR and the Granada experience. *Hispania* 75 (3), 714–722.

Sánchez-Casas, R. and García-Albea, J. (2005) The representation of cognate and noncognate words in bilingual memory: Can cognate status be characterized as a special kind of morphological relation? In J. Kroll and A.M.B. De Groot (eds) *Handbook of Bilingualism: Psycholinguistic Approaches* (pp. 226–250). Oxford: Oxford University Press.

Snodgrass, J. (1993) Translation *versus* picture naming: Similarities and differences. In R. Schreuder and B. Weltens (eds) *The Bilingual Lexicon* (pp. 83–114). Amsterdam: John Benjamins.

Stepanova Sachs, O. and Coley, J. (2006) Envy and jealousy in Russian and English: Labeling and conceptualization of emotions by monolinguals and bilinguals. In A. Pavlenko (ed.) *Bilingual Minds: Emotional Experience, Expression, and Representation* (pp. 208–231). Clevedon: Multilingual Matters.

Trafimow, D., Silverman, E., Fan, R.M-T. and Law, J. (1997) The effects of language and priming on the relative accessibility of the private self and the collective self. *Journal of Cross-Cultural Psychology* 28, 107–123.

Van Hell, J. and De Groot, A.M.B. (1998) Conceptual representation in bilingual memory: Effects of concreteness and cognate status in word association. *Bilingualism: Language and Cognition* 1, 193–211.

Verspoor, M. and Lowie, W. (2003) Making sense of polysemous words. *Language Learning* 53, 547–596.

Weinreich, U. (1953) *Languages in Contact*. The Hague: Mouton.

Chapter 7

Why Gestures are Relevant to the Bilingual Lexicon

MARIANNE GULLBERG

Introduction

What is a chapter on gestures doing in a book on the bilingual mental lexicon? Surely the mental lexicon is only concerned with linguistic representations in the mind, how they are stored, accessed and learned, and how they are deployed in production and comprehension? Well yes, and gestures can contribute to the study of all those domains. Gestures are an integral part of our communicative efforts and when we speak, we typically also gesture. Importantly, gestures are influenced by the details of what we are saying and trying to convey. Although very different from words and speech, gestures reflect views and perspectives on the world that are governed by language and by lexical considerations. The point made in this chapter is that gestures open for a broader view of the mental lexicon, targeting the interface between conceptual, semantic and syntactic aspects of event construal. They offer new possibilities for examining how languages coexist and interact in bilinguals beyond the level of individual surface forms.

A number of caveats must be stated at the outset. The claim is not that gestures are only cognitive, linguistic or lexical in nature. They are not. Gestures are deeply multifunctional and complex. First, gestures are visuo-spatial interactional units that unfold in the physical world between interlocutors. They are therefore mediated and influenced by a host of sociopsychological, contextual and cultural factors that guide human interaction. Second, gestures are imagistic and holistic and therefore convey information of a different type and in a different format from spoken language. Third, gestures perform a range of functions, some of which are linguistic or pragmatic, whereas others are interactional, performative, cognitive, etc. Finally, gestures are not simply a spillover of mental activity beyond speakers' control. Although speakers are mostly not very aware of gesturing, they can and do deploy gestures purposefully to achieve particular communicative goals. Mindful of these qualifications, the point here is nevertheless that gestures are *also* influenced by linguistic concerns, and as such can be informative about what happens when an individual operates with lexical items in more than one language.

Another caveat concerns terminology. The studies reviewed in this chapter represent a range of different disciplines, which use different terminologies to refer to the participants under study who, in turn, have different profiles in terms of acquisition history (e.g. early versus late, simultaneous versus consecutive acquisition), formal proficiency, fluency and usage patterns. To circumvent unnecessary confusion and in the interest of consistency, the term 'bilingual' is adopted throughout this chapter to refer to the study of the 'bilingual mental lexicon'. As in the psychological literature, *bilingual* here refers to knowledge of more than one language, independently of acquisition history, proficiency or usage patterns. However, in discussing empirical studies, the term *second language (L2) learner* is generally used to refer to participants whose acquisition history, proficiency or fluency in a foreign or second language is under scrutiny. This usage reflects the theoretical framework of the majority of studies cited, which are situated in the field of second language acquisition (SLA) research. However, the reader is reminded that the aim of the chapter is not to favor any particular theoretical stance, but rather to highlight what gesture analysis might say about lexical representations across a range of speakers with knowledge of several languages.

The chapter starts with a brief introduction to gestures and how to study them. The next section outlines the current views on the relationship between gesture, speech and language. It also discusses what lexical information gestures reflect and how they reflect it, illustrating gestural consequences in monolingual contexts across a variety of languages. Next, issues and findings concerning the bilingual lexicon are reviewed, looking at what gestures unveil about lexical acquisition and cross-linguistic interaction in the bilingual lexicon. The final section discusses some theoretical and methodological implications and outlines directions for future inquiry.

1.   An Introduction to Gestures and How to Study Them

1.1.   The phenomenon

Modern gesture studies tend to define gesture as a 'visible action [...] used as an utterance or as part of an utterance' (Kendon, 2004: 7), or, put differently, as symbolic movements of hands, arms, heads, eyebrows, etc., related to the expressive effort (Kendon, 2004; McNeill, 1992). Naïve observers are able to determine which movements are a relevant part of an utterance even when watching interlocutors whose speech they do not understand (Kendon, 1978). They recognize conventionalized gestures or emblems like the Victory sign, but also non-conventionalized movements that depict and represent properties of events and objects (e.g. peeling an imaginary banana), pointing gestures, gestures that indicate speakers, and movements that are rhythmically aligned with speech. Observers also recognize what is *not* (necessarily) a gesture: various self-grooming movements or self-regulators (e.g. playing with jewelry), practical actions with real objects (e.g. peeling a real banana) and non-verbal behavior, like blushing (e.g. Ekman & Friesen, 1969; Poyatos, 2002). This definition of gesture excludes non-verbal behavior not because it is not communicative, but because it is not part of what the speaker is trying to convey. In contrast, the definition is inclusive regarding articulators. That is, gestures can be made with hands, arms, head, eyebrows, etc. That said, the review in this chapter will focus chiefly on manual movements because these are best described in connection with language.

As outlined above, gestures thus defined are visuo-spatial phenomena with structural and semiotic properties that can be systematically described and studied. They are multifunctional and sensitive to both communicative and speaker-internal processes. Strikingly, despite con-siderable individual and contextual variation (e.g. Feyereisen & de Lannoy, 1991), there is also consistency in gestural practices within speech communities such that individual gesture production is realized within the boundaries of culturally and linguistically determined repertoires (cf. Gullberg, 2006b). Of particular importance here are the linguistic influences.

The links between gestures, speech and language are manifold (cf. Gullberg, 2008). Of theoretical importance is the observation that gestures are temporally, semantically and pragmatically coordinated with speech (Kendon, 1983; McNeill, 1992). That is, gestures are typically temporally aligned with a coexpressive part of speech: gesture and speech convey the same thing at the same time. The temporal alignment between related meanings in speech and gesture is very fine-grained (e.g. Kendon, 1980; Seyfeddinipur, 2006). 'Coexpressive' means that the modalities express closely related but not identical information. Because gestures are imagistic, spatial and synthetic, they can convey information not easily encoded in speech, such as the speed and direction of an action talked about or the size and shape of a mentioned entity (Beattie &

Shovelton, 2002; Kendon, 2004). For example, a speaker saying '(she) finished her coffee' may perform a gesture lifting a grip hand shape to her mouth. If the grip hand shape is small with thumb and index finger touching, this suggests an espresso cup, whereas a large, loose-grip hand shape suggests a big mug. Although not identical, the spoken and gestural meanings are clearly related. Moreover, no individual part of the gesture can be said to separately convey the meaning elements associated with finishing the coffee, the size or shape of the cup. Instead, all meaning elements are conveyed synthetically by the entire gesture. Speakers distribute information across speech and gesture quite deliberately depending, for example, on visibility (e.g. Holler & Beattie, 2003; Melinger & Levelt, 2004). In language comprehension, gestures affect addressees' interpretation of and memory for speech (Beattie & Shovelton, 1999; Graham & Argyle, 1975; Kelly *et al.*, 1999). For example, information that has only been present in gesture resurfaces in speech, gesture or both (Cassell *et al.*, 1999). And evidence from neurocognitive studies shows that the brain integrates speech and gesture information in the same way as speech (Özyürek *et al.*, 2007; Wu & Coulson, 2005). On all accounts, gestures are intimately linked to speech and language.

1.2. How to study gestures: A methodological excursion

Gesture studies rely both on observational, naturalistic, and on elicited, semi-experimental data. *Gesture elicitation tasks* are designed to promote spontaneous gesture production while keeping (1) the situation and the content of speech constant to facilitate comparisons across participants and (2) speakers' awareness of their own gesture production at a minimum. Participants are typically asked to retell stories, often (animated) cartoons or other video materials, or to solve referential communication tasks (Yule, 1997) involving spatial or action-related topics, such as descriptions of spatial layouts, route descriptions, etc. Task set-ups are typically dyadic because the presence of an interlocutor promotes gesture production (cf. Bavelas *et al.*, 1992).

Gesture coding typically involves the identification, description/transcription and classification of relevant gestural movements (for useful examples of analytical procedures, see McNeill, 1992, 2005). The core movement phase, the stroke, is often structurally identified (Kendon, 1980; Seyfeddinipur, 2006). Further structural descriptions concern the articulator (what moves?) and its configurations (what shape/form does it have?), the place of articulation (where in gesture space?), the form of the gestural movement (how does it move?) and the temporal alignment of the movement relative to speech (when does it move?). Temporal coding requires the analysis of single video-frames (25–40 ms, depending on the system). Gestures are also often classified on semiotic-functional grounds (for taxonomies, see Kendon, 2004). Conventiona-lized, culture-specific gestures (emblems) (e.g. Ekman & Friesen, 1969; Payrató, 1993) are distinguished from nonconventionalized movements, simply labeled gestures or gesticulation. These lack standards of well-formedness and often co-occur with speech. These latter, which are the main focus of current gesture research, are in turn grouped into (1) *representational gestures*, which depict, illustrate or index some aspect of what is being talked about iconically or by contiguity and (2) *rhythmic gestures*. McNeill's (1992) scheme for speech-associated gestures identi-fies four not mutually exclusive dimensions where representational gestures are further categorized as iconic, metaphoric and deictic, whereas rhythmic gestures are labeled *beats*. Most studies reviewed here focus on representational, iconic, gestures.

Analyses of naturalistic gesture data often concern contexts of use as well as the structure and sequence of actions between speakers. In the studies reviewed here, analyses typically focus on the temporal-semantic relationship between speech and gesture, specifically what the gesture (stroke) expresses relative to speech. Given the different nature of the modalities, it is challenging to specify how coexpressivity in speech and gesture is determined. Predictably, multiple terms are found in the literature to characterize different relationships (e.g. match/mismatch, complementary, supplementary, and contradictory meanings, etc.; cf. Kendon, 1983, 2004). Furthermore, interpretations of coexpressivity and views of how best to triangulate speech and gesture data to arrive at a 'full representation' differ across theories. Overall, because standar-dized transcription or coding schemes do not exist, it is vital to be explicit about coding and to provide inter-rater reliability measures to ensure replicability.

2. Gestures, Language and the (Monolingual) Lexicon

Before discussing how (representational) gestures are relevant to the bilingual lexicon, I will review the arguments for considering gestures to be 'lexical'. In this section, I will argue that gestures are lexical in the sense that they reflect information targeted for expression in speech, and the ways in which that information is encoded both in terms of information structure and lexical choices as instantiated in semantics and syntax. Gestures reflect linguistic conceptualization or event construal. The lexical influence is seen in gestural timing and form, and in the distribution of information across modalities.

The observation that speech and gestures are temporally and semantically coexpressive lies at the core of all speech-gesture theories, although the nature of the relationship is not undisputed (for overviews, see De Ruiter, 2007; Kendon, 2004; McNeill, 2000a). Of particular relevance for discussions of the (bilingual) lexicon are those theories that connect with Levelt's speech production model (Levelt, 1989; Levelt *et al.*, 1999) and refer to his processing levels: the Conceptualizer, where the preverbal message is formed; the Formulator, where grammatical and lexical elements are assembled to express the preverbal message; and the Articulator, where overt speech is created. The relevant speech-gesture theories all assume a link between gesture and speech at the conceptual level, based on the argument that gesture and speech must be planned together to account for the detail and flexibility of the semantic and temporal coordination. They differ, however, in the precise role and weight they assign to imagery, linguistic categories and communicative intentions, and also in their view on how late in the encoding process speech and gesture interact.

The Growth Point Theory (McNeill, 1992, 2005; McNeill & Duncan, 2000) considers the departure point of any utterance to be the news-worthy element of thought, the growth point, which has both imagistic and linguistic content. As the thought is expressed, speech and gesture convey the content for which each modality is best suited. Critically, the theory posits that speech and gesture are fully integrated and interact throughout planning and speaking. The Interface Hypothesis (Kita & Özyürek, 2003) is more specific concerning the influence of language. It holds that gestures reflect underlying imagery and 'spatio-motoric' thinking, but are *also* influenced by the precise linguistic means used to convey the imagery. In this framework, the speech formulator is assumed to interact online with an 'action generator' to arrive at a gestural form that satisfies both imagistic and linguistic constraints. The Sketch Model or Postcard Architecture (De Ruiter, 2000, 2007) posits that the speaker's overall communicative intention, as well as imagistic and linguistic properties of the message, drive production in both modalities to form a deliberately coherent multimodal utterance. This model also assumes a 'gesture planner' (cf. the action generator), but does not assume cross-talk between the speech formulator and the gesture planner. Coordination between the modalities instead takes place only at the conceptual level.

What is the consequence of these views for the nature of the conceptually grounded coexpressivity in speech and gesture? Gestures' spoken *lexical affiliates* (Schegloff, 1984) are rarely words. That is, gestures do not typically align with a single word, nor do they, in any simple way, express the meaning of individual lexical items, as exemplified earlier in section 1.1. Instead, because they are imagistic and synthetic, gestures have *conceptual affiliates* (De Ruiter, 2000). That is, gestures reflect the information that speakers target as relevant and select for expression as they prepare to talk in a broader sense (cf. McNeill, 1992: 126), a phenomenon alternatively referred to as macro-planning, linguistic conceptualization, event construal or perspective taking (e.g. Levelt, 1989; Von Stutterheim & Nüse, 2003). It has recently been suggested that, as speakers prepare to talk, their choices are 'filtered' through the linguistic categories that they habitually use to categorize and express events (e.g. Berman & Slobin, 1994; Slobin, 1996; Von Stutterheim & Nüse, 2003), a notion known as the *thinking for speaking hypothesis* (Slobin, 1996). The hypothesis is predicated on the idea that habitually employed linguistic categories guide attention to certain types of information that are then selected for expression, giving rise to language-specific rhetorical styles or perspectives (Slobin, 2004). This view differs some-what in scope from the traditional linguistic relativity or the neo-Whorfian hypothesis (e.g. Gumperz & Levinson, 1996; Lucy, 1992).

A view of gestures and speech as linked and interacting at the conceptual level with further connections through the production stages means that gestures can reflect aspects of information chosen for expression, which, in turn, are (partly) guided by linguistic, lexical representations. Put differently, gestures can reflect information selected for expression (what is newsworthy) and also the way in which it is then (lexically) encoded in speech. Cross-linguistic differences in what is considered newsworthy and how it is expressed – that is, in lexical-ization patterns – will have direct consequences for gestural forms and timing relative to speech.

This view of gestures and speech connects to existing models of the mental lexicon, partly via Levelt's processing levels. More specifically, however, this perspective on speech and gestures is germane to those approaches that challenge traditional narrow boundaries of the lexicon and include syntactic and constructional information, and also to those that argue against the conventional view that lexical items (e.g. *dog, hund, pas*) are language-specific but concepts (e.g. [DOG]) are universal (e.g. Francis, 2005; Pavlenko, 1999, this volume).

2.1. Cross-linguistic lexical consequences

In monolingual contexts, gestures reflect cross-linguistic differences in lexicalization patterns in three ways. First, the *temporal alignment* of gestures relative to speech is sensitive to information structure. Gestures tend to co-occur with spoken elements that represent new or otherwise focused information, such as new referents or actions (Levy & McNeill, 1992; McNeill & Levy, 1993). Cross-linguistic differences in what is considered newsworthy or focused, reflected in different organization of discourse, yield different gesture patterns (cf. Duncan, 1996). For example, Swedish and Dutch speakers treat actions as newsworthy and organize narrative discourse around verbs, aligning gestures with these verbs (*a frog jumped out of a jar*). Japanese speakers, in contrast, also treat settings as important and construct discourse around the introduction of entities making up the setting in existential constructions (*there was a frog and a jar*), therefore, they also gesture about nominal entities (Gullberg, 2003, 2006a; Yoshioka & Kellerman, 2006). These effects are arguably lexical in nature.

Second, lexicalization patterns or the details of the focused lexical information are also reflected in gestures' *shape and form*. For instance, studies drawing on Talmy's (1985, 2000) typological distinction between verb-framed and satellite-framed languages have shown that gestures take different shapes cross-linguistically as a result of how semantic components like path (e.g. *down*) and manner of motion (e.g. *roll*) are expressed morphosyntactically (e.g. Duncan, 1996; Kita & Özyürek, 2003; McNeill, 1992; McNeill & Duncan, 2000). Put differently, gestures convey different types and amount of information depending on how meaning is syntactically mapped in speech. For example, a tight expression of path and manner in one single clause, typical in English (manner verb + path satellite, e.g. *rolls down*), may be accompanied by an equally tight gestural package with path and manner in one gesture (e.g. a circling movement rightwards). In contrast, a looser construction with path and manner in two separate clauses, characteristic of Turkish (path verb + manner verb, e.g. *descends as it rolls*), may be reflected in two separate gestures, each expressing either path (rightwards movement) or manner (circling) (Kita & Özyürek, 2003).

Gesture forms also reflect narrower differences in lexical representations when morphosyntax is kept constant. For instance, cross-linguistic differences in what meaning components are integral to the representation of general placement verbs like the French *mettre* (put) and posture verbs like the Dutch *zetten* (set) and *leggen* (lay) are mirrored in cross-linguistic differences in gesture (Gullberg, in press-a). Information about the displaced object is crucial for posture verb selection in Dutch, which is reflected in gestural hand shapes incorporating the object. This object information is absent from French gestures, which encode only the path of the movement, reflecting a different set of meaning components for the French verb *mettre* (put).

Finally, gestures may reflect language-specific conceptualizations in the *distribution of information across the modalities*. It has been suggested that speakers of verb- and satellite-framed languages have different means of modifying what information is foregrounded (McNeill, 2000b; McNeill & Duncan, 2000). Speakers of verb-framed languages like Spanish can foreground manner by expressing it in gesture when it is absent from speech. Since there is no manner in speech, such manner gestures may blanket the entire clause in so called *manner fogs* or align with other elements like ground expressions (Duncan, 2005). In contrast, speakers of satellite-framed languages like English can foreground manner by expressing it both in speech and gesture, or background it by expressing path in gesture when manner is present in speech. The cross-linguistic empirical support for this hypothesis is somewhat ambiguous, however. For instance, Japanese and French, both verb-framed languages like Spanish, show little evidence of manner fogs (Brown & Gullberg, 2008; Gullberg *et al.*, 2008). Interestingly, both languages have means other than manner verbs available to express manner. The size of the manner lexicon may therefore interact with the typologically constrained modes of distributing information across speech and gesture. This observation strengthens the notion that gestures and speech are lexically linked.

3. Gestures and the Bilingual Lexicon

3.1. Gestures as lexical stand-ins and vehicles of lexical acquisition

Several perspectives on gestures are possible when discussing the bilingual mental lexicon. An obvious lexical perspective is the popular conviction that gestures can stand in for lexical items. Their iconic properties intuitively make gestures suitable for expressing lexical content. Speakers typically produce more gestures when speaking their L2 than their L1 (e.g. Gullberg, 1998; Sherman & Nicoladis, 2004). The reason is assumed to be that they replace sought lexical material with gestures. Although speakers *can* use gestures to compensate for lexical shortcomings, they do not typically substitute spoken lexical items with gestures. Instead, they use gestures in combination with spoken approximations to invite lexical assistance from their interlocutors (e.g. Goodwin & Goodwin, 1986; Gullberg, 1998, in press-b; Mori & Hayashi, 2006). Moreover, as compensatory devices, gestures also do important grammatical and interactional work (Gullberg, 1998, in press-b).

More interesting is the possible relationship between gestures and lexical learning, and their putative impact on the development of lexical labels and lexical representations in a new language. Both seeing (e.g. Allen, 1995) and producing gestures (McCafferty, 2006; Tellier, 2006) may be helpful, although very few studies actually test effects of gestures on adult lexical acquisition (for an overview, see Gullberg, 2008).[1] The accounts for why gestures should promote lexical acquisition are similar for both reception and production. Gestures are assumed to invoke greater depth of processing through semantic redundancy and through grounding of the abstract (speech) in the concrete (gesture) (e.g. Hostetter & Alibali, 2004). Such notions receive support from a range of disciplines showing, for example, that self-enactment improves memory (e.g. Engelkamp & Cohen, 1991), and that seeing an action or a gesture activates the same parts of motor cortex as performing the action or gesture yourself (e.g. Rizzolatti & Craighero, 2004). This is assumed to entrench representations and consolidate memories and learning. However, although these accounts are interesting, we still know very little about the influence of gestures on the development of lexical representations in production, and even less about their effect on the development of language-specific lexical representations in the presence of an existing representation.

3.2. Gestures and cross-linguistic interactions in the bilingual mental lexicon

Much of the L2 and bilingual lexical literature tries to understand how two or more languages interact in the minds of individual speakers, tackling questions like selection and control, but also interaction at the representational level. The lexical processing literature provides overwhelming and compelling evidence for a shared lexicon in which all languages available to a bilingual speaker interact at all times in comprehension (e.g. Costa, 2005; Kroll & Sunderman, 2003; La Heij, 2005). It is less clear how such pervasive lexical interaction functions beyond the single word level, in production, and when the semantic-conceptual interface is considered. Furthermore, the evidence of bidirectional influence in bilingual processing is not easily reconciled with the findings in the field of SLA that mainly focuses on unilateral influence from the L1 on the L2 (cf. Odlin, 2003, 2005).

Several possible consequences of interactions in the lexicon have been posited (cf. Cook, 2003; Pavlenko, 1999, this volume). L1 and L2 representations could be kept entirely separate, assuming that L2 representations are acquired. There could also be unidirectional transfer from L1 to L2, or from the L2 to the L1 (backwards transfer). The L1 and L2 representations could also be restructured, leading to partially overlapping systems. And finally, the L1 and L2 could converge, yielding a system distinct from either monolingual system. Related to these notions are long-standing views on the difficulty of acquisition (and likelihood of transfer) depending on the relationship between languages and representations (cf. Pavlenko, this volume; Stockwell *et al.*, 1965). Absolute equivalence between L1 and L2 categories is considered easiest, followed by merging/coalescing of two L1 categories into one L2 category; abandoning an L1 category; creating a new L2 category; and splitting an L1 category into two L2 categories. All the consequences of interaction outlined have been attested, including effects of the L2 on the L1, restructuring and/or convergence. Categorization studies, for example, show that speakers with knowledge of more than one language may place category boundaries differently from monolingual speakers (e.g. Ameel *et al.*, 2005; Athanasopoulos, 2006; Cook *et al.*, 2006; Graham & Belnap, 1986; see Pavlenko, this volume, for an in-depth discussion). In many cases, bilinguals may converge on common underlying categories in both languages (cf. Ameel *et al.*, 2005).

Many of these studies rely on innovative methodology, reflecting the difficulties in capturing the processes of lexical cross-linguistic interactions as instantiated in actual language use. In this context, gestures can shed new light on the interactions and possible processes observable at the semantic-conceptual interface above and beyond speech. Gesture studies in this domain are guided by the following logic: gestures reflect cross-linguistically different conceptualizations, specifically what information is considered for expression. If speakers learning an L2 shift their conceptualizations from the L1 to the L2, then their gestures – while speaking the L2 – should look different from those of monolingual speakers of their L1 and similar to those of monolingual L2 speakers (if they are to be target-like). If they maintain their L1 representations, then their gestures – while speaking the L2 – will look different from those of monolingual speakers of the L2. The timing of gestures relative to speech, the form of gestures and the distribution of information across speech and gesture all provide information about such changes and shifts. The following sections will briefly review studies targeting each of these three aspects of gesture production as a means to examine lexical representations.

3.2.1. Timing

The first set of studies examines the alignment between gestures and spoken elements in a given language to see whether L2 learners change their lexical representations with regard to what is newsworthy. Spanish, English and Dutch speakers retelling stories about motion all align their path gestures with different elements in speech. Native Spanish speakers predominantly align path gestures with path verbs (*bajar* 'descend'), whereas native Dutch speakers favor particles (*uit* 'out') and ground phrases (*de pot* 'the jar'). Native English speakers vary more, co-ordinating their path gestures with particles (*down*), verbs and particles (*roll down*), verbs (*roll*) and ground phrases (*the street*) (Kellerman & Van Hoof, 2003; McNeill & Duncan, 2000; Negueruela *et al.*, 2004; Stam, 2006b).

To be native-like, Spanish learners of English, moving from a verb- to a satellite-framed language, must shift their perspective on motion from a focus on verbs to a more diversified English-like focus, reflected in a shift of gesture alignment. However, Spanish learners of English at different proficiency levels continue to align their path gestures with verbs when speaking L2 English (Kellerman & Van Hoof, 2003; Negueruela *et al.*, 2004; Stam, 2006b). They persistently regard the path instantiated in the verb as the most newsworthy lexical element of the motion event. All studies interpret this gesture pattern as a case of transfer from L1 to L2 prompted by the habitual focus on verb-path driven by the lexical representations in the L1. However, Kellerman and Van Hoof (2003) found that Dutch learners of English unexpectedly also coordinated their gestures with verbs, even though Talmy's (1985) typology suggests that their satellite-framed L1 Dutch should yield an English-like focus on (verbs and) particles. The authors refrain from interpreting this finding, but the gesture data raise the possibilities that (1) verb-path is the most news-worthy element of motion in all languages and (2) that there are general learner or bilingual effects such that the presence of another language, regardless of its typological properties, promotes a language-neutral event construal. Teasing apart specific cross-linguistic influences from general learner effects is a key task for future studies, that will also need to control for formal proficiency, fluency and actual knowledge of relevant lexical items. It is only when lexical forms are known, that gestures can contribute anything about the lexical representations over and beyond speech. If forms are unknown, gestures could be compensatory and driven by different mechanisms than linguistic conceptualization.

3.2.2. Shape and form

A second set of studies examines the form, shape and content of gestures to uncover (1) what information is packaged together, (2) how it is packaged and (3) whether lexical representations show evidence of adjustment. In a study of Turkish learners of English, only the most advanced proficiency group was able to express manner and path in one clause in L2 English in a typical satellite-framed way (*roll down*) (Özyürek, 2002). Although speech was thus target-like, learners nevertheless produced Turkish-like gestures expressing only manner or only path at least half of the time, rather than both manner and path in one gesture. Based on the gesture patterns, Özyürek argues that the linguistic conceptualization underlying (target-like) speech was Turkish, with a separate focus on path *or* on manner, rather than on both components together, a case of transfer of the L1 Turkish perspective to L2 English.

Similar arguments are made for the expression of ground elements. In a study of Dutch and Japanese, native Dutch speakers were found to introduce grounds with mention of the action in speech, they were also found to gesture mainly about the action (*the frog jumped out of a jar*) (Yoshioka & Kellerman, 2006). Native Japanese speakers introduced grounds in chains of existential clauses (*there was a jar and a frog*) with separate gestures for each ground mentioned (as discussed in section 2.1). Dutch learners of Japanese, moving from a satellite- to a verb-framed language, continued to introduce grounds with actions in L2 Japanese speech and gesture. Again, the pattern was interpreted as lingering L1 representations and transfer of perspective from the L1 to the L2. These two studies highlight that L1 influences are sometimes visible only in one modality (Turkish–English) and sometimes in both (Dutch–Japanese).

A further study probed the popular notion that transitions from a language making many distinctions in a given domain to a language making fewer distinctions in the same domain is straightforward (cf. Pavlenko, this volume). If lexical categories reflect linguistic conceptualization, all transitions – including those from two L1 categories into one L2 category – should require adjustments of representations. However, speech alone may not be informative about such adjustments because it is underspecified. Gestures may provide a fuller picture of the potential interaction. Dutch learners of French very quickly learn to use the placement verb *mettre* (put) accurately in L2 French speech. They seem to have no problems abandoning their two fine-grained L1 posture verbs *zetten* (set) and *leggen* (lay), which call for a focus on the displaced object in addition to the action of movement (Gullberg, submitted). That is, their spoken L2 forms suggest that they have a French-like lexical representation of the general category *mettre* (put). Interestingly, however, when they speak the L2, their gestures reveal Dutch-like, French-like and mixed patterns. That is, some learners continue to produce Dutch-like gestures with object-incorporating hand shapes while speaking French, whereas others produce path-only gestures in French style. The gesture patterns suggest that different learners operate with different representations of placement in the L2, some of which have shifted towards the L2 and some of which show both L1- and L2-like properties. These patterns also suggest that the reorganization of representations is a gradual process with intermediate stages where both L1 and L2 perspectives come into play. Importantly, this study provides evidence that adjustment towards an L2 category is within the realm of the possible because some learners do gesture in a French-like fashion.

3.2.3. Distribution of information across modalities

A third approach examines the distribution of meaning components across speech and gesture in L2. Recall that it has been suggested that speakers of verb- and satellite-framed languages have different means of modifying what information is foregrounded (McNeill, 2000b; McNeill & Duncan, 2000). Verb-framed languages like Spanish and Japanese can foreground manner in gestural manner fogs, that is, express manner in gesture when it is absent from speech. In contrast, English can background manner by expressing path in gesture when manner is present in speech. Two studies have shown that Spanish learners of English tend to produce manner fogs in L2, that is, to express manner in L2 gesture when it is absent from L2 speech (Negueruela *et al.*, 2004; Wieselman Schulman, 2004). Intriguingly, Neguerela *et al.* (2004) found English learners of Spanish doing the same. Although the speech and gesture production of these two groups of learners were similar on the surface, the authors explain the patterns by two different mechanisms for the respective groups.

In the Spanish learners' spoken L2 English, the absence of manner is assumed to reflect transfer from L1 to L2. Because manner of motion is not a core part of their native Spanish representation of motion, they are assumed to have difficulties learning and encoding it in L2 English. They therefore continue to rely on gesture to express manner as in L1. In contrast, the absence of manner in English learners' spoken L2 Spanish is in fact target-like, since Spanish typically does not lexicalize manner of motion. English speakers are accustomed to encoding manner in L1 speech. When English speakers find no readily available spoken lexical category for expressing manner, which is a component of their L1 lexical concept, in L2 Spanish, they instead rely on gesture as a compensatory strategy. These alternative explanations for an outcome that looks similar on the surface of both speech and gesture highlight the dilemma of determining what processes might underlie different types of transitions between lexical representations.

3.2.4. Bidirectional influence

So far the discussions have centered on L2 performance compared to that of native monolingual speakers of the target language, the traditional focus of SLA research. This is also why the discussion has focused on unidirectional transfer from the L1 to the L2 in the traditional sense. However, if languages interact in both directions within the same mind, as the bilingualism and processing literatures suggest (see also Jarvis, this volume; Pavlenko, this volume), then unidirectional effects of the L2 on the L1 or bidirectional effects should also be observable. Only a handful of studies have examined speech and gesture in the same speakers performing in both their languages to gauge such bidirectional influences or effects of the L2 on the L1.

A number of studies have focused on Spanish learners of English living in the USA (i.e. late learners immersed in the target culture who use both languages regularly) and their descriptions of motion events both in the L1 and L2. Two studies have found such speakers to behave the same in L1 Spanish and L2 English, aligning their path gestures with verbs just like monolingual Spanish speakers (Negueruela *et al.*, 2004; Stam, 2006a). Neguerela *et al.* (2004) found the same pattern in English learners of L2 Spanish who aligned path gestures with satellites or ground phrases in both languages. Based on the gesture patterns, these studies suggest that a conservative or L1-based representation, *L1 thinking for speaking*, guides both languages. Crucially, there was no evidence of an influence of the L2 on the L1.

Intriguingly, in another study, Spanish learners of English with the same learning and usage profiles, patterned like monolingual Spanish speakers in speech but showed an English-like pattern in gesture, expressing more path than manner (Wieselman Schulman, 2004). This study suggests a different pattern whereby speech is conservative but gestures show a shift to or an influence of a more L2-based representation. Unfortunately, the author offers no explanation for this result. These conflicting findings raise a number of methodological questions concerning the role of different analytical categories (timing versus information distribution across modalities), proficiency, language usage patterns, etc. Overall, however, these studies suggest that speakers immersed in the target culture may operate with lexical representations of the L1 in both languages, again indicating 'traditional' unidirectional transfer and little evidence of reorganization of lexical representations.

Another set of analyses targets Japanese speakers with only intermediate proficiency in L2 English performing in both their L1 and L2 (Brown, 2007). This study controls for immersion effects by comparing Japanese speakers who reside in Japan and in the USA and who are matched on English formal proficiency. Overall, these learners show evidence of bidirectional transfer. Although the Japanese speakers with knowledge of English do not talk more about manner in their L1 than do monolingual Japanese speakers, they are nevertheless significantly more likely to background manner than monolingual Japanese speakers (Brown & Gullberg, 2008). That is, they gesture more about path when manner is present in speech, which is an English-like pattern of manner modification. Crucially, they are also significantly less likely than monolingual English speakers to background manner in their L2 English. The learners are therefore more similar to themselves in L1 and L2 than to monolingual speakers of either language. Moreover, there is no difference between the groups residing in Japan versus the USA in speech or in gesture, suggesting that cultural immersion may play less of a role than linguistic conceptualization for these patterns.

These findings indicate that very modest contact with another language can influence lexical behavior and prompt bidirectional interactions in which the L1 affects the L2 and the L2 the L1. Non-monolinguals seem to construe motion events differently from monolinguals. Moreover, the study highlights that effects of bidirectional interaction are not necessarily a matter of language shift, loss or attrition following immersion in the L2 setting, or an effect of advanced bilingualism. They may be the normal result of processing lexical items of more than one language as the processing literature suggests. However, again, the conflicting findings from the Spanish–English and Japanese–English studies raise questions. Why do speakers living in the L2 community and using both languages regularly (i.e. functional bilinguals) show only L1 transfer whereas barely proficient foreign language learners in Japan show evidence of bidirectional transfer and effects of the L2 on the L1? Replication studies are badly needed, as are further methodological refinements in the study of cross-linguistic influence on lexical representations and on gestures.

4. Issues and Future Directions

The analysis of gestures raises some important theoretical and methodological questions regarding the relationship between surface forms, lexical representations and the role of gestures as mediating between them. In monolingual contexts, gestures are assumed to tap into semantic-conceptual representations and to reflect the ways in which semantic components map onto morphosyntax at the surface. Overall, gestures provide a fuller picture of lexical representations, of what information is taken into account for speaking than can be gleaned from speech alone. Logically, then, a change in representations should lead to changes both in speech and in gesture. Yet, as seen above, data from L2 learners and bilingual speakers frequently display a dissociation between surface form and gesture. L2 learners are repeatedly found to continue to align their gestures with spoken elements in the L2 in a way that reflects L1 rather than L2 perspectives, such as Spanish learners gesturing with verbs rather than with satellites when talking about motion in L2 English. Similarly, learners express meaning in gesture, reflecting an L1 representation even as they express other meaning in L2 speech. In other words, they gesture one thing and say another.

Even more noteworthy, in most studies gesture is more conservative than speech, i.e. speech is more likely to be target-like than gesture production. Throughout the studies, these patterns are interpreted as indicating transfer of L1 representations, perspectives or *thinking for speaking*. It raises the question of what representations actually under-pin and generate L2 surface forms, especially when these look target-like. This is all the more striking because the focus here is not typically on single lexical items, but rather on more complex constructions. And how dissociated can speech and gestures be and still be said to reflect lexical representations? Put yet another way, is speech or gesture considered to be more directly linked to lexical representations in the triangulation of multimodal data, and if so, how and on what grounds? Answers to such questions are equally crucial to theories of gesture production – which are still based only on monolingual speakers – and to theories concerning the bilingual lexicon when considered multimodally.

These concerns notwithstanding, gestures open many new avenues of inquiry and there is enormous potential for expanding the scope of studies in this domain. Almost everything remains to be done. We need to examine more languages, different data and gesture types. We must expand beyond the domain of motion, in particular because the interaction between semantic-conceptual representations and morpho-syntax may take different forms in other domains. We must consider the possible effects of discourse types (cf. Lucy, 1996), sociocultural and educational backgrounds (cf. Pederson, 1995), and other cultural practices on linguistic conceptualizations. Different developmental trajectories and routes (e.g. simultaneous versus consecutive bilingualism) need to be examined. Multilingual speakers should also be considered. Currently, gesture studies have only examined cases of two coexisting languages, although in reality many participants have probably been multilingual. What happens in speech and gesture when a third, fourth and fifth language enters into the equation, and what role does typological distance play? These are all traditional questions in the language acquisition and bilingualism literatures, but gesture data may reveal new details about these issues.

Finally, methodological rigor and replication are imperative to these endeavors. Background factors like proficiency, language usage patterns, etc., need to be controlled, as is standard practice in other areas of research with bi- and multilinguals. Two issues in particular are crucial. First, studies of cross-linguistic influence need to distinguish transfer from more general learner- or bilingualism effects. To do so, it is necessary to examine speakers of at least two source languages learning the same target language (cf. Jarvis, 2000). Such precautions should refine our understanding of what is truly cross-linguistic influence in the lexicon, and what is not. This is all the more important where gestures are concerned since so little is known about cross-linguistic and cross-cultural influences, as opposed to more general ways of encoding information in gesture.

Second, gesture production is driven by a host of factors, and linguistic conceptualization is only one of them. Any study hoping to reveal something about linguistic conceptualization must take steps to control for and distinguish gestures that hold the floor, for instance, or gestures deliberately performed for the addressee whose form and timing may have been modified to achieve a particular interactional goal (cf. Kendon, 2004). Although such gestures may very well still reflect language-specific conceptualization, it is important to realize that they may not. It is largely unknown at this point how language-specific aspects of gesture production may be influenced by such phenomena. This is yet another domain for future research.

A minor but related point is that gesture coding should ideally be based on structural criteria (with sound turned off), not on semiotic or meaning-related ones, to avoid circularity when gesture information is compared to speech information. Standard practices, such as providing inter-rater reliability measures, are vital. Other methodological issues to consider include sample size and, more interestingly, units of analysis. Some of the conflicts in the findings reviewed above may stem from small sample sizes and from the different units of analysis used (e.g. timing of gesture, gestural form, distribution of information across modalities).

Conclusions

This chapter aimed to demonstrate what gestures can reveal about the core issues for the study of the bilingual mental lexicon. Hopefully, it is by now clear that gestures have something to contribute to the study of lexical representations, their acquisition and development and the way in which they interact in the bilingual lexicon. Gestures reflect lexical representations at the levels of form and meaning over and above the level of speech and thus provide information about the processes of constructing new representations in an L2 or Ln from different starting points. They may also affect lexical learning. Finally, they unveil more details about cross-linguistic interactions and the nature of coexisting representations as they are deployed online in actual language use. In short, gestures provide a fuller picture of the bilingual mental lexicon than speech alone. That said, and returning to the caveats in the introduction, it is important to remember that they are also multi-functional interactive phenomena influenced by individual, situational and cultural factors. Many things are still unknown about how these factors influence the phenomena outlined in this chapter. A definite answer to the question of why gestures are relevant to the bilingual lexicon may therefore seem premature in view of how little we know and how much remains to be uncovered. Yet, the existing evidence suggests that gestures should have a natural place in discussions of the bilingual lexicon, acquisition and bilingual language use.

Acknowledgements

I gratefully acknowledge the financial support of the *Nederlandse Organisatie voor Wetenschappelijk Onderzoek*, grant *MPI 56-384*, *The Dynamics of Multilingual Processing*, awarded to M. Gullberg, P. Indefrey and W. Klein. I also thank the editor and two anonymous reviewers for helpful comments on a previous version of this chapter. All remaining nonsense is my own.

Note

1. The contribution of gestures to (improved) speech comprehension is widely documented (e.g. Riseborough, 1981; Sueyoshi & Hardison, 2005). Although separate from effects on acquisition, the comprehension and acquisition effects obviously correlate in real life, and are probably cumulative. This is true even outside the lexical domain, as seen in a study showing that Spanish-speaking children in an English-speaking school learned more mathematics when English explanations were accompanied by gestures than when they were not (Church *et al.*, 2004).

References

Allen, L. (1995) The effect of emblematic gestures on the development and access of mental representations of French expressions. *Modern Language Journal* 79 (4), 521–529.

Ameel, E., Storms, G., Malt, B. and Sloman, S. (2005) How bilinguals solve the naming problem. *Journal of Memory and Language* 52 (3), 309–329.

Athanasopoulos, P. (2006) Effects of the grammatical representation of number on cognition in bilinguals. *Bilingualism: Language and Cognition* 9 (1), 89–96.

Bavelas, J., Chovil, N., Lawrie, D. and Wade, A. (1992) Interactive gestures. *Discourse Processes* 15 (4), 469–489.

Beattie, G. and Shovelton, H. (1999) Mapping the range of information contained in the iconic hand gestures that accompany spontaneous speech. *Journal of Language and Social Psychology* 18 (4), 438–462.

Beattie, G. and Shovelton, H. (2002) An experimental investigation of some properties of individual iconic gestures that mediate their communicative power. *British Journal of Psychology* 93 (2), 179–192.

Berman, R. and Slobin, D. (1994) Filtering and packaging in narrative. In R. Berman and D.I. Slobin (eds) *Relating Events in Narrative: A Crosslinguistic Developmental Study* (pp. 515–554). Hillsdale, NJ: Lawrence Erlbaum.

Brown, A. (2007) Crosslinguistic influence in first and second languages: Convergence in speech and gesture. Unpublished PhD dissertation, Boston University/Max Planck Institute for Psycholinguistics.

Brown, A. and Gullberg, M. (2008) Bidirectional crosslinguistic influence in L1–L2 encoding of manner in speech and gesture: A study of Japanese speakers of English. *Studies in Second Language Acquisition* 30 (2) 225–251.

Cassell, J., McNeill, D. and McCullough, K.E. (1999) Speech-gesture mismatches: Evidence for one underlying representation of linguistic and nonlinguistic information. *Pragmatics & Cognition* 7 (1) 1–33.

Church, R., Ayman-Nolley, S. and Mahootian, S. (2004) The role of gesture in bilingual education: Does gesture enhance learning? *International Journal of Bilingual Education and Bilingualism* 7 (4), 303–319.

Cook, V. (2003) Introduction: The changing L1 in the L2 user's mind. In V. Cook (ed.) *Effects of the Second Language on the First* (pp. 1–18). Clevedon: Multilingual Matters.

Cook, V., Bassetti, B., Kasai, C., Sasaki, M. and Takahashi, J. (2006) Do bilinguals have different concepts? The case of shape and material in Japanese L2 users of English. *International Journal of Bilingualism* 10 (2), 137–152.

Costa, A. (2005) Lexical access in bilingual production. In J. Kroll and A.M.B. De Groot (eds) *Handbook of Bilingualism. Psycholinguistic Approaches* (pp. 308–325). Oxford: Oxford University Press.

De Ruiter, J.P. (2000) The production of gesture and speech. In D. McNeill (ed.) *Language and Gesture: Window into Thought and Action* (pp. 284–311). Cambridge: Cambridge University Press.

De Ruiter, J.P. (2007) Postcards from the mind: The relationship between speech, gesture and thought. *Gesture* 7 (1), 21–38.

Duncan, S. (1996) Grammatical form and 'thinking-for-speaking' in Mandarin Chinese and English: An analysis based on speech-accompanying gesture. Unpublished doctoral dissertation, University of Chicago.

Duncan, S. (2005) Co-expressivity of speech and gesture: Manner of motion in Spanish, English, and Chinese. In C. Chang, M.J. Houser, Y. Kim, D. Mortensen, M. Park-Doob and M. Toosarvandani (eds) *Proceedings of the 27th Annual Meeting of the Berkeley Linguistic Society, 2001* (Vol. General Session, pp. 353–370). Berkeley, CA: Berkeley Linguistic Society.

Ekman, P. and Friesen, W. (1969) The repertoire of nonverbal behavior: Categories, origins, usage, and coding. *Semiotica* 1 (1) 49–98.

Engelkamp, J. and Cohen, R. (1991) Current issues in memory of action events. *Psychological Research* 53, 175–182.

Feyereisen, P. and de Lannoy, J. (1991) *Gestures and Speech: Psychological Investigations*. Cambridge: Cambridge University Press.

Francis, W. (2005) Bilingual semantic and conceptual representation. In J. Kroll and A.M.B. De Groot (eds) *Handbook of Bilingualism. Psycholinguistic Approaches* (pp. 251–267). Oxford: Oxford University Press.

Goodwin, M. and Goodwin, C. (1986) Gesture and coparticipation in the activity of searching for a word. *Semiotica* 62 (1/2), 51–75.

Graham, R. and Belnap, K. (1986) The acquisition of lexical boundaries in English by native speakers of Spanish. *International Review of Applied Linguistics* 24 (4), 275–286.

Graham, J. and Argyle, M. (1975) A cross-cultural study of the communication of extra-verbal meaning by gestures. *International Journal of Psychology* 10 (1), 56–67.

Gullberg, M. (1998) *Gesture as a Communication Strategy in Second Language Discourse. A Study of Learners of French and Swedish*. Lund: Lund University Press.

Gullberg, M. (2003) Gestures, referents, and anaphoric linkage in learner varieties. In C. Dimroth and M. Starren (eds) *Information Structure and the Dynamics of Language Acquisition* (pp. 311–328). Amsterdam: John Benjamins.

Gullberg, M. (2006a) Handling discourse: Gestures, reference tracking, and communication strategies in early L2. *Language Learning* 56 (1), 155–196.

Gullberg, M. (2006b) Some reasons for studying gesture and second language acquisition (Hommage à Adam Kendon). *International Review of Applied Linguistics* 44 (2), 103–124.

Gullberg, M. (2008) Gestures and second language acquisition. In P. Robinson and N. Ellis (eds) *Handbook of Cognitive Linguistics and Second Language Acquisition* (pp. 276–305). London: Routledge.

Gullberg, M. (in press-a) Language-specific encoding of placement events in gestures. In E. Pederson and J. Bohnemeyer (eds) *Event Representations in Language and Cognition*. Cambridge: Cambridge University Press.

Gullberg, M. (in press-b) Multilingual multimodality: Communicative difficulties and their solutions in second language use. In C. Goodwin, J. Streeck and C. LeBaron (eds) *Multimodality and Human Activity: Research on Human Behavior, Action, and Communication*. Cambridge: Cambridge University Press.

Gullberg, M. (submitted) What learners mean. What gestures reveal about semantic reorganisation of placement verbs in advanced L2.

Gullberg, M., Hendriks, H. and Hickmann, M. (2008) Learning to talk and gesture about motion in French. *First Language* 28 (2), 200–236.

Gumperz, J. and Levinson, S. (1996) Introduction: Linguistic relativity re-examined. In J. Gumperz and S. Levinson (eds) *Rethinking Linguistic Relativity* (pp. 1–18). Cambridge: Cambridge University Press.

Holler, J. and Beattie, G. (2003) Pragmatic aspects of representational gestures. Do speakers use them to clarify verbal ambiguity for the listener? *Gesture* 3 (2), 127–154.

Hostetter, A. and Alibali, M. (2004) On the tip of the mind: Gesture as a key to conceptualization. In K. Forbus, D. Gentner and T. Regier (eds) *The 26th Annual Conference of the Cognitive Science Society* (pp. 589–594). Chicago, IL: Cognitive Science Society.

Jarvis, S. (2000) Methodological rigor in the study of transfer: Identifying L1 influence in the interlanguage lexicon. *Language Learning* 50 (2), 245–309.

Kellerman, E. and Van Hoof, A.M. (2003) Manual accents. *International Review of Applied Linguistics* 41 (3), 251–269.

Kelly, S., Barr, D., Breckinridge Church, R. and Lynch, K. (1999) Offering a hand to pragmatic understanding: The role of speech and gesture in comprehension and memory. *Journal of Memory and Language* 40 (4), 577–592.

Kendon, A. (1978) Differential perception and attentional frame: Two problems for investigation. *Semiotica* 24 (3/4), 305–315.

Kendon, A. (1980) Gesticulation and speech: Two aspects of the process of utterance. In M. Key (ed.) *The Relationship of Verbal and Nonverbal Communication* (pp. 207–227). The Hague: Mouton.

Kendon, A. (1983) Gesture and speech. How they interact. In J. Wiemann and R. Harrison (eds) *Nonverbal Interaction* (pp. 13–45). Beverly Hills, CA: Sage.

Kendon, A. (2004) *Gesture. Visible Action as Utterance*. Cambridge: Cambridge University Press.

Kita, S. and Özyürek, A. (2003) What does crosslinguistic variation in semantic coordination of speech and gesture reveal?: Evidence for an interface representation of spatial thinking and speaking. *Journal of Memory and Language* 48 (1), 16–32.

Kroll, J. and Sunderman, G. (2003) Cognitive processes in second language learners and bilinguals: The development of lexical and conceptual represen-tations. In C. Doughty and M. Long (eds) *The Handbook of Second Language Acquisition* (pp. 104–129). Oxford: Blackwell.

La Heij, W. (2005) Selection processes in monolingual and bilingual lexical access. In J. Kroll and A.M.B. De Groot (eds) *Handbook of Bilingualism. Psycholinguistic Approaches* (pp. 289–307). Oxford: Oxford University Press.

Levelt, W. (1989) *Speaking: From Intention to Articulation*. Cambridge, MA: Bradford Books/MIT Press.

Levelt, W., Roelofs, A. and Meyer, A. (1999) A theory of lexical access in speech production. *Behavioral and Brain Sciences* 22 (1), 1–37.

Levy, E. and McNeill, D. (1992) Speech, gesture, and discourse. *Discourse Processes* 15 (3), 277–301.

Lucy, J. (1992) *Language Diversity and Thought: A Reformulation of the Linguistic Relativity Hypothesis.* Cambridge: Cambridge University Press.

Lucy, J. (1996) The scope of linguistic relativity: An analysis and review of empirical research. In J. Gumperz and S. Levinson (eds) *Rethinking Linguistic Relativity* (pp. 37–69). Cambridge: Cambridge University Press.

McCafferty, S. (2006) Gesture and the materialization of second language prosody. *International Review of Applied Linguistics* 44 (2), 195–207.

McNeill, D. (1992) *Hand and Mind. What the Hands Reveal about Thought.* Chicago, IL: University of Chicago Press.

McNeill, D. (ed.) (2000a) *Language and Gesture.* Cambridge: Cambridge University Press.

McNeill, D. (2000b) Imagery in motion event descriptions: Gestures as part of thinking-for-speaking in three languages. In M. Juge and J. Moxley (eds) *Proceedings of the 23rd Annual Meeting of the Berkeley Linguistics Society 1997* (Vol. General session) (pp. 255–267). Berkeley, CA: Berkeley Linguistic Society.

McNeill, D. (2005) *Gesture and Thought.* Chicago, IL: University of Chicago Press.

McNeill, D. and Duncan, S.D. (2000) Growth points in thinking-for-speaking. In D. McNeill (ed.) *Language and Gesture* (pp. 141–161). Cambridge: Cambridge University Press.

McNeill, D. and Levy, E. (1993) Cohesion and gesture. *Discourse Processes* 16 (4), 363–386.

Melinger, A. and Levelt, W. (2004) Gesture and the communicative intention of the speaker. *Gesture* 4 (2), 119–141.

Mori, J. and Hayashi, M. (2006) The achievement of intersubjectivity through embodied completions: A study of interactions between first and second language speakers. *Applied Linguistics* 27 (2), 195–219.

Negueruela, E., Lantolf, J., Rehn Jordan, S. and Gelabert, J. (2004) The "private function" of gesture in second language speaking activity: A study of motion verbs and gesturing in English and Spanish. *International Journal of Applied Linguistics*, 14 (1), 113–147.

Odlin, T. (2003) Crosslinguistic influence. In C. Doughty and M. Long (eds) *The Handbook of Second Language Acquisition* (pp. 436–486). Oxford: Blackwell.

Odlin, T. (2005) Crosslinguistic influence and conceptual transfer: What are the concepts? *Annual Review of Applied Linguistics* 25, 3–25.

Özyürek, A. (2002) Speech-language relationship across languages and in second language learners: Implications for spatial thinking and speaking. In B. Skarabela (ed.) *BUCLD Proceedings* (Vol. 26; pp. 500–509). Somerville, MA: Cascadilla Press.

Özyürek, A., Willems, R., Kita, S. and Hagoort, P. (2007) On-line integration of semantic information from speech and gesture: Insights from event-related brain potentials. *Journal of Cognitive Neuroscience* 19, 605–616.

Pavlenko, A. (1999) New approaches to concepts in bilingual memory. *Bilingualism: Language and Cognition* 2 (3), 209–230.

Payrató, L. (1993) A pragmatic view on autonomous gestures: A first repertoire of Catalan emblems. *Journal of Pragmatics* 20 (3), 193–216.

Pederson, E. (1995) Language as context, language as means: Spatial cognition and habitual language use. *Cognitive Linguistics* 6 (1), 33–62.

Poyatos, F. (2002) *Nonverbal Communication Across Disciplines*. Amsterdam: John Benjamins.

Riseborough, M. (1981) Physiographic gestures as decoding facilitators: Three experiments exploring a neglected facet of communication. *Journal of Nonverbal Behavior* 5 (3), 172–183.

Rizzolatti, G. and Craighero, L. (2004) The mirror-neuron system. *Annual Review of Neuroscience* 27 (1), 169–192.

Schegloff, E.A. (1984) On some gestures' relation to talk. In J. Atkinson and J. Heritage (eds) *Structures of Social Action* (pp. 266–296). Cambridge: Cambridge University Press.

Seyfeddinipur, M. (2006) Disfluency: Interrupting speech and gesture. Unpublished doctoral dissertation, Radboud University.

Sherman, J. and Nicoladis, E. (2004) Gestures by advanced Spanish-English second-language learners. *Gesture* 4 (2), 143–156.

Slobin, D. (1996) From 'thought and language' to 'thinking for speaking'. In J. Gumperz and S. Levinson (eds) *Rethinking Linguistic Relativity* (pp. 70–96). Cambridge: Cambridge University Press.

Slobin, D. (2004) How people move. Discourse effects of linguistic typology. In C. Moder and A. Martinovic-Zic (eds) *Discourse Across Languages and Cultures* (pp. 195–210). Amsterdam: John Benjamins.

Stam, G. (2006a) Changes in patterns of thinking for speaking with second language acquisition. Unpublished doctoral dissertation, University of Chicago.

Stam, G. (2006b) Thinking for speaking about motion: L1 and L2 speech and gesture. *International Review of Applied Linguistics* 44 (2), 143–169.

Stockwell, R., Brown, J. and Martin, J. (1965) *The Grammatical Structures of English and Spanish*. Chicago, IL: Chicago University Press.

Sueyoshi, A. and Hardison, D. (2005) The role of gestures and facial cues in second language listening comprehension. *Language Learning* 55 (4), 661–699.

Talmy, L. (1985) Lexicalization patterns: Semantic structure in lexical forms. In T. Shopen (ed.) *Language Typology and Syntactic Description* (Vol. 3; pp. 57–149). Cambridge: Cambridge University Press.

Talmy, L. (2000) *Toward a Cognitive Semantics*. Cambridge, MA: MIT Press.

Tellier, M. (2006) L'impact du geste pédagogique sur l'enseignement/apprentissage des langues étrangères: Etude sur des enfants de 5 ans. Unpublished doctoral dissertation, Université Paris VII – Denis Diderot.

Von Stutterheim, C. and Nüse, R. (2003) Processes of conceptualisation in language production: Language-specific perspectives and event construal. *Linguistics* 41 (5), 851–881.

Wieselman Schulman, B. (2004) A crosslinguistic investigation of the speech-gesture relationship in motion event descriptions. Unpublished doctoral dissertation, University of Chicago.

Wu, Y.C. and Coulson, S. (2005) Meaningful gestures: Electrophysiological indices of iconic gesture comprehension. *Psychophysiology* 42 (6), 654–667.

Yoshioka, K. and Kellerman, E. (2006) Gestural introduction of Ground reference in L2 narrative discourse. *International Review of Applied Linguistics* 44 (2), 171–193.

Yule, G. (1997) *Referential Communication Tasks*. Hillsdale, NJ: Lawrence Erlbaum.

Chapter 8

The Tip-of-the-Tongue Phenomenon as a Window on (Bilingual) Lexical Retrieval

PETER ECKE

Introduction: When a Word is on the Tip of the Tongue

"Me puedes pasar la...? [Can you pass me the...?] Espera, no me digas, está cerca... [Wait, don't tell me! It's close...] -*A* -*O?* There is an *A* in it. -*Pañuelo?* [tissue] *K? -Cobija?* [blanket] No... I know it's *Kissen* in German, *pillow* in English... -*Cubierta?* [cover] Hm... -*Pillow*... Gosh, what is it?..."
-*A*... It's *almohada*! [pillow] -What a relief.[1]

The temporary (and often frustrating) retrieval failure exemplified above is commonly known as the tip-of-the-tongue (TOT) phenomenon. The speaker is certain that he knows a momentarily unavailable word (the target), feels close to recalling it and frequently has access to partial target attributes and/or related words (associates) during word search. The phenomenon is, of course, not limited to bi- or multilingual speakers as in the example shown above, but there is some evidence that bilinguals experience more TOTs than monolinguals (to be discussed below). The phenomenon has been investigated empirically for some time, at least since Wenzl's (1932, 1936) collection of naturally occurring TOTs, and Brown and McNeill's (1966) seminal laboratory study that elicited and analyzed TOTs in American college students.

Researchers have investigated TOTs in the hope that this very peculiar kind of slowed down and interrupted word retrieval may reveal some insight into the architecture and constraints of the speech processor that normally operates at speeds that render observation almost impossible. In a TOT, semantic and syntactic information of the desired word has been specified, but phonological encoding fails or is realized only in part. This characteristic of the TOT phenomenon has generally been taken as evidence for a two-stage encoding process with dissociated processing levels that are organized according to different principles (cf. Garrett, 1993). However, the flow of activation from stage to stage has been of much debate in the literature on speech production. Proposals have been made for discrete top-down, cascaded and interactive processing in lexical production. As will be seen, some of the discussion in TOT research concerns the very issues of modularity versus interactivity of processing units as well as activation versus competition/inhibition that are central in the debate about lexical selection and its control in bilingual speech production (cf. Costa & Santesteban, 2006). There has been relatively little research to date on TOTs in bilinguals. Therefore, selected studies on TOTs in monolinguals will be included in the review, where research questions, methodology and findings could be of interest to bilingualism researchers, and hopefully of use in further developing and testing hypotheses about lexical production in speakers of more than one language.

1. Research Questions

What are some of the questions that psycholinguists and psychologists have asked about the TOT phenomenon? We will only review questions in this section, but will return to some of the more relevant issues with respect to bilingual speech production in the section on research findings. Researchers have been interested in the cause(s) of TOTs as well as the ways in which they are resolved. Two main hypotheses have been proposed: the *blocking hypothesis* and the *incomplete activation hypothesis* (cf. Brown, 1991). According to the first view, TOTs occur as a consequence of interfering (usually more frequently or recently used) competitors that are activated prior to the target and subsequently block/inhibit its retrieval (e.g. Jones, 1989; Jones & Langford, 1987). The alternative view is that the target is activated incompletely, and associates are merely a consequence of incomplete target retrieval (e.g. Brown & McNeill, 1966; Meyer & Bock, 1992). Probably the most popular version of the incomplete activation hypothesis is the *transmission deficit hypothesis* proposed by Burke and associates (1991). Under this view, the target word's meaning and syntactic attributes have been specified, but the activation of the target's phonology fails due to weakened connections between the nodes of the two representational levels. According to the authors, meaning-form connections become weak with infrequent or nonrecent target word use and aging. Other research questions that are more or less related to the primary issues of TOT causation and resolution are the following:

The study of TOTs across languages: what are some universal character-istics of TOTs? Are TOT retrieval output patterns in languages other than English comparable to those documented for English words? Providing positive answers to these questions would allow for potential general-izations about the functioning of the human speech processor.

Different speakers' susceptibility to TOTs: are certain groups of speakers more prone to TOTs than others? For example, are older adults and bilinguals, including foreign/second language (L2) learners, more likely to experience TOTs than younger adults and monolinguals, and if so, why? Do TOT search patterns and resolution types differ between these groups, and if so, do they suggest differences in lexical representation and processing between these groups?

TOT target word types: what kinds of words are particularly prone or relatively resistant to temporary retrieval failure and why? Researchers have investigated the impact of frequency of word use, unfamiliar or unusual word forms and the number of phonological and semantic neighbors as potential factors that may affect target retrieval. They have also studied whether certain word types, such as proper names, or words with direct translation equivalents, including cognates in bilingual speakers, may be more or less susceptible to TOTs. What do these differences suggest about peculiarities in the processing of certain word types, and possible advantages or disadvantages that certain speaker types may display to retrieve these words?

Retrieval patterns: what are the retrieval patterns in speakers' TOTs, as reflected by partial target information and interim word associates? What can be inferred from these output patterns with respect to the representational levels involved in lexical production, their interaction or dissociation, and potential principles of their organization? Are these patterns in any way informative with respect to the time course of lexical production and or morphological composition processes?

Effects on TOT resolution: how do speakers retrieve the words that are on the tip of the tongue? To what extent are they recalled through conscious search attempts, spontaneous pop-ups, reference use or environmental cues? Do certain kinds of associates and experimenter-presented cues or primes, e.g. partial target information and phonolo-gically or semantically related words, including those from the non-target language in bilinguals, affect target recall? Are certain states of mind, including stress, tiredness, abrupt changes in topic or switches in language in bilinguals conducive to TOT causation?

TOTs in bilinguals: are there any observable differences in search patterns for TOTs with L1 words versus L2 words or words of a dominant and non-dominant language in bilingual speakers? To what degree do TOT word searches involve intralingual and interlingual (cross-linguistic) associations in bilingual speakers? Could such findings be informative with respect to the structure and control mechanisms of the bilingual lexicon?

Tentative answers to some of these questions will be reviewed in the section on research findings. Before this, however, it is necessary to describe the research methods that have been used to investigate the TOT phenomenon in monolingual and bilingual speakers.

2. Methods of Data Collection and Analysis

TOTs have been investigated through retrospective questionnaires, cognitive diaries and laboratory studies. In *retrospective questionnaires*, participants are asked about their individual experiences with TOTs. They are usually asked to estimate how often they experience TOTs per week or month, what they think they normally know about the words that are on the tip of the tongue, and how they search for or recall the targets (e.g. Burke *et al.*, 1991; Cohen & Faulkner, 1986). Retrospection may help to obtain an initial picture of speakers' perceptions and subjective theories about TOTs, their approximate frequency of occurrence and typical resolution types. However, it will tell us little about online language processing.

In *cognitive diary studies*, participants are asked to keep a diary for a longer period of time, usually four weeks. They are instructed to record TOT experiences at the time they occur, very much like think-aloud protocols (cf. Cohen, 1996). Participants normally take note of fragmentary information about the target word (e.g. any letters, sounds or grammatical attributes of the target, related words that come to mind during TOT word search), and how the TOT is resolved, e.g. through conscious search, environmental cues, reference use or as spontaneous pop-up. Diary studies also have their limitations. Reason and Lucas (1984: 55–56) mention three kinds of bias inherent in diary studies that may affect participants' reports of TOTs and the researcher's inferences about the phenomenon, its frequency, attributes and resolution:

(1) *volunteer bias*: individuals who participate in TOT studies may do so because they think that they are particularly prone to this kind of memory failure;

(2) *selection bias*: usually only the more noteworthy, amusing or memorable slips are likely to be recorded in the diary;

(3) *recording bias*: not all information available to the subject in a TOT is
     recorded, and the reported information may be affected by the
     participants' subjective theories about the recall failure.

Some of these problems may be circumvented by providing participants with explicit instructions and structured diary sheets with
questions to obtain detailed information about the TOT. An advantage
of diary studies is that they usually generate quite comprehensive
records of TOT experiences compared to the more controlled but often
limited laboratory studies, which will be described next.

Laboratory studies have the advantage that they can generate TOTs in
a relatively short time in a large number of participants and under
relatively controlled conditions, i.e. via similar stimuli for the same
potential targets. Through careful selection of stimulus types and target
words, laboratory studies can focus on particular aspects of TOT word
search, e.g. the question whether speakers in a TOT have access to
syntactic properties of the target, such as grammatical gender (e.g.
Vigliocco *et al.*, 1997). Brown and McNeill (1966), who introduced the
TOT elicitation method, presented the participants with definitions of
low-frequency words (such as '*A navigational instrument used in measuring
angular distances, especially the altitude of sun, moon, and stars at sea*') and
asked participants to recall the corresponding word form (*sextant*). Three
response types are possible in such a study: the participants may (1)
immediately recall the target that fits the definition, (2) report that they
do not know the word or (3) indicate that they experience a TOT. In the
last case, participants are asked to rate how well they know the target,
record partial attributes, e.g. the initial letter and number of syllables of
the target, and/or record other words that come to mind during the TOT.
The interim products of recall are analyzed by the researcher with respect
to their similarity to the target.

In a TOT elicitation study with Hebrew–English bilinguals, Gollan
and Silverberg (2001) presented participants with word definitions in
either their L1 or L2, but asked them to recall the corresponding targets
in both the L1 and L2 and report TOTs when they occurred in either
Hebrew or English. In most TOT studies, participants are asked to write
down their retrieval products. Kohn and associates (1987) argued,
however, that transforming recall products into the written mode is
unnatural and may alter TOT search. Therefore, they elicited word recall
and TOTs through spoken definitions and asked participants to
verbalize what would come to mind during the TOT. The participants
were tested individually and their think-aloud protocols were recorded

and subsequently analyzed. Most TOT studies follow Brown and McNeill's (1966) paradigm using definition stimuli to elicit TOTs, but some researchers use alternative stimuli to generate TOTs. These will be described next.

Instead of definitions, several studies used *pictures* as stimuli for word recall (e.g. Maylor, 1990; Yarmey, 1973). Use of pictures is normally limited to recall tasks for concrete words or personal names. Abstract word recall would be difficult to induce through pictures. In an attempt not only to control the targets of TOT search, but also variation in participants' word knowledge and frequency of target word use, Smith *et al.* (1991) introduced a learning-recall paradigm for TOT generation in which participants were first taught a set of imaginary animals (called TOTimals) through paired association of TOTimal pictures and the corresponding names. In a later recall session, they were given only the pictures of the TOTimals, were asked to recall the corresponding words, and report TOTs and target attributes if they occurred. TOTimals reportedly generated very high rates of TOTs in this learning-recall task. It has to be acknowledged though that the retrieval failures generated in the TOTimal studies might be somewhat different from genuine TOTs in that they, at least in part, are a reflection of a learning/knowledge problem and not only an access/retrieval issue.

One study with proficient bilinguals (Ecke, 2004b) and one study with beginning L3 learners (Ecke, 2001) used *translation equivalents* as stimuli for TOT elicitation. In both studies, translation stimuli produced TOT rates comparable to definition stimuli. Ecke (2004a) suggested that translation equivalents are well-suited for TOT studies with bilinguals. They are often less ambiguous than definition stimuli, which frequently also elicit searches for words that are not intended by the experimenter (so-called negative TOTs, which have to be eliminated from the data analysis).

A number of laboratory studies investigated potential effects of target word fragments (e.g. Abrams *et al.*, 2003; Brown & Knight, 1990) and related words (e.g. Brennen *et al.*, 1990; Jones & Langford, 1987) on TOT resolution. In such studies, participants receive definition stimuli to elicit word recall attempts and TOTs; and either immediately after the definition or when speakers indicate that they experience a TOT for a definition, they are presented either with a phonologically related word, a semantically related word, an unrelated word or a target word fragment. The researchers then analyze whether the presentation of such *primes* or *cues* has a positive or negative effect on target recall. One study with bilingual participants presented speakers (immediately after the definitions) with primes of either form-related words, meaning-related words or non-related words both from within the target's language and from the non-target language (Askari, 1999) in an attempt to examine the effect of various intralingual and interlingual primes on target recall (to be discussed below).

Most of what is known today about TOTs is certainly the result of carefully controlled laboratory studies. However, laboratory studies are somewhat artificial with respect to target word selection and stimulus presentation and may be biased toward a certain group of participants. Another problem lies in the limited response time available to partici-pants, especially for those who are tested in a group setting and not individually. Their word search is frequently terminated by the experi-menter before the target is recalled, often after only a minute or two. Consequently, the preliminary recall data will only reflect a small fraction of a TOT experience that under natural conditions may be quite dynamic and could last minutes, hours or even days (Reason & Lucas, 1984). Harley and Brown (1998: 166) pointed out that the frequently reported high rates of TOTs in laboratory studies may represent an overestimation of TOT frequency, whereas TOT rates in diaries are probably an under-representation of naturally occurring TOT rates. They suspect that some of the TOTs reported in the laboratory may rather be instances of feeling of knowing (FOK) than genuine TOTs in which recall is imminent (cf. also Priller & Mittenecker, 1988, for a discussion of FOK versus TOT, and Schwartz *et al.*, 2000 on strong and weak TOTs).

A problem for both diary and experimental studies is the so-called 'fragmentary data problem' (Brown & McNeill, 1966): participants provide different amounts of TOT data, and stimuli elicit different numbers of TOTs for different targets which causes problems for statistical analysis. Brown and McNeill (1966) suggested dealing with the issue by reporting data fully and analyzing them in more than one way. Ideally, diary studies and laboratory studies should be combined to investigate TOTs.

3. Research Findings

A comprehensive review of research findings from TOT studies is beyond the scope of this chapter and the objectives of this book. Interested readers are referred to Brown (1991) and Schwartz (1999, 2002) for excellent reviews of the broad spectrum of TOT research across disciplines. The present discussion will be limited to findings from mostly psycholinguistic studies of TOTs in monolinguals with potential relevance for bilingual production, studies that particularly investigated word retrieval failure in bilinguals, and studies that compared TOTs in bilingual and monolingual speakers and TOTs with targets from dominant and non-dominant languages.

3.1. The cross-linguistic study of TOTs

Most TOT research has been done with English native speakers, although the phenomenon is certainly universal (Brown, 1991). Schwartz (1999) reported that many cultures use a metaphor similar to 'being on the tip of the tongue' for the TOT phenomenon. Researchers have investigated aspects of TOTs in German, Italian, Japanese, Polish, Russian and Spanish (cf. Schwartz, 2002) and the related tip-of-the-finger (TOF) phenomenon in American Sign Language (Thompson *et al.*, 2005). Retrieval patterns appear to be largely similar. TOTs across languages coincide, for example, in speakers' frequent access to a TOT word's first letter/sound (cf. Brown, 1991), but there are also possible areas of difference, e.g. with respect to the importance of syllabic structure in phonological encoding and the availability of morpho-syntactic attributes, such as grammatical gender, in noun targets of various languages (Gollan & Silverberg, 2001).

3.2. Different speakers' susceptibility to TOTs

Diary as well as laboratory studies have shown that TOT occurrence increases steadily with age and is particularly high in old age (Brown & Nix, 1996; Burke *et al.*, 1991; Heine *et al.*, 1999; Lovelace, 1991). Burke and associates (1991) explain the age-related increase as a weakening of form-meaning connections due to the reduced frequency of word use over time, which makes word retrieval more vulnerable to a transmission deficit of activation from semantic/syntactic levels to phonological forms. Older adults, however, were also shown to have a larger vocabulary than younger adults, which could be reason enough for the higher rates of TOT experiences (Schwartz, 2002). Gollan and Brown (2006) argued that an individual's susceptibility to TOTs is affected by vocabulary size. They found that older adults (with larger vocabularies) had more TOTs with difficult words compared to younger adults (with smaller vocabularies), but there was no significant age difference in TOT rate for easy target words. The authors argued that TOTs should not be perceived primarily as failed retrieval (something essentially negative), but instead as partially successful retrieval (something rather positive). Experiencing a TOT (i.e. partially recalling a word) is qualitatively more than not knowing or not recalling a word at all. If (younger) individuals have a smaller vocabulary, they are likely to report fewer TOTs with difficult words, simply because they do not know the words in question.

More relevant to the present discussion is a series of studies that compared TOT rates in monolingual speakers and bilingual speakers. In a laboratory study, Gollan and Silverberg (2001) elicited TOTs in Hebrew–English bilinguals and English monolinguals and found higher rates of TOTs in the bilingual group. In another study using pictures to elicit TOTs, Gollan and Acenas (2004) found that Spanish–English bilinguals and Tagalog–English bilinguals experienced more TOTs in their dominant language English compared to English-speaking monolinguals unless the stimuli depicted cognate targets that the participants were able to translate after the experiment. Gollan and Acenas (2004) also reported that when bilinguals knew the translation equivalent of a target, they were more likely to correctly recall the target word and less likely to experience a TOT. According to the authors, this finding suggests that translation equivalents do not inhibit, but facilitate correct target recall, an argument consistent with a recent proposal against inhibition processes in bilingual lexical production (Finkbeiner *et al.*, 2006).

Gollan *et al.* (2005) conducted a diary study and a laboratory study with Spanish–English bilinguals and monolinguals and again found that bilinguals reported more TOTs overall than the monolinguals. Interestingly, however, bilinguals experienced fewer TOTs with proper names compared to the monolinguals. Normally, proper name recall is considered a more difficult task than recalling nouns, verbs or adjectives. In most diary studies, they are reportedly the words most frequently found to be on the tip of the tongue (e.g. Burke *et al.*, 1991; Cohen & Faulkner, 1986). Bilinguals then performed better than monolinguals on the relatively difficult task of retrieving proper names whereas they performed more poorly than monolinguals on the relatively easy task of retrieving nouns, verbs and adjectives. Gollan and associates (2005) argued that bilinguals do not face a general cognitive processing deficit compared to monolinguals; the increased rate of retrieval failure for nouns, verbs and adjectives merely reflects an increase in processing complexity only for concepts that can be mapped on two or more phonological forms in the bilingual lexicon. When there is no need to select a language-specific form, as in the retrieval of proper names and, perhaps, cognates, bilinguals equal or even exceed monolinguals in recall performance. This interpretation, however, contradicts the above-mentioned translation facilitation effect that was reported by Gollan and Acenas (2004).

Ecke (2004a) compared TOTs in proficient Spanish–English bilinguals of the Southwestern USA who had experienced a shift in language dominance from their L1, Spanish, to their L2, English, with TOTs in Mexican Spanish speakers (quasi monolinguals and beginning learners of L2 English). In a comparative diary study, he found, contrary to expectation, that the bilinguals reported fewer naturally occurring TOTs overall compared to the quasi monolinguals. However, in a laboratory study that elicited TOTs for Spanish words of three frequency ranges, the bilinguals reported more TOTs overall and correctly recalled fewer targets in their non-dominant Spanish L1 than the quasi monolinguals. The different and apparently contradicting rates of naturally occurring and elicited TOTs were attributed by Ecke to bilinguals' frequent use of compensatory strategies, such as codeswitching or appeal for translation in everyday life (cf. Dörnyei & Scott, 1997). Bilinguals use these strategies effectively when in need of lexical resources for immediate communication, thus, avoiding or bypassing retrieval failures before they can convert into TOTs. While the effectiveness of such strategies for communication is uncontroversial, it is possible that codeswitching and the avoidance of difficult-to-access targets may lead to a continuous reduction of individual word frequencies in the non-dominant language, thus further contributing to the attrition of lexical production skills (Bolonyai, 1998).

Ecke (2004a) also showed that bilinguals experience more TOTs with high-frequency words (in their non-dominant language) than quasi monolinguals. He found that English–Spanish bilinguals experienced naturally occurring TOTs more with higher frequency words in non-dominant Spanish (M = 20.4/million) compared to dominant English (M = 6.9/million) and also compared to TOTs in dominant Spanish reported by the Mexican Spanish speakers (M = 12.3/million). The laboratory study (with Spanish target words only) showed a similar picture: the bilinguals experienced more TOTs with low-frequency words (M = 2.2/million), medium-frequency words (M = 10.5/million) and high-frequency words (M = 88/million) than the quasi monolinguals who experienced fewer TOTs in all frequency ranges, but most TOTs with low-frequency words.

The author suggested that, analogous to older adults, the bilinguals displayed an increased vulnerability to lexical retrieval failure in their non-dominant L1 Spanish as a result of weak form-meaning connections due to a relatively low frequency of word use (cf. Burke *et al.*, 1991). Spanish words are less frequently used by the bilinguals compared to the words of the increasingly dominant L2 English, and especially compared to the Spanish L1 words used by the Mexican quasi monolinguals. That bilinguals' dominant languages can also generate higher rates of TOTs compared to monolinguals was shown by Gollan and Acenas (2004) cited above. The TOT data taken together suggest that bilinguals, in general, are disadvantaged in lexical retrieval simply because they use words specific to each language less frequently than monolinguals.

3.3. Retrieval patterns: Fragmentary target information

TOTs generally represent an accessed lexical meaning and syntactic form (lemma) and an inaccessible or only partially accessed corresponding phonological form. Research has shown that speakers in a TOT state can describe or define the meaning of the word and report its syntactic category, e.g. whether (Japanese) TOT targets are nouns or adjectives (Iwasaki *et al.*, 1998). In a TOT elicitation study with English-speaking participants, Vigliocco and associates (1999) found that their participants were able to indicate whether an inaccessible target was a count noun that can be pluralized (e.g. *cucumber*) or a mass noun (e.g. *water*) that is never pluralized. A number of studies provided evidence that speakers of languages such as Italian (Badecker *et al.*, 1995; Miozzo & Caramazza, 1997; Vigliocco *et al.*, 1997) and Spanish (Ecke, 2004a) have access to the grammatical gender of nouns that are on the tip of the tongue. These findings have been taken as evidence for a two-stage architecture of the speech processor and a dissociation of syntactic and phonological encoding (Garrett, 1993; Levelt 1989).

However, in a study of TOTs in Hebrew–English bilinguals, Gollan and Silverberg (2001) found that Hebrew speakers rarely report access to the grammatical gender of TOT noun targets, which the authors explained as a peculiarity of the Hebrew language: there are no prenominal gender markers in Hebrew, i.e. articles and adjectives preceding a noun do not have to be marked for gender (see also Friedmann & Biran, 2003, for similar findings). Ecke (2004a) found that Mexican Spanish speakers reported higher rates of correct grammatical gender guesses of TOT words compared to English-dominant Spanish–English bilinguals living in the USA. He suggested that the lower rate of gender reports in the bilinguals may point to a reduced sensitivity to gender processing that reflects early lexical attrition (Weltens & Grendel, 1993) and/or cross-linguistic influence (CLI) from the dominant gender-less English language, an interpretation that seems consistent with reported gender processing difficulties in studies of language attrition (cf. Ecke, 2004b: 336–337, for a review of relevant studies).

Speakers in TOT states are frequently able to report the initial letter/ sound of the target, they are less likely to report the final letters of the word, and least likely to recall any middle letters (cf. Brown, 1991). Some studies also report a relatively high rate of correctly guessed numbers of syllables of targets (e.g. Koriat & Lieblich, 1974; Yarmey, 1973) or the general rhythmic patterns of the targets (Wenzl, 1932, 1936). The latter reports corroborate Wenzl's (1932) early assumption that TOT recall proceeds from general 'Gestalt' features to more specific attributes and Brown and McNeill's (1966) comparable notion of generic recall. Garrett (1984) suggested that these frequently recalled salient attributes have to be specified first in a linking address before other segments can be retrieved in the process of phonological encoding. Data from sound-related lexical substitution errors also have been interpreted as evidence for the assumption that the first phoneme/first letter and number of syllables are salient phonological attributes which are essential in the planning of an initial phonological or syllabic frame in which other sound segments are filled in later (cf. Fay & Cutler, 1977; Shuttuck-Hufnagel, 1979; Wheeldon & Levelt, 1995).

A number of studies investigated whether the presentation of certain letter or sound fragments of targets would assist speakers in resolving the TOT. Brennen and associates (1990) found that presenting the target's first letter to speakers in a TOT helped them to recall the target. Brown and Knight (1990) reported that first letters were most effective, last letters less effective and middle letters least effective in cueing target retrieval during TOTs. Abrams *et al.* (2003) and White and Abrams (2002) found that presenting speakers with the first syllable of the target facilitated TOT resolution whereas presenting only the target's initial phoneme, middle syllables or final syllables had no effect on target recall. These findings support the view that the phonological lexicon (at least of fluent native speakers of English) is organized according to salient attributes that are frequently known by the speaker in a TOT and that are quite likely to cue target recall if presented by an experimenter. These salient attributes are also detectable in form-related lexical substitutions. When an error substitutes a target, it is most likely to follow access routes corresponding to the beginning letter/sound of the target (Brown & Knight, 1990) which is reflected in the high rate of first letter matches between error and target (cf. Fay & Cutler, 1977).

3.4. Retrieval patterns: Word associates

Speakers experiencing a TOT frequently report related words (associates or 'interlopers') that come to mind during target word search. In fact, most reported TOTs contain word associates (e.g. Reason & Lucas, 1984). Younger adults are more likely to experience TOTs with associates compared to older adults (Burke *et al.*, 1991). TOTs with word associates usually take longer to get resolved than TOTs without any associates (Burke *et al.*, 1991; González, 1996). This raises the question whether the associates play any role in TOT causation or resolution, and whether they can be informative about principles of lexical organization. Analogous to researchers who analyze speech errors' similarity with the replaced targets, TOT researchers approach the issue by analyzing target-associate relations of similarity.

Word associates have been analyzed and compared with target words with respect to their frequency counts. Findings so far are not consistent. Some studies report that associates, on average, are of higher frequency compared to the target (Ecke, 2004a; Reason & Lucas, 1984), others report that they are of equal or even lower frequency (Harley & Brown, 1998). Associates higher in frequency than the target have been interpreted as consistent with blocking (Reason & Lucas, 1984). According to this view, high-frequency words related to lower frequency targets are easier to activate and frequently win amongst similar candidates that compete for activation. Once activated, they may inhibit target recall. On the other hand, associates of equal or lower frequency have been seen as the result of a strategic search process: some speakers in a TOT may think that the inaccessible target is an especially difficult, unusual or rare word. Therefore, they may direct their search to difficult, low-frequency words and, perhaps, discard relatively high-frequency candidates (Harley & Brown, 1998).

The large majority of TOT word associates share properties with the inaccessible target. Most targets and associates share the same syntactic class (between 84% and 93% in Burke *et al.*, 1991). If a target, for example, is a noun, then associates are most likely to be nouns as well. This also is the case in TOTs with L2 words (78% in Ecke, 2001; 79.5% in Ecke & Garrett, 1998). These findings suggest a strong constraint of the (specified) syntactic category on target word search in both L1 TOTs and L2 TOTs. This constraint, however, appears to be somewhat weaker than in lexical substitution errors, probably because of the partial involvement of conscious recall strategies in TOTs that can go beyond automatic retrieval.

Apart from syntactic similarity, most word associates are semantically related to the target. According to Harley and Brown (1998: 164), the high rate of semantically related words reflects stronger overall semantic-phonological activation, compared to occasional phonological-lexical feedback. Unfortunately, relatively little is yet known about the specific semantic relation types of target-associate pairs in TOTs, although their study could potentially be useful for the modeling and testing of psychologically real semantic/conceptual relation types, very much like the study of meaning-related substitution errors (e.g. Garrett, 1992) or the study of word associations (e.g. Chaffin, 1997). Ecke (1996: 165) reported that most semantically related associate-target pairs in a study of TOTs with English, Russian and Spanish native speakers could be classified as members of the same category (*sink – urinal, Nolde – Heckel*) and synonyms (*estante* [Spa. rack, bookcase] – *librero* [Spa. bookcase], *abzats* [Rus. paragraph] – *paragraf* [Rus. paragraph]). In a TOT study with (German) L3 targets, Ecke (2001) found that most associate-target pairs were members of the same category (*vaso* [Spa. glass] – *Flasche* [Ger. bottle]) and event-based (thematically related) pairs (*Wort* [Ger. word] – *buchstabieren* [Ger. spell]), but cautioned that these relation types may merely be representative for objects (nouns), the most frequent TOT word type in his study.

In addition to meaning-related associates, there is also a robust, though usually lower rate of associates similar in sound to the target, and words that are similar in both sound and meaning to the target (e.g. Kohn *et al.*, 1987). Associates similar in sound frequently match the target on the first letter or sound (cf. Brown, 1991) and somewhat less frequently on the number of syllables (Brown & McNeill, 1966; Yarmey, 1973), which again points to the special status of these attributes in phonological encoding. Ecke (1997), comparing TOTs with L1 targets and TOTs with L2 targets, reported that extended search for L2 words involved higher rates of phonologically related associates compared to TOTs with L1 words that involved more semantically related associates.

Campaña Rubio and Ecke (2001) taught learners of L2 English very infrequent animal names in the L2 (words such as *desmostylia* and *rynchophore*) together with pictures and meaningful information in the L2 about the animal; they later tested participants for recall and TOT experience, presenting them with a picture of the animal. They found that TOTs with these very recently learned words involved mostly phonologically related associates (such as *dinámarca* or *decencia* for the target *desmostylia*), whereas meaning-related associations were rare. Another finding of their study was that phonologically related associates were very similar to the targets overall, and frequently matched them in middle letters, initial letters and syllabic stress. Similarly Ecke (2001) found that sound-related target-associate pairs of TOTs with recently learned L3 words frequently coincided not only in the initial sound segment (e.g.

Fleisch [meat] – *Flasche* [bottle]) as in most TOTs with L1 words, but also in middle segments (e.g. *Lehrer* [teacher] – *Beruf* [profession]) and stressed syllable (*'Arbeit* [work] – *'Abfalleimer* [waste basket]).

Ecke and Garrett (1998) suggested that these patterns may reflect developmental changes in lexical retrieval: the retrieval of relatively unstable (often novel L2) words is, in relative terms, more form-focused and has to rely on a greater variety of phonological attributes compared to word retrieval of relatively stable (often L1) words. The retrieval of stable words is primarily meaning-focused and access to their phonology is routed through a limited set of salient form attributes, such as the initial sound segment of the word. The developmental differences in lexical retrieval inferred from TOT studies with L1, L2 and L3 words are similar, in principle, to earlier proposals of developmental changes in the L1 lexicon of children, based on speech error data (Aitchison & Straf, 1981; Vihman, 1981), developmental changes in the L2 learner lexicon, based on speech error data (Henning, 1973; Laufer, 1991; Poulisse, 1999) and changes in the L2 lexicon, based on findings from word association studies with L2 learners of different proficiency levels (Meara, 1982; Söderman, 1993). (For a critical review of research on developmental changes in the lexicon and differences between the L1 and L2 lexicon, see Singleton (1999); for an attempt to capture developmental changes of the L2 lexicon in the laboratory, see Talamas *et al.* (1999).)

Word associations in TOTs of bilingual speakers are also interesting with respect to their language affiliation. Are they from the language of the target or are they 'intrusions' from another language reflecting cross-linguistic influence (CLI) in TOT word search? Ecke and Garrett (1998) reported that 76% of the associates in TOTs with L2 targets were intralingual, i.e. they were of the same language as the target. The TOTs of the proficient Spanish–English bilinguals in Ecke (2004a) also involved primarily intralingual associations (73% overall). However, the TOTs for targets in the non-dominant L1 generated higher rates of interlingual associates (33%) compared to the TOT targets of the dominant L2 (16%). In another study, Ecke (2008) investigated whether speakers' different levels of proficiency in English L2 had any impact on the amount of CLI in their extended search for Spanish L1 targets. He found that most associates were intralingual (of the L1), but that English L2 influence increased with speakers' level of proficiency in the L2.

Language of associates was also analyzed in a laboratory study that elicited TOTs with L3 words (Ecke, 2001). Participants were Spanish native speakers who were proficient in English (L2) and novice learners of German (L3). The associates of the L3 TOTs included the following kinds/sources of CLI: L1 influence: *agua* [Spa. water] – *Flasche* [Ger. bottle], *René* [name] – *Taschenrechner* [Ger, pocket calculator], L2 influence: *fence* – *Fenster* [Ger. window], *seldom* – *manchmal* [Ger. sometimes] and (intralingual) L3 influence: *schlaf* [Ger. sleep] – *Flasche* [Ger. bottle], *Kuli* [Ger. pen] – *Taschenrechner* [Ger. pocket calculator]. The analysis revealed that most associates (75%) were intralingual (of the L3). Fifteen percent of the associates were English L2 words, and only 10% of the associates came from the participants' L1 Spanish. The results of the studies taken together suggest that bilinguals, when in a TOT, primarily search within the target's language, even if the target belongs to a non-dominant language. Search for targets of less dominant languages, however, is more affected by CLI, compared to word search in more dominant languages.

3.5. Effects of word associates on TOT resolution

The patterns of associate-target pairs described above do not say anything yet about possible effects of the associates on target retrieval. Early research on TOTs with L1 words suggested that (experimenter-presented) phonologically related associates inhibit (block) target retrieval (Jones, 1989; Jones & Langford, 1987). However, more recent studies found that phonologically related words assist retrieval or, at least, do not hinder it (Meyer & Bock, 1992; Perfect & Hanley, 1992). In one experiment conducted by James and Burke (2000), phonologically related words presented before a definition-based recall task increased correct target retrieval and decreased TOTs. In a second experiment, presenting phonologically related words after TOT onset increased the rate of TOT resolution. Both findings support the view that experimenter-presented phonologically related primes assist in the retrieval of word forms. In a recent TOT elicitation experiment, Abrams and Rodriguez (2005) manipulated the syntactic class of experimenter-presented phonologically related primes. They found that sound-related primes that differed in syntactic class from the target facilitated target retrieval, whereas sound-related primes of the same syntactic class had no effect on target retrieval.

In an experiment with Farsi–English bilinguals, Askari (1999) investigated the potential effect of phonologically and semantically related words from within and from across languages on target recall and TOT frequency. Askari found that phonologically related words (no matter whether from the L1 or L2) assisted target recall in the non-dominant L2 English. Semantically related words, on the other hand, seemed helpful in the recall of L1 Farsi words, although merely to disambiguate definitions and to create a greater confidence in target recall. She interpreted her findings as support for a shared phonological lexicon for the bilinguals' L1 and L2.

In a diary study with speakers of L1 Spanish and L2 English, Ecke (2008) examined whether the L2 associates generated in naturally occurring TOTs with L1 targets had any effect on TOT resolution. Based on a qualitative analysis of TOT records that contained the speakers' estimation of the time span between associate and target retrieval, the author suggested that most associates have no effect at all on target recall, that phonologically similar associates that share salient form attributes and their position in the word's frame (e.g. *eagle – egolatría*) can assist TOT resolution, whereas phonologically similar associates that differ from the target in the position or sequence of salient form attributes (e.g. *Chamberlaine – Echavarria*) can hinder (block) target retrieval.

Campaña Rubio (2006) in two laboratory studies elicited TOTs with L1 words in a group of Spanish speakers and TOTs with L2 words in a group of Spanish-speaking learners of L2 English. When in a TOT, the participants had the choice to either look up a meaning-related word or a sound-related word that, they were told, could serve as a possible retrieval aid. Interestingly, most cues chosen as aids for the TOTs with L1 words were meaning-related words (75%), whereas most cues chosen in TOTs with L2 words were sound-related words (72%). Moreover, choosing a meaning-related cue almost never led to target recall. On the other hand, choosing a sound-related cue led to target recall in 42% of the cases. Campaña Rubio's (2006) findings suggest that speakers employ attentional resources differently depending on whether they search for words in the dominant or non-dominant language. Search for words of the dominant L1 is, in relative terms, more meaning-driven whereas search for words of the non-dominant L2 is relatively more form-driven.

Summary and Outlook

This chapter reviewed questions that researchers have asked about the TOT phenomenon. It presented naturalistic and laboratory methods of its investigation and discussed selected findings from TOT studies with monolinguals and bilinguals that may be informative to researchers with interest in the bilingual lexicon. A TOT was characterized as a temporary word retrieval failure in which the speaker has activated part of the target (usually its meaning, syntactic specification and salient letters/sounds). Because of its temporary nature and the fragmentary information available to the speaker, a TOT should be seen as a partially successful retrieval attempt in comparison to a complete failure to produce (or know) a word (Gollan & Brown, 2006). Research into TOTs, in general, and TOTs in bilinguals, in particular, has contributed much to our understanding of the organization of the mental lexicon and the functioning of lexical access in speech production. The following are some of the contributions that were discussed in this chapter: TOT research has helped to identify the main processing stages of lexical production and to sketch out its overall time course (Garrett, 1993; Levelt, 1989). By investigating the partially accessed target attributes, reflected in the letters/sounds and words that come to mind during speakers' target word search, TOT research contributed to the identification of salient form attributes (Garrett, 1984) and meaning relations (Garrett, 1992) that are crucial for the organization and processing of lexical information. Similarities and differences in lexical retrieval have been suggested for stable lexis, usually of dominant languages or L1s, and unstable lexis, usually of non-dominant languages or L2s: TOTs with words of less stable L2s generate more sound-related associates and fewer meaning-related associates compared to TOTs of more stable L1s, suggesting that their resolution is more form-driven and less meaning-driven (Ecke, 1997).

By studying the language of word associations that are generated in the TOTs of bilinguals, researchers attempted to determine the degree to which TOT word search activates structures within and across languages. Although word search in naturally occurring TOTs proceeds primarily within the target's language, occasional CLI (Ecke, 2001) and priming effects in TOT elicitation studies (Askari, 1999) point to common conceptual and lexical (form) stores.

A series of experimental studies investigated the effects of letter/sound cues and various kinds of related words (from within and across the target's language) on TOT resolution. Findings suggest that presenting the speaker with the target's initial letter/sound (Brennen *et al.*, 1990; Brown & Knight, 1990), the letters/sounds of its first syllable (Abrams *et al.*, 2003) and sound-related words (James & Burke, 2000) assists target recall. Particularly effective seem to be words that share the first syllable with the target and that differ from it in syntactic class (Abrams & Rodriguez, 2005; White & Abrams, 2002). Phonologically related words can also have a facilitating effect even if they are not of the target language (Askari, 1999; Ecke, 2008).

Empirical data from both monolingual and bilingual speakers suggest that most TOTs are the result of a transmission deficit of activation from the semantic/syntactic levels to the phonological level (Burke *et al.*, 1991) and not a consequence of interference from competing lexical items. Bilinguals, very much like older adults, experience more TOTs in experimental studies than monolinguals (Gollan & Acenas, 2004; Gollan & Silverberg, 2001). They use individual word forms (in their less dominant and more dominant languages) less often than monolinguals in their single language. This reduced frequency of individual word use results in relatively weak form-meaning connections that can become susceptible to incomplete lexical activation. One consequence of such reduced individual word use is that bilinguals experience TOTs with words of relatively high frequency ranges compared to monolinguals that report TOTs mostly with low-frequency words (Ecke, 2004a). Bilinguals are reportedly disadvantaged in the retrieval of nouns, verbs and adjectives in TOT elicitation studies, but the disadvantage disappears for the retrieval of cognate words, proper names, and possibly words of which translation equivalents are known by the speaker (Gollan *et al.*, 2005). Diary studies found that bilinguals do not report more naturally occurring TOTs than monolinguals. In everyday life, bilinguals' word retrieval deficits may not always materialize in TOTs, probably because the speakers apply compensatory strategies, such as codeswitching or appeal for translation, to ensure effective, uninterrupted communication (Ecke, 2004a).

This chapter reviewed research that is based on the view that TOTs can serve as a window on lexical retrieval, in general, and bilingual lexical production, in particular. It focused on psycholinguistic TOT studies that assume that interim recall products will reflect the actual processing steps and representational levels involved in lexical production. While TOTs certainly reflect components of lexical retrieval, they probably are more complex than interrupted instances of lexical retrieval (Schwartz, 1999). Researchers using naturalistic methods (Reason & Lucas, 1984; Wenzl, 1932) have long recognized this complexity and variety of TOTs, and the impossibility of attributing all TOTs and their resolution to only one cause. The challenge of future research will be to differentiate between subcategories of TOTs, including the processes involved in each, and to relate findings to patterns observed in other mono- and bilingual production phenomena, such as lexical substitution errors, codeswitching and word association.

Acknowledgements

I would like to thank Aneta Pavlenko, Chris Hall and two anonymous reviewers for their insightful comments and suggestions on an earlier version of this chapter.

Note

1. The example presented here was a TOT experienced and recorded by the author in a personal TOT diary when he lived in Mexico.

References

Abrams, L. and Rodriguez, E. (2005) Syntactic class influences phonological priming of tip-of-the-tongue resolution. *Psychonomic Bulletin & Review* 12 (6), 1018–1023.

Abrams, L., White, K. and Eitel, S. (2003) Isolating phonological components that increase tip-of-the-tongue resolution. *Memory & Cognition* 31 (8), 1153–1162.

Aitchison, J. and Straf, M. (1981) Lexical storage and retrieval: A developing skill? *Linguistics* 19, 751–795.

Askari, N. (1999) Priming effects on tip-of-the-tongue states in Farsi-English bilinguals. *Journal of Psycholinguistic Research* 28, 197–212.

Badecker, W., Miozzo, M. and Zanuttini, R. (1995) The two-stage model of lexical retrieval: Evidence from a case of anomia with selective preservation of grammatical gender. *Cognition* 57, 193–216.

Bolonyai, A. (1998) In-between languages: Language shift/maintenance in childhood bilingualism. *International Journal of Bilingualism* 2, 21–43.

Brennen, T., Baguley, T., Bright, J. and Bruce, V. (1990) Resolving semantically induced tip-of-the-tongue states for proper nouns. *Memory and Cognition* 18, 339–347.

Brown, A. (1991) A review of the tip-of-the-tongue experience. *Psychological Bulletin* 109, 202–223.

Brown, A. and Knight, K. (1990) Letter cues as retrieval aids in semantic memory. *American Journal of Psychology* 103, 101–113.

Brown, A. and Nix, L. (1996) Age-related changes in the tip-of-the-tongue experience. *American Journal of Psychology* 109, 79–91.

Brown, R. and McNeill, D. (1966) The "tip of the tongue" phenomenon. *Journal of Verbal Learning and Verbal Behavior* 5, 325–337.

Burke, D., MacKay, D., Worthley, J. and Wade, E. (1991) On the tip of the tongue: What causes word finding failures in young and older adults? *Journal of Memory and Language* 30, 542–579.

Campaña Rubio, E. (2006) Fallas en la recuperación léxica por hablantes nativos y aprendices de una lengua extranjera [Lexical retrieval failures in native speakers and second language learners]. Unpublished doctoral dissertation, Universidad Autónoma de Sinaloa.

Campaña Rubio, E. and Ecke, P. (2001) Un estudio experimental sobre la adquisición y recuperación (parcial) de palabras en una lengua extranjera. [An experimental study on the acquisition and (partial) retrieval of foreign language words.] In G. López Cruz and M. Morúa Leyva (eds) *Memorias del V Encuentro Internacional de Lingüística en el Noroeste* (pp. 63–84). Hermosillo, Mexico: Editorial Unison.

Chaffin, R. (1997) Associations to unfamiliar words: Learning the meanings of new words. *Memory & Cognition* 25, 203–226.

Cohen, A.D. (1996) Verbal reports as a source of insights into second language learner strategies. *Applied Language Learning* 7, 5–24.

Cohen, G. and Faulkner, D. (1986) Memory for proper names: Age differences in retrieval. *British Journal of Developmental Psychology* 4, 187–197.

Costa, A. and Santesteban, M. (2006) The control of speech production by bilingual speakers: Introductory remarks. *Bilingualism: Language and Cognition* 9 (2), 115–117.

Dörnyei, Z. and Scott, M. (1997) Communication strategies in a second language: Definitions and taxonomies. *Language Learning* 47, 173–210.

Ecke, P. (1996) Cross-language studies of lexical retrieval: Tip-of-the-tongue states in first and foreign languages. Unpublished doctoral dissertation, University of Arizona.

Ecke, P. (1997) Tip of the tongue states in first and foreign languages: Similarities and differences of lexical retrieval failures. In L. Díaz and C. Pérez (eds) *Proceedings of the EUROSLA 7 Conference* (pp. 505–514). Barcelona: Universitat Pompeu Fabra.

Ecke, P. (2001) Lexical retrieval in a third language: Evidence from errors and tip-of-the-tongue states. In J. Cenoz, B. Hufeisen and U. Jessner (eds) *Cross-linguistic Aspects of L3 Acquisition* (pp. 90–114). Clevedon: Multilingual Matters.

Ecke, P. (2004a) Words on the tip of the tongue: A study of lexical retrieval failures in Spanish-English bilinguals. *Southwest Journal of Linguistics* 23 (2), 33–63.

Ecke, P. (2004b) Language attrition and theories of forgetting: A cross-disciplinary review. *International Journal of Bilingualism* 8 (3), 321–354.

Ecke, P. (2008) Cross-linguistic influence on word search in tip-of-the-tongue states. *TESOL Quarterly* 42, 515–527.

Ecke, P. and Garrett, M. (1998) Lexical retrieval stages of momentarily inaccessible foreign language words. *Ilha do Desterro, Special Issue: Cognitive Perspectives on the Acquisition/Learning of Second/Foreign Languages* 35, 157–183.

Fay, D. and Cutler, A. (1977) Malapropisms and the structure of the mental lexicon. *Linguistic Inquiry* 8, 505–520.

Finkbeiner, M., Gollan, T. and Caramazza, A. (2006) Lexical access in bilingual speakers: What is the (hard) problem? *Bilingualism: Language and Cognition* 9 (2), 153–166.

Friedmann, N. and Biran, M. (2003) When is gender accessed? A study of paraphasias in Hebrew anomia. *Cortex* 39, 441–463.

Garrett, M. (1984) The organization of processing structure for language production: Application to aphasic speech. In D. Caplan, R. Lecours and A. Smith (eds) *Biological Perspectives on Language* (pp. 172–193). Cambridge, MA: MIT Press.

Garrett, M. (1992) Lexical retrieval processes: Semantic field effects. In E. Kittay and A. Lehrer (eds) *Frames, Fields and Contrasts* (pp. 377–395). Hillsdale, NJ: Erlbaum.

Garrett, M. (1993) Errors and their relevance for models of language production. In G. Blanken, J. Dittmann, H. Grimm, J. Marshall and C. Wallesch (eds) *Linguistic Disorders and Pathologies* (pp. 72–93). Berlin: Walter de Gruyter.

Gollan, T. and Acenas, L. (2004) What is a TOT? Cognate and translation effects in tip-of-the-tongue status in Spanish-English and Tagalog-English bilinguals. *Journal of Experimental Psychology: Learning, Memory, and Cognition* 30, 246–269.

Gollan, T., Bonanni, M. and Montoya, R. (2005) Proper names get stuck on bilingual and monolingual speakers' tip-of-the-tongue equally often. *Neuropsychology* 19, 278–287.

Gollan, T. and Brown, A. (2006) From tip-of-the-tongue data to theoretical implications in two steps: When more TOTs mean better retrieval. *Journal of Experimental Psychology: General* 135 (3), 462–483.

Gollan, T. and Silverberg, N. (2001) Tip of the tongue states in Hebrew-English bilinguals. *Bilingualism: Language and Cognition* 4, 63–83.

González, J. (1996) El fenómeno de la 'punta de la lengua' y la recuperación léxica: Estudio de sus propiedades en Castellano y el efecto de la frecuencia del estímulo [The tip of the tongue phenomenon and lexical retrieval: A study of its characteristics in Spanish and the effect of stimulus frequency]. *Estudios de Psicología* 56, 71–96.

Harley, T. and Brown, H. (1998) What causes a tip-of-the-tongue state? Evidence for lexical neighborhood effects in speech production. *British Journal of Psychology* 89, 151–174.

Heine, M., Ober, B. and Shenaut, G. (1999) Naturally occurring and experimentally induced tip-of-the-tongue experiences in three adult age groups. *Psychology and Aging* 14, 445–457.

Henning, G. (1973) Remembering foreign language vocabulary: Acoustic and semantic parameters. *Language Learning* 23 (2), 185–197.

Iwasaki, N., Vigliocco, G. and Garrett, M. (1998) Adjectives and adjectival nouns in Japanese: Psychological processes in sentence production. *Japanese/Korean Linguistics* (Vol. 8; pp. 555–568). Stanford, CA: Stanford University Press.

James, L. and Burke, D. (2000) Phonological priming effects on word retrieval and tip-of-the-tongue experiences in young and older adults. *Journal of Experimental Psychology: Learning, Memory, and Cognition* 26, 1378–1391.

Jones, G. (1989) Back to Woodworth: Role of interlopers in the tip-of-the-tongue phenomenon. *Memory & Cognition* 17, 69–76.

Jones, G. and Langford, S. (1987) Phonological blocking in the tip of the tongue state. *Cognition* 26, 115–122.

Kohn, S., Wingfield, A., Menn, L., Goodglass, H., Berko Gleason, J. and Hyde, M. (1987) Lexical retrieval: The tip-of-the-tongue phenomenon. *Applied Psycholinguistics* 8, 245–266.

Koriat, A. and Lieblich, I. (1974) What does a person in a 'TOT' state know that a person in a 'don't know' state doesn't know. *Memory and Cognition* 2, 647–655.

Laufer, B. (1991) Some properties of the foreign language learner's lexicon as evidenced by lexical confusions. *International Review of Applied Linguistics* 29 (4), 317–330.

Levelt, W. (1989) *Speaking: From Intention to Articulation*. Cambridge, MA: MIT Press.

Lovelace, E. (1991) Aging and word finding: Reverse vocabulary and close tests. *Bulletin of the Psychonomic Society* 29, 33–35.

Maylor, E. (1990) Recognizing and naming faces: Aging, memory retrieval, and the tip of the tongue state. *Journals of Gerontology* 45 (6), 215–226.

Meara, P. (1982) Word associations in a foreign language: A report on the Birbeck vocabulary project. *The Nottingham Linguistic Circular* 11 (2), 29–38.

Meyer, A. and Bock, K. (1992) The tip-of-the-tongue phenomenon: Do experimenter-presented interlopers have an effect? *Cognition* 45, 55–75.

Miozzo, M. and Caramazza, A. (1997) The retrieval of lexical-syntactic features in tip-of-the-tongue states. *Journal of Experimental Psychology: Learning, Memory, and Cognition* 23, 1410–1423.

Perfect, T. and Hanley, R. (1992) The tip-of-the-tongue phenomenon: Do experimenter-presented interlopers have any effect? *Cognition* 45, 55–75.

Poulisse, N. (1999) *Slips of the Tongue: Speech Errors in First and Second Language Production*. Amsterdam: John Benjamins.

Priller, J. and Mittenecker, E. (1988) Experimente zum Unterschied von 'Wort auf der Zunge' und 'Gefühl des Wissens' [Experimental studies on the difference between 'word on the tip of the tongue' and 'feeling of knowing']. *Zeitschrift für experimentelle und angewandte Psychologie* 35, 129–146.

Reason, J. and Lucas, D. (1984) Using cognitive diaries to investigate naturally occurring memory blocks. In J. Harris and P. Morris (eds) *Everyday Memory Actions and Absent-mindedness* (pp. 53–69). London: Academic Press.

Schwartz, B. (1999) Sparkling at the end of the tongue: The etiology of tip-of-the-tongue phenomenology. *Psychonomic Bulletin & Review* 6 (3), 379–393.

Schwartz, B. (2002) *Tip-of-the-tongue States: Phenomenology, Mechanism, and Lexical Retrieval*. Mahwah, NJ: Lawrence Erlbaum.

Schwartz, B., Travis, D. and Castro, A. (2000) The phenomenology of real and illusionary tip-of-the-tongue states. *Memory & Cognition* 28 (1), 18–27.

Shuttuck-Hufnagel, S. (1979) Speech errors as evidence for a serial order mechanism in sentence production. In W. Cooper and E. Walker (eds) *Sentence Processing: Psycholinguistic Studies Presented to Merrill Garrett* (pp. 295–342). Hillsdale, NJ: Erlbaum.

Singleton, D. (1999) *Exploring the Second Language Mental Lexicon*. Cambridge: Cambridge University Press.

Smith, S., Brown, J. and Balfour, S. (1991) TOTimals: A controlled experimental method for studying tip-of-the-tongue states. *Bulletin of the Psychonomic Society* 29, 445–447.

Söderman, T. (1993) Word associations of foreign language learners and native speakers: The phenomenon of a shift in response type and its relevance for lexical development. In H. Ringbom (ed.) *Near-native Proficiency in English* (pp. 91–182). Åbo: Åbo Akademi University.

Talamas, A., Kroll, J. and Dufour, R. (1999) From form to meaning: Stages in the acquisition of second language vocabulary. *Bilingualism: Language and Cognition* 2 (1), 45–58.

Thompson, R., Emmorey, K. and Gollan, T. (2005) 'Tip of the fingers' experiences by deaf signers: Insights into the organization of a sign-based lexicon. *Psychological Science* 16, 856–860.

Vigliocco, G., Antonini, T. and Garrett, M. (1997) Grammatical gender is on the tip of Italian tongues. *Psychological Science* 8, 314–317.

Vigliocco, G., Vinson, D., Martin, R. and Garrett, M. (1999) Is 'count' and 'mass' information available when the noun is not? An investigation of tip of the tongue states in anomia. *Journal of Memory & Language* 40, 534–558.

Vihman, M. (1981) Phonology and the development of the lexicon: Evidence from children's errors. *Journal of Child Language* 8, 239–264.

Weltens, B. and Grendel, M. (1993) Attrition of vocabulary knowledge. In R. Schreuder and B. Weltens (eds) *The Bilingual Lexicon* (pp. 135–156). Amsterdam: John Benjamins.

Wenzl, A. (1932) Empirische und theoretische Beiträge zur Erinnerungsarbeit bei erschwerter Wortfindung [Empirical and theoretical contributions on recall during impeded word finding]. *Archiv für die gesamte Psychologie* 85, 181–218.

Wenzl, A. (1936) Empirische und theoretische Beiträge zur Erinnerungsarbeit bei erschwerter Wortfindung [Empirical and theoretical contributions on recall during impeded word finding]. *Archiv für die gesamte Psychologie* 97, 294–318.

Wheeldon, L. and Levelt, W. (1995) Monitoring the time course of phonological encoding. *Journal of Memory and Language* 34, 311–334.

White, K. and Abrams, L. (2002) Does priming specific syllables during tip-of-the-tongue states facilitate word retrieval in older adults? *Psychology and Aging* 17 (2), 226–235.

Yarmey, A. (1973) I recognize your face but I can't remember your name: Further evidence on the tip-of-the-tongue phenomenon. *Memory and Cognition* 1, 287–290.

Chapter 9
L1 Attrition and the Mental Lexicon

MONIKA S. SCHMID and BARBARA KÖPKE

Introduction

The bilingual mental lexicon is one of the most thoroughly studied domains within investigations of bilingualism. Psycholinguistic research has focused mostly on its organization or functional architecture, as well as on lexical access or retrieval procedures (see also Meuter, this volume). The dynamics of the bilingual mental lexicon have been investigated mainly in the context of second language acquisition (SLA) and language pathology. Within SLA, an important body of research is devoted to vocabulary learning and teaching (e.g. Bogaards & Laufer, 2004; Ellis, 1994; Hulstijn & Laufer, 2001; Nation, 1990, 1993). In pathology, anomia (i.e. impaired word retrieval), one of the most common disorders in aphasia (e.g. Basso, 1993; Kremin, 1994), has given rise to a considerable number of investigations, including those conducted with bi- and multilingual patients (e.g. Goral *et al.*, 2006; Junqué *et al.*, 1995; Kremin & De Agostini, 1995; Roberts & Le Dorze, 1998). Less attention to date has been paid to more subtle changes and to the evolution of the bilingual lexicon over longer time spans. It is only recently that these phenomena have been investigated in the context of research on lexical retrieval in aging (see the overview in Goral, 2004) and first language attrition.

That such dynamics of the nonpathological bilingual lexicon have not received more attention as yet is somewhat surprising, as the principal models of the bilingual mental lexicon clearly allow for a dynamic perspective. The Revised Hierarchical Model developed by Kroll and colleagues (e.g. Kroll, 1993; Kroll & Tokowicz, 2001, 2005) claims separate lexicons for each language, but does capture the bidirectional and asymmetric relations between these lexicons (Goral *et al.*, 2006: 236). Furthermore, the links between the lexicons can vary in strength (depending on proficiency and language use, e.g. Kroll & Tokowicz, 2005: 546) indicating that there may be changes in the connections between word forms and meaning in the different languages over time (for a more detailed description, see Pavlenko, this volume).

In connectionist models like the Bilingual Interactive Activation Model (BIA, Grainger & Dijkstra, 1992 or BIA+, Dijkstra & van Heuven, 2002; for detailed descriptions, see Marian, this volume) or the Bilingual Interactive Model of Lexical Access (BIMOLA, Grosjean, 1997), cross-linguistic links between items (such as phonetic or orthographic features, word forms, lemmas, concepts or a language subsystem) are regulated by activation and inhibition mechanisms that are dependent on frequency of use and may account for dynamic aspects of the bilingual lexicon, which can be observed in all situations of bilingual language use and development.

1. First Language Attrition

1.1. What is attrition?

The term *first language (L1) attrition* refers to a change in the native language system of the bilingual who is acquiring and using a second language (L2). This change may lead to a variety of phenomena within the L1 system, among which are interferences from the L2 on all levels (phonetics, lexicon, morphosyntax, pragmatics), a simplification or impoverishment of the L1, or insecurity on the part of the speaker manifested by frequent hesitations, self-repair or hedging strategies. As such, L1 attrition may be a phenomenon that is experienced by all L2 users, from the earliest stages of L2 development. For the purpose of the present discussion, we assume the case of bilingual development that has most often been investigated in attrition research: that of late bilinguals who experience a drastic change in their linguistic habits as adults, i.e. postpuberty migrants.

Given the stability of the native language system in mature speakers, it has long been assumed that L1 attrition is an extreme and relatively rare development, which only occurs under certain specific circumstances. These include emigration to a different linguistic environment, an adaptation to this environment in most areas of daily life, an extreme reduction in L1 input and use, and the persistence of these circumstances over a prolonged time span (decades). In such a situation, it was postulated, L1 attrition might eventually 'set in', particularly when compounded by attitudinal factors such as a rejection of the L1.

More recently, it has been suggested that attrition may not be such an extreme or such a discrete phenomenon (Cook, 2003, 2005; Schmid & Köpke, 2007). Drawing a line which separates the attriter from the nonattriter has proven a daunting task in the past (see Köpke & Schmid, 2004), which might indicate that L2 influence on L1 is a natural consequence of the competition of more than one linguistic system in the same mind/brain. In situations where the L2 is used more extensively than the L1 over a long period of time, these influences may merely be more pronounced and more clearly visible.

On the other hand, the process we refer to as L1 attrition is probably due to two factors: the first one is the presence, development and (eventually) dominance of the L2 system. This factor may lead to increasing L2 interference across all linguistic levels, but it is probably something that all bilinguals experience to some degree. The ensuing change that can be observed in the L1 system has been labelled *externally induced* language change (Seliger & Vago, 1991: 10), as it is dependent on competition and cross-linguistic influence (CLI). Such language contact phenomena can be witnessed in all bilinguals to some extent. The second factor is the dramatic reduction in L1 use and input, which is specific to the emigrant's situation and may then lead to *internally induced* language change (Seliger & Vago, 1991: 10): due to the absence of input and confirming evidence, the language system undergoes a structural reduction and simplification.

Neither factor alone would therefore lead to what we might term 'attrition proper': competition from L2 without a break in linguistic tradition (as in the case of a bilingual who continues to use the L1) or lack of exposure without competition (in the hypothetical desert-island-situation, which might lead to a kind of language 'atrophy'). It is only when both processes conspire that language attrition occurs.

1.2.   Attrition and the lexicon

Although attrition effects can be witnessed across the full range of an individual's linguistic knowledge and use, the lexicon is an area of predominant interest for investigations of L2 influence on L1. It has often been suggested that this is a 'vulnerable' or 'sensitive' part of the linguistic system, where attrition manifests itself first and most extremely (Andersen, 1982; Köpke, 2002; Weinreich, 1953; Weltens & Grendel, 1993).

This is an intuitively convincing assumption: numerically, the lexicon is a much larger system than other areas of language knowledge (i.e. we know far more words than we have, for example, phonetic or morphological items). Furthermore, the lexicon is a network of items that are far less densely connected and interdependent than, for example, the phonological inventory. While relatively minor changes to the phonological or morphological system can have far-reaching ramifications that lead to an overall restructuring, the lexicon can tolerate a certain amount of change, loss or interference. A certain amount of flexibility may even be an intrinsic characteristic of open-class systems such as the lexicon.

An interesting perspective on the effects of loss in the lexical system involves the computer simulations of vocabulary loss provided by Meara (2004). His models are relatively small and loosely interlocking systems of 2500 items, each of which is connected to two other items from which it receives input, and each of which has a binary activation status ('on' or 'off'). The activation of the two other items that a particular item is connected to determines its own activation status: once input falls below a certain threshold, the item will be deactivated.[1] A series of simulations with different 'attrition events' on such networks demonstrates that the loss of a certain amount of lexical knowledge can take place without dramatic consequences for the overall system: in most cases, the trajectory of loss shows an initial period of great stability, followed by a dramatic cascade where a great proportion of information is lost in a relatively short period of time, after which the (reduced) system stabilizes again.

While these findings provide food for very interesting speculations on language attrition in real life, the widely made suggestion that the lexicon is the most vulnerable area of linguistic knowledge remains problematic for two reasons. Firstly, the claim that attrition will affect the lexicon 'first' is unwarranted, as there are virtually no longitudinal studies that would make it possible to charter the chronology of the attritional process. Secondly, the assumption that attrition will affect the lexicon most dramatically of all linguistic areas presupposes that it is possible and meaningful to compare the degree of L2 influence or L1 reduction across linguistic systems. However, it is hard to see what measuring stick should be used to make such a comparison. How does the 'forgetting' of a certain number of lexical items score in relation to the erosion of some morphological rule? We would suggest that, at the present state of knowledge, it is futile to imply comparisons across linguistic levels with respect to the speed and degree with which they will be affected by the attritional process.

1.3. Types of lexical attrition

One of the most common fallacies of research on L1 attrition is that any indication of CLI is interpreted as evidence for attrition, particularly in the area of the lexicon. However, an approach that wants to distinguish L2 influence on L1, as it is experienced by all bilinguals, from L1 attrition, which is compounded by internal restructuring due to lack of input, should exercise caution in this respect, and give some consideration to what attrition is and what it is not. A very useful classification is provided by Pavlenko (2004), who proposes five types of CLI (see also Pavlenko, this volume):

(1) *Borrowing.* The process of borrowing involves the use of L2 elements that are typically morphologically and phonologically integrated into the L1 system. This is a phenomenon which is frequent in the language of immigrants, particularly where political or social phenomena are concerned that are not identical to what the immigrant was used to in the country of origin (see Ben-Rafael & Schmid, 2007, for examples from the spoken French of immigrants in Israel who had joined a Kibbutz). Arguably this type of CLI constitutes a semantic enrichment of the system, and cannot be taken as evidence for attrition: it is not an indication of previously existing elements no longer being available to the speaker, but of the vocabulary of the speaker (or of the immigrant community) being extended to encompass new concepts and items.

(2) *Restructuring.* In the process of restructuring, existing L1 items are reanalyzed according to the semantic scope of the corresponding L2 item. In other words, while the item itself remains a part of the language, its meaning is changed. Pavlenko cites the example of the Spanish verb *correr* 'to run', which is (infelicitously) used by Cuban immigrants in the USA in phrases such as 'running for office' (Otheguy & Garcia, 1988, ct. by Pavlenko, 2004: 51).

(3) *Convergence.* The process of convergence refers to the merging of L1 and L2 concepts, creating one single form that is different from both the L1 and the L2 one. The example quoted by Pavlenko (2004: 52) is color categories, where it has been shown that bilinguals can have norms that diverge significantly from the monolingual ones in both languages.

(4) *Shift.* The process of shift describes the changing of L1 items or structures towards norms specified by the L2, for example in the area of emotion terms and scripts (Pavlenko, 2005).

(5) *Attrition.* The process is characterized by the fact that the L1 system is not merely changed in the ways described above (which, as was pointed out, may often be considered an enrichment or extension of an otherwise intact overall system), but is simplified or 'shrunk' to some degree. This process may imply internal restructuring of the

system by way of processes such as analogical levelling of grammatical features, loss of vocabulary and an overall reduction in complexity (see Schmid, 2004).

The terminology used above may appear to be slightly misleading, since distinguishing the *internally* induced restructuring/loss under (5) from the *externally* induced processes described under (1)–(4) implies that these do not constitute attrition, i.e. that changes in the L1 system which can be ascribed to language contact are not part of the overall attrition process. Actual research practice, however, usually lumps all of these processes together under the general heading of 'attrition'.

The methodological challenge that arises from this classification, then, is how to distinguish indications of the processes described under (1)–(4) from attrition as it is understood under (5) in experimental practice. For example, it is often not evident from the available data whether a speaker codeswitches intentionally in order to make a pragmatic or semantic point, or whether the switch is triggered by the fact that access to the corresponding L1 item has been compromised. Even if the speaker overtly indicates that he/she cannot locate a particular lexical item, this may not indicate that the word has been permanently lost. All speakers experience such word-finding difficulties from time to time (see Ecke, this volume).

Investigations should therefore rely not only on superficial scans of data for codeswitches, borrowings and other infelicitous or non-target-like use of the L1, but apply more holistic and controlled measures that may reveal a more accurate overall picture of the linguistic repertoire of the speaker.

2. Research Designs and Findings

Research on language attrition has always been characterized by strong interdisciplinarity. This is reflected in the somewhat eclectic collection of research tools that have been borrowed from various other research fields and applied more or less rigorously in the hope that they may be suited to detect attrition. Despite the indisputable progress made with respect to methodological questions over the past decade (see for example the contributions in Schmid *et al.*, 2004), methodological inconsistencies still abound. This is why this section will present an overview of the most important tasks that have been used with respect to lexical aspects of L1 attrition, focusing on methodological aspects, theoretical assumptions and findings.

2.1. Verbal fluency

2.1.1. Method

The *verbal fluency task* (VFT) is one of the most popular tools in language attrition research, partly because it is very simple to administer across languages, since it does not use linguistic material that would have to be adapted. A further advantage is that it has been reported to be highly reliable in a variety of populations (Roberts & Le Dorze, 1998). In the VFT, the subject is invited to produce as many words as possible from a particular semantic category (e.g. animals, clothes, food) during a period of time usually lasting 60 seconds. An alternative is to elicit words based not on semantic but on formal criteria, by asking the respondent to produce words which begin with a certain letter (e.g. the letter *p*, *l* or *t*). The instructions, typically, are as follows: 'I would like to see how many different animals (or words starting with the letter *p*) you can call to mind and name for about a minute. Any animal will do. For instance you can start with *dog*'.

The responses are recorded and all words which are part of the given category and language are counted as correct responses. The score is the total number of correct responses produced during the 60-second period. Formal verbal fluency is usually found to be slightly more difficult than semantic verbal fluency; it gives rise to more variation within normal populations (Roberts & Le Dorze, 1998) and seems to be more sensitive to aging effects (Evrard, 2001: 182).

2.1.2. Assumptions

The VFT is used to measure the rate of lexical retrieval. This task has frequently been applied in neuropsychology for the assessment of lexical performance in aphasia (Goodglass & Kaplan, 1983; Nespoulous *et al.*, 1986), dementia (Martin & Fedio, 1983) and to assess the effects of aging in monolinguals (Cardebat *et al.*, 1990) and bilinguals (cf. the reviews in Goral, 2004). In the context of multilingualism, the VFT is assumed to reflect the dominance pattern of the languages (Gollan *et al.*, 2002; Roberts & Le Dorze, 1997). However, it has been shown that lexical productivity is largely dependent on category choice: in semantic verbal fluency some categories (e.g. animals, clothes) obtain higher results than others (e.g. toys, tools or weapons) since those categories contain more items, and more frequent ones, than others (cf. Evrard, 2001; Sabourin, 1988). Similarly, in formal VFTs, the recommendation is to choose a frequent word-initial consonant (this criterion, of course, varies across languages, but is relatively easy to assess on the basis of standard dictionaries).

2.1.3. Findings from attrition studies

The VFT has been used in a number of studies on L1 attrition. The format of the task used most often in attrition studies is semantic, in particular the categories animals and fruit and vegetables (Keijzer, 2007; Schmid, 2007; Waas, 1996; Yağmur, 1997: 91). Ammerlaan (1996: 94f) used three different semantic and three different phonological criteria for each language.

Generally speaking, language attrition is a research area where findings are often ambiguous and unsatisfactory. In this context, the VFT appears at first glance to be quite a rewarding tool, since it has (so far) invariably produced significant findings: attriters have lower scores than control groups (Keijzer, 2007; Schmid, 2007; Waas, 1996: 110; Yağmur, 1997: 91) and they perform better in their L2 than in their L1 (Ammerlaan, 1996: 112).

However, the initial enthusiasm in view of these results is often tempered when the findings are investigated in more detail: while between-group differences are clear-cut and easy to detect, all attempts to account for within-group variation have failed so far. Waas (1996) and Yağmur (1997) tried to establish whether there was a correlation between the L1 VFT results on the one hand and the attitudinal component (which Waas measured on the basis of 'ethnic affiliation' and Yağmur by means of a Subjective Ethnolinguistic Vitality Questionnaire) on the other, but neither correlation was significant. Schmid (2007) assessed the impact of the frequency of exposure to and the use of the L1 in various settings, equally to no avail. Similarly, it appears that educational level is a factor that plays a minimal role for this task in the context of L1 attrition: Yağmur (1997: 77) and Dostert (2007) found that educational level was not a strong predictive factor on the VFT. This is an interesting result, since more metalinguistic tasks, such as the C-Test, are typically strongly dependent on individuals' education levels.

Furthermore, while in fact being a highly specific test of lexical retrieval, the VFT has often been interpreted along the lines of a measure of overall proficiency. This overgeneralization of VFT scores is unwarranted because they are not necessarily related to measures in other linguistic domains. Schmid (2006) demonstrated a very weak correlation between VFT and lexical diversity and fluency (accounting for less than 10% of the variance observed across the sample), and Yağmur (1997) did not find any correlation between the VFT and the scores on the syntactic test (a relative clause formation task).

In other words, the VFT may indeed be able to detect differences in speed of retrieval between attrited and nonattrited populations.

However, it is very difficult to draw any conclusions as to what these differences relate to. If attriters are consistently outperformed by control subjects, but if their performance is unrelated to the frequency of exposure to and use of L1 or to their attitudes towards L1, then what causes attrition in the first place? Additionally, VFT studies with bilingual populations in general have shown that bilinguals may be less fluent than monolinguals in each language, both in semantic and in formal fluency (Gollan *et al.*, 2002; Rosselli *et al.*, 2000). There may therefore be an effect of the L2 on the L1 which all bilinguals experience to some degree, and which impacts on their performance on the VFT. It is unclear to what degree the poorer performance found in attriters can be ascribed to this general bilingualism effect, and to what degree it is the outcome of language attrition.

2.2. Picture naming and matching

2.2.1. Method

Tasks investigating lexical retrieval by means of picture stimuli fall into two categories: those that investigate recall and those that investigate recognition. In both cases, subjects are presented with a series of pictures (usually black-and-white line drawings; a set of standardized pictures for this purpose is presented by Snodgrass & Vanderwart, 1980). In the retrieval task (*picture naming*), the subject is asked to name the word as quickly as possible. In the *recognition task*, the name of the item either has to be identified in forced choice, or the subject is asked to indicate whether the word presented together with the picture is the accurate name for the object in the picture.

Such tasks typically measure two things: accuracy and response time. Accuracy is relatively unproblematic to establish (a pilot study among the target population can be helpful in eliminating problematic pictures and identifying target responses). If reaction time (RT) is to be measured, it is advisable to use specialized equipment and software that can accurately gauge the interval between presentation and response. However, sophistication of measuring methods in picture naming and matching experiments in language attrition research varies considerably. One study used an untimed task (Schoenmakers-Klein Gunnewiek, 1998), while two others measured the interval with a hand-held timer (Isurin, 2000; Soesman, 1997). In Ammerlaan's (1996) study, the onset of the picture presentation was marked by means of a beep that, together with the response, was taped so that the interval could later be measured. To date, in attrition research, only Hulsen (2000) has used fully appropriate and reliable means of measuring by the use of specialized soft- and hardware, including a voice-key.

2.2.2. Assumptions

The naming of a picture, object or line drawing triggers at least three steps: (1) analysis of the structural characteristics of the object or the picture, (2) activation of the semantic representation and (3) activation of the corresponding phonological representation. All three steps have been shown to be liable to selective impairment in different kinds of pathologies (see Gérard, 2004, for a review). Qualitative analysis of errors occurring in such tasks allows the identification of the locus of the failure either at the semantic level – where an inappropriate (or partially inappropriate) semantic representation may be activated – or at the form level – where difficulties in activating the corresponding phonological form may arise.[2] Alternatively, Ferrand (1997) claims that naming consists of the selection of a linguistic form corresponding to a visual representation and does not necessarily involve the activation of the corresponding semantic information. Although the first view is probably more common, both views may account for the major findings from bilingual lexical retrieval and access studies. The most robust effects observed in such investigations, i.e. frequency and cognate effects, have been located at the form rather than the semantic level (Jescheniak & Levelt, 1994). Frequency effects have been explained in terms of activation threshold as a function of frequency and recency of an item's activation (Paradis, 2004). Accordingly, more frequent lexical items are easier to activate. Cognate effects are clearly located at the phonological (or orthographical) form level, since cognates may have very different meanings in the two languages. Facilitation effects have been explained by the cumulative effect of their frequencies, similar to what is observed in intralingual homographs or homophones (Jescheniak & Levelt, 1994).

Matching tasks are frequently conducted with the same material as naming tasks and are supposed to be easier because the phonological form only has to be recognized and associated with the picture and not 'actively' retrieved. According to Paradis (2004), matching tasks are easier to accomplish than naming tasks even in cases where the activation threshold of an item is higher due to low frequency, lack of use or pathology. Recognition of items involves external stimulation and thus requires fewer neurological impulses than retrieval of items where the only stimulation is internal semantic or visual representation.

2.2.3. Findings from L1 attrition research

Picture naming and/or matching tasks have been used in both quantitative (Albert, 2002; Ammerlaan, 1996; Hulsen, 2000; Schoenmakers-Klein Gunnewiek, 1998; Soesman, 1997) and qualitative (Isurin, 2000; Olshtain & Barzilay, 1991) investigations of L1 attrition. Among the quantitative studies, Albert (2002), Hulsen (2000) and Schoenmakers-Klein Gunnewiek (1998) established a reference group of unattrited native speakers against which findings were compared, while Ammerlaan (1996) and Soesman (1997) investigated within-group variation, comparing more and less attrited speakers.

Most of the quantitative investigations listed above classify their stimuli as high- and low-frequency (with the exception of Albert, 2002), and as cognate or noncognate in L1 and L2 (with the exception of Soesman, 1997). Some apply further criteria, such as single-stem versus compound items (Ammerlaan, 1996; Hulsen, 2000), morphological similarity (measured in number of syllables, Ammerlaan, 1996) and so on. Albert (2002) used a timed picture-naming task in L1 where compound nouns were primed by their L2 counterparts.

High-frequency items were found, without exception, to be retrieved faster (where a timed setup was used) and more accurately than low-frequency ones. With respect to cognates, overall findings are slightly more ambiguous: while Ammerlaan and Hulsen found a facilitating effect in cognates, Schoenmakers-Klein Gunnewiek's results are inconclusive as to the role of similarity. A case study of a 10-year-old Russian orphan in the process of forgetting her L1 (Isurin, 2000) even found that cognates were more difficult to retrieve; however, as this study is based on the observation of a single subject and the number of cognate and noncognate items in the stimuli was not controlled, these results may not be generalizable. In Albert's (2002) priming experiment, cognate status of each part of the compounds was the main variable, with the result that cognates with similar meaning in both languages facilitated naming, whereas *faux amis* increased both error rates and RTs.

Olshtain and Barzilay (1991) investigated naming in the context of narrative speech by means of *Frog, Where Are You?* (Mayer, 1969), a picture-based booklet frequently used in linguistic research to elicit spontaneous descriptive and narrative speech (cf. Berman & Slobin, 1994). They found much larger variation in words used to express infrequent specific nouns (such as 'pond', 'deer', 'gopher', 'jar' etc.) for a group of Americans living in Israel than for the American control group. Yağmur (1997) obtained similar results with the same material for Turkish immigrants in Australia.

The overall findings suggest a long-term effect of emigration on both RTs and accuracy in lexical retrieval: in Soesman's (1997) data, the best results were achieved by those immigrants who had the shortest length of residence and the largest amount of contact with the L1 in daily life. Hulsen (2000), who investigated three generations of immigrants, found an increase in RTs and a decrease in accuracy across generations. Interestingly, the overall RTs in her first generation of subjects did not differ from those of the control group, but their responses were significantly less accurate, and there was greater interindividual variation in response time.

Ammerlaan (1996) and Hulsen (2000) went on to present the same stimuli to the subjects in a picture-matching experiment subsequent to the picture-naming task, in order to test whether those items that subjects had been unable to recall might be recognized. In a forced-choice task (with the correct word plus five distractor items), Ammerlaan (1996) found that subjects were still unable to identify the correct item in one third of the cases that they had been unable to recall. Hulsen (2000), who presented the picture together with one word and asked subjects to indicate whether it was the correct item or not, found that her first generation immigrants did not perform differently from the control group on this task. Schoenmakers-Klein Gunnewiek (1998), who used different items in the naming and in the matching tasks, found no overall difference between her experimental groups and the control group. Similarly, Jaspaert and Kroon (1989) found no attrition with a vocabulary test where the subjects had to give a definition or translation of a number of low frequency L1 words.

In sum, picture-naming tasks appear to be a valid measure for detection of lexical retrieval difficulties among attriters, as indicated by the loss of accuracy and increased RTs. Lexical recognition appears to be less prone to attrition: the only study which found a group effect in a matching task (Ammerlaan, 1996) includes a group of participants who emigrated at a younger age than those investigated in the other studies (from six years onwards); and age proved to be an important predicting variable in this study. This suggests that attrition may affect recognition skills only in the most severe cases: it has recently been pointed out that the effects of the so-called Critical Period may be much stronger and more clear-cut in L1 attrition than in L2 acquisition (Köpke & Schmid, 2004: 20). Attrition in speakers for whom input in the L1 is dramatically reduced before puberty (e.g. children of migrants) or even ceases entirely (e.g. international adoptees) has been shown to be on an entirely different scale from what can be found in older migrants (for an overview and discussion see Köpke & Schmid, 2004: 9f).

On the other hand, longer latencies in picture naming alone are not necessarily a sign of attrition. Bilinguals have repeatedly been shown to be slower than monolinguals in such tasks (Mack, 1983; Mägiste, 1979) and RT is frequently taken as a measure of language dominance. More recent studies, however, have evidenced increased response times in naming even with bilinguals being tested in their dominant language (see Gollan *et al.*, 2005; or the review in Michael & Gollan, 2005). So, once again, limits between 'normal' bilingualism and attrition appear to be fuzzy.

2.3. Spontaneous speech

The role of free data in investigations of language attrition is a rather controversial one. On the one hand, it is argued that using language spontaneously is what people do naturally. If the goal of an investigation is to judge to what degree language attrition is a 'real' phenomenon that might impact on people's lives and their ability to communicate, then millisecond differences in RTs in a picture-naming task may be of little relevance, irrespective of their value for psycholinguistic-theoretical investigations of language processing. On the other hand, phenomena that occur in free speech are difficult to quantify and interpret (Schmid, 2004).

Spontaneous speech is a less targeted and specialised method of elicitation than the ones mentioned above, in that it allows the analysis of large and varying areas of the linguistic repertoire (Schmid, 2004). For the purpose of the present overview, however, the application of spontaneous speech for investigations of the mental lexicon will be focused on.

2.3.1. Method

The first issue to be decided by any investigation that wishes to use free data is: how free? To what degree is it possible to avoid the observer's paradox and obtain truly naturalistic data? There are cases of investigations of L1 attrition that have recorded naturally occurring conversations between potential attriters (Ben Rafael, 2004; Brons-Albert, 1994; Jarvis, 2003) or children at play (Bolonyai, 1999; Schmitt, 2001), but most often the data used are semistructured (often autobiographical) interviews (De Bot & Clyne, 1994; De Bot *et al.*, 1991; Gross, 2004; Leisiö, 2001; Schmid, 2002; Søndergaard, 1996), picture descriptions or retellings of picture-book stories (Köpke, 1999; Yağmur, 1997) or film retellings (Dewaele & Pavlenko, 2003; Keijzer, 2007; Pavlenko, 2004; Schmid, 2007). Two case studies (Hutz, 2004; Jaspaert & Kroon, 1992) and one group study (Laufer, 2003) also investigate 'spontaneous' written production in written correspondence or in a composition task.

The second issue is what aspect of the spoken data obtained in this manner is to be analyzed. In this respect, the classification of CLI phenomena proposed by Pavlenko (2004, see above) is extremely relevant. The speech of most bilinguals will contain immediately visible and noticeable phenomena indicating her processes (1)–(4) (borrowing, restructuring, convergence and shift). Many investigations have therefore focused on codeswitching, codemixing, codemerging and other types of interferences or 'errors', classified according to various criteria, e.g. more formal borrowings versus semantic transfer (Hutz, 2004).

It has been argued, however, that accounts of such phenomena may not provide an accurate and holistic picture of an individual's L1 proficiency: for some speakers, using L2 items may be a communicative strategy, which may have many purposes (such as flagging a bilingual identity or expressing concepts which are felt to be L2-specific). Other speakers may make an effort not to codeswitch because they disapprove of mixing languages, while for others still, such switches may indeed signal a retrieval problem in the L1. Any large-scale investigation of language attrition will find that these strategies vary considerably across informants; but they may not be an indication of L1 proficiency at all unless clear instructions had been given to avoid switches.

It has therefore been proposed that investigations of free data should not only focus on error analysis, but attempt to include phenomena that will be less susceptible to communicative strategies. For the purpose of investigations of the mental lexicon, two measurements are of particular relevance: lexical diversity and fluency.

The concept of lexical richness and diversity focuses not only on the size of the active vocabulary at a speaker's disposal, but also on how this is deployed in actual discourse. Traditionally, this was measured by the type-token ratio (TTR), which simply calculated how many words a speaker had used in total (types), and how many of these were different lemmata (tokens). More recently, it has been shown that this measure is not stable if applied to data samples of varying length: TTRs decrease in longer text samples. A measure of lexical diversity that compensates for this factor, called 'D', has therefore been proposed by Malvern and Richards (2002; also Richards, 1987).[3]

The second measurement of relevance here is fluency. Fluency in both native and non-native speakers is a complicated and controversial concept (see the overview in Cucchiarini *et al.*, 2000), however, it has most often been linked to the frequency and distribution of phenomena such as speech rate, hesitations, filled pauses, repetitions and self-repairs (e.g. Lennon, 1990; Möhle, 1984). Nakuma (1997a, 1997b) argues for a combined rate of communicative competence through which individual attrition levels could be measured, and which is calculated on the basis of speech rate, pause duration, repetitions and gap filling as well as the more 'traditional' measures of errors, syntactic complexity etc. A further factor that should be taken into account, however, is that the distribution of hesitation markers might change not only quantitatively but also qualitatively during the attrition process. It has been proposed that native speakers employ hesitations predominantly for purposes of macroplanning, that is, information retrieval and inference, while microplanning issues of converting this information into actual linguistic output are largely automatized (Kess, 1992; Levelt, 1989). While both attriters and non-attriters can be expected to employ hesitation phenomena for macroplanning purposes, microplanning should have become less automatized for attriters, and more intraconstituent hesitation markers should therefore be found (e.g. Yukawa 1997).

2.3.2. Assumptions

For the most part, the investigation of the occurrence, nature and distribution of 'error' phenomena in the speech of attriters (or bilinguals in general) has been theory-neutral. Most of the studies followed the general CLI hypothesis investigating the claim that the lexicon is more vulnerable to interference from L2 than other linguistic domains (see overview in Köpke & Schmid, 2004).

Predictions as to lexical richness are very similar to the ones made with respect to picture naming above: it is assumed that language attriters consistently underuse their L1, and that this nonactivation and inhibition will lead to a higher activation threshold. This will be particularly the case with respect to less frequent lexical items, so that the prediction is that attriters will not only have a reduced lexicon, but one that consists mainly of items that are frequent in unattrited speech.

Investigations of fluency present an interesting perspective, as in L2 learners these phenomena develop towards the native-speaker norm as the L2 system develops (Towell *et al.*, 1996). It is possible that more detailed investigations of hesitation or self-repair phenomena might indicate specific areas of linguistic knowledge in general and the mental lexicon in particular, which become problematic in the process of attrition.

2.3.3. Findings from investigations on L1 attrition

2.3.3.1. Errors.
Investigations of errors in free-spoken data collected from language attriters often attempt to assess the relative degrees of

'erosion' of the overall system across linguistic levels. Of relevance here is the assumption – first made at a very early stage of attrition research – that the lexicon is the most vulnerable area (Andersen, 1982). Some evidence for this assumption is provided by analyses of different error types in natural conversations (Brons-Albert, 1994; Jarvis, 2003), in picture descriptions (Köpke, 2002) and in written correspondence (Hutz, 2004). On the other hand, a longitudinal case study of a corpus of letters by Jaspaert and Kroon (1992) suggests that lexical attrition is less prevalent than generally expected. However, as this study provides no comparative baseline, either from other linguistic domains or from investigations of other populations, this is a claim that remains difficult to substantiate.[4]

More specific predictions regarding lexical errors can be made within particular frameworks or models of language learning or the mental lexicon. The 4-M Model (Myers-Scotton & Jake, 2000) predicts a hierarchy wherein 'content morphemes' are more vulnerable to attrition than 'early system morphemes', such as gender, which is directly elected when a noun is accessed. These in turn are more vulnerable than 'late system morphemes', such as case or plural, which are contextually activated. Investigations among both adults (Gross, 2004) and children (Schmitt, 2004) seem to provide support for such a prediction. Adopting Levelt's (1989) Speaking model, Brons-Albert (1994) analyzed speech errors involving compounds with varying degrees of cross-language transparency and concluded that typologically similar languages, such as German and Dutch, are linked at the form level with respect to morphological and phonological representations. With the exception of these studies, however, to date most approaches to lexical errors in attrited speech have remained descriptive (e.g. Hutz, 2004; Jaspaert & Kroon, 1992).

2.3.3.2. Diversity. Investigations of lexical diversity in free speech are rather scarce to date. The earliest study to include an assessment of the development of TTRs is De Bot and Clyne (1994). In this study, the TTRs calculated on the basis of free-spoken data collected from L1 German immigrants in Australia were contrasted with earlier data from the same sample, collected two decades previously. No difference was found between the measures at the two points in time. This, however, does not preclude the possibility that lexical diversity had suffered at an earlier stage, and that a comparison against a non-attrited baseline might reveal differences. Laufer (2003) similarly investigated the development of lexical diversity (in this case in written production) across the emigration span. She contrasted data from three groups of Russian immigrants to Israel with different emigration spans, and concluded that with increased length of residence the percentage of high frequency words increases, while overall TTRs decrease.

Two investigations of L1 German long-term immigrants to the USA and the UK (Schmid, 2002, 2004) and to Anglophone Canada and The Netherlands (Schmid, 2007), which contrasted TTRs against a nonattrited baseline, revealed a significant decrease between the control and the experimental groups. Interestingly, the former study, an investigation of three groups of immigrants with different overall proficiency levels in L1, found that lexical diversity was the only area in which the group with the highest proficiency level differed from the control group, while their performance on various other morphological and syntactic measures appeared largely unimpaired. This finding provides some corroboration for the assumption that the lexicon is the area of the linguistic system that will be affected earliest and most drastically by attrition.

On the other hand, Dewaele and Pavlenko (2003) report that the data produced by a group of L1 Russian speakers on a film-retelling task did not differ from those elicited from a monolingual group of Russian speakers, either in lexical diversity[5] or in overall productivity. However, the group investigated had a comparatively short emigration span (between 1.5 and 14 years, with the majority of speakers having lived in the USA for 3–8 years).

Taken together, the results presented here indicate that lexical diversity is indeed a feature of language use that may gradually show some decline in the attritional process, but that may also stabilize again at a later stage. No decline was found in the very early (Dewaele & Pavlenko, 2003) or very late (De Bot & Clyne, 1994) stages, while Laufer (2003) and Schmid (2004, 2006)[6] do find significant decrease, which in the former case appears to be related to emigration length.

2.3.3.3. Fluency. The development of fluency indicators, such as speech rate, hesitation phenomena etc. is one of the more radically under-researched areas of language attrition. A case study of three young attriters of Japanese (Yukawa, 1997) reports variable findings as to the development of hesitation markers, with only two of the three speakers showing a slight increase towards the end of the attrition period (between five and 16 months). The only investigation that systematically compares the frequency of pauses, filled pauses, repetitions and retractions (self-corrections) between attriters and nonattriters is Schmid (2007). She reports a significant difference between her two experimental groups, L1 German speakers in Anglophone Canada and The Nether-lands, on the one hand, and the control group on the other, on all of these measures except filled pauses. With respect to this latter phenomenon, the Canadian group behaves very similarly to the control group, while the average number of filled pauses in the Dutch group is almost twice as high. Preliminary results in a reanalysis of older data (Köpke, 2007) also suggest reduced fluency in attriters (Germans in France and Anglophone Canada) compared to control subjects.

Given these findings and the results reported by Dewaele and Pavlenko (2003), who found no difference in overall productivity between the attrited group and the control group, it appears vital to conduct further investigations on fluency markers in attrition. Here it should also be taken into account that it may not be wholly appropriate to investigate each of the measures enumerated above separately: while an increase in each separate phenomenon may indicate a reduction in overall fluency, there may also be high degrees of individual differences: one speaker may have the tendency to pause and reflect when he/she experiences retrieval difficulties, while another may repeat the previous word several times or prefer a filled pause. It may therefore be profitable to look at the combined incidence of hesitation markers per speaker, taking into account the positions in the sentence at which these markers occur, since these may provide indications of where particular grammatical problems are located (Schmid & Beers Fägersten, forthcoming).

2.4. Judgment tasks

2.4.1. Methodology

The last group of tasks involve *judgements of semantic distinctions*, usually on verbs, as these tend to show more language-specific usage than other lexical items, such as nouns. In particular, such judgments have investigated idiomatic verb use (Altenberg, 1991), metaphoric verb sense and opaque expressions (Pelc, 2001) and collocations used with verbs (Laufer, 2003). The expressions to be judged are presented within the context of a sentence in writing (Altenberg, 1991; Laufer, 2003) or in two modalities, aurally and in writing (Pelc, 2001). Both binary acceptability ratings (Laufer, 2003; Pelc, 2001) and preference indications on a five-point Likert-scale (Altenberg, 1991) have been used. Addition-ally, Altenberg (1991) conducted a post-test interview where she invited the participants to comment upon their own judgments.

2.4.2. Assumptions

It is generally supposed that semantic aspects of vocabulary use as reflected in metaphorical or idiomatic verb use and collocations are indications of the structure of the mental lexicon. Hence, any change in use can be taken as evidence of structural changes in the mental lexicon as a consequence of attrition. In other words, these tasks are aimed at capturing phenomena that fall under Pavlenko's (2004) categories of restructuring or convergence (see above). Following this rationale, it is possible to distinguish changes in the structure of the mental lexicon that have been completed (resulting in a permanent change with stable performance) and others that are still ongoing (resulting in variation of performance). Unfortunately, this latter point has not yet been addressed by attrition studies.

2.4.3. Findings

The first study to apply this type of semantic judgment in an attrition context was Altenberg's (1991) case study of two German–English bilinguals. While these two subjects gave non-target-like judgments in a number of cases, the post-test interviews indicate that judgement tasks (which are generally supposed to be offline tasks and as such less sensitive to performance effects) are far from reflecting stable competence: in many cases, the participants indicated surprise at their judgement when they were confronted with their answers. This variation in semantic judgements indicates that attrition might affect linguistic confidence, so that attriters become somewhat insecure with respect to native norms of their L1.

Altenberg's initial impression that the accuracy of semantic judgments might be affected by the process of language attrition is confirmed by quantitative investigations of Greek–English (Pelc, 2001) and Russian–Hebrew (Laufer, 2003) bilinguals. Laufer's (2003: 20) analysis of collocation judgements is based on the claim that 'when an incorrect collocation is judged correct, the reason is likely to be a change in the way words have become related to other words in the mental lexicon'.

The issue of what judgment tasks actually measure, and what interpretations and conclusions they allow, is highly controversial (cf. the discussion in Altenberg & Vago, 2004). Among the most frequently expressed critiques is that these tasks might reflect metalinguistic skills rather than linguistic proficiency, and that these metalinguistic skills are less prone to attrition (De Bot *et al.*, 1991). However, Köpke and Nespoulous (2001) showed that (grammaticality) judgement tasks may be more sensitive in detecting attrition than online production tasks. Concerning semantic distinctions – which are the most frequently investigated aspect of lexical representation within the context of attrition – these assumptions appear to be corroborated by the findings reviewed above.

3. Discussion

The findings presented in this chapter reveal that the mental lexicon has consistently been found to be affected by the language attrition process. These findings are striking in the context of investigations of attrition on other levels of linguistic knowledge, such as the grammatical or phonological system, which typically find very little change (at least in postpuberty migrants, see Köpke & Schmid, 2004). They do suggest that the lexicon – or at least its semantic aspects, which have been mainly studied – may indeed be more susceptible to change than other areas of language. To what degree that susceptibility is specific to attrition, as opposed to bilingual development, remains an open question.

It is noteworthy that many of the areas in which investigations of language attrition have detected differences between experimental and control populations tally with differences which are often observed in bilinguals in general: more tip-of-the-tongue phenomena (see also Ecke, this volume), weaker results in VF and longer RTs in picture naming (e.g. Gollan *et al.*, 2005; Michael & Gollan, 2005). Two alternative explanations of the differences observed between bilinguals and monolinguals with respect to lexical retrieval have recently been proposed:

(1) cross-language interference arising directly from competing lexical representations across languages;
(2) weaker links between semantic and phonological representations due to the fact that bilinguals use the words of each language less often compared to monolinguals. (Michael & Gollan, 2005: 395–397)

Interestingly, this classification reflects the two processes that from a more structural point of view have been labelled *internally* versus *externally* induced change, and as such have played an important role in accounts of language attrition. From a psycholinguistic perspective, too, attrition has been interpreted on the basis of the two cognitive processes of L2 influence on the one hand and lack of use on the other (Köpke, 2004: 17): The Activation Threshold Hypothesis (Paradis, 1993, 2007; see also Gürel, 2004; Köpke, 2002) predicts that non-use of the L1 will raise activation thresholds in this system, leading to both L2 interference and weaker links.

On the basis of the similarity of results based on observations of bilingual populations in general and of attriting populations in particular, it can be speculated that the same mechanisms (mainly related to processing costs) may assert themselves in diverse situations such as the simultaneous processing of two or more languages, L2 influence on L1 and language attrition. It is therefore possible that the process of restructuring of the L1, which we perceive as attrition in long-term immigrants, is a gradual one which starts far earlier than previously assumed. We should even entertain the possibility that the onset of attrition coincides with the onset of bilingualism; that bilinguals know and use language in a way that is fundamentally and irreversibly different from that of monolinguals (Cook, 2005).

Two methodological issues arise from this assumption:

(1) Studies of bilingualism in general, that usually seek to investigate highly proficient bilinguals, should allow for the possibility that some of their findings on the apparent processing costs of bilingualism are, in fact, due to the presence of attriters in the sample.
(2) Studies of language attrition will have to reassess the selection principles for control group subjects: comparing monolingual controls with bilingual experimental subjects may yield a distorted picture. While the practical difficulties in establishing a baseline of active bilinguals against which attriters can be compared are daunting, such reference groups are indispensable.

One theoretical implication of this is that models of the bilingual mental lexicon should be discussed more systematically with respect to their capacity to account for dynamic variation over time. Consider for example the Modified Hierarchical Model (Pavlenko, this volume): the size of the boxes corresponding to L1 and L2 words, L1- and L2-mediated concepts and shared representations may vary according to dominance patterns within bilingual development. But most importantly, the variation in the strength of the connections between L1 and L2 words on the one hand and L1 and L2 words and concepts on the other – one of the most interesting aspects also distinguishing the Revised Hierarchical Model (e.g. Kroll & Tokowicz, 2005) – should be able to account for even subtle changes in these dominance patterns, with an additional link between L1 words and the conceptual representations shared by L1 and L2 getting stronger within the attrition process.

A further important methodological issue is *task dependency*. L2-dominant bilinguals in general, and language attriters in particular, appear to be experiencing traffic from L2 to L1 in two main areas with respect to the mental lexicon:

- *retrieval and access modalities* (slower and perhaps less accurate, e.g. fluency task, naming task, hesitation and fluency phenomena in spontaneous speech);
- *restructuring* of the mental lexicon (judgments, errors in spontaneous speech or in naming tasks).

Both these processes are a reflection of the structure of the mental lexicon and show that processing and control issues may assert themselves differently, depending on the task at hand. In this respect, interesting findings are presented by Jarvis (2003) in a case study of a Finnish woman in the USA. In this study, a qualitative analysis of deviations observed in spontaneous speech (natural conversation) shows that the majority of these deviations were lexico-semantic or idiomatic in nature. When the same structures were elicited in a more formal film-retelling task, the subject did not reproduce her own errors. However, in a more metalinguistic judgement/correction task, she accepted nine out of 15 of the deviant structures she had produced spontaneously (but not in the more formal film-retelling task). This variation between tasks within a single subject indicates that task choice is an important issue in attrition research.

Regrettably, research on attrition has not yet been conducted with what is probably the most popular paradigm in research on lexical access: the lexical decision task (for a recent research review see Dijkstra, 2005). The reason for this is that the focus of attrition studies is generally on production, which many theoretical frameworks (e.g. the Activation Threshold Hypothesis) assume to be more vulnerable to attrition than receptive skills. As the lexical decision task has been shown to provide intriguing results for bilingual populations, it is quite likely that this tool may be sufficiently sensitive to give insights into the more subtle dynamics of the bilingual mental lexicon as evidenced by attriters.

In conclusion, it appears possible that attrition is merely the emerging part of the iceberg of bilingualism. The more subtle effects of L2 influence on L1, which are probably experienced by all bilinguals, usually remain under the waterline and cannot be detected except by targeted psycho- and neurolinguistic investigations. The chief benefit of two decades of research on language attrition, then, is to point out the particularities of the bilingual – who, as Grosjean (1989) so famously noted, is not two monolinguals in one person.

Acknowledgements

The authors wish to express their thanks to Aneta Pavlenko and two anonymous reviewers for their excellent critical suggestions on an earlier version of this text. We feel that this paper is much improved as a result. Any remaining inadequacies are ours alone.

Notes

1. Meara acknowledges that these simulated networks are not to be confused with an accurate representation of an actual mental lexicon, but 'a stripped-down, greatly oversimplified "lexicon" with a tiny number of elementary properties' (Meara, 2004: 138f), which nevertheless provide interesting insights into how such a process might work.
2. Problems that occur in the first step and are not linguistic in nature, are outside the scope of this review and will not be treated here.
3. The calculation of D is less straightforward than that of the simple TTR, but for text samples that have been coded in CHAT format according to the CHILDES conventions (http://childes.psy.cmu.edu/), D can be calculated with the help of the freely downloadable program CLAN.
4. The question of how to quantify and qualify the amount of attrition is relevant here: Jaspaert and Kroon observe that 5% of the main verbs in their corpus have undergone interference. Whether or not this should be considered 'substantial' remains an open question.
5. Dewaele and Pavlenko (2003) calculated lexical diversity on the basis of the Uber formula proposed by Dugast (1980) in order to compensate for varying text length.
6. Similar results are obtained in L2 attrition, e.g. in Japanese returnees where reduced diversity seems to be related to age (Fujita, 2002; Reetz-Kurashige, 1999; Yoshitomi, 1999).

References

Albert, R. (2002) La representation des connaissances morphologiques chez les bilingues dans deux langues voisines [The bilingual representation of morphological knowledge in two neighboring languages]. In J. Müller-Lancé and C.M. Riehl (eds) *Ein Kopf – viele Sprachen: Koexistenz, Interaktion und Vermittlung [One Head – Many Languages: Coexistence, Interaction and Transmission]* (pp. 15–30). Aachen: Shaker Verlag.

Altenberg, E. (1991) Assessing first language vulnerability to attrition. In H. Seliger and R. Vago (eds) *First Language Attrition* (pp. 189–206). Cambridge: Cambridge University Press.

Altenberg, E. and Vago, R. (2004) The role of grammaticality judgements in investigating first language attrition: A cross-disciplinary perspective. In M.S. Schmid, B. Köpke, M. Keijzer and L. Weilemar (eds) *First Language Attrition: Interdisciplinary Perspectives on Methodological Issues* (pp. 105–129). Amsterdam: John Benjamins.

Ammerlaan, T. (1996) "You get a bit wobbly..." – Exploring bilingual lexical retrieval processes in the context of first language attrition. Unpublished doctoral dissertation, Katholieke Universiteit Nijmegen.

Andersen, R. (1982) Determining the linguistic attributes of language attrition. In R. Lambert and B. Freed (eds) _The Loss of Language Skills_ (pp. 83–118). Rowley, MA: Newbury House.

Basso, A. (1993) Le manque du mot aphasique: Revue de la littérature [Word-finding problems in aphasics: A literature review]. _Revue de Neuropsychologie_ 3 (2), 133–155.

Ben-Rafael, M. (2004) Language contact and attrition: The spoken French of Israeli Francophones. In M.S. Schmid, B. Köpke, M. Keijzer and L. Weilemar (eds) _First Language Attrition: Interdisciplinary Perspectives on Methodological Issues_ (pp. 165–187). Amsterdam: John Benjamins.

Ben Rafael, M. and Schmid, M.S. (2007) Language attrition and ideology: Two groups of immigrants in Israel. In B. Köpke, M.S. Schmid, M. Keijzer and S. Dostert (eds) _Language Attrition: Theoretical Perspectives_ (pp. 205–226). Amsterdam: John Benjamins.

Berman, R. and Slobin, D. (1994) _Relating Events in Narrative: A Crosslinguistic Developmental Study_. Hillsdale, NJ: Lawrence Erlbaum.

Bogaards, P. and Laufer, B. (eds) (2004) _Vocabulary in a Second Language: Selection, Acquisition and Testing_. Amsterdam: John Benjamins.

Bolonyai, A. (1999) The hidden dimension of language contact: The case of Hungarian-English bilingual children. Unpublished doctoral dissertation, University of South Carolina.

Brons-Albert, R. (1994) Interferenzfehler in der Muttersprache von in den Niederlanden lebenden Deutschen [L2 induced native language interference among Germans living in The Netherlands]. In B. Spillner (ed.) _Nachbarsprachen in Europa_ [_Neighboring Languages in Europe_] (pp. 96-104). Frankfurt: Peter Lang.

Cardebat, D., Doyon, B., Puel, M., Goulet, P. and Joanette, Y. (1990) Evocation lexicale formelle et sémantique chez des sujets normaux: performances et dynamiques de production en fonction du sexe, de l'âge et du niveau d'étude [Formal and semantic verbal fluency tasks among normal subjects: Performance and production dynamics in relation to sex, age and education level]. _Acta Neurologica Belgica_ 90, 207–217.

Cook, V. (2003) _Effects of the Second Language on the First_. Clevedon: Multilingual Matters.

Cook, V. (2005) The changing L1 in the L2 user's mind. Keynote address at the 2nd International Conference on First Language Attrition, Vrije University, Amsterdam, August.

Cucchiarini, C., Strik, H. and Boves, L. (2000) Quantitative assessment of second language learners' fluency by means of automatic speech recognition technology. _Journal of the Acoustic Society of America_ 107 (2), 989–999.

De Bot, K. and Clyne, M. (1994) A 16-year longitudinal study of language attrition in Dutch immigrants in Australia. _Journal of Multilingual and Multicultural Development_ 15 (1), 17–18.

De Bot, K., Gommans, P. and Rossing, C. (1991) L1 loss in an L2 environment: Dutch immigrants in France. In H. Seliger and R. Vago (eds) _First Language Attrition_ (pp. 87–98). Cambridge: Cambridge University Press.

Dewaele, J.M. and Pavlenko, A. (2003) Productivity and lexical diversity in native and non-native speech: A study of cross-cultural effects. In V. Cook (ed.) *Effects of the Second Language on the First* (pp. 120–141). Clevedon: Multilingual Matters.

Dijkstra, T. (2005) Bilingual visual word recognition and lexical access. In J. Kroll and A.M.B. De Groot (eds) *Handbook of Bilingualism. Psycholinguistic Approaches* (pp. 179–201). Oxford: Oxford University Press.

Dijkstra, T. and Van Heuven, W. (2002) The architecture of the bilingual word recognition system: From identification to decision. *Bilingualism: Language and Cognition* 5, 175–197.

Dostert, S. (2007) The concept of 'native speaker' within SLA and FL attrition. Paper presented at the EuroSLA 17 Conference, Newcastle University, September 11–14.

Dugast, D. (1980) *La statistique lexicale* [*Lexical Statistics*]. Genève: Slatkine.

Ellis, N. (1994) Vocabulary acquisition: The implicit ins and outs of explicit cognitive mediation. In N. Ellis (ed.) *Implicit and Explicit Learning of Languages* (pp. 211–282). London: Academic Press.

Evrard, M. (2001) Contribution à l'étude de l'accès lexical aux noms propres chez des adultes d'âges différents en situation de dénomination [Contribution to the study of the lexical access of proper nouns in naming tasks among adults of different ages]. Unpublished doctoral dissertation, Université Toulouse-Le Mirail.

Ferrand, L. (1997) La dénomination d'objets: Théories et données [The naming of objects: Theories and data]. *L'Année Psychologique* 97, 113–146.

Fujita, M. (2002) Second language English attrition of Japanese bilingual children. *Dissertation Abstracts International, Section A: The Humanities and Social Sciences (DAIA)* 63 (1), 59–60.

Gérard, Y. (2004) Mémoire sémantique et sons de l'environnement [Semantic memory and environmental sounds]. Unpublished doctoral dissertation, Université de Bourgogne.

Gollan, T., Montoya, R., Fennema-Notestine, C. and Morris, S. (2005) Bilingualism affects picture naming but not picture classification. *Memory & Cognition* 33 (7), 1220–1234.

Gollan, T., Montoya, R. and Werner, G. (2002) Semantic and letter fluency in Spanish-English bilinguals. *Neuropsychology* 16, 562–576.

Goodglass, H. and Kaplan, E. (1983) *The Assessment of Aphasia and Related Disorders*. Philadelphia, PA: Lea & Febiger.

Goral, M. (2004) First-language decline in healthy aging: Implications for attrition in bilingualism. *Journal of Neurolinguistics* 17 (1), 31–52.

Goral, M., Levy, E., Obler, L. and Cohen, E. (2006) Cross-language lexical connections in the mental lexicon: Evidence from a case of trilingual aphasia. *Brain and Language* 98, 235–247.

Grainger, J. and Dijkstra, T. (1992) On the representation and use of language information in bilinguals. In R. Harris (ed.) *Cognitive Processing in Bilinguals* (pp. 207–220). Amsterdam: Elsevier.

Grosjean, F. (1989) Neurolinguists, beware! The bilingual is not two monolinguals in one person. *Brain and Language* 36, 3–15.

Grosjean, F. (1997) Processing mixed language: Issues, findings, and models. In: A.M.B. De Groot and J. Kroll (eds) *Tutorials in Bilingualism. Psycholinguistic Perspectives* (pp. 225–254). Mahwah, NJ: Lawrence Erlbaum.

Gross, S. (2004) A modest proposal: Explaining language attrition in the context of contact linguistics. In M.S. Schmid, B. Köpke, M. Keijzer and L. Weilemar (eds) *First Language Attrition: Interdisciplinary Perspectives on Methodological Issues* (pp. 1–43). Amsterdam: John Benjamins.

Gürel, A. (2004) Selectivity in L2-induced L1 attrition: A psycholinguistic account. *Journal of Neurolinguistics* 17 (1), 53–78.

Hulsen, M. (2000) Language loss and language processing. Three generations of Dutch migrants in New Zealand. Unpublished doctoral dissertation, Katholieke Universiteit Nijmegen.

Hulstijn, J. and Laufer, B. (2001) Some empirical evidence for the Involvement Load Hypothesis in vocabulary acquisition. *Language Learning* 51, 539–558.

Hutz, M. (2004) Is there a natural process of decay? A longitudinal study of language attrition. In M.S. Schmid, B. Köpke, M. Keijzer and L. Weilemar (eds) *First Language Attrition: Interdisciplinary Perspectives on Methodological Issues* (pp. 189–206). Amsterdam: John Benjamins.

Isurin, L. (2000) Deserted island: Or, a child's first language forgetting. *Bilingualism: Language and Cognition* 3 (2), 151–166.

Jarvis, S. (2003) Probing the effects of the L2 on the L1: A case study. In V. Cook (ed.) *Effects of the Second Language on the First* (pp. 81–102). Clevedon: Multilingual Matters.

Jaspaert, K. and Kroon, S. (1989) Social determinants of language loss. *Review of Applied Linguistics (I.T.L.)* 83/84, 75–98.

Jaspaert, K. and Kroon, S. (1992) From the typewriter of A.L. A case study in language loss. In W. Fase, K. Jaspaert and S. Kroon (eds) *Maintenance and Loss of Minority Languages* (pp. 137–147). Amsterdam: John Benjamins.

Jescheniak, J. and Levelt, W. (1994) Word frequency effects in speech production: Retrieval of syntactic information and of phonological form. *Journal of Experimental Psychology: Learning, Memory, and Cognition* 20 (4), 824–843.

Junqué, C., Vendrell, P. and Vendrell, J. (1995) Differential impairment and specific phenomena in 50 Catalan-Spanish aphasic patients. In M. Paradis (ed.) *Aspects of Bilingual Aphasia* (pp. 177–209). Oxford: Pergamon Press.

Keijzer, M. (2007) First language attrition: An investigation of Jakobson's regression hypothesis. Unpublished doctoral dissertation, Vrije Universiteit Amsterdam.

Kess, J. (1992) *Psycholinguistics: Psychology, Linguistics and the Study of Natural Language*. Amsterdam: John Benjamins.

Köpke, B. (1999) L'attrition de la première langue chez le bilingue tardif: implications pour l'étude psycholinguistique du bilinguisme [L1 attrition among late bilinguals: Implications for psycholinguistic investigations of bilingualism]. Unpublished doctoral dissertation, Université de Toulouse-Le Mirail.

Köpke, B. (2002) Activation thresholds and non-pathological first language attrition. In F. Fabbro (ed.) *Advances in the Neurolinguistics of Bilingualism* (pp. 119–142). Udine: Forum.

Köpke, B. (2004) Neurolinguistic aspects of attrition. *Journal of Neurolinguistics* 17 (1), 3–30.

Köpke, B. (2007) Proficiency measures in language attrition research: A reanalysis of data. Paper presented at the EuroSLA 17 Conference, Newcastle University, September.

Köpke, B. and Nespoulous, J.L. (2001) First language attrition in production skills and metalinguistic abilities in German-English and German-French bilinguals. In T. Ammerlaan, M. Hulsen, H. Strating and K. Yağmur (eds) *Sociolinguistic and Psycholinguistic Perspectives on Maintenance and Loss of Minority Languages* (pp. 221–234). Münster: Waxmann.

Köpke, B. and Schmid, M. (2004) First language attrition: The next phase. In M. Schmid, B. Köpke, M. Keijzer and L. Weilemar (eds) *First Language Attrition: Interdisciplinary Perspectives on Methodological Issues* (pp. 1–43). Amsterdam: John Benjamins.

Kremin, H. (1994) Perturbations lexicales: Les troubles de la dénomination [Lexical difficulties: Naming disorders]. In X. Seron and M. Jeannerod (eds) *Neuropsychologie humaine [Human Neuropsychology]* (pp. 375–389). Liège: Mardage.

Kremin, H. and De Agostini, M. (1995) Impaired and preserved picture naming in two bilingual patients with brain damage. In M. Paradis (ed.) *Aspects of Bilingual Aphasia* (pp. 101–110). Oxford: Pergamon Press.

Kroll, J. (1993) Accessing conceptual representations for words for words in a second language. In R. Schreuder and B. Weltens (eds) *The Bilingual Lexicon* (pp. 54–81). Amsterdam: John Benjamins.

Kroll, J. and Tokowicz, N. (2001) The development of conceptual representation for words in a second language. In J. Nicol (ed.) *One Mind, Two Languages: Bilingual Language Processing* (pp. 49–71). Cambridge, MA: Blackwell.

Kroll, J. and Tokowicz, N. (2005) Models of bilingual representation and processing. Looking back and to the future. In J. Kroll and A.M.B. De Groot (eds) *Handbook of Bilingualism. Psycholinguistic Approaches* (pp. 531–553). Oxford: Oxford University Press.

Laufer, B. (2003) The influence of L2 on L1 collocational knowledge and on L1 lexical diversity in free written expression. In V. Cook (ed.) *Effects of the Second Language on the First* (pp. 19–31). Clevedon: Multilingual Matters.

Leisiö, L. (2001) Morphosyntactic convergence and integration in Finland Russian. Unpublished doctoral dissertation, University of Tampere.

Lennon, P. (1990) Investigating fluency in EFL: A quantitative approach. *Language Learning* 3, 387–417.

Levelt, W. (1989) *Speaking: From Intention to Articulation*. Cambridge, MA: MIT Press.

Mack, M. (1983) Psycholinguistic consequences of early bilingualism: A comparative study of the performance of English monolinguals and French-English bilinguals in phonetics, syntax, and semantic experiments. Unpublished doctoral dissertation, Brown University.

Mägiste, E. (1979) The competing language systems of the multilingual: A developmental study of decoding and encoding processes. *Journal of Verbal Learning and Verbal Behavior* 18, 79–89.

Malvern, D. and Richards, B. (2002) Investigating accommodation in language proficiency interviews using a new measure of lexical diversity. *Language Testing* 19 (1), 85–104.

Martin, A. and Fedio, P. (1983) Word production and comprehension in Alzheimer's disease: The breakdown of semantic knowledge. *Brain and Language* 19, 124–141.

Mayer, M. (1969) *Frog, Where Are You?* New York: Dial Press.

Meara, P.M. (2004) Modelling vocabulary loss. *Applied Linguistics* 25 (2), 137–155.
Michael, E. and Gollan, T. (2005) Being and becoming bilingual. Individual differences and consequences for language production. In J. Kroll and A.M.B. de Groot (eds) *Handbook of Bilingualism. Psycholinguistic Approaches* (pp. 389–407). Oxford: Oxford University Press.
Möhle, D. (1984) A comparison of the second language speech production of different native speakers. In H. Dechert, D. Möhle and M. Raupach (eds) *Second Language Productions* (pp. 26–49). Tübingen: Narr.
Myers-Scotton, C. and Jake, J. (2000) Four types of morphemes: Evidence from aphasia, codeswitching and second language acquisition. *Linguistics* 8 (6), 1053–1100.
Nakuma, C. (1997a) A method for measuring the attrition of communicative competence: A pilot study with Spanish L3 subjects. *Applied Psycholinguistics* 18 (2), 219–235.
Nakuma, C. (1997b) Loss of communicative competence: Measurability and description of a method. *International Review of Applied Linguistics in Language Teaching* 35 (3), 199–209.
Nation, P. (1990) *Teaching and Learning Vocabulary.* New York: Newbury House.
Nation, P. (1993) Vocabulary size, growth, and use. In R. Schreuder and B. Weltens (eds) *The Bilingual Lexicon* (pp. 115–134). Amsterdam: John Benjamins.
Nespoulous, J.L., Lecours, A., Lafond, D., Lemay, A., Puel, M., Joanette, Y. *et al.* (1986) *Protocole Montréal-Toulouse, Version M1 Beta.* Montréal: Laboratoire Théophile Alajouanine.
Olshtain, E. and Barzilay, M. (1991) Lexical retrieval difficulties in adult language attrition. In H. Seliger and R. Vago (eds) *First Language Attrition* (pp. 139–150). Cambridge: Cambridge University Press.
Otheguy, R. and Garcia, O. (1988) Diffusion of lexical innovations in the Spanish of Cuban Americans. In J. Ornstein-Galicia, G. Green and D. Bixler-Marquez (eds) *Research Issues and Problems in U.S. Spanish: Latin American and Southwestern Varieties* (pp. 203–242). Brownsville, TX: University of Texas.
Paradis, M. (1993) Linguistic, psycholinguistic, and neurolinguistic aspects of interference in bilingual speakers: The activation threshold hypothesis. *International Journal of Psycholinguistics* 9 (2), 133–145.
Paradis, M. (2004) *A Neurolinguistic Theory of Bilingualism.* Amsterdam: John Benjamins.
Paradis, M. (2007) L1 attrition features predicted by a neurolinguistic theory of bilingualism. In B. Köpke, M.S. Schmid, M. Keijzer and S. Dostert (eds) *Language Attrition: Theoretical Perspectives* (pp. 121–134). Amsterdam: John Benjamins.
Pavlenko, A. (2004) L2 influence and L1 attrition in adult bilingualism. In M.S. Schmid, B. Köpke, M. Keijzer and L. Weilemar (eds) *First Language Attrition: Interdisciplinary Perspectives on Methodological Issues* (pp. 47–59). Amsterdam: John Benjamins.
Pavlenko, A. (2005) *Emotions and Multilingualism.* Cambridge: Cambridge University Press.
Pelc, L. (2001) L1 lexical, morphological and morphosyntactic attrition in Greek-English bilinguals. Unpublished doctoral dissertation, City University of New York.

Reetz-Kurashige, A. (1999) Japanese returnees' retention of English-speaking skills: Changes in verb usage over time. In L. Hansen (ed.) *Second Language Attrition in Japanese Contexts* (pp. 21–58). Oxford: Oxford University Press.

Richards, B. (1987) Type/token ratios: What do they really tell us? *Journal of Child Language* 14, 201–209.

Roberts, P. and Le Dorze, G. (1997) Semantic organization, strategy use, and productivity in bilingual semantic verbal fluency. *Brain and Language* 59, 412–449.

Roberts, P. and Le Dorze, G. (1998) Bilingual aphasia: Semantic organization, strategy use, and productivity in semantic verbal fluency. *Brain and Language* 65, 287–312.

Rosselli, M., Ardila, A., Araujo, K., Weekes, V., Caracciolo, V., Padilla, M. *et al.* (2000) Verbal fluency and repetition skills in healthy older Spanish-English bilinguals. *Applied Neuropsychology* 7, 17–24.

Sabourin, L. (1988) Processus lexico-sémantiques et hemisphere droit: etude de la fluence verbale à partir de critères formels et sémantiques [Lexical-semantic processes and the right hemisphere: Investigations of formal and semantic verbal fluency]. Master Thesis, Université de Montréal.

Schmid, M.S. (2002) *First Language Attrition, Use and Maintenance: The Case of German Jews in Anglophone Countries.* Amsterdam: John Benjamins.

Schmid, M.S. (2004) First language attrition: The methodology revised. *International Journal of Bilingualism* 8 (3), 239–255.

Schmid, M.S. (2006) Problems of measurement in language attrition research. Paper presented at the workshop 'Measurement of Bilingual Proficiency' at the 16th Sociolinguistics Symposium, Limerick, July.

Schmid, M.S. (2007) The role of L1 use for L1 attrition. In B. Köpke, M.S. Schmid, M. Keijzer and S. Dostert (eds) *Language Attrition: Theoretical Perspectives* (pp. 135–154). Amsterdam: John Benjamins.

Schmid, M.S. and Beers Fägersten, K. (forthcoming) The development of disfluency markers in L1 attrition. *Applied Linguistics.*

Schmid, M.S. and Köpke, B. (2007) Bilingualism and attrition. In B. Köpke, M.S. Schmid, M. Keijzer and S. Dostert (eds) *Language Attrition: Theoretical Perspectives* (pp. 1–8). Amsterdam: John Benjamins.

Schmid, M.S., Köpke, B., Keijzer, M. and Weilemar, L. (eds) (2004) *First Language Attrition: Interdisciplinary Perspectives on Methodological Issues.* Amsterdam: John Benjamins.

Schmitt, E. (2001) Beneath the surface: Signs of language attrition in immigrant children from Russia. Unpublished doctoral dissertation, University of South California.

Schmitt, E. (2004) No more reductions! – To the problem of evaluation of language attrition data. In M.S. Schmid, B. Köpke, M. Keijzer and L. Weilemar (eds) *First Language Attrition: Interdisciplinary Perspectives on Methodological Issues* (pp. 299–316). Amsterdam: John Benjamins.

Schoenmakers-Klein Gunnewiek, M. (1998) Taalverlies door Taalcontact? Een onderzoek bij Portugese migranten [Language loss through language contact? An investigation of Portuguese migrants]. Unpublished doctoral dissertation, Katholieke Universiteit Brabant.

Seliger, H. and Vago, R. (1991) The study of first language attrition: An overview. In H. Seliger and R. Vago (eds) *First Language Attrition* (pp. 3–15). Cambridge: Cambridge University Press.

Snodgrass, J. and Vanderwart, M. (1980) A standardised set of 260 pictures: Norms for name-agreement, image agreement, familiarity, and visual complexity. *Journal of Experimental Psychology: Human Learning and Memory* 6 (2), 174–215.

Soesman, A. (1997) An experimental study on native language attrition in Dutch adult immigrants in Israel. In J. Klatter-Folmer and S. Kroon (eds) *Dutch Overseas: Studies in Maintenance and Loss of Dutch as an Immigrant Language* (pp. 181–194). Tilburg: Tilburg University Press.

Søndergaard, B. (1996) Decline and fall of an individual bilingualism. *Journal of Multilingual and Multicultural Development* 2 (4), 297–302.

Towell, R., Hawkins, R. and Bazergui, N. (1996) The development of fluency in advanced learners of French. *Applied Linguistics* 17 (1), 84–119.

Waas, M. (1996) *Language Attrition Downunder*. Frankfurt: Peter Lang.

Weinreich, U. (1953) *Languages in Contact*. The Hague: Mouton.

Weltens, B. and Grendel, M. (1993) Attrition of vocabulary knowledge. In R. Schreuder and B. Weltens (eds) *The Bilingual Lexicon* (pp. 135–156). Amsterdam: John Benjamins.

Yağmur, K. (1997) *First Language Attrition Among Turkish Speakers in Sydney*. Tilburg: Tilburg University Press.

Yoshitomi, A. (1999) On the loss of English as a second language by Japanese returnee children. In L. Hansen (ed.) *Second Language Attrition in Japanese Contexts* (pp. 80–111). Oxford: Oxford University Press.

Yukawa, E. (1997) L1 Japanese attrition and regaining. Unpublished doctoral dissertation, Stockholm University.

Author Index

Numbers in roman refer to text citations; those in italics refer to reference citations

Subject Index

PSYCHOLOGY SERIES

Albert T. Poffenberger, Ph.D., Editor

Professor of Psychology, Columbia University

ABNORMAL PSYCHOLOGY—ITS CONCEPTS AND THEORIES
H. L. Hollingworth, Ph.D., Professor of Psychology, Barnard College, Columbia University.

CONTEMPORARY SCHOOLS OF PSYCHOLOGY
Robert S. Woodworth, Ph.D., Sc.D., Professor of Psychology, Columbia University

INTRODUCTION TO PHYSIOLOGICAL PSYCHOLOGY
Graydon LaVerne Freeman, Ph.D., Assistant Professor of Psychology, Northwestern University

INTRODUCTION TO COMPARATIVE PSYCHOLOGY
C. J. Warden, Ph.D., Associate Professor of Psychology, Columbia University; T. N. Jenkins, Ph.D., Assistant Professor of Psychology, New York University; and L. H. Warner, Ph.D., Research Associate, Department of Zoölogy, Pomona College

GENETIC PSYCHOLOGY
Adam Raymond Gilliland, Ph.D., Professor of Psychology, Northwestern University

PSYCHOLOGY—AN EMPIRICAL STUDY OF BEHAVIOR
Frederick H. Lund, Ph.D., Professor of Psychology, Temple University

THE PSYCHOLOGY OF DRESS
Elizabeth B. Hurlock, Ph.D., Instructor in Psychology, Columbia University

GESTALT PSYCHOLOGY—FACTS AND PRINCIPLES
George W. Hartmann, Ph.D., Associate Professor of Educational Psychology, Teachers College, Columbia University

COMPARATIVE PSYCHOLOGY
C. J. Warden, Ph.D., Associate Professor of Psychology, Columbia University; T. N. Jenkins, Ph.D., Assistant Professor of Psychology, New York University; and L. H. Warner, Ph.D., Research Associate, Department of Zoölogy, Pomona College
PRINCIPLES AND METHODS. VERTEBRATES.

PRINCIPLES OF EDUCATIONAL PSYCHOLOGY
W. D. Commins, Ph.D., Instructor in Psychology, Catholic University of America

THE SCIENCE OF HUMAN BEHAVIOR
Wallace T. Wait, Ph.D., Professor of Educational Psychology, Colorado State College of Education

The SCIENCE *of* HUMAN BEHAVIOR

By

WALLACE T. WAIT, Ph.D.

PROFESSOR OF EDUCATIONAL PSYCHOLOGY,
COLORADO STATE COLLEGE OF EDUCATION

PSYCHOLOGY SERIES ✓ ALBERT T. POFFENBERGER, EDITOR

THE RONALD PRESS COMPANY ✓ NEW YORK

PREFACE

This book has grown out of an attempt, during the past ten years, to bring together the material about human behavior that will most satisfactorily answer the questions that young adults ask about themselves and about those they know. It has been my experience that more than any logical and systemic treatment of human behavior in the abstract, there is need for a direct approach to an understanding of the why and how of everyday behavior. Young adults have learned many things about human behavior before they enroll in their first course in psychology, and this book is intended to enable them to consolidate and systematize the knowledge they already possess as much as it is to furnish them with new information.

My chief aim has been to present a generalized account, on the college freshman level, of the factors governing human behavior, with a view to providing the readers with simple explanations, in terms of natural law, of the phenomena of everyday experience. Thus, although these explanations are based upon scientific principles, abstruse, technical terminology has purposely been avoided.

The chief question in the course out of which this book has grown has been, "How do we get that way?" I have attempted to supply an answer to this question that will presuppose neither an exceptional aptitude for dealing with abstractions nor any previous formal study of psychology. I have tried to go on from the point where the reader's previous observation and thinking about human behavior has taken him and at the same time to furnish him with the basis for further systematic generalization. By this means it is hoped that better prediction and greater control of human behavior can be made possible to the thoughtful reader.

In assembling and organizing the material I have deliberately departed from the traditional outline of texts in general psychology. In a very real sense the book is intended to be a sampling of the various fields of psychology and a means of orienting the reader to the whole field. For this reason it cuts across the entire psychological area; but, because of the limitations imposed upon a book that is to serve as a text in college courses of one semester or quarter, it has had to confine itself to those topics most necessary to the accomplishment of its aim.

The illustrations, both verbal and pictorial, are drawn chiefly from human rather than sub-human experience. The exercises are intended to be merely means of assuring further application of the principles discussed elsewhere in other instances of common human experience. The references have been chosen primarily for their interest and their general appeal.

I am indebted to many persons for suggestions and criticisms which are largely responsible for whatever merit this book may have. Additional experience and more numerous criticisms might have resulted in further improvement of the book; I must, however, accept the responsibility for its present form and for any errors and inadequacies it may have.

I am particularly indebted to President G. W. Frasier for making it possible for me to put my ideas into practice in such a course as this book represents. I am indebted also to Professors Robert Davis, Thomas Howells, Karl Meuensinger, S. L. Crawley, W. R. Griffith, and E. R. Guthrie, and to Mr. Fred Couey, for reading the manuscript in whole or in part and for the criticisms they have offered. I am also greatly obligated to the Misses Ferree and Smith for the hours of painstaking effort they have given to the details of the several revisions of the manuscript.

I deeply appreciate the kindness of several publishers whose willingness to permit their publications to be quoted is acknowledged elsewhere. I am also indebted to numberless investigators and writers whose works have furnished the basis for many of the statements in the book. In a certain sense, little of this material can be said to be my own. I freely acknowledge my indebtedness to others for much of the content and I willingly accept the responsibility for its organization and presentation.

Finally, I am obligated to the many classes of freshmen at Colorado State College of Education who have used this material in a preliminary form and whose criticisms have done much to give this book such value as it may have.

WALLACE T. WAIT

Greeley, Colorado
May, 1938

CHAPTERS

ix

ILLUSTRATIONS

PLATES

THE SCIENCE OF
HUMAN BEHAVIOR

Chapter 1

AN INTRODUCTION TO THE STUDY
OF HUMAN BEHAVIOR

What Is Psychology?—Psychology has been defined and described in many ways. It is likely to mean something very different for the "man on the street" than for the student who has undertaken even an elementary study of this science, while for the advanced student it is to be expected that the definitions might well be refined still further to show more distinctly some of the subtle shades of meaning of the word.

For the reader of this book, who is presumably approaching a study of the science of psychology for the first time, the definition must be one that will indicate clearly the nature of the knowledge which the field includes. It must divest the term "psychology" of the mystery with which it has been surrounded in the advertising matter of the quack, who employs it as a means of arousing the interest of the public and, at the same time, of hiding the real motives and methods of procedure he is using. It must also avoid the highly technical points of discussion that are of interest chiefly to the advanced student and the professional academic psychologist. In other words, this preliminary statement must be one that makes common sense to the beginning student.

Psychology, then, may be defined as a systematic study of the behavior of the individual member of a species for the purpose of predicting and controlling such behavior. In this book the essential concern will be with human psychology, and wherever the term "psychology" is used it will be thus limited in meaning, except in such instances as the behavior of lower animals shall be specifically included. By the term "behavior" will be meant anything that the individual does as a whole person. This will include not only the responses which can be readily seen by an observer, but also those subtle responses that in everyday language go by

3

such names as perceiving, thinking, sensing, and imagining. A brief examination of some of the typical problems that confront the psychologist will give a clearer idea of the wide variety of behavior included in this field of study.

What Are Some of the Types of Problems of Concern to the Psychologist?—In each of the several problems selected to show the full extent of the meaning of psychology, there are two ways in which the psychologist might appropriately approach his subject. One of these is frequently called the theoretical approach. The psychological investigator or observer who chooses this method seeks to answer all possible questions concerning the behavior involved, such as : which organs are affected, what caused the response at all, and similar questions centering in an investigation of the nature of the behavior itself.

The other method of approach is sometimes called the practical or applied, because it aims to study the problem in terms of its immediate importance in a practical life situation. The "applied psychologist" has to do with that part of the whole problem which makes the most direct appeal to popular interest, but he would be helpless if he did not have available to him the results of the studies made by the psychologist who has followed the first of these two lines of approach. In each of the psychological problems listed below, both the theoretical and the applied aspects will be emphasized in the statement of the problem as well as in the brief discussion. Some of these problems are now fairly well solved. Others still await further investigation.

1. How much change in the intensity of a stimulus is required to produce a change in the response made to it? Does the intensity of pain double if the voltage of an electric current applied to the skin is doubled? How much will efficiency in a factory be increased if the intensity of the lighting is doubled? What should the intensity be to produce the maximum of efficiency? Can the psychologist help solve this problem?

2. How long after a stimulus is applied does the response get started? More practically, why do so many automobile accidents occur in the which the driver strikes a pedestrian who steps into

the lane of traffic immediately ahead of the car even when the speed is low and the brakes are good? A certain taxi-cab company wished to reduce the number of accidents that had accumulated on the records of some of the men it employed. If it could determine before hiring and training its drivers which ones would most probably have accidents, it could reduce the number of these mishaps. The company secured the services of a psychologist who devised means of measuring applicants' *reaction time*. By refusing to hire those whose reaction time was slow, the company greatly reduced its number of accidents.

3. What are the characteristics of differences among individuals when compared on the basis of any given trait? How valuable would the answer to such a question be to the merchant or buyer concerned with the sizes and styles of merchandise? Of even greater importance to the reader, individually, is the question of the selection of a suitable vocation. Such a problem can be more intelligently solved by the person who knows the characteristics of individual differences.

4. What are the psychological conditions that determine how learning takes place? A very practical problem for any student is that of how to make his or her learning more efficient. In the factory, too, the manager is very much concerned with employing those who can learn most readily to do the assigned tasks for which they are hired. How can the employer know whom to hire? One psychologist was able to devise tests for predicting how rapidly and how well the applicant could learn to perform the required task.

5. What takes place in the mind of the thinker who is solving a problem in mathematics, in social etiquette, or in bridge construction? Would a knowledge of the essential processes involved in thinking enable the reader to do a better job of problem solving?

6. Why does a baby not learn to walk before he is about one year old? Why is it not profitable to try to teach the average child to read before he is about six years old? Would the teacher who knew how bodily structure and behavior developed be able to determine more wisely the type of school activities to be employed?

7. Why are men of eminence, such as those listed in *Who's Who,* so much more likely to have relatives also listed in such a book than those who are not of sufficient distinction to be included? What makes many behavior traits common to several successive generations of certain families? Why do such undesirable traits as delinquency and insanity often run in families? Are the answers to such questions important in choosing the person one is to marry or in determining the kind of environment in which to rear one's children?

8. What sets behavior into action? What is the nature of the drives or urges that compel people to do things? Would one have better success in trying to control the behavior of oneself or of others if one knew the nature of such drives? How can one sell oneself in getting a job? Which appeals will be most effective in selling a car and which in selling a package of breakfast food?

These are only samples of the limitless problems of predicting and controlling behavior. The reader will be able to add to this list indefinitely. It should also be evident to him by this time that there is a very great deal that is of practical value in the study of psychology, but it must be remembered that before the practical applications can be made, the underlying principles must be understood.

In this connection another point is worth noting. Not only can psychology be applied to ordinary life situations by persons who do not possess an exhaustive knowledge of the subject of psychology, but the very knowledge of the principles to be applied grows out of everyday experience. By the time early adulthood is reached or even before, everyone is compelled to become a psychologist of sorts. It is a mistake to assume that all knowledge of psychology comes from books, lectures, and courses in the subject. Since this science deals with human behavior, one must have acquired a rather considerable working knowledge of it by observing the behavior of oneself and of others long before meeting the first course or the first book on psychology. This is an important point for the beginner to remember, since there is such a frequent human tendency to dread and avoid that which is new and unknown. If the reader will remember that he or she is already a psychologist of considerable experience, this dread will be greatly lessened. The purpose of this book is merely that of extending and organizing the knowledge of psychology already possessed by even the most inexperienced beginner. At the same time an attempt will be made to aid these beginners to apply their knowledge and experience in solving such psychological problems as may arise in their everyday living.

What Are the Characteristics of Behavior in the Psychological Sense?

Behavior Considered by Psychologists, Physiologists, and Sociologists.—Psychological behavior differs from the aspects of behavior studied by the physiologist. The psychologist is concerned with the relationship of the whole individual to his or her stimulating environment, while the physiologist deals mostly with the relationships of the various organs of the body. Probably there is no very sharp dividing line between these two branches of human science. To be complete each must consider some of the characteristics of the other.

In a certain sense sociology is also concerned with behavior; but for the sociologist, the unit to be considered is not the person. Instead, the essential unit is some social organization such as the family, the state, or any socialized group considered as a whole. As psychology is based in part upon a knowledge of the function of the separate bodily organs, so sociology is based upon a knowledge of the behavior of the individual. Thus, all three of these sciences are concerned with human behavior, but each limits its field arbitrarily as it borders upon the others.

Some Important Factors of All Behavior.—Some of the most important factors of behavior are common to all animal life, even to the simplest one-celled creatures. Three such traits will indicate nicely some of the qualities of human behavior. These three are: first, *irritability,* by which is meant the capacity to be aroused by stimulation from the environment; second, *conductivity,* or the capacity to conduct the results of the irritation to a remote part through its tissue; and third, *motility,* which is the general name for the capacity to move bodily tissue in whole or in part as the result of stimulation from the environment. There are other capacities too, but these are among the most important for the study of behavior.

In the simplest forms of animal life there is little specialization of either structure or function. The one-celled organism does all these three things about equally well. As one goes further along the line of progressively more complex structures of the higher forms of life, one finds a greater degree of specialization of function. In man, the most complex of all creatures, certain tissues are highly specialized in irritability and are called sense organs. Others are specialized in conductivity and make up the nervous system; while the bulk of the body is highly developed in motility as it is found in the muscles.

All behavior, in the psychological sense, must be accounted for in terms of these three elements: irritability, conductivity, and motility.[1] The more this specialization has progressed, the more complex is the behavior which is possible for the members of that species. Man, as the possessor of the most specialized structure, has the most complex behavior of all animals. But even in this very complex behavior, the elements of irritability, conductivity, and motility are clearly seen. Responses always result from some stimulation of the organism through one or many sense organs. The results of such stimulation are conducted through the nervous system, often in a very complex manner, to remote parts of the body. This results in the responding of the muscles and glands. A fundamental general principle of psychology is that no behavior takes place except in response to stimulation.

It should be noted and constantly remembered that the behavior differences between man and other species, so far as psychology is concerned, are differences in degree and not in kind. Moreover, the behavior differences observable along the line from the amoeba to man make a fairly continuous series.

---

[1] This, of course, takes no account of the effects of the secretions of the glandular tissues, which have considerable significance in problems of behavior.

The progressive increase in complexity of the same basic factors in behavior is stressed here to emphasize the fact that, whatever the definition of mind may be, in a psychological, as distinguished from a theological sense, it must be possessed in some degree by all species of animals.

What Is Mind?—It has been common practice in the past to define psychology as the study of the mind. There need be no objection to this if the term "mind" can be defined in a satisfactory manner. There has been considerable disagreement among psychologists about what mind really is—a disagreement that is ages old. The next chapter will discuss some of the developments of the concept of mind. Here the reader must be content with some of the simple and common-sense concepts that find acceptance today.

Another characteristic of all animal life, in addition to the three already mentioned, might well be called modifiability. By this is meant the ability of the organism to have its possibilities of response influenced by its previous behavior. This is true of the amoeba, as has been shown experimentally. After ingesting a grain of carmine and repeatedly excreting it as useless to its needs, the amoeba finally profits from its previous experience by rejecting and avoiding the carmine grain. It is this ability to profit by experience which Guthrie has called an important characteristic of mind.

Psychologists nowhere depart further from common sense than in their notion of the nature of minds. The man on the street acknowledges that minds are rather mysterious but he is definitely sure that mind is something that you either have or you haven't. Bricks haven't. He has, and he knows that he has. Dogs also have minds. Angle-worms? Here he becomes a little doubtful. Angle-worms seem very definitely to resent indignities in a way that a brick does not. And their daily round of activity seems to have something of a plan and a purpose behind it. A brick reacts to a kick by moving over, but there is a distinctly passive and helpless air about the brick's behavior. . . .

But do angle-worms have minds? Are growth and reproduction and defensive reaction enough to qualify the worm for that distinction?

Plants also grow and multiply and defend themselves not only by their structures but in many cases by movement. Common sense is inclined to deny that plants have minds, for this is an opinion shared by only a very few detached sentimentalists.

What is it then that plants lack that is to be found in creatures which common sense endows with minds? Strangely enough, common sense will be found to offer a very good answer to this question. Growth and reproduction and defense reactions are life, but they are not mind. Mind is these and something more: it is growth and reproduction and reactions serving these ends plus something that common sense might call profiting by experience. . . .

. . . The ability to learn, that is, to respond differently to a situation because of past response to the situation, is what distinguishes those living creatures which common sense endows with minds. This is the practical descriptive use of the term "mind." . . . Mind must be for us a mode of behavior, namely, that behavior which changes with use or practice, behavior, in other words, which exhibits learning.[2]

How Is "Mind" Related to Body?—Man's early attempts to explain mind all took the form of assuming an extranatural being or force which has never successfully been brought within the recognized limits of science. Gradually this concept of mind changed until at present the best and most satisfactory explanations of man's behavior are to be found in terms of the relationships of man's organic structure to the forces and forms of energy of his environment.

In the uncritical terminology of everyday life, mind and body are considered to be more or less distinct entities, related, it is true, but still distinct and separable. Thus, when the man on the street says that he has "made up his mind" to buy a house, just what does he mean? What was involved in "making up his mind"? If one has been watching him for a few days, he will have been seen walking or driving around the house under consideration. He has probably gone through the house in some detail. This behavior is quite different from the kind he manifests if he is calling at this house for other purposes. He probably has exam-

[2] E. R. Guthrie, *The Psychology of Learning*, New York, Harper & Bros., 1935. Reprinted by permission of the publisher.

ined the condition of the floors and their finish, and has inspected all fixtures. He undoubtedly has looked the furnace over with some care and has asked questions about the amount of fuel needed to heat the house. Then, too, he probably has gone to the court-house or to an abstractor's office and has spent some time in examining the legal title to the property. He may have taken the abstract to an attorney for his advice. He may have discussed the matter with his banker. Undoubtedly, he has not only talked about it to his family, but he has brought some members of the family to examine it with him. Then, as the result of all of this activity and much more like it, he announces that he has "made up his *mind*" to buy the house.

If an observer has been watching this man, he will have noticed the activity which has been described. There is another kind of activity which will have escaped notice, that which is commonly called consciousness. If he is asked to tell what has been going on in his consciousness, he will, unless he is a trained introspectionist, tell much of what he was seen to do. He will not be able to add very much that could not be guessed pretty well from careful observation of his overt behavior. This thing called mind which he says he "has made up" seems, after all, to be a more or less complex kind of behavior of the man as a whole, and that will probably be about as near to a satisfactory explanation of it as can be had even though the investigation be carried on indefinitely. In fact, that is about where psychologists, after all these centuries of attempted definitions, are forced to leave the answer to the question : "What is mind?"

Mind may be defined for the purpose of this book as the sum total of all of the capacities of the organism to respond to his environment as a whole individual. Note particularly that only those capacities to respond are meant which involve the reaction of the organism as a unitary, integrated individual. This whole organism may be considered to be made up of parts, but the capacities of the parts to respond as such do not constitute mind, although it may be necessary to understand these part responses in order to understand the nature of mind as here defined. This does not imply that any part has a fixed and permanent relationship to the whole response. The whole response may change from time to time without seeming to involve more than a minimum of change in terms of the respective part activity. Neither is it true that all parts are equally involved in all adjustments, but in this capacity for behavior called mind integration is the essential feature.

Such a concept of mind, though it lacks something of the completeness necessary for all possible uses of the term, does have the distinct advantage of being readily workable. Such a definition makes no assumption of a thing superior to the body or directing the body's behavior from without. No supernatural or mysterious substance or force is introduced to describe or explain man's activity. No one part of the total of man's behavior is singled out as being of more significance than any other part. All the various aspects of man's capacity to respond as a single unit are regarded jointly as a function of the body.

At first, this definition may seem to be a very great departure from the usual sense in which the word mind is used. But is there really so much difference? Consider the case of the man who has "made up his mind" to buy the house. What is meant by such an expression? Is it not essentially that he is now capable of an act of which he was not capable before? Just what happened to his bodily mechanism is not known, but something, that presumably has taken place in this bodily organism, makes him a different man. Possibly something else may occur to this man in the next few hours that will "change his mind" again, i.e., will make him capable only of some other activity than that of buying the house.

There is another use of the term "mind," one in which the meaning is quite like the term "intelligence." One sometimes hears a person say "John has a fine mind." What does such an expression mean? Is it not implied that John has an unusually large range of capacities to react and to modify his behavior in terms of experience? On the other hand, to say that John's mind is dull implies that John's capacity to respond to his situations in life is somewhat limited and that he does not profit readily from experience.

A problem arises from this definition. The term "mental activity" should presumably be the activity of the mind. But this is possible only if mind is something which itself can act. When mind is defined as the function of the organism as a whole, the term "mental activity" becomes absurd unless it can be given a meaning that will be useful and convenient. The common-sense use of the term may well be examined to discover if the layman's everyday use of it has a significant meaning.

How does mental activity differ from the type of activity usually called physical or motor? The answer provided by common sense is that these activities cannot be distinguished from each other except in terms of some arbitrary definition. As the term "mental activity" is usually employed, it designates those responses which do not involve overt and easily observable behavior. In the school task commonly referred to as "mental arithmetic" the pupils are observed to be stimulated by the oral reading of the problem and then to give the answer without anything very noticeable happening in the interval. If a person be asked to visualize a house, some few minimal movements of the visualizer's eyes, lips, and neck may be noticed, but there is usually nothing that will provide the observer with a clue as to the color or size or kind of house that is imagined. The person who has visualized may be able to describe his image in detail, so that, if the report be regarded as an honest one, some complex activity must have taken place. This is the kind of activity which is customarily called mental.

A little experiment will show this point of view to advantage. Most people would agree that multiplying one three-place number by another without any writing surface or writing instrument would be a "mental" task. This is the experiment. Get a friend to try such a task in arithmetic and *at the same time* chew a piece of candy. Close watch should be kept of movements of the eyes, hands, and other parts of the body. The eating of the candy will in all probability interfere with the arithmetic problem. Why? Possibly the answer lies in the fact that the lips, tongue, and throat muscles cannot manipulate the candy and at the *same* time carry out the sub-vocal speech involved in multiplying. The less practiced in mental multiplication the subject of the experiment may be, the more likely it is that the eating will interfere with the multiplication. Eye movements are frequently important parts of visual imagery, and they may be involved as the subject moves his eyes around over the imaginary surface upon which the problem is set in his visual image.

At the other extreme, probably none of the activity commonly called physical is entirely devoid of these less easily observable response elements. The whole range of activity from the extreme called purely "mental" to that commonly called purely "physical" can be represented as having a place somewhere on a straight line, as shown in Figure 1. At the end of the line marked M would be placed such an activity as that of the multiplication problem mentioned. Here very little of what goes on in the way of activity can be observed, though when the answer is reported it is apparent that some activity has occurred. The farther to the right one goes on this line, the more observable would be the total pattern of activity.

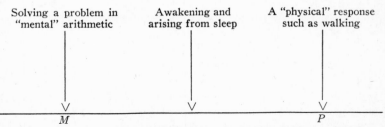

Figure 1. Representation of the Activity Range Through the Range of Observability from "Mental" to Motor Activity

Near the right end of the line, at P, might be placed such an activity as walking, tying one's shoes, or mowing the lawn. In all of these there is a readily observable pattern of response which in everyday language is called motor or physical. Of course, there are important elements of the whole pattern which cannot readily be observed, just as at the other extreme there are some elements that are observable. In other words, there is no activity which may be properly called either purely physical or purely mental.

Note, therefore, that Figure 1 indicates one level of activity and not two.

Since the only definitely known characteristic of the activity called mental is this quality of not being easily observed, why not let it be plainly understood that when this term is used it simply means that some important parts of the activity cannot readily be seen? That is exactly what the term will mean when it appears hereafter in this book.

Convenient Grouping of the Factors That Determine Behavior

Two Groups of Factors.—What must be known before it is possible to predict the response which any human being will make at any specified time? The answer is complex indeed. In fact, much of the discussion of the following chapters will be concerned with the several parts of the answer to this question. The whole answer may be said to fall into two rather distinct divisions: (1) the nature of the total stimulation impinging upon the person at the moment, and (2) the structure of the organism of the person at that particular time.

Factors of Stimulation.—The first group of factors is of interest to the psychologist only in a limited sense. They are of much more direct concern to the physicist, to the chemist, and possibly to the physiologist. The psychologist is concerned with them only to the extent that they are the necessary agents for releasing the potential energy of the human organism. As factors influencing behavior, they are like the trip mechanism which releases the energy of the hammer head of the pile driver. Strictly speaking, they can neither determine the nature nor the direction of the response. Neither can they determine the extent or amount of the behavior except in a limited sense.

All stimuli to which the human being can respond are forms of natural energy. Each kind of stimulation differs from every other kind in some natural characteristics. This differentiation corresponds to the specialization of the sense organs. The function of these forces is simply to set going in the sense organs another kind of energy called the nerve impulse. So far as is known, the nerve impulses, no matter what sense organ originates them, are exactly alike. The sole business of any sense organ when it is affected by an appropriate stimulus is to generate a nerve impulse and discharge it into the nervous system.

For convenience it is sometimes assumed that a single stimulus may act alone in generating a response. This never actually happens. Everyone is at all times being affected by a host of different stimuli, and an explanation of his total response at any one instant must take into account the total pattern of stimulation. An illustration may help to make this clear. Disregard for the moment the factors of bodily structure. It is obvious even to the most casual observer that what a person will do in response to a pin prick will depend in part upon what other stimuli are acting upon him at the instant when the pin prick is administered. If applied in a laboratory situation, one kind of response might be obtained. If given by a friend in a playful manner, a somewhat different response might be expected. Still a third kind of response might be obtained if it were administered by an enemy or as part of a hostile situation. Still further, it might make a considerable difference whether it was the first or the thirtieth in a series of pin pricks in quick succession, all of them of equal but low intensity.

Factors of Organic Structure.—As complex as the factors of stimulation may be in producing a response, even more complex are the factors of bodily structure. Anything which influences the structure of the organism, presumably influences its behavior when the organism is stimulated. These factors fall into at least four large and fairly distinct groups: the factors of heredity, maturity, and experience, and those due to certain periodic cycles of bodily function which are distinctly physiological in nature. These will be discussed briefly at this point and in detail in later chapters.

1. The problem of inheritance of behavior resolves itself into the question of the inheritance of organic structure, since it is

evident from biological research that only the potentialities of developing bodily structures can be inherited. Either heredity has no influence upon behavior, or such influence must be accounted for in terms of hereditarily influenced structure. No new principles or hypotheses are needed to account for the latter. The facts of biological transmission of structural traits from generation to generation are already well established. More detailed consideration of the influence of heredity on behavior must await the chapter dealing with the question, "Why Do Certain Behavior Traits Seem to Run in Families?"

2. Another chapter, entitled "How Does Maturity Modify Behavior?" will deal with the second of these groups of factors. No parent would think of expecting a six-months-old child to walk and run, because even the layman would recognize the child's lack of sufficient strength to permit such behavior. In a similar manner, the pre-adolescent is not expected to behave like the later adolescent or adult in the matter of mating and reproduction. The reason for this is again the immature state of the pre-adolescent's bodily structure. In this book the term maturity is restricted to that meaning of the word which deals with sheer growth of the structure. It does not include the effects of experience which are included under this term by some psychological experimenters.

3. Concerning the structural changes involved in learning, the psychologist must to a great extent depend upon hypotheses. The exact nature of such changes is not known. It is of considerable significance, however, to recognize the rather marked agreement among neurologists and psychologists that some structural changes are basic to learning, that there is some sort of a "neurological trace" whereby the person is structurally different before and after learning. The best hypotheses at present point to this effect as taking place chiefly in the central nervous system. It is difficult to study the nervous system in the living organism, but while awaiting the discovery of the facts, reasonable and satisfactory hypotheses may be employed. Further discussion of this group of factors will be found in the chapter, "What Is the Effect of Experience Upon Behavior?"

4. The other group of factors affecting the structure, and hence the behavior, of the organism includes such periodical changes of the body as those involved in hunger, thirst, sex, and fatigue. In each of these instances there seems to be essentially an equilibrium, the disturbance of which by internal bodily changes results in an internal type of stimulation at present not well understood. This stimulation is closely related to some of the problems of motivation and as such will find fuller treatment in the chapter, "What Are the Mainsprings of Behavior?"

It is possible that there are factors determining the structure and hence the behavior of an individual that will not fit conveniently into any one of these four categories. It is also probable that there are certain factors which might conveniently be considered under more than one of these headings. Such facts need not be alarming in the least. Any classification is usually valuable in terms of how convenient it is rather than how exclusive it may be. This classification will furnish a convenient basis of attack upon the complexities of the problems of the how and why of human behavior, which, after all, is the most important quality it could possess for the purposes of this book.

The Psychologist at Work

The Task of All Science.—The fundamental task of all science is to gather data, to classify those data, and to explain them. Science attempts to reduce its explanations to as few general principles as possible. Furthermore, it confines the observations, classifications, and explanations to natural phenomena. This means that it steadfastly refuses to deal with events which demand an explanation in terms of extranatural or supernatural causes. It is true, of course, that some events which in times past have seemed extranatural have now been brought within the compass of natural law, and it is possible that similar explanations may be found in the future for phenomena considered extranatural today.

Science and superstition are alike in that both assume cause and effect relationships and both seek to understand and explain what is observed. In other respects they differ greatly. Science seeks to reduce all explanations to a few general principles, while superstition seeks a new explanation for each event observed. In addition, science insists upon rigid control of all factors which might contribute to the event observed, and presents an explanation only when all possible tests of its findings have convinced the experimenter of the correctness of his observation. Superstitious man, on the other hand, tends to accept as true the first explanation that suggests itself. He often fails, yet he flatly refuses to put his explanation to a controlled test. He may go so far as to refuse to accept the failure of his explanation, even in cases when the explanation proves to be contrary to fact.

Psychology as a Science.—All the sciences have had their origin in philosophy. Some separated themselves from philosophy earlier than others. Mathematics and chemistry were among the earliest to become independent sciences. Psychology was one of the latest to develop, despite the fact that philosophy's earliest problems dealt with the explanation of man and his behavior. The long period of development which psychology underwent before it became a science will be traced in the next chapter. Here it is enough to note that not only has psychology had the same origin as other sciences, but it has also had the same general course of development and employs the same general methods as do all other true sciences.

Each science deals with a restricted part of the whole field of natural phenomena. In fact, within each field there is a great deal of specialization, all dealing with the same great general principles, but concentrating the attack upon special areas within the whole field. Thus, in chemistry, certain experimenters confine themselves to the discovery of new organic compounds and new ways of developing familiar compounds from new sources. In the same way, some psychologists spend their lifetimes experimenting with rats, dogs, and monkeys by exploring the results upon behavior of the destruction of parts of the brain. Others work with equal industry in their nursery-like laboratories, studying children's behavior in many different situations. Still others spend their time in discovering the optimum conditions of learning.

In the process of developing their general laws all sciences employ hypotheses. Since primitive times man has been making guesses to explain what he observed. As man learned more about himself and his world, these guesses became more accurate. The ones that did not check with further observations were either changed or dropped altogether. As man's knowledge developed into the sciences, these guesses came to be called hypotheses. Often these hypotheses were so definitely proved that they were no longer guesses and were then called laws. Every science attempts first to set up hypotheses and then to verify them to the point where they become fundamental principles or laws.

Psychology, like other sciences, is attempting the same task. The field of psychology presents greater difficulties of observation than do other fields of natural science. Hence, in psychology the development of hypotheses into laws has not progressed to the point that has been reached in the other fields. There are some hypotheses in this field, however, that seem to be well on the way to verification. It is probably better to continue for the present to regard them as hypotheses rather than to call them laws. They seem to check with the observed facts and are extremely useful as means of explaining other facts.

A Hypothesis Which Is Fundamental to Psychology.—One such hypothesis refers to the first general group of factors determining behavior and emphasizes the importance of the stimulus. It commonly goes by the name of the *reaction hypothesis*. Briefly stated, it is that every reaction is the result of a stimulus acting upon the body through the sense organs. No action is to be thought of as occurring spontaneously, i.e., without some stimulus to give it impetus.

This hypothesis has far-reaching implications. It may seem to the beginning student of human behavior to be contrary to fact, especially in the case of the more subtle types of behavior such as thinking, imagining, and perceiving. A thought, an image, or a percept may seem to occur without any causally related preceding stimulus, and it may be difficult to discover what was the initiating incident or object. The failure in such cases may be due to a lack of skill and insight on the part of the observer.

An illustration may be helpful. As this is written I am reminded of an uncle whom I have not seen for some time. I am not aware of having even thought of him recently. The question naturally arises why this particular person should be called to mind at this particular moment. What was the provoking stimulus? An examination of the responses immediately preceding gives the following as a fairly complete account of the chain of events that ensued. The name of the city of Seattle was mentioned by a radio speaker. This brought an immediate response, due probably to my familiarity with that city. In turn there followed the recollection of the University of Washington campus where I spent some time as a student. This recalled a recent visit to that campus, at which time I noted particularly the removal of some of the old Exposition buildings. This recalled visit suggested the Exposition, which in turn suggested the uncle who used to entertain me with tales of the exhibits. I was then a small boy in a rural community where exciting incidents from the outside world made a profound impression. Here, then, was a whole chain of responses, subtle and hard to ascribe to particular parts of the bodily mechanism. Nevertheless, it seems clear that each of the succession of responses produced a stimulus which in turn called out the next succeeding response. A parallel situation involving a chain of responses in which the whole process can easily be observed will indicate more exactly what is meant by the statement that each response produces a stimulus which in turn initiates another response.

If the cheek of a three-months-old infant be stimulated, a usual response is the turning of the head toward the point stimulated. If the infant is in the regular nursing position, the lips may thereby be brought into contact with the nipple. This is a normal stimulus for a seizing and sucking movement of the lips. This response normally results in a flow of liquid into the mouth and throat. This is the usual stimulus for swallowing, and so on through the whole process of digestion, including both muscular and glandular responses. It is not correct to think of the increased activity of the gastric glands in the stomach as resulting directly from the touch on the cheek of the infant, but the orderly sequence of stimulus, response, stimulus, and response is here clearly shown. In the case of the recalled uncle the situation is exactly the same, but the intervening processes of stimulus-response are not so easily or completely observable. Otherwise they are alike. In any event these illustrations will indicate the far-reaching significances of this basic hypothesis.

Psychology Uses Data from Other Fields of Science.—The interrelationship of all fields of science has already been indicated. It is often expedient to employ facts which have been obtained by experimenters in other fields. Psychology freely acknowledges its debt in this respect to such sciences as biology, medicine, physics, and chemistry.

The effect of heredity upon behavior has been made clear by the employment of the laws of heredity developed in the field of biology. Until these were available, many erroneous notions were held by students of behavior. One of these was the idea that the behavior, including the thoughts and temperament of the unborn child, was influenced by what the mother said and did during pregnancy. Instinctive behavior was also explained as the result of the inheritance of habits of many successive generations of the members of the species.

The effect of normal and abnormal secretion of the endocrine glands is only now coming to be known in the field of medicine, and already this knowledge is being used by psychologists to explain normal and some abnormal behavior. In early times a certain kind of defective mentality known as cretinism was explainable only as an act of a creative divinity. Later, the cause, although unknown, was assumed to be a natural one. Only within recent years has it been discovered to be due to subnormal functioning of the thyroid gland. Now the cretin child can be assured of a reasonably normal development of body and behavior through glandular treatment while still an infant.

The study of emotional behavior has similarly become partly

a study of human chemistry, and a knowledge of the function of the members of the body, particularly of the limbs, is greatly enhanced by a knowledge of the principles of mechanics.

Many of the experimental techniques employed in a psychological laboratory today have had their origin in ideas borrowed from the laboratories of the other sciences. To be a successful experimenter in a modern psychological laboratory demands more than a chance acquaintance with the procedures of other scientific fields.

Psychology Employs Its Own Experimental Methods to Secure Data.—It must not be inferred from the preceding paragraphs that psychology is dependent upon other sciences for all of its data. It has experimental techniques and special tools and devices by which it secures much data for itself. Parts of this experimentation can be carried out directly with human beings; other parts can be better accomplished by using some of the lower animals as subjects of experiment. An illustration of each of these methods is given below followed by a brief synopsis of the cautions necessary in conducting scientific psychological experimentation.

1. HUMAN EXPERIMENTATION. T. R. Garth of the University of Denver's department of psychology is trying to find an answer to the question, "Are the higher average intelligence test scores of white children compared with Indian children due to differences of heredity or to differences of experience?" It is not enough to measure the intelligence of large groups of children of each race. Other factors must be considered. Indian children tend to live different lives and have different experiences than do children reared in the homes of white parents. Therefore, Garth is gathering data relative to the intelligence quotient of many Indian children who have lived intimately in the homes of white foster parents for several years. These instances are not numerous and another caution must be exercised. There is the possibility that those Indian children selected to be reared in a white home are originally superior children. Furthermore, how do these white homes compare with the average of all such homes

in furnishing experiences to be sampled by the intelligence test? This is a kind of psychological experiment that takes years to accomplish and which must be repeated several times before the problem can be considered really solved.

2. ANIMAL EXPERIMENTATION. Some kinds of psychological experiments cannot employ human subjects because of obvious social disapproval. Lashley has been working for years with rats and other lower animals to determine the effect upon behavior that will result from the destruction of parts of the brain. Similarly, society would not approve of putting a human child in the environment of the higher apes to see how much its developing behavior would be influenced by heredity and how much by an unusual type of environment. The Kelloggs partly solved this problem by taking a female gorilla infant into their home and rearing it as a child, not as a pet, along with their own infant son for a period of nine months.

In other instances it is profitable to study lower animals either in comparison with human beings or by themselves. The principal reason for this is that the relative simplicity of the behavior of such animals gives the effect of a slow-motion picture study. Besides, the lower animals can often be controlled experimentally more easily than humans, since they are less influenced by social contact with others of their species. Moss and other investigators have tried to discover the relative forcefulness of such inborn physiological drives as hunger, thirst, sex, and fatigue. This would be very difficult to do with human beings because of the effect of social experience.

Human beings are the most highly specialized of all animals, and consequently due caution must be employed in interpreting human behavior on the basis of animal experimentation. Nevertheless, this type of study bulks large in the psychological literature. It should be remembered that the best source of information about man is the study of man himself. Anything else is only a substitute. In this book experimental data derived from the study of human beings will be employed for the most part. This applies particularly to the anecdotes used for purposes of illustration.

Some Difficulties of Psychological Experimentation.—The scientific method of obtaining data is a rigorous one, demanding exactness and care in the employment of its procedures and techniques. The general types of cautions applicable to all science will be mentioned first and these will be followed by a brief discussion of a particular difficulty confronting students of psychology.

In any scientific experiment the experimenter must first carefully state his problem. He should consider any previous effort on the part of himself, or of others, in order to avoid all possible pitfalls. He must select the subjects for his experiment in such a way as to insure that they are representative samples of the whole class for which conclusive evidence is sought. He must secure or construct the necessary apparatus and measuring instruments, making sure that they will actually do with accuracy what he wants them to do. He must control all possible factors, holding all but one of them as constant as possible and allowing only one to be the experimental variable. This is necessary if he is to discover the exact cause of such results as he may obtain. He must insure a permanent and complete record of his procedures and results. He must carefully and objectively weigh his results in drawing his conclusions and provide for the repetition of the experiment by himself or others.

This is an exacting procedure. Is it any wonder that scientific facts are obtained at such great cost of effort and ingenuity? And is it any wonder that facts obtained by means of such procedures have considerable weight and influence?

Reread the very brief account of Garth's experiment, and note how his procedure takes into account the several points mentioned here. These factors apply in any kind of experimentation in any field of science. Few experiments actually meet these ideal conditions. Certainly, much of the informal experimentation of the beginner will fall short of such conditions. But as the psychologist approaches this ideal, his discoveries will increase in reliability.

One difficulty is of utmost importance to the amateur psychologist and hence deserves special comment. It is relatively easy for the chemist to view his reagents in his test tubes and retorts in an impersonal manner. After all, they are something independent of himself. But, when the psychologist observes human behavior, whether of himself or of another, he is dealing with something that is directly or indirectly personal. It is most difficult at times for the psychologist to assume and maintain a detached attitude. It is relatively easy to understand that physical and chemical phenomena have natural causes. It is sometimes much more difficult to understand that equally natural causes underlie psychological phenomena.

An Outline Summary

Eleven points developed in this chapter are basic to the discussion of the chapters which follow:

1. Psychology is the study of behavior for the purpose of predicting and controlling the behavior of the individual.

2. The problems of psychology are varied in form and touch upon many aspects of everyday life.

3. The psychologist's interest in behavior is confined to behavior of an integrated sort that is significant as the response of an individual. In this respect it differs from the interests of the physiologist and the sociologist.

4. There are certain factors of behavior that are common to all animal life. As the structure of bodily organisms increases in complexity and specialization, the corresponding possibilities of behavior show a similar increase.

5. For this book, mind is to be regarded simply as a mode of behavior, i.e., mind is what the body does as the integrated and modifiable behavior of the individual as a whole unit.

6. The common-sense examination of behavior called "mental" reveals that it is as truly the activity of the organism as the behavior called "physical." Since the only significant difference is in terms of the ease of observation and localization, such difference will be taken frankly as the basis of a definition of "mental" behavior.

7. Prediction and control of behavior will be possible in terms of how accurately two groups of complex factors are known.

A. It is necessary to know what stimuli are acting upon the person at the time of and immediately before the response which is to be predicted or controlled.
B. It is necessary to know as exactly as possible what is the organic nature of the mechanism. To do this, at least four groups of factors must be considered.
   (a) The individual's heredity must be known in order to know the possible limits of his structural development.
   (b) The individual's maturity must be known in order to determine how much of his potential growth has taken place.
   (c) The individual's previous experience must be known in order to determine what changes this has produced in his behavior.
   (d) Finally, a variety of periodic physiological conditions of the organism must be known in order that their respective influences may be considered in prediction or control.

8. The task of psychology is simply a specialized part of the whole task of science, which is to gather data, to classify them, and with these data explain natural phenomena.

9. In explaining natural phenomena, hypotheses are developed, and, when necessary, are used in the explanation of other phenomena. One such hypothesis, which is of basic importance in psychology, is the reaction hypothesis which states that no response of the organism is possible except as a reaction to a stimulus.

10. Psychologists borrow freely from the experimental data of other fields of science. They also do much experimentation for themselves in seeking new data with which to explain behavior. Where the direct attack of the study of human behavior is impossible, the psychologist substitutes the indirect study based mostly upon animal experimentation.

11. Like all other sciences, psychological experimentation adheres rigidly to the scientific method and scientific attitude. This is done in the face of the difficulties of all scientific experimentation and in addition under the handicap of the difficulty of maintaining an objective attitude where the thing being studied is of vital personal interest to the experimenter.

Problems for Further Thought

1. Make a list of twenty or more kinds of human behavior that might be of interest to the student of psychology, and which illustrate as wide a variety of human activities as possible.

2. Mention ten or a dozen kinds of information that the physiologist must supply to the psychologist in order that the latter may explain behavior. Do the same for information that the psychologist must supply the sociologist.

3. List the chief aims of science. Show how these aims are involved in psychology.

4. Suggest several explanations for some bit of commonplace behavior of your own which you have observed, and select from these that one which best explains it and which involves the fewest assumptions.

5. Suggest several kinds of information, in securing which the psychologist must employ animal experimentation. Include several different types. Point out, in each case, the more important limitations in applying the results in interpreting human behavior.

6. Secure, if possible, a chart or other device used by a phrenologist and critically examine it to discover how reasonable it is. This will require also that you compare the chart with a diagram, drawing, picture, or model of the brain that shows the division of its working parts. Write out your conclusions from your examination.

7. Make a list of a variety of activities arranged in order of increasing difficulty of observation of the essentially significant parts of the response. Then consider this list in the light of the suggested definition of "mental" and "physical" kinds of activity. Does the definition seem to correspond to a common-sense interpretation of facts?

8. Make an examination of the mental experiences preceding some unexpected recall of a person, place, or incident where the immediate stimulus for the recall is not readily recognized. The illustration on page 21 will suggest the procedure.

9. Explain in your own words the two chief reasons why students of human behavior must be particularly careful to be scientific in their explanations of what they observe. Illustrate from your own experience.

Suggested Readings

Bingham, W. V. (Editor). Psychology Today. Chicago, University of Chicago Press, 1932. Ch. I, "Psychology: Today," J. R. Angell, pp. 3–10; Ch. II, "Psychology: A Modern Science of Human Management," W. P. Miles, pp. 11–19.

Martin, E. D. Lectures in Print: Psychology. New York, The Peoples Institute Publishing Co., 1924. Lecture I, "What Psychology Really Is—Its Uses and Abuses," pp. 1–11.

Murphy, Gardner. A Briefer General Psychology. New York, Harper & Bros., 1935. Ch. I, "Psychology as a Science," pp. 1–14.

Robinson, E. S. Man as Psychology Sees Him. New York, The Macmillan Co., 1934. Ch. VIII, "What Is Psychology," pp. 289–309.

Schoen, Max. Human Nature. New York, Harper & Bros., 1930. Ch. I, "What Psychology Is," pp. 3–16.

Wiggam, A. E. Exploring Your Mind with the Psychologists. New York, Bobbs-Merrill Co., 1928. Chs. II and III, "Your Mind, What It Is—How It Works. Some Present-Day Theories." E. L. Thorndike, pp. 27–58.

Chapter 2

MAN'S WAYS OF EXPLAINING HIS BEHAVIOR

This chapter will discuss the great general trends in the development of man's efforts to explain his behavior. Present-day explanations are related to those of the past in two important ways. Some of the present explanations are directly carried over from former times. All the rest have their roots in those of the past and have developed from them.

Some form of chronological arrangement must be employed because each stage of development has been based upon those preceding. However, a strictly chronological treatment might fail to emphasize the important trends in this development of the understanding of behavior because it is the understanding of behavior and not the behavior itself that has undergone a fundamental change through the ages. Certain great general developments of the common social heritage will be outlined to trace the many specific influences they include. These several developments are inherent in the evolution of the whole cultural civilization of Western Europe and America.

Five of these general developments will be examined in turn to show how each has contributed to present-day explanations of behavior in the two ways already suggested: (a) animism, (b) the philosophy of the classical Greeks, (c) the Christian religion, (d) the pre-scientific psychology, (e) the birth and growth of psychology as a science.

Prehistoric Beginnings of Man's Belief in the Dual Nature of Himself.—Very, very primitive man was probably entirely unable to distinguish between spirit and matter.

But at last the day did come when, like the stealthy climb of a slow dawn, the idea of spirit crept into man's head. It came to him almost unavoidably. Of a morning he awoke, looked up bewilderedly, at the familiar rocks of his cave, and gasped, "Hello, that's queer!"—or sounds to that effect. For there he was just where he had been when he had stretched out and fallen asleep the night before—and yet he knew he had wandered very far from that place during the interim. He was certain of it! Very vividly he remembered fighting huge beasts during the night, or hurtling down ravines, or devouring whole mastodons, or flying. . . . And yet there he was, still lying in his smelly cave, for all the world as though he had never for a moment left it! . . .

Of course, we civilized folk would explain the mystery by simply saying the fellow had had a dream. (Which is perhaps not so much of an explanation at that.) But he, poor savage, could not even guess at such an explanation. The idea of a dream was as foreign to his mind as the idea of a monocle or a wardrobe trunk. No, the only explanation he could offer himself was the obvious one that he was dual: that he possessed not merely a body but also a spirit, and that while his body had that night remained decently at home, his spirit had gone a-roaming. . . . Why not?

There were other experiences which that answer seemed to explain. There was, for instance, death. Here was a body erect and vibrant one moment, and prostrate, inert, the next. What had happened to it? . . . Obviously the same answer fitted: its soul had fled.[1]

Browne's account is only one man's guess as to what may have been the beginning of man's supposition that he had a dual nature. But it is as good a guess as any and seems to fit satisfactorily into the known facts about primitive man. It is considerably oversimplified. Probably all members of the primitive group had many such experiences and in talking it over among themselves sought for an explanation for such occurrences. In the course of time it can be seen how primitive man might have developed the belief that his nature was twofold, consisting of the physical body and a something else which he has never been able to define satisfactorily or to account for in any other way.

Primitive man's lack of knowledge of himself was largely responsible for his inability to explain what he observed of his behavior. He was unable to stand off and look at himself in an objective way. Even if he had been able to do so, he would still

---

[1] From Lewis Browne, *This Believing World*, pp. 30–32. By permission of The Macmillan Co.

have been unable to explain himself any more satisfactorily than he was able to explain the thousand and one things of his daily environment.

Animism as a Primitive Method of Explaining Control of Behavior.—Animism may be defined as belief in spirit domination; principally, the belief in the idea that certain natural objects are possessed of spirits. Each object is supposed to have its own peculiar spirit. This might be described in another way by saying that the object is assumed to consist of two parts—a material part through which the object is expressed to the senses, and another having the nature of a spirit. These spirits are believed to be detachable from the material substance of the object. Man is one of these objects. A man's spirit is assumed to be able to leave his body under certain conditions, or the spirit from some other object may come into man's body and influence or dominate the behavior of that particular person. Man's control of his own behavior, therefore, is to be gained by preserving the proper relationship with these spirits. He seeks the aid of friendly spirits as a means of gaining his own ends, while he attempts to prevent the unfriendly ones from interfering with his behavior.

Among primitive peoples, almost all objects, animals, plants, inorganic things like rocks and rivers, and even forces and forms of energy such as light, darkness, and fire are presumed to possess these spirits. Peoples a little less primitive distinguish living and moving things from those not living and moving. They attribute spirits mostly to living things and certain forces of nature.

In a number of places in the world there are today races of people who may be thought of as still possessing these characteristics of primitive times. Sometimes they have numerous contacts with other civilizations but maintain their primitive behavior in spite of these contacts. An example of the animistic beliefs of such a primitive people will furnish an excellent illustration of the way primitive man has explained and still does explain himself and his behavior.

In the island of Haiti there exists today a civilization which in some respects furnishes a very good picture of the life and behavior of primitive man. The habits and beliefs of the simple peasant people of this island constitute an excellent example of the efforts of primitive man to explain how his behavior is controlled. The religion of the Roman Catholic church is supposedly the belief of the Haitian people. In actual fact, however, much of the population expresses its belief in the Voodoo worship commonly found there. This religion is an amazing system of credence, a compound of the African beliefs of the blacks brought there as slaves and the tenets of the Roman Catholic church. The Voodoo worship is as pantheistic as any of the religions of primitive times. According to Voodoo, all spirits have their abode in natural objects of the environment, but any of them may be incarnated in the bodies of the human beings and may thus control human behavior.

The control of these spirits is often obtained through the use of fetishes and the working of magic. Seabrook, who spent some time among the Voodoo worshippers of Haiti, gives an interesting account of how a friendly priestess, Maman Célie, made for him an "ouanga" packet to preserve him safe from all harm.

It was the realization of this, I think, that enabled me to see, somewhat with their eyes, as more than mummery, the ceremony of the *ouanga* packet's making.

In a small, bare room . . . a large cowhide was spread, hairy side upward, on the earthen floor, and around it in a circle sat solemnly a dozen negroes. . . . The only light flickered upward on their faces from small candles arranged as a geometric pentagram on the cowhide. . . .

Spread in the center of the candle pentagram, on the cowhide, was a square red cloth, like a napkin, which was to be the covering of my *ouanga* packet. Bright ribbons, red and yellow, lay beside it, and also feathers brilliantly dyed. In little, separated piles upon the cowhide were balsam leaves, leaves of the castor-bean plant, roots of the lime tree; a saucer of flour, a saucer of ashes, a bottle of clairin, a bottle of perfume, a tiny iron crucifix.

Maman Célie and I sat on one side in the circle, Papa Théodore facing us. While they chanted . . . old Théodore took some of the roots and leaves, mixed them in a brazier, charred them over a fire . . . then pounded them together in a mortar. . . . Atop these leaves he now laid the crucifix, also a tuft of hair (tied together with thread) which had been cut previously from the central crown of my head; a paring from my right thumb-nail, and a small square cut from a shirt which had been worn next my skin. . . . Articles intimately connected with the individual to be affected . . . are used variously as a substitution for himself. . . .

Maman Célie handed me a copper coin and instructed me to place it on the packet. And now, before it was tied up, she told me to make a prayer (wish). I hesitated, then stood with both arms stretched straight out before me, palms downward, as I had seen them do and said in English:

"May Papa Legba, Maitresse Exilée and the Serpent protect me from misrepresenting these people, and give me power to write honestly of their mysterious religion, for all living faiths are sacred." [2]

A quotation from another source will indicate still further the psychological effect of this sort of primitive control of man's behavior.

Jungle magic is never for effect. It is purposeful, studied. When famines, pestilences, and evils come upon the forest people, it is magic that wards them off. It deals with things—with medicines, potions, and ideas—which, in the forest, are more real than steel and far more dangerous. Magic saves. Then it is white. Magic kills. Then it is black. It is the science of the jungle.

The way of an enemy is never direct. The mysterious ways of jungle death are the only ways down which death comes. Sometimes a Bushnegro, out of jealousy, anger, or fear, wishes another dead. So he sets his fetishes against his enemy, invokes the *winti* of the bush to set upon and destroy him. It is dangerous business, for the murderer knows that in time he will himself be almost inevitably destroyed. But there are stronger passions even than fear.

The spirits of evil are set in action. The one against whom they are working learns of his mortal danger. He attempts propitiation, seeks to make his protective fetishes stronger than the destructive fetishes of his enemy. But almost surely, soon or late, he dies, and his family know that he has been murdered. That is the forest way. [3]

---

[2] W. B. Seabrook, *The Magic Island*, New York, Harcourt, Brace & Co., 1929, pp. 49–53.
[3] John W. Vandercook, "White Magic and Black," *Harper's Magazine*, October, 1925, pp. 548–553.

It is evident that these animistic beliefs play a very important part in the control of a primitive person's behavior and that of his friends and enemies.

Animism, or something closely resembling it, is evident in much of the believing and thinking of present-day modern civilizations. In the first place, there are many beliefs which are called superstitions by some but which are important determiners of behavior of their believers. Many of these represent a type of animism not far removed from that of primitive man. In addition, there are many superstitions and some religious beliefs that have not developed much beyond the stage of animism. In other words, modern social believing and thinking are shot through with this sort of social heritage.

Two Theories Explaining Control of Human Behavior in the Times of the Classical Greeks.—The Greeks were much more systematic than was animistic primitive man in their attempts at explaining themselves and the world which they observed. In this respect they differed from their ancestors. They were more cautious in developing their explanations and more willing to employ a sort of controlled imagination, somewhat akin to that shown by the modern scientist in his present-day attempts to explain what he observes. These Greeks began to separate their religion from their explanation of natural events and thus to develop what has since come to be called philosophy.

Philosophy in this primitive sense may be defined as a systematic attempt to explain things which the philosophers themselves have observed or which they know from the observations of others. It differs from animism chiefly in that it is much more systematized. The animist explains each individual observation separately. The philosopher attempts to develop a broad system of explanations which will serve in a wide variety of instances. In their explanations, however, both employ imagination in the form of more or less shrewd guesses in addition to facts already known. Another characteristic difference between the animist and the philosopher is the ability of the philosopher to assume a more detached and objective point of view than does the animist.

The philosophy of the early Greeks was probably centuries in the building; there is no record of its earliest development, nor was it confined to the Greeks alone. It simply had its culmination in the teachings of the great philosophers who lived in classical Greek times. The development of a systematic knowledge of the world around them and their explanation of it was still in an elementary state 500 years B.C. About that time Greek philosophers began to formulate an explanation which was logical and which seems to have been the forerunner of the logical philosophies of today. It should be remembered that these philosophers were attempting to establish a universal means of explaining the supposed dual nature of man. At the same time, they were attempting to explain the structure of all substances and the relationships between substances.

Very briefly, their teachings were that all the universe was composed of atoms. These atoms were exactly alike as to substance but differed in shape and in size. They were believed to be driven by an unknown force, so that they were always in motion. When the larger atoms came together, they formed the various kinds of material substances which were the familiar sensed objects of the environment. The mind or soul, for which there seemed to be several terms, was not believed to be composed of this same substance. It was made up of another very subtle substance which could not be sensed directly. The very small atoms which composed it penetrated between the larger atoms that made up the material of the physical body.

Some philosophers taught that different kinds of mental activities were due to the motions of these very small atoms. The particular kind of mental activity was determined by the part of the body involved. It was thought that desire was located in the liver, anger in the heart, and reason in the brain. The atoms which made up the soul were believed to be not only very small, but spherical in shape and practically identical with those which made up fire. For these early philosophers, this explained the warmth of living bodies.

Two Greek philosophers are of particular interest in any attempt to trace the development of man's explanation of himself.

These men lived in the third and fourth centuries B.C. They are important because of the influence that some of their teachings have had since their time upon systematic explanations of man's behavior. They differed in at least one very important respect, and it is this difference that is pertinent to this discussion.

Plato was the first of these two philosophers in point of time. He does not seem to have developed a connected system of philosophy of his own, but he largely reflects the teachings of the most advanced thinkers of his own time and of those preceding him. He attempted to explain the human soul or mind as an active substance, made up of the small atoms already mentioned. This soul was believed to be imprisoned within the body during life and was the means by which the acts of the body were controlled. The soul was also the element of the body which obtained knowledge by means of what are now known as sense organs. He divided the soul into several parts and assigned them locations in the body much as did his predecessors. The important thing to note in regard to the teachings of Plato and his predecessors is that the mind or soul was thought to be a material substance which inhabited the body during life and which was presumably more or less free to come and go. While it was in possession of the body, it had complete control over it.

Aristotle's span of life overlapped that of Plato's but extended a few years beyond. He has probably exerted more influence upon all kinds of later scientific and philosophical thought than any other of the early philosophers excepting, possibly, Plato. His teachings are of interest to psychology because of the accuracy of his observations and his shrewd insight into human behavior and because of his influence upon psychological theory. The most important difference between Aristotle's explanation of human behavior and that of his predecessors, including Plato, lies in his explanation of the nature of the mind or soul. According to Aristotle, the soul was not a substance at all. He used the Greek word which is best translated as "form." He thought of the soul as the form of the matter composing the body. Probably the word "function" as it is used in mathematics today would be a satisfactory equivalent of Aristotle's concept of the soul. In other words, the soul was what the body did. In modern terminology it might be explained by saying that the soul was the activity of the body. The particular kind of activity of the soul was determined by the character of the structure of the body. If the whole body were eye, the soul would consist only of seeing. The soul could not exist except in and through the activity of the body.

Aristotle is thus seen to be the revolutionary thinker of his day. His teachings and writings are properly considered to be pioneer influences in the development of the sciences and scientific thinking. Not for centuries, however, was the full significance of this pioneer influence felt. Much that was known and written by him was lost to the civilization of Western Europe until the revival of learning in the Middle Ages. With due allowances for the inaccuracies of the knowledge of his day, the influence of Aristotle can be seen in the scientific activities of modern times. His particular beliefs may not be important or even valid today, but modern scientific attitudes and methods find in him one of their earliest advocates.

On the other hand, Plato's significance in modern life consists not so much in his direct contribution to modern thinking as in the indirect contribution he has made through the doctrines of the Christian religion which has borrowed freely from the concepts formulated and emphasized by him.

Christian Religion—Psychology of the Early Christian Church.—It is believed by many laymen that all the doctrines and teachings of the Christian church have developed since the beginning of the Christian era. This is now known to be an incorrect assumption. Many of the doctrines and teachings incorporated in the Christian faith have developed from, and are the modifications of, the philosophy and teachings that prevailed prior to Christian times. It is easy to understand that the thinkers and teachers of the early Christian centuries could not fail to be influenced by the knowledge and beliefs of their own time, and that the early Christian fathers had to choose between the different points of view expressed by Plato and Aristotle. It is also easy to see why the modified teachings of Plato were the more acceptable to the thinkers and leaders of the early Christian church. The soul that was a substance could easily be related in their thinking to a divine soul, whereas it was difficult for them to conceive of an all-soul in Aristotle's sense of the term.

The early Christian writers were not primarily concerned with either the physiology or the psychology of man. Their sole concern was with that side of human life which deals with man's eternal salvation. Early Christian writers from the time of St. Paul to that of St. Augustine made no significant contribution to man's understanding of his own behavior. Having accepted the Platonist theory as the foundation of their own thinking about the soul, they proceeded to make man's soul the only thing about him that was of importance. Their very definition of soul, which follows that of Plato, makes it an extremely difficult concept to examine and study.

The Christian church did not encourage independent thinking, as the experiences of Copernicus and Galileo bear witness. The essential teaching of the church was that man was the most important object in the universe, and that the soul was the most important part of man. Anything that seemed to detract from the importance of man's soul was thoroughly disapproved. Only with the reintroduction of Aristotle's teachings into Europe was the reawakening of scientific thinking made possible.

The essential nature of the age-old conflict between science and religion is one of method rather than of content. The central concept of much of religious thinking is the assumption of revealed truth, truth that is complete and given with authority. Science, on the other hand, seeks to discover the truth through experience with a natural world, always remaining open-minded, never accepting any truth as complete or final. It is of some interest to speculate on what might have happened if the early church fathers had adopted the methods and concepts of Aristotle rather than those of Plato. It might reasonably be supposed that the whole domain of human behavior would not so long have remained outside the field of science. As it is, the influence of the early church was such as to delay a scientific explanation of human behavior. Even today, both the layman and the professional churchman tend to deny the importance of the scientific method in the field of religion.

The Philosophical Beginning of Psychology.—Not until the latter part of the sixteenth century were philosophers found who were essentially concerned with man's behavior in a way that differed from the prevailing teachings of Christian theology. During the seventeenth and eighteenth centuries, however, many philosophers did attempt to explain man and his behavior rather definitely in terms of natural laws. Three of these who have had an important influence upon the later developments of psychology will be briefly mentioned: Descartes, Leibnitz, and Locke.

Descartes is often regarded as the first psychologist of the modern period. Descartes recognized two separate and distinct substances—mind and body. This dual nature of man, according to Descartes, did not particularly concern the religious considerations of the soul. In fact, it may be said that with Descartes psychology had at least begun to lose its soul.

Descartes knew more about anatomy than did those philosophers who preceded him, although his knowledge was very incomplete. He thought of the body simply as a machine. The mind or soul (he still used the word) was the thinking substance, but he recognized it as a substance nonetheless. To explain its control of the body, he thought of it as being located in what is now known to be the ductless gland called the pineal body. The mind was supposed to act upon the body by means of "animal spirits," defined as a "certain subtle air or breath" flowing from the brain through the nerves, which he believed to be hollow. This will be seen to be a rather shrewd forerunner of present-day descriptions of the nerve impulses.

. . . According to Descartes, the mind sits in this organ and is moved by the animal spirits, and may also move the animal spirits when occasion requires. When one sees, a movement is started in the eye that drives the animal spirits inward over the optic nerve to the third ventricle; this inclines the pineal gland and produces in mind a picture of the object. On the other hand, when the mind desires to move a member, it (the gland) can direct the animal spirits to the proper muscles and they produce the movement. Thus body acts on mind and mind acts on body directly.[4]

Descartes was surprisingly modern in many of his teachings. He was probably the first to recognize what is now called a conditioned response. He catalogued and classified the emotions, but he did not make much effort to work out the laws of mental action. Descartes' teachings plainly indicate a conception of mind-body relationship in terms of interaction of the two.

In Germany at about the same time, Leibnitz developed another theory of the relation of mind and body. This theory is commonly called parallelism. Leibnitz believed that every kind of thing in the universe was an entity in itself, and as such possessed both natural substance and thinking substance. He still recognized the soul as a substance, but he thought of animals other than human beings as also having this thinking substance. Like Descartes, he was not primarily concerned with the religious concept of the soul. He was more keenly interested in the way in which the soul was responsible for the behavior of the body. The important thing about Leibnitz's material substances and thinking substances was that they were entirely independent of each other except in so far as they existed simultaneously in each individual and in each thing. Whatever happened to one happened simultaneously in the other, but without any cause and effect relationship. Mind and body, as Leibnitz viewed them, were set going in the beginning by God and have gone on thus at the same rates ever since. He compared body and mind to two perfectly-timed clocks without any common control. Whatever was registered in one would be registered in the other. Thus, events in consciousness were parallel to, but otherwise unrelated to, the events in the body. In fact, Leibnitz was not very much concerned about the body. How the mind worked was his chief if not his only concern. His theory of parallelism is not seriously accepted today, but it had a very definite importance in his time.

About the same time, John Locke, an English philosopher,

---

[4] W. B. Pillsbury, *The History of Psychology*, New York, W. W. Norton & Co., 1929, p. 58.

dealt with the problem of man's behavior. He differed from his contemporaries in the one very important respect: he was concerned only with ideas, i.e., with mental content and with the problem of how knowledge is acquired.

One of the important points of Locke's teachings was that man has no ideas at all at birth. This was absolutely contrary to the generally prevailing belief at that time. He likened the human mind at birth to a clean sheet of paper, a *tabula rasa*. What was to be written on this clean sheet would be determined entirely by experience. This theory has had a very great influence upon later educational development.

Locke is called an empirical philosopher because he approached his problems through the observation of experience rather than in terms of pure deductive reasoning. The principal method of discovering truth in Locke's time was to take some earlier teacher as an accepted authority and from this point go wherever one would so long as one could proceed logically. Locke, therefore, made a very real contribution in terms of method as well as in terms of content of his explanations.

It is not important for the purpose here to trace in detail the development of any of these philosophical theories through the years that followed. The only reason for mentioning these three philosophers is that they were so largely responsible for the beginning of the present-day interest in understanding human behavior.

In explaining human behavior they were, in a sense, the forerunners of the scientific movement. In a fuller sense, however, they cannot be regarded as scientists so much as logicians. Their method was most certainly not experimental. They were the forerunners of what came to be called "arm-chair psychologists." The influence of this mode of thinking is much in evidence today. Oftentimes it is much easier to sit back comfortably and speculate and theorize than to submit the problem of human behavior to rigorous scientific experimentation. Such procedures are likely to be frowned upon by the scientist, but the arm-chair psychologist draws his consolation from the example of these and other eminent philosophers and is not much concerned about the outcome of his thinking, except to make certain that it be exactly logical.

Psychology as a Science—the Beginning of Experimental Psychology.—The method of obtaining knowledge about man's behavior had changed from the purely deductive, logical procedure to one that was concerned principally with data resulting from the actual observation of man. It was only a step from this to the beginning of a truly experimental attack upon the problem of human behavior. This process of development was slow. In Germany during the last half of the nineteenth century, before a laboratory devoted entirely to psychology had been opened, certain physiologists in German universities began to be interested in experimental work in psychology. Most of the early experimentation had to do with sensation. This field was one that seemed to lend itself well to attack by physiologists who already possessed a good knowledge of the physical structure of the sense organs. These physiologists were interested in seeing what happened in the conscious experiences of the individual when the sense organs were stimulated in certain known ways.

Wundt was not the originator of the experimental method in psychology, but to him goes the credit for extending it greatly and making its importance generally recognized. He opened the first laboratory that was devoted exclusively to psychological experimentation. His contribution to the development of psychology consists in the great number of his original studies and in his training of many men from other countries in his laboratory.

Wundt was among the first to combine a sound knowledge of man's bodily structure with that of his behavior. His aim was to subject all hypotheses concerning man's behavior to rigid experimentation and to base his conclusions upon the results of these experiments. This marked a very distinct step forward.

Someone has facetiously remarked that first of all psychology lost its soul, then it lost its mind, finally it lost consciousness, and now it has only its behavior left. Some regard this as a tragedy. Actually it is an achievement that has taken ages to accomplish, and closer examination will show that much of worth that has presumably been lost is actually retained in the complete concept of behavior.

An Outline Summary

1. Explanations of human behavior from earliest times to the present show considerable continuity and overlapping. Each succeeding explanation has been the product of two sets of factors:

   A. New discoveries and the advancement of knowledge.
   B. Previously accepted explanations based on older knowledge.

2. Several great influences have had their effect upon man's explanations of his behavior and each is still in some degree involved in present-day explanations.

   A. Animism assumes that many creatures, including man, are twofold in nature, possessing a physical body and a spirit which inhabits and controls the body.

   B. The Greek philosophers differed importantly among themselves but all attempted to explain human behavior systematically in terms of observed natural phenomena.

   C. The early Christian church was concerned only with the human soul and with spiritual behavior. The body and all of its behavior was regarded as of little importance except as it was governed by the soul which in turn was considered to be a fragment of a supernatural "all-soul."

   D. The philosophers of the Middle Ages developed logically deductive methods of explaining human behavior but employed very little controlled observation and experimentation as a check upon the truth of their explanations.

   E. Psychology became a science in the nineteenth century when it began to explain human behavior in terms of carefully controlled observations and experimentation, and sought its explanations in terms of predictable natural phenomena. Psychology is now established as a natural science but with certain characteristics of its own.

Problems for Further Thought

1. What are the outstanding similarities and differences between a superstition of a primitive people and a hypothesis employed by a group of scientists?

2. List a dozen or more superstitions that you have known to be taken seriously by one or more persons. Why do such superstitions prevail in a civilization such as ours?

3. Point out a number of resemblances of the animistic beliefs of primitive people to some of the beliefs and practices of current usage in our own civilization.

4. What are the advantages of an attempt to explain man's behavior as suggested in the previous chapter, i.e., in terms of stimulus and organic structure, over those involving a dualistic concept of mind and body such as most of those receiving emphasis in the past?

5. What are the most important reasons why man still prefers to use the term "mind" in the animistic sense instead of more readily choosing the newer point of view?

Suggested Readings

No readings are provided for this chapter. It is intended that it shall serve as a means of furnishing a background of understanding and a kind of perspective for the age-old problem confronting man in his attempts to explain, predict, and control his own behavior. The material contained herein may reasonably serve such a purpose without more extensive reading. Here the only purpose is to develop an appreciation of the magnitude and the difficulty of discovering how man has arrived at his present point of view in explaining himself.

Chapter 3

WHY DO CERTAIN BEHAVIOR TRAITS SEEM TO RUN IN FAMILIES?

Some Family Traits of Behavior.—Family traits of behavior are very common. Sometimes they take the form of minor peculiarities of personality. Again they may assume such major proportions as to mark all or nearly all members of the family group in some conspicuous manner. Experience with one's own family will furnish illustrations of this fact. To ask why these behavior traits run in families is to begin the study of the way in which human behavior is determined and controlled.

Social and genetic studies have been made of certain families. Some of these families have been highly esteemed socially, while others have ranked very low in the social scale. The Jukes and the Kalikak families have been contributing social problems to their communities for several generations. On the other hand, there is the Edwards family in America and the Darwin family in England which have freely supplied their social groups with splendid accomplishments.

The question arises: What explanation can be given for the facts which have been scientifically observed and carefully recorded? Are such behavior traits really inherited, or are they the result of other factors which are inherited? Or finally, can they be accounted for without calling heredity into the question at all? The answer to these questions and to others like them will require some knowledge of human inheritance. It will also require a knowledge of the way environment affects those biological factors which in themselves are determined by heredity.

A lively controversy has been raging for years between two groups of scientists. One would emphasize the importance of the individual's heredity and minimize the influence of the environment. The other group would reverse this emphasis. As is usually true in controversies, the truth probably does not lie at either extreme. No factors concerning heredity have practical significance except in terms of the individual's environment. On the other hand, no factors of environment can be completely understood unless they are also viewed in the light of the individual's heredity.

The first question to be considered is what actually can be inherited. The knowledge of human heredity possessed by the average person is usually limited to the old inadequate definition of heredity as the resemblance of one generation to another. Ordinarily heredity is not much concerned with fundamentals such as the number of arms, legs, or eyes.

> In fact, these things are so much a matter of course that they are not even thought of as being a part of the child's heredity. No one remarks that John has two legs just as his father has, or that Jane resembles her mother in having an ear on each side of her head. But John may be said to have unusually long legs like his father or Jane to have particularly small and beautiful ears like her mother.[1]

Knowledge of the manner and extent of inheritance has been gained by giving particular attention to individual differences. Mendel, in his monastery garden, noticed that some pea vines were characteristically short and other pea vines were tall. When two differing strains were crossed, he watched to see which characteristics were present in the offspring. This is only an illustration of the procedure basic to one line of present-day knowledge of inheritance of traits. With man the control of mating is, of course, outside the realm of laboratory technique. Moreover, the number of offspring is small, and the human life span is very long. Therefore, it is necessary to note the presence of certain characteristics in several generations of one family stock and to check these findings with what is otherwise known about the nature of inheritance.

The zoölogist is unable to explain how behavior can be inherited unless behavior is defined as the responses of the bodily

---

[1] Paul Popenoe, *The Child's Heredity*, Baltimore, Williams & Wilkins Co., 1929, p. 12.

mechanism. In other words, *behavior traits,* as such, cannot be inherited. The resemblance of the behavior of children to that of their parents may, therefore, be accounted for in part in terms of the similarity of structure, which in turn may be partly due to inheritance. In reality, not even the bodily mechanism is inherited. Rather it is only the possibility of the development of specific kinds of structure which is inherited.

The child does not inherit any definite thing; he inherits merely a *potentiality of developing to a certain degree under normal conditions.* He can never exceed the limits of his potentiality, but he may and often does fall short of them. He does not get the most out of his heredity because the conditions are not favorable to the development of his possibilities. This is fortunate if the possibility is an injurious one, unfortunate if the possibility is a useful or desirable one.[2]

The really surprising thing is that there is so little difference in the characteristics of successive generations, and not that there are a few striking similarities. This will be made clear through a better understanding of the chance events that take place in germ cells during the process of maturing. The variations that appear in both anatomical traits and behavior traits from generation to generation are of two kinds. First, there are the slow changes that take place over thousands of years, and which constitute what is sometimes called evolution. Second, there are the changes which cause variations within each species. These are due to the combination of characteristics of the parents, represented in their germ plasm. It is this last group of variations that is of particular importance in the tracing of family resemblances. In order to understand how these parental characteristics may be combined, it will be necessary to have an elementary understanding of the process of development and fertilization of the germ cells.

The Biological Mechanics of Inheritance.—Each child has its beginning in the union of the germ cells of its parents. These

---

[2] *Ibid,* pp. 5–6.

germ cells contain bits of protoplasm called chromosomes, which are the real bearers of heredity. Each chromosome is composed of many units, called "genes" or "determiners." The latter term is especially significant, since these genes actually determine the potentialities of the individual. Each germ cell of a human being has 24 pairs of these chromosomes.[3] This is a human characteristic. Other species of animals may have other numbers of chromosomes, but they always occur in pairs. When one cell (the ovum) unites with another cell (the spermatozoön), the new cell would have double the original number of chromosomes unless something happened to prevent it. What actually happens is that, before the germ cell reaches the stage where fertilization can take place, the 24 pairs of chromosomes in the cell are reduced to 24 chromosomes, by the division of each pair. In the process of fertilization the chromosomes are again paired. However, each pair is now made up of one chromosome from each of the parent cells, so that the fertilized ovum, which is the beginning of a new individual, has the normal 24 pairs characteristic of the human being, supplied equally by each parent.

Chance plays an important rôle in determining the combination of the chromosomes in the fertilized ovum from which the new individual develops. The factors of chance operate at two points. In the first place, chance determines which particular chromosomes of each pair shall go to the cell which is to take part in fertilization. Although the chromosomes of each pair are similar, they are not always identical. One member of the pair may carry certain determiners in a dominant manner, while the other may carry them in a recessive manner. Sometimes, of course, both may be dominant or both recessive, but unless they are identical, the two germ cells which result from the division will not have identical possibilities of determining structure. Chance again enters as a determining factor in the process of fertilization itself. Of the large number of germ cells which are actually matured during the lifetime of either a man or a woman, only two are involved in each process of fertilization from which

---

[3] There are actually 23 pairs and an odd one in one sex and 24 pairs in the other, but for the purpose here they can be conveniently considered as 24 pairs.

an embryo develops.[4] Chance alone seems to determine which of the countless number of different germs cells will be selected for fertilization.

As an example, let us consider a simplified case in which only three pairs of chromosomes are involved. For convenience let these three pairs be called Aa, Bb, and Cc. When the reduction referred to above takes place, what possible different combinations of chromosomes may result? In such a case there are eight different possible combinations: ABC, ABc, AbC, Abc, aBC, aBc, abC, and abc. The same process takes place in both the male and the female. In fertilization therefore, there is the possibility of *any* one of these eight different combinations in the male germ cell uniting with *any* one of the eight different combinations in the female germ cell. Thus there would be possible 64 combinations of chromosomes in the fertilized ovum having only three pairs of chromosomes.

This is shown graphically in Figure 2. It may also be shown by the formula $(2^n)^2$ where n is the number of pairs. If n equals 3, as in this case, the computation of the formula yields 64, just as in Figure 2. It would be impractical to show the number of combinations in the case of the human germ cell by a process similar to Figure 2 because such a procedure would be extremely complex. However, it is possible to compute how many combinations there would be by means of the formula which in this case would be $(2^{24})^2$. Such a number is incomprehensibly large, being approximately 281,000,000,000,000.

As will be seen by an examination of Figure 2, not all of the 64 combinations are different. For example, all of the small squares from the lower left-hand corner to the upper right-hand corner are identical. However, of the 64 possibilities, 36 are different, and in the human being there would be more than 141,000,000,000,000 different possibilities. The significance of all of these meaninglessly large numbers is simply that the chance that brothers or sisters will have exactly the same inheritance can be discounted entirely.

---

[4] In the case of multiple identical siblings, only two germ cells are involved, regardless of the number of siblings.

MALE
Aa Bb Cc

WHEN REDUCED BECOMES

ABC, ABc, AbC
Abc, aBC, aBc
abC, or abc

when *any* one of these UNITES WITH *any* one of these

IT FORMS A FERTILIZED OVUM WITH ONE
OF THE 64 COMBINATIONS SHOWN BELOW.

FEMALE
Aa Bb Cc

WHEN REDUCED BECOMES

ABC, ABc, AbC
Abc, aBC, aBc
abC, or abc

Male ABC \ Female	ABC	ABc	AbC	Abc	aBC	aBc	abC	abc
ABC	AABBCC	AABBCc	AABbCC	AABbCc	AaBBCC	AaBBCc	AaBbCC	AaBbCc
ABc	AABBCc	AABBcc	AABbCc	AABbcc	AaBBCc	AaBBcc	AaBbCc	AaBbcc
AbC	AABbCC	AABbCc	AAbbCC	AAbbCc	AaBbCC	AaBbCc	AabbCC	AabbCc
Abc	AABbCc	AABbcc	AAbbCc	AAbbcc	AaBbCc	AaBbcc	AabbCc	Aabbcc
aBC	AaBBCC	AaBBCc	AaBbCC	AaBbCc	aaBBCC	aaBBCc	aaBbCC	aaBbCc
aBc	AaBBCc	AaBBcc	AaBbCc	AaBbcc	aaBBCc	aaBBcc	aaBbCc	aaBbcc
abC	AaBbCC	AaBbCc	AabbCC	AabbCc	aaBbCC	aaBbCc	aabbCC	aabbCc
abc	AaBbCc	AaBbcc	AabbCc	Aabbcc	aaBbCc	aaBbcc	aabbCc	aabbcc

Figure 2. The Possibilities of Variation in a Trait Dependent Upon Three Pairs of Chromosomes Which Show Mixed Dominance in Both Parents

The possibility of considerable variation in the offspring of two parents is clearly evident in everyday observation. Yet this principle of variation operates hand in hand with another important general principle which may seem at first to be quite contradictory to it. Despite the wide range of variations possible, it is nevertheless true that "like tends to beget like." There is a greater probability that children will be like the average of their parents than that they will resemble any other individual. The important truth follows that the kind of family traits that go into the mating will determine the nature of the traits of the offspring. Inbreeding may, therefore, be generally good or generally bad, depending upon the qualities of the family stock that enter into the process.

"Social Inheritance."—The term "social inheritance" is frequently used to designate certain aspects of family resemblance that cannot be accounted for in terms of biological factors. There are probably some dangers in the use of such a term that need to be guarded against. Actually, there is no such thing as the transmission from one generation to the next of any social factors by means of the germ plasm. The kind of inheritance here involved is much the same as that implied in saying that Mr. Brown inherited his farm from his father. The term "inheritance" may thus be used with two somewhat different meanings, and care must be exercised in discriminating between the two. Both of them are important in answering the question which heads this chapter.

Do the offspring of a Jukes or a Kalikak family inherit the socially undesirable behavior which is so much in evidence in the studies made of them? The answer will depend upon how the word "inherit" is used. They cannot inherit any kind of behavior in the biological sense, but they may biologically inherit very limited potential capacities for behaving in a way that society generally prizes. Their "social inheritance" is, of course, undesirable, and coupled with limitations of biological inheritance it makes an unfortunate combination. Both of these sets of factors must be considered in seeking an explanation of their behavior.

Impossibility of Inheriting Characteristics Acquired by Parents.—To the above-mentioned facts concerning heredity must be added certain others having to do with the continuity of the germ plasm through successive generations. In all higher forms of animal life the germ plasm develops separately from the rest of the body cells. When the fertilized germ cell begins to develop, it divides into two cells, each with chromosome content exactly like itself. Each of these in turn divides, and the process is repeated several times before any differentiation of cell structure begins. Before differentiation does begin, very early in the life of the embryo, one of these cells, which has a chromosome structure exactly like that of the fertilized cell from which the embryo began, is left in an undifferentiated form. Eventually, through further development, this gives rise to the gonads of the individual, from which the germ cells will later develop. The body develops anew for each generation, while the germ plasm continues from one generation to the next. The statement is sometimes made that one is more nearly related to one's grandparents than to one's parents. This is a figurative statement, of course, but it does throw light upon the frequently observed phenomenon that children in a family may sometimes rather strikingly resemble a grandparent in one or a few characteristics.

The facts of heredity and development all point to the impossibility of transmitting biologically from one generation to the next those characteristics that are the result of accident or habit. The nature of the future germ cells is determined at the moment of fertilization, and hence the possibility of transmitting characteristics acquired as a result of experience simply does not exist.

A similar problem is involved in "prenatal" culture, which was, at one time, in good medical repute. According to this belief, the mother could influence the future development of the unborn child by what she thought and did during pregnancy. This is now recognized as impossible. The only way in which the activity of the mother can influence the unborn child is by means of substances which could be passed through the placenta to the blood stream of the child. Unless the mother's activity produces such substances in her own blood stream, no such influence would be possible.

Characteristics of the Behavior and Appearance of Twins.— It seems hardly necessary, in view of what has just been said, to point out that there may be a wide variation in the traits of structure inherited by children of the same parents. This would mean that the behavior traits of children in the same family might also readily be expected to differ to a considerable degree, since differences in structure might easily account for differences in behavior.

In the human species, most births are single. Twinning is not at all unusual, but cases in which more than two children are born at a time are exceedingly rare. These plural births are of two kinds. *Monozygotic* or identical twins are individuals that are presumably born as a result of the fertilization of a single ovum. There seems to be excellent evidence that the Dionne quintuplets are identical, all having developed from the fertilization of a single ovum.[5] The *polyzygotic* or non-identical plural births are matured from two or more ova fertilized at approximately the same time. In the identical twins the division of the original fertilized ovum takes place within a very short time after fertilization and before differentiation of structure begins. The two resulting parts each develop as an individual, but since they were derived from a single fertilized ovum they must have identical heredity. In the case of non-identical twins, the situation is exactly the same as that of brothers and sisters. The only difference is the accident of being born at the same time. They may differ in their heredity as much as any other children born of the same parents. Identical twins are always of the same sex; non-identical twins may be of the same or opposite sex.

A study of similarities in twins, as compared with other children in the same family, has been a very fruitful means of discovering the effects of heredity. The environment of twins is, in most cases, more nearly alike than is the environment of chil-

---

[5] W. E. Blatz, *et al., Collected Studies on the Dionne Quintuplets,* Toronto, University of Toronto Press, 1937.

dren in the same family born at different times. These similarities of environment may lead to confusion, since parents often emphasize the similarities of twins in their treatment of the children, especially in their dress, in providing toys, and in other matters of family care. This similarity of environment may have something to do with the similarities of behavior of the individuals as they grow up. At the present time it is not clear, even after extensive study of twins, exactly how much the hereditary factors contribute to the appearance of family behavior traits in successive generations.

Recently Newman [6] and associates at the University of Chicago have been studying the mental traits of identical twins who have been raised in separate homes. Up to the present time some eight or nine pairs of such twins have been studied rather carefully. In all these cases the twins were separated in early life and frequently did not even know that they had a twin until the early formative period of life was past. These twins have been measured in terms of intelligence, emotion, and temperament. Remarkable similarities have been found in the matter of intelligence, but the similarities of emotions and temperament are not so great. This may be due partly to the fact that the instruments for measuring emotions and temperament are not so reliable as those for measuring intelligence. On the other hand, it may be possible that emotional and temperamental differences can be more readily influenced by environmental factors.

A Study of Quadruplets.—The Keys quadruplets, born in the United States, have furnished psychologists with very interesting data bearing on the problem of inheritance. They have been extensively studied, and rather exact measurements have been made of their psychological and physical traits. A most complete series of mental and physical measurements was made at the time they were twelve years of age. Mona and Roberta are apparently identical or monozygotic twins. They are brunettes and in general looked remarkably alike at the age of twelve. They differed

---

[6] H. H. Newman, "Identical Twins," *The Eugenic Review*, XXII, April, 1930, pp. 22–23.

THE KEYS QUADRUPLETS

Aged 5 months, 2 years, 12 years, and 16 years. Can you pick out the identicals, Roberta and Mona, and the non-identicals, Mary and Leota, from the description in the text?

THE KEYS QUADRUPLETS

The pictures on this and the preceding page were furnished by the courtesy of *Look,* in which magazine they appeared with several other pictures of these quadruplets on January 18, 1938.

only slightly in physical measurements. Mary and Leota, the other two girls, differed very much in their appearance. Leota was fair-skinned, light-haired, shorter, and lighter in weight than the other three. Mary was dark and resembled Mona and Roberta in general physical proportions and appearance, but she was readily distinguishable from these two. In intelligence, Mona, Roberta, and Leota were much alike. All three were distinctly superior individuals. Mary was also above the average in intelligence, but was somewhat different in this respect from her sisters. Their records in the elementary school showed a great similarity in the primary grades. Their achievement test scores in the upper grades also showed marked similarities for Leota, Mona, and Roberta. These three were distinctly accelerated in terms of achievement. Mary also was slightly accelerated, but the achievement test scores seemed to confirm those of intelligence.

Brintle concludes in part as follows :

Roberta and Mona are strikingly alike in form of face, color of hair and eyes, and in bodily build. Mary and Leota are distinctly different from each other in these respects. Mary resembles Roberta and Mona but has a decidedly different form of face and bodily build. Leota, with her blond hair and blue eyes, and distinctly different form of face and bodily build, is no more like her three sisters than if she were an ordinary sibling. It seems, therefore, that Roberta and Mona are identical twins and that the four individuals developed from three eggs.

Assuming Roberta and Mona to be identical twins, a comparison may be made of the results of their traits that were measured. Although there were slight differences in the physical measurements, the two are as nearly alike as identical twins ordinarily are. From the results of the series of measurements represented here, we do not find any striking differences between Roberta and Mona. On the other hand, the results of both the achievement and the psychological measurements show a marked degree of similarity. It seems, therefore, that with this particular set of twins, random and environmental influences have had no marked effects on the traits measured.

In studies of identical twins, their identical similarities are sometimes attributed to the identical environment. Therefore, from the study of a set of quadruplets in which we have both a set of the identical twins and a set of fraternal twins who were in reality under the same environmental conditions, it appears that random and environmental influences have had very little or no effect in causing the identical twins to grow more unlike. Furthermore, it does not seem that the fraternals have become more like the identicals, but rather the factors of heredity have been most influential.[7]

Inheritance of Special Talents.—It is frequently noted that certain special abilities or so-called "talents" appear successively in several generations of the same family. Can this appearance best be accounted for in terms of inheritance or in terms of environmental conditions? It will be worth while to consider one special talent and attempt to apply to it the principles of biological heredity. A very appropriate one for this purpose is musical talent, because it has been studied in relatively great detail. Seashore [8] and others have succeeded in picking out a number of fairly simple elements which, taken together, may constitute what is called musical talent. The analysis, while fairly complete, probably does not take into consideration certain elements as yet not clearly recognized. One or two of the elements which have been isolated will suffice as illustrations.

The first of these is pitch discrimination. Two tones, differing in pitch by only a small amount, are sounded one at a time with only a short interval between. Individuals are then asked to indicate whether the first tone had a higher or lower pitch than the second. A few persons can discriminate correctly every time a comparison is made; others will insist that the same tone has been sounded twice. If one of the tones is changed so that the difference becomes greater, more persons can discriminate correctly. If the difference is made large enough, anyone who can hear the tones will be able to make a correct discrimination. A few individuals can distinguish between the pitches when they are very nearly alike. For others there must be a large difference before they can discriminate surely. The interesting

---

[7] Shirley L. Brintle, "Mental and Physical Measurements of a Set of Twelve-Year-Old Quadruplets," *Pedogogical Seminary and Journal of Genetic Psychology,* Vol. 39, p. 100. These girls are now adults and have recently graduated from college. The similarities and differences shown when they were twelve in general seem to be about equally evident today.

[8] C. E. Seashore, *The Psychology of Musical Talent,* New York, Silver, Burdett & Co., 1919.

thing about this phenomenon is that training produces very little improvement.

The organic basis of this difference is not definitely known. It is supposed to be due to minute differences in the structure of the inner ear. These differences, whatever they are, might very readily be accounted for in terms of factors of inheritance. To this extent then, one may be said to inherit varying degrees of this ability, which undoubtedly is an important attribute of musical talent. However, it is a potentiality only. Certainly not all individuals who may have inherited it to a degree that enables them to make fine pitch discriminations develop recognizable musical talent, but it can readily be understood that a person who lacks this potentiality would have very real difficulty in playing any musical instrument that demanded fine pitch discriminations.

Not all the factors measured by Seashore's test are so little influenced by training; hence musical talent is not entirely determined by heredity. Tonal memory, consonance, and discrimination of intensity are elements of musical talent which do show the effects of training. Even in these cases heritable differences in structure are of basic significance in musical behavior. The inheritance of what might be called musical talent probably depends upon many hereditary factors. The potentiality is all that can be accounted for in terms of inheritance. A musically talented individual, therefore, is the result, first, of a combination of chromosome factors which have resulted in the development of structural characteristics that make possible the various elements of talented musical behavior. In the second place, the appearance of such musical talent is dependent upon desirable environmental stimulation. Different degrees of inherited potentialities of this sort might require different types and amounts of environmental influence.

In the case of the musically talented family, the fact that the parents were talented would mean that they had a bodily structure which made such behavior possible. This would increase the probability of their children having a structure somewhat similar. Moreover, the environmental stimulation in such a family would do much to insure the development of the musical ability to a point somewhere near the highest level of possibilities determined by inheritance. It is a characteristic of ordinary human observation that instances of the appearance of such a trait as musical talent in successive generations of a family are looked for and remembered, while other members of the family who do not carry on the family tradition are easily overlooked.

Other Inherited Traits Which Are Particularly Likely to Influence Behavior.—Three groups of traits will illustrate how the behavior of an individual may be potentially determined in part by inheritance. These groups show progressively more complex combinations of factors of inheritance.

1. TRAITS DUE TO KNOWN ODDITIES OF INHERITED STRUCTURE. Color-blindness is an inability to distinguish certain colors. It exists in two varieties and in varying degrees of completeness. The most common kind is called red-green color-blindness. Persons affected with this particular sort of incapacity are more or less incapable of distinguishing certain shades of red from certain shades of green. In the other kind there is complete inability to recognize colors. Very few persons are thus afflicted. It is presumed that such persons see only what the individual with normal color vision recognizes as different shades of gray.

Color-blindness is definitely known to be due to an absence of certain minute structures in the retina of the eye. It is not a disease, although it may be called a defect. The condition is heritable and behaves as a sex-linked recessive. This means that it is recessive in the same way that blue-eyedness is recessive to dark-eyedness. It is sex-linked in the sense that it appears to be linked with the genes in the chromosome which determines the sex of the offspring. The pattern of inheritance is a peculiar one and involves an apparent skipping of the males of every other generation.

Other relatively simple oddities of human structure which in some degree might influence behavior are congenital dislocation of the hip, some forms of dwarfism, several varieties of short-fingeredness, stiff-jointed fingers, a condition of extreme brittleness of all the bones in the body, an extra digit on each hand and

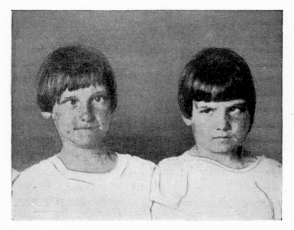

FOUR SQUINTERS IN ONE FAMILY

Mrs. C. S., age 46, had had 14 children, of whom 9 were living at the time of this study (*Journal of the American Medical Association*, May 22, 1926). Her right eye had always turned out. Her three youngest children, shown above, have eyes that turn in. The boy's right eye has been turning in since age 2; the older girl's right eye since age 2; the younger girl's left eye since age 1. Although no history of strabismus could be found on either paternal or maternal side of this family, the tendency is found from careful studies to be inherited. Photograph from Dr. Frank H. Rodin, Stanford University Medical School, San Francisco, Calif. (By permission from Paul Popenoe, *The Child's Heredity*, Williams & Wilkins Co., Baltimore, Md.)

foot, hernia, and some forms of harelip and cleft palate. The list could be greatly extended. Some of these peculiarities are more clearly inherited than others. Some behave like dominants, while others have the characteristics of recessives. Many, if not most of them, seem to depend upon the cumulative effect of two or several genes in different chromosomes. However, all are heritable in the strictly biological sense, and the presence or absence of any one might have a definite effect on the behavior and personality of the individual who inherited them.

2. DOMINANCE. A somewhat more complex behavior characteristic is the matter of dominance of one side of the body over the other, most commonly manifested in what is called handedness. In all civilizations of the world most persons show a preference for the use of the right hand. This trait appears in such widely scattered places and in so many kinds of civilizations that it would be very difficult to account for it in terms of learning alone. Moreover, such dominance is usually not limited to that of hand and arm but involves many parts of the body. Until recently it was believed that man was the only animal to show such dominance. However, some evidence has recently been brought forth to indicate that even lower animals have something resembling the human preference for the use of one side of the body.

Preference in handedness is usually well recognized by the individual. Some are very dominantly right-handed while others show equal dominance of the left hand. However, a very large number of individuals are not so completely one-handed, using some implements with the right hand, and others with the left.

The matter of right-eyedness or left-eyedness is another interesting feature of dominance. Many more individuals are dominantly right-eyed than left-eyed. It is apparent, too, that the degree of dominance is stronger in some individuals than in others. It is possible that many readers have never been aware of the fact of dominant eyedness because so little social attention is paid to it as compared to handedness.

Left dominance seems to appear much more frequently among the members of certain families than in others. It is not known exactly what is the nature of this heritable tendency nor just how it behaves. However, even after all allowances are made for the learned elements in dominance, there still remains considerable evidence to show that this trait is inherited. It may be a matter of inherited brain structure, although this has not been completely established.

3. TEMPERAMENT. A still more complex behavior trait commonly goes by the name of temperament. This is not a unitary trait, but a complex of several simpler components. Neither is it exclusively a result of hereditary potentialities, for learning is undoubtedly of great importance in its development. A case in point is that of a father who assumes that his son's violent temper is the outcropping of a family trait. Such a possibility may exist. But the evidence is not entirely convincing when the father assumes that the family trait in question comes from the wife's family stock. Fortunately, more reliable evidence than this is available.

It is frequently noted that two children in the same family, although not far apart in age, show distinctly different temperaments. Consider the case of two children four and six years old in the same family. The four-year-old is a lively, vivacious, talkative person. The six-year-old is distinctly different in temperament, being reserved and talking very little. The behavior patterns of these two children have been characteristic throughout their lives. Both are apparently equally bright, but there is a distinct difference in their personalities which cannot be accounted for in terms of age or known differences of experience. It is possible that the differences manifested in such a case are actually due to inherited differences in structure. Such differences may easily be accounted for in terms of the chance combination of genes in the fertilized ova from which these two children of the same parents have sprung.

Much more noticeable differences appear when the children of different families are compared. In such a case, differences in family environment and in procedures of child training must be considered. However, much the same variety of differences is noticeable even in orphanages where the environment is somwhat similar for all individuals. In all such cases observation may be faulty or actually misleading. The assumption that family or racial differences in temperament do exist may cause observers to look for those data that seem to prove the assumption. At the same time, it may cause some rather obvious exceptions to be overlooked. Nevertheless, it is possible that the exceptions here noted may be due to the already emphasized fact that all children born of the same parents do not have the same hereditary potentialities.

An additional difficulty is that human beings possess an organism which is more easily modified by its reactions to environment than that of any of the lower forms of animal life. The geneticist is compelled to get much of his information about temperamental traits from the study of lower animals. This he must supplement by the accumulation of all data available from observations and measurements of human beings. Some of the data used by the geneticist in making his conclusions will be summarized from Popenoe.[9] These, in turn, are drawn from a wide variety of original sources.

In the first place, distinct characteristics of temperament make their appearance in the individual's behavior during very early childhood and seemingly even during the prenatal period of life. Secondly, temperamental differences are noticeable in different family strains of the same animal species. For example, white rats are normally lacking in wildness and savageness, whereas wild rats, *even when raised from birth in captivity,* manifest these traits to a marked degree. Thus, the wildness and savageness cannot be accounted for entirely in terms of the life experience of the rats. Offspring of a white rat and a wild rat raised in the entire absence of the wild parent show wildness and savageness approximately midway between the behavior manifested by the parents. A recent experiment with tame white mice and wild mice show somewhat similar results.[10]

In the third place, it may be noted that racial differences in temperament are extremely difficult to explain in terms of en-

---

[9] Popenoe, *op. cit.,* Ch. XX, p. 197 ff.
[10] F. A. Moss, *Comparative Psychology,* New York, Prentice-Hall, Inc., 1934, Ch. III, C. P. Stone, pp. 58–59 ff.

vironmental and cultural conditions. Students of Negro life in the remote parts of the deep South, where the Negro stock is almost pure, have noted some distinct racial characteristics of temperament of the Negro as compared with the temperamental characteristics of whites of a similar socio-economic level.

A fourth fact of importance is that an outstanding temperamental trait is occasionally noted in successive generations, with about as great frequency as would be expected for corresponding anatomical traits. The marked resemblance of temperamental traits in identical twins has frequently been noted. In such cases it is difficult to determine how much of the resemblance is due to heredity and how much to similarity of environment. The temperamental and emotional similarities of identical twins are too striking to be readily accounted for in terms of environmental influences.

Finally, there is the association of types of temperament with types of bodily structure. Different types of bodily structure are recognized as being largely determined by heredity. It is only fair to note that much of the evidence is not very clear and there is considerable confusion about the classifications employed in describing bodily types. The same is true of types of temperament. However, some studies suggest that temperamental traits may frequently be found in their extreme forms in individuals who have distinctly different bodily structure. Introversion (preoccupation with one's own inner mental life) according to Popenoe, tends to be found most frequently in tall, thin individuals. Extraversion (preoccupation with external affairs and things) seems to go more frequently with rotund, thick-set persons.

Although the modern scientist's knowledge of the function of the endocrine glands is still incomplete, the evidence available seems to point clearly to the conclusion that temperamental differences are related to differences in the functioning of several of these glands. Such functional differences may depend upon structural differences and these in turn may have an hereditary origin. Therefore, heredity may conceivably have a distinct bearing upon the appearance of temperamental traits in successive generations of a family.

The Heredity-Environment Problem.—In conclusion, the problem of the relative importance of heredity and environment needs another word. It is not a question of which one is the more important in determining the behavior of the individual. Rather, it is a question of the way in which each influences the other. No one can exist without either a reasonably satisfactory heredity or a reasonably adequate environment. The very fact that the individual is born and lives throughout childhood and later life implies that both heredity and environment have at least been sufficient to satisfy the minimum requirements of life. The real relationship of those two sets of factors might be stated somewhat in this manner. Heredity determines the potentialities within which the individual's development may proceed. Environment determines the degree to which the individual develops within the limits set by heredity. The importance of both heredity and environment must be recognized. All changes occurring in the behavior of the individual must be brought about by means of environmental stimulation. On the other hand, no amount of environmental influence can produce in the behavior of the individual a change that transcends the limits determined by heredity.

An Outline Summary

1. Inheritance in the biological sense must not be confused with the frequently employed figurative use of the term "social inheritance."
2. Behavior traits can be inherited only in the sense that behaving structure can be influenced by inheritance.
3. Heredity can only determine the limits within which bodily structure can develop.
4. The great complexity of the human germ cells and of the processes involved in their development and fertilization make it probable that the children of two parents will inherit somewhat different potentialities of structure and hence of behavior.
5. The experience of the parents cannot influence their germ cells nor the inherited characteristics of their offspring.
6. The importance of the influence of both heredity and experience is well indicated by the study of the behavior of identical twins as compared with that of fraternal twins.

7. Experience, as it is determined by the environment, may modify any behavior trait within the limits set by heredity.

8. The "heredity vs. environment" problem is really not so much a question of which is the more important, as it is one of determining how each set of factors influences the other.

PROBLEMS FOR FURTHER THOUGHT

1. In the light of the discussion contained in this chapter, what will determine the advisability of cousin marriages?

2. Briefly describe some behavior trait, such as walking or vocal inflection, that is a peculiarity of some family you know. Then enumerate some of the difficulties involved in determining the relative influence of heredity and environment.

3. Briefly describe some family talent known to you, such as artistic ability. What evidences can you discover that this is dependent upon biological heredity? Upon environmental influences, particularly in early life?

4. The question is often asked: "Is insanity inherited?" If insanity is defined briefly here as so gross a deterioration and maladaption of the individual's behavior as to endanger the safety and welfare of the individual or of society, what must be the nature of the answer in the light of the discussion found in this chapter? What might be the actual hereditary basis of such maladjustment? What kind of environmental influences must also be considered?

5. Tests show many adults who have a left-sided dominance, but who shake hands, write, and do other things of a social nature with the right hand. Show how this may illustrate the modification of innate behavior tendencies through environmental influences. Some persons do not yield easily to social pressures. To what extent may this indicate the differences in the limits of modifiability set by inheritance?

6. Such a complex trait as musical talent seems to depend upon and include a fairly large number of specific traits which may be unrelated among themselves. Show how the appearance of such a talent may depend upon both inherited capacities and fortunate stimulating situations.

7. Since the determiners of a child's heredity are fixed at the instant of fertilization, of what importance is it to the teacher or parent to know something about the child's inheritance?

8. Since there is nothing that can be done about changing the heredity of a child after conception, why is it particularly important that the parent and teacher should understand the significance and limitations of the influence of environment?

9. Explain how such behavior patterns as personality and temperament can be influenced by heredity.

10. Of what significance for the problem of the relationship between heredity and environment is the study of the behavior of fraternal and identical twins?

Suggested Readings

Arlitt, Ada H. Psychology of Infancy and Early Childhood. 2nd Ed., Mc-Graw-Hill Book Co., Inc., 1930, Ch. II, pp. 10–36.

Gilliland, A. R. Genetic Psychology. New York, The Ronald Press Co., 1933, Ch. VI, pp. 93–113.

Goodenough, Florence. Developmental Psychology. New York, D. Appleton-Century Co., 1934, Ch. III, pp. 27–59.

Guyer, M. F. Being Well Born. Indianapolis, Bobbs-Merrill Co., 1916.

Murphy, Gardner. A Briefer General Psychology. New York, Harper & Bros., 1935, Ch. II, pp. 13–28.

Wiggam, A. E. The Fruit of the Family Tree. New York, Bobbs-Merrill Co., 1934.

Chapter 4

SOME WAYS IN WHICH BEHAVIOR DEPENDS UPON STRUCTURE—WHAT ARE INSTINCTS?

Characteristics of Instinctive Behavior.—A casual observation of the behavior of many species of animals makes it evident that all members of a given species behave in some respects remarkably alike. There seems very little, if any, possibility that such behavior can be properly thought of as entirely learned.

It is a well-known fact that mother cats normally show great solicitude for their kittens for a period of several weeks after the kittens are born. Cats do this with their first kittens even when they have never had the opportunity of learning. If they are deprived of their kittens, they frequently show a kind of behavior that to the human being is most readily interpreted as mourning. It may last several days or even weeks. Sometimes they have been known to "adopt" either kittens from another litter or the young of some other animal. They have even been known to nurse young rats and squirrels, whereas the normal behavior of a cat would be to eat them. Such "maternal instinct" appears among a large number of mammals. The question arises : Why do these mother cats behave in such a way?

Among human beings instinctive behavior is not so obvious, but there are some behavior patterns which appear early in life without opportunity for learning. These are called either reflexes or instincts. If a small rod slightly larger than a pencil is placed in contact with the palm of an infant a few days old, its behavior can be predicted. The thumb and fingers close tightly around the rod with the thumb on the same side as the fingers. This is called the grasping reflex and it may be strong enough to support the entire weight of the infant's body. Why does the infant grasp the rod in this particular manner and with such evident tenacity? It will be the function of this chapter to answer this question and similar ones about the behavior traits of lower animals and human beings.

A variety of explanations have been offered by psychologists to account for the behavior noted in these illustrations. The word "instinct" is frequently employed by those who present explanations that differ widely. Hence, to say that the behavior is instinctive is not a satisfactory explanation. From the psychologist's point of view, to say that an act is the result of an "instinct" is often equivalent to saying that the cause of the act is unknown.

Most descriptions of instinct have two characteristics in common, unlearnedness and universality. The lower animals are supposed to have much of their behavior made up of instincts. Man, too, is often said to have a long list of such unlearned, universally appearing behavior traits. Instincts and reflexes are usually thought of as inborn tendencies to make certain responses under certain conditions. These tendencies are frequently regarded as mysterious and even as outside the realm of natural law.

It has been shown that organic structures of the body may be influenced by heredity. This offers a partial explanation of the similarity of behavior of successive generations of the species. As a means of understanding the real nature of instinctive activity, it is necessary to examine first the simplest of these acts.

Reflexes.—Reflexes resemble instincts in that they manifest themselves in the absence of opportunity for learning. They are universal within a species. The chief difference between them lies in the fact that reflexes are less complex than instincts. The grasping behavior of the human infant should be regarded as reflexive rather than instinctive, since the name reflex is usually reserved for such relatively simple activities. Reflexive activity usually involves the movement of a localized part of the body. Another well-known reflex in human behavior is the knee jerk. If one sits on a table, with the lower part of the leg suspended, the knee jerk can be produced by firmly but gently striking the tendon just below the kneecap with the edge of a book or with the hand. The usual response is an involuntary kicking movement.

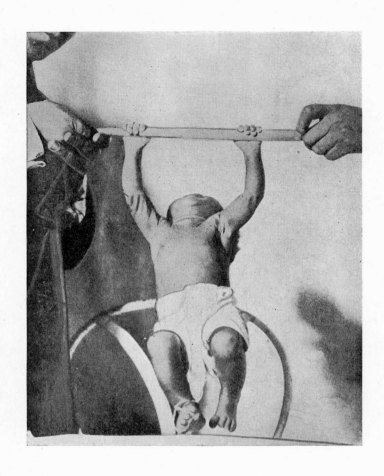

SUPPORTING HIMSELF

This young infant nicely illustrates the tenacity of the grasp reflex of early childhood. Note the position of the thumbs. (By permission, from Paul Popenoe, *The Child's Heredity,* Williams & Wilkins Co., Baltimore, Md.)

Another human reflex is the involuntary winking in response to a touch in the vicinity of the eye. It occurs with normal infants at birth. The wink produced by the visual stimulus of an object approaching the eye may also be a reflex, although it may involve some learning.

Glandular activity is largely reflexive in nature. The salivary glands secrete without previous learning when food and other substances are placed in the mouth of a new-born child. Most of the glands of the body are ready to function in some degree by the time of birth, but their growth continues, and their later behavior may also be influenced by learning.

In each of these reflexes as well as in others it is to be noticed that the activity appears promptly and uniformly when the appropriate stimulus is presented.

Within narrow limits these reflexes may be modified by learning, but they usually persist throughout life with little modification. Very few such responses involve the cortex or gray matter of the brain when they appear in their unlearned form.

Reflexive Activity of Human Infants..—It will be worth while to list a few of the reflexive activities in the human infant at birth. The list on page 74 is confined largely to those reflexes in which both the activity and the stimulus can be observed.

The stimulus is largely internal or organic in nature in such activities as coughing, gasping, yawning, hiccoughing, sneezing, and vocalizing. All of these and many more are illustrative of the behavior called reflexive. They are all relatively simple responses to simple stimuli. Each response normally includes only a small group of mechanisms, such as a related group of muscles or a gland. Some of these groups remain almost constant throughout life, and are changed very little by either maturation or learning. Others are modified in varying degrees, while still others tend to disappear entirely. All involve the central nervous system, but none depend upon the higher complex neural mechanisms of the brain. Many are ready to function without learning, depending upon the innate development of the structure.

Activity	Stimulus
Wink.	Tactual, upon or near the eye itself. Later, approach of an object to the eye, i.e., visual stimulus.
Pupilary or iris reflex.	Change in the intensity of light.
Turning the head.	Light touch on the cheek when child is hungry.
Sucking movements of the lips.	Touching the lips with nipple or other object.
Increase in salivary activity.	Presence of food in the mouth.
Swallowing and gulping.	Presence of a substance in the back of the mouth or at the base of the tongue.
Spitting.	Noxious substance in the mouth.
Eye movements. Fixation.	A light or object at short distance.
Grasping.	Contact of rod-like object across the palm of the hand.
Babinsky reflex. (A fanning-out movement of the toes, quite different from the curling-in movement characteristic of later life.)	Stroking the sole of the foot with a blunt object.
Movement of arms, legs, and head, including withdrawal and defensive movements.	Numerous stimuli, external ones tactual in nature.
Smiling, laughing, and cooing.	Tickling certain areas of the body.

Instincts.—Instincts are like reflexes in that both appear promptly when the structure is sufficiently mature and the organism is appropriately stimulated. Both are essentially uniform for the whole species and are relatively uninfluenced by learning. Both may be absent at birth and may appear later, and both often seem to serve a definite purpose in the individual's life economy. When the responses are localized and only slightly subjected to the effects of learning, they are usually called reflexive. When the responses are complex, involving general adjustment of the whole organism to its surroundings, the term "instinctive behavior" is more appropriate.

The similarity of these responses in all respects except that of degree of complexity and modifiability suggests at once that they are only different phases of the same process. If all types of reflexive and instinctive behavior were to be arranged along a straight line, the simplest and least modifiable reflex could conveniently be placed at one extreme. The more complex and more modifiable behavior patterns would be placed toward the other end of the line. Hence, only arbitrary distinctions can be drawn between reflexes and instincts or, as will be shown later, between instincts and habits. Some modifiability through learning seems to be possible for even the simplest reflex. On the other hand, the most complex habit has its origin in responses which are innately within the scope of the organism, when stimulated.

Is Instinctive Behavior Purposeful?—Among the several ways in which instinctive behavior has been classified, the purpose of the activity furnishes the most usual basis for classification. Thus, one frequently hears or reads about instinctive food-seeking activity, instinctive self-preservation, and instinctive species-perpetuation. A careful study of some of these activities arouses one's suspicions about the supposed purposefulness of the activity. This suspicion is especially valid if the purpose is thought of as some loosely described inner urge, presumably the result of an inherited memory.

It will be worth while to note some of the studies that have been made of this problem. The behavior of some of the lower animals has been used most frequently for two reasons. First, such animals are freer from social inhibitions than are humans. Hence, their behavior is more easily observed and analyzed. In the second place, it is in these lower animals that instincts are presumably found in a "pure" form, and they supposedly play a more important part in the animal's behavior.

First, observe some of the instinctive behavior of insects. One species of butterfly lays its eggs upon a certain shrub where the larvæ hatch in the fall. They pass the hibernating stage on the shrub not far from the ground. When a certain degree of warmth is supplied in the spring, these larvæ *always move up* the stem and feed on the leaves at the highest tip. One may ask, "Why do they always go up the stem to their food instead of down the stem to starvation and certain destruction?" These caterpillars have a certain bodily condition which is designated by the term *positive heliotropism*. A tropism is a forced movement. The prefix *helio* refers to the sun or to light in general. Thus, to be positively heliotropic means to have a forced movement toward the light.

When these caterpillars are placed in a horizontal glass tube before a window, they proceed at once *toward the window*. They do not turn back when they reach the closed end of the tube nearest the window. The food which is at the other end of the tube is completely out of reach, for it lies in the direction away from the light. In their normal environment, going toward the light brings them to the first leaves at the tip of the branch. Having eaten of these, the bodily chemical condition is changed, positive heliotropism disappears, and they can then move in any direction.

Another group of interesting and significant facts which apparently has some bearing upon this question has to do with the influence of the endocrine glands. It is well known that a female dog shows maternal solicitude for her young only during a period of a few weeks after they are born. At the end of four to six weeks she will no longer permit them to nurse, nor does she show maternal solicitude.

Gustavson,[1] among others, has isolated, in pure chemical form, one of the female sex hormones. When this hormone is injected into the body of a non-pregnant female dog which has never given birth to pups, she develops the signs of maternal solicitude and the mammary glands secrete as long as this hormone is kept in her body. Gustavson has also shown by his experiments that when this substance is injected into male barnyard fowls they lose their male characteristics of appearance and in some respects behave like the hen.

From this account, it will be clear that while instinctive behavior does serve a useful purpose for the species, it is not a purposeful activity on the part of the individual. Rather, it seems

---

[1] R. G. Gustavson, *The Journal of Experimental Zoology*, Vol. 64, No. 1, p. 133.

probable that through the ages of natural selection those members
of the species which were so constituted organically and physiologically that they responded with these forced movements lived
and perpetuated their kind. Members of the species with slightly
varying organic constitutions responded to the stimuli of the
environment with other types of behavior and consequently died
without propagating offspring. No claim is made that these internal organic conditions are the final explanation of the behavior
called instinctive, but they do suggest a part of such an explanation.

Other Characteristics of Instinctive Behavior.—Instinctive
behavior patterns may be brought into action by a great variety
of stimuli. Most frequently it is necessary to take into account
whole patterns of stimulation in order to understand the complex
characteristics of the instinctive behavior pattern. The stimulation often involves elements that are quite diverse, some depending upon the condition of the organism at the moment, others
upon factors of environment. The latter may be either social
or non-social, depending upon whether or not they involve other
human beings. The condition of the organism may change from
moment to moment or from year to year. The conditions of the
environment are extremely mobile so that very great changes
may be expected among them from time to time. It must be noted,
too, that a change in any single element in the total group of
stimuli may result in the formation of a significantly different
pattern of stimulation and hence of response.

For example, consider the manifestation of human mother
love, much of which unquestionably depends upon learned social
factors of stimulation. The sight and contact of the child provides an external source of organic stimulation, while at the
same time there are intraorganic factors which must also be
considered as sources of stimulation, although the mother may
not be aware of them at all. One such factor, most frequently
recognized during the period of lactation, is the distention or discomfort caused by the increased accumulation of milk in the
mammary glands. These and many other sources of stimulation

may simultaneously form parts of the total pattern which may undergo noticeable changes from time to time.

Another significant characteristic of instinctive behavior is the great complexity of the response itself. Instinctive responses normally represent an adjustment of the person as a whole to his environment. Since both the stimulating environment and the human organism are extremely complex, it would be unreasonable to expect to find a simple explanation for the whole response, which could be labeled an "instinct."

Assume that you observe a boy running across a field. Such running behavior might be the result of an instinct of curiosity, of hunger, of fear, or of many other assumed motives of an instinctive kind. It might simply be called running behavior, but usually the psychologist is interested in knowing what makes the boy run. The only way such a question can be answered is to examine the behavior pattern itself in the light of the whole external situation in which it is exhibited. Only through such a procedure is it possible to discover why the boy is running.

In order to understand why the mechanism behaves in the particular manner observed, it is necessary to know more than merely the nature of the stimulus, the nature of the response, and the nature of the organism at the moment of response. Each must be considered in the light of the others. By way of illustration, consider the case of the pendulum-regulated clock, all wound up and ready to go. There it stands motionless until the pendulum is touched in a particular manner, whereupon it starts ticking, the hands move, and it is said to be running. Was it the touching of the pendulum that made it move? Only in a limited sense. After all, it is the adjusted, wound-up condition of the mechanism as related to the touch that makes it respond as a clock is expected to respond. Suppose that the mechanism is out of its usual adjustment so that no tension exists; then the clock will react differently or may not react at all, in spite of being stimulated in exactly the same manner. Or suppose again that it is ready to go, but instead of touching the pendulum the observer sits down in front of the clock and talks to it. No response takes place, of course. The nature of the stimulus, though adequate for other mechanisms, is not appropriately related to this one.

Instinctive Behavior Is Not Entirely Uniform or Unlearned.

—Universality and uniformity have come to be accepted as significant characteristics of instinctive behavior by most laymen and by some psychologists. Often only a few casual observations are made, and these may tend to overstress the importance of *seeming similarities* and to overlook *important dissimilarities*. A closer examination of such behavior will show that the responses of two individuals of the same species may be far from exactly identical or the similarities of accomplishment may be noted, but the diversity of the behavior itself may be overlooked. When prevented from carrying out the behavior first attempted, the animal can be expected to attempt some modification of the original response. The farther up the scale of animal life one goes, the greater this modifiability seems to be. Man, standing at the top of the scale, is the species showing the greatest degree of modifiability.

No one who knows the habits of birds would mistake the nest built by a robin for that of a Baltimore oriole. But not all robins' nests are made in the same kind of places or even of the same materials. On the other hand, man has a wide variety of sheltering structures, but no one has suggested that the similarity of structure observed among the shelters of primitive tribes is due to any inborn tendency to build that kind of house because it is simply assumed that man's behavior is modifiably adaptable to his environment.

It has not been determined whether or not young orioles raised entirely apart from their species would build nests of the oriole type. However, experiments have been carried out to test the instinctive character of the song of birds. Scott [2] raised young orioles so that they never had opportunity to hear the songs of the adult birds. All of them learned to sing, but they developed a song quite different from birds brought up with the wild

---

[2] W. E. D. Scott, "Songs in Birds," *Science*, 14:522; "Data on Songs in Birds," *Science*, 15:178; "The Inheritance of Song," 19:154.

APE AND CHILD USING SPOON

Note the difference in the manipulatory skill of the two. (From
W. N. and L. A. Kellogg, *The Ape and the Child*, McGraw-Hill
Book Co., Inc.)

APE AND CHILD PLAYING

Note the comparative skills in handling the play objects; Donald 18 months, Gua 16½ months. (From W. N. and L. A. Kellogg, *The Ape and the Child*, McGraw-Hill Book Co., Inc.)

orioles. He repeated this experiment with a number of other species of birds, with similar results in every case. Conradie [3] brought up young English sparrows with canaries. He found at first that the vocalization of the sparrows was characteristically that of sparrows, but later they developed a song resembling that of the canaries. Still later, when they were placed with normal sparrows, they soon took up the usual sparrow chirp. Finally, he returned them to the company of the canaries and reports that they adapted themselves to the canary type of song. Such experiments, although involving only a few kinds of behavior and a few species of animals, cast serious doubt upon the unlearned character of so-called "instincts," even where such behavior is quite universal with the species. It is probable that much of the universality of behavior in the human species is also largely due to learning. Such learned activities, although they greatly resemble those called instinctive, might better be thought of as *universal habits*.

A good deal of the similarity of behavior that is observed in human beings must be accounted for in two ways. In the first place, all human beings have certain marked similarities of structure. In the second place, they are stimulated in a common manner, especially during infancy and early childhood. These two factors together easily explain much of the similarity of behavior that is commonly thought of as instinctive.

Kellogg [4] carried out a very unique experiment in an attempt to discover the relationship between inherited structural characteristics and the effects of environment during infancy. Since it is socially impossible to raise a human child in the environment of an ape, he brought an ape into his home for a period of nine months. The ape was seven and one-half months old at the time the experiment began. His own child was ten months old. The ape was treated exactly like a child, never as a pet. During these nine months, the ape and the child played together, were tested together, and, in general, lived like brother and sister. During the experiment, tests were employed to show the nature of the

---

[3] E. Conradie, "Songs and Calls," *Journal of Psychology*, 16:190.
[4] W. N. and L. A. Kellogg, *Ape and Child*, New York, McGraw-Hill Book Co., 1933.

responses of the two individuals. In such an environment the ape behaved very much more like a human being than do young apes raised in the usual ape environment. The ape did not become a human being, for structurally the child and the ape were different, and these structural differences were as clearly apparent at the end of the experiment as at its beginning. For example, the ape learned to respond to a very large number of words but never learned to reproduce the words. The boy's behavior was also somewhat different from that of boys of the same age who had been raised exclusively in the company of humans. This experiment, the first of its kind, must be repeated with other individuals, over longer periods of time, before the final answer to the question of the relative influence of nature and nurture can be answered, even in such limited situations.

Are There Any Human Instincts?—If instincts are to be regarded as definite, inborn, unlearned patterns of response, they must necessarily be very few in number for the human species. Human instincts are therefore best thought of as inborn urges to behave according to certain patterns which are determined by the inherited nature of the structure. However, there is no reason for thinking of these patterns as being unmodifiable. Such would be a contradiction of terms and a dynamic impossibility.[5] These patterns of human behavior may be considerably modified through the changes in the organic structure resulting from growth and experience common to the species. Since human beings have an organic structure which is more modifiable than that of any other species, it is not surprising to find that their behavior patterns are much less fixed and less uniform than are those of the lower animal species.

Finally, it must be remembered that instincts do not differ from habits in any very significant manner. The term "habit" is usually used to designate the behavior resulting from a modification of the pattern of one's structure, as it is differentiated by individual differences of experience, so that once the habitual

---

[5] R. H. Wheeler and F. T. Perkins, *Principles of Mental Development*, New York, T. Y. Crowell Co., 1932, p. 200. See also p. 122.

behavior has been established the individual is literally compelled to respond in terms of his modified organic structure. Any tendency to behave in a particular manner, therefore, tends to be called either a habit or an instinct depending upon whether it is essentially a differentiated response or one that is common to the whole species. The "dynamicness" of behavior and the effect of experience upon behavior will be further discussed in later chapters, as these factors pertain to human motivation and human learning.

An Outline Summary

1. The characteristics of instinctive and reflexive behavior.
   A. Because members of the same species have similar structures, their instinctive and reflexive behavior patterns will show close similarities. This accounts for the universality of instinctive traits within a species.
   B. Such behavior is purposeful only in the sense that it serves a useful end for the members of the species in the usual environment. It does not imply an inborn purpose of the individual to behave in a particular manner.
   C. Instinctive behavior (and reflexive behavior to a lesser degree) may be set into action by a variety of stimuli and may manifest itself in a variety of ways.

2. Instinctive and reflexive behavior is determined by the nature of the structure as it exists at birth or as it is modified by the processes of anatomical and physiological development.

3. The differences between instinctive and reflexive behavior.
   A. Instincts are more complex patterns of behavior, normally involving adjustment of the body as a whole, whereas reflexes usually involve only adjustments of restricted parts of the body.
   B. The larger instinctive patterns are usually more modifiable than the ones called reflexes.

4. Limitations of the term instinct when applied to human behavior.
   A. Instinctive behavior is normally influenced to an important degree by experience, so that after the period of very early infancy has passed all behavior must in part be accounted for in terms of experience. To the extent that

learning plays a determining rôle, the behavior is no
longer called instinctive.
B. Human beings are probably more modifiable by experience
than any other species. Hence the term instinct has a
very limited application in describing human behavior.
However, the term does tend to stress the point that
habits are dynamic in themselves.
C. An important characteristic of instinctive behavior is its
dynamic quality sometimes called an "urge." This quality it shares with behavior patterns called "habit."

PROBLEMS FOR FURTHER THOUGHT

1. If "instinct" is defined as follows, why is it inappropriate to
use the term when speaking of human behavior: An instinct is an
inborn pattern of behavior appearing uniformly for all members of
the species, independently of structure and experience?

2. Explain the only meaning that may be given the word "instinctive" if it is to be used appropriately in describing human
behavior.

3. Show by illustration how some bit of human behavior may
serve a useful purpose and yet not be purposeful in the sense that
the behavior was actually planned.

4. The emphasis in this chapter has been placed upon an explanation of instinctive behavior in terms of both the stimulation and the
organic condition prevailing at the time the action takes place. Point
out the difficulties entailed in employing this explanation when accounting for any particular instinctive response. Show also how
these difficulties compare with those involved in any other kind of
explanation of instinctive behavior.

5. Illustrate one of the kinds of human behavior formerly classified as instinctive, such as "self-preservation," and show how important the learned elements really are to the whole response.

6. Show by an illustration involving human behavior how
similarities of the inherited nature of structure and similarities in
the early environment are sufficient to account for similarities in
behavior patterns that have been so strongly stressed in the older
notions of instinct.

7. During a recent football season the sports editor of a metro-
politan newspaper, in calling attention to the several games to be

played during the next week-end, said, "Every fan will have ample opportunity to exercise his football instinct." This is obviously an entirely different meaning of the word "instinct" from that developed in this chapter. Make a list of other uses of the word "instinct" that will illustrate the truth of the statement that when the word is used by the non-psychologically trained person, it usually is employed as a means of admitting that the cause of the behavior in question is not clearly understood.

Suggested Readings

DASHIELL, J. F. Fundamentals of Objective Psychology. Boston, Houghton-Mifflin Co., 1928. Ch. VII, "Reflexes and the Integration of Action," pp. 154–157.

McDOUGAL, WILLIAM. Social Psychology. New York, John W. Luce & Co., 1921. Ch. II, "The Nature of Instincts," pp. 20–46; Ch. III, "The Principal Instincts," pp. 47–92. This reference is suggested as an example of the older and now generally abandoned view of human instincts.

PERRIN, F. A., and KLEIN, D. B. Psychology. New York, Henry Holt & Co. Ch. III, "Psychological Foundations of Behavior: The Instinct Hypothesis," pp. 122–130.

SANDIFORD, PETER. Educational Psychology. New York, Longmans, Green & Co., 1929. Ch. VI, "Reflexes and Instincts," pp. 116–128.

SCHOEN, MAX. Human Nature. New York, Harper & Bros., 1930. Ch. IV, "Reflexes," pp. 103–115; Ch. V, "Instincts," pp. 116–128.

SMITH, STEVENSON, and GUTHRIE, E. R. General Psychology in Terms of Behavior. New York, D. Appleton-Century Co., 1921. Ch. II, "Instinct," pp. 48–69.

WATSON, J. B. Behaviorism. New York, W. W. Norton & Co., 1930. Chs. V and VI, "Are There any Human Instincts?" pp. 93–139.

Chapter 5

SOME OTHER WAYS IN WHICH BEHAVIOR DEPENDS UPON STRUCTURE—WHAT ARE EMOTIONS?

Characteristics of an Emotion.—The theory has been insist-ently advanced in the past that emotions were nothing more than states of consciousness and were composed of sensations origi-nating in various parts of the body. Muscular and glandular responses were either believed to cause, or to result in, emotions. For a time the chief issue was whether such responses came be-fore or after the state of consciousness called an emotion. More recently, however, psychologists have tended to minimize the rôle played by consciousness in emotions, preferring to study objectively the responses of the muscles and glands themselves. This is the point of view taken in the following discussion.

Comparison of emotional and instinctive behavior reveals both similarities and differences. Instinctive responses have been shown, in the preceding chapter, to be those that characteristically involve the adjustment of the person as a whole to his external environment. Emotional responses are those in which the inter-nal adjustments predominate. Emotional and instinctive be-havior are alike in that both are, to some extent, innate, and both may be extensively modified by experience. Instinctive behavior involves primarily the muscles attached to the skeleton, while emotional behavior affects mostly the non-skeletal muscles and the glands.

The muscles not attached to the skeleton are called *visceral* or smooth muscles. The largest of these are found in the digestive tract, but they appear also in many other places in the body. Tiny muscles of this sort control the ducts of the glands, such as the perspiration ducts. Others are so arranged in the skin that when they contract, the "hair stands on end," as in fear or anger. Visceral muscles are slower in their response to stimulation than are skeletal muscles. They can also remain contracted for a longer time without fatigue.

The glands are composed of cells which secrete certain substances. Glands are scattered throughout the body and may be classified conveniently into two groups, those that have ducts and those that are ductless. The glands of digestion and perspiration are duct glands. The ductless or endocrine glands pour their secretion directly into the blood as it circulates through them. The thyroid and the adrenals are examples of this kind of gland.

"Emotions" or Emotional Behavior?—The term "emotion" should not be regarded as a name for a type of response that is entirely different from non-emotional behavior. Behavior is a continuous, complex process involving simultaneous activity in many parts of the body. Man does not respond now with an emotion, then with an instinct, and at some other time with a habit. These names do not designate distinctly different types of behavior; they are merely abstractions which are necessary for convenience of study. The behavior commonly called emotional is an "emotion" in pure form only within a textbook. The same is true of an "instinct" or a "habit." Some of the characteristics of emotional activity are present at all times in everyday life and comprise what is sometimes called one's *emotional tone*. These emotional elements intensify, inhibit, and otherwise modify the behavior in process at any given time and are integral parts of the whole pattern of behavior.

Emotional responses may differ in intensity, but when a particular one is being experienced it literally dominates all the organs of emotional response. One might say a person instinctively withdraws the right arm from the prick of a pin, but one would never speak of being angry in the right arm. This "all-over-ness" is a very important characteristic of emotional behavior.

Emotional responses change readily from one into another. Under unusual circumstances a person may pass rapidly from the heights of elation to the depths of despair and back again, but ordinarily this change does not touch the extremes. Only one emotional pattern can be experienced at a time. The individual is never angry with one part of his body and happy with another part.

Difficulties in Studying Emotions.—Because of at least two factors, emotional responses are difficult to analyze. Most of the parts of the body involved in an emotional response are hidden from observation. Changes in the activity of the glands can sometimes be inferred from observation, as in the case of increased perspiration. But for the most part, emotional changes can be detected only by chemical examination of the blood or by experiments involving removal or alteration of certain glands. Obviously, this last cannot be done except under controlled conditions, and with lower animals as subjects; and in such cases all possibility of verbal report is of course out of the question. Another difficulty is that an emotional response is normally a complex and widely scattered pattern. Observation of more than a few of the part-responses is impossible, whether the emotional response is studied introspectively or is recorded by mechanical devices.

Introspection as a method of studying emotions is not reliable. Who can tell by examining his consciousness whether his adrenal glands are functioning rapidly or slowly? Moreover, the sort of self-analysis required by introspection calls for an attitude of calmness and a lack of emotional bias which is impossible to maintain when one is influenced by strong emotions.

An objective study of emotions is also difficult. In an attempt to study emotional responses objectively a subject was strapped firmly into a chair, and recording devices for measuring parts of his emotional response were adjusted. He was asked to write in detail an account of his most intimate and embarrassing personal experience, with positive assurance that no one would know what he had written. This insured that the response would be genuine, and the experiment proceeded to its conclusion. While discussing the results, the instructor picked up what the subject had written and began to read the contents aloud. The emotional response was almost instantaneous, but an objective record was not obtained. The subject left the room with his paper, dangling various pieces of apparatus behind him.

Briefly then, emotions may best be described as complex patterns of response which involve predominantly activity of the glands and the visceral muscles. They are diffused responses comprising a total complex whole. *Their function may be said to be that of adjusting the individual internally* to the needs of a particular situation, much as instinctive behavior adjusts the individual to his external environment.

Nervous System Controlling Emotional Responses.—In order to understand how these complex internal adjustments are brought about, it will be necessary to know something of the structure and function of certain parts of the nervous system.

All responses of the skeletal muscles result from nerve impulses distributed *directly* to them from the brain or spinal cord. In the case of the visceral muscles and the glands, there is an *intervening link* between the central nervous system and these organs of response. This intervening link as a whole is called the autonomic nervous system. It is composed of *ganglia,* each made up of many nerve cells. A series of these ganglia lies in two rows, parallel to, but outside of the spinal column. They are connected by chains of nerve fibers. From these ganglia other nerve fibers pass to the various glands and groups of visceral muscles all over the body, so that the whole system may function in an integrated manner.

Other ganglia are scattered throughout the body. Some are very close to the organs they supply, as is the case with those in and near the heart and lungs. These groups of ganglia are sometimes called plexuses, viz., the solar plexus in the upper abdomen near the surface of the body.

Within the autonomic system there is provision for two different kinds of adjustment. First, it is itself divided into two functional divisions which in general operate in an opposing manner. Every visceral muscle and every gland has a connection with both these divisions. This makes it possible for each organ to be a part of two essentially different patterns at different times. For instance, under emotionally satisfying conditions digestion is accelerated, while during anger it is inhibited.

A second type of adjustment involves the grouping together of the responses of all of the organs involved in emotion into two essentially different patterns. These will be called "emergency" emotions and "appetitive" emotions. The names are only roughly descriptive, but they will serve to call attention to the chief characteristics of each.

The "emergency" emotions are so called because they serve to prepare the body to meet primitive emergencies, as in rage, fear, and strong excitement. During this type of emotional response the glands and muscles of the digestive tract are inhibited, while the heart and adrenal glands are speeded up. The appearance of adrenalin in the blood causes more blood sugar to be released from the liver. The walls of the arteries in the abdominal region are constricted, forcing more blood into the skeletal muscles. Metabolism is heightened; the rate of respiration is increased; the amount of perspiration increases noticeably. In short, a whole pattern of responses is "thrown into gear" preparing the body for an emergency, hence the name "emergency" as supplied by Cannon.[1]

On the other hand, when the other functional division of the autonomic nervous system is dominant, the digestive activities are heightened, respiration is decreased, the heart beat is lessened, and the blood pressure drops. Adrenal activity is decreased, and in general there is a state of well-being that is here designated by the general name of "appetitive emotions."

From the functioning of this autonomic nervous system there results an integration of behavior of the widely scattered and otherwise independent vital organs of the body that would be impossible by any other means.

The conservative view of the autonomic is that it is a system of motor relays from the cerebrospinal axis to the visceral organs, chang-

---

[1] W. B. Cannon, *Bodily Changes in Fear, Hunger, Pain, and Rage*, New York, D. Appleton-Century Co., 1929.

ing the character of the innervations supplied to these organs. Reactions in the viscera differ in character from the reactions of striped muscles. Possessed of some capacity for independent action, these organs—that is to say the muscular and glandular tissue found in them—may be thought of as controlled by the nervous system only in the sense of having their *tonus* steadily *maintained* and also, on occasion, by increase or decrease. The neural impulses in autonomic innervation (arising originally at receptors, of course) pass through the autonomic relays. The smell of food in this way comes to excite secretions in the stomach. The sight of a wild beast or a coiling snake arouses a whole concurrence of a changed activity in the heart, in the blood distribution, in the gastro-intestinal movements of digestion, in the breathing, the perspiration, the mouth (dry) and changes of other sorts—making in all an emotional response.[2]

To Understand Emotions the Total Bodily Response Must Be Considered.—All the activity of daily life is emotionally toned in one way or another. The emergency type of emotional response is more often noted and better remembered than the appetitive. This is because emergency responses are more unusual and more intense. However, the fact that one is not aware of an emotional response does not indicate that there is none.

It should be noted that there are many different names for emotional responses which are very much alike when considered from the point of view of nervous control. Thus, fear and anger are practically alike as far as the internal elements of response are concerned. The response is called fear when it causes the individual to withdraw from the stimulus. It is called anger when it prompts the individual to take a defensive or aggressive attitude. These responses are given different names only because in each case different impulses stimulate the skeletal muscles to activity. In other words, the total emotional pattern to which a name is usually assigned in everyday life involves more than just the internal adjustment of the individual. It includes not only responses brought about directly by the central nervous sys-

---

[2] J. F. Dashiell. *Fundamentals of Objective Psychology,* Boston, Houghton-Mifflin Co., 1929, pp. 147–148.

tem, but also those brought about indirectly by means of the autonomic nervous system.

Whether the soldier on the battlefield is a hero or a coward will often depend upon whether he gets started forward or to the rear. Many a panic has been brought about by some little incident in the total situation which initiated a precipitate flight. The heroes on such occasions are likely to be those who have got started with a behavior pattern of an opposite sort.

Genetic Approach to the Emotions.—The approach to the study of emotions as outlined above represents the attitude of the physiologist or of the physiological psychologist. Thus far it has yielded some valuable and interesting data. Another point of attack is that employed by the genetic psychologist.

It would be interesting to follow an adult through the experiences of a day or a week. During this time there would be manifested a number of instances of behavior which would be recognized as due to emotional responses. Yet from simple observation alone, it would often be impossible to be sure what name to give these responses; and if the person himself were asked to report, he would not be of much assistance. The reason for this is, partly, the fact that there are no standards of behavior to which any of the names of emotional responses can be attached. Two different persons may be enraged. This implies that their behavior has something in common, but it certainly does not mean that their behavior will be identical.

By the time a person has reached adult life, he has had many experiences which have not been shared exactly with anyone else. For example, the fear response may be produced in one individual at the sight of a snake coiled up in a path. Another shows no fear response at all to this particular stimulus. If he recognizes it as a harmless sake, he may even catch it and put it in his pocket. On the other hand, both may show responses which they themselves would call fear, but which to an observer may not seem at all alike. Long before one becomes an adult, his emotional responses have become too mixed with each other and too heavily overlaid with learning to permit of exact analysis by verbal report. It is impossible to tell what the original response might have been. Consequently, it will be worth while to follow the genetic psychologist in his attempts to understand the behavior of adults by tracing the development of this behavior from infancy to adult life.

Emotional Responses of the Infant Which Are Independent of Learning.—In seeking to solve his problems, the genetic psychologist is anxious to know, first of all, what is the original emotional behavior of the infant. This is necessary in order to recognize the significance of the changes that may take place later. To discover the facts about infant emotional behavior, the genetic psychologist must study the infant's behavior in a wide variety of situations.

Watson was among the first to conduct laboratory experiments with the emotional responses of young infants. His subjects were children up to one year of age, many of whom had been observed from birth so that their emotional experience was well known. In order to discover which fear responses were unlearned, these young children were presented one after another with such stimuli as animals, birds, darkness, and fire. A passage from one of Watson's lectures will illustrate his methods.

We first took the children to the laboratory and put them through the routine of tests with various animals. We had the laboratory so arranged that they could be tested in the open room, alone; with an attendant; with the mother. They were tested in the dark room, the walls of which were painted black. This room was bare of furniture. It offered an unusual situation in itself. In the dark room we had conditions so arranged that we could turn on a light behind the infant's head or illuminate the room with the light in front of and above the infant. The infants were always tested one at a time. The following group of situations was usually presented:

First, a lively black cat, invariably affectionately aggressive, was shown. The cat never ceased its purring. It climbed over and walked around the infant many times during the course of each test, rubbing its body against the infant in the usual feline way. So many false notions have grown up around the response of infants to furry animals that we were surprised ourselves to see these youngsters *positive always* in their behavior to this proverbial "black cat." Reaching out to touch the cat's fur, eyes, and nose was the invariable response.

A rabbit was always presented. This, likewise, in every case called out manipulatory responses and nothing else. Catching the ears of the animal in one hand and attempting to put it in its mouth was one of the favorite responses.

Another furry animal invariably used was the white rat. This, possibly on account of its size and whiteness, rarely called out continued fixation of the eyes of the infant. When, however, the animal was fixated, reaching occurred.

Airedale dogs, large and small, were also presented. The dogs were also very friendly. The dogs rarely called out the amount of manipulatory response that an animal the size of the cat and rabbit called out. Not even when the children were tested with these animals in the dark room, either in full illumination or with a dim light behind their heads, was any fear response evoked.

These tests on children not emotionally conditioned proved to us conclusively that the classical illustrations of hereditary responses to furry objects and animals are just old wives' tales.[3]

According to Watson, the kinds of emotional responses of early infancy and childhood are limited to three. These he calls fear, rage, and love, but he particularly suggests caution in the use of these terms in their customary sense. The outwardly observable elements of what he calls the fear response are

. . . a jump, a start, a respiratory pause followed by more rapid breathing with marked vasomotor changes, puckering of the lips. Then occur, depending upon the age of the infant, falling down, crawling, walking, or running away.[4]

Of the rage response he says,

The unlearned behavior elements in rage behavior have never been completely catalogued. Some of the elements, however, are easily observed, such as the stiffening of the whole body, the free slashing movements of the hands, arms, and legs, and the holding of the breath. There is no crying at first, then the mouth is opened to the fullest extent and the breath is held until the face becomes blue.[5]

---

[3] J. B. Watson, *Psychologies of 1925*, Worcester, Mass., Clark University Press, 1927, pp. 42-44.
[4] *Ibid.*, p. 46.   [5] *Ibid.*, p. 48.

The *love* response

. . . in an infant depends upon its state; when crying, the crying will cease and a smile begin. Gurgling and cooing will appear. Violent movements of the arms and trunk with pronounced laughter occur in even six to eight-months-old infants when tickled. It is thus seen that we use love in a much broader sense than it is popularly used. The responses we intend to mark off here are those popularly called "affectionate," "good-natured," "kindly," etc. The term "love" embraces all of these as well as the responses we see in adults between the sexes. They all have a common origin.[6]

Watson has pointed out three kinds of innate emotional responses. A preceding section suggested only two kinds of emotions, the emergency and the appetitive. An examination of what Watson calls fear and that which he calls rage will show that they are both of the emergency type. In other words, there seems to be no contradiction here of general principles.

Stimuli Which Produce Unlearned Emotional Responses in Infants.—Each of the types of emotional responses mentioned by Watson can be produced in the infant by only a limited variety of stimuli. Those producing fear responses are of two kinds. One is the sudden loss of support which results from dropping the infant or suddenly jerking the blanket upon which it is lying. The other is a sudden sharp sound such as may be obtained by striking a steel bar with a hammer. Not all infants respond in the same manner to these stimuli. Several experimenters have reported finding young children who did not show the usual fear response when thus stimulated.

Rage is essentially the response to restriction of activity. Hampering of movements by clothing, or holding the head or hands will usually produce this response in young infants. The author has succeeded on several different occasions in producing a response similar to that described by Watson as rage, in infants less than one week old. This was done by gently holding the feet and legs in an outstretched position while restricting the move-

---

[6] *Ibid.*, p. 49.

ment of the arms, head, and trunk. Distinct rage responses have thus been called out in as little as thirty seconds. Throughout life, forms of physical restriction seem to have the power to produce some sort of rage response.

The love response in an infant can be obtained by stroking the skin or by tickling. This is especially effective in the regions upon or around the lips and nipples, and in the region of the external genitals. The same stimulus is effective to a lesser degree in the armpits, over the ribs, and around the mouth or chin. These responses are probably very early associated with objects and individuals in the infant's experience. Fondling by the mother, such as is normally involved in nursing, might reasonably be expected to result in the mother's being able to call forth the love response more readily than others. Possibly the feeding response itself may be, from early infancy, closely associated with the love response. In the appetitive emotional states it must be remembered that the digestive processes are going on at an optimum rate. This fact may have a direct bearing upon the process of taking food into the body and may be responsible for the normal adult's emotional response to food taking.

The external or visible parts of emotional responses and the stimuli by means of which they are obtained from infants are probably, at this stage, largely innate. Marquis, in experimenting with infants one month old, demonstrated that an emotional response to a sudden loud sound was present and could be modified by the process known as conditioning.[7] It is a long way from these simple responses and these limited stimuli to the complex, emotional behavior observable in the average adult. Two factors largely account for the changes that take place. One is the process of growth, while the other concerns the problem of learning. As the child grows to adulthood, these factors become more complex and consequently more difficult to follow and measure.

Emotional Responses of the Adult.—When the emotional behavior of the adult is compared with that of the infant, some

---

[7] Dorothy P. Marquis, "Can Conditioned Responses Be Established in the Newborn Infant?" *Journal of Genetic Psychology,* December, 1931, p. 479 ff.

very significant differences can be noted. These differences concern both the nature of the emotional response and the type of stimulating situation which calls it forth. The adult fear behavior, for example, seldom includes weeping. Probably the most significant characteristic of the fear response of the adult is a temporary loss of control of the usual motor responses of intelligent behavior. When adults are badly frightened, they frequently do most unintelligent things. The oft-observed behavior of the person who is frightened upon discovering that his home is on fire is a case in point. Under such circumstances intelligent adults have been known to throw dishes and mirrors out of the window and then carry an armful of pillows out of doors.

The agitation of fear is often accompanied by a marked decrease in the salivary response. Such a person is sometimes spoken of as being dry-mouthed with fright. This lack of salivary response in fright is the basis of the ordeal of rice, a means sometimes still employed in certain oriental countries for determining whether or not a suspect is guilty of a particular crime. The ordeal consists of giving the suspected person a mouthful of dry rice to chew and swallow. For one who is not frightened this is not a difficult task at all. But the guilty person, fearing that he will be detected, is unable to swallow the dry rice because of a lack of a normal salivary secretion. Similar discomfort is frequently felt by an inexperienced speaker when he finds himself facing an audience. His mouth is dry, and he may frequently attempt to moisten his lips, which will be difficult unless he is supplied with the conventional glass of water.

The stimulating situation that calls forth a fear response in adults is often very different from that to which the infant reacts. Although the infant's customary response to sudden loss of support is also fairly common in the adult, many adults, as a result of their life experiences, have become negatively adapted to these loss-of-support situations and show no fear response to them. Steel workers, engaged in erecting the framework of modern skyscrapers, have become so accustomed to their precarious positions that no fear is apparent in their behavior. On the other hand, adults show fear responses to many kinds of situations that

PERFECT COMPOSURE HIGH IN THE AIR

This picture was made during the construction of Rockefeller Center, New York. Would you feel equally secure and at ease in this worker's place? Explain the reason for any difference. (An Ewing Galloway Picture.)

are not frightening to infants and young children. A four-year-old girl may be prevailed upon to pick angleworms in the garden, yet most girls by the time they are fourteen are very much more inclined to fear them. The fear response to sudden sharp sounds tends to persist in some degree for most individuals throughout life. Here again, however, negative adaptation resulting from many experiences of this sort may completely eliminate such fear responses.

Several years ago the author observed a party of amateur mountaineers crossing a river. It was much too deep and swift for wading, but a good suspension bridge was found. It was stoutly made and hung from two strong steel cables. The foot path was two planks wide. The sides were tightly enclosed with a fine mesh wire to about shoulder height. It would have been difficult to climb off that bridge, to say nothing of falling off. On the side of the river from which the party approached, the bridge extended back from the river bank for nearly fifty feet. Here the branches of the trees had grown close to the mesh screen. They really offered no support, but they gave a substantial appearance to the sides of the bridge. The members of the party did not hesitate to walk along the bridge to the edge of the trees. But at that point trouble began. Most of the women and some of the men showed very evident distress at having to cross the two hundred feet of open bridge. It did very little good to call attention to the fact that the bridge was exactly the same ahead of them as behind them.

Emotional Responses Become Attached to New Stimuli.— Most objects and situations eliciting adult fears have acquired their significance largely as the result of learning. Watson and Jones showed conclusively that infants who did not originally show fear to a particular stimulus—a white rat, for example—could be made to show fear to that stimulus if it were presented on several occasions when the child was frightened by some other stimulus.

In the laboratory this emotional conditioning is accomplished somewhat as follows: First the child is tested with the white rat to see if any evidences of fear are present. If the child has never been frightened in the presence of a similar object, it is safe to predict that no fear response will be evidenced. Then, while the child is playing with the rat, the experimenter without any warning strikes an iron bar with a hammer. Almost invariably the infant responds to this stimulus with the behavior which Watson has designated by the name of fear. After two or three repetitions of this procedure, the child shows a definite change in his reaction to the white rat. Instead of approaching, reaching for, and playing with the rat, the child now cringes, withdraws, and avoids it. He may even turn and creep or scamper away as quickly as possible. Very often shrieking or crying accompanies this retreat even when the bar is no longer being struck.

When the author's son was about one year old, he was presented one morning with a toy balloon while he was in his mother's arms. He reached for it with both hands, but just as he was about to touch it, the author allowed his fingers to rub the surface of the tightly inflated rubber, causing a sharp sound. This was the boy's first experience with the balloon situation. His response changed instantly from the approaching and reaching one to that of retreat and withdrawal. He could not be induced to have anything to do with the balloon, even though it was in his playroom for several days. He would not even go near it to get a familiar toy. The single simultaneous presentation of the two stimuli gave the sight of the balloon the same power to provoke an avoidance response as the sound had at first called out. Probably most emotional responses are acquired or modified in some such fashion as this, beginning very early in life and multiplying as the individual grows older.

The brackish taste of green olives is to an infant apparently a natural stimulus for avoidance. Many adults will recall having to "learn to like" green olives. Why is it so frequently true that adults do like them? Probably it is largely because most frequently one's first experiences with green olives occur under very pleasant surroundings when one is enjoying a party or a picnic. In the same way, other substances that are very unpleasant to most persons may be made a rare treat to others. Cod liver oil is a good example. It is usually given to a child who is unwell and out of sorts by an adult who already has a more or less profound disgust for it, and who shows this emotional response by word or gesture. Sometimes it is even given as a punishment. Is it any wonder that it becomes the stimulus that will call out undesired responses? If it is given only when the child is happy, without evidence of disgust from the one giving it and as a reward instead of a punishment, a very different type of emotional response can be established. It is much easier and more fortunate if the desirable response can be established without having first to break down the undesirable one.

One morning some years ago the author appeared at the kitchen door of a neighbor's house. Sitting on a chair in the middle of the kitchen was the father of the family, holding his three-year-old son in his lap. The boy's legs were firmly held between the father's. One of the father's arms encircled the boy's body and held his hands firmly. The other was used to restrict the movements of the child still further, when necessary. Nearby stood the mother, holding a large spoonful of cod liver oil in one hand, and trying to get the boy's mouth open with the other. Even under these heroic circumstances, more oil was sprayed on the wall than the boy was induced to swallow. Is it any wonder that the boy showed a strong dislike for cod liver oil from that time on?

In the family of another neighbor a five-year-old boy was given his cod liver oil only under the most enjoyable and favorable of circumstances. Great care was exercised to avoid anything that might produce an undesirable emotional response. The young lad thus developed a positive fondness for cod liver oil and even succeeded, when the parents were out for the evening, in coaxing an extra spoonful from the girl who was caring for him.

Most adult rage responses probably grow out of being hampered in some manner. At first, the rage response comes only from a hampering of physical movements, but as the individual matures so-called "mental" and "social" hampering frequently produces the same results.

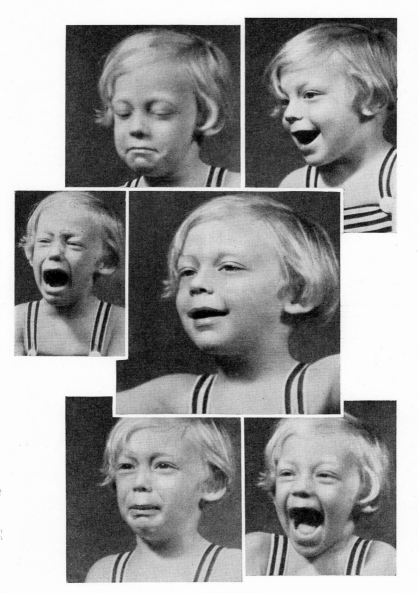

EMOTIONS

What names would you give the emotions expressed here.
See footnote on page 104.

Two small boys, about equally matched for physical strength, were wrestling and scuffling, all in good fun. Finally, one of them got the other one down and sat upon him, preventing his getting up and still further hampering his movements. The good-natured play activity of the boy who was underneath quickly gave way to rage and a genuine fight began, each one, of course, fully believing that the other fellow started it.

At the adult level, restriction of a social sort frequently produces the same result. A man may show no desire to see a moving picture show until the censor closes it, and then becomes rather loud in his insistence that he has a right to see whatever show he wishes. He may get angry and drive to a nearby city to see it, remarking that "no censor can tell me what show to see."

Names of Emotions Are Not Very Accurate.—In order to name an emotion it is not enough merely to be able to observe the responses. The nature of the stimulation must also be known. A group of observers were shown motion pictures of children and adults manifesting various kinds of emotional behavior. As each appeared, the observers were asked to record an appropriate name for the response. When no information was given about the nature of the stimulus, there was very little agreement among the judges. If the pictures were accompanied by a description which told the observer what the stimulus had been, there was considerable agreement in the names assigned to the various emotional patterns.[8] In the same series of experiments, the same general results were obtained when the sound of infants crying was heard by the observers without their knowing the nature of the stimulus that had caused it. It is thus evident that the adult names for emotions are largely the names for responses to certain kinds of situations, more than for certain kinds of responses in themselves.[9]

[8] Mandel Sherman, "Differentiation of Emotional Responses in Infants," *Journal of Comparative Psychology,* 1927, Vol. VIII, pp. 265–284.

[9] (Picture of emotions shown on page 103.) Statement of the photographer who was the father of this boy: "The boy knew that I wanted to photograph him but while playing with his mother he was so fascinated that he completely forgot the camera. His mother played with him, telling him that he was a bad boy and that she would take away his ball. His expression changed very fast until he cried. Then she calmed him explaining that it was only in fun and he was soon happy again. The whole thing lasted only a couple of minutes."

How Emotional Responses Become Detached from Old Stimuli.—How does one go about detaching an emotional response from a stimulus which is capable of producing it? Persons frequently deplore the fact that they are frightened or enraged by some situation and express a wish that it were possible for them not to be emotional in those situations. Is it possible to control the process of conditioning so that undesirable emotional patterns may be detached from these situations? Is it possible to go farther and substitute another emotional response in place of the undesirable one?

Jones, following Watson's technique of emotional conditioning, gives an account of such a change in emotional behavior.[10] Many others have substantiated her results. At the beginning of this experiment it was proved that Peter had no fear of a rabbit. By the procedure described above he was made to fear the rabbit. Several plans had previously been suggested for eliminating fear, such as allowing the child to forget his fear, practicing the fear response to "wear it out," and removing the fear by inducing the child to talk freely about the fear-provoking stimulus.

All these methods have serious shortcomings. In the case of the first suggestion, it is sometimes impossible to keep the individual out of the fear-provoking situation for the weeks or even years necessary for complete forgetting. Aside from its inconvenience, this procedure involves too large an element of time, since fear responses have been shown to establish themselves rather thoroughly and become long-lasting after only a few repetitions. The trouble with the second suggestion is that it does not work. If the child is actually frightened repeatedly by the same stimulus, the fear response is at least as likely to become worse as to become better. The third procedure has the disadvantage that the child may be trained to talk freely about the rabbit, but will still show a fear response when actually confronted with the rabbit.

---

[10] Mary Cover Jones, "The Case of Peter," *Journal of Genetic Psychology,* 1924, Vol. 31, pp. 308–315.

Jones attempted to develop experimentally a more satisfactory technique for the elimination of fear responses. The procedure was somewhat as follows: Each day at the time of the mid-morning lunch, the child was seated in his high-chair far from the door of the nursery. The first day the rabbit was brought into the room in a cage and set down on the far side of the room. This was done while the child was happily engaged with the meal. The child stopped eating and fixed his attention on the rabbit, but otherwise gave no response indicative of fear. Note here that the rabbit was kept far enough away so as not to be a disturbing stimulus for the child.

The second day, the rabbit was again brought in, under similar conditions, but this time it was placed just a trifle nearer the child. This continued for several days, and great care was taken to avoid calling out a fear response to the rabbit. On the other hand, emphasis was placed upon the importance of having the child *respond with a more desirable emotion at the time when he was being stimulated by the sight of the rabbit.* In the course of time, as this process continued, the rabbit could be placed upon the tray of the high-chair with the child happily dividing his attention between his lunch and the rabbit.

In this experiment, two or three points are of particular significance. First, the fear-provoking stimulus is presented simultaneously with another calling forth a desirable emotion. Second, the strength of the stimulus producing the fear must be kept low enough to prevent a response to it, while the stimulus for the desired emotion must be at its maximum possible strength. Third, with successive repetitions of these simultaneously presented stimuli, the fear-provoking stimulus must be gradually increased in intensity. In doing this, however, care must be exercised to prevent this stimulus from becoming strong enough to call forth the fear response. This procedure is essentially the one followed in the case of the boy who learned to like cod liver oil. Probably all one's changes of emotional response to any particular life situation can be accounted for in exactly this way, through employing the principles of emotional conditioning and unconditioning.

In carrying out such an experiment with emotions, note that, first of all, the individual must be *desensitized* emotionally to the particular stimulus which elicits the emotional response. This "getting used to" a stimulus has very appropriately been called "unconditioning." Very frequently it will be desirable, as in the case of Peter, to carry the conditioning farther, so that an actual substitution may be achieved of the desired emotional response for the undesired one. This has been called "reconditioning."

By means of such techniques it is possibly to modify emotional behavior with a considerable degree of assurance of success. The only difficulty that will be encountered by those who understand the technique adequately will be that of controlling the intensity of the stimuli for each response.

Relationship Between Internal and External Components of an Emotional Response.—A question of some interest concerns the relationship between internal and external elements of a total emotional response. What is the relationship between those parts of the response that are controlled directly through the central nervous system and those that are autonomically controlled? Actors and others are probably very adept at producing indications of profound emotional responses without experiencing more than the outward elements of the emotions involved; on the other hand, some persons become very adept at concealing emotion by limiting its observable elements.

There seem to be at least two distinct ways in which the outwardly visible signs of emotional response are of importance. In the first place, they have a marked influence upon the behavior of others. Many a man has fully made up his mind to ask his boss for a raise or a vacation only to have his behavior totally changed by the frown on the boss' face when he approached to ask the question. In the second place, these outward evidences of emotion seem to exert an influence upon the profoundness of the emotion as it is experienced inwardly or consciously. Because these external manifestations normally accompany the internal elements of the total response, any stimulus that will call out the former tends to involve the latter as well. The internal responses are aroused chiefly through the autonomic nervous system and, hence, are involuntary. The external responses, controlled through the central nervous system, are more or less subject to voluntary control. Therefore, this relationship between the external and internal elements of the total response provides a satisfactory means of modifying its intensity.

If the reader has ever read Robert Burns' "Tam-O-Shanter," he may recall the picture the author paints of Tam's wife waiting for his homecoming and "nursing her wrath to keep it warm." What was she probably doing to keep her emotion going? What does one do when one wishes to keep one's anger alive and glowing? Probably Tam's wife banged the pots and pans. She stirred the fire with more than necessary vigor. The door was slammed in no uncertain fashion and, through all the late evening, she could be seen walking around the house with a firm step and with a stern expression on her face. She nursed her wrath by emphasizing the voluntary behavior that usually accompanied it.

Possibly the necessity for maintaining one's anger is infrequent, but at the other extreme many have literally "whistled to keep their courage up," and have assumed the outward appearance of bravery in order to keep from being afraid. When one is "feeling blue," one sometimes makes a deliberate attempt to adopt an attitude of cheerfulness. At first this is forced but gradually it becomes more genuine, due to the fact that in previous experience the outer and inner elements of a total response have accompanied each other. The significant point about all of this is that, since there is no direct voluntary control over some of these emotional responses, *an indirect control over them can best be attained by means of those elements over which control is in some degree possible.*

Emotions and the Endocrine Glands.—The foregoing is not a complete statement of emotional behavior. Not very much has been said of the rôle of the glands, particularly of the endocrine glands, which are believed to play a very significant part in these responses. The word "probably" is used because as yet so little is known with certainty about their influence upon emotional behavior. Hence, it must be sufficient to note that those long-time emotional tendencies, commonly called traits of temperament, are the ones most profoundly influenced by the endocrine glands. They deserve a more thorough consideration than can be included here.

An Outline Summary

1. The nature of an emotional response.
   A. Emotional responses tend to be concerned primarily with the problem of internal adjustment. They involve:
      (a) The smooth muscles (non-skeletal),
      (b) The duct and ductless glands, and
      (c) The autonomic nervous system.
   B. Emotional responses tend to be diffuse, all-pervasive responses because:
      (a) The muscles and glands chiefly involved are widely distributed throughout the body, and
      (b) Whole groups of these organs are thrown into action simultaneously through the autonomic nervous system.

2. The genetic approach to the study of the emotions.
   A. Such an approach is important in order to discover:
      (a) The original nature of such behavior before it is complicated by maturation and experience, and
      (b) How experience modifies emotional behavior.
   B. The infant's original, unlearned emotional responses are:
      (a) Few in number,
      (b) Aroused by only a few kinds of stimuli, and
      (c) Easily modified by experience.
   C. Adults' emotional responses are:
      (a) Very divergent in specific details for different persons, and
      (b) Closely related to each individual's experience.

3. Emotional control.
   A. Control of emotional responses involves two types of factors.
      (a) Emotional responses may be established and removed by conditioning and reconditioning as described by Watson and Jones.

(b) The close association of the autonomically controlled elements and those controlled through the central nervous system makes it possible to increase or diminish the former by voluntary control of the latter.

PROBLEMS FOR FURTHER THOUGHT

1. Mary is not invited to a party given by her chum with whom she has recently had a quarrel and she is very miserable about it. A sympathetic teacher learns of the matter and suggests that the best thing she can do is to have a good cry and thus "get it out of her system." What two good reasons can you suggest why the teacher was mistaken?

2. John is in the fourth grade and has developed a pronounced dislike for arithmetic. This is so very bad that it threatens to cause his failure to "make his grade" this year in school, although the boy has at least the average mental development of his grade. Assume that you are his teacher and that you are going to employ Jones' reconditioning procedure. Explain rather specifically how you would go about this process. In doing so, be sure to keep in mind the several steps suggested by the case of Peter.

3. Ralph is eighteen months of age. He has never been afraid to go to sleep in a dark room. One night a sudden strong wind caused the window shade of his room to make a noisy rattling sound until he was wakened by it. From then on, he showed a great emotional protest against being left in his crib in the dark. How do you account for this emotional response which contrasts so sharply with his previous behavior?

4. As in Problem 2 show how you would go about reconditioning Ralph's behavior mentioned in the preceding problem.

5. Would it be possible for professional actors of such great tragic rôles as Othello, Shylock, or Lady Macbeth *really,* inwardly to experience the tragic feelings as they are apparent from the outwardly visible evidences of such emotions and, at the same time, continue in good health week after week and year after year? Why or why not?

6. In what respects is the situation in the preceding problem different from that of the amateur actor who has to "live his rôle" in order to portray it vividly on the stage?

7. In light of the two preceding problems, state the general principle by means of which the average non-actor might reasonably control the inner experiences of an emotional response, so as to make this feeling either more or less vivid as the occasion demanded.

8. Give several illustrations from your own experience of the way in which your behavior has been modified by the "expression of an emotion" of someone to whom you were reacting. These need not be striking or unusual events, but rather the usual, everyday sort of incidents of life.

9. Assume that you, as an adult, are responsible for the emotional training of a child. What procedure would you suggest as a means of developing a feeling of confidence in, and even enjoyment of visits to, the doctor's or dentist's office or to a barber shop? When should such training begin?

10. A teacher returning to a room after a short absence finds an annoying prank has been played. She punishes the culprit by making him remain after school and learning many lines of poetry. From the points of view of this chapter, why was this procedure psychologically unfortunate?

Suggested Readings

Dashiell, J. F. Fundamentals of Objective Psychology. Boston, Houghton-Mifflin Co., 1928. In Ch. VII, "Native Reaction Patterns—Special Studies of Emotional Patterns in the Adult," pp. 205–228. A systematic treatment of the problems of emotion.

Morgan, J. J. B. Child Psychology. New York, Richard R. Smith, 1931. Ch. V, "Emotional Development," pp. 127–157. This reading deals with emotions from the point of view of their development during childhood.

Oliver, J. R. Fear, The Autobiography of James Edward. New York, The Macmillan Co., 1931. This is a full length story of the encroaching fear, the succeeding nervous breakdown in the life of one man, and one way in which a disorder might be treated.

Watson, Goodwin B., and Spence, R. B. Sketches In and Out of School. New York, 1927. Ch. XI, "Problems of Emotional Conditioning," pp. 143–177. This contains excellent problem materials for further study of the application of the principles brought out in this chapter. It also contains an interesting bibliography for further reading.

Watson, J. B. Behaviorism. Rev. ed., New York, W. W. Norton & Co., 1930. Chs. VII and VIII, pp. 104–195. This reading contains a full but informal account of Watson's experimental genetic studies of emotions.

Wiggam, A. E. Exploring Your Mind with the Psychologists. New York, Bobbs-Merrill Co., 1928. Chs. VII to IX inclusive, "What Are You Afraid of?" Contains interesting and valuable suggestion of Dr. David Mitchell concerning the problems of fears of adult life.

Chapter 6

WHAT ARE THE MAINSPRINGS OF BEHAVIOR?

The importance of the dynamic quality of both instincts and emotions has been stressed repeatedly. The problem of motivation cannot be divorced from these and other aspects of human behavior, but it deserves special consideration in order to understand the more complex aspects of behavior.

The most obvious answer to the questions forming the title of this chapter is that man behaves like a human being because he has the structure of a human being. It will therefore be appropriate to describe the most pertinent characteristics of this structure, emphasizing in general the manner in which it works. The more specialized problem of motivation will then be considered in some detail.

Why and How Does Man Respond to His Environment?— For purposes of convenience in explaining the how and why of his responses, most of man's organs may be divided into three groups. First, there are the *receptors,* or sense organs. A second group are the *effectors,* or response mechanisms, which include all of the muscles and all of the glands. The organs of the third group are often called *connectors.* They include all of the nervous system by means of which the stimuli acting upon the sense organs bring about responses in the muscles and the glands. In a limited sense, the blood stream may also be called a connector, since it carries the secretions of the ductless glands.

1. RECEPTORS. By means of the sense organs man is in touch with the world of which he is a part. Various kinds of energies from the natural world about him are brought to bear upon his structure, each through a different kind of sense organ. There are some kinds of natural forces to which man cannot respond directly because he does not possess organs that are sensitive

to such energies as radioactivity, X-rays, and cosmic rays. However, there are sense organs that respond to most known kinds of physical energy. There are at least four kinds of sense organs in the skin alone : pain spots, touch spots, cold spots, and warm spots. There are probably thousands of each kind. Each organ is complete in itself and is connected with the brain or spinal cord by a sensory nerve fiber. Each is highly specialized in the kind of stimulus to which it normally responds.

Experiences of warmth and cold are obtained only as the corresponding sense organs are appropriately stimulated. Beneath the skin, in the muscles and the lining of the joints, even in the tendons, there are thousands of other sense organs which are called pressure capsules. In the retina of the eye there are the specialized sense organs, called rods and cones, upon which vision depends. In the inner ear are the sense organs by means of which hearing is possible. Close to the inner ear are others that are important in maintaining balance. Other kinds of specialized sense organs are scattered throughout the body.

The sole and specialized business of each of these sense organs is to start a nerve impulse going in the nervous system. Normally a sense organ does not respond to a stimulus which is not appropriate to it. The rods and cones in the eye do not start nerve impulses when sound waves are present.

2. CONNECTORS. The central nervous system and its closely related autonomic nervous system are connected with each sense organ by *sensory* nerve fibers and with each muscle and gland by means of *motor fibers*. The anatomy of this vast complex system is still only partly explored, and the way in which each specific part operates is even less well known. The nervous system is the organic means of controlling and coordinating the vast possibilities of response that are man's heritage as a human being. The nervous system has sometimes been likened to a complex telephone system in which the nerve impulse is comparable to the electrical impulse in the telephone. Beginning at any sense organ, the impulse may be dispatched by means of the complex connections within the nervous system to any gland or muscle in the body. As the blood stream circulates through the body, it

carries the product of the endocrine glands to each of the other parts of the body. It is thus roughly comparable to a vast, complex postal system, actually carrying a substance from one place to another. When these substances reach certain parts of the body, they have a direct stimulating or depressing effect upon those parts.

An illustration will help to make this clear. When the adrenal glands are aroused to activity they discharge into the blood stream a substance called adrenalin. This substance is carried by the blood to all parts of the body where it has a different effect upon different tissues. It has the direct effect of causing the liver to set free increased amounts of blood sugar for use in increased muscle action. It causes the walls of the arteries to contract, which results in increased blood pressure. It also makes the blood itself clot more readily when exposed to the air. Hormones from other glands have their effect upon various other organs of the body and so help to determine the nature of behavior.

3. EFFECTORS. When the nerve impulses make their way through the nervous system, they arrive eventually at some muscle or gland. Each of these muscles or glands has a special function. They differ greatly in size and position and in other ways, but they are all alike in being limited as to the kind of responses they can make. The only change in their state of being that can be produced in response to nerve impulses is that of *responding either more or less actively* than before. The salivary glands can produce only more or less saliva in response to the appropriate stimulus and resulting nerve impulse. They cannot produce tears.

Out of this "more and less" factor in the response of each of the millions of muscle and gland cells in the body is built that enormously complex thing called human behavior. Myriads of different combinations of these minute responses are possible and these become part of the many patterns of response involved in man's behavior.

What Are the Motives of Men and How Do They Come to Be as They Are?—In this chapter the problem of motivation will be divided into two parts dealing with overlapping but not identical phases of human motivation. These two phases will be called *physiological motivation* and *socially conditioned motivation.* Some psychologists prefer to consider the two phases together. Their reasons for so doing and a word of caution are in order at this point.

All motives, as they are here considered, are both physiologically and socially determined, at least for the human adult. Some are primarily physiological and are more or less innate. Others are primarily socially conditioned, depending for their forcefulness in a large degree upon man's social relationships. It is convenient to consider these two groups of motives somewhat separately, recognizing, however, that there is no sharp distinction between them. Each group partakes of the characteristics of the other. Therefore, a motive will be considered as falling into the first group if its innately determined characteristics are the most prominent and into the second group if its qualities as a motive are predominantly determined through experience with other human beings. In the nature of things there will be some motives that might properly be considered in either of these classifications, and in discussing a motive in one group it will sometimes be advisable to consider the qualities it possesses that characterize the other.

Such a grouping of motives will also serve another purpose in the plan of this book. The consideration of the physiological type of motivation is a continuation of the discussions occurring in the chapters preceding, while that pertaining to the socially conditioned variety will relate this discussion to a chapter that comes later and deals more specifically with the way in which behavior is modified by experience.

Motives Arising Directly from Man's Bodily Conditions

A Well-known Motive Examined.—Jean Valjean, the principal character in Victor Hugo's immortal story, *Les Misérables,* was sentenced to nineteen years' imprisonment in convict ships for stealing a loaf of bread. Whether such a man ever actually received such a sentence is beside the point. Men will do almost anything for food under certain conditions. Why? The answer will be found in terms of both physiological and social motivation. Here the physiological aspect will be considered, since in this instance it is a physiological response that is chiefly involved.

When a normal individual has gone without food for three or four hours, certain types of stomach movements begin. These movements of the empty stomach have been shown to occur simultaneously with what are recognized consciously as hunger pangs. They are accompanied by a general condition of restlessness. Wada [1] in her experiments showed that, whether the individual was awake or asleep, this restlessness was observable. The strength of grip of the hands is greater at the time of this condition called hunger, and the ability to do mental work is increased. These characteristics are only a few of the results of the hunger drive.

Habit has a great deal to do with one's being *aware* of these hunger pangs. For those who are habituated to a 12:00 o'clock lunch and are asked to attend a 1:00 o'clock luncheon, the feeling of hunger is a very conspicuous part of their behavior. They have an unusual amount of restlessness; they enter into animated conversation and move about animatedly; they light their cigarettes and puff on them in an almost feverish way. They give evidence of a tension, of which they are probably not aware, by the very way in which they sit forward in their chairs, the way they talk, and the restless way they glance around or move from place to place.

Notice the same group after they have eaten. To all casual appearance, they may be doing the very same things that they had done before luncheon. Some may be smoking, but notice the difference in the way they attack their cigars or cigarettes. The conversation may be animated, but nevertheless there is noticeably less tension, and less restless movement than there was before luncheon. Drowsiness may be very evident within a short time.

---

[1] Tomi Wada, "An Experimental Study of Hunger in Its Relation to Activity," *Archives of Psychology*, 1922, No. 57, pp. 1–67.

To show that such activity as this is not altogether socially conditioned, it is only necessary to observe an infant who has gone without food for a few hours. There are vigorous arm and leg movements. Crying begins; it is intermittent at first, then becomes more regular and more intensive. Note the same infant after it has finished feeding. If sleep does not follow immediately, at least the observable behavior is different. Arm and leg movements are fewer and different in character, and if there is vocalization, it is almost sure to be of the gurgling, cooing kind.

It is extremely difficult to measure quantitatively in human beings the behavior caused by such a motive as the hunger drive, because socialized experience complicates human motives. Civilized human beings, no matter how hungry they may be at such a luncheon as was described above, do not rush up to the table and grab food from the plates to appease their hunger. There are too many socially conditioned motives or drives acting in the other direction. Hence it is difficult to approach such human motives with measuring devices.

The problem is simpler with lower animals. Some experiments have been carried out by Moss and others to measure the intensity of the drive due to hunger, in rats. Moss [2] made a cage consisting of two compartments separated by an electrically charged grid over which the rats could pass, but only at the expense of being electrically shocked. The rats were placed in one compartment, food in the other. The voltage could be measured and the length of time which the rats would stay away from the food before crossing the grid was taken as a measure of the forcefulness of the drive. In the same way the forcefulness of other kinds of motives was measured. However, very few conclusions can be drawn from these experiments as to the forcefulness of the hunger drive in man, largely because of differences in the two species which are due to social conditioning, but they do indicate that such a motive as hunger has a very definite physiological basis.

---

[2] F. A. Moss, "Study of Animal Drives," *Journal of Experimental Psychology,* 1924, Vol. 7, pp. 165–185.

THE DESPAIR OF THE BREADLINE

How long will the hungry man's socially conditioned pride keep him out of the "breadline" when he is destitute? Would it be longer for some persons than for others? Why?

General Characteristics of a Motive.—It is now possible to state the general characteristics of motives. There is room for an honest difference of opinion concerning what a motive is, but the following definition is one which seems to fit the facts and has the advantage of being workable. *A motive is an urge to begin or to continue a characteristic type of action which leads to the reestablishment within the body of a balance, the disturbance of which sets the motive into action.* Some psychologists make a distinction between the "drive" and the "motive." However, no attempt will here be made to distinguish from each other the terms drive, urge, craving, and motive.

According to this definition the basis of every motive is an upsetting of some organic balance which has been previously established at least temporarily. These balances may be involved in what Dashiell [3] calls "tissue needs," or they may be the result of learned or acquired types of behavior. Hunger, thirst, and sexual tension are examples of physiological conditions involved in "tissue needs." Social approval and gregariousness are examples of learned or socialized habits, which will be discussed more fully later.

There is a forcefulness about any type of activity once begun which tends to make it persist. Once a motive becomes active, it dominates the individual's behavior until either the disturbed equilibrium is reestablished, or some other powerful motive interferes and dominates the behavior. One of the most important characteristics of either habits or the so-called instincts is this tendency to continue when once started.

A number of systems have been outlined to explain human motivation, but most of them have employed too much simplification to deserve much credence. Any scheme which seeks to explain the general characteristics of human motivation must be broad enough to fit all sorts of behavior and must at the same time remain within the limits of natural law.

What the reader must understand is that man is endowed, not with a few fundamental and universal drives to action, but

---

[3] J. F. Dashiell, *Fundamentals of Objective Psychology*, p. 233 ff.

with a great variety of motives. The reader will be aided in understanding himself if he can see that he behaves as he does because he possesses a particular kind of organic structure. This organic structure is the joint product of what he has inherited, what he has experienced, and the state of maturity he has reached.

Other Motives Primarily Due to Organic Conditions.—Sensations of thirst can be rather definitely localized. The mucous membranes of the pharynx, nasal passages, and mouth seem to be the points most noticeably affected. The mucous glands of the throat and nose secrete less freely than usual, and the result is a feeling of dryness in these parts. If thirst goes unquenched for a long time, those mucous membranes that can be observed become dry and inflamed. The flesh underneath becomes swollen, and extreme discomfort results. There are fewer socially conditioned factors in the satisfaction of the thirst motive than in the case of hunger. As yet, however, no one has attempted to measure the forcefulness of this motive for human beings.

Another physiological condition within the common experience of everyone is the craving for rest when fatigued. The feeling of fatigue may include the whole body or it may be somewhat localized when certain muscles have been overstrained in a fatiguing exercise. The exact physiological cause for this is not definitely known, but it is assumed to be the accumulated by-products of metabolism.

When the normal individual is rested, there is an urge toward increase of activity. The physiological basis of this urge is even less understood than it is in the fatigue motive. But whatever the underlying conditions may be, the need for activity, like the need for rest, is subject to individual and social conditioning.

Effects of Drugs as Motives.—There is another kind of acquired mode of behavior that deserves special attention. "Drug habits" can only partly be accounted for in terms of the usual explanations of habit formation. The drug substances themselves play a rôle similar to the chemical factors common to motives that are essentially physiological in nature. An extreme example is the person addicted to an opiate. Anyone familiar

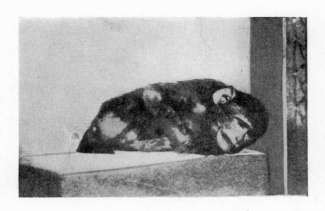

A DRUG ADDICT

This monkey has been experimentally habituated to large doses
of morphine. Above, after 25 hours since the last dose. Below,
30 minutes after receiving a large dose of the drug. (Reprinted
by permission from *Comparative Psychology,* edited by F. A.
Moss. Copyright 1934, Prentice-Hall, Inc., New York.)

with a case of this sort is well aware of the almost terrifyingly dynamic qualities of such a habit. There seems to be literally nothing that one thoroughly accustomed to the use of such a drug will not do, when deprived of it, to obtain a supply of the substance. In a "drug habit," aside from the usual effects of learning, there are physiological effects similar to those involved in fatigue or illness. The drug has a different kind of effect upon certain tissues of the body than that involved in the usual learning process.

Somewhat related to the habits of using opiates are such habits as the drinking of coffee, tea, and other drinks containing caffeine and similar substances. The fact that the effect of caffeine is roughly in inverse proportion to the body weight of the user indicates that the chemical substance has some significant physiological effect upon body tissues. A man who is accustomed to a cup of coffee upon arising in the morning may have a miserable time if circumstances prevent him from obtaining it.

Another example of the forcefulness of a habit of this sort is smoking. Here both physiological and socially conditioned factors are involved in an important sense. Consider the case of a man who is accustomed to his after-dinner cigar. He arises from the dining table and goes to his smoking stand only to be reminded that he forgot to replenish the supply. The nearest cigar store is several blocks away, and a storm is raging. He goes to the door and looks out, but decides that it is foolish to go out into the storm for a cigar. He decides to use this occasion to assure himself that he is master of the habit. Note how he is attempting by his rationalizing to motivate himself to behave as his good judgment tells him he ought to behave. He goes to his accustomed chair, takes the evening paper, and settles himself as usual to read. In half the usual time he throws the paper aside and wanders around the room. He notices a pencil mark on the wall and gets himself all worked up emotionally about the misbehavior of his young son. His remarks about his wife's ability to control the child might better have been left unsaid. She resents the statement, and a warm argument ensues until she goes to her room, leaving him with no one to abuse. He tries to read a book but finds it uninteresting. He tries the radio, but the programs are "all rotten." Finally he remembers that there was a minor business matter that he has not attended to. He decides to take the car and finish it. Incidentally, he drives by the store and remarks to himself, "As long as I'm going this way anyway, I might as well stop and get some cigars." Having lighted the cigar and puffed contentedly on it for a minute or two, he feels that the world is a little more rosy. He thinks, "Maybe I was a bit short in speaking to Mabel; I'll take her that box of candy. That's the kind she likes particularly." And so, having conformed to habit, he is free to resume a more or less routine type of behavior.

Individual Habits as Motives.—The importance of the effects of learning in the motivation involved in the preceding incident raises the question : To what extent is habit, in the sense of being the result of learning, a type of physiological motive? The physiological and anatomical factors involved in ordinary habit formation are not precisely known, but it is fairly well agreed that certain structural changes do occur during learning. Although it is certain that most human learning takes place in social situations, it is enough for the present to consider habits as motives in a physiological sense, leaving to a later section of this chapter a discussion of the socializing effect of group activity in determining the nature of socialized motives. This is an instance of a motive that might appropriately be considered in either group.

Almost any kind of a routine habit may, when interfered with, produce a result similar to that of cigar smoking. The man who comes home and finds the furniture moved, unless he is habituated to having it moved, and the woman who looks in the accustomed place for the scissors only to find them gone are both in for an unfortunate few minutes. The more thoroughly the habit is established, the more forcefully it operates as a dynamic factor in controlling behavior, as the following example illustrates.

Several years ago a teacher of home economics arranged a meat-cutting demonstration for the members of her classes and their mothers. The butcher brought a fore and a hind quarter of beef to the classroom. Everything proceeded beautifully until he reached for his saw. As was his habit, he put his hand over his head to get it, but, of course, it was not there. He laughed that off satisfactorily. In the course of the next twenty minutes he did it no less than eleven times. By that time he was definitely embarrassed and confused. In that embarrassment he finally cut his hand severely, a thing which he had not done for several years. His entire series of composed, coordinated movements had been upset by interference with a single point in his routine.

Relationship Between Endocrine Glandular Activity and Motives.—In several of the motives which have been discussed, such as the hunger, sex, and maternal drives, the glands have been shown to play an important rôle. The endocrine glands seem to be especially important. As examples, two of these glands and their products, the thyroid glands and the gonads or sex glands, will be briefly discussed. The influence of these particular glands upon behavior is fairly well understood.

When the thyroid gland is overactive, providing more thyroxin than is needed for the smooth running of the body, certain general characteristics of behavior become evident. The hyperthyroid person is easily excited, has a tendency to excesses of emotional response, and has poorly coordinated muscular responses. The whole of such a person's behavior is typified by instability, and this is so conspicuous as to color his entire personality.

In an extreme case of this sort, a patient in a prison hospital was unable to pick up a key from a flat narrow surface. In his attempt to do so he knocked the key to the floor where he eventually secured it by getting it against his foot. This patient was a deserter from the army in peace time. His army record had been good until a few months before his desertion. Gradually he began to do things not expected of the professional soldier. He would start to carry out an order or an errand and might end up by doing something entirely different. This, of course, got him into military difficulties. His officers lost patience with him and subjected him to the usual punishment at their command. He always seemed to be penitent for his military misdeeds, but he insisted that he did not know why he behaved as he did. Finally the situation became unbearable to him, and he simply walked away from his post. Several months later he was picked up by railroad police while attempting to board a freight train. According to his own account, the intervening months had been spent in starting to do a number of different things only to abandon them without apparent reason. In fact, his statement was that usually things were going well enough, and he did not know why he changed his mind. He was hospitalized and treated surgically and otherwise for an overgrown and overactive thyroid. He was discharged from the army much improved in general health and apparently also in the general stability of his behavior.

The female gonads secrete several substances. One of these, *oestrin,* is now fairly well known. When the female gonads are removed or destroyed by disease, the woman's femininity is soon replaced by a more masculine physical aspect and a more or less masculine mode of behavior. In reality the tendency is toward a neutral kind of behavior closely approximated by the male whose gonads no longer function as endocrine glands. Experiments with some of the lower animals indicate the possibility of alternating male and female types of behavior by controlling, surgically, the presence of these substances within the body.

It should be evident by this time that anything that influences the anatomical and physiological aspects of man's organism has a direct influence upon his behavior. The stimulus that sets a motive going may be any natural energy to which man's organism can respond. How man will respond to the stimulus depends upon the organization of his whole system of energy, including the influence of his inheritance, his maturity, his experience, and the bio-chemical conditions of the organism as a whole.

Motives Arising from Man's Social Experience

Another Well-known Motive Examined.—On an island off the coast of South America in the Caribbean Sea is a French penal colony. Here are sent convicts who usually live in groups.

Occasionally, as a special punishment, a prisoner may be sentenced to spend a period in solitary confinement. He is then put in a dungeon where he does not even see the guards or the person who brings his food and water. It is the most dreaded of all punishments, and it is reported that prisoners thus confined often "go mad" or even die of lack of companionship.

Why does the deprivation of human companionship so seriously disturb the normal person's habits of living? In the past, it has been customary to assume, by way of explanation, that man like the lower animals has an instinct for gregariousness. But to use the term "gregarious instinct" as a means of explaining why man is normally more contented in the company of his fellows is simply saying that man tends to live in groups because man tends to live in groups. It does not explain anything.

Instead of accepting such an unsatisfactory explanation, an effort should be made to find a better reason why men group themselves into social communities. Such an effort should include an examination of the infantile and childhood experiences of normal people. The human infant at birth is completely helpless, and if left to itself it would die in a few hours. Its very life, to say nothing of its happiness and well-being, depends upon care by adults. It is fed, warmed, and protected by adults. It is praised, warned, and punished by them. Almost everything the infant and child does is socially conditioned; that is, all its responses depend in some degree upon the stimulation provided by the behavior of its social group.

Parents are often heard to remark, "I don't see why John won't play in the sand pile by himself. He must always have someone around to talk to." There may be differences in degree of inherent sociability, but it is not strange that the child should insist upon being around or near others. All his short waking life is normally spent in the presence of others. One cannot, therefore, reasonably expect him to be otherwise than habituated to the presence of others. Nor is there any reason for supposing that such a habit is less important as a motive than are those considered in the preceding section of this chapter.

Frequently it may be noted that a child is contentedly engaged in some apparently solitary play activity; then suddenly the child notices that the other children or the adults who were near have gone. Very soon, sometimes immediately, the child becomes uneasy and restless. The play activity no longer arouses in him the same enthusiasm as before. What has happened? Simply that a very important part of the total environment has changed. The child is habituated to the almost constant presence of others. When this habit is interfered with, the same thing happens, in a general way, that occurs when any other regular habit is disturbed.

During youth and adult life this habit of being with others is usually intensified. Need it be surprising then, knowing what is known about habits as important motives, to find the child is uncomfortable when he is by himself? As the child grows older, he normally becomes habituated to being alone for short periods of time, especially if he knows that others are within reach. But the average person of any age, if deprived of the society of others, will require a very considerable readjustment to enable him to endure his own company. Several college students have reported that they cannot even study alone in their rooms for an hour without at least having the door open as a means of suggesting the presence of others.

Thus it is evident that man during the entire period of infancy, youth, and adulthood is required to control much of his behavior in terms of the actions or the presence of others. This controlling force may be called gregariousness, but whatever it is called it should be recognized that it is largely learned and that it is an important means of motivating behavior.

Man's Need for the Attention and Approval of Others.— Children constantly seek to gain the attention and approval of others. Several years ago in a city school system there was a seventh-grade teacher who at the beginning of the year drew up a set of rules for conduct. One of these authoritatively forbade the chewing of gum in the schoolroom. For several reasons, aside from these rules, she became quite unpopular with her pupils. One day there was a knock on the door of the superintendent's office, and one of the boys from this teacher's room entered. When asked what he wanted, he said that the teacher had sent him there because she thought he had been chewing gum, although he maintained that he had not been doing so. He was told to sit down and wait until the end of the period. About five minutes later another boy appeared with much the same story to tell. He was also asked to wait. Before the end of the period a third boy from the same classroom appeared. When asked, "You weren't chewing gum, either, were you?" he seemed surprised, but he also insisted that he was innocent. No one knows how many more would have been sent to the office had the period not soon ended.

Investigation cleared up what little was not already apparent. The teacher had detected a girl in the act of chewing gum and had commanded her in an imperious manner to march to the front of the room and put the gum in the waste basket. One after another these three boys had thereupon made themselves conspicuous by appearing to be chewing gum. When commanded to come forward, they had done so, but had no gum to deposit. The first time there were suppressed titters from the other pupils. This increased to open snickers when the second boy was detected and to a full laugh when the third boy came forward without any gum.

That poor, unfortunate teacher was quite unable to see that her disapproval of gum-chewing was of absolutely no avail as compared with the attention and approval that these three boys were able to get by playing up to the situation she had created. They had secured the coveted approval of their group. Her disapproval did not matter. They were even willing to risk punishment from the superintendent rather than forego the satisfaction of approval of their fellows.

Why will athletes endure long hours of training and violent physical exertion, sometimes for months at a time, for the sake of making a place on the team or even on the substitute's bench? The answer may be partly that they enjoy the physiological exhilaration of the exercise of a physically well-conditioned body.

Partly, also, it may depend upon another socially conditioned motive, the desire for mastery; but undoubtedly for most athletes much of the motivation would be lost if the contests were held behind locked gates, if the newspapers published no pictures and no accounts of the games, and if no pins, sweaters, or emblems were given to the participants. They are, in this respect, like the boys mentioned in the preceding incident. It is the approval of the group that counts.

The bully at school often gets his attention in an asocial or even anti-social manner as a compensation for the usual attention available to the brighter or less socially restricted pupil. Temper tantrums are not often resorted to by children or adults as a means of getting attention, but some persons make a practice of that sort of behavior when it brings them the desired results. Extreme argumentativeness sometimes works the same way. The term "exhibitionism" is usually reserved for certain abnormal sex practices of adults and children. With children, at least, the prime motive of such behavior is usually that of seeking attention that is not easily obtained by more usual methods.

During illness a great deal of attention is usually given to the one who is ill. As recovery nears completion, this excessive attention is withdrawn. The convalescent has a set of habits to break or a readjustment to make following an illness of any considerable period. This sometimes becomes a very important part of convalescence, both for children and adults.

Another interesting way in which some adults get attention is through membership and office-holding in secret ritualistic organizations. They attend faithfully, perform routine duties, and eventually are elected to a minor office. This often automatically carries them to the higher offices where they have a chance to become somebodies of importance. Their periods of office-holding over, they then retire to the mild glory of being Past Great and Exalted Something-or-Others.

The origin of this motive of gaining social attention and approval seems to be about the same as that of gregariousness; that is, it can be explained in terms of social conditioning in infancy, childhood, and youth. Many of man's physiological needs are gained by getting the attention and approval of his social group. This is true in the family, in the school, and in the groups out of school. When the group approves, he gains his end: when the group disapproves, he fails. He comes to know through experience what will and what will not get approval. Thus by conditioning, the securing of approval comes gradually to be associated with emotional responses.

There are some seeming exceptions to such a general principle. There are those who live in a world more or less apart from their fellows. They spend hours or even years in perfecting some invention, in securing some experimental data, or in doing some other piece of scholarly work. Usually in such cases the approval of a small group is to them of more worth than the approval of the larger group. There are now a dozen or more professional journals in the field of psychology. Editors of these journals say that there is more good material offered for publication than they can possibly print. It is only fair to recognize that one of the motives behind much of the experimentation and writing is the approval that is sought from one's fellow-workers.

There are also the recluses who seem to have withdrawn from society as a whole, and apparently care very little for the approval of others. The hermit, for example, seemingly cares nothing for the approval of society. A closer examination of how he spends his time will reveal that it is a case of emphasizing one habit almost to the exclusion of another. Sometimes he engages excessively in the habit of reading. In some cases religious zeal induces a person to withdraw from society and neglect the approval of the world at large in favor of a restricted group within the church. In addition the presumed approval of a Supreme Being may come to be habitually substituted for the approval of society. Thus are martyrs made. Even such seeming exceptions emphasize the importance of social conditioning.

An Outline Summary

1. Man's behavior as related to his structure.
   A. The structure determining behavior in the psychological sense can be conveniently classified as:

      1. Receptors—the sense organs through which natural forces initiate responses,

      2. Connectors—the nervous system through which the responses are integrated, and

      3. Effectors—the muscles and glands which actually make the response.

   B. All of man's behavior can be accounted for in terms of the variation and integration of the activity of these structures.

2. In general, motivating forces are of two kinds:

   A. Physiological motives

      1. Have their origin in the functioning of the original organic structure, and

      2. Are modified to an important degree by experience and by maturation.

      3. Some substances (drugs) when taken into the body have an important effect upon the structure and hence upon the behavior.

   B. Socialized motives

      1. Have their origin in terms of learning (habits are characteristically dynamic).

      2. Some habits are individually unique and their exact origin differs among individuals, while

      3. Some habits are practically universal, arising out of common social experiences with common stimuli.

PROBLEMS FOR FURTHER THOUGHT

1. What is the most probable reason why some people do not hear such high-pitched sounds as that made by a cricket chirping? Why do not those who are color-blind see the colors seen by others? Explain why such persons are often quite unaware of their deficiencies.

2. Look up material relative to the effect upon behavior of abnormalities of any one of the endocrine glands and report the results of your findings. Pay particular attention to the matter of behavior. (In the suggested readings below, note how Berg, Dorsey, and Hoskins treat this point.)

3. From among your circle of acquaintances select two, one of whom is extremely distressed and annoyed by even the thought of possible disapproval. Select another who is as much the opposite as you can find. Compare their behavior in social situations that are as alike as possible. Note the behavior differences themselves and the differences in the way the groups react to them. Explain as fully as your information about these two persons will permit "how they got that way."

4. Cite several instances from your experience or your observation of the operation of the urge to rest and recuperate when fatigued and to be vigorously active when well rested.

5. When one has developed a habit of working vigorously for certain fixed hours each day, and of resting at certain other fixed hours, what significant modifications of the innate urges mentioned in Problem 4 above are clearly observable? Illustrate.

6. How can the rather universal type of behavior that is commonly called curiosity be explained as an instance of "universal habit"? Explain how the common characteristics of every person's life in childhood would tend to produce this effect. Explain also the differences in degree of curiosity shown by different people.

7. Illustrate the dynamic quality of habit from several experiences or observations of your own. They need not be striking or unusual instances but should clearly embody evidence of the tendency of habit patterns to go through to completion when once they have been set in motion. It may be helpful here to recall acts automatically carried out when one is "absent-minded."

8. Some of the instances cited in Problem 7 may have been somewhat embarrassing because the habitual behavior pattern was inappropriate when it appeared. But are all habitual repetitions disadvantageous? Make a list of a dozen or more habitual acts that are socially or individually useful because they do go through to completion unattended when once they have been set going.

Suggested Readings

Berg, Louis. The Human Personality. New York, Prentice-Hall, Inc., 1933. "The Glandular Basis of Personality," Ch. IV, pp. 48–81. A discussion of the rôle of the endocrine glands in determining general behavior characteristics.

Cannon, W. B. Bodily Changes in Pain, Hunger, Fear, and Rage. New York, D. Appleton-Century Co., 1922. Ch. XIII, "The Nature of Hunger," pp. 232–266. Describes some of the experimental work and presents results showing the nature of the bodily changes that take place in hunger.

DORSEY, GEORGE A. Why We Behave Like Human Beings. New York, Harper & Bros., 1925. Ch. IV, "The Endocrine Glands," pp. 201–262. Discusses in a popular and easy style some of the influences of the endocrine glands upon behavior.

GATES, A. I. Elementary Psychology. Rev. ed., New York, The Macmillan Co., 1928. Ch. II, "The Reaction Hypothesis and the Receiving Mechanisms," pp. 33–58; Ch. III, "The Connecting Mechanisms," pp. 59–80; Ch. IV, "The Reacting Mechanisms," pp. 81–105. These three chapters furnish a simplified statement concerning the bodily mechanisms of behavior which is included in the introductory section of the present chapter. Ch. VIII, "Dominant Human Urges," pp. 216–244. This chapter discusses in a similar simple way the variety of urges or mainsprings of human activity.

HOSKINS, R. G. The Tides of Life. New York, W. W. Norton & Co., 1933. This is the most up-to-date and authoritative statement available to the reader concerning the complex rôle of the endocrine glands in determining human behavior.

KRUEGER, E. T., and RECLESS, W. C. Social Psychology. New York, Longmans, Green, and Co., 1931. Ch. IV, "The Theory of Motivation," pp. 142–170. Discusses the general problem of motivation, including the place of the social motives.

MURPHY, GARDNER. General Psychology. New York, Harper & Bros., 1933. Ch. IV, "The Simpler Motives," pp. 46–64. Deals only with the physiological motives.

PERRIN, F. A. A., and KLEIN, D. B. Psychology. New York, Henry Holt & Co., 1926. Ch. IV, "The Motivation of Behavior," pp. 137–150 and 183–193. These sections of this chapter deal with the physiological drives and social motives, respectively.

SMITH, STEVENSON, and GUTHRIE, E. R. General Psychology in Terms of Behavior. New York, D. Appleton-Century Co., 1921. Ch. IV, "Coenotropes" (Universal Habits), pp. 134–157. Emphasizes the rôle of learning in many of the motivating forces previously called instincts.

THOMSON, M. K. The Springs of Human Action. New York, D. Appleton-Century Co., 1927. This is a general treatise on human dynamics. A number of chapters are especially pertinent to the problem of this chapter.

Chapter 7

HOW DOES MATURITY MODIFY BEHAVIOR?

How Did Betty Learn to Walk So Rapidly?—Betty was almost a year old and had begun to pull herself up to her feet alongside of chairs, when her parents discovered that her right hip was dislocated. The doctor was called at once, and for nearly a year Betty was confined in a heavy cast which was so constructed that it was impossible for her to stand on her feet or put any weight on her right hip. Betty was apparently as happy and active as any other child during her second year of life, except that she could not run, walk, or even crawl in the usual baby fashion. She did get around the house with a peculiar rolling, hitching movement that was as efficient as it was unusual. She even managed to get up and down stairs by herself before the end of the year.

When she was nearly two years old, the cast was removed, and within a week one would not have suspected that she had never walked before. With a week of practice she was apparently as efficient in her method of walking and running as were children of her own age with the usual normal experiences. She started to walk at once after the removal of the cast, although her first steps were somewhat like the first steps of a normal child several months to a year younger than she. The significant thing is that the improvement was so rapid. The question naturally arises: How could this child master the process of walking so rapidly that in less than a week she had caught up with the norms for her age in this particular kind of behavior?

It is the purpose of this chapter to answer this question and to examine the effect upon behavior of maturation of the bodily structure. In the course of this examination, it will be difficult and often impossible to distinguish the results of maturation— the pure, innately determined growth—from the effects of learning, because in the usual experience of the normal child the structural changes in the body due to learning and those due to maturation go on at the same time.

Some Experiments with Lower Animals.—Many experiments have been conducted with the lower animals because of the freedom with which such animals may be subjected to an experimental environment. Spaulding kept four swallows confined in a cage so small that it prevented any possibility of wing action even faintly resembling flying. These young birds were confined from the time they were hatched until those of the same brood left in the nest had grown up and were flying with the skill of the adult bird. When the birds which he had kept in close confinement were released, two of them were able to fly nearly as well as those reared in the usual way. The other two were also able to fly at once, and while they were noticeably less adept, in a very short time even this difference was indistinguishable.

When chicks first come out of the shell, a trait of behavior that is universally present is the pecking response. Newly hatched chicks will not only peck at grains of food, but will indiscriminately peck at the toes of their companions or at ink spots on a paper under their feet. They will even peck at the eyes of the chicks about them. However, this pecking is far from accurate. At first they are hardly 50 per cent successful in seizing a grain of food in their bills so that it can be swallowed. As the days of the first week go by, chicks under normal conditions improve so rapidly that by the seventh day of life they average above 80 per cent of success in the pecking response. Here again the question is whether the improvement is the result of learning or of maturation. Breed and Shepard first, and others since, have endeavored to answer this question. A group of chicks from a newly hatched brood were prevented from pecking during the first days of life by keeping them in total darkness and feeding them by hand. Some were subjected to these conditions for one day, some for two, some for three, and some for as long as four days. When these chicks first began to peck, they were in each case distinctly less perfect in their response than were those of the same original lot which had been permitted to live and grow under normal conditions. The longer the chicks were kept in the dark the more retarded they were, as compared with the control group, but in each case the handicapped chicks were more successful in their first pecking response than the control group had been when first hatched. Even without any experience in pecking, their performance had improved somewhat, but it had not been able to reach the degree of efficiency attained by the chicks with normal experience. A most interesting observation is the fact that by the end of one week of life the chicks from all the groups in the experiment were about equally successful in their pecking responses.

In these experiments with forms of animal life other than human beings, the results seem to be substantially the same as in the case of Betty. An experiment of another kind is described below dealing with human infants in the development of a relatively complex type of behavior.

Gesell's Experiment with Twins.—Gesell [1] used as the subjects of an experiment a pair of identical twins. These twins were called in the experimental report twin T and twin C. When they were 46 weeks of age, twin T began a six weeks' period of training in climbing stairs consisting of four treads leading to a crib. The speed and coördination of movements in climbing showed a very definite improvement during this period of training. In the early stages three or four complete trips up the staircase in a ten-minute session represented a typical performance. In the 25th session, during the fifth week, twin T reached a maximum of ten trips up the staircase in the ten-minute practice period. During the six weeks' period of training, twin T scaled the staircase a total of 126 times and showed a skill considerably greater than twin C's. These twins were also trained in a similar manner to handle cubes. At the close of the training period, the performances of the twins were very similar.

From this and similar experiments Gesell suggests that growth of the individual due to changes in maturity cannot be

[1] Arnold Gesell, "Learning and Growth in Identical Twins," *Genetic Psychology Monographs*, 1929, No. 1.

permanently offset by training. The effect of training may be very important; in fact it usually is. However, if the training is at the marginal level of maturity, it seems to be less productive than the effect of sheer maturation. Thus, one twin by reason of practice seems to become superior to the other in the motor performance involved in this experiment. This gain in efficiency at the end of a long period of training is, however, quickly offset by training the other twin, who in the meantime has also been maturing. This seems to be true only when the behavior is sampled at the lower margin of possible performance. In this respect, it is quite like the case of Betty.

Factors Involved in Maturation Difficult to Discover and Measure.—In such experiments as Gesell's and in the case of Betty, observation of improvement in the absence of opportunity to learn is limited to a single case or two. Consequently, the results are not very convincing. But they do agree with each other and with the experiments with the animals, in which larger numbers were used. In the case of both lower animals and children, there may have been some learning. Betty had been very active during the time she was in the cast. She had certainly had much practice in whatever is involved in keeping one's balance and in other phases of motor activity. These indirect learning factors are impossible to single out and control in an experiment. Added to this general difficulty is the ever-present one of the unwillingness of parents to permit their infants to be hampered in their movements over the period of time necessary for such experiments.

It will be well now to return to the question raised above and state it in a somewhat different way. How much of the improvement in Betty's ability to walk, during the year in which she was in the cast, was due to pure maturation and how much was due to the kinds of indirect experience just mentioned? Or, stating the question in a still more general form, How much of the change, of behavior occurring before the individual reaches the mature, adult level is due to maturation, and what part of it can best be accounted for in terms of learning?

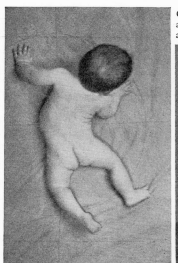

Child pivoting; age 32 weeks; characteristic behavior of children of this age.

First steps; age 52 weeks; note the lack of sureness in maintaining balance that is characteristic of learning to walk.

Testing an infant; age 16 weeks; note the relation of the thumbs to the fingers and the child's attitude to the block on the table.

THREE INTERESTING STAGES OF INFANT BEHAVIOR

(By courtesy of Arnold Gesell, The Clinic of Child Development, Yale University.)

Nature of Changes in Structure During Maturation.— Changes in behavior due to maturation may be classified into two groups, although it is possible that these are simply two different ways of looking at the same kind of change. In any event, the changes of behavior are undoubtedly due to changes in bodily structure. One group of changes seems to be due to the growth in size and change of shape of the parts of the body. The other seems to be characterized by an increased *ease-of-operation* or *ease-of-arousing* a bodily response. This second phase of maturation manifests itself in an increased smoothness and integration of the responses. It is probable that this second phase depends chiefly upon the functional maturing of the nervous system. Through the period of infancy and early childhood, these two aspects of maturation are more easily distinguishable than in later life.

All the organs of the body are present at birth. This presence of structure extends to very minute details. At the time of birth many of the cells and organs are far from mature in size and are far from their mature ability to react. Maturation is a process of development of the structures already potentially present from the time of fertilization. Even a casual observation of the body of the infant at birth will indicate the impossibility of walking. The legs are altogether too undeveloped to sustain the weight of the body. The infant's body must mature in the sense of increasing its size and strength before walking can take place.

As for the other phase of maturation, one must be content with an examination of the increasing complexity of responses. The inner structure of the nervous system cannot be examined. From the first few days of life the normal infant responds to pressure on the soles of the feet by a down-thrusting movement. This is only one of the necessary elements of the total pattern of behavior involved in walking. One may also note that there is very early evidence of some coordination of leg movements. At first there seems to be more of a tendency for the legs to move simultaneously than alternately, but this is soon reversed. By the age of three weeks the child may make walking movements if the body is supported so that the feet just touch a surface. Here there is further evidence of integration of increasingly complex behavior that cannot be accounted for simply by an increase in size and strength. In the same way, progressively more coordinated movements can be observed in the trunk and neck and other parts of the body involved in maintaining balance.

Mothers and nurses frequently observe that the infant begins to walk suddenly. Often, less than a week from the time of the first step taken alone, the infant is making its way successfully, walking where it crept before. This suddenness indicates the necessity of the completion of a certain minimum level of maturity in both these phases of growth. Often in the normal course of events the size and strength of the muscular parts are sufficiently mature before the necessary coordination is present for such a complex muscular activity as standing or walking without support. Occasionally the reverse is true, and the infant is prevented from walking, not by inability to make the necessary movements, but by lack of sufficient strength. This is relatively rare and is most often the result of gross malnutrition or disease. In any event, the child does not walk until both phases of maturation are sufficiently advanced.

In the case of Betty, opportunity was denied for practicing walking for a year. During this time Betty's body had been growing quite normally both in size and to some extent in strength of muscular response. Presumably, too, the various parts of the nervous system were developing in the normal manner. In spite of this, it is very important to note that, both in this case and in the other experimental studies cited, some practice was necessary to perfect the response.

These two phases of development will be called *gross bodily maturation* and *functional maturation of the nervous system.* It must be recognized, of course, that these two names are a bit misleading because not all the structural characteristics included in the former are in any sense gross. It must also be recognized that the functional maturation of the nervous system is after all just as much structural as the development of the muscles or the skeleton. Much more is known about the maturation of the body in its gross structural sense than about the functional maturation of the nervous system. A few of the known facts about each of these two phases of maturation will be summarized in the following paragraphs.

Gross Bodily Maturation.—Gross structural maturation is not a single unitary thing. There are many phases of maturation going on at the same time but at different relative rates. The ossification of the skeleton has progressed by the time of birth to the point where most of the long bones of the body consist of true bony tissues. This ossification continues through childhood, and by taking radiograph pictures of the wrist, the relative degree of its progress in the wrist bones is sometimes used as a measure of maturity.

At birth the head measures approximately one-fourth the total body length, while in the adult it measures about one-eighth. The head reaches almost maximum size by middle childhood. In the new-born infant the muscles of the head and trunk comprise about 40 per cent of the total volume of muscular tissue. In the adult the percentage is from 20 to 30 per cent. The lower limbs in the new-born infant make up about 40 per cent of the weight, but by adult life this has increased to about 55 per cent.

The sense organs are relatively well developed at birth. They increase rapidly in sensitivity after birth, gradually slowing down in the early school years as these organs approach their maturity. The glands, both duct and ductless, are all present and most of them are functioning actively at the time of birth. The endocrine glands effect the development of each other. The thymus develops rapidly, and is at its largest a year or more before puberty. The gonads, on the other hand, do not develop rapidly until about the time of puberty. At present it seems probable that an important function of the thymus gland is that of acting as a check upon the development of the gonads and the secondary sex characteristics.

It should be evident by this time that there is no single rate of maturation. Instead, there are many rates of growth, nor are these rates uniform. For the particular function of each organ there is usually an early period of very rapid growth followed

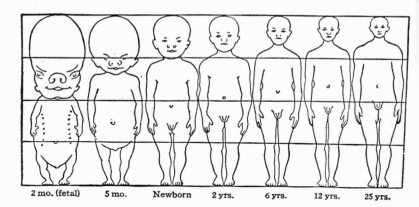

2 mo. (fetal)   5 mo.   Newborn   2 yrs.   6 yrs.   12 yrs.   25 yrs.

Figure 3a. Figures Representing the Changes During Prenatal and
Postnatal Growth
(From Morris, *Morris's Human Anatomy.* Copyright P. Blakiston's Son & Co., Inc.,
Publishers)

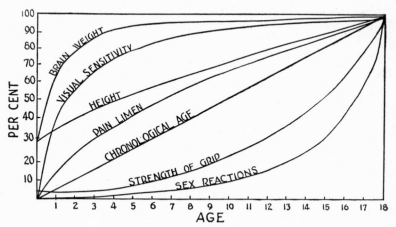

Figure 3b. Various Curves of Growth
(Modified from Gates, *Psychology for Students of Education,* The Macmillan Co., 1930)

by one of diminished rate. Maturity in one respect does not necessarily imply similar maturity in other respects. This is a fact that parents and teachers are very likely to overlook.

Figure 3 will indicate in graphic form some of the characteristics of maturation which have just been presented. Notice that by the late teen age nearly all the functions included in this figure are shown to be practically mature, but that not all of them have reached maturity at the same rate.

In recent years several cases of *puberty praecox* (unusually early reproductive maturity) have been reported for both sexes.[2] In these cases the secondary sex characteristics have also appeared. Size and strength are greatly in excess of the average for the child's age. Interestingly enough, the growth of mental function is apparently not affected, indicating that the latter depends upon factors which are not specifically influenced by those that control the factors of gross bodily maturation. Such cases as these support the view that maturation is of two somewhat distinct sorts.

The processes of maturation, viewed as a whole, can be seen in the change from month to month and year to year, even though the specific changes may not be individually apparent. It is significant, however, to consider how these changes in structural development are involved in the gradually changing behavior of the child as he grows older.

Functional Neural Maturation.—There are only two avenues of approach to the study of neural function. One of these is comparison of the brain and nervous tissues of individuals after death, the brains being chosen from those whose death arrested development at different ages. The other is the drawing of inferences relative to brain development as related to the increasing complexity of the behavior of the individual. The latter will be discussed in some detail, with many illustrations, later in this chapter. Consideration will first be given to neurological structure.

---

[2] Arnold Gesell, "Precocious Puberty and Mental Maturation," *Twenty-Seventh Yearbook of National Society for the Study of Education*, Part I, Ch. 19, pp. 399–409.

At birth the frontal lobes of the cerebral hemispheres are relatively the least developed part of the infant's brain. These areas have to do mostly with motor control. The parts of these frontal lobes, whose functions are not definitely known, are believed to be made up largely of motor association tracts and areas. This would seem to explain the relatively low order of motor coordination of the infant at birth, since the muscular and skeletal development is relatively complete as compared to the development of the frontal lobes. The rate of growth of these frontal lobes is proportionately greater than that of the rest of the brain during infancy and early childhood.

The whole brain grows very rapidly in size and weight during the first few years of life. By the age of two, the brain is about 70 to 75 per cent of its adult weight. By four, this percentage is almost 90. This increase in size may or may not indicate a corresponding increase in the ability of the brain to function in a mature manner. Certainly, this rapid growth would seem to explain some of the increase in neural function. This question, however, cannot be completely answered by any known procedure and only in part by a study of the microscopic structure of the brain from stage to stage of development.

It is known that, as the child grows older, the neural fibers of the nervous system became enveloped in a sheath of substance which has an important relation to the function of the neurons. For example, the optic nerve increases rapidly in size immediately after birth and is practically full grown by the end of the first year. Much of this increase in size is due to the addition of this sheath to the nerve fibers. This change is particularly rapid in the first few weeks of life and probably accounts for the high degree of maturation of visual behavior in early infancy.

By the third or fourth month of fœtal life, the number of cells in the cerebral cortex is as great as it ever will be. Consequently, any growth changes that take place beyond that time do not result from an increase in the number of cells. Instead, the changes are concerned chiefly either with size or shape, or with the number and structure of the fibers which develop as a part of the cells. At birth many of the cells of the cortex when examined under the microscope are imperfect and immature. As the child grows older, changes occur in the cell bodies of these cortical neurons and more especially in the nerve fibers related to them.

These facts have been further substantiated by microscopic studies of tissue from the brains of adults whose intelligence during life has been known. Such studies have shown that certain kinds of low-grade feeble-mindedness are accompanied by only rudimentary development of certain brain cells. Maturation, therefore, apparently involves minute changes in the internal structure. These microscopic changes, however minute they may be, seem to have great significance in determining the kind of behavior of which the person is capable.[3]

Care must be taken to recognize that some changes in brain tissue are probably the result of learning. In spite of this, there seem to be sound reasons for attributing much of the increased maturation of behavior to changes which continue beyond the point of rapid brain growth. Since the changes due to maturation and those due to learning go on simultaneously, one cannot be sure about the relative proportions of each.

Changes in Overt Behavior Showing Maturation.—Gesell has studied the development of infants and young children very extensively. Much of the following is summarized from accounts of his observations.[4] Gesell distinguishes four types of responses, two of which, motor responses and vocal responses, will be traced here through the early years of childhood. It is not implied that the sequence of appearance of the following series of complex responses is solely the result of maturation. The influence of learning is, of course, important, but in the responses considered here it may be assumed that all infants have approximately equal opportunities to learn, and that the differences in age at which the several levels of response make their appearance are due primarily to the degree of maturation present.

1. MOTOR DEVELOPMENT AS AN INDEX OF MATURITY. Infantile behavior cannot be described in words. Nothing short of

---

[3] See Figure 4, Chapter 8.
[4] Arnold Gesell, *The Mental Growth of the Pre-School Child*, New York, The Macmillan Co., 1925.

actual observation of the child or of a motion picture of his behavior will do the child justice or show the differences in the behavior of different infants.

At birth the child shows relatively little in the way of postural or motor activity of a coordinated type. The term "random movement" best describes much of the activity observed. Fairly well-coordinated arm and leg movements do appear within the first few days and coordinated eye movements are established very early. Rhythmical sucking movements of the lips usually appear within 24 hours, so that the nursing response is established without much difficulty within a short time thereafter. But on the whole, the infant manifests only a limited type of observable coordinated movement. The internal activities which are innervated through the autonomic nervous system are apparently much more matured at birth than are those depending directly upon the central nervous system.

Yawning, sneezing, and crying are all well developed within a very short time after birth. The hands may be thrust into the mouth even within the first few hours of life. The head moves from side to side. When the palm of the hand comes in contact with a rod or the finger of an adult, the infant's fingers and thumb close in a tight grip that may on occasion be strong enough to support the child's whole weight for several seconds. When placed on its face and abdomen, the infant's legs may be flexed in such a way that they suggest crawling movements, but the head cannot be raised from the supporting surface. Within a month much change takes place. Gesell says of this period of development: "The rate of growth during the first week of life, if we could measure it, doubtless far exceeds that of any comparable interval of growth in later infancy." [5] The statement would probably have been true of an even longer period of time.

At the four-month level the normal infant holds his head erect and the neck muscles will resist pressure from either side of the head. Most infants of this age, when laid on their backs, will make an effort to sit up, and a few can succeed with some support.

---

[5] *Ibid.*, p. 198.

When laid on the stomach, the infant raises his head from the supporting surface. In this position, too, there are usually some squirming, wriggling movements indicative of the creeping responses that will develop more fully later. When the infant is held in an upright position with the feet touching the floor or table, there are often thrusting movements with the feet. The beginning of the thumb opposition can be noted, and many infants at this age can pick up an inch cube when placed within reach on a table before them. In the bath, most four-months-old infants show kicking responses and some hand splashing, though the splashing lags behind the kicking.

We are concerned with many of the same responses in the behavior of infants six months old, but greatly different degrees of nicety and completeness of the responses are evident. The majority of infants at this age can sit up with only slight support, a few can sit alone, and a few can creep or hitch themselves along the floor. At this age more infants can pick up a cube than at four months, but still not all can do this. Some will hold a cube in each hand temporarily without dropping them and a very few will accept a third after dropping one of those already held. In reaching for objects, the six-months-old infant tends to employ the whole body, activity of the head and mouth as well as that of the hands entering into the response. When a small pellet is placed on the table before the infant, he ordinarily disregards it, but if he does secure it, it is done with a sort of palm scoop. It is rare for the infant of this age to use precise thumb and finger prehension. Only a few six-months-old infants show a definite tendency to throw, cast, or brush an object aside. Splashing with the hands in the bath, however, is common by this age.

By the age of twelve months, many of the responses which showed differences before are well established for all infants, making it necessary to observe new types of coordinated behavior. At this age, nearly all can stand with some help, a smaller number can stand alone, and most of them can make stepping movements. Some can walk with help, a few can walk alone, nearly all can creep, and many can climb at this age. Most of these infants will now take a third cube without dropping either of the other two, and nearly all will secure the pellet from the table with fine prehension. A preference for one hand with inhibition of the other is well developed. When given a piece of paper, a large crayon, and a demonstration of scribbling, two-thirds of all one-year-old infants will imitate the scribbling. Only occasionally does scribbling take place spontaneously.

The motor behavior of the two-year-old child is found to be significantly more complex and more coordinated. Most of the previously noted responses no longer show many differences, since all have been well developed during the ensuing year. The two-year-old can seldom succeed in copying a circle or in imitatively making a bold horizontal line, but he is somewhat more likely to succeed with a similar vertical line. Children of this age will usually be able, upon command, to secure a small shot from a saucer and place it in a narrow-necked bottle, and then to remove it in imitation of the response of an adult. This shows a considerable advance in muscular coordination.

At the four-year-old level nearly all children can copy a circle, nearly as many can copy a cross, but few can copy a square or a triangle. Two-thirds of them can trace a diamond and some can trace a cross. The drawings of four-year-old children show a considerable degree of muscular coordination which continues to improve through succeeding years. From this time on, however, the improvement in motor responses becomes more difficult to distinguish from other elements in the total response. Thus, normal four- to six-year-old children are not highly successful in drawing a picture of a house or of a man, but this seems more a matter of lack of perception of significant elements than of the muscular coordination necessary for fairly good drawing.

Improvement in motor response as a result of maturation need not be traced beyond this point. Primary school teachers generally recognize the necessity of employing movements involving the large muscle groups instead of the smaller ones. In a well-equipped kindergarten the building blocks are of the size of bricks and larger, though light in weight. In most homes where parents do not understand the significance of immature muscular coordination, children of the same age are expected to play and build with blocks often as small as an inch on each side.

2. LANGUAGE DEVELOPMENT AS AN INDEX OF MATURITY. Among the first evidences of life is the birth cry. This has been variously interpreted by philosophers, but the meaning to the infant is beside the point here. Within a few weeks this response has been so differentiated as to enable the mother to recognize frequently what she calls a hunger cry, a pain cry, an anger or rage cry, and several others.

In addition to the response called crying, there are some few lip and respiration sounds which appear shortly after birth. These, together with the vocal sounds of crying, form the basis of what later become language responses. At the age of six months these have been multiplied extensively. Gesell [6] reports an accurate and detailed observation of one six-months-old infant by Malmberg. Seventy-five different sounds and combinations of sounds were used by this infant during a 24-hour period. He estimated that about 3 per cent of the waking time of this infant was employed in vocal activity. Three months later this percentage had more than doubled. Many of the sounds are probably quite unpronounceable to the adult. It is significant to note that in the progress of learning to use language, the child first learns to repeat what he hears himself say. This auto-imitation undoubtedly precedes the imitation of sounds heard from others.

By the time the child is a year old, he can, on the average, use four or five words singly. The most frequently occurring words are *dada* and *mama* followed in frequency by terms of greeting and farewell. As early as nine months of age one commonly finds the ability to make adjustments to some words spoken by others. Comprehension is evidenced by the behavior of the infant even before the child can use words in its own response. By eighteen months of age the child is using two or more words together, and a few can point to objects in a picture or name them when pointed to by others.

---

[6] *Ibid.*, p. 216.

By two years of age, the child is using simple sentences, can name familiar objects, and can obey commands involving prepositions such as *in, on, under,* or *behind,* but rarely uses pronouns or plurals. Most children two years of age can point to familiar-named objects or name familiar objects pointed to in pictures. A few at this age can repeat three or four syllables after hearing them once.

By four years of age infantile inaccuracies of articulation are pretty much a thing of the past. The average child of this age can repeat ten or twelve syllables from memory after a single oral stimulation. A very few can repeat five digits, but most can repeat only four. Most children can use descriptive words or phrases by this age, and somewhat fewer can define by use such common objects as chair, house, and doll.

The spontaneously spoken vocabulary of the child increases greatly from four or five words at the age of one year, to several hundred or a thousand by the age of six. A number of studies have been made of the vocabularies of children, and in general they agree. They show a remarkably rapid increase during the years from one to six or eight.

Other Ways in Which Maturation May Be Shown.—Two different types of responses have been shown to become progressively more complex as the individual becomes more mature. The implication is that the greater complexity of response is causally related to greater general maturation of the structure of the child as he grows older. This seems reasonable in terms of the particular responses which have just been examined. Other types of responses might have been used in addition to the ones employed here. Gesell has stressed the increasing complexity of the child's adaptive behavior and the similar increase of complexity in his personal-social responses as he becomes more and more mature.

There are, of course, wide ranges of difference in the general rates at which individuals mature. These, like differences in intelligence, which will be considered in detail in the next chapter, seem definitely to be dependent upon inherited potentialities.

Other differences relate to more specific behavior patterns and presumably may be more the result of differences in environment. Hence, it is evident that learning as well as maturation is of great importance in modifying the behavior of the individual.

Some of the ways in which maturation is made evident in the early years of childhood have been pointed out, because, during these early years the rate of increase in maturity is relatively great enough to permit of careful examination and analysis. It is characteristic of most of the phases of maturation that the rate of development becomes progressively slower. Consequently, if an attempt is made to note the differences in levels of maturity beyond the early years of childhood, confusion results because of the relatively small increases from month to month and year to year. The confusion is made greater by the fact that changes due to experience have by this time accumulated to the point where learning tends to obscure the process of maturation.

An Outline Summary

1. Maturation as a factor in behavior.
   A. Maturation is difficult to study because:
      (a) From birth learning and maturation proceed simultaneously,
      (b) Social objections make possible only a limited type of experimentation with human infants, and
      (c) Experiments with lower animals give evidence that is only partially applicable to human behavior.
   B. Several kinds of experiments revealing the significance of maturation have been employed, including:
      (a) Controlled experiments with young animals, such as chicks, birds, rats, and apes, and
      (b) A few controlled experiments of a limited nature with identical twins.

2. Nature of changes during maturation.
   A. Such changes fall into two categories:
      (a) Gross structural maturation involving chiefly changes in relative and absolute size and shape of organs.

        (b) Functional maturation probably involving for the most part minute changes in the structure of the nervous system and is concerned with muscular coordination and integration of behavior.

    B. Differences in rates of maturation are of two general kinds:

        (a) Maturation generally tends to show a progressive slowing down as age increases, and

        (b) Different organs have rates of growth and different ages of final maximum maturity.

3. Kinds of overt behavior that indicate degrees of maturity.

    A. Motor development as shown by postural control and several other kinds of muscular coordination and integration.

    B. Language development as shown by the mastery of vocal responses and the employment of language symbols.

    C. Other types, such as adaptive behavior and personal-social responses.

4. The relationship of the effects of maturation and experience.

    A. The appearance of a behavior pattern is impossible before a minimum degree of maturity is attained.

    B. The effect of experience upon behavior depends upon the degree of maturity attained.

    C. No amount of experience before the attainment of the necessary minimum of maturity has any great or permanent effect upon the individual's behavior. Increased maturity after this minimum of maturity has been reached tends to lessen the amount of learning necessary to produce a given degree of improvement.

PROBLEMS FOR FURTHER THOUGHT

    1. Observe, for at least half an hour each, children of the ages of six months, one year, and two years. Compare the motor behavior of these on the basis of the material in this chapter, summarized from Gesell.

    2. Make a list of presents that would be suitable for a niece or nephew at the following ages, paying no attention to the matter of cost, but emphasizing the matter of their appropriateness to the maturity of the child's age: (a) three years; (b) five years; (c) eight years; (d) twelve years; (e) seventeen years.

3. What is the chief source of difficulty in discriminating between the results of innately determined maturation and those of learning?

4. This chapter has emphasized the fact that the whole program of maturation of behavior evidently follows a pattern of regularity that is similar for all children. What is the most significant practical value of these facts?

5. A child is reported to have cut only two teeth at one year of age. At that age he began to creep. He did not walk until twenty months of age, although body size was near normal. The Babinski reflex was still present at nine months of age. He was able to follow with his eyes an object moving slowly before his face in a horizontal direction for the first time at about four months of age. At his present age of two years he can say a few words but does not make even short sentences.

(a) What sort of development rate does this picture present?
(b) What will be the most probable state of his development (i.e., retarded, average, or advanced) when he is four years of age; at eight years of age; at the end of adolescence?

6. A teacher of seventh grade pupils in a school on the prairies of eastern Colorado complained that she could not make her pupils appreciate a poem which was included in the course of study. It was "The Chambered Nautilus," by Holmes. The chief objects described are the sea and the sea shell. The theme of the poem is suggested by the line, "Build thee more stately mansions, oh my soul!" What objection might appropriately be raised against the use of this poem under the circumstances, aside from the unfamiliarity of these children with things pertaining to the sea?

Another poem that is often included in elementary readers is Whittier's "Barefoot Boy" on the ground that it is about a small boy. In reality it is a poem of retrospective reflections and the envious wish of a man to be a boy again. Does the same objection apply to this poem's use in elementary school as to the "Chambered Nautilus"?

SUGGESTED READINGS

GESELL, ARNOLD. Infancy and Human Growth. New York, The Macmillan Co., 1928. Ch. VII, "The Tempo and Trend of Infant Development," pp. 136–163. Note particularly p. 143 ff.

GESELL, ARNOLD. The Mental Growth of the Pre-School Child. New York, The Macmillan Co., 1925. Ch. II, "The Significance of Pre-School Development," pp. 9–14; Ch. III; "Development and Duration," pp. 15–23; Ch. IV, "The Scientific Study of Development," pp. 24–36.

GESELL, ARNOLD, and THOMPSON, HELEN. Infant Behavior, Its Genesis and Growth. New York, McGraw-Hill Book Co., Inc., 1934. Ch. V, "Mental Growth and Maturation," pp. 293–322.

GESELL, ARNOLD. "Learning and Growth," Genetic Psychology Monographs. Worcester, Mass., Clark University Press, 1929, No. 1.

HOLLINGWORTH, H. L. Mental Growth and Decline. New York, D. Appleton-Century Co., 1927. Ch. II, "The Nature of Development," pp. 8–16; Ch. III, "General Features of Development," pp. 17–32; Ch. IV, "Stages of Human Growth," pp. 34–48. Several other chapters will also be of interest dealing with the several stages of growth.

JORDAN, A. M. Educational Psychology. New York, Henry Holt & Co., 1928. Look in index under "maturity" and "reading interest."

KELLOGG, W. N. and L. A. The Ape and the Child. New York, McGraw-Hill Book Co., Inc., 1933. Look in index under "maturity."

Chapter 8

WHAT IS INTELLIGENCE?—HOW CAN IT BE OBSERVED AND MEASURED?

It is appropriate at this point to consider the topic of intelligence, since it very nicely illustrates a special phase of general maturation, and because problems pertaining to intelligence are themselves of great importance.

Intelligence as an Abstract Quality.—Intelligence, as it is usually defined in psychology, is one of the most debated issues in that field. Everyone thinks that he or she knows what an intelligent person is. Why should psychologists have so much trouble in discovering and measuring intelligence? What the psychologist has done often seems such a long, roundabout way of defining and measuring that which is fairly well known to everybody.

Many psychologists have tried to discover a means of measuring intelligence, but Binet was the first to arrive at a satisfactory method of attacking the problem. Instead of looking for the *intelligence* of an individual, he began to look for indications of *intelligent behavior*. Instead of regarding intelligence as a thing, Binet advanced the idea that it was a way of behaving. He was not concerned with finding a single mental trait or faculty of the mind. He began to observe the behavior of individuals who were known to be feeble-minded and to compare this behavior with that of persons of the same age and with approximately the same experience who were known not to be feeble-minded. He was looking for evidences of intelligent behavior as distinguished from unintelligent behavior. In other words, he regarded intelligence as a characteristic of behavior comparable, as an abstraction, to such qualities as goodness or honesty. It was something that existed only as an abstract quality.

What Are the Characteristics of Intelligent Behavior?—Before the measurement of intelligence can be discussed it is necessary to answer the question: What are the characteristics of intelligent behavior? Psychologists' attempts to answer this question do not show perfect agreement in all particulars, but there are some general aspects about which there is a fair accord.

To begin with, intelligent behavior does not follow a fixed and unvarying pattern. What might be intelligent behavior in one total situation might not be such an intelligent way of behaving in another. The way in which an eight-year-old boy manipulates a simple problem situation might give evidence that he was of average brightness, but if a twelve-year-old boy responded to the same problem situation in the same manner it might be a reasonable cause for suspecting that the child was of low intelligence. Nevertheless, no matter what the age of the person may be, there are certain characteristics of intelligence which manifest themselves in increasingly greater degree with increasing maturity.

One of these characteristics is the ability to center one's attention on a particular task or problem until success is achieved or proves to be impossible. Another is the ability to analyze and discover significant elements in the problem situation. A third is the ability to disregard insignificant elements and relationships. Still another is modifiability. The unintelligent person, using an unprofitable method, keeps on doing a thing in the same way over and over again, while the intelligent person in the same situation discovers a more economical way of accomplishing the same end. Observation of this characteristic type of behavior has sometimes caused intelligence to be defined as the capacity to learn. The capacity to learn is, indeed, an important factor, but at the higher levels of maturity the most important characteristic of intelligence is the ability to utilize abstract ideas. The intelligent individual is capable of utilizing ideas obtained from previous experiences even in the complete absence of the physical facts of that experience.

As one watches a group of persons of about the same age and experience solving mechanical puzzles, it will soon be evident that some fix their attention very definitely on the problem itself and continue to do so over relatively long periods of time. Others soon find their attention distracted, and begin to respond to things which have no bearing upon the problem at all. This indicates, as characteristic of intelligence, not only the fixing of attention upon a problem, but also the ability to disregard non-pertinent elements in the whole situation.

It will also be observed that some continue doing the same thing over and over again with a sort of random manipulation of the parts of the puzzle. Eventually they may stumble on the solution, in which case they will probably be surprised at the results. On the other hand, some, having tried a particular manipulation once or twice, discover that it is not successful, and thereafter, avoiding repetition of this useless procedure, seek to discover other manipulations. When they finally arrive at the solution, they have an understanding of the relationships involved and can reproduce the solution more or less at will. Finally, in this mechanical puzzle situation it will be evident that some persons are continually manipulating the parts, while others move them very little. When asked what they are doing, some, at least, will be able to describe some part of their behavior in terms of ideas. In fact, some will be found who have examined the puzzle and have laid it to one side to "think out" the solution without more manipulation of the different parts.

Of course, it should not be inferred from this illustration that mechanical puzzles are the only means of estimating intelligence. It is characteristic of all intelligence tests since the time of Binet that a complete test consists of a number of samples of different kinds of situations from the individual's life experiences. No reliable measurement or estimate of intelligence can be made on the basis of a person's reaction to a single situation.

Basis of Intelligent Behavior.—Intelligent behavior, like behavior in general, is dependent upon the inheritance of the individual. The structure most significantly involved seems to be the nervous system, particularly the cerebral hemispheres. It is not known in detail exactly which elements of brain structure distinguish the feeble-minded person from the normal or superior ones. Studies have been made which seem to show decided structural differences in the cerebral cortex of the low-grade feeble-

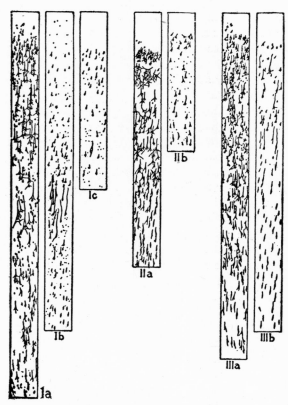

Figure 4. Structural Differences in the Cerebral Cortex of a Feeble-Minded Person Contrasted with the Corresponding Part of a Normal Individual
(Herbert Woodrow, *Brightness and Dullness in Children,* Philadelphia, J. B. Lippincott Co., 1919, Fig. 5, p. 76)

minded person when contrasted with the corresponding part of the cortex of the normal individual. Figure 4 shows the differences in the structures as shown in these studies. It should be noted, however, that as yet little is understood about the structural differences of the brain as related to differences in intelligence.

Environment, too, is important in the understanding of intelligent behavior, for only through environmental factors can behavior be made evident. The degree to which any behavior is intelligent can be judged only in terms of how well this behavior adjusts the individual to his own environment. Let this point be very clear. It is not the environment that makes one intelligent; rather it is the nature of one's responses to the environment that calls forth such degree of intelligence as one possesses.

By any kind of a measure the late Thomas A. Edison would be regarded as an intelligent man because of what he accomplished in the environment of a modern world. Suppose that, with exactly the same inherited structure, he had been born in feudal times. It is improbable that under feudal conditions of life he would have invented electric lights and the phonograph. But it is altogether probable that he would have been a superior individual in terms of the craftsmanship of his times and of the demands made upon his inventive genius by the environmental conditions of that day. Or suppose that Leonardo da Vinci had been born in the twentieth century. He might not have painted the particular pictures that have come from his brush and he might not have been interested in the particular kinds of mechanical inventions that have been credited to him. However, it would be safe to say that, whatever the time or the country in which he had found himself, he would most certainly have been regarded as an exceedingly intelligent man.

It should be clear, therefore, that intelligence is concerned with the manner of behavior rather than with the particular thing that is done. How intelligently one behaves, i.e., how successfully one adjusts to his environment, depends very largely upon the structural conditions of the bodily mechanism. The limiting capacities of bodily mechanism are presumably inherited; at least they depend upon inheritance as an important factor.

Intelligence as a *capacity to learn* or as an *aptitude for adjustment* must be carefully distinguished from *what one learns* or *which particular adjustment one makes*. Herein lies the reason for much of the confusion experienced by many persons in approaching the question of whether present-day intelligence tests really measure intelligence. Since the time of Binet and, more particularly, since the use of intelligence tests has become widespread, many have argued that these tests could not possibly be regarded as measures of intelligence in the generally accepted sense of the word. They have asked, for example: How could it possibly be true that the ability to repeat a sentence or to count thirteen pennies could be considered a measure of a child's intelligence? These critics have failed to recognize the difference between what one learns and the aptitude or capacity for learning. The only known way in which to determine a person's capacity to learn is to compare his behavior with the behavior of those who have had similar experiences.

Tests of Intelligence Are Really Aptitude Tests.—The term "intelligence test" is unfortunate. It implies to most persons something about which they are inclined to be "touchy." One ordinarily runs no risk of offense in telling a man that his boy is a bit below average in height. One may even flatter a woman by saying that she is a bit below average in weight, although the fashion in that respect seems to be changing. But suggest to either a man or a woman that his or her children are a bit below average in intelligence, and things will take a different turn.

Intelligence tests are tests of a rather undefined kind of aptitude. As most of them are now constructed, they attempt to measure aptitude for dealing with abstract language situations. Their results are of genuine significance when properly used. They are extremely useful for predicting success in situations that involve a high degree of general abstract language ability, but they must not be thought of as complete measures of all kinds of aptitudes. They are not to be regarded as of more than incidental value in the matter of predicting vocational aptitude and no properly trained psychologist would make such claims for them. It is only the partially trained or untrained "tester," whose enthusiasm regarding the use of these tests is probably his greatest professional vice, who will make these extravagant claims.

ADMINISTERING AND INTERPRETING INTELLIGENCE TESTS
REQUIRES MUCH TRAINING AND EXPERIENCE

Intelligence tests are made up of samples of problem situations. They are based upon the assumption that the capacity to learn can be measured by what one has learned, or that aptitude for adjustment can be determined by the adjustments which one can make in the test situation. But the responses of those tested must be properly evaluated. For example, there is nothing about the ability to count thirteen pennies that makes a child four years of age seem to have normal intelligence. The significance of such a performance lies in the fact that the average four-year-old child can do this, while most three-year-old children fail to do it. Stated in still another way, no measures employed in an intelligence test have any significance in themselves. Whatever significance they have comes entirely from a comparison of the responses of various persons who have been measured in the same test situation.

A further condition of the value of these tests as measures of intelligence must be made clear. Binet very early recognized that the problem situations to be included in a test should be those with which all the participants had had approximately equal experience. Every good intelligence test therefore includes only test situations which are drawn from experiences equally familiar to all who might be measured by the tests.

Interpreting Intelligence Test Scores.—Two concepts which are frequently employed in evaluating and interpreting the results of intelligence tests are "mental age" and "intelligence quotient." Considerable confusion often arises from the use of these terms, due apparently to lack of understanding of the meaning and limitations of each.

By mental age is meant the degree of maturity of mental function that is evidenced by the person tested. It is expressed numerically as the average of the ages of all those who have a similar degree of mental maturity. It indicates *how much* the individual has matured mentally, but in itself it furnishes no information at all as to *how rapidly* the growth is taking place. Thus, to say that a person has a mental age of eight years does not indicate whether the person is a very bright child of five or a feeble-minded adult.

The intelligence quotient (I.Q.), on the other hand, is a device for indicating *how rapidly* the individual is maturing mentally, but in itself it does not indicate *how much* growth has already occurred. It is obtained by dividing the mental age by the chronological age and multiplying by 100 to avoid dealing with a decimal fraction. It should not be thought of as a kind of percentage, since the units of mental age are not constant for the entire chronological range of development. The intelligence quotient obtained for a person whose mental age and chronological age are the same would, of course, be 100, and since such is the case with the average person, an I.Q. of 100 is said to be average. The same result is obtained if the intelligence quotients of a very large number of randomly selected persons are averaged. It is customary to interpret intelligence quotients approximately as:

I.Q. below 20............................ Idiots
I.Q. from 20–50.......................... Imbeciles
I.Q. from 50–70.......................... Morons
I.Q. from 70–80.......................... Borderline deficiency
I.Q. from 80–90.......................... Dull
I.Q. from 90–110......................... Normal
I.Q. from 110–120........................ Superior
I.Q. from 120–140........................ Very superior
I.Q. from 140 & above.................... "Near" genius or genius

It should not be imagined, however, that sharply defined dividing lines distinguish one classification from another. The divisions are merely means of convenient definition that correspond to common-sense observations.

Mental maturity is reached relatively early in life, probably by middle adolescence for the average person. Hence, the concept of the intelligence quotient *loses its meaning* if applied to persons who have gone beyond the point where one's mental age reaches its maximum. In order to distinguish degrees of mental level in those older than the high school age, it is therefore necessary to employ other devices.

Among such devices, the one most frequently used is the percentile scale. Percentile norms are computed from large groups of scores by determining which scores in the group are equalled or surpassed by each percentile point from 1 to 99. Thus, a per-

CHILDREN'S DRAWINGS

Can you tell how old these four children are mentally? All have intelligence quotients that are near average. After you have made your estimates, turn to the footnote on page 166. (From Florence Goodenough's *Measurement of Intelligence by Drawings*. Copyright 1926 by World Book Co., Yonkers-on-Hudson, New York.)

centile score of 25, 50, or 80 would indicate that the person having such a score was as good or better than 25, 50, or 80 per cent, respectively, of the group used for determining the norm.

Most tests of intelligence commonly employed by college personnel departments use scores which are reported in terms of percentiles. The American Council Psychological Examination bases its percentile scores upon the scores of a large number of college freshmen from several types of colleges in different parts of the United States. Suppose, then, that a certain freshman makes a percentile score of 25 on this test. Just what does such a score mean? Principally, it means that this person has made a score as good as 25 per cent of the large test group of heterogeneous college freshmen.

The question is then frequently asked: What degree of intelligence would such a percentile score represent, if expressed in terms of I.Q.? In the light of the foregoing discussion, it will be seen that there is no satisfactory answer to this question, since college freshmen have gone beyond the age where the intelligence quotient is significant. School progress is a highly selective process. The further the group proceeds through the grades and classes, the greater is the likelihood that those with lower levels of mental ability will drop out. As a result, each succeeding higher level of school is attended by an increasingly select group. It is at present impossible to determine which level of the original unselected group that began school in the first elementary grade is represented by the average at the college freshman level. But it must be apparent that the average college freshman is much above the middle level of the general population. All college freshmen are graduates of high school before the selective process of college entrance begins. Probably persons who are very much below the average of intelligence of the whole population do not graduate from high school. Hence the college freshman with a 25 percentile score on the college entrance test is undoubtedly above the general population average.

Relationship of Intelligence to Anatomical and Physiological Traits.—There is a common but false belief that persons who are particularly well endowed with intelligence are for that reason especially prone to have poor health or to be lacking in good looks, or to have certain traits that are not socially desirable. This has probably grown out of the wishful thinking of persons who are not particularly gifted with intelligence. They try to compensate for their feeling of deficiency by pointing out that they are not socially lacking in other traits. Such a belief has no justification in terms of the evidence now available.

Terman and his assistants made a very intensive study of a number of traits of about a thousand children with very superior intellects. The findings show that, as a group, these children were also distinctly better than average in such traits as health, freedom from physical defects, height, and weight.[1] Similar results have been shown by others who have made special studies of gifted children.

On the other hand, many students and observers of feeble-minded children have been impressed by the socially undesirable traits that appear in such a group. Feeble-minded children, as a group, are below the average of normal children in height and weight. They are distinctly below the average in social development. Compared with groups of near-average individuals, these feeble-minded persons are much more frequently ill, and physical defects are decidedly more numerous among them. In fact, among the very low-grade feeble-minded, marked physical abnormalities are very common.

Despite these observations, it is not at all safe to depend upon physical traits as indicators of intelligence. A high forehead is still wrongly believed to be indicative of a high degree of intelligence. Instead, it may be only an indication of rickets in childhood. In the same way the size of the head and the distance between the eyes are only fanciful indications of the degree of intelligence. One group of idiots is called *macrocephalic*. Literally, this means giant-headed idiots. At the other extreme are

---

[1] L. M. Terman, *et al., Genetic Studies of Genius,* Vol. 1, Stanford Univ. Press, 1925. Drawings on page 164.

Drawing	M.A.	C.A.	I.Q.	Sex
A	5-0	5-4	94	Girl
B	7-3	7-4	99	Boy
C	9-9	9-7	103	Boy
D	13-3	12-9	104	Boy

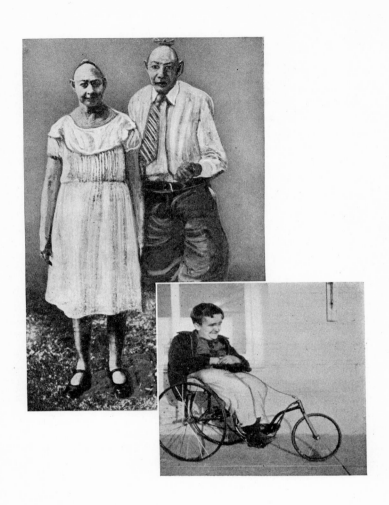

TWO TYPES OF MENTAL DEFECTIVES

How much does extreme head size indicate the level of intelligence?

the "pin heads," the *microcephalic* idiots. Numerous studies have been made of the weight of the brains of individuals whose intelligence in life has been fairly well known. Very large brains, as well as very small ones, have been possessed by individuals of almost every level of intelligence.

Similarly numerous studies have been made to discover the relationship between general physical appearance and intelligence. In some cases the observations were made of the persons themselves, while in other cases photographs were used. In no case has it been shown that even the most experienced judges of intelligence are able to judge with any accuracy either high or low intelligence. But when these same persons have been observed *while they were behaving,* somewhat better results have been obtained. In other words, when the behavior itself is examined, more reliable evidence of intelligence is obtained than is the case when only the anatomical features are employed as a basis of judgment.

Relationship of Intelligence to Other Behavior Traits.—A problem that is of particular interest to social workers is the relationship of intelligence to delinquency. A mass of evidence has been accumulated over a period of years, but not all of it has been well interpreted. It is doubtless true that the average intelligence of juvenile delinquents is below that of the average of school children of the same age. However, one may easily be misled by such evidence. Many investigators have interpreted their data to imply that there is a special tendency for the individual of low-grade intelligence to be antisocial. But it does not necessarily follow that the facts establish a close cause and effect relationship. Certainly, there are large numbers of children of low intelligence who do not show antisocial behavior, while large numbers of intellectually superior children are antisocial.

Children of low intelligence are most frequently found in homes of the lower social and economic levels, and in such cases the low intelligence is in large part due to the inheritance of a low general aptitude level. The relatively poor social and economic features of their environment might also be expected to be re-

flected in their somewhat greater tendency toward antisocial
behavior. Of course, this antisocial tendency does not extend to
all individuals, either parents or children, nor is it confined to the
lower ranges of intelligence.

Another significant factor in antisocial behavior can be observed in the schools. Pupils who are intellectual misfits tend to
become antisocial. School children of low intelligence are unable
to meet the demands made upon them, and the school and social
pressures brought to bear upon such pupils are often important
causes of the beginnings of antisocial behavior.

In another way, intelligence has an interesting relationship to
other aspects of behavior. Since socially desirable traits tend to
be positively related to each other, one might reasonably expect
that financial, social, school, and political attainments would
most frequently be found in those of greatest intelligence. As a
matter of fact, several studies of both children and adults confirm this expectation. Thus Terman's [2] study clearly showed the
superiority in school attainment and social adjustments of a
group of intellectually superior children. It seems to be a case
of "to him that hath shall be given, and from him that hath not
shall be taken away even that which he seemeth to have."

How Does Intelligence Change During the Span of Life?—
At birth the infant can make very few adjustments to his environment. Within a few days after birth he learns to cry to be picked
up. By the time he is half a year old he is able to reach for objects.
One of Watson's [3] experiments with such an infant shows a clear
case of adjustment. The child was seated in his mother's lap. A
lighted candle was held within reach. The child made several efforts to reach and grasp the candle flame. The experimenter took
care that the child was not burned, but he was allowed to get his
hand uncomfortably hot. When the candle was presented again,
the child hesitated, then made a movement that was distinctly
different from the previous reaching and grasping. This new
movement was decidedly in the nature of a slapping motion.

    [2] *Ibid.*
    [3] J. B. Watson, *Psychology from the Standpoint of a Behaviorist,* Philadelphia, J. B.
Lippincott Co., 1924, p. 299.

Another illustration involves a child of about thirteen months of age. A bright new yellow pencil was held before him. He grasped and held it in his right hand. Another pencil was presented. He first reached for this one with his right hand while still holding the first pencil with that hand. Then he transferred the pencil to the left hand and reached for the second with the right. When a third pencil was offered, after a slight hesitation he transferred the first to his mouth, the second to his left hand, and reached for the third with his right hand. He could not go beyond holding three pencils at a time. When a fourth was offered, he dropped the one in the left hand, transferred the third one to that hand and took the new one in the right. This is clear evidence of adjustment to a fairly complex situation.

It would be interesting to trace the increasing ability to make such adjustments throughout later ages by the use of similar illustrations. However, it is only necessary to watch children of different stages of development to see that this ability gradually increases to the point where the child can adapt its responses to complex life situations. It will also be helpful to refer to the discussion of maturity in the preceding chapter.

Another characteristic of increasing ability to behave intelligently is seen in children's drawings, when artistic value is not involved.[4] Here the examiner is dealing with the ability to discover pertinent elements in a situation and the relationships between them. When a three-year-old child is given a piece of paper and a pencil and is asked to draw a man, the result is likely to be little more than a circle with some marks in it. When questioned, the child replies that the circle is the man's head and the marks in it are eyes. At a little later age the child spontaneously adds arms and legs directly to this circle representing the head. A hat may be included, often above but not on the head. Later the body is drawn, and still later the neck is represented. All this has been in terms of a front view. Finally, the profile drawings begin to appear, although at first front views and profile elements are often found in the same drawing.

---

[4] F. Goodenough, *Measurement of Intelligence by Drawings*, Yonkers-on-Hudson, World Book Co., 1926.

These boys are of the same chronological age but differ widely in their intelligence quotients.

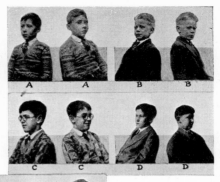

Examine the pictures carefully and rank the twelve boys pictured on this page in order of your judgment of their intelligence.

Then turn to the footnote on page 179. (By permission, from Paul Popenoe, *The Child's Heredity,* Williams & Wilkins Co., Baltimore, Md.)

Drawing a house shows similar stages of growth. At first it is little more than a rectangle. When doors and windows are added, they are frequently put on the side of the house so that they stick out from what adults take to be a side view. Only much later does the child discover the relationship involved in representing the roof and the gabled ends. Not infrequently two gabled ends are shown on opposite sides of the building. Finally, there is a fairly complete representation of the respective elements of the house, with their proper relationship indicated. This increasing insight or ability to perceive relationships and specific elements is one of the characteristics of the increase in the general aptitude called intelligence. It is manifested in terms of a great variety of adjustments and continues to increase to the maximum level of each individual's capacity. It is this increased ability to recognize relationships and to adjust to complexities that is the chief characteristic of the change in intelligence as the child matures. Later in life this tendency is reversed, resulting in the inflexibility of old age.

Relationship Between Rate and Final Level of Intelligence. —Dvorak [5] and others have demonstrated an interesting fact concerning the relationship of rate of growth of intelligence and the time in life when the high point in the curve is reached. Dvorak's study shows that those with an I.Q. at or near normal have a growth curve that follows the one represented by the middle line in Figure 5. The I.Q. remains approximately constant with increased age up to middle adolescence.

On the other hand, for persons with an I.Q. distinctly below normal, the growth curve becomes progressively flatter, and the final high point is reached earlier in life than for the normal individual. This is represented in Figure 5 by the lower line. The I.Q. of the inferior individual tends to decrease as he grows older.

For those individuals who are distinctly superior, the curve also becomes flatter as age increases; but this increasing flatness

---

[5] A. Dvorak, "Relation of I.Q. to the Prognosis of Special Class Pupils," *School and Society*, June 21, 1924, Vol. XIX, No. 495.

appears at a slower rate, and the final high point is reached at a later age. This is represented by the upper line in Figure 5. Here the I.Q. tends to increase with increasing age. Such individuals are not only brighter than normal, they mature more rapidly; and they actually continue to grow for a longer period

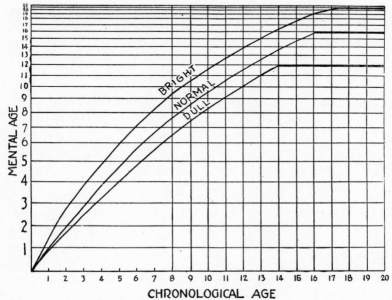

Figure 5. Progress of Mental Maturity at Three Levels of Intelligence

of time. A dull individual, on the other hand, is not only duller than the average, but seems to get duller as he gets older and reaches his maximum of intelligence relatively early in life.

The average person, considering his mental endowment as a whole, reaches approximately full capacity between the ages of fourteen and sixteen. Terman [6] in his revision of the Binet-Simon test says that sixteen is the age of mental maturity, while Pintner [7] believes it to be fourteen. Thorndike,[8] on the other

[6] L. Terman, *Measurement of Intelligence,* Boston, Houghton Mifflin Co., 1916.
[7] Rudolph Pintner, *Intelligence Testing,* New York, Henry Holt & Co.. 1931.
[8] E. L. Thorndike, *Adult Learning,* New York, The Macmillan Co., 1928, Ch. XI.

hand, has evidence to show that intelligence probably continues to increase until the middle or late twenties. He suggests, however, that the increase from the middle of adolescence until maturity is at such a very slow rate that it cannot readily be measured by intelligence tests now available.

Can One's Intelligence Be Changed?—Such questions as the following are often asked, particularly about children whose I.Q.'s are below normal: "Will the child outgrow this dullness?" "Can anything be done that will increase the child's capacity for intelligent behavior?" The first of these questions has already been answered in the negative. In fact, the tendency seems to be in the opposite direction, though the decrease may not, on the average, be great.

Around the second question has raged a storm of controversy. The answer, based on several extended experiments, seems also to be in the negative, at least as far as large increases are concerned. Itard, long ago, sought to increase the capacity of the Wild Boy of Aveyron. This boy was found roaming wild in the forest and was taken by Itard into his own home. There, for several years, Itard gave him every attention and sought to show that his uncouth habits and apparent low mental capacity could be changed to a marked degree. Finally, however, he was forced to conclude that it could not be done, and that the boy was destined to remain an idiot all his life.

Society and social attitudes prevent the carrying out of experiments that would conclusively answer this question, but approximations have been attempted by Freeman [9] and others. Children who were placed for adoption were measured by intelligence tests before adoption and after having lived in the foster home for several years. The assumption is that homes that are open to the adoption of children provide an environment somewhat better, on the average, than do the homes from which these children come. In the case of children placed when very young there is

---

[9] F. N. Freeman, "The Influence of Environment on the Intelligence, School Achievement, and Conduct of Foster Children," *27th Yearbook of National Society for the Study of Education,* Part I, pp. 103–218. Summary, p. 209.

some evidence of an increase in I.Q. But this increase is not large and does not appear to a noticeable degree if adoption takes place after the age of about ten years. *In no case* was there any evidence of feeble-minded children becoming normal, or of a normal child becoming distinctly superior.

It would not be fitting to end this discussion of intelligence without mentioning a point of view emphasized several years ago. Bagley [10] suggested that growth of intelligence ought to be regarded as having two dimensions. It might increase both vertically and horizontally. By the vertical development he seems to mean about whatever is measured by present-day intelligence tests. By horizontal growth he means the almost limitless amount of knowledge and number of skills and adjustments that are possible at each successive level of vertical growth.

Consider the case of a person with a mental age of eight years. He has the capacity to learn and adjust which is common to the normal eight-year-old. He cannot learn certain things that the normal ten- or twelve-year-old child can learn, nor can he make some of the adjustments of behavior characteristic of the person who is older mentally. However, there are many possibilities for new adjustments at the *eight-year* level. His development of the vertical type may stop at the mental age of eight years, but there are countless adjustments that normal eight-year-old children *can make* that many never have an opportunity to make at that age. If they do make them, it is often at a later age. This point of view seems sound enough and has the great advantage of giving hope of increased and enriched living to every person whatever his mental level may be.

An Outline Summary

1. The nature of intelligence.
    A. Intelligence is a specific aspect of the general problem of maturation of behavior.
    B. Intelligence is an abstraction; it does not exist as a concrete thing.

[10] W. C. Bagley, *Determinism in Education*, Baltimore, Warwick & York, 1925, Ch. 1.

    C. Intelligence is best regarded as a generalized aptitude for adaptation to new situations in terms of previous experience.

    D. Some important characteristics of intelligent behavior:
- (a) Ability to learn from experience.
- (b) Ability to keep a problem in mind.
- (c) Ability to employ a variety of approaches in solving a problem.
- (d) Ability to disregard unimportant and irrelevant details in solving a problem.
- (e) Ability to deal with abstract ideas.

2. The neurological basis of intelligence.

    A. Is not well known but presumably depends upon complex structural characteristics of the cerebral cortex.

3. Tests of intelligence.

    A. Have grown out of attempts of psychologists to obtain quantitative measures of human adaptability.

    B. Are really measures of what an individual has achieved as compared with what others have achieved in situations where previous experience with the test items is closely similar.

    C. Comparison with others is the basis of all interpretations of intelligence test scores:
- (a) Mental age is the measure of an individual's mental maturity expressed as the average of the chronological ages of those who have developed to an equal degree.
- (b) Intelligence quotients compare the rate of individual mental growth with that of the average.
- (c) Percentile scores express the relative degree of mental growth in terms of the per cent of a large group who have scores which the individual equals or surpasses.

4. Intelligence as related to other traits.

    A. Anatomical traits:
- (a) Show too little significant relationship to intelligence to permit an estimate of intelligence from a knowledge of such traits.

(b) Some studies show a small but positive relationship between bodily development and the development of intelligence.

B. Behavior traits:

(a) Mental development shows a small positive relationship to other socially desirable behavior traits.

5. The growth curve of intelligence.

A. Rate of growth:

(a) The rate of individual growth decreases with advancing age.

(b) Compared to general averages of rate of growth, the individual's rate tends to remain constant, i.e., the dull stay dull and the bright remain bright.

(c) The final level of mental growth is inversely proportional to the rate of growth.

(d) Only extreme changes in bodily structure or in environment will produce even slight changes in the mental growth curve.

Problems for Further Thought

1. A twelve-year-old boy is in the elementary school. He is given an intelligence test from which it is determined that his mental age is ten years. In discussing this matter with the parent, which of the following lines of reasoning is justifiable? (a) The boy is feeble-minded. (b) He is dull enough to make it probable that he will have difficulty in doing school work of the usual kind at the usual rate. (c) He has an intelligence quotient of 120 and this would indicate that he should receive extra promotion. (d) He should be trained to be either a barber or an auto-mechanic. (e) He should be taken from school entirely.

In each case explain why the implied interpretation of intelligence test scores is sound or why it is not.

2. In a novel by the name of *Job,* written by Roth a few years ago, one of the characters is a feeble-minded boy who is left in Poland by the family when the others emigrated to the United States. Several years later he turns up in New York as a talented, intelligent individual. Indicate the reasons why such a plot is or is not within the realm of probability.

3. Mary is six years old this month. An intelligence test indicates that her I.Q. is 100. What will be the most probable mental age of Mary when she is ten years old?

4. Harry has an I.Q. of 137 obtained from reliable intelligence testing. He is now fourteen years old. Approximately how much longer can he be expected to continue to grow mentally? Would the answer be the same if the intelligence quotient were 63? What is the basis for your answer?

5. Would it be reasonable to expect that college students who were very deficient in reading ability would increase their intelligence test scores significantly by greatly improving their reading ability? Explain why or why not. If the answer is in the affirmative, would such an improvement in intelligence test score indicate a genuine increase in abstract intelligence or would it merely mean that the test was showing more truly the intelligence which was there all the time? Why?

6. In the following table are given the *averages* of the raw scores made on the Army Alpha tests by persons who reported the corresponding occupations in civil life.

40– 49	Farmer—teamster
50– 59	Tailor—barber—baker—bricklayer
60– 69	Machinist—blacksmith—auto-mechanic
70– 79	Receiving clerk—stockkeeper—shipping clerk
80– 89	Electrician—telegrapher
90– 99	Railroad clerk—filing clerk
100–109	Bookkeeper—nurse
110–119	Draftsman—accountant—civil engineer

This list is very incomplete and it should be remembered that these represent only the averages of scores for these occupational groups. Within each group there would be a wide variation.

How much justification was there for the following procedure? A veterans' rehabilitation adviser looked up an ex-soldier's Army Alpha score and found it to be 65, and said to the applicant, "All right, in which would you prefer training, machine shop practice, blacksmithing, or as an auto mechanic?" Explain why you think this was or was not a proper use of an intelligence test score.

7. In the American Council Psychological Examination there is one section which involves an artificial language. In view of the emphasis upon the importance of having all intelligence test items

sample experiences which are reasonably common to those tested, what is the justification for this material? Would zero or near zero experience be a basis for equal experience?

SUGGESTED READINGS

FREEMAN, F. N. Mental Tests. Their History, Principles, and Applications. Boston, Houghton Mifflin Co., 1926. Ch. II, "Early Experimentation with Tests," pp. 32–57; Ch. XIII, "The Bearing of Mental Tests upon Mental Growth," pp. 327–364.

GATES, A. I. Psychology for Students of Education. Rev. ed., New York, The Macmillan Co., 1930. Ch. XV, "Individual Differences in Intelligence," pp. 487–527.

MURPHY, GARDNER. General Psychology. New York, Harper & Bros., 1933. Ch. XXI, "Intelligence Tests," pp. 430–448.

PINTNER, RUDOLPH. Intelligence Testing. Rev. ed., New York, Henry Holt & Co., 1931. Part I, Chs. I-IV, "Historical and Theoretical."

TERMAN, L. M. The Measurement of Intelligence. Boston, Houghton Mifflin Co., 1916. Ch. II, "Description of the Binet-Simon Method," pp. 36–50.

WIGGAM, A. E. Exploring Your Mind with the Psychologists. New York, Bobbs-Merrill Co., 1928. Ch. X, "How Smart Are Your Children?" by L. M. Terman, pp. 215–235; Ch. XI, "The Psychologist Looks at the Bright Child," by L. M. Terman, pp. 239–272; Ch. XII, "Have You a Future Genius in Your Home?" by Elizabeth Cox, pp. 275–300.

WOODWORTH, R. S. Psychology. 3rd ed., New York, Henry Holt & Co., 1934. Ch. IV, "Intelligence," pp. 49–86.

KEY TO INTELLIGENCE QUOTIENTS OF THE BOYS PICTURED ON PAGE 171

A....	95	C....	127	E....	80	G....	121	I....	137	K....	133
B....	111	D....	92	F....	118	H....	105	J....	116	L....	100

Chapter 9

WHAT IS THE EFFECT OF EXPERIENCE UPON BEHAVIOR?

A Simple Instance of Learning.—A favorite occupation of a certain three-year-old boy was digging earthworms from the garden. He had no hesitation about picking them up, handling them, or putting them in his pocket. A year later he seemed very reluctant to touch them. It took some urging and demonstration to get him even to make the attempt. Then he cautiously picked one up only to drop it and jump back when it wriggled.

What had happened during the interval? Could it be possible that the change was due to increased maturity? A comparison of the play activities of this boy during the intervening year with the activities before that time suggests a much more satisfactory explanation. All his play with earthworms before his third year had been solitary. During the intervening year he had been playing with other children who screamed and ran at the sight of an earthworm. The best explanation, therefore, seems to be in terms of this intervening experience with the general situation of which the earthworms had constituted one important part. In other words, he had learned.

What Is Learning?—The incident described above is commonly said to be an evidence of learning. Learning usually designates a kind of modification of a response in which the change is brought about through the influence of the response itself upon the organism.

In line with the general point of view of this book, such changes in behavior must presumably depend upon corresponding changes in the structure of the total organism. Psychologists are in fair agreement that some organic changes probably do take place in learning and that these changes are probably to be found in the central nervous system, but up to the present time there is very little agreement as to the nature of such changes. A discussion of the many points of view would be beside the point here. A much more satisfactory procedure for present purposes is to accept tentatively the general hypothesis of a structural change as basic to behavior changes and to turn to the problem of how learning can be controlled.

This does not imply that the problem of the organic basis of learning is unimportant. It simply means that for the beginning student of psychology such a problem ranks in importance below those concerned with controlling the conditions which produce the desired learned modifications.

Methods of Describing Conditions of Learning

During the course of time, several methods have been devised for describing the conditions under which learning takes place. Three of these will be discussed here because each emphasizes an important characteristic of the learning process. The first places emphasis upon the feeling tone within the learner during learning. The second emphasizes the relationship between stimuli from the environment and the learned reaction. The third has its greatest importance in emphasizing the rôle of organization of the whole learning process. If these points are kept in mind, it will be evident that there is no essential conflict between these descriptions of the learning process.

Thorndike's Laws of Learning.—The first of these descriptions of the conditions of learning was formulated chiefly by Thorndike and has had a very widespread acceptance in educational circles. Thorndike originally experimented with cats in puzzle boxes, and on the basis of these experiments formulated the now famous laws of readiness, use, and effect. Because they involve such matter-of-fact terms and are so readily interpreted, they have had widespread acceptance among non-psychologically trained educators. They were and still are extremely useful and adaptable rules-of-thumb by which the learning process in schools and elsewhere could be guided. They are usually stated in some such manner as the following.

THE LAW OF READINESS. When an organism is ready to act, for it to do so is satisfying, and for it not to do so is annoying. When an organism is not ready to act, for it to do so is annoying, and for it not to do so is satisfying. This principle has been criticized freely and can probably be defended by the scientist only in a very general way. It should be emphasized, however, that the criticisms lose much of their force when this law is roughly related to those conscious experiences which might be called states of readiness. It still remains a simple statement of fact that when a person is ready to learn, he will learn. It urges the importance of "striking while the iron is hot." It says nothing about heating the iron.

THE LAW OF USE. Other things being equal, that connection (between stimulus and response) is most firmly fixed which is exercised the most. This is sometimes stated in the converse form in the law of disuse as follows: Other things being equal, that connection (already established) which is not exercised tends to disappear or lose its effectiveness. A corollary of the law of use is the law of frequency, usually stated as: Other things being equal, that connection is most firmly fixed which is most frequently exercised. In a similar manner, the law of recency states that: Other things being equal, that connection is most firmly fixed which has been most recently exercised. These statements taken together are frequently referred to as the law of exercise. The most significant criticism of this general law is that it seems to be true only in a limited degree. Practice does not always make perfect. In fact, unless the practice involves more than mere repetition, it apparently is not a very significant factor in learning. Thorndike's recent writings indicate that he places relatively little importance upon this principle.

THE LAW OF EFFECT. This may be stated as follows: Those responses which result in a painful or annoying state tend to be eliminated or made weaker. Those connections which result in a pleasant or satisfying state tend to be retained and made stronger.

These general statements are important and in a rough way do seem to be essentially true in terms of the layman's uncritical acceptance of the words or phrases descriptive of his behavior. It is possible to point out some rather significant objections and exceptions to these laws. Considerable experimental work has been done, some of which seems to verify one or more of these laws. On the other hand, other experimental work very definitely puts some objections in the way of their acceptance as universal statements of fact.

The chief objection to using these general statements of observed fact lies in the difficulty of controlling the states of satisfaction and annoyance as these terms are used by the non-psychologically trained layman. What may be a pleasure-provoking situation at one time or for one person may provoke annoyance at another time or for someone else. In other words, it is necessary to go beyond the situation itself in order to understand the "why" and "when" of the conscious states of pleasantness and annoyance.

Conditioned Response Method of Describing Learning.— At about the time that Thorndike was experimenting with his cats in puzzle boxes, a Russian physiologist, Pavlov, was studying glandular reactions in dogs. He was measuring the amount of the salivary response to different substances placed in the mouth when he noticed that the sight and smell of food and certain stimuli other than the presence of a substance in the mouth would produce a flow of saliva. Upon investigation he found that this flow could be produced by almost any conceivable stimulus under certain experimental conditions. He therefore called a response produced by any other than the original stimuli a "conditional response" to distinguish it from the response inherently made by the animal. Such responses are now generally called "conditioned responses."

The elements essential for the establishment of a conditioned response can be well illustrated by one of Pavlov's early experiments. A buzzer was sounded simultaneously with the putting of food into the dog's mouth. This double stimulation was repeated several times. Then the buzzer was sounded without the food, and there followed an intense salivary response. Further experimentation revealed a wide variety of stimuli that could be used in place of the buzzer. In fact, it has been found justifiable to generalize to the extent that any response which the individual is capable of making may be attached (conditioned) to any stimulus to which he is sensitive.[1]

This method of conditioning has been widely applied in experimental studies of human beings. Mateer was one of the early experimenters to use this method with young children. Feeding chocolate was the original stimulus in her experiment. Opening of the mouth for the chocolate was the response studied. Ten seconds before the chocolate was given a blindfold was slipped down over the eyes. After several repetitions of this double stimulation the children opened their mouths as soon as the blindfolds were applied. In other words, the application of the blindfold was "conditioned" to become a stimulus for a response which it could not previously call out. Infants, children of all ages, and adults have many conditioned responses. For example, if the reader has not eaten for several hours, the very mention of food may call out a profuse flow of saliva. It is common to speak of one's mouth "watering" at the thought of a particularly well-liked delicacy.

It must not be thought that all conditioned responses primarily involve glandular behavior. Both simple and complex motor responses may be attached to new stimuli by this method. Ideational learning may also be explained as conditioning. This is illustrated by the customary learning of a simple number combination in school. The verbal response *four* is variously obtained from the pupil to the situation of two objects and two more objects *plus* the sound of the teacher saying "four." When this has been repeated a number of times, the response "four" to the non-verbal part of the stimulating situation is established. Emo-

---

[1] Florence Mateer, *Child Behavior,* Boston, Richard G. Badger, 1918.

tional responses are also readily conditioned. Recall Watson's experiment with the fear responses of the boy named Peter. As was pointed out in the discussion of emotions, what is feared by adults is largely the result of learning and can be accounted for in terms of conditioning where the facts about the individual's previous experience are known.

Conditioned response experiments have been conducted with infants as young as three months of age.[2] The principle seems to hold true for all kinds of learning and for human beings of all ages as well as all levels of animal life, from the one-celled creatures to apes and man. Conditioning does not explain what goes on in the nervous system, but it does describe the conditions under which learning takes place without the use of pleasure and pain or satisfaction and annoyance. All that is necessary for a description of the conditions of learning by this principle is to note the responses which the individual makes, the stimuli which call out the response, and the means at hand to substitute another stimulus for the one originally employed. Many present-day psychologists favor this description because of this greater objectivity.

Gestalt Method of Describing Learning.—First of all it will be necessary to state briefly ways in which the Gestalt school of psychology differs from other schools. In attempting to describe a pattern of behavior, most other schools of psychologists would analyze it into a series of simpler responses and would think of the whole pattern as made up of the sum or the serial arrangement of the smaller units. The food-getting behavior of the very young infant could aptly be described as a series or chain of reflexes. It is believed by many psychogists that this is true of most human behavior. They admit that up to the present most of the complex behavior patterns have not yielded entirely to analysis. But still more important is the fact that, after behavior has been analyzed and broken up into its smaller units, there still seems to be something left that defies analysis. Thus, when a complex motor act, such as playing the piano or peeling and eat-

---

[2] H. E. Jones, "The Retention of Conditioned Emotional Responses in Infancy," *Pedagogical Seminary and Journal of Genetic Psychology,* December, 1930, 37:485–498.

ing an apple, is analyzed into a series of reflexes, there is still no picture of the total behavior pattern.

The Gestalt psychologist insists that the whole behavior pattern is more than the sum of the reflexes and habits and that the very *wholeness* or *patternness* is itself an important element that must be taken into consideration for a complete description of the behavior. The Gestalt psychologist is concerned with discovering the conditions under which these several unitary acts, all of which are already familiar to the individual, are brought together in the relationships necessary to make a new whole act. Köhler,[3] one of the leaders of this school of psychology, carried out some extensive experimentation with apes. Many of these experiments have been repeated by Alpert,[4] using pre-school and kindergarten children as the subjects, with results for human beings that are startingly like those obtained by Köhler with his apes.

The Gestaltists object, too, to the usual maze experiments of other psychologists. They insist that such experimental set-ups do not permit the subject of the experiment to employ his capacity to discover relationships. They insist that a learning experiment should be made in such a manner that it will enable the subject to utilize the significant parts of the situation in order to gain an insight into the whole of it. They contend that this gaining of insight is the chief element of learning. It might even be permissible to use the word "understanding" in place of insight, since gaining an insight means essentially understanding the relationships within a stimulating situation as a whole in terms of the previous experience of the learner. When such insight is gained, the solution of a problem is essentially complete.

In the work of Alpert, the usual situation consisted of some variation of the following conditions: A child is separated from some familiar and favorite toy. The only means of obtaining the toy is through some roundabout method. The object of the experiment is to determine whether the child can see the necessary

---

[3] W. Köhler, *The Mentality of Apes,* New York, Harcourt, Brace & Co., 1925.
[4] A. Alpert, *The Solving of Problem Situations by Pre-School Children,* New York, Teachers College, Columbia University, 1928.

relationships of the familiar objects which are conveniently placed nearby.

In one experiment, a three-year-old girl was placed in a play pen that was too high for her to scale. She could reach between the upright bars but could not crawl between them. A favorite toy was placed on the floor just beyond reach. Inside the pen was placed a light bamboo stick with which the child was already familiar as a general plaything, although it had not previously been used as a tool for securing objects. The experimenter then withdrew to a point where she could watch, but she did not assist the child in her attempts to secure the toy. At first the child tried to secure it by reaching. When this failed, she called upon the experimenter and even showed some emotional responses when she was ignored. Then she began to play with the stick, but at first without using it as a tool for getting the toy. Suddenly— and the suddenness is apparent in many Gestalt experiments— she seemed to understand the relationship between the stick and the toy and forthwith promptly pulled the toy to her with the stick.

Not every instance of insight results in complete success. In fact, in many instances the relationships discovered may not be pertinent to the solution. Sometimes these insights lead to solutions that are correct enough but impossible to carry out. The satisfactory solution must be one that is both correct and possible of execution. It is significant to note that no new motor acts of a unitary kind need be involved. The several acts involved in the solution of a problem are often already familiar. The learning consists of gaining an insight into the total situation and of putting the individual parts of the whole into their correct functional relationship.

The Gestaltists insist—and in this they are joined by some other psychologists—that every instance of learning is the result of activity on the part of the learner. The essential characteristic of this learning activity is the putting together of the parts. It might be better described by saying that it consists of "seeing together," or perceiving the relationship between the several parts of the whole situation. Mere frequency of repetition is of no particular significance to the Gestaltist. The new situation must take on meaning as it is learned. In the absence of meaning, learning is very difficult and, indeed, may be of a very limited kind and usefulness. It is quite possible that there is no learning at all in the absence of the development of some kind of meaning. In memorizing a list of nonsense syllables which have been so constructed as to prevent their having any recognized meaning, the act of learning may consist of discovering or inventing meaning in terms of rhythms, cadences, and sequences.

The following illustration is drawn from a schoolroom task of the elementary grades and is an excellent example of the suddenness and permanence of learning that comes when the problem situation is so arranged, and its elements so emphasized, that the learner has an opportunity to discover the meaningful relationships.

A boy in the fourth grade was having difficulty in memorizing his number combinations in the order from one to ten. Each new table seemed to be more difficult than the preceding one, and the boy, possibly feeling very sorry for himself, was complaining bitterly about the very hard number combinations in the tables of nines and tens. More by way of encouragement than anything else, his father wrote out the table of tens in irregular order, and pointing to it asked the boy: "Do you see anything interesting or unusual about this table?" After the boy had made several irrelevant comments, the father pointed to the zeros in the column of products. An expression of delight at the discovery of this relationship revealed itself in the boy's face as he exclaimed: "They all end in zeros." He was then asked if he could see anything else that was interesting. This time without any further assistance he discovered the relationship between the first digit in the product and the multiplier. Again there was an expression of delight, almost of amazement, whereupon the boy dashed off to his mother, in another part of the house, exclaiming, "Mother! I know my tens. I know my tens." As a matter of fact, the whole table was completely learned in permanent form without a single repetition.

In the case of the other tables, the boy had seemed to show a remarkable ability to forget the combinations almost as fast as learned. With the table of tens, the combinations were available at any time. The discovery of the significant relationships, the gaining of an insight, as the Gestaltist would describe it, resulted in learning because the new meaning had been gained through organization of the various elements. The difficulty that the boy encountered with the multiplication tables was probably much the same as the adult encounters in trying to memorize a series of nonsense syllables. The fact that they are meaningful to the adult does not insure that they have meaning to the child.

The boy's father then attempted to utilize the same method with the table of nines. This time there was greater difficulty in getting him to see the important relationships because of the complete abstractness of all his previous number experiences in school. Few adults seem to have discovered for themselves the relationships in this table by means of which the learning of the combinations becomes somewhat meaningful.

$$9 \times 4 = 36 \qquad 9 \times 3 = 27$$
$$9 \times 7 = 63 \qquad 9 \times 6 = 54$$
$$9 \times 2 = 18 \qquad 9 \times 1 = 9$$
$$9 \times 8 = 72 \qquad 9 \times 5 = 45$$
$$9 \times 9 = 81 \qquad 9 \times 10 = 90$$

What relationships can you discover that aid in organizing this table?

In commenting upon this method of describing learning, it is well to make clear the contribution of the Gestalt emphasis. In addition to all the individual parts that go into learning an act as a whole, there is a significant further factor which may be called the organization of these parts into the whole. Playing a scale on the piano is more than striking the right individual keys. It involves both a sequential relationship and that relationship expressed by rhythm. If a bar of any familiar melody is played in one key, it is recognized not only as a series of notes; it has meaning as a whole, that is, as a melody. This melody may be transposed into another key so that, actually, different notes are involved, but if the same sequence of notes and the same rhythm is kept, it will still be recognized as the same melody. Here the essential nature of the whole is much the same, although the parts making up the whole may be very different. But if the *same notes* are played in *different rhythms,* the result may be interpreted either as "Yes! We Have No Bananas" or "My Bonnie Lies Over the Ocean." In this case the different rhythmic organization of the parts makes the essential difference.

On the other hand, to say that all learning is the result of discovering relationships seems to be going beyond demonstrated facts. The facts as they have been substantially demonstrated by the experimenters with other points of view seem to indicate that analysis is unquestionably of importance. The Gestaltists have made a real contribution to the understanding of the conditions of learning, but they have hardly supplanted all other attempts to describe learning. In fact, it is possible to explain the process of the discovery of new meaning in old situations in terms of the Thorndikian psychology and in those of the Pavlovian conditioned response. The contribution of the Gestalt movement lies in the emphasis that it has placed upon the importance of the discovery of meaningful relationships in the whole learning situation. This implies that teaching is the process of arranging the learning situation in such a way that the learner can easily discover important relationships.

There are other ways, too, of describing what happens during learning as far as conditions within and without the learner are concerned. The three mentioned above are the most important for the purpose here.

FORMATION OF COMPLEX HABITS

Grouping of Simple Responses into Larger Patterns.—Another important problem of learning concerns the formation of larger patterns of habits from simpler acts. If the responses of a skilled typist are compared with those of a beginner, one sees that there are, indeed, very great differences. In writing a word the beginner makes several distinct responses, each to a relatively simple stimulus. In writing the word "study," there are at least five separate responses. The skilled typist sees the word as a whole or may see it only as part of a phrase of several words. As a matter of fact, it is not at all uncommon for the typist to reproduce correctly a word that is misspelled in the copy. The most satisfactory way of explaining this is that the typist is not responding to the individual letters at all but to the word as a whole, which acts as the appropriate stimulus for a pattern of response in spite of the errors in spelling.

All three of the characteristics of learning already emphasized are important in understanding what happens in such cases as learning to typewrite, but the second and third are the most useful. This part of the process of learning is sometimes called foreshortening and overlapping. By means of conditioning one can understand much of this foreshortening process. The original response of striking each key is made to a visual stimulus of seeing each letter separately. But as these responses follow each other, there is present, for each letter after the first, another significant group of stimuli. These are the mechanical forces applied to the sense organs in the muscles, tendons, and joints by the changes in shape and position of these parts of the body. Consequently, there are always present the two stimuli necessary for conditioning a response. One of these is the sight of the letter. The other is the group of kinesthetic stimuli produced by the response of the preceding letters. In this way, making one response in a series tends to set off the ones which follow, and the more thoroughly habituated these responses become in that order, the more likely is the complete series to follow from the beginning.

On the other hand, the Gestaltists emphasize the point that the formation of large habits from simpler responses depends upon the learner's discovery of further relationships between the parts of the whole stimulating situation. Until one gains an insight into these relationships, increase in skill of performance is limited. An illustration from a high school course in geometry will make this clear. A pupil may learn to demonstrate a particular theorem with only an insight or recognition of which statement in the printed solution follows the preceding one. He may not have any insight at all into the geometrical or logical relationships. In such a case the performance is of a very limited type. Gaining more significant insight into the relationship of the several parts of the whole situation is of much greater importance in this case than the mere foreshortening as in the case of playing a piano scale or using the typewriter. Gaining such an insight into the more significant relationships is an important contributing factor in making a smooth, fast-running pattern of the several parts, each previously understood by itself.

Can a Learned Response Be Used in a New Situation?— This is really a very important question. Stated in other words it means: Can one benefit by past experience when one meets new situations?

Common observation makes it evident that this can and does happen at least to some degree. But observation also leads to the conclusion that there are many times when past experience is not utilized in new situations even though the new situation seems to be quite similar to the old. Consequently, the question naturally arises as to what determines the conditions under which transfer of learning can take place. Is there anything that can be done during learning that will tend to make the results more usable in a wide variety of situations?

Thorndike has answered these questions concerning transfer in terms of what he calls *identical elements*. An identical element is one which belongs to both responses, the old one which has been learned and the new one which demands a solution. Consider the following case: During the World War I was thoroughly drilled in the act of saluting. In fact, a great deal of stress was placed on it. If I was standing, it was required that I stand up straight with feet together, head up, chest out, etc. About a year after separation from the service I was standing on a street corner talking to a friend. The conversation was extremely informal, and so was my position, with one foot sustaining my weight, the other thrust forward and raised somewhat to the curbing in front of me. A woman of my acquaintance passed, and I tipped my hat in the manner prescribed by custom.

After she had gone, my friend called attention to my action in tipping my hat. He told me I had "come smartly to attention" before bringing my hand to my hat. There were some identical elements in the army and civilian situations. The total responses were similar but not identical. In the army the response consisted merely of bringing the hand to the brim of the hat in the prescribed fashion. The civilian salutation consisted of taking hold of the hat, in this case not by the brim but by the front of the crown. It was the accompaning behavior only that was identical, and this part of it was less essential in civilian life than in the army.

It has been pointed out by a number of psychologists that the mere presence of identical elements in the new and old responses does not in any sense guarantee that they will be utilized. They must be brought distinctly to the learner's attention in some manner before this is possible. In high school physics, one may have studied the important laws and principles governing the application of force. But even with this hint only a very few can correctly state the physical law explaining why the common revolving water sprinkler revolves. When one of Newton's laws of force is cited—"to every action there is an equal and contrary reaction"—some will at once recognize that it applies, but will say, "We did not study about water sprinklers. We studied about the recoil of guns." That is just the point of this illustration. Until the elements of two situations which are identical have been pointed out, one is not able to use previous information in solving a problem.

It should be noted that such employment of previously learned responses is often either wholly inappropriate or at least partly unsuited to the new situation. Such instances might be called cases of *negative transfer,* i.e., cases in which previous experience interferes with rather than aids in the correct response to the new situation. Examples of this are very frequent in everyday life. The experienced tennis player takes up handball and finds that his old habits of hitting the ball with the racket must be partly remade. They interfere with his success in hitting the ball with the hand.

Judd [5] has emphasized a somewhat different point of view regarding this question of training transfer. He stresses the importance of building up generalizations, i.e., a generalized and complete understanding of the principles or elements common to the two situations. Such a generalization can be developed by experiencing a number of situations, all of which deal with the particular principle involved. Out of the experience of discovering these similar elements among the many dissimilar ones will evolve a more complete generalized knowledge of the principle which thus becomes available in a wider variety of situations and can be used in the solution of new problems. Hence, Judd would not teach the child a ready-made rule and follow it by several applications for purposes of illustration. Instead he would advocate giving the learner experience with a wide variety of activities employing this principle, encouraging and directing the learner in discovering for himself the pertinent principle. This, he believes, would develop a better generalization, by means of which the learning would be more transferable than if dependence were placed upon the mere presence of identical elements. It might be said that it is important to learn how to *discover* identical elements as well as how to *use* them once they have been discovered.

An Outline Summary

1. The characteristics of a learned response.
   A. Learning consists of a modification of a response as the result of experience.
      (a) Learning, so far as behavior can be observed, consists of changes in already existing responses.
      (b) Learning presumably depends upon some change in organic structure, probably in the nervous system.
2. Methods of describing learning.
   A. Thorndike's "Laws of Learning."
      (a) The most significant general characteristic of this description is the importance attached to the conscious states of satisfaction and annoyance as determiners of learning.

[5] C. H. Judd, *The Psychology of Secondary Education,* Boston, Ginn & Co., 1927, Ch. 19.

B. The conditioned response.
    (a) Here the chief characteristic is the complete objectivity of control of the learning process. Control is entirely in terms other than the consciousness of the learner and has to do largely with factors outside the learner.
C. The formation of configurations (Gestalt).
    (a) Here the chief characteristic is the emphasis upon learning in terms of whole, meaningful patterns by a reorganization of experience previously devoid of the particular meaning that comes from the reorganization.

3. Formation of complex habits.
  A. Several simple responses may be grouped and associated to form a more complex response where only simpler and partial responses existed before.
    (a) Here the different methods of describing the control of learning also apply, although particular importance should probably be attached to the reorganization of meaningful, whole experiences.
    (b) Learning may be aided or hindered by what has been previously learned. Here too the several methods of describing learning may be applied, and here again the Gestalt emphasis probably has particular significance.

PROBLEMS FOR FURTHER THOUGHT

1. Why does it make relatively little practical difference to the parent or teacher what the neurological changes in learning may be?

2. Describe in some detail the results of your observation of a child's efforts to learn or solve a new problem. It should involve a problem that is not solved so easily as to make the learning behavior difficult to observe.

3. From your own experience or observation cite several instances in which repetition did not play an important part in the learning process. Cite several others in which there was much repetition in practice without very much improvement.

4. A basketball star player "goes stale." He can no longer hit the basket with his former assurance. The harder he tries and the

more he practices, the worse he seems to get. The coach orders him to "lay off" practice for a week, assuring him that he will then be all right. After a week of not practicing he is again in his old form. How do you explain this result of not practicing?

5. Cite several experiences of your own efforts at learning which did not seem to be going well until you "saw the point," after which the problem was solved to a degree that represented near perfection. Problem situations involving rules of grammar in English or a foreign language, in the sciences, in mathematics, and with mechanical puzzles should furnish experimental material for this exercise.

6. It usually happens that a person learning to skate attempts to use the habits already well learned in walking. The extremely well established walking habits tend to transfer (negatively) to the skating situation so that they interfere with the new skill. Cite other examples from your experience of both positive and negative transfer. For some of the instances use situations that involve insight into the principles involved as in the case of Newton's law of force and the explanation of the working of the revolving water sprinkler.

Suggested Readings

Gates, A. I. Psychology for Students of Education. Rev. ed., New York, The Macmillan Co., 1930. Ch. VIII, "Laws of Learning," pp. 253–288. This is a good elementary discussion emphasizing a modified form of Thorndike's point of view.

Guthrie, E. R. The Psychology of Learning, New York, Harper & Bros., 1935. This is a brief and very readable discussion of learning, emphasizing the conditioned response method of explaining the conditions of learning. For a briefer treatment, see Smith and Guthrie below.

Heidbreder, Edna. Seven Psychologies. New York. D. Appleton-Century Co., 1933. Ch. IX, "Gestalt Psychology," pp. 328–375. This is a simple account of the principles emphasized by Gestalt psychologists. For a more comprehensive discussion of learning from this point of view, see Wheeler below.

Smith, Stevenson, and Guthrie, E. R. General Psychology in Terms of Behavior. New York, D. Appleton-Century Co., 1921. Ch. III, "Learning," pp. 75–133. This is an elementary and simple discussion of the conditioned response method of learning written several years ago. For a brief statement it is still an extremely satisfactory statement of this point of view.

Wheeler, R. H., and Perkins, F. T. Principles of Mental Development. New York, T. Y. Crowell Co., 1932. Ch. II, "The Laws of Human Nature," pp. 16–38; Chs. XIII to XVIII incl., "Analysis and Control of the Learning Processes," pp. 239–347. There is no satisfactory brief statement of the principles of learning from the point of view of Gestalt psychologists. This is probably the most satisfactory statement available. For a brief account of Gestalt psychology as a whole see Heidbreder above.

Chapter 10

SOME OF MAN'S WAYS OF BEHAVING NOT EASILY OBSERVED

Introduction.—The preceding chapters have dealt with those phases of behavior which are most easily observed and are therefore familiar to most people. It is necessary now to give attention to some of the more subtle phases of man's complex behavior.

"Consciousness" may be just a convenient name for those aspects of man's behavior which cannot be attributed to the observable operation of muscular and glandular parts of his organism. The exact nature of consciousness often escapes the attention even of the person possessing it. The most frequent method of examining it is that of introspection—the process of looking critically into one's own consciousness. The most serious difficulty involved in introspection is that the thing being observed is purely personal. No one else can observe it or know of it except as the observer makes available the results of introspection by means of verbal report; and since there is often great variance in the terms employed by different observers to describe states of consciousness, confusion frequently results.

The behavior involved in thinking is a response of certain muscles and glands, and the simultaneous employment of these same parts by other activities definitely interferes with thinking. Thus, one may carry on any kind of motor response so long as it does not involve the muscle groups most necessary to thinking. One may ride a bicycle, walk through a crowd in the street, hoe one's garden, or engage in any similar activity without materially interfering with thinking. But it is difficult or impossible to carry on a conversation about one topic and think clearly about another. Some people even find it difficult to think and, at the same time, do anything else that involves the speech apparatus. A smoker's pipe often goes out when he is in deep thought.

A large part of thinking can best be accounted for in terms of sub-vocal speech. If one can talk aloud about a problem, either to oneself or to someone else, the solution is thereby often brought nearer. Individuals undoubtedly differ very much in the degree to which they reduce the thinking process below the threshold of an observable response. Some can think clearly about abstract problems only when they can formulate all their thoughts orally, while others succeed in their thinking with only a minimal amount of sub-vocalization. The effectiveness of the thinking cannot be judged by the amount of observable vocalization employed.

What is true of thinking seems to be true also of other kinds of activity such as imagining, dreaming, perceiving, and reading. It is probable that many responses of this sort occur in the everyday activities of every person. To omit from an analysis of human behavior these important ways of responding would result in a very incomplete picture. And, since it is a part of many of the other more complex kinds of behavior, perception will be the first to be discussed.

What Kind of Response Is Perception?—The word *perceive* literally means "to see into." Familiar synonyms for perception are "insight" and "recognizing." Perception is a very brief kind of response; in fact, the response itself is characteristically of such short duration that it is difficult to study directly. An illustration of a rather familiar experience may serve to throw further light on its fleeting character.

Everyone is familiar with the kind of drawing, frequently found on puzzle pages of magazines for children, which portrays some familiar landscape scene with many trees and shrubbery. The legend beneath the picture says that a person or animal has been lost and is to be found somewhere in the detail of the picture. The reader is asked to look for it. After scrutinizing the outlines of the landscape, there are suddenly to be seen the features of the missing person (or animal), so placed as to be an integral part of the scene as a whole. When once perceived it becomes difficult to avoid seeing that part of the picture which could not be seen before. In fact, it stands out so clearly that it seems impossible

Sir Francis Drake

The natives take Drake across the Isthmus of Panama
and he has his first view of the Pacific

Puzzle—

Find His Comrade John Hawkins, His Nephew Francis,
Queen Elizabeth, and His Enemy King Philip of Spain

By Helen Hudson

A PUZZLE PICTURE

(From *Our Puzzle Book*, by Helen Hudson, copyright 1933
by Rand McNally & Company.)

that the figure could so long have remained hidden in the intricacies of the drawing.

The simple example of the act of perceiving involves, of course, recognizing, understanding, and interpreting the whole picture of the landscape. But in such responses familiarity with the object represented causes the process of perceiving to become so automatic that it is difficult to recognize the perceiving response itself. However, when the new perception is produced in this unusual way, it makes a significant change in the total pattern.

In other words, the total response to the stimulation now differs from the total response previously provoked by the same group of stimuli. Of course, in this instance, two different perceptions are involved. Perception is just as truly present in the first interpretation of the picture as in the second. What really occurs is that one experiences two perceptions of the same stimulation in so far as the actual lines on paper constitute such stimulation. What has happened in the process of changing is that the person, in making the new perception, completes a new organization of the elements which make up the stimulating pattern. This process of organization is always involved in perception and constitutes one of its most essential characteristics.

Ordinarily perception is a complex response to a complex stimulating situation. It is only rarely that in situations outside the laboratory the activity of perceiving can be simplified into an elementary experience. In the laboratory a number of devices are used to simplify the process. One of these is called a *tachistoscope*. The tachistoscope presents stimuli to the subject under highly controlled conditions. It consists primarily of a window in a screen, which is closed by a shutter. This shutter can be so operated as to expose the stimuli for very brief periods of time.

It is a characteristic of vision that one sees only while the eye is momentarily stopped and fixed upon a particular point in the environment. This point of attention may shift very rapidly, but perception does not take place during the movement of the eyes from one point to another. If the shutter on the tachistoscope is open for a period of approximately one-tenth of a second, it will insure that the subject can see only during one fixed position of attention. Using that length of exposure, the subject may be presented with a variety of visual stimuli and be required to reproduce what is perceived during the short time of exposure. The importance of organization in perception is nicely shown by such an experiment.

One such study will be used here for purposes of illustration. All the stimuli presented were numbers or letters typewritten on cards. First a series of evenly spaced capital X's were presented, and the subject was asked to indicate how many were seen. When there were from one to four he was positive of the number. When there were five or more in the series, he was unable to state the correct number positively. Numerical digits were then substituted for letters. The subject could reproduce the digits exactly in their correct order if there were no more than four. Increasing the number of digits beyond that point resulted in lack of certainty. It is interesting to note that there is a considerably greater degree of accuracy of the digits at either end of a long series than at the middle. Next mixed capital letters were substituted for digits with practically the same results. Notice that when the material consisted of more than four unrelated or relatively unrelated units, the subject was unable to reproduce them accurately. The next step was to use familiar words. Here the subject recognized accurately words up to nine and ten letters long with the length of exposure remaining the same as before. When unfamiliar words were substituted for the familiar ones, the subject was again confused and inaccurate for words of more than five or six letters. Finally, short sentences of familiar words were exposed as in the preceding parts of the exercise. The first sentence consisted of two words, "good morning." This was clearly reproduced. Increasingly long sentences were employed with perfect reproduction up to the sentence, "I am going at two o'clock." This was the full capacity of the shutter on the particular tachistoscope employed.

Notice some of the significant factors in this little experiment. When the material to be perceived had only a limited possible meaning, the act of perceiving involving the organization of these limited meanings had very narrow limits. Thus, with the X's the only possible normal meaning would have to be expressed in terms of the nature and the number of the units. When dissimilar letters were employed, the number of units perceived at a single exposure remained approximately the same despite the fact that the units themselves were different. In this case, however, the units were familiar to the person; that is, they had the usual limited meaning of numbers and the letters of the alphabet. When familiar words were employed, the organization could encompass a much larger absolute number of units, because they could readily be organized into units familiar as a result of previous organizations. This clearly indicates that the words were perceived as units and not in terms of letters. The same is true of the sentences composed of short familiar words. Here the organization in perception is still more complex. The words themselves are units in larger organizations.

Organization is the keynote of the activity called perceiving. By means of this organization the individual interprets the stimuli presented in such a way that the whole thing becomes a meaningful experience. Thus it becomes evident that acts of perceiving are based upon previous experiences. Any new or unfamiliar sensory experience is difficult to perceive and when perceived requires interpretation in terms of familiar or apparently related previous experiences. This involves the whole question of false or incorrect perceptions, called illusions, which will be discussed later.

It must not be thought, however, that perception takes place only through the sense of vision. Perception may involve any of the numerous kinds of sensory experience of which the human being is capable. Auditory perception, for example, involves the organization of auditory experience. As this is being written, an auditory stimulus is interpreted as the slamming of a door at the other end of the corridor. Other auditory stimuli are given the meaning of someone walking on the floor of the room above. Still others are interpreted as meaning that two persons are talking some distance down the hall. In fact, in this last instance, the identity of the individuals is included in the perceptions, although no names are heard.

WHAT FIGURE CAN YOU ORGANIZE FROM THIS PATTERN OF
BLACK AND WHITE?

See footnote on next page. (From Street, *A Gestalt Completion Test,*
by permission of Bureau of Publications, Teachers College, Columbia
University.)

In a similar way olfactory and gustatory perceptions are involved in everyday experiences. Certain odors are interpreted as meaning the presence in the environment of certain objects, even though the objects themselves are not present to any other sense organs. Much of the enjoyment of eating is directly and indirectly dependent upon olfactory and gustatory perception. In the dining-room situation there are additional visual stimuli, so that the total perceptual response may involve a meaningful organization from stimuli present to several senses simultaneously.

The kinesthetic or muscle sense organs play an important rôle in motor responses, but are ordinarily overlooked. Many familiar gestures and organized motor responses are involved in such everyday activities as conversation, walking, and other movements of locomotion. The muscular tensions resulting from the stimulation of the kinesthetic sense organs in the muscles, tendons, and joints are interpreted by the individual in terms of previous experience, so that appropriate muscular responses are made as in complex motor habits. Only when there is a disturbance of these sense organs does one appreciate the importance of kinesthetic perception. Without them, organized motor habits of even the simplest nature would be impossible. Because the kinesthetic sense organs are so numerous and so widespread throughout the muscular parts of the body, they cannot be studied as easily as can the sense organs of vision, audition, and olfaction, and are therefore not as well understood at the present time.

Illusions.—Illusions are false or incorrect perceptions. When a sensory stimulus is interpreted as something other than its usual self, the response is called an illusion. Much of the information about perception has been gathered from studies of illusions. When the same stimuli are interpreted in two or more ways alternately, it is possible to understand the significance of the "set" or direction taken in the process of organizing the response. Look at Figure 6 (chair illusion). A chair will probably be recognized, at first facing forward with the seat below the eye level; consequently the upper surface of the seat will be seen. Now

Picture on page 203. Can you see a knight on horseback?

look at it again and see if it can be perceived in another way. The most probable successful response in this case will be one in which the chair is seen from behind, facing away and to the right. This time, however, the chair is above the eye level and the under surface of the chair seat will be seen.

This second perception of the same black lines on a light surface will be more difficult for most persons to attain and maintain than the perception first described. The reason for this seems to

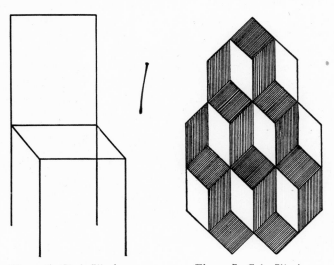

Figure 6. Chair Illusion   Figure 7. Cube Illusion

be that the usual experience of a person looking at a chair is more likely to be from the front than from the back and from above the level of the seat rather than from below. In other words, the most common experiences from previous similar situations will most easily be organized with the present stimuli of the figure to produce the total response of perceiving a chair.

Figure 7 is another familiar double figure. Can you see in this figure either six or seven cubes alternately?

Look at the shadows in the picture on the surface of the tank of the locomotive in Figure 8. Do these shadows represent indentations or bulges on the surface? Now turn the book upside down and look at the figure again. How do you account for what you have seen? In answering this question notice the direction of light in the picture and remember how light would normally fall upon such a surface as a cylindrical tank. Does it come from above or from below? Will the answer to this question

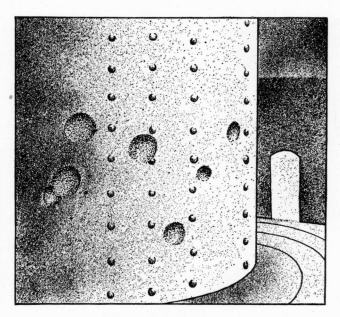

Figure 8. Tank Illusion

make it possible to explain why, in one position, the shadows appear to be caused by protrusion from the surface and in the other position by indentation into the surface?

Figures 9 and 10 are other illustrations of well-known visual illusions. Figure 9 can be seen either as a garden vase or as the profile of two faces. Figure 10 can be perceived as the head of either a duck or a rabbit.

Auditory illusions are involved in many cases of ghostly tapping, stair climbing, and door slamming. Natural phenomena probably cause the auditory stimulations which are organized by the hearer to mean the sounds of the passing of some ghostly visitor. As beautiful an illustration as one could wish occurs in Kipling's *My Own True Ghost Story,* in which the author tells how he lay awake all one night and listened to a game of billiards in the next room, played by the ghostly former inhabitants of the bungalow. He knew this room to have been a former billiard

Figure 9. Vase Illusion

room, but he also knew that, at the time, it contained no billiard table. In the bright sunlight of the next day he discovered that the whir of the balls on the tables had been the scurrying of a rat in the ceiling cloth, and the click of the balls, a loose window sash rattling in the storm. In this incident the process of organization of previous experiences, sometimes called mind-set, is clearly evident. In the morning light, when this mind-set or direction of organization had been changed, it was impossible to interpret the stimuli as before. This is a rather unusual incident, but its very unusualness makes clear the process involved in perception.

Illusions of disturbed balance may arise from an incorrect perception of a stimulus affecting the sense organs of equilibrium. An illusion involving a combination of sound and equilibrium is the old parlor trick of blindfolding a person and directing him to step on a board which has been placed two or three inches above the floor. Thereupon, two persons seize the ends of the board and proceed to jiggle it as if they were lifting it. In the mean-

Figure 10. Duck or Rabbit?

time the other members of the group crouch down close to the floor and continue the conversation without interruption. The subject is then commanded to jump. The board is actually only an inch or two from the floor but the subject's behavior in jumping from it clearly indicates his illusion of being a considerable distance in the air. In this performance the direction of the auditory stimuli contribute a very important part of the total stimulating pattern that is incorrectly perceived.

Imagery.—Imagery is the name commonly given to a subtle type of behavior in which the response is in some measure the re-creation of a response previously experienced. Images may be said to be reenacted responses to a sensory stimulus arising at a time when the material substances involved in the previous experience are not actually present to the senses. Imagery may involve any type of previous sensory experiences—visual, auditory, kinesthetic, and others. They may differ in the vividness of their reenactment from almost exact reproductions of the previous experience, on one hand, to vague, indefinite, and incomplete forms, on the other. Some persons declare that they have no imagery at all, while others give behavioral evidence of the fact that they can re-create accurately some previous experience.

In the image, regardless of the type of sense organ involved, the most significant factor seems to be the element of re-creative organization of the previous experience. Nothing new may be added and nothing old omitted, although usually the image is not nearly so exact a reproduction of the previous experience. This reorganization of experience has the same general characteristics as has the process of organization involved in perception. Differences in vividness of imagery depend largely upon how much the previous organization in perception directs the reorganization in the image. Studies of phenomena of imagery are by no means adequate, but evidences of significant motor responses can be detected in the behavior of the person reporting the image. These responses may be so subtle and so commonplace as to escape the attention of any but a carefully trained observer. Although they may be detected in some persons to a noticeable degree, they cannot be observed so readily in the behavior of others. There seems to be little doubt that the essential nature of the total behavior involved in imagery includes a significant amount of muscular and glandular activity which serves to reenact the original behavior. Problem 7 at the end of the chapter provides an opportunity to experiment informally with this phenomenon.

Verbal stimulation may call forth a reproduction of a previous response that was largely non-verbal, but if one has had only limited experience with the words used for the stimulus there seems to be difficulty in creating any image at all. For example, what visual image is suggested to the reader by the term "Dodo bird"? In what way is the image related to previous experience? The author's image of a "Dodo bird" is limited to a vague reproduction of an illustration in a book read years ago.

Imagination may be definitely creative. In fact, all imagination involves some variation from the original. Certainly all creative work requires imagination, as is evident in literature, painting, sculpture, and music. Stark realism soon loses its interest, and a work of art that is merely an exact reproduction of some very familiar experience soon loses its appeal because it provides no opportunity for the play of imagination. It is important to recognize, however, that in this creative use of the imagination, what is created is a new arrangement or a new combination of the old experiences of the artist. The elements involved may come from a considerable range of the artist's experiences, but they are brought together by him in this new arrangement. Only in that sense has something been created.

Some persons have pronounced auditory imagery, while others enjoy a highly developed kinesthetic kind. In the latter instance the imagery seems to involve chiefly muscular responses, and this kind of imagery is frequently combined with that which is predominantly visual or auditory. The person who is imagining the sound of a piece of music often seems to employ a kinesthetic type of response which had previously been called out in the actual presence of the auditory stimulus. A master violinist reports practically no visual imagery of the notes of a piece of music. Asked to play an all-but-forgotten piece, he can be observed fingering the strings with the left hand. Soon the music comes, but he says he has no idea of what lies more than a measure ahead. Here the imagery is dependent upon kinesthetic responses involving the muscles of the hand and arm. In a similar way some persons seem to have very definite olfactory and gustatory imagery, although these are rarely reported.

Reading.—Certain phases of reading are very closely related to the process of perception. For convenience, the process of learning to read may be divided into two somewhat distinct groups of skills. One of these depends almost exclusively upon the development of appropriate sensory-motor skills such as the movement of the eyes in a succession of jumps and pauses across the page.

On the other hand, there are some subtler phases of reading which cannot be observed readily, but which are important in the more advanced types of reading. It is necessary for the reader to perceive, recognize, or understand the successive groups of printed symbols. However, even when the reader can do this correctly, he may still be unable to understand satisfactorily a paragraph of such symbols. In other words, reading requires not only the perception of each symbol on the page; it also requires the organization of the meanings represented by the complex groups of words and sentences.

Students of secondary school and college level frequently report that they can read a whole page of print, recognizing every word, perhaps even subliminally pronouncing the words, only to be chagrined at the end to discover that they have not really understood the meaning of what was read. Such a difficulty clearly indicates the importance of the process of the perception of the large related groups of words making up the sentence, the paragraph, and the topic. It implies that the development of skill in reading demands, in its upper levels, considerable emphasis upon training in organizing such of the reader's experiences as are related to the symbols on the printed page.

Perception in reading takes place during the pauses of the eye as it moves along the page. These pauses are very brief and correspond approximately to the exposure of the material in the tachistoscope. Meaningful subject matter is much more easily read than material that has little meaning. That is the principal reason why it is so difficult to read an author whose vocabulary or style is unfamiliar. Many persons, for example, find the English translation of Sigrid Undset's *Kristin Lavransdatter* very slow and difficult reading, even though it is interesting. In this case the translation has carried over the idiom of the Norwegian language to such an extent that the English reader finds himself handicapped by unfamiliarity with the style.

Thinking and Problem Solving.—Both thinking and imagination are based upon previous experience. Thinking, like imagination, is the result of new combinations of this previous experience.

Thinking differs from imagination in several important respects. One of these is the differences in control through sensory stimuli either directly involved from the environment or result-ing from recalled experiences. In imagination, recalled ideas are allowed to go on more or less unchecked and uncontrolled by what the individual is immediately experiencing or remembering. This freedom from control may vary all the way from extreme random fantasy to the controlled imagination of creative art. When the control is still more restrictive, the resulting activity is called thinking. Hence, the imagination of the creative artist stands midway between the uncontrolled imagination of fantasy and the cautiously developed, carefully controlled thinking of the mathe-matician engaged in solving a problem. In thinking, then, the rigorousness of control not only serves as a characteristic of good thinking, but it distinguishes thinking from imagination.

Like imagination, abstract thinking involves the manipula-tion of ideas. It also resembles trial-and-error motor learning. In a motor activity such as solving a mechanical puzzle, there is usually considerable manipulation of the objects present to the senses. The clever thinker, confronted with a mechanical puzzle, will manipulate the parts of the puzzle less than will the poor thinker. Instead of manipulating the parts themselves, the clever thinker manipulates them in terms of ideas. This means that he can imagine the parts moving into different relationships with-out actually moving the parts. Such manipulation of ideas may, like the manipulation of the parts, result in errors, but the good thinker, in manipulating his ideas, is able to check and verify or reject the results of the manipulation in exactly the same way as in the manipulation of the concrete objects themselves. In other words, trial and error are usually involved in solving any kind of problem which requires creative imagination or thinking, but the person who is capable of manipulating ideas is not encum-bered by the necessity of manipulating the substances represented by the idea. This, of course, makes for greater efficiency, since it eliminates much of the awkwardness and difficulty of mechan-ical manipulation which often stands in the way of the solution of the problem.

An actual problem with which the author was faced some years ago may help to make this clear. The problem arose as a result of dropping a pair of pliers through a crack in the board steps leading to the porch of his house. The porch was enclosed at the side with lattice work, providing no opening between the porch level and the ground. The pliers were plainly visible through the crack from above or through the openings in the lattice work. Neither of these openings, however, was large enough to permit a hand to reach the pliers. In solving this problem there was considerable manipulation of ideas with only a minimum of significant movements. This manipulation of ideas resulted in the formulation of several possible solutions. Each of these was in turn rejected, at least tentatively, and further search was instituted for other possible solutions until a satisfactory one was hit upon. The first suggested solution was obviously borrowed from closely similar experiences of boyhood, such as dropping a coin into a crack in a sidewalk. This solution would have made it necessary to secure tools and remove one of the boards from the step, but this would have meant defacing the newly painted woodwork. Hence, the tentative rejection of this suggested solution, with the recognition that it would serve as a last resort if other means failed.

The pliers had fallen in such a position that one side of the handle lay free from the ground. The perception of this fact suggested the possibility of slipping a noose on the end of a string over the handle and pulling up the pliers. This solution was rejected without attempting to carry it out because it seemed probable that it would be difficult to make the noose tighten around the handle sufficiently to enable the pliers to be lifted through the narrow crack.

The next suggestion was to allow the pliers to remain there and to replace them with another pair. This seemed to be a satisfactory solution, but by this time the problem itself had become fascinating. Furthermore, the pliers would probably be needed before they could be replaced. Looking over the whole situation again, it was noticed that the ground near the lattice work was unplanted. This suggested the possibility of making a small excavation and slipping a shovel under the lattice work to scoop up the pliers and draw them to the edge, where they could be secured. This seemed to be the most reasonable solution. Notice that up to this time there had been no effort at actual, overt manipulation of any of the objects involved in the problem situation. The last suggestion was followed and proved satisfactory.

In this particular instance success resulted from the first activity that involved manipulation of a material substance, but there had been considerable manipulation of ideas preceding the verification of the fourth in the succession of suggested solutions. Each manipulation of ideas resulted from a new perception of relationships involving both present sensory data and recalled experiences. Each manipulation resulted in an hypothesis. Then came the significant characteristic of reasoning, i.e., checking and verifying in terms of the present circumstances. If it had been only an imaginary situation, mere invention might have sufficed without checking against the facts in hand.

Rôle of Muscular Response in Thinking—an Explanation of "Mind Reading."

—Careful observation of one's own thinking or that of others indicates that some muscular responses are present even when the thinker is totally unaware of them. The muscles most involved are those of the speech apparatus. Hence, thinking has sometimes been defined as a process of sub-vocal speech. Other kinds of muscular responses are often also involved, such as gesture and posture, and emotional responses involving flushing and blanching of the skin and changes in rates of respiration.

It is interesting to note, in connection with these observations, that the process of "mind reading," so far as it has any demonstrable basis, consists of the appropriate interpretation of these slight responses. Some persons become skilled in such perception and consequently are enabled to make very practical guesses as to what another person is thinking. This is especially true in cases where the "mind reader" is very familiar with the person whose "mind" is being read.

The story is told of a certain professional showman who made a specialty of this sort of thing and used his performance for advertising purposes. It was in the days of the horse and buggy. The "mind reader" asked a locally selected committee to take a certain object and, driving by any route they pleased, hide it in a spot of their own choosing. In the meantime he remained blindfolded, closely guarded by the watching crowd. When the committee returned, the showman took the driver's seat, still blindfolded, and drove the team, sometimes at a full gallop, over the exact route followed by the committee. His only request was that one of the members of the committee should sit in the front seat with him, keep his hand on the left wrist of the driver, and stop him if he were about to run over anyone. Arriving at the spot, he dismounted from the buggy, still accompanied by the committeeman with his hand on the showman's wrist, went to the lumber pile where the object was hidden, and promptly removed it, much to the amazement of the committee. Here, surely, was a wonderful exhibition of mind reading. The committeeman, riding in the front seat with the blindfolded driver, had unintentionally given him slight muscular clues which enabled the trained "mind reader" to accomplish his task. Much the same kind of explanation can be applied to the many interesting ways in which one person often elusively but effectively modifies the behavior of those about him, sometimes without awareness on the part of the others of the nature of the stimuli which have controlled their behavior.

Other interesting facts concerning the rôle of muscular response in thinking have been evolved from experimental studies such as those of Jacobson,[1] who developed techniques for teaching individuals to relax. He found that in states of almost complete relaxation thinking activities were greatly reduced and the affective or emotional aspects of behavior considerably minimized. Certainly, common observation would seem to verify the fact that a person in process of solving a problem is decidedly active, at least to the extent that he experiences an unusual degree of muscular tenseness. He may be sitting quietly and may appear to be comfortably relaxed; nevertheless, there is a vast difference in the very posture and appearance of the person who is actively thinking and one who is merely sitting and resting. An experi-

---

[1] Edmund Jacobson, *Progressive Relaxation,* Chicago, University of Chicago Press, 1929.

enced professor has no difficulty in singling out in his classroom those students who are actively engaged in some kind of thoughtful activity. Of course, it does not necessarily follow that the listener is thinking about what the speaker is saying, but, whatever his thoughts may be, the student who is thinking behaves differently from the one who is merely sitting quietly in the presence of the speaker.

Intuitions, Hunches, and Premonitions.—The processes involved in intuition are, with some exceptions, the same as those involved in reasoning. The good reasoner takes care to verify each hypothesis before accepting or rejecting it. In intuition, this process of verification is either reduced to a minimum or is absent altogether. Another difference is often, but not always, present. In the process called reasoning, the reasoner is likely to be aware of the stimuli to which the response is made. In intuition, the stimuli are often subtle and sometimes masked by other facts.

The latter difference is even more evident in the responses that are called "hunches." One sometimes hears it said, "I have a hunch that Fred is coming over tonight." What the person really means is that there is a pretty good chance that Fred will come, but that the actual evidences of the prospect of his coming have not been carefully examined. Consequently, the hypothesis is not verified. It is also important to remember that hunches and premonitions are rather more likely than not to be evident in situations involving frequently recurring acts. Really, then, there is nothing mysterious about these phenomena. Roughly they resemble reasoning, but they usually represent an inadequate and faulty type of reasoning. That they so frequently seem to be correct is due to the fact that they occur in habitual situations. Moreover, it is easy to remember the cases where the hunches have been right and correspondingly easy to forget those that have turned out to be wrong.

Abstracting and Generalizing.—In several respects, these two types of behavior closely resemble certain aspects of thinking. Abstracting is the "drawing out" of a particular element of experience because of its significance and uniqueness. Nothing is ever abstracted as a unique element of experience if it occurs always with the same accompanying elements.

An illustration from childhood concerns the abstraction of the element of "orangeness" from the many groups of spherical objects of many sizes and colors. The child's actual perception of an object can be determined only by his complete response to the object. This includes not only his verbal behavior but also reaching, handling, and manipulating. One very young child called any spherical object a "wow," apparently a generic name for all such objects as apples, oranges, rattles, and balls. It was soon noticed, however, that this name was applied only to yellow or orange-colored objects. Still later the name "wow" was applied only to oranges, the child having learned to discriminate between an orange and other objects of the same general size, shape, and color. This name persisted for months and was obviously the child's original effort at pronouncing the word "orange." Clearly this is evidence of the fact that the child abstracted the concept of orangeness first from sphericalness, then from sphericalness and color, and finally from sphericalness, color, and other characteristics by which oranges differed from other objects of his experience.

Abstraction has been discussed before giving thought to generalization, because generalization cannot take place until some degree of abstraction has preceded it. What happens in actual life situations is that the generalizations develop simultaneously with the continuing process of abstraction. Generalization may be defined as the discovery of a general truth which governs two or more specific situations, with the implication that this general truth will also apply in new situations as they arise. In its highest form generalization involves a very large number of specific situations. Any rule or definition is a generalization. Thus, "a noun is the name of a person, place, or thing" and "objects in space are attracted to each other in direct proportion to their masses and inversely in proportion to the distance between them" are generalizations which have grown out of experience with many situations. In order to be able to formulate abstractions and generalizations, it is necessary that the investigator experience the element to be abstracted or the principle to be generalized in a variety of situations. Thus, if "dogness" and "animalness" always accompany each other, no abstraction of one of these elements from the other can take place. And in order to develop the rule of grammar just cited as a meaningful generalization of his own, it is necessary for the learner to experience a variety of situations from which this principle may be abstracted and generalized. It is worthy of note that when one has discovered the essential element in an abstraction, it does more than merely add to all the other elements already perceived; it adds new meaning to the whole situation. This enlargement of meaning is the essential basis of generalization.

An Outline Summary

1. Perceptions.
    A. The characteristics of perception:
        (a) Perception literally means to "see into"; synonyms are insight, recognition, and understanding.
        (b) The perceptual response consists essentially of the organization of the stimulation present to the senses, in terms of previous experience.
        (c) Perception may involve any one kind of sensory experience or a combination of several.
    B. Illusions:
        (a) A perception that differs materially from the usually accepted organization of any group of stimuli is called an illusion.

2. Imagery.
    A. Characteristics of imagery:
        (a) An image consists essentially of a minimal reproduction of a former response, particularly of a former perception, in the absence of the concrete stimuli for the previous response.
        (b) In imagery several or many previous experiences may be employed in a variety of new combinations.

B. Imagination:
    (a) Imagination consists of the organization of previous experiences into new patterns in such a manner that the newness of the pattern may conceal the essential nature of the original responses.

3. Reasoning.
    A. Characteristics of reasoning:
        (a) Reasoning resembles imagination in that it employs old experiences in new patterns.
        (b) It differs from imagination in that reasoning employs a much greater degree of control in checking the resulting new organization against other experiences.
    B. Intuitions, hunches, and premonitions:
        (a) These all resemble reasoning except that the person responding is much less aware of the experiences; hence the control is less rigid.

4. Abstraction and generalization.
    A. Abstraction:
        (a) Is the result of discovering a common element in many different situations.
        (b) The abstraction is often a response to a quality or a relationship that does not exist in a material form.
    B. Generalization:
        (a) Is the result of the discovery of a general governing principle from several or many different situations with at least an implied extension of the discovered principle to similar situations not yet experienced.

Problems for Further Thought

1. Recall an experience involving an illusion such as mistaking a bush for a human figure. Write down as much of the detail of the whole situation and mind-set as you can recall. Do these circumstances help to explain the nature of the activity? In what way? Could you regain the illusion when the mind-set was different? Explain.

2. After reading this chapter through once, how successfully can you *organize* the whole chapter in terms of the main points discussed without looking through it again? Can you go so far as to phrase the most important subtopics under the main topic headings? Try it and compare your results with those of others in the class and with the outline summary. How successful have you been? What does this suggest in terms of the development of perception?

3. Ask the instructor for a simple mechanical puzzle, or work out a crossword puzzle, noting the processes of thought activity mentioned in this chapter. A jigsaw puzzle is very useful here. Note how different individuals differ in their ability to select the right piece from the many on the board. Note, too, the cues you use to check the results of your attempts to solve each part of the problem.

4. Why do readers often find the illustrations of a piece of fiction so annoying? One often hears the remark in such a case: "That isn't at all the way I had it pictured." Explain.

5. How can you account for the illusions of movement in certain neon signs when in reality there is no actual movement of the light from one part of the field to another.

6. Select three articles or short chapters from three books representing easy, moderate, and very difficult reading material. Read each through once and then write out the essential ideas of each selection. Check the articles again for content and compare with your written report. Note how important a part organization plays, especially in the more difficult selections.

7. Without warning the subject of this experiment about the nature or purpose of it, get some friend to visualize for himself while you slowly read to him the following description. Better yet, have someone else do the reading so that your attention will be entirely directed to discovering subtle movements of which the person doing the visualizing may be entirely unaware.

"Imagine yourself seated on the ground after dark in front of an open campfire. The fire is rather small so that you are sitting close to it. You reach out with a stick and poke up the fire so that a cloud of sparks sails off into the darkness of the night. See how they soar away, some of them going directly upwards for a great distance in the still night air."

As you have watched the person while this description was being read, have you been able to observe any evidence of muscular movements? These may take the form of slight eye movements, usually upward, slight inclination of the head in an upward direction, or possibly even the general but slight tendency on the part of the individual to lean backward as if watching these sparks flying away at a great height almost directly overhead. Make a record of these responses and compare your results with those of others in the class.

SUGGESTED READINGS

ARLITT, ADA H. Psychology of Infancy and Early Childhood. 2nd ed., New York, McGraw-Hill Book Co., Inc., 1930. Ch. IX, "Sensation and Perception," pp. 206–255.

CURTI, MARGARET W. Child Psychology. New York, Longmans, Green & Co., 1930. Ch. IX, "The Organization of Meaning in Thinking and Reasoning," pp. 251–286. The preceding two chapters dealing with the origin and growth of meanings are useful also.

FRANZ, S. I., and GORDON, KATE. Psychology. New York, McGraw-Hill Book Co., Inc., 1933. Ch. X, "Perception," pp. 341–383. This reference is very rich in illustrative material.

GILLILAND, A. R.; MORGAN, J. J. B.; and STEVENS, S. N. General Psychology. Boston, D. C. Heath & Co., 1935. Ch. VI, "Perception," pp. 172–206. Also contains much good illustrative material.

MURPHY, GARDNER. A Briefer General Psychology. New York, Harper & Bros., 1935. Ch. XVI, "Thought," pp. 314–342; Ch. XVII, "Imagining, Dreaming, Inventing," pp. 343–363.

Chapter 11

SOME OF MAN'S WAYS OF BEHAVING
AS A PART OF A SOCIAL GROUP

Nature of Social Behavior.—In Chapter 1 it was pointed out that psychology is closely related to sociology in that sociology is primarily interested in the nature and functioning of the social group and social institutions while psychology is interested in the behavior of man within these social groups and institutions. The connecting link between sociology and psychology is sometimes called social psychology. This branch of psychology deals with the characteristics of man's behavior toward his fellow men.

Everything in man's environment, both animate and inanimate, has a stimulating effect upon him, but the particular kind of stimulation that he receives from the presence of other human beings is of special importance to him. It involves an interaction that is usually lacking in other kinds of stimulation.

A similar phenomenon can be observed among those lower animals that form social groups. Some animals have characteristics of behavior that are distinctly social in the human sense of the word. Notice, for example, the communal activities of insects, or the cooperative social activity of some of the higher forms of animal life. Man's social life is far more complex and extends into many varied fields of behavior. This greater complexity can be attributed in part to the very long period of human infancy. The long period of dependence and development in close contact with the highly organized life of his elders provides for the human infant a very extensive period of social conditioning. Many of these socially conditioned habit patterns persist through later life.

In order that the child may survive and be able to get along with the older members of the group, it is necessary for him to learn certain modes of behavior. The human being has many possible ways of reacting to any situation, and the young person may develop any one of a variety of habits of meeting his difficulties. The particular habits that are thus developed tend to persist, as do all habits, although this does not imply that later modifications are impossible.

Socially established habits tend to control behavior even in the apparent absence of the social situations in which they were learned. This is illustrated by the habits that are sometimes called morals. One who has been thoroughly habituated to honest behavior can be depended upon to behave honestly even when there is no probability that dishonest practices would be detected. The persistence of habits under such circumstances insures the continuance of a well-established behavior pattern.

The governing factor in such a situation is sometimes called "*conscience.*" One is frequently told to "Let conscience be your guide." But what is conscience? Is it anything other than certain habits of acting and thinking about certain social situations that have been established within the individual? This may not be all that is involved in the concept of conscience, but habit certainly plays an important rôle in it. These habits usually become fixed in the early years of life, and thereafter remain as a powerful guiding and controlling influence upon behavior.

Complexity of Social Behavior.—The social behavior of any human being is very complex and difficult to analyze. Not the least important reason for this is the very complexity of the *social inter-stimulation* of all the members of the group of which he is a part. In order to understand the social behavior of the individual, it must be studied as part of the behavior of the whole group. Slight changes in the behavior of other members of the group may have an important effect upon the behavior of the one being studied.

The complexity of the human organism and the wide range of possibilities in the response of any one person to a given situation make prediction of social behavior extremely difficult. A sudden loud noise, for example, may cause different individuals to react in very different ways. One may flee in panic, another may simply stand and tremble, while a third may strike out violently at those around him.

Previous experience is another important factor in social behavior, but since this previous social experience has invariably been complex it is almost impossible to know which part of a person's experience will predominantly influence the present response.

Because it is so very difficult to analyze, social behavior has, in the past, been often attributed to other than natural forces. Such an attitude destroys all possibility of understanding, predicting, and controlling such behavior. To avoid so erroneous an attitude, it is necessary to examine an important means of inter-stimulation within the social group; namely, communication.

Rôle of Communication in Social Stimulation and Response.

—Communication in the form of language, gesture, facial expression, and posture plays two important rôles in social inter-stimulation—that of producing desired responses in others, which is the real communicative rôle of language, and that of bringing about a change in one's own behavior.

Language is a series of habits employing certain symbols whose meanings are determined by the common social experience of those employing them. Human beings are equipped with a speech apparatus and a controlling nervous system which, within certain limits, is the same for everyone. The experiences to which different individuals are subjected will determine the need for the acquisition of any particular set of language symbols. This applies not only to the learning of different languages but also to the development of different vocabularies within the same language. It is not unusual for young children to invent language symbols to represent some idea, but these are normally soon forgotten. Idioms and other peculiarities of speech acquired in early childhood often persist throughout life, even when the individual is transposed to a different social group with different norms of speech behavior. The social significance of language is evident in the language changes which children display while maturing. At different stages of development, these language changes correspond to changes in the social nature of the developing child.

When the child first begins to employ language, the vocalizations probably have no deeper significance than do other random movements of the body. These sounds of early infancy acquire meaning as a result of the interplay of behavior between the child and his family, but it has been shown by experimentation that the child makes the sounds before the adult meaning is attached to them. Situations similar to this recur in some degree throughout life.

The development of language is a means of becoming socialized. At the same time, it provides a means of controlling the behavior of others. These two factors together represent the essence of socialization which is, after all, only the interaction of the individuals comprising a social group. Without language, socialization would be largely impossible, since communication would then be limited to gestures and movements of much the same order as those employed by some of the lower animals.

However, certain gestures and movements of parts of the body have come to have meaning as standardized symbolic representations of ideas, and they pass for the equivalent of speech in ordinary social life. Among the most obvious of these are the shakings of the head in negation and affirmation. Other instances are beckoning with the hand or head, pointing with the finger, or directing the gaze toward a point for the purpose of attracting the attention of another to that point.

There are still other individual characteristics of behavior which are not quite so universally used. These range from bodily posture and facial expressions, which are fairly common, to individual mannerisms which can be interpreted only by those of the group who are thoroughly familiar with the idea represented by the gesture.

Imitation—The Similarity of Stimulus and Response.—Certain similarities of behavior, such as are always found among the members of any large social group, have frequently been described under the heading of imitation. The most commonly accepted layman's concept of imitation implies that human beings have a capacity to behave like each other that cannot be explained in terms of natural phenomena. This is unfortunate, and indicates that a better explanation of imitative behavior is needed. In imitative behavior the response of one individual is not only similar to that of another, but normally results from the similarity of stimulation of both. Suppose that a number of men are standing on a street corner gazing at the cornice of a many-storied building. The very fact that many are doing the same thing is often said to be an example of imitation. But, as one continues to observe this group, it will probably be noticed that other persons approach and begin to behave in a like manner. This can mean only that imitative behavior not only resembles the behavior of others, but also acts as a stimulus in calling forth like behavior.

Such an interpretation does no violence to principles of scientific explanation. The similarity of structure and the similarity of the learning experiences of human beings is sufficient to explain the phenomena of imitation. All the members of the sidewalk group have, as human beings, similar bodily structure. Previous experience has taught each of them that whatever is attractive to a group of human beings will probably be attractive to him, and the very fact that all those present are doing the same thing increases the probability that the object of their attention will be interesting to the newcomer. Imitation, then, might be described as suggestion. The behavior of a group suggests a particular kind of activity to the newcomer and this suggestion acts as a stimulus to similar behavior on his own part.

Social Significance of Imitation.—There is a special social significance in doing and being like others. Eagerness to conform to the social mode is a strongly enforced result of the processes of social conditioning. One learns to be and to act like the other members of one's group in order to avoid the unpleasant consequences of the disapproval of the group.

Although different families provide their members with different kinds of early childhood experiences, certain fundamental similarities and even identities nevertheless exist. Nearly all children are raised in a family situation in which their well-being and continued happiness depend upon their conforming to certain modes of behavior established by the family. For example, about one-third of the world's population habitually use knives, forks, and spoons in eating; another third use chopsticks in place of the fork and spoon; and approximately the remaining third still use fingers as a means of conveying food to the mouth. For the child who is raised in a family under social conditions where forks and spoons or chopsticks are regarded as the appropriate implements of eating, using the fingers will result in disapproval by the family group. Consequently, the child adopts his family's customs. Eventually such behavior develops as a habit to the point where it becomes extremely distasteful to be obliged to dispense with such implements. For the child who is raised under family conditions under which fingers alone are employed for the conveyance of food, an entirely different set of habits is developed. It can thus be seen that experience is an important factor in determining the mode of behavior employed by a whole group.

Social customs, modes of dress, methods of salutation, and, in general, habits involved in social intercourse develop for the individuals of the group in proportion as common social pressures are brought to bear upon all members of that group. This concept can be extended further to include superstitions and beliefs. As societies and civilizations become more complex, the social pressure brought to bear upon its members becomes more and more varied. In general, it is probably true that the more primitive the society the more unvariably alike are the behavior patterns of the members of the group.

Suggestion—an Elementary Process of Social Control.—Essentially, suggestion is a matter of stimulation. The particular kind of stimulation called suggestion implies that the person is being stimulated indirectly. This indirectness may vary considerably in degree. It may be carried to such an extreme that the

Don't blame this poor camel for putting on airs"... Oshkosh luggage seems to have that effect on man or beast.

Nowadays most people who take wardrobe trunks like them big. The Oshkosh "Chief" at left has 16 hangers plus a completely organized drawer section and costs $200. Round hat box for women, $32.50. The third piece with leather straps is a large carry-all case with tray, surprising in capacity allwit light in weight. $35.

OSHKOSH
TRUNKS AND LUGGAGE

OSHKOSH TRUNKS, INC. 40 EAST 31TH STREET, NEW YORK

THE SUGGESTION OF SUPERIORITY

(By permission, from *The New Yorker*, June 26, 1937.)

person being stimulated is not at all aware of the stimulus controlling his behavior. It is important to remember that, however indirectly it may be applied, suggestion is still a process of stimulation.

The psychology of advertising is largely the application of principles involved in the concept of suggestion. Many a purchaser comes to accept and believe certain statements because they are presented frequently in a variety of advertising media. A number of years ago, when a certain brand of cigarettes was selling at a slightly higher price than other brands, the advertising of that brand was centered around the slogan, "What a whale of a difference a few cents makes." Many persons actually believed that there was such a "whale of a difference." With at least one smoker this belief persisted even after he had been unable, while blindfolded, to tell the difference between the cigarettes from his own package and those from packages of several other varieties. In this case, the repeated suggestion that there was a difference had come to be accepted as so patent a fact that even the evidence of a new experience had little effect on his firmly established belief.

A well-known food product had for years been advertised under the slogan, "None genuine without this signature." In reality, the actual food value and desirability of that particular food product was not even mentioned directly in this slogan. But the implication was that a food product of a similar sort that did not come in a package bearing this signature would be inferior. The implication was so strong that this line of advertising was continued for years. What the advertiser had succeeded in doing was to suggest to the purchaser that genuineness and desirableness meant the same thing. Genuineness in this particular case referred only to the fact that the product was manufactured by one particular firm.

One of the most noted examples of suggestion in advertising was employed in recent years by a cigarette manufacturing company, until it was compelled by court action to modify its line of advertising. The effectiveness of this particular slogan depended upon the national fad of feminine slimness prevailing at the time.

It read : "Reach for a —— instead of a sweet." This slogan was often accompanied by another slogan, "Coming events cast their shadows before." The latter suggestion was usually illustrated by the representation of either a masculine or feminine figure (more often the latter) of a most desirable youthful trimness and slimness, casting a shadow which could only be made by an unfashionably rotund person. The implication, in this advertising, was very definitely that the use of this particular brand of cigarettes would make one slimmer or enable one to retain one's slimness. Actually, nothing to that effect was said, but in this case the suggestion was so direct as in the opinion of the court to be the equivalent of an actual statement of fact.

It is not only in the matter of the market that suggestion is of social importance. It is significant also in a variety of other social situations. The dietitian in a hospital must be ever-conscious of the desirability of suggesting hunger to the patient by means of good food, attractively prepared. Crosses erected on the highway at points where fatal accidents have occurred suggest to the passing driver the desirability of caution. Wearing apparel is frequently designed to suggest certain personality traits.

Probably the most outstanding examples of wholesale or mass suggestion are to be found in the old-fashioned religious revivals, political rallies, mob actions, and similar social gatherings. Here, of course, we have instance of the repeated reenforcement already discussed under the heading of imitation. But there is a forceful suggestion in seeing someone else "hitting the sawdust trail" during a revival meeting that can have a profound effect upon those members of the congregation who are a bit undecided. A skilled revivalist knows this and therefore places certain of his assistants at strategic points in the audience so that at the appropriate moment, upon urgent invitation of the speaker, they can come forward. Their action in going forward becomes a powerful suggestion and oftentimes may be the deciding factor in provoking the response desired by the revivalist. The political or collegiate rally has much the same character. The leader in charge attempts to evoke an enthusiasm in certain persons in the crowd, because such a response frequently acts as a suggestion which may be all that is necessary to bring about similar activity on the part of the entire group.

Hypnosis is a phase of suggestion. The most outstanding characteristic of the behavior of a person who has been hypnotized is that he becomes more suggestible within a narrow range. At the same time, he becomes almost completely non-suggestible to stimulations by anyone other than the hypnotist. It might be said that hypnosis is essentially a process of narrowing the range of normal stimulation so that the field includes only the hypnotist. His commands and suggestions are then carried out completely by the one who has been hypnotized. However, there are limits to the suggestibility of any hypnotized person. The evidence points to the fact that the one hypnotized cannot be induced while in the hypnotic state to follow suggestions which are strongly contrary to his previously well-established habits. The good showman keeps this in mind and in producing his bizarre results on the stage, carefully avoids suggesting to his hypnotized subject a type of behavior against which strong inhibitory habits have been established. There is, therefore, nothing particularly startling about hypnosis, many of the beliefs about it being entirely unfounded. The subject must cooperate by following the directions of the hypnotist.

Not all hypnotists are equally successful in getting their subjects to respond to their suggestions, and some persons are less suggestible than others, since they are much keener in their perception of the hidden implications involved in the suggestion. The extremely non-suggestible person is sometimes called negativistic. Such a one, instead of responding positively to the suggestion, behaves in a very contrary manner. This tendency toward negativism may be advantageously employed by the person who is aware of this tendency in human behavior. The well-known story of Tom Sawyer getting the fence whitewashed is an excellent example of this fact.

Social Inter-Stimulation Within the Group.—There are other ways in which the individual, when in the presence of his fellows, is stimulated to a different kind of behavior than would result if he were alone. The young college man who on a warm summer day proudly wears a heavy sweater bearing an athletic emblem is probably trying, through such behavior, to attract the attention of others in his group.

Rivalry is also recognized as an important factor of social control. This may involve competition with other persons or the checking of oneself against certain objective standards. It is a well-known fact that in track events the conference and national records are achieved on the basis of rivalry. The absence of a rival has a decided effect in lessening the quality of the performance. This is particularly true of motor performances, but it is also evident in such mental activity as imagination and problem solving.

Participation in the activities of face-to-face situations, such as committee meetings, is largely a matter of adjustment between individual ascendance and submission. If the committee is composed of those of approximately equal tendencies toward dominance, the discussion is largely a give-and-take affair. Where such activity does not result in a clear agreement, a compromise is almost sure to result. In such a group the influence of each committee member upon the others is clearly seen. In some committees, however, the tendency toward dominance is not equally distributed. Often one member is the dominant influence in the group. In such a situation the discussion will still be based on general inter-stimulation, but because there is one dominant pole around which the activity of the others tends to center the conclusion reached by the group will usually be colored in large measure by the opinions of the ascendant personality.

In any event, group activity has a stimulating effect upon the thinking of all the members of a discussion group, even when one personality dominates. The thinking of each participant is significantly influenced by any activity on the part of other members of the group. The necessity of convincing others tends to stimulate thinking and imagination, for when one is confronted with listeners it is necessary to consider the effect of one's ideas upon these listeners. They may not even be actually present, as in the case of the one who expresses himself in writing, but the results tend to be essentially the same. The most effective creative imagination and thinking is that which is done with listeners of some sort in mind.

When the Group Gets Larger—The Audience and the Mob. —A crowd is defined by Allport as "a collection of individuals who are all attending and reacting to some common object, their reaction being of a simple, prepotent sort and accompanied by strong emotional responses." [1] A large college class attending a lecture differs markedly from a mob of strikers, but the difference is almost entirely one of the degree of emotional response.

The crowd differs from the face-to-face group in several important respects, and resembles it in others. It resembles it chiefly in that the behavior of each individual is affected to some extent by that of his fellows in the crowd. This is true even in a college class. It has been shown from experimental studies that students near the center of the class are more actively stimulated by those around them and attain a higher average standing than students who are at the fringe of the class. This difference is due to group inter-stimulation rather than to differences in the way in which the various parts of the class are stimulated by the speaker. The same sort of thing can be observed in large revival groups or in crowds gathered to witness a spectacle such as a ball game. The individuals tend to lose some of their identity in being members of the crowd. This is true chiefly in the sense that all are tending to stimulate each other to a similar kind of behavior.

An interesting example of the emotional reenforcement produced by crowd activity is furnished by an incident that occurred on the first anniversary of the signing of the Armistice that ended the World War. It happened in a small Western city, a few miles distant from the scene of an Armistice day riot in which several ex-service men in uniform had been killed at the hands of a labor organization. As the news of this incident reached the city, the ex-service men congregated in their clubhouse. Here was a crowd in the complete sense of Allport's definition. All were reacting

---

[1] F. H. Allport, *Social Psychology,* Boston, Houghton Mifflin Co., 1924, p. 292.

directly, and with considerable emotional reenforcement, to the death of other ex-service men at the hands of what was regarded as an un-American organization. While emotions were running high someone suggested a parade. The idea was immediately adopted. The American flag and other banners were brought out and carried at the head of a column of men who proceeded to march through that portion of the local community which was inhabited mostly by members of the opposing group. A few minutes of brisk marching served to cool the ardor of all but the most fiery spirits. However, as they were returning to the hall, one of the marchers noticed that a bystander did not doff his hat as the flag was carried by. He first called from the marching ranks commanding the man to take off his hat. It is possible that the man, who was a foreigner, did not understand the command. In any event, he did not take off his hat. Thereupon the ex-soldier proceeded to the sidewalk and forcibly removed it. Fortunately, the man thus accosted offered no resistance. Had he done so, violent mob action might have resulted.

All the general characteristics of crowd activity were brought into play in this incident: (1) the simplicity and directness of behavior, (2) the similarity of the behavior of all in the crowd, and (3) the emotional reenforcement resulting from inter-stimulation within the group as the members individually react both to the common source of stimulation and to each other. The tendency of the individual to lose his identity in the mass activity of the group as a whole is also seen here. "Shorty had his gang with him," was the remark that was made in referring to the incident a week later. Shorty was no coward under any circumstances, but it is extremely improbable that he would single-handed have accosted this bystander who was physically more imposing in appearance than Shorty himself.

It has frequently been remarked that the emotions manifested in crowd activity are most often of the "primitive survival-value" type. The tendency for the more civilized and more highly moral activities to disappear in a crowd situation is probably due to the fact that none of the learned inhibitions which function habitually in everyday life can withstand the force of the intensive inter-stimulation of those within the group. The "mob mind" is only a convenient figure of speech, and the individuals in a crowd are still behaving in accordance with their individually acquired habits or inherited dispositions. All that the crowd situation does is to provide a strong stimulus for a kind of behavior which would normally be inhibited.

During the World War the whole American public became a crowd and almost a mob. People said and did and believed things which they now blush to recall. Independence of thought and action was virtually impossible. Anyone who dared to express himself by word or action in terms of the usual habits of average American conservatism was actually in danger of mob violence, at times, and of social disapproval always.

Each person within the crowd tends to multiply by his own reaction the effect of the stimulation received from some focal point, for example, from the leader. He does this because the members of the crowd are acted upon, through suggestion, by at least those with whom they come personally into contact. The leader's commands and entreaties become magnified through the action of the listeners, so that each one of them is affected not only by the leader himself but also by the suggestive effect of the behavior of those surrounding him.

Social Attitudes and Social Consciousness.—An attitude may be defined as an emotionally reenforced habitual pattern of behavior usually affecting the person as a whole and evoked by a specific kind of life situation. Not all attitudes can properly be regarded as social, but we are particularly concerned here with those that involve social situations. Attitudes change as one takes part in the activities of different groups. The old adage, "When in Rome do as the Romans do," is an admonition which is often both consciously and unconsciously adopted in going from one social group to another. In this sense a person may be said to have several social personalities which sometimes are so distinctly different that acquaintances from different social groups have opposing opinions of the individual's personality. Many a business man is known to have an attitude of brusqueness with his business associates but is kindness personified in his home. On the other hand, the reverse of this is sometimes evident.

These attitudes have a rather important effect upon both oneself and one's associates. Habits of any sort enable one to meet familiar situations with a minimum of effort. An attitude toward a particular kind of social situation enables one to adjust to that situation readily and with a minimum of conscious attention. Success in adjusting to a social group frequently depends in part upon creating a satisfactory impression upon the group. It is oftentimes more important to be impressive than to be logical, since being impressive may modify the behavior of others in a way that being logical sometimes fails to do. Being impressive may be accomplished in terms of manners of dress and speech, mannerisms of posture and gesture, breadth or apparent breadth of information, and by other similar means.

One often fails to analyze specifically many of his social attitudes. Such analysis is important only in so far as it makes possible the modification of an attitude to meet the requirements of the social situation. Many of the most useful social attitudes have become so habitual that they are no longer a part of consciousness, although they are definitely parts of personality. There are situations, however, in which one may become socially conscious of his rôle in the group. Social consciousness might be defined as awareness of one's attitude toward his social group and his feeling of belonging to it. In the latter respect the individual becomes a member of the crowd and to some extent loses his identity and individuality.

Another characteristic of social consciousness is awareness of the value of behaving like the group, and for the good of the group. This is a significant part of the social consciousness of fraternity and sorority membership. It does not necessarily imply that the identity of the member is lost or completely submerged in that of the group, but it does presuppose awareness of the value and the importance of behaving in the approved group manner even though it should involve some individual loss of identity.

The importance to the child of the consciousness of being recognized as a part of his own family and school group can hardly be exaggerated. It is often characteristic of a young child when punished to imagine himself not a member of that family, but someone who has been taken into it by mistake. Similarly, the consciousness of being a member of a particular class in school is oftentimes of great importance to the pupil. One of the most extreme forms of punishment that a teacher can employ is to create a situation that causes the rest of the class to shun or avoid one of its members. Children on a playground sometimes do this spontaneously as a result of incidents outside the knowledge of the teacher.

One of the things that will probably always make war and military duty bearable, if not actually popular, is the opportunity it affords for experiencing the social consciousness of being part of a very large group. There is no denying the thrill that comes to the trained soldier in any large review or mass movement of troops under a single command. Several writers have mentioned the element of unity that seems to be recognized in the regular retreat formation which is a part of the military ceremonies at the close of the day's activities. Much the same sort of thing is experienced by the soldier in any kind of military enterprise, and the reason for it is essentially that these enterprises are group activities. The group may vary from a squad to an army, but the soldier who is part of it can hardly escape a social consciousness of belonging to a closely unified group. It is this satisfaction that makes bearable many of the distressing, annoying, or even disgusting features of military duty.

Finally, there is the social consciousness of being a member of a particular race or nationality. To a certain extent one loses ones' identity as a member of the large racial group, and only to the extent that there is a merging of the individual's identity with that of the others is it possible to develop a social consciousness of being an integral part of the larger racial group.

It is apparent that, however large or small the social group may be, no matter how it may vary from time to time or place to place, the social attitude of its members depends upon the development of the social consciousness within that group. The sense of solidarity, the sense of belonging to the group, adds something of great significance to the individual's sense of security—a security which can be obtained only at the sacrifice of something of the individual's own identity, although the degree of loss of individuality will differ from one type of group situation to another. It is not suggested for a moment that the truly desirable and worthwhile persons in any social group are those who are the least important as individuals. Even in a military organization, the most important are those who stand out as individualities, each possessing a striking personality.

An Outline Summary

1. The characteristics of social behavior.
    A. Behavior in situations involving other human beings implies a reciprocal element that is absent from other stimulating situations:
        (a) Human beings react to other human beings in terms of what will the other fellow do.
        (b) These responses include behavior in which habits are the only trace of the presence of others.
        (c) This reciprocal element is present in human beings to a much greater extent than in any other species.
    B. Social behavior is usually very complex:
        (a) It is usually behavior that has its basis of habit in very many previous and somewhat different social situations.
        (b) It may even be the reaction to a complex abstraction.

2. The nature of communication in social behavior.
    A. Communication may take many different forms, such as:
        (a) Speech, written and oral,
        (b) Gesture of hands, shoulders, face, etc., and
        (c) Posture.
    B. The origin of the meaning of the symbols employed in communication lies in the social experience common to all those who use them.

3. The rôle of communication in social behavior.
   A. Communication has a dual rôle:
      (a) It results in the modification of the behavior of others.
      (b) It is involved in the changing of the behavior of the speaker (thinking and imagination).

4. The social significance of imitation.
   A. The response resembles the behavior of others and acts as a stimulus for others.
   B. Imitation is a form of social conformity and as such is important for the individual's well-being.

5. Suggestion.
   A. Suggestion is essentially an indirect stimulus in which the one responding usually fails to see the whole significance involved.
   B. It plays an important part in determining behavior in all social situations.
   C. Hypnosis is an extreme degree of hyper-suggestibility within a narrow range and is marked by an uncritical acceptance of the stimulus as presented.

6. Social inter-stimulation.
   A. In the face-to-face situation the interaction is direct and in some degree reciprocal (as in rivalry).
   B. In the audience and the mob the interaction is less direct but the multiplication of the interaction may greatly increase the total stimulation of each member.

7. Social attitudes and social consciousness.
   A. The nature of such responses:
      (a) They are emotionally reenforced responses which have their origin in, and are concerned with, social situations.
      (b) They may change as the individual passes from one group to another.
      (c) They stress the importance of being like the group and of acting for the good of the group.
      (d) They involve giving up some of one's own identity in exchange for identification with the group as a whole.

Problems for Further Thought

1. Try this little experiment on a busy street or on the campus when many people are passing. Stand and stare at a high building, or at the sky at a fixed point; or stoop over and look fixedly at the ground as if watching something of great interest. You need not say a thing, at least after the first two passers-by have joined you. Simply vary your behavior in such a manner as further to stimulate the group as it gathers. Contradict no one and supply no definite information. You will soon have a large group gathered around. It may even be possible for you to slip out of the group and be a spectator from a little distance.

In such a case how do you account for the high degree of interest that these people have shown without knowing what it is that has aroused their responses? How do you account for the similarity of behavior displayed by the many people involved? Does it aid your explanation to call it imitation?

2. Gather a dozen or more advertisements from magazines, preferably those employing a well-known slogan, such as Ivory Soap's "99 $^{44}/_{100}$% pure. It floats." Examine each to see just what is claimed specifically and how much is left to inference supplied by the reader. Do not fail to include some patent-medicine advertisement. Tabulate the results of your analysis in three columns. In the first put the slogan or statement from the advertisement; in the second, the actual statement of reasonably substantiated facts; and in the third, the implied fact or facts. Below is illustrated this treatment of the slogan quoted above.

Statement	Stated Facts	Implications Not Specifically Stated
"99 $^{44}/_{100}$% pure. It floats."	This soap floats	Floating is related to purity—hence this soap is highly desirable.

3. Visit an old-fashioned revival meeting or a football rally and observe the techniques employed by those in charge to secure the desired responses of the members of the group. Record your observations. Were chance factors relied upon to secure the desired results or did the leader show evidences of having planned to obtain these results?

4. A number of years ago a woman was not well dressed unless she wore shoes that came well above the ankles. Now it would be difficult to find such a pair of shoes outside the antique shops. The style began with shoes of a moderate height. It soon got to a point where the stylishness of the shoe was largely measured by its height. More recently it has become the proper thing for young men, particularly on college campuses, to disdain hats and caps. How do you account for the appearance and change of men's and women's styles? Indicate the place, in such a development, of the factors of imitation and suggestion and inter-stimulation within the group.

5. During the closing days of the war, when trench fighting was largely over, a platoon commander of infantry on the Western Front reported the following incident. His platoon had found the going easier than expected and had advanced beyond the units on either flank, which had been completely halted. His platoon was in a hot spot, receiving fire from both flanks as well as from the front. His company commander ordered him to bring his platoon back several hundred yards across an open, bare, unprotected hillside. As soon as the retirement began, it became difficult to prevent it from becoming a flight. In fact, when about half way back some men got out of control and began to run. This spread to some of the others in the platoon and even to the adjoining organizations. Only by a slight margin was a rout prevented. Making an orderly retreat under a hot fire is recognized by military commanders as one of the most difficult of battle maneuvers. Explain why. In the situation described above enumerate the factors discussed in this and other chapters which are useful in explaining the incident.

6. The following problem is intended to show the wide variations in certain social attitudes existing among members of a relatively homogeneous group. No exact measurements are here intended.

Let each member of the class write out a *very short* statement (not more than one short sentence) which will express his or her belief concerning each of the following social topics and institutions: (Each should be on a separate sheet of paper and should be left unsigned.)

The church	Trial marriage
War	Divorce
The Negro race	The League of Nations
The white race	Prohibition
The yellow race	Social security by legislation

Add other topics of local interest. When as many statements as possible on each of these topics have been secured, divide the group into as many committees as there are topics. Let each committee arrange a list of statements, including all that are notably different. Let the chairman of each committee read these to the whole class, pausing after each one to give the members a chance to indicate either personal agreement or disagreement. Some will be hard to decide, but one reaction or the other should be secured from each person to each item. When all have been read, collect the papers and compare the results in the separate committees. These committees should then have an opportunity to report to the class the general agreement and disagreement shown by the group as a whole.

In this exercise it must be kept clearly in mind that even a majority agreement does not necessarily indicate anything but a similarity of attitude.

SUGGESTED READINGS

ALLPORT, F. H. Social Psychology. Boston, Houghton Mifflin Co., 1924. Part II, "Social Behavior." Chs. VII to XV, incl. Some chapter headings will indicate the general nature of the contents of this book. This is one of the few social psychologies written essentially from the point of view of psychology rather than sociology. Ch. VII, "The Nature and Development of Social Behavior"; Ch. VIII and IX, "Social Stimulation"; Ch. X, "Response to Social Stimulation, Elementary Forms"; Ch. XI, "Response to Social Stimulation in the Group"; Ch. XII, "Response to Social Stimulation in the Crowd"; Ch. XIII, "Social Attitudes and Social Consciousness"; Ch. XIV, "Social Adjustments"; Ch. XV, "Social Behavior in Relation to Society."

BOGARDUS, E. S. Fundamentals of Social Psychology. New York, D. Appleton-Century Co., 1924. Several chapters of this book bear upon the topics of interest here. Among them are: Ch. X, "Communication," pp. 111–123; Ch. XI, "Suggestion," pp. 124–140; Ch. XII, "Imitation," pp. 141–150; and several others. Dr. Bogardus is a sociologist.

GAULT, R. H. Social Psychology. New York, Henry Holt & Co., 1923. Ch. VI, "Suggestions and Suggestibility," pp. 122–154; Ch. VII, "The Crowd and Allied Phenomena," pp. 155–178; Ch. VIII, "Convention, Custom and Morale," pp. 179–201.

KREUGER, E. T., and RECKLESS, W. C. Social Psychology. New York, Longmans, Green & Co., 1931. Chs. X and XI, "The Nature of Attitudes," pp. 237–320.

YOUNG, KIMBALL. Social Psychology. New York, Alfred A. Knopf, 1930. Ch. XX, "The Behavior of Crowds," pp. 505–521; Ch. XXI, "Crowd Behavior and Personality," pp. 522–536; Ch. XXII, "The Psychology of the Audience," pp. 537–551.

Chapter 12

SOME DIFFERENCES BETWEEN INDIVIDUALS AND BETWEEN TRAITS

Characteristics of Differences Within a Group.—Casual observation is sufficient to convince the most skeptical that all men are not created equal. In this chapter the chief concern will be the extent and nature of these differences, particularly as regards behavior traits.

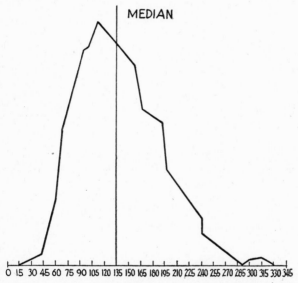

Figure 11. Curve Representing the Distribution of Scores Made by 4,491 High School Seniors on the American Council Psychological Examination

Intelligence is an interesting behavior trait to demonstrate differences among individuals. Figure 11 shows the scores made by 4,491 high school seniors on the American Council Psychological Examination.

The numbers below the base line represent the raw scores made on the test. High school seniors are a selected group. Pupils of low intelligence drop out in large numbers before the senior year. Therefore, the curve does not extend as far in the lower direction as it does toward the upper levels. A few make scores that are very high, but most of the scores are not very far from the median [1] which is shown by the heavy vertical line near the center of the figure. The closer the score approaches the median, the

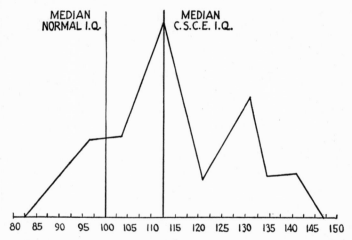

Figure 12. Curve Representing the Intelligence Quotients of a First Grade in the Experimental School of Colorado State College of Education

greater is the number of students with that score; and the farther the individuals deviate from the central tendency, the fewer there are of them.

Figure 12 shows the distribution of intelligence quotients of children entering the first grade. Note that the curve here has about the same general shape as that for college freshmen. These intelligence quotients are from a school charging tuition, which enrolls a rather select group. Hence there is a tendency for the

---

[1] The median is a point on the scale of scores on either side of which half of the scores will be found.

group to average higher than the usual first grade. The median intelligence quotient here is 112, as compared with about 100 for for the usual first grade.

If any anatomical trait like height or eye color, or a behavior trait like emotionality, motor coordination, or speed of reaction is measured, much the same kind of curve is obtained when the group, in which the measurements are made, is a large, unselected one, and the measuring instrument is reasonably exact. This characteristic shape of the curve is due to the *chance* distribution of the amounts of the trait present in the individuals of the group. Psychologists recognize that even where it is impossible to make

Figure 13. Curve Representing the Theoretical Normal Distribution

exact measurements of a human trait, the results would probably follow this kind of a distribution.

In each of the figures above, or in other similar figures from other series of measurements that might have been used, it will be found that a smoothed curve that most nearly fits the scores obtained would approximate the smooth, bell-shaped figure commonly called the *normal curve* or the *curve of chance*. Figure 13 is such a theoretical curve. An understanding of the significance of this curve as it is related to the distribution of human traits will aid greatly in understanding the problems of individual differences.

Normal Distribution as the Result of Chance.—When a coin is flipped, it is usually said that *chance* determines whether it shall fall heads up or tails up. Some readers may misunderstand this meaning of the word chance. They may think of the resulting position of the coin as due either to no cause at all or to the intervention of some extranatural or supernatural agency. Things do not happen without some sort of cause, and it is necessary to seek the causative factors within the realm of natural law. A chance event is therefore defined as one which is caused by several factors, each working independently of the others, but all operating simultaneously. Thus, in the case of the coin, the final position will depend among others, upon the following factors: the side of the coin which is uppermost before it is flipped; the way the coin is held; the force and manner with which it is tossed; the relative air resistance offered by the two faces of the coin; and the nature of the surface upon which it alights. These are only a few of the factors involved, but the result is called a chance event.

Now instead of one coin, take six, preferably all alike. Pennies will do nicely. Shuffle them in a small box or a cup and toss them, all six at once, upon a surface such as a rug. It is possible to have six heads up at the same time, or there may be five, four, three, two, one or no heads at all resulting from the throw. Continue this tossing of the six coins until there is a total of 64 throws.[2] Tabulate the number of times that each of the seven possibilities mentioned occurs. From the results a figure can be made like Figure 13, dividing the horizontal line into seven equal parts and using any convenient unit on the vertical scale. The figure resulting may differ somewhat from Figure 13, but they will approximate each other. Any other number of coins could have been used, and any other number of tossings would have been satisfactory. The larger the number of chance factors operating, the larger will be the number of repetitions required for close approximations of the normal curve. Figure 14 was constructed with the results of one series of 64 tossings of six pennies.

It might be well to emphasize two important characteristics of individual differences in the possession of anatomical and be-

---

[2] This number is used since it is the sum of the exponents when the binomial $(x + y)$ is raised to the sixth power.

havior traits. One of these is the normally wide range between
the highest and the lowest scores in the group. Thus, in the first
grade group shown in Figure 12, there is considerable difference
in the intelligence quotient between the brightest and the dullest
pupil. The other characteristic needs only to be restated more
specifically. The scores from the measurements within a group
tend to cluster around a midpoint and the more any score differs
from the midpoint, the fewer such scores there will be. For
example, imbeciles are lower in the scale of intelligence than are
morons, but there are fewer imbeciles than morons. Similarly,

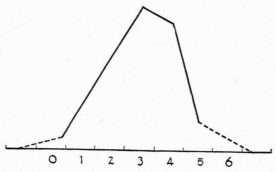

Figure 14. Curve Representing the Results of Tossing Six Coins 64 Times

idiots are still lower in the scale and there are still fewer of these.
The same condition exists at the other end of the scale of intelligence and likewise in every scale of differences in human traits.

**Convenient Method of Showing Differences Between Two
Groups.**—For the convenience of later discussion, it will be well
to have a means of comparing two separate groups which have
been measured by the same scale. Of the several ways of making
such comparisons, the simplest is the one called the "percentage of
overlapping" method. The name arises from the fact that if a
distribution of scores is made for two separate groups for the
same trait and on the same coordinates, the result will be two
curves which will usually overlap. Figure 15 represents the dis-

tributions of the height of all the men and of all the women in a college freshman class plotted as two separate curves on the same coordinates. The lines M_1 and M_2 designate the median heights

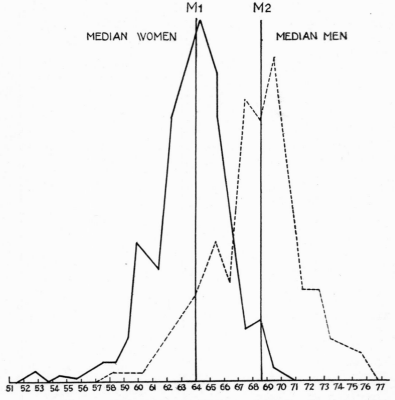

Figure 15. The Distribution of Men and Women of a College Freshman Class on the Basis of Height

of the groups of women and men, respectively. In this case about 4 per cent of the women are as tall as or taller than the man of median height in the group. Therefore, there is an overlapping of the men's group by the women's group of about 4 per cent. If the two medians coincided, 50 per cent would be overlapping.

The Influence of Heredity and Environment Upon Individual Differences

There are several ways of classifying differences among individuals, but we shall confine ourselves to a few of the most significant. We are concerned mostly with behavior differences. It is easy to fall into the error of confusing differences of gross anatomical structure with differences of behavior. In each of the kinds of differences to be discussed here and in the next section, it should be noted that the observable differences of bodily structure are often more conspicuous and more easily measured than are the differences of behavior.

Racial Differences.—There are some very conspicuous differences in anatomical traits between races and, to a less extent, between nationalities. Such traits as skin pigmentation, hair and eye color, facial features, and average height and weight need only be mentioned. However, it is difficult to know when pure racial stocks are involved, and this greatly complicates the problem.

Among the psychological or behavior differences that are sometimes assumed to exist between races are intelligence, emotional characteristics, and sensory acuity. In considering such differences, especially when trying to determine whether they are due to heredity or to environment, it is difficult to be very sure of the reliability of the evidence. One reason for this can be found in the limitations of the present method of measuring most behavior traits. Since there are no fixed units of measurement available in psychology, such as are available to the chemist or physicist, measurements must be made in terms of comparison of the behavior of different individuals. This, it will be recalled, is exactly the procedure employed in measuring intelligence. Comparison of behavior for the purpose of determining intelligence has been found to be valid only when the individuals compared have had practically equal experience in the test situation. Therefore, it can readily be seen that, in comparing the behavior of individuals of different races and different nationalities, it will be difficult to find a means of determining whether or not the behavior differences are, strictly speaking, differences in the biological sense of the word, or whether they are due to environmental factors.

Garth [3] found that pure-blooded Indians, as a group, did less well on an intelligence test than did similar groups of mixed Indian and white blood or groups of pure white stock. But what can be concluded from such an experiment? There seems to be no doubt that in the kind of situation represented by these tests there were reliable differences between the groups, and that the differences favored the white race. But can it be said from this that one race is more intelligent than the other? The answer is no, unless intelligence is defined simply as ability to do well on these tests. There is a tendency for the whites and the Indians to live in somewhat different kinds of environments. In the mixed racial groups, those with a larger proportion of Indian blood tend to live like the pure-stock Indians, while those with a large proportion of white blood in their racial mixture tend to live like the white group. Such behavior differences undoubtedly exist, but it does not follow that they have a biological foundation. They may be caused by differences of experience. Possibly they are caused in part by each.

Studies have been made of the first and second generations of immigrants of different races and nationalities in the United States. These studies largely concern intelligence, because better measuring instruments exist for this trait than for any other. Significant differences have been found which favor sometimes one race or nationality and sometimes another. In trying to interpret the cause of the differences which are found, exactly the same difficulty is encountered as that mentioned in connection with Garth's study. There are also other troublesome factors. One has to do with the problem of sampling. Can any justifiable conclusions be drawn about the race from which immigrants came on the basis of the showing made by the immigrants themselves? Again the answer is no. The necessary data are not

---

[3] T. R. Garth, *Race Psychology*, New York, McGraw-Hill Book Co., Inc., 1931, pp. 75–76.

available to determine whether the group that emigrates is inferior, equal, or superior to those who are left behind. Nor is it certain that the factors that select those who emigrate are the same in each of the countries from which these people came.

Another group of racial studies has been made comparing the Negro and the white races. Here, too, there are some reliably determined differences, but there is the same difficulty of determining the cause of such differences. Even though the races are living in the same geographical area, they may, and often do, have vastly different life experiences. It is contrary to the first principle of science to attribute a result to a more speculative cause when a less speculative one is available. Certainly, many racial and nationality traits can be accounted for in terms of social conditioning.

For example, consider the stolidity which is attributed to the British people or the volatility of the Latin races. These need no biological explanation. The social characteristics of the national life are sufficient to account for the existence of these traits to the extent that they may be shown actually to exist. Of course, it is conceivable that significant biologically inherited differences do exist. Only several large-scale experiments can answer such a question. Such experiments would require raising children born of parents of one race in the homes of parents of another race and in the country and social setting of the race of the foster parents. This transfer of culture would have to begin very early in life. Even then, unless these foster children were raised exactly as other children in the foster homes, the results might not be conclusive.

Family Differences.—In nearly every community there are families who are outstanding in political, business, and professional life. The children from these families, more often than not, continue on the same general social level as their parents. It is also rather usual to find that there are some families in the same communities who are nearly always on the verge of poverty, if they are not actually dependent upon the community for their existence.

A number of studies have been made of eminent families like the Edwards family in America and the Darwin-Wedgwood family·in England. Other studies have been made of the Kalikaks, the Hill Folk, and other degenerate stock. There can be little doubt that behavior traits do have a strong tendency to continue in families, generation after generation. The question of even greater interest here is whether this persistence of family traits in a matter of biological inheritance, or is due to so-called "social inheritance." Here again, as in the studies of racial differences, there are two factors that vary simultaneously, and the argument cannot be said definitely to favor either nature or nurture to the exclusion of the other. (See Chapter 3.)

Differences Due to Sex.—There are some very observable sex differences in the behavior of human beings. Some of these differences are directly dependent upon the greater average physical strength and size of the male. In other cases it is impossible to be sure that the differences are innate. When a certain boy was four years old, he received as a Christmas present a set of cotton-filled dolls representing the Three Bears and Goldilocks. Of all the things he possessed, those dolls were his favorites. One day he was delightedly showing them to an elderly gentleman caller who exclaimed, "What! A great big boy like you still playing with dolls!" This is only one illustration of the way in which social influences operate to insure the appearance of behavior that is approved for one sex or for the other. The play behavior of very young children does not show very great sex differences. Such differences as may appear can be accounted for largely in terms of the treatment by society of the behavior of boys and girls respectively. By the time of adolescence, however, both the *innately determined* and the *socially conditioned* differences have begun to show up distinctly. However, these two sets of factors, operating simultaneously as they do, cannot be satisfactorily separated at the present time.

Some of the behavior responses in which significant sex differences have been shown will be noted briefly. Schoolboys, on the average, do better than schoolgirls in mechanical work, in mathematics, and in physical science. Girls, on the average, somewhat surpass boys in the language arts and in the courses which directly or indirectly bear upon social relationships. Women fatigue more easily in terms of absolute amounts of initial strength, but proportionately to their weight women's ability to withstand fatigue seems as great as men's. In naming colors, women are better than men, but this can undoubtedly be accounted for in terms of frequency and intensity of experience. There seems to be no reliable evidence of sex difference in ability to discriminate colors except for the greater frequency of color-blindness among men and boys. In intelligence test scores, there are no large differences in the locations of the central tendencies or in the amount of variation within the two groups.

It is true, of course, that more men than women reach levels of attainment and distinction that mark them as highly superior individuals. At the other extreme, it is known that there are more feeble-minded men and boys than women and girls in institutions for the feeble-minded. Both of these facts, however, seem to be adequately accounted for in terms of socially determined factors. On the one hand, society has compelled even very able women to spend their time and energies in the home. Whether this is as it should be is beside the point here. On the other hand, society has traditionally expected that the man shall leave the home and at least support himself economically. Also, he is usually expected to support a family. This results in the frequent failure of the feeble-minded man, while the feeble-minded woman often escapes this difficulty within the shelter of the home. Thus there seems to be no conclusive reason for believing that men are more variable than women in their capacity to behave intelligently.

In differences in the acuity of the senses, emotional stability, and in most personality traits, there is no evidence of the superiority of one sex over the other. The reader may be reminded that biological inheritance, which determines the sex, also determines the potentialities of the individual. Moreover, the factors of experience greatly influence the development of the inherited potentialities and the experiential factors differ between individuals and especially between men and women.

Differences Due to Maturity.—These differences are so apparent as to need no special attention where the levels of maturity compared are not close together; but when the levels are close together, some means is needed whereby the differences may be made apparent. Parents, teachers, and social workers frequently overlook significant differences of maturity, blinded by the factor of chronological age.

Gesell's method of direct comparison of two individuals in a controlled situation is a very useful and reasonably convenient method. The two individuals are put into the same situation simultaneously or independently. Then the differences in the behavior of the two children are noted and the conclusions drawn.

If the problem situation can be standardized, and the characteristics of the responses of many individuals of each chronological age noted, a means is secured of determining the level of maturity of an individual at any time within the range of the scale thus formed. This is the essence of a standardized test procedure. By one or the other of the two methods suggested, it is possible to determine characteristic differences in the behavior of individuals or groups. The potentiality of rapid, average, or slow development must be recognized as being largely dependent upon the individual's heredity. Hence the importance of a knowledge of heredity in attempting to understand the process of maturation.

Conclusion.—In the various kinds of individual differences which have been considered, it is not so much a question of deciding whether heredity or environment is the most important, or even of determining exactly how much influence each has in controlling the behavior of the individual. The essential thing to remember is that *both* groups of factors are important. The heredity of the individual cannot be changed, but the limits set by heredity must be recognized. The environment can be changed as a means of modifying the individual's behavior, but in so doing, an effort should be made to have such environmental factors fall in line with hereditary potentialities.

AMOUNT AND SIGNIFICANCE OF INDIVIDUAL DIFFERENCES

Differences Are Quantitative, Not Qualitative.—It should be noted, first of all, that individual differences are in terms of amount and not of kind. In every kind of trait each individual stands somewhere between zero and the maximum. In comparing the total behavior of two persons, differences in personality are often erroneously believed to be due to the possession of different traits. All persons possess some degree of every trait.

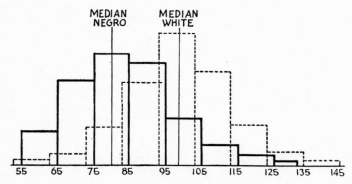

Figure 16. The Intelligence Quotients of White and Negro Children

It should be noted also that there is usually a direct or positive relationship between desirable traits. If an individual is possessed of a high degree of one desirable trait, such a trait is usually accompanied by a better than the average degree of other desirable traits. The notion of negative relationship embodied in the old saying that a "pretty girl could not have much sense" has been definitely disproved. Of course some relationships between socially desirable traits are closer than others, but all of them are positive.

How Large Are Differences Among Individuals and Groups?
—Many persons find it surprising that when groups are compared by the "overlapping of groups" method, the differences are usually not large. Figure 16 shows the results when intelligence

test scores of one group of Negroes and whites are plotted on the same coordinates.[4] Here the median for the Negroes is about 82, while that for the whites is about 100. The data for the Negroes are from a table of Garth's. The solid line represents the distribution of the scores from the Negro group. About 20 per cent of this group equals or surpasses the median of the white group. The medians of the two groups are about 18 points apart. The difference between the highest and lowest scores for the

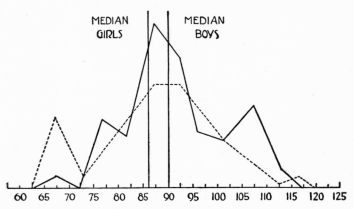

MEDIAN
GIRLS

MEDIAN
BOYS

60 65 70 75 80 85 90 95 100 105 110 115 120 125

Figure 17. Scores by Boys and Girls on Stanford Arithmetic Reasoning Test (Seventh, Eighth, and Ninth Grades)

Negro group is about the same as that for the white group and is about 90 points. Thus it is apparent that these wide ranges of difference within either group make the small difference between the medians seem much less important than it is usually supposed to be. In this case, the difference between the best and the poorest in either group is about five times as great as that between the medians of the groups.

Much the same results are obtained if we compare the scores made by the two sexes in a trait that is supposed to be possessed to a much greater degree by males than by females. Figure 17 shows the difference between the sexes on the arithmetic reasoning sec-

tion of the New Stanford Achievement Test when administered
to a group of junior high school pupils. The percentage of overlapping is very large, and the difference between the median
scores of the two groups is very small compared with wide ranges
of scores within either group. Similar relationships are found
when family differences are compared. Such a large amount of
overlapping should not be expected if the best type of family, like
the Edwards family, is compared with the poorest type known,
such as the Kalikak family.

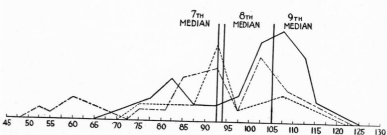

Figure 18. Scores by Seventh, Eighth, Ninth Grade Pupils on the Stanford
Language Usage Test

Individual differences due to maturity may be demonstrated
in the proficiency in language usage of junior high school pupils
as is shown by one part of the New Stanford Achievement Test.
Note the small differences between grade medians as shown in
Figure 18 as compared with the range of scores within each of
the three classes. Some pupils in the seventh grade are better
than the median of the ninth grade, and some of the ninth graders
fall below the seventh grade median.

These facts may be startling to those not already aware of
them. Racial, sex, and family prejudices have been built up
largely by unfair comparisons. It is often the practice to pick out
the most intelligent members of one race and compare them with
the least intelligent members of another. The same is done for
other race, family, and sex comparisons. To be valid, a comparison must be made between the averages of large groups, and the
difference between such averages should then be compared with

the range of scores in either group. This is only one of the simpler means of making comparisons.

It should be clear by this time that, on the whole, the differences between groups of individuals are, more often than not, rather small. But what of the differences among individuals within the group? How much better is the best of the group than the poorest of the same group? Fortunately, there are some data on this subject. Starch [5] has shown that in the eighth grade a comparison of the best and poorest scores made on tests covering the common branches of the school curriculum indicates that the best student is from 1.5 times to 26 times as good as the poorest student in the grade. Limp [6] provides further information. On the basis of 34 psychological tests covering a wide variety of behavior traits, the best is from 1.9 times to as much as 19 times as good as the poorest.

Hull [7] also has collected information from several sources relative to the ratio of best to poorest performance in a variety of vocational occupations. The best was from 1.4 times to 5.1 times as good as the poorest. In this group of data, Hull correctly calls attention to the fact that elimination of the obviously unfit from vocational occupation results in somewhat lower ratios. He concludes: "We shall probably not be greatly in *error if we conclude that among individuals ordinarily regarded as normal in the average vocation the most gifted will be between three and four times as capable as the poorest."* [8] Differences of such magnitude are significant when one considers that the overhead in an industry is as great for a poor worker as for a good one. In fact, it may even be greater.

Differences Among Behavior Traits

How Do a Person's Traits Differ Among Themselves?—So far, consideration has been given solely to the quantitative differences of a given trait when that trait has been measured for groups of individuals. It is now time to consider the differences

---

[5] Daniel Starch, *Educational Psychology*, New York, The Macmillan Co., 1919.
[6] Limp, quoted from C. L. Hull, *Aptitude Testing*, Yonkers, World Book Co., 1928.
[7] *Ibid.*, pp. 34–35.   [8] *Ibid.*, p. 36. Italics in the original.

that exist when the individual is the constant factor and the differences are those between the several traits of the same person. The suggestion that desirable traits tend to accompany each other does not mean that all traits will be present in the same degree. Everyday observation of one's own and one's friends' behavior reveals some behavior traits which stand out above the average level of traits in that one personality. In fact, if it were possible to measure quantitatively all the traits of any personality, an approximation of the normal distribution would result. There would be a very few traits in which the person was either exceedingly high or exceedingly low, but most of his or her trait measures would cluster around the average of all of that person's traits taken together. Compared with the curves obtained when individual differences were discussed, these curves from the distribution of trait differences would have a narrower range, probably not over 80 per cent of the range of individual differences.[9]

There would also be differences among the averages of the traits of two different persons if an attempt were made to compare them. But again, the differences between the averages of the traits of these two individuals would be small as compared with the range of trait differences within either person.

This raises the question of certain specific abilities or talents, such as markedly superior ability in music or art, unusually retentive memory, mathematical ability, and mechanical ingenuity. The history of politics, literature, and science is full of instances of those who have shown a marked superiority in one field or in a group of somewhat closely related fields. Such superiority often makes the person's other capacities seem poor by comparison. Apparently, "the average individual's best vocational potentiality must be between two and a half and three times as good as his worst." [10] Hence the importance of capitalizing upon one's best traits both in ways of making a living and of getting along socially with one's fellows.

How Shall Aptitudes Be Discovered and Evaluated?—The problem of discovering one's own best aptitudes is an important

---

one, both for the sake of vocational and economic efficiency and for the sake of preventing undue wear and strain in living. How poor the world of science would be today if Darwin had not discovered himself and his own aptitudes after the schools he attended had called him dull! Similarly how different our mechanical and industrial world would be if Edison had not discovered his own aptitudes! Undoubtedly millions of square pegs have been trying to fill round holes, because they lacked the ability of these men to discover the work for which their aptitudes were best adapted.

Intelligence tests are recognized as one kind of aptitude test, but, unfortunately, there are few other tests of aptitude that are as well developed. Among the few ways that may be of some assistance in discovering one's greatest and one's poorest aptitudes, the following might well be included.

First of all, a complete and thorough examination by a competent physician is to be recommended. This should show up organic defects and structural peculiarities which might be disqualifying or might serve as a means of limiting the degree of reasonably expected success in certain vocational activities.

For many kinds of activities, it is now known approximately the amount of the aptitude called intelligence that is considered a minimum. Therefore, an intelligence test *administered and interpreted by a competent psychologist is of distinct value*. Such a test is merely useful in determining whether or not one has a minimum degree of this aptitude to make success in the chosen vocation reasonably possible.

In a few lines of activity specific aptitude tests are now available. There are tests for musical ability, mechanical ingenuity, and a variety of clerical tasks such as filing, taking dictation, and typing. Some of these are as yet hardly out of the experimental stage, while others are fairly well developed.

Another method that is useful, within certain limitations, is that of getting frankly critical evaluations of one's aptitudes from those who know one best and who, *at the same time,* know the requirements of the field of endeavor being considered. The two chief faults with this plan are in getting the friends to be frank, and accepting their evaluation for what it is worth after it has been given. Men and women are often prone to consult those who are most likely to give satisfying and pleasing advice. A critical evaluation of those not so friendly may also be of value, since such advisers will not be merely flattering. Such advice must be carefully evaluated without rationalizing to escape its unpleasantness.

Then there is a frankly critical self-evaluation, difficult as that may be. Many persons are incapable of a very detailed examination of this sort and, of course, many are very prone to be prejudiced, timid, and uncertain.

Another means that has much to recommend it, although it has serious faults, is that of trying out the activity. The best time to follow this procedure is in youth while there is still time to try something else. This method is employed in some junior and senior high schools. Its chief disadvantage is the length of time required to try out adequately several different activities.

Finally, one may utilize his avocations as a means of discovering his aptitudes. A highway engineer is reported to have worked at his vocation for a number of years with only a fair measure of success and happiness. During this time he developed a hobby of amateur photography. In this side interest he developed considerable skill and reputation. Finally, he discontinued his engineering work and established himself successfully as a commercial photographer. He is happier now than he was in the highway work and is doing just as well financially. He had the opportunity, through his avocation, to try out an activity rather thoroughly before changing it to a vocation.

There are undoubtedly other ways of getting information about personal aptitudes. The important point here is that one must recognize that there is a considerable range between a trait or group of traits in which one has the highest capacity and those that mark the lower limit of one's own aptitudes. It is important to make as complete a self-diagnosis as possible before choosing a vocation. But this diagnostic self-analysis will be of little value unless the proposed vocation is also analyzed to discover the peculiar aptitudes that are demanded by that field of endeavor.

An Outline Summary

1. The characteristics of the differences among individuals when compared on the basis of any one trait.
   A. All random·groups show the same general qualities regardless of the trait measured.
      (a) There is a wide range between the extreme scores.
      (b) Most scores tend to fall near the center of the group.
      (c) The farther away from the center of a group a score is found, the fewer similar scores there will be.
      (d) All distributions of scores of random groups for any measured trait approximate a "normal" distribution obtained from "pure chance" events.

2. Kinds and amounts of individual differences when groups are compared on the basis of any one trait.
   A. Anatomical trait differences generally tend to be greater than behavior trait differences.
   B. Differences between the medians of two groups are usually small as compared with the differences within either group.
   C. Heredity and environment are both important determining factors of individual differences and each must be considered in the light of the other.
   D. Differences in behavior traits may be conveniently classified as
      (a) Racial differences,
      (b) Family differences,
      (c) Sex differences, and
      (d) Differences due to maturity.

3. Differences among behavior traits of the same person (i.e., trait differences).
   A. Distributions of trait differences show the same general characteristics as do individual differences.
   B. Vocational and personality adjustments require the discovery of the socially most and least desirable traits by means of :
      (a) Standardized tests,
      (b) Physical and psychological examinations,

(c) Objective self-analysis and the analysis of acquaintances, and
(d) Employment and avocational activities of several
kinds involving aptitudes.

PROBLEMS FOR FURTHER THOUGHT

1. Carry out the experiment of penny tossing as explained in
this chapter. If you are more ambitious use ten pennies and toss
them 1,024 times. In either case, graph the results and compare with
the normal curve, Figure 13. Compare your results with those obtained by others. In this experiment it will be easier if one acts as a
recorder while another does the tossing and counting of the number
of heads.

2. This is a class exercise. Let everyone measure the strength
of grip of the right hand with a dynomometer. Tabulate the results
for the sexes separately and compute the average for the two groups.
How much difference is there between these averages? How does
this difference compare with that between the best and the poorest
scores in each group? Note. If a dynomometer is not available, substitute some other feat of strength that will be measurable, such as
lifting a weight from the side straight out to a position at arm's
length from the body, taking the number of times the weight is
lifted as the measure of strength.

3. Booker T. Washington was unquestionably a most able representative of the Negro race. One sometimes hears his name used as
a basis of comparison between the Negro and white races. Without
even raising the question of which race, if either, is superior to the
other, criticize the comparison involved in the argument.

4. Make an analysis of the personality characteristics that are
of greatest importance in several occupations. Committees in the
class may well devote their time to a single profession or occupation.
Let each individual make an analysis of his or her own aptitudes by
any means available. Care must be exercised in both these analyses
that the processes be as objective and as unbiased as possible. If the
committee reports of the analysis of occupations are posted, each
person may well check his or her own self-analysis against each of
these. It will probably be found that for most persons the self-
analysis reveals more than minimum aptitudes for several vocations.
Interests and other factors, such as ability to finance the necessary

professional training, will have to determine the course of action beyond this point. It should be noted that the chief purpose of this problem is to point the way for a beginning of a satisfactory vocational adjustment. Nothing more than that should be expected. It should aid in making the student more conscious of the importance of matching aptitudes with vocational requirements.

Suggested Readings

Individual Differences

Gates, A. I. Elementary Psychology. Rev. ed., New York, The Macmillan Co., 1928. Ch. XVII, "Individuality," pp. 530–557. A discussion of individual differences and their characteristics.

Jordan, A. M. Educational Psychology. New York, Henry Holt & Co., 1928. Ch. X, "Individual Differences," pp. 283–310; Ch. XI, "Family Environment," pp. 311–340.

Aptitude Differences and Vocational Adjustment

Griffitts, C. H. Fundamentals of Vocational Psychology. New York, The Macmillan Co., 1924. Ch. XVII, "Choosing a Vocation," pp. 344–355.

Hollingworth, H. L. Vocational Psychology and Character Analysis. New York, D. Appleton-Century Co., 1929. Ch. VI, "Self-Analysis," pp. 81–100; Ch. XI, "General Competence and Special Ability," pp. 165–176; Ch. XIII, "Interest as Vocational Determinants"; Chs. XVI to XVII, "Vocational Tests," pp. 272–293; Ch. XX, "Vocational Aptitude of Women," pp. 392–350.

Hull, C. L. Aptitude Testing. Yonkers-on-Hudson, World Book Co., 1928. While this book does involve more statistics than will be within the scope of the beginner, parts of it will be found exceedingly interesting and informative.

Husband, R. W. Applied Psychology. New York, Harper & Bros., 1934. Several chapters will make good reading along the line of the discussion of this chapter.

Kornhauser, A. W., and Kingsbarry, F. A. Psychological Tests in Business. Chicago, University of Chicago Press, 1925.

Laird, D. A. The Psychology of Selecting Men. New York, McGraw-Hill Book Co., 1925. Ch. XII, "Group Comparisons to Find Characteristics of Fitness," pp. 220–236; Ch. XIII, "The Use of Psychological Tests in Selection," pp. 237–252.

Stenquist, J. L. Measurements of Mechanical Ability. New York, Columbia University Press, 1923. Teachers College Contributions to Education, No. 130.

Chapter 13

BEHAVIOR THAT IS ABNORMAL

1. DAY DREAMS. Joe was an orphan of twelve who had been placed for adoption in several homes in succession. His latest foster father made a great point of truth-telling and on this point was dissatisfied with Joe. The following incident will illustrate one of Joe's difficulties:

One Saturday afternoon in winter, Joe was given permission to take the shotgun and go hunting for rabbits, of which there were many on the farm. His parents reminded him to be home before dark, but darkness was complete before he returned, thoroughly chilled and with no rabbits. He had enthusiastic tales to tell of the exciting hunting he had enjoyed that afternoon, not for the lowly rabbit, but for much more exalted game heretofore unknown in that broken, rocky, sage-covered district. When his attention was called to the fact that he still had intact all of the shells with which he started, he was not confused in the least, but enlarged his account of his adventures with tales of finding a more suitable weapon, which had apparently been used with telling effect. No questioning or obvious displeasure on the part of his foster parents resulted in anything but increasingly impossible accounts of his afternoon's adventure. What had probably happened was that he had approached the first straw stack looking for rabbits, and not finding any there, had seated himself on the sunny side of the stack, out of the wind. Here he had done the rest of his hunting in his imagination. When the sun had gone down and he had become thoroughly chilled, he was recalled from the world of his fantasy only by the cold realities of a winter night. He showed almost complete lack of ability to distinguish the events of reality from the more thrilling imaginary adventures of that afternoon.

2. A TYPE OF DELUSION—PERSECUTION. A married woman of about forty complains that a man of her acquaintance has hypnotized her and is pursuing her, attempting to make her think and do "improper things." Further questioning reveals that this has all been done by "remote control," since the man does not even live in her community. In fact, she has seen him only a few times, and has never conversed with him or even met him. The man asserts that he does not know her by sight though he knows of her by name. The woman, however, blames him for her loss of several positions and for what she insists was her dismissal from a commercial business school. The director insists that the school never knew why she withdrew except that her work was obviously of poor quality. She blames the sinister influence of this man for her social difficulties in her community as well as for her marital difficulties and is incapable of recognizing the improbability of her explanations.

Characteristics of Abnormal Behavior.—There are several ways in which the word abnormal is sometimes used. The best use of the term is in its literal meaning—away from the normal. In a previous chapter, the terms "norm" and "normal" were employed to designate the average of many measures of a trait or the degree of a trait which occurred most frequently. Accordingly, an abnormal trait would be one that was different from the average or which did not frequently occur in the group. As a matter of fact, the more abnormal a type of behavior may be, according to this definition, the less frequently it may be expected to occur. Thus the illustrations cited above describe behavior so atypical, so abnormal, that one seldom encounters instances of them.

A word of caution is needed at this point. It is customary to think of abnormal behavior as socially undesirable behavior. A moment's thought will make clear the fact that wherever an average is recognized, there must be about as many instances which are above average as there are those below. This fact is sometimes overlooked, with the result that the term abnormal is often thought of only in the sense of worse than normal.

Society tends to frown upon any behavior that is very unusual. Nearly all persons feel uncomfortable about any of their
behavior traits that they recognize to be conspicuously different
from those of the other members of their social group. It has
therefore become difficult to distinguish between the terms, "abnormal" and "socially undesirable." In this chapter the term
"abnormal" will be used in its literal sense, as meaning away
from the normal, but at the same time the common practice of
regarding unusual behavior as socially undesirable will be kept
in mind.

There are many degrees of abnormality. Actually, the average
of any distribution of trait measures would be only a single point.
Ordinarily all those measures of a trait that are fairly near the
central tendency are called average in everyday usage. When the
trait-measure goes beyond a certain degree of difference from the
average, it is recognized as being abnormal. The practical difficulty lies in trying to fix the points between what may be called
normal and abnormal. These points must be determined more or
less arbitrarily, and social usage plays a large part in fixing them.
Literally then, nearly everyone is abnormal in some degree in
respect to every trait, since the measurements of very few, if any,
are actually at the central tendency of the group. However, it is
only when the individual's behavior departs largely from this
mythical midpoint that such a person is said to behave abnormally. Note, too, that one may be distinctly abnormal in one or
a few traits and yet behave in a satisfactorily normal manner in
all other respects.

What Is Insanity?—"The insane are just like the rest of us,
only more so." When a person behaves in a manner so unusual
that he or she becomes a menace or a nuisance, society has agencies and institutions for their care. It is usually surprising to
one who visits a modern mental hospital for the first time to find
that it is sometimes difficult to distinguish between the patients
and assistants in the hospital. The patients are often normal
enough in all but a few respects. The instances cited at the beginning of the chapter are cases of this sort. Moreover, delu-

sions, day dreams, rationalizations, and such behavior traits are common to nearly all persons in mild degree.

The term insanity is purely a legal one, not a psychological one. It is used by lawyers, courts, and social agencies. The psychological and psychiatric method of designating extremely abnormal behavior is to call it a psychosis, a neurosis, or a psychoneurosis. Note the ending of all of these terms. *Osis* means illness. These abnormalities of behavior are regarded by the psychologist and the psychiatric physician as forms of illness. They are comparable in many respects to other kinds of illness, although they have some interesting characteristics of their own as does every kind of ailment.

Why Study Abnormal Behavior?—The foregoing discussion should help to explain why it is important to study abnormal human behavior. Because abnormal behavior is unusual, it tends to be conspicuous and interesting. Because it is an exaggeration of normal behavior, studying it is equivalent to examining normal behavior under a magnifying glass. The characteristics of the behavior pattern become more easily recognizable. Thus, by seeing these characteristics of himself manifested in an unusual and often in an exaggerated manner in other persons' lives, the normal person is better able to understand his own motives, habits, and inhibitions.

Convenient Classification of Abnormalities of Behavior.— Behavior abnormalities may take a very wide variety of forms. In fact, any kind of behavior which is manifested by human beings is probably distributed through the whole range represented by the normal curve. In approaching the study of abnormalities of behavior, this very great range may seem confusing. It is therefore advisable that some sort of a systematic approach be attempted by means of a convenient classification.

Sometimes a conspicuous breakdown in the organic structure is accompanied by a corresponding disturbance of normal behavior. The cause and effect relationship in such cases is fairly evident. However, in many severe abnormalities of behavior and usually in the less pronounced cases, careful examination of the organism fails to show any such conspicuous breakdown or destruction of organic tissue. In order to account for the latter group of abnormalities, the cause must be sought in the previous experience of the individual. This raises again the point emphasized in a previous chapter that, at present, the nature of changes in structure resulting from experience are not known. These abnormalities of behavior not due to conspicuous organic causes are probably the result of subtle organic modifications resulting from learning.

It is customary to refer to the former class of abnormalities as "organic," while the latter group usually goes by the name "functional." This nomenclature may be a bit confusing since it implies that the functional abnormalities have no structural basis. Nevertheless, it is less confusing to use the terminology already well established than to attempt to develop another.

ABNORMALITIES OF BEHAVIOR DUE TO UNUSUAL CONDITIONS OF MAN'S ORGANISM

A CASE OF AMNESIA RESULTING FROM AN ACCIDENT. A young college man collided with another player while practicing baseball and was knocked to the ground, violently striking his head. After a few minutes he resumed practice but seemed to his teammates to be a bit dazed. Within a few minutes he threw his glove on the field and, walking across a tennis court where a game was in progress, went to his room in the dormitory. This behavior was so unusual for him that one of the players was sent to see what was the matter. He found him in bed with his baseball clothes on. A short time later he was aroused, assisted in dressing, and taken to the college dining-room for dinner. There his behavior was noticeably unusual. He answered questions, but his answers were entirely irrelevant, and his conversation in general seemed much confused. Soon after dinner he was missed by his now anxious companions and a search was begun. He was found being brought back to the campus by an older acquaintance whose residence he had visited and where he had caused his host much concern by his unusual behavior and conversation. This time he was put to bed, and watch was kept over him until he went to sleep. In the morning he seemed normal enough but had no recollection of anything that he had done since the preceding morning, several hours before the accident. The *amnesia,* for the period following the accident until the next morning, was complete and permanent. For the interval of a few hours before the accident, the amnesia was not quite complete and was partly recovered later. For several weeks after the accident the young man experienced considerable difficulty with fusion of vision for near objects, such as print. This gradually cleared up.

Characteristics of Abnormalities of Behavior Called "Organic."—The case described above is an illustration of the group of abnormalities called "organic." A characteristic of all organic disturbances is that they accompany and are presumably caused by destruction or impairment of some member or members of the body. Very often these are portions of the central nervous system. This destruction may be due to physical destruction of a part of the brain, as in the case of a war wound or industrial accident; or it may be caused by disease, as in paresis. Where paresis is present there may be considerable destruction of portions of the cerebral hemispheres. This is sometimes called "softening of the brain."

Other causes of behavior disturbances of an organic nature may be the accumulation of poisons and poisonous after-effects and such substances as alcohol, lead, opium, and the like, which may cause an actual degeneration of nervous tissue under some circumstances and hence bring about disturbances in the behavior of the individual.

Another group of organic behavior disturbances is due to brain tumors or to similar malignant growths within other parts of the nervous system. These malignant tissues may grow to a certain size and then cease their growth. In such cases behavior is definitely impaired and may remain so for the rest of the afflicted person's life. In other cases, the destruction may increase and cause death.

Somewhat closely allied to these disturbances are the paralyses due to hemorrhages within the central nervous system. Blood escapes from its proper channels into the surrounding nervous tissue, where it clots and impairs or prevents the functions of that portion of the nervous system. This blood clot may be reabsorbed and the nervous function may return to normal or, if the injury is very severe, it may result in either permanent disturbance of function or death.

The group of behavior disturbances discussed above are generally called psychoses, i.e., diseased minds. The term psychosis is reserved for abnormalities of behavior that are so severe that the personality is appreciably disintegrated and the resulting behavior differs strikingly from that exhibited prior to the onset of the disorder.

Still another group of organic abnormalities of behavior is due to defects of the several kinds of sense organs in the body. Many of these defects are of relatively slight degree. A striking instance of this is the case of color-blindness discussed in an earlier chapter. Tone deafness, a condition in which certain tones are inaudible, is another example. Any kind of sense organ may apparently be involved and in turn cause abnormalities of that part of one's behavior which directly or indirectly depends upon its functioning. Helen Keller's childhood illness resulted in the loss of sight and hearing. It can easily be seen how this interfered with the normal development of speech behavior even though the speech apparatus was left intact.

The endocrine glands are rapidly coming to be recognized as playing an enormous rôle in determining changes in bodily structural and corresponding behavior patterns. Some of these, like the thyroid gland, are fairly well known. The nature of behavior abnormalities resulting from the disturbances of others is not so well known. It will have to suffice here to cite one case from the literature now rapidly developing in the field.

Anna Stone was the mother of a six-weeks-old baby girl. She was driving with the child and her husband when they crashed head-on into another car coming around a sharp curve. Anna and the child were apparently uninjured, but the mother was shocked and panicky for days after the accident. She became very nervous and irritable, going into rages over trifling disturbances in the household routine. She began to perspire and lose weight; in a few months, she declined from 140 to 90 pounds. Her eyes became prominent and seemed about to pop from her head. She developed attacks of palpitation and dizziness. For the most part, she was very depressed, although sometimes she would be elated. She could not sleep and complained of always feeling "as if I were on the go." She began to worry about her loss of weight and could not understand it in view of her ravenous appetite. She thought at times that "she was seeing things." But she felt she could get well "if only this thing in me which drives me on would let me go."

Anna's condition was so serious that it was necessary to operate upon her and remove most of the thyroid gland. After this, she began to gain weight and to become placid, and she left the hospital a "new woman," as she expressed it.

But within six months she returned. Her change was astounding; she had become enormous, having gained seventy pounds; her skin was dry and a pasty yellow, her eyes dull; she felt sleepy all the time and said, "I don't care whether school keeps on or not." She admitted she had not taken thyroid extract for more than two weeks after leaving the hospital; "it was too much trouble and, anyhow, I felt perfectly well."

It was obvious that she was a victim of a myxoedema, or a thyroid deficiency due to the removal of most of the gland and to a failure of the portion remaining to supply her with sufficient secretion for normal functions. With the gland feeding, she rapidly lost weight and has remained normal up to the present time.[1]

The thymus, the pituitary, and the parathyroids, the gonads or sex glands, and many other endocrine glands are undoubtedly intricately involved in large areas of human behavior. Changes in behavior invariably accompany changes in the function of any and all of these glands. The greater the change in the gland, the greater the change in the behavior.

Other kinds of "organic" abnormalities might be noted, such as those basic to the different degrees of intelligence or as they are manifest in such conditions as epilepsy, some of them only

---

[1] Louis Berg, *The Human Personality*, New York, Prentice-Hall, Inc., 1933, pp. 57–58.

poorly understood. The factors involved in differences in intelligence have already been discussed in a previous chapter, and
those involved in some of the other abnormalities are too little
understood to justify their inclusion in this discussion.

ABNORMALITIES OF BEHAVIOR DUE TO UNUSUAL
WAYS OF ADJUSTMENT

What Are Functional Abnormalities?—These disorders are
called *functional* to distinguish them from the organically caused
disorders already mentioned. A functional disorder is one for
which no organic disturbance can be found as a cause. Organic
and functional disorders may be thought of in terms of an
analogy.

Suppose my watch fails to keep proper time and I take it to a
repair shop where the watchmaker finds that a piece of the ma-
chinery is broken or bent. This corresponds to the situation
found in the case of an organic disturbance of behavior. The
behavior is irregular or different from the normal because some
organic part of the mechanism is defective.

But suppose when I take the watch to the shop the repair man
can find nothing wrong with the mechanism? It is all there. He
may tell me this, but still I know the behavior of the watch is different from that of other watches. When he examines it further,
he may find that the tension on the regulating spring is not correct. It may be that that particular watch is not so constructed
as to be able to adjust itself automatically to differences in temperature. In either case, the situation corresponds to what may
be called a functional disorder. In the first case the watchmaker
may adjust the tension on the regulating mechanism so that hence-
forth it behaves according to normal expectations. In the second
place, he may tell me to keep it always in a place where the environmental conditions (temperature in this case) will not require the
watch mechanism to make an adjustment that is impossible, because of its construction. In other words, the adjustment must
be made by adjusting the relationship of the behavior of the
parts or by adjusting the behavior of the whole mechanism to

its environment. The adjustment cannot be made by replacement or repair of parts of the mechanism.

Any analogy has its limits of usefulness and breaks down when pressed too far. Therefore, it will be well to turn to an illustration from the field of human behavior for a case of a functional disorder.

As I entered the spacious but somber room where Miss M. and her crutch spent their days, I caught at first sniff that unmistakable scent which always accompanies a certain type of invalidism. The ingredients emanate from oranges which, like a stage property, seem never to be eaten; roses which have been kept too long; mentholated ointments which are forever being rubbed on—all dissolved in stale atmosphere. There appears to be a fixed incompatibility between this sort of invalidism and ozone.

It was my first meeting with Miss Emma M., although I knew her sisters. The elder was a successful wife and mother and a participant in civic activities. The younger was a violinist. This unfortunate middle sister I had heard spoken of as leading what is popularly called a "life of suffering."

She received me with a wan smile. Something about the smile was so familiar that I could hardly believe I had never seen her; later on I realized that I had merely caught the strong family likeness which appears in all the wan smiles of all the world's noble army of martyrs.

"It is such a pleasure to see someone from the outside world." (Her pensive voice certainly didn't suggest pleasure.) "A shut-in longs so for any mental breeze."

Wishing to be agreeable, I took the hint and, for a solid forty-five minutes, I toiled womanfully to breeze her up. I chatted about my trip to California, my climbing of the Grand Canyon, a prize play, an English author, the wet and dry issue; with might and main I pumped my mental bellows in a heroic effort to create that longed-for breeze. Utter failure.

For my every topic was turned, by a quick, deft twist, to point to her own affliction. Thus:

"California! Land of sunshine! And here in my north room the sun never peeps! The south rooms were needed by the others, you see."

Again, "You scaled the Canyon afoot! And I never leave this floor! It would have inconvenienced the family to have an elevator installed."

It was weeks later that I happened on an elderly physician I know well who has long been the M.'s family doctor. "I wish you'd throw a light on that situation," I said.

He hesitated. Then, "It's only fair to the rest of the family to do so. The truth is, they've used every means short of binding and gagging to drag Emma into the best south room in the house. Will Emma? Emma won't. She hangs on to her gloomy room with talons, so that she can feel abused. As for the automatic elevator which would permit her to get about, they'd gladly tear the house to pieces if necessary to install it. Let 'em? Not she. It would deprive her of another grievance. Grievances are her three meals a day and a snack between."

"How on earth," I marveled, "with sisters so wholesome, so genial, so altogether delightful, did she come to be as she is?"

"That's just it," he replied. "It's their being so that's the matter with her. Even her leg."

I was quite at sea by this time. How Miss M.'s leg could be paralyzed by the fact that her sisters were charming, I confess I did not see.

"It's like this," he went on. "From childhood the others were uncommonly popular, and Emma was left out. Not their fault; they were always lugging her forward, but they couldn't make people like her. She had a whining voice and she was dull and disagreeable. Now, see how it worked out. She saw her sisters shining while she was left in the background. Instinctively she fought to gain attention, to be important. Not knowing how to achieve her end by legitimate means, she resorted to others. She magnified every slight ailment, she complained of every grievance. The family kept on their toes to please her, and indulged her as being *delicate*. Still, no medical examination could find anything the matter. At last she had a fall. Slight fracture—healed quickly. But she has never since been able to walk."

"You mean she *thinks* she can't walk?" I puzzled.

He shook his head. "No. I mean she *can't*. Understand, in the judgment of all consulting surgeons that leg is absolutely well. But she has a genuine ailment. The point is that it's not in her leg; it's in *her*. In her effort to convince others, she has convinced herself until she has created a reality. My dear," concluded the veteran doctor, "there's no disease so sad as that of the wretched human being who, endowed with life's two greatest blessings, sound brain and sound body, is so physically diseased that he can't can."[2]

---

[2] Sarah Comstock, "On the Eating of Worms," *Harper's Magazine,* January, 1931, pp. 229–230.

In this case the disorder of Emma's leg was functional. Physicians could find nothing whatever organically wrong with the member or with the nervous system pertaining to it. Nevertheless, the paralysis was there and continued to be there in spite of medical treatment. In fact, medical treatment in the ordinary sense was quite inappropriate in such a case. To be able to do anything in treating such a case it is necessary largely to disregard the symptom, in this case paralysis, and seek for underlying causes. These causes will often be found entirely outside of the patient's organism itself. They lie in the individual's habits of reacting to his environment. The paralysis served to provide Emma with a lot of satisfying attention which she had not succeeded in getting in competition with her sisters. In order for any treatment to be successful, it will have to proceed from this point.

Functional Disorders Are Different from Malingering.—It must be emphasized that these functional disorders are genuine. They are to be differentiated sharply from malingering, in which the sufferer definitely pretends to be ill and recognizes that his behavior is not in keeping with the real facts.

During the war there were a good many cases of "shell shock." In these cases the soldier characteristically "went all to pieces." His total behavior pattern was shattered. As a soldier he was at least temporarily but genuinely unfitted for further combatant military service, although nothing seriously wrong could be found with the man's organic mechanism. On the other hand, there were innumerable cases in which the soldier attempted to be placed on "sick call" in order to escape some dangerous or unpleasant duty. He might even deliberately maim himself by a self-inflicted wound so that there would be no question about insuring at least temporary absence from the dangers of the front line.

In times of depression like those of recent years a similar type of functional neurosis sometimes develops. An interesting newspaper account of such cases is here taken from the Associated Press dispatches:

Depression shell shock is the newest ailment confronting medical men. It is brought on in victims of hard times in much the same way as the familiar shell shock attacked soldiers in the World War.

A victim of this "disease" unconsciously magnifies some minor ailment into a disabling sickness in order to escape the worst difficulties of poverty and unemployment without losing his own self-respect and the respect of others. It is described by Dr. Roscoe Hall, clinical director of St. Elizabeth's Hospital, federal institution for mental ills.

A man suffering from "depression shell shock" undergoes exactly the same mental processes as a war shell shock victim, Dr. Hall explains. In many instances, however, his case is more difficult to handle because the fears built up by battling enormous economic odds often are greater than those inspired by the horrors of battle.

A wartime shell shock victim was torn between two desires—one for self-preservation and the other for self-respect by his fellow soldiers. To run away would be disgraceful, yet to face the dangers of battle seemed unbearable.

The depression victim is faced with much the same dilemma, says Dr. Hall. Under the American scheme of things, it has been considered disgraceful to be unable to earn one's own living. A man out of a job has two alternatives: to keep up the fight for a job, going hungry and, worse still, seeing his family suffer; or to apply for public relief.

To many, however, asking for charity seems as cowardly as running away from battle. The solution, for both the soldier and the unemployed man, is the unconscious one of developing an illness.

The soldier knows it is not disgraceful to leave the front lines if he is too ill to fight. The depression victim can avoid the futile struggle for existence if he is too ill to walk the streets. Usually the victims do not realize that they have followed this course of reasoning, and their illnesses are real, but caused almost entirely by a mental process rather than by some physical disorder.

The depression shell shock victims, like those of the war, probably in many cases will continue to need treatment and care long after the emergency that caused their trouble is over, Dr. Hall believes. At the start of the present depression, relief agencies still were rehabilitating victims of the previous depression of 1920.[3]

Functional Disorders Are the Result of Two Sets of Incompatible Habits.—In the discussion of the functional disability of

---

[3] Associated Press, *Greeley Daily Tribune,* July 12, 1934.

the "shell shocked" soldier above, it might be said that there is a conflict between the subconscious and the conscious ideas, but it will be possible to come closer to grips with the treatment of the case if such a verbal entanglement is avoided. Let it be recognized, then, that the patient has two or more patterns of habits and reflexes which are mutually incompatible. The soldier, for example, cannot carry out the two sets of habits simultaneously. One must be shelved to make room for the other, or a general disorganization of behavior may and often does result. This soldier is in somewhat the same fix as the dog which is stimulated to produce a scratch reflex on both right and left shoulders at the same time. The dog cannot scratch his right shoulder with the right hind foot and at the same time employ that same hind foot to sustain the body's weight while he scratches with the left hind foot.

The case of Anrep's dog is also a close parallel. Anrep first trained the dog to approach and feed from one box. At the same time he trained the same dog to stay away from the punishment always attached to another box. The boxes were identical except that one was surmounted by a circle and the other by an ellipse with the short axis equal to the diameter of the circle on the other box. After thus establishing two different habits to two different stimuli, he gradually shortened the long axis of the ellipse to a point where the dog could not distinguish between it and the circle. Here he reports that the dog's general behavior broke down. He manifested many of the symptoms of a "nervous breakdown" of a human being. He became cross, ugly, and very irritable, although before the experiment he had had what might be called a friendly, happy disposition that made him something of a pet in the laboratory. It was even necessary to send him to the country for a few weeks for a "rest cure." This is a clear case of two incompatible sets of habits elicited by what *to the dog was the same stimulating situation* with the two boxes. The parallel to human behavior is close enough to be at least suggestive.

Characteristics of Functional Abnormalities.—Ordinarily this type of abnormality presents a number of characteristics by which it can be recognized. First there is the point, already stressed, that no organic disfunction can be found which will satisfactorily and directly account for the abnormal behavior. It is universally true, however, that the patients believe that the cause is organic. They usually resent even the implication that the distresses they are suffering exist only in their thinking and not in their legs or arms or hearts or other parts of their organisms.

Another common characteristic of functional disturbances of behavior is the suddenness with which these symptoms appear and disappear. The onset of the disabilities is often sudden, and in cases where they do disappear the recoveries are usually almost miraculous. These are the kinds of disabilities that are cured in the excitement of public demonstrations of "faith healing."

It is also characteristic of such abnormalities of behavior that they serve a purpose useful to the patient, although this purpose is often difficult to determine. Not that the patient recognizes the purpose or even believes it when it is pointed out, but nevertheless the purpose is universally present. These abnormalities represent attempts on the part of the patient to escape from some difficult problem. The solution is usually an inadequate one, but is the most satisfying one available to the patient. The case of Miss Emma M. (see page 274) is an excellent illustration. Her functional paralysis was the solution to her problem of getting the attention that she had never otherwise been able to get. At the same time it enabled her to avoid unfavorable comparisons with her sisters. Solutions of this kind have a way of being very inadequate to the patients and they are usually an annoyance to those who must live with these sufferers.

Some Common Types of Functional Abnormalities.—Only a few of the most striking types of functional abnormalities will be cited. When a person's behavior is disturbed so that it differs from the normal behavior of the social group to the extent that the whole personality is distorted, the resulting state is called a psychosis as with organic abnormalities. Psychopathic hospitals have many cases of functional psychosis. Pronounced delusions often appear as important parts in the disturbed behavior of psychotic patients. The Emperor Napoleons and Queen Marys that are found in almost any state hospital for the insane are usually suffering from functional psychoses. The neuroses and psychoneuroses are lesser departures from normal behavior. In these categories are found the neurasthenias, hypochondrias, shell shocks, and depression psychoneuroses.

Neurasthenia is the name given to that type of an abnormality in which the person feels perpetually tired when there is no sufficient physiological cause. College students' spring fever is probably a mild kind of neurasthenia. The student is motivated to do the work that is waiting to be done and at the same time to loaf and enjoy the spring weather. All would be well if one could do both or do one without being distressed by not doing the other. A frequent solution is to rationalize one's tiredness so that the studying may be conscientiously set aside.

Hypochondria is a type of abnormal behavior in which the person is overly anxious about every little ache, pain, and organic sensation. Such a person can read the label on a patent-medicine bottle and immediately identify in his own person all the symptoms described. They are the world's army of martyr sufferers— "never understood" by the succession of physicians and healers who are called in. One eminent medical diagnostician has remarked that if, in his diagnosis, he discovered that the patient had undergone more than two major surgical operations, he immediately called in a psychiatrist because such a case almost always needed the treatment of such a specialist.

Functional amnesias (loss of memory for certain parts of past experience) are frequently reported in the newspaper. They usually represent persons who would "like to get away from it all" and who have found this the only method of escape that appears to be available. Closely parallel to this are the functional paralyses and functional anesthesias (loss of sensation) such as the reduction of acuity of vision, hearing, and sense of pain and touch. In all such cases there is usually little disturbance of the personality as a whole. Sometimes a general distintegration is avoided by dissociations into a split personality. In these cases the patient organizes the two or more incompatible patterns of behavior into separate compartments and by completely dissociating them from each other avoids the difficulty, after a fashion. The fictional case of Dr. Jekyll and Mr. Hyde represents the type of disorder in which a complete dissociation has taken place, although the author's explanation of how it was brought about is highly fanciful.

Other Means of Escaping from Unpleasant Reality.—Not so far from the normal are found some commonly occurring behavior traits that can scarcely be considered abnormal at all. They frequently appear in the lives of nearly everyone. Who, for example, has not at some time engaged in "wishful thinking" to the point that the thing wished for has been believed true? The "tall" stories of one's own exploits and experiences are familiar cases of this sort. It has previously been pointed out that the so-called insane are just like everyone else, only more so. This should now be quite clear. As the above discussions and illustrations have been followed, many readers will have noted the similarities between this or that description and instances of their own behavior.

Rationalization and projection are essentially the same in that both are activities involving some degree of failure to recognize the real reasons for doing what is done. Rationalization is the process of sorting out the reasons, accepting only those which coincide with one's desires, and failing to recognize contrary ones.

A college woman is trying to decide whether or not to visit her home during a four-day holiday. She recalls that her mother has been ill. It is six weeks since she has been home. She needs some clothes and books that are at home. A good rest will be very beneficial, and so on at great length. She fails to recognize that the trip will be expensive and an inconvenience at home, that she could have the things sent by parcel post, and that she will get very little rest. She sifts the arguments for and against and accepts only those in favor of doing what she wants to do. In this respect her arguments differ from genuine reasoning.

Projection is very similar. Here, too, a *good* reason is sought in preference to the *real* reason. It differs from rationalization in that, in projection, the individual places the blame for something already done onto an immaterial cause and overlooks the real causative factor. A girl is carrying a bucket of milk from the barn to the house. She stumbles and spills the milk and blames the rock in the road. The material factor here is that she was not watching the path. The child late for school says the clock at home must be slow. Maybe it is, but he overlooks the fact that he stopped to play on the way to school.

The author witnessed an interesting case of this sort a year or so ago. A neighbor driving his car past the author's house had to stop because he ran out of gas. He examined the tank, found it dry, and protested to high heaven that someone had stolen his gasoline. Probably he had forgotten to fill the tank, as he keeps his car securely locked in his garage in the basement of his own house. In fact, the very loudness of his protestations was indicative of the fact that he was trying to convince himself as well as his neighbors that his predicament was due to no carelessness on his part. If he can believe that the gasoline was stolen, he is relieved of the blame or chagrin that goes with a recognition of his own carelessness.

Day dreams of both the suffering-hero and conquering-hero types are common experiences. The case of Joe, cited earlier in this chapter, is an illustration of the latter type in an aggravated stage. Then there is the type of behavior that is sometimes called the "sour grape" attitude and another that is the opposite which is sometimes called "sweet lemon" behavior. A schoolgirl is not invited to a party. She tells her companions that she did not want to go to "that old cat's party anyway." Another girl gets a new pair of shoes for Christmas and announces that it is just what she wanted all the time, although a few days before she has been heard to wish for a new dress. Dreams during sleep also provide a means of escape from what would otherwise be unpleasant ways out of a difficulty. Yawning and sleep may even be forms of defending one's self from tiresome and annoying situations. Finally it is a matter of record that young persons in school, from the elementary to the college level, show more frequent illness at the time of examinations than at any other times of the year. The illness in such cases is often the pupil's attempt to solve a difficult situation when motivated by two incompatible sets of habits. One of these makes him fear the results of making a poor showing, while the other makes him eager to conform to the social expectations of his group. Of course, if he were ill, no one would really expect him to take the examination. Thus, he can avoid running counter to the social expectations and at the same time can at least temporarily be relieved of the possibility of making a poor showing on the examination. To be sure, he must convince himself that he is sick in order to maintain his own sense of personal integrity. Hence the functional illness. This is essentially the course of events in functional abnormalities, whether the behavior shows relatively large or small departure from the norms of the group of which one is a part.

The important element in all these types of escape behavior is that they are more pleasant than the real facts of the life situation. They provide a substitute for reality and a way out of annoying difficulties although it must be recognized that the means of escape is usually rather unsubstantial. In any case, it is necessary that the individual convince himself of the reality, if there is to be any satisfaction at all in such a way out of a difficult problem.

It should be noted again that such kinds of behavior are not abnormal. They are not in themselves even dangerous. The abnormality exists in allowing such activities to become habitual to a point where they become so satisfying that a *real solution of the difficulty becomes impossible.* In other words, the danger lies in developing a set of habits of dealing with life situations which are incompatible with the biological demands of life and the demands of living successfully with others in a complex social order.

The problem of preventing undesirable abnormalities of behavior and of remedying them when they do occur is an important one and will constitute a large part of the discussion in the chapter that follows.

An Outline Summary

1. The nature of abnormal behavior.
    A. Abnormal behavior resembles normal behavior in being a response of an organism to a stimulus.
    B. Abnormal behavior differs from normal behavior only in being unusual or less frequent than that ordinarily found in similar situations. Behavior is not regarded as abnormal until it departs from normal by a considerable degree.
    C. The dividing line between normal and abnormal behavior is always an arbitrary point fixed by social usage.

2. For convenience, abnormal behavior is classified according to its cause.
    A. Organically, where it can be directly accounted for in terms of a known breakdown of organic structure, and
    B. Functionally, where the abnormality cannot be accounted for directly in terms of a structural fault. Such abnormalities often show evidence of the incompatibility of two or more established responses aroused simultaneously by the same stimulating situation.

3. The degrees of abnormality.
    A. Abnormalities so severe as to disturb the integration of the whole personality are called psychoses.
    B. Neuroses and psychoneuroses are type names for abnormalities severe enough to disturb the normal behavior of the patient in one or more important respects without excessively disrupting the general personality.
    C. Minor functional abnormalities such as day dreams, rationalizations, projections, and "sour grapes" delusions are more frequently found and are not especially dangerous except as they become exaggerated or greatly multiplied in frequency.

Problems for Further Thought

1. Do you know any persons who have become partially deaf and whose general behavior has come to be different from the average by reason of such abnormality? What are the usual differences in such cases? Note especially any evidences of such behavior traits

as delusions and unusual compensations. Write up a case of this sort, noting the ways in which this person has adjusted to the affliction (whether the adjustment be wholesome or not).

Consider also the case of any person you may know in which there are evidences of a supernormal sense of hearing (any of the other senses will serve equally well). Write up an account of the manifestations of this kind of abnormality.

2. It is not always true that very unusual deviations from average height (or weight) cause deviations from average behavior, but these cases do appear frequently. Undoubtedly, you know of such instances from your circle of acquaintances. Make a list of unusual characteristics of behavior which you have noticed—of unusually tall women and unusually short men. Why are these deviations of structure more significant than unusual tallness of men and unusual shortness of women? In the same way, why is unusual heaviness or fatness more significant, especially for women, than unusual thinness as a factor governing behavior in social situations? Can you imagine social conditions where the reverse might be true? Describe them.

3. From your own experience, recall an occasion of rationalizing which is now clearly such, rather than good reasoning. Show what was the real reason in this case. Do the same for a case of your own projection of a blame onto someone or something else, or recount some significant day dream and point out the motive really involved.

4. Faith healing is as old as man's history. Would such healing be more likely to succeed in the case of functionally caused or organically caused abnormalities? What evidence can you find that they are not always cases of functional abnormality? Remembering that individuals with a functional abnormality always believe it to have an organic basis, what credibility can be placed in the testimony of the functionally ill on the point of whether their illness is functionally or organically caused?

5. The "sweet lemon" or Pollyanna type of behavior, in which a person "kids himself" into believing that no matter what happens it is always for the best, is frequently advocated as an ideal way of meeting life's disappointments. What are the difficulties in securing such behavior? Of even more importance, what are the shortcomings or even dangers of such a mode of behavior?

6. Probably all readers will know of one or more cases of "nervous breakdown." Examine carefully a case of this type and pick out the two conflicting drives (usually involved in separate habits) that cause the conflict. Show how these habits become incompatible, i.e., how they come to be called out in the same stimulating situation.

7. "Spring fever" is a mild form of neurasthenia that bothers many people. Show how the conflicting drives in such a case develop. Why do most people who get this "fever" get over it after a few days or weeks, usually without knowing what has happened? Suggest means that a person may employ to arrive at an effective solution of the conflict involved.

SUGGESTED READINGS

BERG, LOUIS. The Human Personality. New York, Prentice-Hall, Inc., 1933. Ch. IV, "The Glandular Basis of Personality," pp. 48–81; Ch. VI, "Maladjustment," pp. 93–117; Ch. XI, "Personalities in Conflict," pp. 189–221; Ch. XIII, "The Psychoses: Personalities in Flight," pp. 236–282.

CONKLIN, E. S. Principles of Abnormal Psychology. New York, Henry Holt & Co., 1927. Ch. II, "Sensory Abnormalities," pp. 22–42; Ch. IV, "Distorted Thinking" (Paranoia), pp. 60–77; Ch. V, "The Psychoses," pp. 78–112; Chs. VI and VII, "The Psychoneuroses: Psychasthenia, Neurasthenia, Compulsion, Neurosis, Anxiety Neurosis, Hysteria," pp. 113–159; Ch. VIII, "Shell Shock," pp. 160–177; Ch. XVII, "The Abnormally Endowed," pp. 388–421.

FISHER, V. E. An Introduction to Abnormal Psychology. New York, The Macmillan Co., 1929. Ch. I, "Some Typical Problems in Abnormal Psychology," pp. 1–9; Ch. IV, "The Conscious, Subconscious, Conscious and Unconscious," pp. 57–73; Chs. V to VII, "Some Common Modes of Reaction to Difficulties," pp. 74–153; Chs. VIII to XI, "The Psychoneuroses," pp. 154–370; Chs. XII to XIV, "The Psychoses," pp. 271–354.

HART, BARNARD. The Psychology of Insanity. 4th ed., New York, The Macmillan Co., 1931. This is another small book that has had a long and interesting life as a book. It is essentially Freudian in point of view and sympathy.

HOLLINGWORTH, H. L. Abnormal Psychology, Its Concepts and Theories. New York, The Ronald Press Co., 1930. Ch. I, "Meaning and Use of Abnormal Psychology," pp. 3–21; Ch. IV, "Contemporary Viewpoints—The Neuro-Anatomical," pp. 69–91; Chs. X and XI, "Psychological Origins of Functional Disorders," pp. 214–256. Several other chapters in this book will be found to be of interest to the reader without previous background in this field.

MORGAN, J. J. B. The Psychology of Abnormal People. New York, Longmans, Green & Co., 1938. Ch. I, "Introduction," pp. 1–32; Ch. II, "Disorders of Sensation," pp. 33–68; Ch. VIII, "Motor Disorders," pp. 268–309; Ch. IX, "Abnormalities of Intelligence," pp. 310–348; Ch. XIII, "Hysteria," pp. 472–505; Ch. XIV, "Disorders of Regression," pp. 506–533; Ch. XV,

"Compensatory Disorders," pp. 534–564; Ch. XVI, "Episodic Disorders,"
pp. 565–592.
Moss, F. A., and HUNT, THELMA. Foundations of Abnormal Psychology.
New York, Prentice-Hall, Inc., 1932. This whole book is written with
emphasis upon the organic phases of abnormal behavior. It thus forms a
good companion reference to such texts as Morgan, Hollingworth, and
Conklin. Note particularly Part II, Chs. XI to XXI, inclusive, "A Consideration of Specific Diseases."

Chapter 14

DEVELOPMENT OF MENTAL HYGIENE AND ITS APPLICATION TO EVERYDAY LIFE

What Is Mental Hygiene?—Everyone is well aware of what is meant by bodily disorders or diseases. But there is another phase of health which may be called mental health. Mental health may be defined as that state of mental well-being in which the individual is adequately adjusted to the facts of his social environment and is capable of making further adjustment to such new situations as may arise. Mental health is characterized by a flexibility of power to adjust, a contact with reality, and a satisfactory integration of the whole personality.

In man's attempt to combat and prevent organic diseases, there has been developed a branch of medical science which is called physical hygiene. Its aim is to prevent and combat the infections and ravages of the diseases of the organic mechanisms of the body. In recent years a similar science called mental hygiene has developed parallel to this. Its aim is to prevent and combat the disorders of behavior commonly called mental.

Historical Résumé of the Treatment of the Insane.—In ancient times the insane were almost universally believed to be possessed of evil spirits or devils. In one of Christ's miracles, it is told that he cured an insane man by commanding the "legion" of devils to depart from him. Whether or not one believes in the miraculous deliverance of the afflicted man, this serves as a typical example of the prevailing concept of insanity in the time of Christ. There are several other instances in Biblical literature of persons who are "possessed" of evil spirits. This belief is characteristic of primitive peoples and still persists to a certain extent.

Medical science grew slowly through the Middle Ages, only gradually gathering momentum as knowledge of the body increased. The medical treatment of physical disorders, even as late as the beginning of the nineteenth century, seems now to have been woefully haphazard. George Washington died probably as much from the blood letting that his physician thought necessary for him as from the effects of the severe cold he had contracted. It is not surprising, therefore, that treatment for mental ill health was almost wholly unknown, even as late as a hundred years ago.

Until 1773 there was no such thing in this country as a hospital exclusively for the mentally ill. Prior to that time and for some time afterward the insane were confined in "madhouses," which at their best were little better than jails and for the most part were infinitely worse. The violent patients were heavily manacled, while the harmlessly insane were allowed to roam at will and get along as best they could. These were the "Tom o' Bedlams" of England and the witches and warlocks mentioned in the literature of the Scottish countries. The care of those who were confined in "madhouses" consisted only of providing an inadequate supply of food and shelter. No one cared how they fared. They were outcasts of society and were in a sense the living dead. They were confined only for the safety and convenience of society until death released them from the terrible burden of life.

About the year 1800 Pinel in France became convinced that this procedure was entirely wrong. He advocated kindliness, elimination of almost all restraint, and an attempt to restore the patient to normal social life through individual understanding and treatment. He was regarded as a bit "mad" himself even to advocate such things. However, Pinel's teachings gradually began to have effect. Even as late as the beginning of the nineteenth century it was customary to allow visitors to see the inmates of one of these "madhouses" in Philadelphia upon payment of a small fee. The idle and the curious might go there much as people today go to see the curious creatures in a zoological garden.

At the beginning of the present century nearly all the state institutions for the insane were indoctrinated with the idea of restraint and treatment by force. Medical treatment was very meager; exercise, at least for the more violent ones, was almost completely lacking; sanitation was often very bad, and no one had even heard of occupational therapy. Such patients as could be occupied for the profit of the institution might have something active to do if they were not violent, but if they were violent they were placed in a solitary, padded cell or possibly even in a "strait jacket." In a few private institutions conditions were somewhat better. Psychiatry had just begun to get its terms defined, and much of the time and energy devoted to the study of psychiatry was still being spent in classifying symptoms and tabulating data.

Contrast these conditions with those of a modern psychopathic hospital. It is usually housed in a building whose appearance is no different from any other large modern hospital. There are locks, it is true, but the bars, the padded cells, and the strait jackets are conspicuous by their absence. The hospital staff is made up of a corps of competent psychiatrists, psychologists, psychiatrically trained nurses, and other specialists. Each patient, when admitted, is given a complete medical, psychological, and psychiatric examination. All are housed in rooms or dormitories which are models of cleanliness and sanitation, to say nothing of comfort and cheerfulness. Trained social workers gather needed information about the patient's home, business, and community life. Occupational therapy is employed as an important part of the treatment in many cases. This consists of suitable employment, not for the gain of the institution, but for the recovery of the patient. In a very genuine sense it is a hospital, a place where those who are ill may go to regain their health.

Origin and Growth of Mental Hygiene Movement.—In 1903 and 1904 Clifford W. Beers was confined first in a private and then in a state institution for the insane. He recovered, more because the disturbance had run its course than as the result of the treatment he received in those institutions. Then, while the experience was fresh in his memory, he wrote a remarkable book, *A Mind That Found Itself*. In this book he traces his own experiences from boyhood as they were later related to his psychosis. He tells with remarkable clearness the incidents of the beginning, duration, and recovery from his mental illness. Out of his experience in these institutions was born the determination to do two things. His first aim was to correct the conditions that commonly existed and that he had experienced in institutions for the insane. Second, he hoped to do something that would prevent others from having to suffer experiences like his own.

Interest in Beers' effort grew, and in 1908 the Connecticut Society for Mental Hygiene was formed. A year later the National Society for Mental Hygiene was organized. Now such societies exist in many states, all of them branches of the national organization. In 1930 an International Congress for Mental Hygiene was held in America. Thus the movement has outgrown all local or national boundaries.

The history of the National Society's activities is divided into three parts. The first lasted until the entry of the United States into the World War. During this pre-war period its major efforts were directed toward reforms and improvement of the teatment of the mentally ill. Effort in this direction still continues. During the war its efforts were directed chiefly toward reducing the amount and intensity of mental ill health in the armed service. Since the war its major aims have been the education of the public in matters of preventive mental hygiene, and the establishment of clinics outside of psychopathic hospitals, but serviced by experts, for the purpose of discovering and remedying behavior problems before they become so severe as to need hospitalization.

Relationship of Mental Health to Physical Health.—There is a relationship between mental health and the organic functioning of the body which should be quite apparent after the discussion in the previous chapter. Sometimes even fitting a person with glasses when they are needed will contribute materially to the reduction of general nervousness and instability. The clearing up of focal infections in the cases of bad teeth or tonsils will sometimes have the effect of clearing up behavior problems. Treatment for glandular imbalance or malnutrition can also do much to remedy certain mental conditions.

It must not be inferred from the above that a person cannot be in reasonably good mental health if he is afflicted with such bodily infirmities. "A sound mind in a sound body" is a very creditable objective for every human being, but lack of the sound body does not make a sound mind impossible. Often it is the habits of the individual that get him into his worst behavior difficulties.

Every competent practicing physician recognizes that in many cases a large part of his success depends not only on his treatment of the physical disorder but on his advising the patient as to the best way of adjusting to his malady. This is particularly true in cases where the physical handicap is of a permanent nature.

Relationship of Success and Failure to Mental Health.—If the author were making a child's bill of rights, the first item on the list would be a demand that every child be provided with an opportunity for a reasonable degree of success and approval by society within the range of that particular child's capacities. This, of course, is equally important for adults. Almost invariably children are brought up in such a way as to make social approval in some form a thing greatly to be sought. To be able to do something that will be approved by others constitutes for most persons one of the most important elements of what is called success. The demands that are made by society are sometimes entirely out of proportion to the capacity of some of its members to meet these demands. The less intelligent child in school and the less competent business man or laborer in commercial and industrial life often fail to succeed because society has expected what is literally impossible. This is true in normal times, and during periods of unusual stress it becomes acutely so.

There may be tragedies in life, as great as, but there is none greater than, that of the child in school or the man or woman in business, in professional or social life, who is below average in capacity to succeed in these fields, and who at the same time is expected to uphold the traditions of a brilliant family.

Allan Williams, 22 years of age, was employed by a firm of wholesale jewelers as a messenger. His salary was not sufficient to enable him to support himself had he not lived at home. His work was simple, but it involved responsibility for the carrying of jewelry, often of considerable value. He seemed to be competent, and his employers were satisfied with his work. However, Allan was not happy, largely because his work and his low salary made it impossible for him to get away from home and live his own life.

His father was a professional man of considerable ability. His mother and an aunt who lived in the home also came from a professional family. The adults of the family were united in their desire that Allan should attend the state university and enter some profession. Therein lay the difficulty. Allan had a mental age equivalent to about that of the average twelve- or thirteen-year-old boy. How he had finally, after six years of patient plodding, accumulated enough credits to be graduated from high school will always be something of a mystery. At any rate, Allan had no wish for more schooling. His ambition was to go to live on a farm and learn the poultry business. This probably represented more of a desire to be away from the parental disapproval than any fondness for chickens. The parents could not be made to see that Allan was anything more than a "bit timid." The young man will be doomed to the unhappiness of attempting what is impossible for him until circumstances free him or until he finds the home situation intolerable and takes matters into his own hands.

Mental Health and Learning to Face Reality.—Everyone finds it hard at times to distinguish the real from the imagined in the various ways that imagination manifests itself. We sometimes say, "Pinch me to see if I am awake," or "Can this possibly be real?" The child is more easily to be excused for mistaking reality and fantasy than is the normal adult, because of the difference in the adult's maturity and the greater amount of previous experience he has had. When an adult continues to make such mistakes, he or she is said to be childish. Nevertheless, adults do continue to mistake fantasy for reality to a remarkable degree. Such activities as rationalization, projection, and day dreaming are not essentially dangerous or even mentally unhealthy, so long as one has frequent opportunities for success in terms of real situations. These escape activities are employed because they do restore an equilibrium of tension, however imperfect that restoration may be. The danger to mental health lies in the fact that the habit of seeking success in terms of fantasy "steals upon us ere we are aware." Having firmly established the habit, one is motivated more easily in that direction than in the direction of reality.

The following case will serve as an example. A woman who was dissatisfied with a rather prosaic married life attended all the motion pictures exhibited in a small city. She enjoyed particularly stories of love and romance. Eventually she became dissatisfied with her husband and her home, although both were probably as good as the average. She complained that she "couldn't see why they [her family] couldn't have things nice and do interesting things like other people do." She had got her ideas in these matters largely from the screen, and she had acquired the habit of confusing the events on the screen with real events of her life to the point where it interfered with her adjustment to her real problems of living.

Mental Health and Preventive Hygiene—Critical Points in the Life of the Individual.—As in other fields of hygiene, the modern emphasis in mental hygiene is being placed upon prevention. It is deemed wiser that the individual be rightly habituated in the first place, than that he or she be allowed to establish faulty habits and thus make it necessary to be reeducated. In the following paragraphs it will be possible to point out and to discuss very briefly only a few of the points in the life of a person in which the importance of preventive mental hygiene is emphasized.

Immediately after birth the child begins to form habits that are of importance throughout life. Among the most important of these are the habits of adjusting to others. *Consistency* and *regularity* are to be emphasized in all dealings with the infant and young child. If at one time the child is given satisfying attention for showing off and at another time is punished for the same activity, how is he to become rightly habituated? Many of the inconsistencies of the child are merely reflections of those of the parents.

The establishment of adequate foundations for proper emotional and social habits is of the utmost importance. It seems to be significant that nursery and pre-school classes for very young children are becoming more numerous in recent years. These schools have arisen to meet the demands of life in the modern home, where the child has fewer companions and fewer home occupations than in years past. Possibly parents are beginning to recognize the importance of proper social habituation in these early years and the loss, through modern conditions of life, of much that formerly served this important purpose.

Another point that is stressed by mental hygienists concerns the experience of beginning school. The school supplies a new source of authority, new routines to be adopted, and new allegiances to be formed. This is a problem for the parents as well as the child, and some parents tend to resent the division of authority and the establishment of allegiances outside the home. These adjustments for the child, unless properly prepared for through like experiences before entering school, may precipitate a crisis which may later have far-reaching effects upon the child's adult personality.

The period of adolescence presents a number of critical situations. The one which merits the greatest stress from the viewpoint of mental hygiene is that which Dr. Leta S. Hollingworth [1] has so aptly termed "psychological weaning." What was said in regard to the child entering school is also applicable to the adolescent entering or preparing to enter adult life. The parents so often find it difficult to "let go." They continue to advise, prohibit, enjoin, and instruct as in earlier childhood.

A mature unmarried woman reports that if she invites a gentleman friend to the house for the first time, he is welcomed by the parents. If he is invited again the welcome is less cordial, and

---

[1] L. S. Hollingworth, *The Psychology of the Adolescent,* New York, D. Appleton-Century Co., 1928.

by the third time that particular friend's welcome is worn out. This has happened repeatedly. To make matters worse she has been so trained as to be miserable if she meets gentlemen friends by appointment elsewhere than at home. The parents have probably not admitted to themselves that they want her to keep on living with them instead of marrying.

Parents are frequently heard to say of the young adolescent, "Don't you just hate to see them grow up?" thereby expressing a wish to keep their children as they are. The adequately adjusted adult must sooner or later establish an independence from the home. Where this independence cannot be achieved gradually and normally, it must be established later, at the death of the parents if not before. It then becomes a very painful ordeal, involving great stress and a difficult process of rehabituation. The basis of the ever-popular "mother-in-law" jokes is exactly this inability of many mothers to "let go" of their children when they marry. They still feel that their advice and care is needed. Naturally this leads to friction in the newly established home.

Other critical points or problems of adolescence have to do with adjustments in matters of sex, religion, economic independence, establishing moral or ethical codes, philosophy of life, and the like. Mental hygiene recognizes these as critical points of habituation and through its educational programs and its behavior clinics attempts to prevent mental ill health from accompanying such habituation. Certainly adolescence must not be overlooked in any program of mental hygiene.

For adults, maladjustments seem to center around the home and the social-business life, with the greater frequency in the former group. Mental hygienists in their preventive program pay more attention to the periods of childhood and adolescence. The adult period marks the time where the attention is most frequently directed at attempts to cure or correct the results of earlier faulty habits. This probably should not be the case. Prevention is as important in adult life as in earlier years.

Mental Health and Remedial Mental Hygiene—Significance of Symptoms.—It has already been intimated that the symptoms observable in abnormal behavior may be misleading. In the case of a boy who frequently plays truant from school, the truancy is often taken as a point for the application of remedial treatment. The boy is whipped, kept after school, or otherwise punished for the truancy. This may lead to a cessation of truancy from school, but if the underlying causes are not treated simultaneously it may reappear or the behavior of the boy may take some other equally abnormal or even more undesirable turn.

Medical practice has about given up the idea of treating symptoms. Now it is customary to regard a fever only as an indication that there is an organic disturbance within the body. Actually the fever is only a manifestation of the body's efforts to bring about a normal condition. This is exactly parallel to the psychiatrist's attempt to remedy the abnormalities of the patient's behavior. He notes the symptoms carefully as a means of diagnosing the patient's difficulty, but does not apply treatment to the symptom itself. Parents and teachers are often not so wise in their methods of handling such cases.

Characteristics that are apparent in any abnormality of behavior are often best regarded merely as symptoms that something is wrong. In the case of a neurasthenic person, is is important to recognize the perpetual weariness and irritability as an indication that the person is maladjusted. Rest cures have been tried with some apparent immediate success, only to result in a relapse when the patient returns to the old family, school, or business environment.

A number of years ago a young woman was graduated from a liberal arts college and began to teach school. She wished to go into the business world, but this was regarded by her family and friends as beneath the dignity of her social station in life. Within the first school year she had a "nervous breakdown" and was treated in a hospital. She apparently had recovered and at the urging of her family took another teaching position. Again she came to the verge of a nervous breakdown within a few months. She then took matters into her own hands, resigned her position, and secured another in a dry-goods department of a large mercantile establishment. Here the physical energy demanded was great, but within a year she was promoted to an important position in that establishment, where she was very happy.

Here is a clear instance of a symptom, i.e., the "nervous breakdown," which was simply an indication of a maladjustment. The underlying cause of the maladjustment lay as much in the woman's environment as in herself. She was an intellectually superior person with well-developed habits of being annoyed at the immature intellectual responses of her pupils. At the same time she had well-developed habits of doing what her parents and her social group regarded as "proper." Hence the inevitable conflict of habitual responses. Her solution was not necessarily the only suitable one, but it did remedy fundamental causes of the disturbance and not merely the symptoms.

From the standpoint of remedial mental hygiene, then, it is evident that it is important to use the symptom of the inappropriate behavior as a means of discovering the underlying factors which cause it. From this diagnosis it is possible to proceed rationally to a solution of the difficulty. Very often these remedial measures involve a change in the environment more than immediate attention to the individual himself.

Remedial Mental Hygiene as a Problem of Reeducation.— If the readjustment is to be genuine and of a lasting character, it must include some reeducation which most commonly and most importantly involves the patient himself. It may also involve changing the habits of others who form a part of the patient's environment. Situations which necessitate rehabituation occur when one is entering school, leaving home, or being married. When a child is born into the home, not only must the child be habituated to many social routines, but the parents must also be rehabituated in certain important respects. When an adolescent leaves home for school or for a home of his own, the parents must in some measure be rehabituated to the new situation.

It is desirable from the point of view of good mental health that rehabituation shall be as gradual and as progressive as possible. Parents should recognize the necessity for eventual separation of the adolescent from the home and begin a gradual process of emancipation years before the final separation is made. In such a case the actual separation will be a mentally healthy one for all concerned. On the other hand, separation due to such a cause as death is often followed by a period of mental ill health during the process of reorganization of habits. In some cases where the unfortunate person cannot manage alone, assistance must be sought from competent psychiatrists.

Religion and Mental Hygiene.—Religion has been considered an important agency in bringing peace of mind and happiness to those who embrace its teachings. This may be true in general, but it is certainly equally true that religious beliefs and unbeliefs have been the source of much of the world's turmoil and of individual maladjustment and unhappiness.

Much of the religious teaching of the world has been reduced to little more than a series of doctrines and dogmas. The really dangerous thing about these dogmas is that they are given all the authority and weight of approval of a Supreme Being and their acceptable interpretations are kept in the hands of a few selected persons. These religious doctrines and teachings are to be believed, but they are not to be subjected to the rational judgment of the believer.

In the days of limited knowledge and of few opportunities to know personally very many items of information, much had to be accepted as the truth simply because it appeared to be the truth. As time went on men learned to check the truth of statements in the secular world. It was only natural that similar attempts should be made in the field of organized religion. This attempt, however, has been consistently repulsed by many religious leaders and teachers. The attitude of organized religion has consistently been that layman and priest alike should believe the established doctrines as revelations from a Supreme Being.

In religious as in other types of situations, many persons are found who develop two mutually incompatible sets of habits. According to one they are required to behave as rational beings, subjecting all sorts of statements to the critical analysis of reasonableness and common experience. They are required by an increasingly strong tendency of social stimulation to be thoughtful and deliberate in their rational judgments. On the other hand, their habits of religious belief demand another and different type of mental activity. Here *acceptance* of the doctrine is the chief requirement. The individual is even encouraged "not to question, but rather to believe." This, of course, brings about varying degrees of functional disintegration of personality. Probably the most common form of this breakdown of behavior is that represented by the person who dares not allow himself to doubt and so shuts off his religious beliefs from the rest of his mental experience. This is sometimes called a "logic-tight" mind and is the only way that some people can gain any semblance of satisfactory mental adjustment. At best such an adjustment can be only partly satisfactory, and at its worst it leads to serious disintegration of personality.

Another valid criticism of much of the world's present and past religious teaching is that such teaching encourages the devout to flee from the realities of everyday life problems. He sees constantly held out to him the reward of a future life where all is just and no worry exists. He is encouraged to accept these promised intangible and unworldly rewards in lieu of the satisfactions that normally result from solving the problems of life in a present and very real world. This tends to encourage the believer to rationalize his actions and project his failures and shortcomings upon other "wicked persons" or even upon the Devil himself. In many organized religious efforts too little emphasis is placed upon the present realities of life.

The mentally unhealthy aspects of religious behavior have so far been given the greatest emphasis, but this tells only part of the story. More and more the modern tendency in the development of religious thought leans toward a mentally helpful and healthful program. The humanitarian and social service aspects of religion have been receiving much more attention in recent years. Greater emphasis is being placed upon life in the present and upon behaving in accordance with social codes that have much to be said in their favor. Religious leaders are recognizing the fact that, as the social order changes, the specific social codes must change with them. Organized religion is encouraging its followers to face the realities of this world and are placing less emphasis upon the ideas of future reward and punishment. This makes religion more truly a hygienic device for assisting its adherents in meeting life's difficulties and in making a satisfactory life adjustment.

Mental Hygiene and Sex.—Sex is a perfectly normal form of human motivation, just as much so as hunger and thirst. Sex behavior, however, differs from hunger and thirst behavior in that it has a greater social significance. This fact alone creates the need for even greater emphasis upon a rational consideration of sex problems than upon other less powerful motives. Sex habits involve much more than the behavior immediately concerned with reproduction. The other phases of sex education have been greatly neglected. All young people need training in habits, ideals, and attitudes concerned with the routine living together of the two sexes in the social group. Such habits, ideals, and attitudes are usually years in the building. When they are expected to develop suddenly, mental disturbance will invariably follow. Again, in the case of such a suddenly expected development, one is the victim of two sets of incompatible habits, and the usual result is some degree of personality disturbance.

Something needs to be done both individually and socially to desensitize people in the matter of irrational emotionality concerning sex. Relatively little can be done about changing the attitudes of the older members of this generation. Attitudes have the characteristics of habits. Those which are of concern here are habits of thinking which for many adults have long been established and which are often strongly reinforced emotionally.

The typical sex education program, where one does exist in the home or school, centers too exclusively upon matters of the biology and hygiene of reproduction. This is unquestionably important, but it is not so important as to justify the exclusion of training to meet the demands made upon young men and women in their adjustment to members of the opposite sex in the give and

take of ordinary social life. Children and adolescents need training in all the imaginable ways in which individuals of one sex
adjust themselves socially, in the large sense, to members of the
other sex.

An Illustrative Case.—By way of illustrating the significant
effects of mental ill health upon the behavior of one person, let
us consider the case of a college girl chosen because this girl's
maladjustment involves so many of the factors already mentioned
in this chapter.

Mary had apparently led a very secluded life until she came
to college. Her religious teaching had been abundant and strictly
orthodox, in accordance with the teachings of her parents' faith.
These teachings involved ideas of the sinfulness of dancing, card
playing, theater attendance, and the like. Consequently her experience in social adjustment had been very limited.

Her instruction in the matter of sex had been woefully inadequate. Even her knowledge of the simple biology of sex was very
limited. Her ideals and attitudes of sex in a larger sense were
badly in need of readjustment. In some respects there were indications of fixation upon the father as an ideal. There seems to
have been an almost complete lack of normal social contacts with
members of the opposite sex during high school. She had been
taught that all men were to be regarded with caution, if not with
actual suspicion.

There was evidence of only one case of an adolescent love
affair, and that was with an older man and was confined to ad-
miration from a distance. There were apparently some very close
friendships with one or two girls which bordered upon what are
sometimes called crushes, although she did not recognize them
as thwarted sex responses. She had never been away from home.
Mother or father always directly or indirectly made all her decisions of even minor importance.

Thus prepared, Mary went to college. She had to rebel almost
openly to get there without her mother going along to keep house
and care for her. However, she stood firm, but afterward had
qualms of conscience about her behavior to her mother. In col-

lege she made new friends, mostly among the girls. During her first year her "dates" with college men consisted exclusively in walking home from church with one or another of them.

She was very soon in doubt about her religion, not so much from any teaching in her college classes as from a recognition that other college men and women did not believe as she did. She was compelled to decide whether her parents were right in their teachings about men and about her religious beliefs, or to doubt whether the friends she came to know were, after all, decent and respectable young men and women. She was too intellectually honest to doubt the latter, but it was a painful jolt to believe the former.

Added to her other difficulties was an organic defect of only moderate importance, discovered by the college physician. She was worrying much about her other troubles and simply added this physical defect to the list. All in all, Mary was a most miserable and unhappy young woman. She admitted afterward that she had seriously contemplated suicide as the easiest solution. Probably only her own uncertainty and lack of initiative prevented this unhappy solution of her difficulty.

Several years have passed since she found herself in these complicated situations. She has succeeded very well, with help, in establishing herself emotionally by emancipating herself from her home with a minimum of discomfort to herself and her parents. She fell into and out of love several times and developed habits, ideals, and attitudes about sex that should have been part of her normal development before the time when she entered college. She has married and is a happy and successful wife and mother. She is now part of a group who regard her as a very fine, well-balanced young woman. The organic difficulty is unchanged, but is no longer a cause for worry.

All in all, Mary has gained a degree of mental health that would hardly be credible to those who knew her only in college. But how much distress, how sad the delay of good mental health, how much discomfort to herself and others resulted from the deplorable mental hygiene conditions in which she spent her childhood and most of her adolescence.

Characteristics of a Mentally Healthy Person.—Good mental health is necessary to a socially efficient and dependable life and to the attainment of a satisfactory degree of genuine and lasting personal happiness. If this statement is a fair evaluation of the importance of mental health, it would seem desirable to attempt to discover the characteristics of the mentally healthy person.

It has been brought out in this and the preceding chapters that mental health is largely dependent upon certain habits of behaving. The mentally healthy individual is therefore characterized by *habitually:*

1. Attending primarily to the present situations, being free from worry about the past and future except as they are vitally related to the present.

2. Facing facts as they really exist without distorting them through imagination. (Failure or refusal to recognize facts as they exist and imaginary distortion of facts to make them either more or less favorable than they are is conducive to mental ill health.)

3. Keeping physically fit through a desirable regime of work, rest, and recreation, giving special attention to the removal or correction of remediable defects.

4. Compensating in a *constructive* way for those unpleasant facts in life which are unalterable.

5. Seeking to discover all possible facts about his own personal capacities and inadequacies without undue feelings of superiority or inferiority.

6. Adjusting his environment and ways of life to his personal capacities and inadequacies.

7. Having a variety of interests, one or a few of which constitute the basis for vocational adjustment, the remaining ones forming the bases of avocations.

8. Finding a desirable and adequate means of self-expression as an outlet for emotionally toned drives. (Includes outlets for creative activity.)

9. Achieving some successful and satisfying social relationships.
10. Developing a good balance between self-reliance and a normal sense of social dependence.
11. Learning to recognize evidences of unhealthy reactions in himself and to deal with them effectively.

Such a list of habitual modes of living is of importance only as it furnishes the reader with a means of checking upon himself and upon those to whom he must adjust socially. A discovery of the area within which readjustments must be made is the necessary first.step in the direction of a more mentally healthy way of getting along with oneself and with one's associates.

An Outline Summary

1. The development of treatment of the insane.
    A. In ancient times the insane were regarded as being possessed of evil spirits and were social outcasts, confined in institutions and given care only when they were dangerous to society.
    B. At present the insane are regarded as persons who are mentally ill and are treated in hospitals for the purpose of restoring them to their place in society.
2. The organized mental hygiene movement:
    A. Began through the influence of Clifford W. Beers and his book, *A Mind That Found Itself,*
    B. Has grown to international proportions with active programs in many countries, and
    C. Has its present efforts directed primarily toward prevention rather than to remedial measures.
3. The task of the mental hygiene program involves:
    A. Keeping behavior in line with the characteristics of the mentally healthy person, and
    B. Assisting in the restoration of mental health when it has been impaired.
4. Mental health difficulties require:
    A. Analysis of:
        (a) The difficulty itself as represented by symptoms,

      (b) The needs and possibilities of rehabituation of the person involved, and

      (c) The environment of the one concerned, with special reference to the possibility of modification to relieve strain.

  B. Treatment, which may take the form of :

      (a) Reeducation (rehabituation) or

      (b) Readjustment of the environment to relieve strain and to make possible a limited adjustment within the limited possibilities of the patient.

5. Special problems of the program of mental hygiene.

  A. Certain social problems are frequently involved in mental ill health and deserve special consideration. Among these are :

      (a) Religious beliefs and religious education, and

      (b) Sex education in its most comprehensive sense.

  B. Certain points in the chronological development of the human being deserve special attention as potential danger spots. Among these are :

      (a) Early infancy with its problems of wholesome beginnings of social adjustments and routines,

      (b) Beginning school—establishing new social contacts, and

      (c) Adolescence with its problems such as that of "psychological weaning."

PROBLEMS FOR FURTHER THOUGHT

1. We usually enjoy a short story or a novel because of one of two rather different reasons. It may be a means of escape from the realities of life or it may be a means of interpreting and understanding certain phases of life which to a great extent have fallen outside the realm of our experiences. Probably any piece of literature may, in some measure, serve both functions at the same time, but ordinarily one or the other is clearly recognizable as a chief reason for reading the story. Thus when I read the *Adventures of Sherlock Holmes,* it is probably chiefly as a means of relaxation and escape from the toils of the day. On the other hand, when I continue through a book like *Kristin Lavransdatter, Ultima Thule,* or *The Seven Pillars of Wisdom,* it is because they contribute to me some-

thing of a better understanding of certain phases of life not so fully experienced in person.

Make a list of all the books you have read within the last year and classify it on the basis suggested here. What does the result suggest? Is there any significance in a preponderant number of "escape literature" items on your list? Explain. Of what significance would the absence of any such motives in reading be (if any)?

2. Suggest several specific ways in which religion may be involved in severe cases of mental ill health. Make your suggestions on the basis of experience or very carefully considered observation of acquaintances. Why are cases so often found in psychopathic hospitals in which the patient has convictions of having committed the unpardonable sin? How is this feeling of grave guilt related to mental health?

Make a list of as many mentally hygienic activities as you can that are encouraged and fostered by religious institutions. What are the most important ways by which such institutions can encourage healthy-mindedness?

3. How dependent are you upon forms of recreation which are essentially commercialized and "looker-on" activities? Make a list of all the recreations in which you have engaged for the last month. Define recreation here as activities in which you have participated just because you wanted to. Now classify them (five classifications) on the basis of: First, are they solitary or do they essentially involve others? Second, do they demand equipment to the extent that the recreational facilities are owned by a commercial interest and rented to you? Third, were they activities in which you were essentially a participant or a looker-on? Fourth, if they were group activities did they involve members of your own sex only or are they essentially bi-sexual activities? Fifth, did they require skill obtained by previous practice? Note that under each classification there are two possibilities for each activity.

Before going further mark in some significant way the activities on the list that you most enjoyed. Now compute the approximate percentages under each of the five classifications suggested above. Note how many of the preferred activities fall within each group.

Further continuation of this exercise would suggest a compilation of the results of the whole class so that each member would have a basis of comparison of himself with the average of the group.

4. The most frequently encountered problem of adolescents is that of establishing, at the proper time, a sense of independence. It manifests itself in a variety of ways. Make a compilation of the unsigned answers of all the members of the class to the following questions. (Indicate sex, since there are sex differences in some of the following.)

(1) How many children are there in your family younger than yourself?

(2) Have you ever had an allowance, definite as to time and amount?

(a) How old were you when it was first supplied? (b) Was it yours to do with as you saw fit or did someone tell you how it should be used? (c) Were you made to save it or was that a problem for you to decide?

(3) When did you first have a latch key so you could come in at night without making someone wait up for you?

(4) When did you first have a "date" with one of the other sex with the knowledge and approval of your parents?

(5) When did you first have a voice in the matter of the choice of your clothes? Do you now have the full responsibility of choosing what you will wear?

(6) When were you first trusted with the family car when no other member of the family was along?

(7) When were you first given responsibilities in the home such as caring for the house and yard and similar chores without supervision from your parents?

When the results have been compiled compare your answers with the average of the class. Then write a short paragraph on "Things I Wish My Parents Wouldn't Do." How many of these unliked things pertain to the difficulty of making parents realize your maturity? Before leaving this list, answer for yourself the question, "Am I really capable of guiding and directing myself in these matters without having to pay too great a price for learning by experience?"

5. Sex education is another problem that offers difficulty during the period of adolescence. In a manner similar to that suggested in Problem 4 above, answer the following questions pertaining to obtaining information about sex.

(1) How old were you when you first knew the basically essential facts of bi-sexual reproduction?

(2) Who supplied you with your first information about sex? (Parents, other relatives, doctor, or playmates?)

(3) What courses in elementary school and high school added to your sex education?

(4) What other courses in college have made a contribution in this respect?

(5) Were questions pertaining to sex ones that you could ask your parents without embarrassment to them or to you?

(6) What factors have contributed (within the scope of your knowledge) to your embarrassment in matters pertaining to sex? To your lack of embarrassment in such matters?

(7) To what extent have your various experiences in home, school, and church tended to make you regard things pertaining to sex as shameful, sinful, or disgusting? Answer by checking the one most appropriate term in the following list: (a) very much, (b) to a considerable extent, (c) moderately, (d) very little, (e) not at all.

6. Read one of the following books dealing with first hand experiences of the writers as inmates of hospitals for the mentally very ill. Write your reaction to the account indicating what *new points of view* it has given you about such patients and such institutions.

A Mind That Found Itself, by C. W. Beers.
Reluctantly Told, by Jane Hillyer.
Asylum, by William Seabrook.

A recent novel that presents a good picture of the life of the patients and a staff of such an institution is Phyllis Bottome's *Private Worlds* and Brand's *The Outward Room.*

Remember that Beers' book describes conditions that do not now generally prevail. *Asylum, Private Worlds,* and *The Outward Room* give a much better picture of modern conditions.

Suggested Readings

Berg, Louis. The Human Personality. New York, Prentice-Hall, Inc., 1933. Ch. XIV, "The Quest for Happiness," pp. 283–308.

Burnham, W. H. The Normal Mind. New York, D. Appleton-Century Co., 1924. One of the earlier books on mental hygiene by one of the pioneers in the field.

ELKIND, HENRY (Editor). The Healthy Mind. New York, Greenburg, Publisher, 1929. This is a series of papers by seven outstanding leaders in the field of mental hygiene, each of whom has contributed a chapter.

GROVES, E. R., and BLANCHARD, PHYLLIS. Introduction to Mental Hygiene. New York, Henry Holt & Co., 1930. This book covers many different aspects of mental hygiene problems in its several chapters, each dealing with a separate problem. It is more comprehensive than most, including some phases of the mental hygiene program that are of greater social than individual significance.

HOWARD, F. W., and PATRY, F. I. Mental Health. New York, Harper & Bros., 1935. This book is essentially a text and is one of the most recent in the field. It covers the whole field with emphasis upon the application of principles of remedial and corrective purposes.

KIRKPATRICK, EDWIN A. Mental Hygiene for Effective Living. New York, D. Appleton-Century Co., 1934. This is another recent textbook. Here the emphasis is upon personal adjustment.

MORGAN, JOHN J. B. Keeping a Sound Mind. New York, The Macmillan Co., 1934. This book is particularly directed to the individual's problems of mental health. The title suggests the essential characteristic of the book.

OLIVER, J. R. Psychiatry and Mental Health. New York, Chas. Scribner's Sons, 1932. This particular book on psychiatry is cited in preference to any other because it is probably the most readable and understandable for the layman of the many that are available. Dr. Oliver is not only a physician and psychiatrist but is also an ordained priest in the Protestant Episcopal Church. This gives the book an unusual point of view but adds rather than detracts from its readableness and interest-holding power. It originated as a series of lectures designed to meet the need of individuals only meagerly trained in psychology.

STRECKER, E. A., and APPEL, K. E. Discovering Ourselves. New York, The Macmillan Co., 1931. Especially Part II, "The Psychology of Everyday Life—The Conflicting Urges of Thought, Feeling and Action."

WOODWORTH, R. S. Adjustment and Mastery, Problems in Psychology. Baltimore, Williams & Wilkins Co., 1933. This is a small volume that will prove helpful to many readers.

AUTOBIOGRAPHIES AND FICTIONAL ACCOUNTS

By Former Asylum Inmates

BEERS, C. W. A Mind That Found Itself. New York, Longmans, Green & Co., 1908.

BOTTOME, PHYLLIS. Private Worlds. New York, Houghton Mifflin Co., 1934.

BRAND, MILLEN. The Outward Room. New York, Simon & Schuster, Inc., 1937.

HILLYER, JANE. Reluctantly Told. New York, The Macmillan Co., 1926.

SEABROOK, WILLIAM. Asylum. New York, Harcourt, Brace & Co., 1935.

Chapter 15

THE INTEGRATION OF PERSONALITY

Purpose of This Chapter.—In Chapters 1 to 14, a number of the individual characteristics of man's behavior have been examined separately and each has been treated as if it were an independent factor. This procedure was necessary for a better understanding of each specific phase of human behavior. In the present chapter we shall assemble again that which has been taken apart for separate examination, with a view to obtaining some understanding of that vaguely defined thing that is commonly called personality. An attempt will be made to present a picture of the whole personality—that which makes each person someone apart from all others. This will not be an easy task, for the reason that it is usually easier to examine the parts of a thing separately than to study the complex integrated whole. But the only really worthwhile result of the study of man's behavior comes from an understanding of his behavior as a whole person.

Difficulties in the Study of Human Personality.—The axiom of geometry which states that the whole is equal to the sum of its parts is oftentimes assumed to be equally true in all other fields. However, even a casual examination of a personality will indicate that when that person's behavior is examined bit by bit the results of the analysis do not yield an adequate picture of that thing which identifies him as a person. In so far as personality is concerned, the whole can be said to be equal to the sum of its parts only if the relationship between the parts is also considered as an integral factor.

Another difficulty that is encountered in the study of personality is the great complexity of the factors which contribute to the development of the thing as a whole. It has been repeatedly noted in the previous chapters that the behavior of the individual is determined by everything that influences his or her organic mechanisms. To this must be added the effect of the total stimulating environment which is present at the time of the response and immediately preceding it. What a personality is will be determined by the amount and kind of influence contributed by each factor, as that factor is related to and acted upon by each of the others. The mutual relationships of these several factors are so complex and so varied for different individuals that it is difficult to draw many significant general conclusions. About all that can be said is to repeat that biological inheritance seems to set the limits of development and the potentialities of behavior. Whether or not these limits are reached will depend in large measure upon the experiences resulting from the individual's "social inheritance." But in accounting for an individual's personality it is not enough to examine hereditary and social factors independently of each other. Each must be considered as it is related to and is acted upon by the others. This necessity presents itself repeatedly in the study of personality and is a requirement that must be reckoned with.

Maturity must also be considered in both its biological and its social aspects. By their early twenties most persons are at their maximum capacity, considered biologically. Social maturity is a different matter. Maximum flexibility and modifiability are probably related to early life, yet it is true that as long as life lasts some flexibility and modifiability of behavior persists. Maturity of personality must, therefore, be regarded as something relative.

Personality Related to Anatomical Traits.—The question is frequently asked, "Can one's personality be determined from analysis of one's physical features?" "Do blondes have a different kind of personality than brunettes?" The answer to such questions deserves some attention, since the emphasis upon the relationship of behavior to organic structure may have led some readers to faulty conclusions.

There can be little doubt that one's anatomical features play an important rôle in determining personality. This topic has already been considered in terms of the manifestation of these anatomical features in abnormal degrees. The overly tall or overly short person tends to behave differently from the average by reason of his extreme stature. These differences are noticeable enough to make it apparent even to a person without specific training in personality analysis. Probably much the same thing is true of any other anatomical trait. It should be pointed out, however, that the unsuspecting person may easily be misled by the charlatan character analyst who flits from town to town reaping a financial harvest as the result of the gullibility of the uninformed. These character readers usually insist that they can and do analyze the personality of their subjects by means of such features as the color of hair and eyes, prominence of chin, height of forehead, distance between the eyes, facial lines, and a variety of other specific anatomical traits. It is possible that some of them really believe that their results are achieved in this manner, but most of their pronouncements are little better than mere guesses. Some of the success that such analysts sometimes have is only a matter of coincidence. For the rest, it is undoubtedly based upon shrewd observation, resulting from training and years of experience in interpreting the minimal responses that the subject makes in their presence.

Personality as Shown by Different Ways in Which One Behaves.—Instead of continuing to analyze behavior into the factors forming the topics of previous chapters, it will be worthwhile to think of the different aspects of one's personality as shown by the different ways in which one behaves as a person. This analysis does not attempt to break down behavior into its component parts; instead, it is a classification into a series of pictures of the individual's behavior when observed from different points of view. *In each case the picture is of a whole person behaving.*

When an attempt is made to classify these different ways of behaving, the same difficulties are encountered as have been met in segregating factors of behavior in the previous chapters. Therefore, any classification that may be employed must be recognized as a classification of convenience only. The one used here is not the only one that could have been used, but it will serve the purpose. It should further be pointed out that this classification is not the result of exhaustive analysis. Many additional habits which are important parts of personality should suggest themselves to the reader after examination of the ones here mentioned. In this analysis the various kinds of behavior are classified as motor, intellectual, emotional, socio-economic, and health habits. In many of the specific habits there will be overlapping. The part that each characteristic plays in the *whole* personality and the way in which that characteristic is related to others in the same personality is the important thing to note.

1. MOTOR HABITS. There are many motor habits that are significant as personality traits and which contribute something important in distinguishing one personality from another. Only a few of these will be mentioned and these mainly by way of illustration. One's posture in walking, sitting, and standing contributes to one's personality as it is known to friends. By means of these significant habits it is often possible to recognize acquaintances at a distance too great to permit identification by means of facial features.

Many persons develop the use of specific gestures. In fact, some social groups, racial and otherwise, are often characterized by the extent to which these gestures play a part in their total behavior. The popular supposition that members of the Jewish race use their hands in a peculiar fashion while talking amounts almost to a belief that this trait is characteristic of that race. It is possible, of course, that Jews do use their hands more in talking than do other races, although it is very doubtful if this would constitute an important racial difference.

Closely akin to gestures are facial expressions. Individuals differ widely in what might be called expressiveness of facial responses. Some betray their thoughts and feelings very frequently by subtle changes in the responses of the facial muscles. At the other extreme, there are those who are sometimes called "poker faces." Some develop set habits of facial expressions for certain life situations. Others may develop a distinctly different kind of habit for the same kind of situation. All such habits help to distinguish the personality of one person from another.

Vocal habits might well be mentioned along with these other motor responses. Particular characteristics of pitch and tone of voice as well as habitual peculiarities of enunciation and inflection readily distinguish certain acquaintances from others. Undoubtedly the characteristic habits involved in speech as a whole contribute significantly to what is regarded as one's personality.

2. INTELLECTUAL HABITS. An amplification of the list of traits here mentioned and many illustrations of them will immediately be suggested to any thoughtful reader. One of these habits is open-mindedness, or, at the other extreme, closedmindedness. Another intellectual trait fairly well distinguished from open- and closed-mindedness, but which is often confused with it, is immediately suggested by the pair of words, decisive and indecisive.

Persistence of individual effort in problem situations is another important trait of personality. Here again, a wide range is found among the members of any group. Its emotional accompaniments might warrant the classification of this trait under another heading. Attentiveness and keenness in observing important details is another outstanding personality trait. This is closely related to still another, that of maintaining a point of view throughout some of the complexities of diverse life situations, as, for example, in solving a problem. Not long ago the author was speaking with a student who had been reading arguments in support of several different and somewhat conflicting schools of psychology. The student said, "Every argument sounds so plausible that I am first a Behaviorist, then a Purposivist, then a Gestaltist, and I am limited in my points of view only by the number of the contending views presented. I am incapable of reading a defense of Purposivism and at the same time maintaining any other point of view." Probably a better illustration is the case of the college co-ed who allowed herself to be dated to a certain formal function by no less than four different college men. Each one of them seemed to her more attractive than the preceding ones, until she found herself in the dilemma of having to explain to at least three men why she would not be able to accompany them.

One other intellectual trait should be maintained before leaving this topic. This is general modifiability or flexibility of habits of thinking and imagining. Some people think "in a groove." It was said of President Wilson by some of his opponents that he had a single-track mind. This trait will, of course, be recognized as being very much like the habit of maintaining a mind-set. A modification of this trait that is much encouraged by scientists is that of a questioning attitude, or of actually seeking more evidence before drawing a conclusion, instead of waiting passively for evidence to present itself.

The relationships of many of these traits to each other will have become obvious by this time. Some of the terms will seem to apply to the same behavior, but there are some important differences in each. This lack of preciseness in the definition of terms illustrates nicely one of the important difficulties involved in any analysis of personality. It is difficult to be certain that different persons who employ the same term are talking about the same thing. Also, it is important to note that the extremes of any of these traits are very likely to get one into personality difficulties, and hence contribute to difficulties of social adjustment.

3. EMOTIONAL HABITS. The close relationship between intellectual habits and emotional habits has already been mentioned. In fact, one of the most significant things about emotional responses is that they are usually parts of larger patterns of behavior. Emotional habits may be thought of as those elements of behavior that contribute colorfulness and feeling tone to the whole behavior pattern.

Among these traits special attention should be given to the habit of making the emotional response appropriate to the life situation. Emotional control is one of the factors involved in this although control and appropriateness do not necessarily imply the same thing. The kind of man or woman whose personality is most annoying to his or her associates is the one whose emotional response is not appropriate to the situation arousing it. Such a one is described by a college student who, in complaining about a roommate, said, "I never know whether she is going to be angry or not. Sometimes she gets very angry at what seem to me to be trifling incidents, and then again, when I fully expect her to be angry, she doesn't get angry at all. She may even laugh about the incident."

Associated with this personality trait is another having to do with general emotional responsiveness. Modern experimental medicine has suggested the dependence of emotional excitability upon the active functioning of certain of the endocrine glands. Important as the organic basis of this trait may be, due consideration must be given to the effect of habituation. In the case of either marked excess or marked deficiency of certain glandular secretions, the personality would be marked by corresponding excesses or deficiencies in the arousal of emotional responses. But not all such emotional differences can be accounted for in terms of glandular abnormalities. Training and habit formation undoubtedly play a very important part, particularly in the early formative years of childhood. Such cases may simply be instances of the sort of trait that runs in families and that is, at the same time, dependent more upon the social than upon the biological heritage of the individual.

4. HEALTH HABITS. Health habits have been included as a separate part of this classification because of their importance to the whole personality. Both physical and mental health should be considered. Consequently, the first personality trait to be mentioned will be that of recognizing and facing reality as it exists instead of submitting to an imaginary means of escape from unpleasant life situations.

Mental health and bodily health are so closely interrelated that it is difficult to distinguish the significance of the one type of health habit from the other. A certain man was known to the author for many years as one who rarely smiled and who almost never had been known to laugh. If it rained for three days in succession, he was gloomy and pessimistic about too much moisture. If the sun were to shine three days in succession, he would be equally downcast at the prospect of a drought. When he was without work for some time he was considerably downcast at the prospect of living without an income, and when he had what would seem to be steady work, he worried for fear the work would soon end. His wife was an excellent cook, but the list of dishes that he could enjoy was so limited that the artistry of her cooking was largely lost upon him. He suffered a very great deal from indigestion, and it would be extremely difficult to determine whether the indigestion was the result of his worry or the worry the result of his indigestion. Quite aside from the matter of his health, however, his personality is such as to make it rather unpleasant to associate with him, and his friends were extremely few. His bodily health and his personality had both been definitely affected by his unhygienic mental health habits over a period of years.

Aside from habits that have reference essentially to mental health, it would be appropriate to note the importance of such specific habits as those related to bodily cleanliness, food preferences, and elimination. A sound, clean, healthy body is a great asset to any one's personality. Examination of the advertising in current magazines will furnish evidence of the general recognition of this fact. This advertising has probably caused a good deal of worry and concern to some persons who might have been better off without such opportunities to indulge their habits of worry. On the other hand, it has undoubtedly made many people conscious of bodily cleanliness, and may have done much to improve the development of habits conducive to personal health and wholesome personality.

5. SOCIO-ECONOMIC HABITS. Very much of what is ordinarily meant by the term personality refers to that part of one's total behavior which is evident in social situations. Broadly speaking, therefore, any habitual pattern of behavior having to do with the way a person responds to others of his social group might be called a social personality trait. In this category are found pairs of words designating the opposite extremes of certain habitual modes of behavior. Ascendancy-submission behavior refers to the varying degrees of the tendency to be either submissive to the commands and suggestions of others or to be assertive and dominating in such behavior. A casual examina-

tion of one's circle of acquaintances will provide illustrations of varying degrees of such a trait.

There is also a group of generalized terms used to designate certain habitual modes of behavior such as honesty, dependableness, and responsibleness. Each of these describes a complex group of habits which differ in many details though all have certain characteristics in common. This point if often overlooked in applying the generalized term to a specific kind of response. A man may be absolutely honest in matters pertaining to his neighbor's property, but this would not necessarily imply that he is equally honest in the matter of his neighbor's reputation. In making a complete analysis of any personality, it would therefore seem to be necessary to break down such general terms as honesty in order that the more specific phases of this general trait may be determined. Other traits of this kind are neatness, sociability, variability, and cooperativeness.

On the other hand there are some much more specific social habits that reflect one's personality and greatly influence responses of the person-to-person type. A few years ago Laird published a little book entitled, *Why We Don't Like People*.[1] In this he presents the results of an analysis of some of the traits that make some people liked and some disliked. Perhaps it might be well to cite his list of nine habits which have the greatest influence in determining whether a person will be liked or disliked. They are, in the order in which he lists them, as follows:

1. Be depended upon to do what you say you will do.
2. Go out of your way to help others.
3. Do not show off your knowledge.
4. Do not let yourself feel superior to your associates, and be careful lest they get the impression that you do.
5. Do not reprimand people who do things that displease you.
6. Do not exaggerate in your statements.
7. Do not make fun of others behind their backs.
8. Do not be sarcastic.
9. Do not be domineering.

---

[1] D. A. Laird, *Why We Don't Like People*, New York, A. L. Glaser & Co., Inc., 1933.

Laird lists other traits of lesser significance which might be considered to advantage by the person who is anxious to be better liked by other people. A check-list compiled by Laird for evaluating your own likableness will be found at the end of this chapter. Most of the traits that have been mentioned are definitely on the social rather than on the economic side, although, of course, one's economic status is often dependent upon some of the social traits already mentioned. Certain economic personality traits that seem to be the result of habituation have come to be identified with certain nationalities. The old facetious definition of an optimist as a "man who would buy from a Jew and sell to a Scot and expect to make a profit on both ends," makes definite reference to the assumed personality traits of these two nationalities. The difficulty of trying to separate the economic factors from the social ones is so great as to make the distinction not worth while in ordinary circumstances. In the case just mentioned, it would be difficult to determine whether the factors were essentially economic or essentially social if, as a matter of fact, they actually do exist as racial characteristics.

The Integration of Personality.—The fact is worth emphasizing that many of the traits mentioned are groups of habits which have enough of a common element to give them a common classification. So long as one's habits contribute to the unity and distinctness of one's individuality, one will under ordinary circumstances be regarded as having a satisfactorily *integrated* personality. The word "integrate" literally means "to make one" or "to bring together into a whole." The integrated personality, therefore, is one in which the various habits are related or brought together in such a way that each contributes to the whole personality.

Sometimes one's habits are not compatible with each other. In such cases there may be interference of the habits to the point where the personality disintegrates. It may then become a split personality such as that depicted in the famous story of Dr. Jekyll and Mr. Hyde. It is not the fact that in one of its phases it is so socially reprehensible that causes a split personality to be regarded as unwholesome. Other cases of split personality, of actual medical record, do not involve such socially undesirable behavior. It is the distintegration that is more important than the nature of the two warring groups of personality traits themselves.

On the other hand, a personality may be very well integrated and still be socially undesirable. In such a case the whole pattern of habits tends to center around characteristics that are socially unpleasant and sometimes even socially menacing. A fictional character that nicely illustrates such unpleasantness is Scrooge, as depicted by Dickens in the *Christmas Carol*. Silas Marner is another example of an integrated personality that was not a socially desirable one during the time of his miserliness.

Integration, then, is a matter of mental good health, and the process of reintegrating traits of a personality which shows signs of disintegrating is one of the very frequent tasks of the psychiatrist. Usually the remedial measures consist essentially of rehabituation. This is the process of changing some of the patient's habits to make them more compatible with each other and more acceptable to the social groups of which the patient is a part. In this process the particular habits that are causing the difficulty are discovered by careful diagnosis of the patient's total behavior, and the offending habits are then made the special object of retraining.

What, Then, is Personality?—So far, much of this discussion of personality has seemingly continued the process of analysis which characterized the previous chapters. In spite of this, however, it is possible now to begin to distinguish that important factor called integration. Considered from all angles, personality is that which characterizes the individual and distinguishes him from others of his species. It is the sum total of all his behavior traits as a person, and in addition, it involves the relationship of these traits to each other when the person's behavior is considered as a whole. Any process of determining personality that depends solely upon analysis of traits will be found to give an inadequate picture. It then becomes apparent that any changes in personality which are to be made must be effected in one of two ways. Either the specific traits involved must be modified, or else the relationships between the respective traits as they exist must be altered.

Process of Changing One's Personality.—Can one's personality be changed, and if so, how can it be done? The answer to the first part of this question seems to be that undoubtedly personality can be changed within certain limits. These limits are twofold in nature. In the first place, the proposed changes must be within the limits determined by the biological inheritance. In the second place, they must fall within the limits that can result from changing the stimulating environment. In other words, the only way of changing a person's behavior is by changing some significant aspect of his environment in order that his habits may thereby be modified.

The second part of the question is more complex. First of all, the offending trait or traits must be discovered. In doing this, careful self-analysis in as unprejudiced a manner as possible may be a convenient starting place. It often happens that a man or woman recognizes that his or her personality is not satisfactory, that it is resulting in the dislike of too many people. In viewing personality as a whole the task seems so hopelessly large as to be discouraging. Most people do not know specifically which are the things that cause their personalities to be socially unsatisfactory.

The chief difficulty often lies in finding out which are the offending habits, and it is in these cases that the findings of such workers as Laird are particularly useful. If only the offending habits can be discovered, the sufferer is already well on his way to recovery. From this point the process is essentially one of habit formation. The conditions of learning, as discussed in a previous chapter, will be the best aids in establishing the new habits to replace the old.

The motivation necessary for carrying through the process of rehabituation is usually provided by the intense desire to be better liked. In the absence of such a motivating force, it is first necessary to obtain the active cooperation of the learner.

A case of this sort has been reported by Laird:

A certain boy turned out by his own rating to have the worst score in the collection. Now it happened that this boy possessed, in spite of that, numerous advantages and talents which would seem to make it comparatively easy for him to be liked. He had wealth and social accomplishments, dressed well, played the piano like a wizard, and was good as an amateur in several popular forms of athletics. All to no avail. By the admission of all the other students in the group who knew him, as well as by his own description of himself, he was shown to be the most disliked.

For sixteen months he had been in close contact with a group of about fifteen boys of his own age. For sixteen months, in the manner of boys, they had been telling him that he was "all wet," and that he was a "pain in the neck." He knew well enough that he was disliked, but he honestly did not know why. The analysis which he made for himself in ten minutes in the laboratory pointed out definite traits as the reasons why he was disliked. Thus, in place of a vague realization of his misfortune he secured a diagram of the weak points which were to blame and which he knew he must correct.

Two weeks after this boy had made his self-analysis, one of the others of his group was working for me for a few hours. In the course of conversation, he remarked, "Say, what did you do to Smithers? We have razzed him and been after him continually for almost two years now, and here something happened up in the laboratory—I don't know what, whether it was serum or an injection of horse sense, but he is a changed fellow. We are beginning to like him immensely."

One of the traits of this boy had been showing off his knowledge. He never spoke of salt except as sodium chloride, partly in fun but also with an underlying desire of displaying his learning. Another trait was the habit of trying to get others to do things for him. He had the reputation of buying one package of cigarettes a month and smoking two packages a day. The analysis had pointed out traits like these which even the boys who disliked him did not realize were the cause of their dislike.[2]

It is often necessary to know how these habits came to be formed since this makes it possible to know what changes in the environment will have to be made to change the habit. By follow-

---

[2] Laird, *op. cit.*, pp. 27–28.

ing the conditioned response procedure described in the chapter on emotions, environmental situations can often be so arranged that the desired reconditioning can be effected. It is exactly the process employed by Watson and Jones in reconditioning the fear response of the boy to the rabbit. It would be advantageous at this point to review this experiment as recounted in the chapter on emotions.

Objective Attitude as a Desirable Personality Trait.—The objective attitude may best be understood by contrasting it with the subjective attitude. The latter is concerned chiefly with feelings, emotions, and other personal experiences. In contrast to this, the objective attitude is mostly concerned with those things which lie outside of oneself, and enables men and women to consider themselves in an impersonal way. The objective attitude is illustrated by the scientist in his own laboratory, by the merchant as he deals with the customer, and by the farmer as he plans his rotation of crops. Of course, in each of these situations there is also room for some degree of the subjective attitude. The scientist or merchant or farmer normally may be expected to have something of a glow of pride in his own possession and his own work. The wholesome personality represents a balance between the extremes.

The question naturally arises: How is the objective attitude to be developed? The key to the answer is found in the normal development of human beings through childhood into adult life. Children are essentially egocentric in the early years of infancy and childhood. This gradually gives way to a point of view in which one is able to see oneself as a member of a social group. This is usually brought about by the incidental and normal activities of life by means of which one is made to assume larger social responsibilities. If one is to live satisfactorily with others, one must learn to see things from the other person's point of view. Consequently, for the adult who is lacking in an objective attitude, the suggested means of attaining it might very well be that of learning to see things connected with oneself from the point of view of others.

An Outline Summary

1. Difficulties in dealing with the problems of personality.

   A. The sum of all the separate traits which result from an analysis of a personality fails to give an adequate representation of that personality because,

      (a) The traits themselves are so complex as to make it difficult to analyze them or to classify them properly, and

      (b) The relationships between the separate traits are themselves important determining factors in any personality.

   B. Knowledge of the various factors of behavior gained from a study of each one by itself in the previous chapters must be reassembled in such a manner as to show the way in which each factor influences and is influenced by each other factor. One convenient way of doing this is by a classification of the behavior of a person into habitual responses. The more important of these for the understanding of a personality are:

      (a) Motor habits,

      (b) Intellectual habits,

      (c) Emotional habits,

      (d) Health habits, and

      (e) Socio-economic habits.

2. Characteristics of an integrated personality.

   A. The several habitual tendencies toward response are mutually compatible, showing no important conflict in general life situations.

   B. A well-integrated personality may be either socially desirable or socially undesirable depending upon the social acceptableness of the dominant trend of the integration.

3. Personality can be changed by:

   A. Changing one or more of the separate habitual responses that are involved in the personality as a whole, or by

   B. Changing the significant relationships as they exist between the dominant responses without important changes in the habitual responses themselves.

Problems for Further Thought

1. Many people are dismayed and distressed to find themselves so much disliked. Being at a loss to know why they are disliked, they are powerless to do anything to remedy the matter. Laird in his book, *Why We Don't Like People,* devotes two chapters to this problem. Below is a list of 45 questions taken from that book, and Laird's suggestions about scoring the answers. Remember that the value of this exercise to you lies in the fact that this inventory will help you take stock of yourself. Hence it is important that you maintain an objective attitude toward your own behavior if the results are to be of any value.

Traits Which Make Us Liked

Give yourself a score of 3 for each of these questions to which you can honestly answer "Yes":

(1) Can you always be depended upon to do what you say you will?

(2) Do you go out of your way cheerfully to help others?

(3) Do you avoid exaggeration in all your statements?

(4) Do you avoid being sarcastic?

(5) Do you refrain from showing off how much you know?

(6) Do you feel inferior to most of your associates?

(7) Do you refrain from bossing people not employed by you?

(8) Do you keep from reprimanding people who do things that displease you?

(9) Do you avoid making fun of others behind their backs?

(10) Do you keep from domineering others?

Give yourself a score of 2 for each of these questions you can answer "Yes":

(11) Do you keep your clothing neat and tidy?

(12) Do you avoid being bold and nervy?

(13) Do you avoid laughing at the mistakes of others?

(14) Is your attitude toward the opposite sex free from vulgarity?

(15) Do you avoid finding fault with everyday things?

(16) Do you let the mistakes of others pass without correcting them?

(17) Do you loan things to others readily?

(18) Are you careful not to tell jokes that will embarrass those listening?
(19) Do you let others have their own way?
(20) Do you always control your temper?
(21) Do you keep out of arguments?
(22) Do you smile pleasantly?
(23) Do you avoid talking almost continuously?
(24) Do you keep your nose entirely out of other people's business?

Give yourself a score of 1 for each of these questions you can answer "Yes":

(25) Do you have patience with modern ideas?
(26) Do you avoid flattering others?
(27) Do you avoid gossiping?
(28) Do you refrain from asking people to repeat what they have just said?
(29) Do you avoid asking questions in keeping up a conversation?
(30) Do you avoid asking favors of others?
(31) Do you avoid trying to reform others?
(32) Do you keep your personal troubles to yourself?
(33) Are you natural rather than dignified?
(34) Are you usually cheerful?
(35) Are you conservative in politics?
(36) Are you enthusiastic rather than lethargic?
(37) Do you pronounce words correctly?
(38) Do you look upon others without suspicion?
(39) Do you avoid being lazy?
(40) Do you avoid borrowing things?
(41) Do you refrain from telling people their moral duty?
(42) Do you avoid trying to convert people to your beliefs?
(43) Do you avoid talking rapidly?
(44) Do you avoid laughing loudly?
(45) Do you avoid making fun of people to their faces?

"The higher your score by this self-analysis the better liked you are in general. Each 'No' answer should be changed through self-guidance into a 'Yes' answer. The highest possible score is 81. About 10% of people have this score. The lowest score made by a person who was generally liked was 56. The average young person has a score of 64. The average score of a person who is generally disliked is 30. The lowest score found was 12." [3]

2. In Wiggam's book, *Exploring Your Mind with the Psychologists* (listed below), are two chapters of an interview with Adams which deal with the problems of judging ourselves and our fellows. Adams sets up an easy and interesting technique by means of which a group of any nine individuals who know each other very well can get fairly reliable analyses of their personality on the basis of 63 traits. For more extended analysis than that provided in the problem above, this will serve the purpose. It will be necessary to have at least one copy of the book.

3. Below is a list of 20 questions that are to be answered with "Yes" or "No." They are designed to measure your ability to be objective in your attitude as that attitude has been discussed. Put your answers on an unsigned sheet. Let these be collected and the average number of affirmative answers be computed for the class. Then compare your own score with this class average. In addition, let the committee compute the number of affirmative answers for each question. This will enable you to compare yourself in terms of the class replies. No large-scale norms are available, nor is it known whether sex and age make any difference in the results.

Directions: Here is a list of questions to be answered by either "Yes" or "No." Think of situations from your own experience but try to get as honest an estimate as possible of the average of the situations represented by the questions. There is no time limit but nothing is gained by overmuch study of the questions. Do not sign your name to the slip you hand to the committee that will compile results, but keep a copy of your answers for use in making your own comparisons later.

_____ (1) Can you accept philosophically the destruction of a treasured keepsake? (not "weeping over spilt milk").

_____ (2) When you do things for the pleasure of others do you recognize your own gain in so doing?

_____ (3) Are you able readily to recognize and assume responsibility for failure in a group enterprise in so far as you have, in reality, been to blame?

---

[3] Laird, *op. cit.*, pp. 30-32.

_____ (4) Do you regularly avoid putting the blame on the cards or on the referee, when you lose a card game or an athletic contest?

_____ (5) Do you evaluate the praise you receive for that which you have done well, even when you may behave with modesty?

_____ (6) Do you recognize the motives for your own acts even when you keep them hidden from others?

_____ (7) Does your estimate of your own ability agree substantially (not much higher or lower) with the estimate of those who know you well?

_____ (8) Can you cheerfully adjust your manner of living to meet a loss of a sum of money or a job, without playing for the condolences and sympathy of your friends?

_____ (9) Can you recognize what justice there actually may be in the voiced criticism of your behavior without rationalization on your part?

_____ (10) Can you fail to get the grade in a course that you have expected, without putting the blame on the course or the instructor?

_____ (11) When you are being cajoled or urged to act contrary to your best interest, in the name of friendship, do you usually recognize the motives of those urging you?

_____ (12) Do you allow yourself to be persuaded to act as you desire to act, against your better judgment?

_____ (13) Do you go to shows when you know there is important pressing work to be done?

_____ (14) Can you recognize a considerable degree of justice in the criticism of those who know you well, when these criticisms are made in a keen but friendly manner?

_____ (15) Do you avoid prolonged mourning at the loss of loved ones or of very dear friendships, even though you miss them very much?

_____ (16) Do you avoid a sour grapes or a sweet lemon attitude when you fail to establish a friendship or fail to attain a reward which you wish very much?

_____(17) Do you usually refuse to take credit which is attributed to you but which you *honestly* believe you do not deserve?

_____(18) Do you usually refuse to buy things which you very much want but which you know you could not afford?

_____(19) Can you usually avoid thinking that your opponents are unfair when their arguments are more logical than your own?

_____(20) Do you usually recognize the true cause of an extreme lack of energy when there is not a sufficient organic basis for such fatigue?

SUGGESTED READINGS

BERG, LOUIS. The Human Personality. New York, Prentice-Hall, Inc., 1933. Ch. I, "Personality and the Body," pp. 1–12. Other chapters will be of interest as collateral reading for special topics.

BOWERS, E. F. Charm and Personality—How to Attain Them. New York, National Library Press, 1934.

BURNHAM, W. N. The Wholesome Personality. New York, D. Appleton-Century Co., 1932. Among the many parts of this book that are related to the whole problem of personality adjustment, the following are cited especially: Ch. I, "The Background of Personality," pp. 1–27; Ch. III, "Other Factors of Personality," pp. 53–83; Ch. VI, "The Wholesome Personality," pp. 176–220; Ch. VII, "The Objective Attitude."

HAWKES, E. W., and JOHNS, R. L. Orientation for College Freshmen. New York, The Ronald Press Co., 1929. Ch. XVII, "Personality and Character," pp. 192–203.

LAIRD, D. A. Why We Don't Like People. New York, A. L. Glaser & Co., 1933. Ch. I, "People We Like," pp. 3–14; Ch. II, "Why We Like Some People and Don't Like Others," pp. 15–32; Ch. XII, "Look to Your Personality," pp. 178–198. Several other chapters are pertinent also. This is interesting and easy reading for the non-professional reader.

VALENTINE, P. F. The Psychology of Personality. New York, D. Appleton-Century Co., 1927. A systematic textual discussion of the problems of personality.

WIGGAM, E. A. Exploring Your Mind with the Psychologists. New York, Bobbs-Merrill Co., 1928. Ch. IV, by D. A. Laird, "How to Make an Inventory of Our Personality," pp. 61–85; Chs. V and VI, by H. F. Adams, "How We Judge Ourselves and Fellow Men," pp. 89–123.

WRIGHT, MILTON. Getting Along with People. New York, McGraw-Hill Book Co., Inc., 1935. This recent book is written in a popular and easy manner. It will be found to be interesting collateral reading and factually important.

AUTHOR INDEX

SUBJECT INDEX